P9-CDL-318

2.00

BOOK MARKET
Marketplace Center
18001 Bothell Hwy S.E.
Bothell, WA 98012
481-1322

A HISTORY
OF THE
CHRISTIAN CHURCH

A HISTORY
OF THE
CHRISTIAN CHURCH

Williston Walker

ONE-TIME PROFESSOR
OF ECCLESIASTICAL HISTORY
IN YALE UNIVERSITY

THIRD EDITION

REVISED BY
Robert T. Handy OF UNION THEOLOGICAL SEMINARY, NEW YORK

SECOND EDITION REVISED BY
Cyril C. Richardson, Wilhelm Pauck, and Robert T. Handy
OF UNION THEOLOGICAL SEMINARY, NEW YORK

CHARLES SCRIBNER'S SONS · NEW YORK

THIRD EDITION
Copyright © 1970 Charles Scribner's Sons

FIRST AND SECOND EDITIONS
*Copyright 1918, © 1959 Charles Scribner's Sons;
renewal copyright 1946 Amelia Walker Cushing and
Elizabeth Walker*

This book published simultaneously in the
United States of America and in Canada—
Copyright under the Berne Convention

All rights reserved. No part of this book
may be reproduced in any form without the
permission of Charles Scribner's Sons.

9 11 13 15 17 19 V/C 20 18 16 14 12 10

PRINTED IN THE UNITED STATES OF AMERICA
SBN 684-41471-6 (cloth)
Library of Congress Catalog Card Number 70-108358

TO MY WIFE

Preface to the Third Edition

A NUMBER of significant events in church history took place in the 1960's. Therefore, though it was not advisable fully to revise this useful volume again so soon after the thorough revision of 1959, it was decided to make some changes in the latter part of the book, to add an additional chapter, and to update the bibliographical suggestions. It is instructive to observe how much of the history that is recounted in this long-standard work has been reconsidered again in the epoch-making deliberations and actions of the Second Vatican Council and the Third and Fourth Assemblies of the World Council of Churches.

ROBERT T. HANDY

Union Theological Seminary
September 1969

Revisers' Preface

For nearly half a century Walker's *History of the Christian Church* has been a standard textbook. It was written by a scholar of ripe learning, who profited especially from the rich fruits of German historical scholarship in the later 19th and early 20th centuries. Its rare combination of clarity, compactness and balance has been responsible for its unparalleled success. Moreover, despite the advances made in historical scholarship, the main text of Walker has held up remarkably well. Nevertheless, sections have inevitably become out of date, and especially in the later portions has extensive rewriting been necessary. It has been the aim of the revisers to retain the main structure of the original, and only to revise those parts where there were errors of fact or where the interpretation was seriously questionable. Occasionally sections have been added to introduce a better balance or to take note of modern discoveries. In the modern period a more radical reworking of the material has been necessary in order to bring the text up to date.

The division of labor between the revisers has been as follows: Professor Richardson has been responsible for the work to the early Middle Ages (pp. 1–215), Professor Pauck through the Reformation (pp. 219–401), and Professor Handy from Puritanism to the Modern Day (pp. 402–545). Grateful thanks are due Dr. Edward R. Hardy of the Berkeley Divinity School, New Haven, for his scholarly help on the section dealing with the Greek Orthodox Church. It is our hope that by bringing the text up to date we have added to its usefulness and so prolonged the life of a worthy and popular volume.

CYRIL C. RICHARDSON
WILHELM PAUCK
ROBERT T. HANDY

Union Theological Seminary
September 1958

Contents

Period Three

THE IMPERIAL STATE CHURCH

Period Four

THE MIDDLE AGES TO THE CLOSE
OF THE INVESTITURE CONTROVERSY

Period Five

THE LATER MIDDLE AGES

Period Six

THE REFORMATION

Period Seven

MODERN CHRISTIANITY

List of Maps

A HISTORY
OF THE
CHRISTIAN CHURCH

Period One

FROM THE BEGINNINGS
TO THE GNOSTIC CRISIS

The General Situation

*T*HE BIRTH of Christ saw the lands which surrounded the Mediterranean in the possession of Rome. To a degree never before equalled, and unapproached in modern times, these vast territories, which embraced all that common men knew of civilized life, were under the sway of a single type of culture. The civilizations of India or of China did not come within the vision of the ordinary inhabitant of the Roman Empire. Outside its borders he knew only savage or semicivilized tribes. The Roman Empire and the world of civilized men were co-extensive. All was held together by allegiance to a single Emperor, and by a common military system subject to him. The Roman army, small in comparison with that of a modern military state, was adequate to preserve the Roman peace. Under that peace commerce flourished, communication was made easy by excellent roads and by sea, and among educated men, at least in the larger towns, a common language, that of Greece, facilitated the interchange of thought. It was an empire that, in spite of many evil rulers and corrupt lower officials, secured a rough justice such as the world had never before seen; and its citizens were proud of it and of its achievements.

Yet with all its unity of imperial authority and military control, Rome was far from crushing local institutions. In domestic matters the inhabitants of the provinces were largely self-governing. Their local religious observances were generally respected. Among the masses the ancient languages and customs persisted. Even native rulers were allowed a limited sway in portions of the empire, as native states still persist under modern empires. Such a land was Palestine at the time of Christ's birth. Not a little of the success of Rome as mistress of its diverse subject population was due to this considerate treatment of local rights and prejudices. The diversity in the empire was scarcely less remarkable than its unity. This variety was nowhere more apparent than in the realm of religious thought.

Christianity entered no empty world. Its advent found men's minds filled with conceptions of the universe, of religion, of sin, and of rewards and punishments, with which it had to reckon and to which it had to adjust itself. Christianity could not build on virgin soil. The conceptions which it found already existing formed much of the material with which it must erect its structure. Many of these ideas are no longer those of the modern world. The fact of this inevitable intermixture compels the student to distinguish the permanent from the transitory in Christian thought, though the process is one of exceeding difficulty, and the solutions given by various scholars are diverse.

Certain factors in the world of thought into which Christianity came belong to universal ancient religion and are of hoary antiquity. All men, except a few representatives of philosophical sophistication, believed in the existence of a power, or of powers, invisible, superhuman, and eternal, controlling human destiny, and to be worshipped or placated by prayer, ritual, or sacrifice. The earth was viewed as the center of the universe. Around it the sun, planets, and stars ran their courses. Above it was the heaven; below the abode of departed spirits or of the wicked. No conception of what is now called natural law had penetrated the popular mind. All the ongoings of nature were the work of invisible powers of good and evil, who ruled arbitrarily. Miracles were, therefore, to be regarded not merely as possible; they were to be expected whenever the higher forces would impress men with the important or the unusual. The world was the abode of innumerable spirits, righteous or malevolent, who touched human life in all its phases, and who even entered into such possession of men as to control their actions for good or ill. A profound sense of unworthiness, of ill desert, and of dissatisfaction with the existing conditions of life characterized the mass of mankind. The varied forms of religious manifestation were evidences of the universal need of better relations with the spiritual and unseen, and of men's longing for help greater than any they could give one another.

Besides these general conceptions common to popular religion, the world into which Christianity came owed much to the specific influence of Greek thought. Hellenistic ideas dominated the intelligence of the Roman Empire, but their sway was extensive only among the more cultivated portion of the population. Greek philosophic speculation at first concerned itself with the explanation of the physical universe. Yet with Heraclitus of Ephesus (about B. C. 490), though all was viewed as in a sense physical, the universe, which is in constant flow, is regarded as fashioned by a fiery element, the all-penetrating reason, of which men's souls are a part. Here was probably the germ of the Logos (λόγος) conception which was to play such a rôle in later Greek speculation and Christian theology. As yet this shaping element was undistinguished from material warmth or fire. Anaxagoras of Athens (about B. C. 500–428) taught that a shaping mind (νοῦς) acted in the ordering of matter and is independent of it. The Pythagoreans, of southern Italy, held that spirit is immaterial, and that souls are fallen spirits imprisoned in material bodies. To this belief in immaterial existence they seem to have been led by a consideration of the properties of numbers—permanent truths beyond the realm of matter and not materially discerned.

To Socrates (B. C. 470?–399) the explanation of man himself, not of the universe, was the prime object of thought. Man's conduct, that is morals, was the most important theme of investigation. Right action is based on knowledge, and will result in the four virtues—prudence, courage, self-control, and justice—which, as the "natural virtues," were to have their eminent place in mediæval Christian theology. This identification of virtue with knowledge, the doctrine that to know will involve doing, was indeed a disastrous legacy to all Greek thinking, and influential in much Christian speculation, notably in the Gnosticism of the second century.

In Socrates' disciple, Plato (B. C. 427–347), the early Greek mind reached its highest spiritual attainment. He is properly describable as a man of mystical piety, as well as of the prófoundest spiritual insight. To Plato the passing forms of this visible world give no real knowledge. That knowledge of the truly permanent and real comes from our acquaintance with the "ideas," those changeless archetypal, universal patterns which exist in the invisible spiritual world—the "intelligible" world, since known by reason rather than by the senses—and give whatever of reality is shared by the passing phenomena present to our senses. The soul knew these "ideas" in previous existence. The phenomena of the visible world call to remembrance these once known "ideas." The soul, existing before the body, must be independent of it, and not affected by its decay. This conception of immortality as an attribute of the soul, not shared by the body, was always influential in Greek thought and stood in sharp contrast to the Hebrew doctrine of resurrection. All "ideas" are not of equal worth. The highest are those of the true, the beautiful, and especially of the good. A clear perception of a personal God, as embodied in the "idea" of the good, was perhaps not attained by Plato; but he certainly approached closely to it. The good rules the world, not chance. It is the source of all lesser goods, and desires to be imitated in the actions of men. The realm of "ideas" is the true home of the soul, which finds its highest satisfaction in communion with them. Salvation is the recovery of the vision of the eternal goodness and beauty.

Aristotle (B. C. 384–322) was of a far less mystical spirit than Plato. To him the visible world was an unquestioned reality. He discarded Plato's sharp discrimination between "ideas" and phenomena. Neither exist without the other. Each existence is a substance, the result, save in the case of God, who is purely immaterial, of the impress of "idea," as the formative force, on matter which is the content. Matter in itself is only potential substance. It has always existed, yet never without form. Hence the world is eternal, for a realm of "ideas" antecedent to their manifestation in phenomena does not exist. The world is the prime object of knowledge, and Aristotle is therefore in a true sense a scientist. Its changes demand the initiation of a "prime mover," who is Himself unmoved. Hence Aristotle presents this celebrated argument for the existence of God. But the "prime mover" works with intelligent purpose, and God is, therefore, not only the beginning but the end of the process of the world's development. Man belongs to the world of substances, but in him there is not merely the body and sensitive "soul" of the animal; there is also a divine spark, a Logos (λόγος), which he shares with God, and which is eternal, though, unlike Plato's conception of spirit, essentially impersonal. In morals Aristotle held that happiness, or well-being, is the aim, and is attained by a careful maintenance of the golden mean.

Greek philosophy did not advance much scientifically beyond Plato and Aristotle, but they had little direct influence at the time of Christ. Two centuries and a half after His birth, a modified Platonism, Neo-Platonism, was to arise, of great importance, which profoundly affected Christian theology, notably that of Augustine. Aristotle was powerfully to influence the scholastic theology of the later Middle Ages. Those older Greek philosophers had viewed man chiefly in the light of his value to the state. The conquests of Alexander, who died B. C. 323, wrought a great change in men's outlook. Hellenic culture was planted widely over the Eastern world, but the small Greek states collapsed as independent political entities. It was difficult longer to feel that devotion to the new and vast political units that a little, independent Athens had, for instance, won from its citizens. The individual as an independent entity was emphasized. Philosophy had to be interpreted in terms of individual life. How could the individual make the most of himself? Two great answers were given, one of which was wholly foreign to the genius of Christianity, and could not be used by it; the other only partially foreign, and therefore destined profoundly to influence Christian theology. These were Epicureanism and Stoicism.

Epicurus (B. C. 342–270), most of whose life was spent in Athens, taught that mental bliss is the highest aim of man. This state is most perfect when passive. It is the absence of all that disturbs and annoys. Hence Epicurus himself does not deserve the reproaches often cast upon his system. Indeed, in his own life, he was an ascetic. The worst foes of mental happiness he taught are groundless fears. Of these the chief are dread of the anger of the gods and of death. Both are baseless. The gods exist, but they did not create nor do they govern the world, which Epicurus holds, with Democritus (B. C. 470?–380?), was formed by the chance and ever-changing combinations of eternally existing atoms. All is material, even the soul of man and the gods themselves. Death ends all, but is no evil, since in it there is no consciousness remaining. Hence, as far as it was a religion, Epicureanism was one of indifference. The school spread widely. The Roman poet Lucretius (B. C. 98?–55), in his brilliant De Rerum Natura, gave expression to the worthier side of Epicureanism; but the influence of the system as a whole was destructive and toward a sensual view of happiness.

Contemporarily with Epicurus, Euhemerus (about B. C. 300) taught that the gods of the old religions were simply deified men, about whom myths and tradition had cast a halo of divinity. He found a translator and advocate in the Roman poet Ennius (B. C. 239?–170?). Parallel with Epicureanism, in the teaching of Pyrrho of Elis (B. C. 360?–270?), and his followers, a wholly sceptical point of view was presented. Not merely can the real nature of things never be understood, but the best course of action is equally dubious. In practice Pyrrho found, like Epicurus, the ideal of life one of withdrawal from all that annoys or disturbs. With these theories Christianity had little in common, although the Apologists made use of Euhemerus' views in their attacks on pagan mythology, and the Fathers availed themselves of arguments from scepticism to enforce their conviction that human reason had severe limits.

The other great answer was that of Stoicism, the noblest type of ancient pagan ethical thought, the nearest in some respects to Christianity, and in others remote from it. Its leaders were Zeno (B. C.?–264?), Cleanthes (B. C. 301?–232?), and Chrysippus (B. C. 280?–207?). Though developed in Athens, it flourished best outside of Greece, and notably in Rome, where Seneca (B. C. 3?–A. D. 65), Epictetus (A. D. 60?–?), and the Emperor, Marcus Aurelius (A. D. 121–180), had great influence. It was powerfully represented in Tarsus during the early life of the Apostle Paul. Stoicism was primarily a great ethical system, yet not without claims to be considered a religion. Its thought of the universe was curiously materialistic. All that is real is physical. Yet there is great difference in the fineness of bodies, and the coarser are penetrated by the finer. Hence fine and coarse correspond roughly to the common distinctions between spirit and matter. Stoicism approximated, though it much modified, the view of Heraclitus. The source of all, and the shaping, harmonizing influence in the universe, is the vital warmth, from which all has developed by differing degrees of tension, which interpenetrates all things, and to which all will return. Far more than Heraclitus' fire, which it resembles, it is the intelligent, self-conscious world-soul, an all indwelling reason, Logos (λόγος), of which our reason is a part. It is God, the life and wisdom of all. It is truly within us. We can "follow the God within"; and by reason of it one can say, as Cleanthes did of Zeus: "We too are thy offspring." The popular gods are simply names for the forces that stream out from God.

Since one wisdom exists in all the world, there is one natural law, one rule of conduct for all men. All are morally free. Since all are from God, all men are brothers. Differences in station in life are accidental. To follow reason in the place in which one finds oneself is the highest duty, and is equally praiseworthy whether a man is an Emperor or a slave. So to obey reason, the Logos, is the sole object of pursuit. Happiness is no just aim, though duty done brings a certain happiness purely as a by-product. The chief enemies of a perfect obedience are passions and lusts, which pervert the judgment. These must resolutely be put aside. God inspires all good acts, though the notion of God is essentially pantheistic.

The strenuous ascetic attitude of Stoicism, its doctrine of the all-pervading and all-ruling divine wisdom, Logos (λόγος), its insistence that all who do well are equally deserving, whatever their station, and its assertion of the essential brotherhood of all men, were profoundly to affect Christian theology. In its highest representatives the creed and its results were noble. It was, however, too often hard, narrow, and unsympathetic. It was for the few. It recognized that the many could never reach its standards. Its spirit was too often one of pride. That of Christianity is one of humility. Still it produced remarkable effects. Stoicism gave Rome excellent Emperors and many lesser officials. Though it never became a really popular creed, it was followed by many of high influence and position in the Roman world, and modified Roman law for the better. It introduced into jurisprudence the conception of a law of nature, expressed in reason, and above all arbitrary human statutes. By its doctrine that all men are by nature equal, the worst features of slavery were gradually ameliorated, and Roman citizenship widely extended.

The ancient systems of philosophy underwent some notable changes in the period which saw the advent of Christianity. A syncretic spirit was abroad, and the various schools influenced each other. The original rigorous ethic of the Stoa, for instance, was modified by the Aristotelian mean, and the celebrated Stoic philosopher Poseidonius (B. C. 135–51), betrays influences of Platonism. His, indeed, was one of the most universal minds of antiquity. To rational and mystical interests he added those of the historian and geographer. Again, in Plutarch (see below) the eclectic character of Middle Platonism is very clear. Stoic, Aristotelian and Pythagorean themes are blended with Plato. This syncretic quality of Hellenistic thought becomes evident in many of the Church Fathers.

One may say that the best educated thought in Rome and the provinces, by the time of Christ, in spite of wide-spread Epicureanism and Scepticism, inclined to pantheistic Monotheism, to the conception of God as good, in contrast to the non-moral character of the old Greek and Roman deities, to belief in a ruling divine providence, to the thought that true religion is not ceremonies but an imitation of the moral qualities of God, and toward a humaner attitude to men. The two elements lacking in this educated philosophy were those of certainty such as could only be given by belief in a divine revelation, and of that loyalty to a person which Christianity was to emphasize.

The common people, however, shared in few of these benefits. They lay in gross superstition. If the grip of the old religions of Greece and Rome had largely relaxed, they nevertheless believed in gods many and lords many. Every town had its patron god or goddess, every trade, the farm, the spring, the household, the chief events of life, marriage, childbirth. These views, too, were ultimately to appear in Christian history transmuted into saint-worship. Soothsayers and magicians drove a thriving trade among the ignorant, and none were more patronized than those of Jewish race. Above all, the common people were convinced that the maintenance of the historic religious cult of the ancient gods was necessary for the safety and perpetuity of the state. If not observed, the gods wreaked vengeance in calamities—an opinion that was the source of much later persecution of Christianity. These popular ideas were not vigorously opposed by the learned, who largely held that the old religions had a police value. They regarded the state ceremonies as a necessity for the common man. Seneca put the philosophical opinion bluntly when he declared that "the wise man will observe all religious usages as commanded by the law, not as pleasing to the gods."

It was to the masses that the Cynic preachers of this period made their appeal. The moral corruption of the Empire provoked a revival of this ancient creed of independence and self-sufficiency, which had been championed by Diogenes of Sinope (B. C. 400?–325?). While many of these itinerant preachers were vulgar and even obscene, there were honorable ones, too, such as Dio Chrysostom (A. D. 40?–112?). He harangued against vice and lust, he idealized the rustic's life over against that of the rich townsman, and he proclaimed a message of world-harmony and true piety, based on a universal, innate idea of God. The wandering and ascetic life of the Cynic had, perhaps, some influence on the development of Christian monasticism.

The abler Emperors strove to strengthen and modify the ancient popular worships, for patriotic reasons, into worship of the state and of its head. This patriotic deification of the Roman state began, indeed, in the days of the republic. The worship of the "Dea Roma" may be found in Smyrna as early as B. C. 195. This reverence was strengthened by the popularity of the empire in the provinces as securing them better government than that of the republic. As early as B. C. 29, Pergamum had a temple to Rome and Augustus. This worship, directed to the ruler as the embodiment of the state, or rather to his "genius" or indwelling spirit, spread rapidly. It soon had an elaborate priesthood under state patronage, divided and organized by provinces, and celebrating not only worship but annual games on a large scale. It was probably the most highly developed organization of a professedly religious character under the early empire, and the degree to which it ultimately affected Christian institutions awaits further investigation. From a modern point of view there was much more of patriotism than of religion in this system. But early Christian feeling regarded this worship of the Emperor as utterly irreconcilable with allegiance to Christ. The feeling is shown in the description of Pergamum in *Revelation* 2:13. Christian refusal to render the worship seemed treasonable, and was the great occasion of the martyrdoms.

Men need a religion deeper than philosophy or ceremonies. Philosophy satisfies only the exceptional man. Ceremonies avail for more, but not those whose thoughts are active, or whose sense of personal unworthiness is keen. Some attempt was made to revive the dying older popular paganism. The earlier Emperors were, many of them, extensive builders and patrons of temples. The most notable effort to effect a revival and purification of popular religion was that of Plutarch (A. D. 46?–120?), of Chæronea in Greece, which may serve as typical of others. He criticised the traditional mythology. All that implied cruel or morally unworthy actions on the part of the gods he rejected. There is one God. All the popular gods are His attributes personified, or subordinate spirits. Plutarch had faith in oracles, special providences, and future retribution. He taught a strenuous morality. His attempt to wake up what was best in the dying older paganism was a hopeless task and won few followers.

The great majority of those who felt religious longings simply adopted Oriental religions, especially those of a redemptive nature in which mysticism or sacramentalism were prominent features. Ease of communication, and especially the great influx of Oriental slaves into the western portion of the Roman world during the later republic, facilitated this process. The spread of these faiths independent of, and to a certain extent as rivals of, Christianity during the first three centuries of our era made that epoch one of deepening religious feeling throughout the empire, and, in that sense, undoubtedly facilitated the ultimate triumph of Christianity.

One such Oriental religion, of considerably extended appeal, though with little of the element of mystery, was Judaism, of which there will be occasion to speak more fully in another connection. The popular mind turned more largely to other Oriental cults, of greater mystery, or rather of larger redemptive sacramental significance. Their meaning for the religious development of the Roman world has increasingly been brought home to us. The most popular of these Oriental religions were those of the Great Mother (Cybele) and Attis, originating in Asia Minor; of Isis and Serapis from Egypt; and of Mithras from Persia. At the same time there was much syncretistic mixture of these religions, one with another, and with the older religions of the lands to which they came. That of the Great Mother, which was essentially a primitive nature worship, accompanied by licentious rites, reached Rome in B. C. 204, and was the first to gain extensive foothold in the West. That of Isis and Serapis, with its emphasis on regeneration and a future life, was well established in Rome by B. C. 80, but had long to endure governmental opposition. That of Mithras, the noblest of all, though having an extended history in the East, did not become conspicuous at Rome till toward the year A. D. 100, and its great spread was in the latter part of the second and during the third centuries. It was especially beloved of soldiers. In the later years, at least of its progress in the Roman Empire, Mithras was identified with the sun—the *Sol Invictus* of the Emperors just before Constantine. Like other religions of Persian origin, its view of the universe was dualistic.

All these religions taught a redeemer-god, and had their origin in nature cults. Under varied mythologies, generally of a dying and rising god, the natural cycle of birth and decay was celebrated and applied to the rebirth of the soul so that it could overcome death. All these cults held that the initiate shared in symbolic (sacramental) fashion the experiences of the god, died with him, rose with him, became partakers of the divine nature, usually through a meal shared symbolically with him, and participated in his immortality. All had secret rites for the initiated. All offered mystical (sacramental) cleansing from sin. In the religion of Isis and Serapis that cleansing was by bathing in sacred water; in those of the Great Mother and of Mithras by the blood of a bull, the *taurobolium,* by which, as recorded in inscriptions, the initiate was "reborn forever." All promised a happy future life for the faithful. All were more or less ascetic in their attitude toward the world. Some, like Mithraism, taught the brotherhood and essential equality of all disciples. There can be no doubt that the development of the early Christian doctrine of the sacraments was affected, if not directly by these religions, at least by the religious atmosphere which they helped to create and to which they were congenial.

In summing up the situation in the heathen world at the coming of Christ, one must say that, amid great confusion, and in a multitude of forms of expression, some of them very unworthy, certain religious demands are evident. A religion that should meet the requirements of the age must teach one righteous God, yet find place for numerous spirits, good and bad. It must possess a definite revelation of the will of God, as in Judaism, that is an authoritative scripture. It must inculcate a world-denying virtue, based on moral actions agreeable to the will and character of God. It must hold forth a future life with rewards and punishments. It must have a symbolic initiation and promise a real forgiveness of sins. It must possess a redeemer-god into union with whom men could come by certain sacramental acts. It must teach the brotherhood of all men, at least of all adherents of the religion. However simple the beginnings of Christianity may have been, Christianity must possess, or take on, all these traits if it was to conquer the Roman Empire or to become a world religion. It came "in the fulness of time" in a much larger sense than was formerly thought; and no one who believes in an overruling providence of God will deny the fundamental importance of this mighty preparation, even if some of the features of Christianity's early development bear the stamp and limitations of the time and have to be separated from the eternal.

The Jewish Background

THE EXTERNAL COURSE of events had largely determined the development of Judaism in the six centuries preceding the birth of Christ. Judæa had been under foreign political control since the conquest of Jerusalem by Nebuchadrezzar, B. C. 586. It had shared the fortunes of the old Assyrian Empire and of its successors, the Persian and that of Alexander. After the break-up of the latter it came under the control of the Ptolemies of Egypt and then of the Seleucid dynasty of Antioch. While thus politically dependent, its religious institutions were practically undisturbed after their restoration consequent upon the Persian conquest of Babylonia; and the hereditary priestly families were the real native aristocracy of the land. In their higher ranks they came to be marked by political interest and religious indifference. The high-priesthood in particular became a coveted office by reason of its pecuniary and political influence. With it was associated, certainly from the Greek period, a body of advisers and legal interpreters, the Sanhedrim, ultimately seventy-one in number. Thus administered, the temple and its priesthood came to represent the more formal aspect of the religious life of the Hebrews. On the other hand, the feeling that they were a holy people living under Yahwe's holy law, their sense of religious separatism, and the comparative cessation of prophecy, turned the nation to the study of the law, which was interpreted by an ever-increasing mass of tradition. As in Mohammedan lands to-day, the Jewish law was at once religious precept and civil statute. Its interpreters, the scribes, became more and more the real religious leaders of the people. Judaism grew to be, in ever-increasing measure, the religion of a sacred scripture and its mass of interpretative precedent. For a fuller understanding and administration of the law, and for prayer and worship, the synagogue developed wherever Judaism was represented. Its origin is uncertain, going back probably to the Exile. In its typical form it was a local congregation including all Jews of the district presided over by a group of "elders," having often a "ruler" at its head. These were empowered to excommunicate and punish offenders. The services were very simple and could be led by any Hebrew, though the arrangements were in the hands of "a ruler of the synagogue." They included prayer, the reading of the law and the prophets, their translation and sometimes an exposition (sermon), and the benediction. Because of the unrepresentative character of the priesthood, and the growing importance of the synagogues, the temple, though highly regarded, became less and less vital for the religious life of the people as the time of Christ is approached, and could be totally destroyed in A. D. 70, without any overthrow of the essential elements in Judaism.

Under the Seleucid Kings Hellenizing influences came strongly into Judæa, and divided the claimants for the high-priestly office. The forcible support of Hellenism by Antiochus IV, Epiphanes (B. C. 175–164), and its accompanying repression of Jewish worship and customs, led, in B. C. 167, to the great rebellion headed by the Maccabees, and ultimately to a period of Judæan independence which lasted till the conquest by the Romans in B. C. 63. This Hellenizing episode brought about a profound cleft in Jewish life. The Maccabean rulers secured for themselves the high-priestly office; but though the family had risen to leadership by opposition to Hellenism and by religious zeal, it gradually drifted toward Hellenism and purely political ambition. Under John Hyrcanus, the Maccabean ruler from B. C. 135 to 105, the distinction between the religious parties of later Judaism became marked. The aristocratic-political party, with which Hyrcanus and the leading priestly families allied themselves, came to be known as Sadducees —a title the meaning and antiquity of which is uncertain. It was essentially a worldly party without strong religious conviction. Many of the views that the Sadducees entertained were conservatively representative of the older Judaism. Thus, they held to the law without its traditional interpretation, and denied a resurrection or a personal immortality. On the other hand, they rejected the ancient notion of spirits, good or bad. Though politically influential, they were unpopular with the mass of the people, who opposed all foreign influences and stood firmly for the law as interpreted by the traditions. The most thoroughgoing representatives of this democratic-legalistic attitude were the Pharisees, a name which signifies the Separated, presenting what was undoubtedly a long previously existing attitude, though the designation appears shortly before the time of John Hyrcanus. With his reign the historic struggle of Pharisees and Sadducees begins.

As a whole, in spite of the fact that the Zealots, or men of action, sprang from them, the Pharisees were not a political party. Though they held the admiration of a majority of the people, they were never very numerous. The ordinary working Jew lacked the education in the minutiæ of the law or the leisure to become a Pharisee. Their attitude toward the mass of Judaism was contemptuous.[1] They represented, however, views which were widely entertained and were in many respects normal results of Jewish religious development since the Exile. Their prime emphasis was on the exact keeping of the law as interpreted by the traditions. They held strongly to the existence

[1] John 7:49.

of spirits, good and bad—a doctrine of angels and of Satan that had apparently received a powerful impulse from Persian ideas. They represented that growth of a belief in the resurrection of the body, and in future rewards and punishments which had seen a remarkable development during the two centuries preceding Christ's birth. They held, like the people generally, to the Messianic hope. The Pharisees, from many points of view, were deserving of no little respect. From the circle infused with these ideas some of Christ's disciples were to come. The most learned of the Apostles had been himself a Pharisee, and called himself such years after having become a Christian.[2] Their earnestness was praiseworthy. The great failure of Pharisaism was twofold. It looked upon religion as the keeping of an external law, by which a reward was earned. Such keeping could easily lead to obscuring an inward righteousness of spirit, and a warm personal relation to God. It also shut out from the divine promises those whose failures, sins, and imperfect keeping of the law made the attainment of the Pharisaic standard impossible. It disinherited the "lost sheep" of the house of Israel. As such it received the well-merited condemnation of Christ.

The Messianic hope, shared by the Pharisees and common people alike, was the outgrowth of strong national consciousness and faith in God. It was most vigorous in times of national oppression. Under the earlier Maccabees, when a God-fearing line had given independence to the people, it was little felt. The later Maccabees, however, deserted their family tradition. The Romans conquered the land in B. C. 63. Nor was the situation really improved from a strict Jewish standpoint, when a half-Jewish adventurer, Herod, the son of the Idumean Antipater, held a vassal kingship under Roman overlordship from B. C. 37 to B. C. 4. In spite of his undoubted services to the material prosperity of the land, and his magnificent rebuilding of the temple, he was looked upon as a tool of the Romans and a Hellenizer at heart. The Herodians were disliked by Sadducees and Pharisees alike. On Herod's death his kingdom was divided between three of his sons, Archelaus becoming "ethnarch" of Judæa, Samaria, and Idumea (B. C. 4–A. D. 6); Herod Antipas "tetrarch" of Galilee and Peræa (B. C. 4–A. D. 39); and Philip "tetrarch" of the prevailingly heathen region east and northeast of the Sea of Galilee. Archelaus aroused bitter enmity, was deposed by the Emperor Augustus, and was succeeded by a Roman procurator—the occupant of this post from A. D. 26 to 36 being Pontius Pilate.

With such hopelessly adverse political conditions, it seemed as if the Messianic hope could be realizable only by divine aid. By the time of Christ that hope involved the destruction of Roman authority by supernatural divine intervention through a Messiah; and the establishment of a kingdom of God in which a freed and all-powerful Judaism should flourish under

[2] *Acts* 23:6.

a righteous Messianic King of Davidic descent, into which the Jews scattered throughout the Roman Empire should be gathered, and by which a golden age would be begun. To the average Jew it probably meant little more than that, by divine intervention, the Romans would be driven out and the kingdom restored to Israel. A wide-spread belief, based on *Malachi* 3:1, held that the coming of the Messiah would be heralded by a forerunner.

These hopes were nourished by a body of apocalyptic literature, pessimistic as to the present, but painting in brilliant color the age to come. The writings were often ascribed to ancient worthies. Such in the Old Testament canon is the prophecy of *Daniel,* such without are the *Book of Enoch,* the *Assumption of Moses,* and a number of others. A specimen of this class of literature from a Christian point of view, but with much use of Jewish conceptions, is *Revelation* in the New Testament. These nourished a forward-looking, hopeful religious attitude that must have served in a measure to offset the strict legalism of the Pharisaic interpretation of the law.

Other currents of religious life were moving also in Palestine, the extent of which it is impossible to estimate, but the reality of which is evident. In the country districts especially, away from the centers of official Judaism, there was a real mystical piety. It was that of the later Psalms and of the "poor in spirit" of the New Testament, and the "Magnificat" and "Benedictus" [3] may well be expressions of it. To this mystic type belong also the so-called *Odes of Solomon.* From this simpler piety, in a larger and less mystical sense, came prophetic appeals for repentance, of which those of John the Baptist are best known.

The discovery of the Dead Sea Scrolls has cast a flood of light on this piety and on the existence of a body of Judaism to be distinguished from the Sadducees and Pharisees. The library and the monastic ruins of the community of Qumran, on the northwest shore of the Dead Sea, have revealed the location of a Brotherhood, associated in some way with the Essenes of whom Philo, Josephus and Pliny the Elder wrote in the first century of our era. It is probable that many such communities existed, living a semimonastic life (sometimes, as with the Essenes proper, disavowing marriage, sometimes, as at Qumran, permitting it) in protest against the official Judaism of Jerusalem. These "Puritans" or "Covenanters" (as they might be called) believed that they were the true Congregation of Israel, the faithful remnant. They esteemed the Law and interpreted it in their own way, claiming to be especially "enlightened" and to preserve its right meaning against current perversions. They venerated a "Teacher of Righteousness" (whose historical identification remains obscure) as its true expositor. They observed periodic lustrations, an annual rite of entering and renewing the Covenant, and a sacred meal of bread and wine. Furthermore, they

[3] *Luke* 1:46–55; 68–79.

exercised a strict discipline when the community's rules (preserved in the *Manual of Discipline*) were infringed. Their noble, though somewhat legalistic, piety is evident in this document, while its more mystical side is to be seen in their *Psalms of Thanksgiving*, which have survived. Their organization included various officers, "overseer," "priests of Zadok," "the twelve perfect men" or "elders," "judges" and others. Finally, they looked fervently toward the redemption of Israel. They believed a new Prophet, a new Teacher, a High Priest and a King (some four messianic figures) would arise to gather the scattered hosts of Israel together, to defeat her enemies and inaugurate the age of the Kingdom.

The influence of these groups upon John the Baptist and primitive Christianity has been much debated. It is, however, clear that there are many points of contact; and while the New Testament is curiously silent about this sectarian stream in first-century Judaism, Christianity derived no little from it. It is not impossible that John the Baptist and some early disciples of Jesus had once belonged to such communities.

One further conception of later Judaism is of importance by reason of its influence on the development of Christian theology. It is that of "wisdom," which is practically personified as existing side by side with God, one with Him, His "possession" before the foundation of the world, His agent in its creation.[4] It is possible that the influence of the Stoic thought of the all-pervading divine Logos ($\lambda \acute{o} \gamma o \varsigma$) is here to be seen; but a more ethical note sounds than in the corresponding Greek teaching. Yet the two views were easy of assimilation.

Palestine is naturally first in thought in a consideration of Judaism. It was its home, and the scene of the beginnings of Christianity. Nevertheless the importance of the dispersion of the Jews outside of Palestine, both for the religious life of the Roman Empire as a whole, and for the reflex effect upon Judaism itself of the consequent contact with Hellenic thought, was great. This dispersion had begun with the conquests of the Assyrian and Babylonian monarchs, and had been furthered by many rulers, notably by the Ptolemies of Egypt, and the great Romans of the closing days of the republic and the dawning empire. Estimates are at best conjectural, but it is not improbable that at the birth of Christ there were five or six times as many Jews outside of Palestine as within its borders. They were a notable part of the population of Alexandria. They were strongly rooted in Syria and Asia Minor. They were to be found, if in relatively small numbers, in Rome. Few cities of the empire were without their presence. Clannish and viewed with little favor by the heathen population, they prospered in trade, were valued for their good qualities by the rulers, their religious scruples were generally respected, and, in turn, they displayed a missionary spirit which made their religious impress felt. As this Judaism of the dispersion presented

[4] *Prov.* 3:19; 8; *Psalms* 33:6.

itself to the surrounding heathen, it was a far simpler creed than Palestinian Pharisaism. It taught one God, who had revealed His will in sacred Scriptures, a strenuous morality, a future life with rewards and punishments, and a few relatively simple commands relating to the Sabbath, circumcision, and the use of meats. It carried with it everywhere the synagogue, with its unelaborate and non-ritualistic worship. It appealed powerfully to many heathens; and, besides full proselytes, the synagogues had about them a much larger penumbra of partially Judaized converts, the "devout men," who were to serve as a recruiting ground for much of the early Christian missionary propaganda.

In its turn, the Judaism of the dispersion was much influenced by Hellenism, especially by Greek philosophy, and nowhere more deeply than in Egypt. There, in Alexandria, the Old Testament was given to the reading world in Greek translation, the so-called Septuagint, as early as the reign of Ptolemy Philadelphus (B. C. 285–246). This made the Jewish Scriptures, heretofore locked up in an obscure tongue, widely accessible. In Alexandria, also, Old Testament religious ideas were combined with Greek philosophical conceptions, notably Platonic and Stoic, in a remarkable syncretism. The most influential of these Alexandrian interpreters was Philo (B. C. 20?–A. D. 42?). To Philo, the Old Testament is the wisest of books, a real divine revelation, and Moses the greatest of teachers; but by allegorical interpretation Philo finds the Old Testament in harmony with the best in Platonism and Stoicism. The belief that the Old Testament and Greek philosophy were in essential agreement was one of far-reaching significance for the development of Christian theology. This allegorical method of Biblical explanation was greatly to influence later Christian study of the Scriptures. To Philo, the one God made the world as an expression of His goodness to His creation; but between God and the world the uniting links are a group of divine powers, viewed partly as attributes of God and partly as personal existences. Of these the highest is the Logos (λόγος), which flows out of the being of God Himself, and is the agent not merely through whom God created the world, but from whom all other powers flow. Through the Logos God created the ideal man, of whom actual man is a poor copy, the work of lower spiritual powers as well as of the Logos. Even from his fallen state man may rise to connection with God through the Logos, the agent of divine revelation. Yet Philo's conception of the Logos is far more philosophical than that of "wisdom" in *Proverbs*, of which mention has been made; and the source of the New Testament Logos doctrine is to be found in the Hebrew conception of "wisdom" rather than in the thought of Philo. He was, however, a great illustration of the manner in which Hellenic and Hebrew ideas might be united, and were actually to be united, in the development of later Christian theology. In no other portion of the Roman world was the process which Philo represented so fully developed as in Alexandria.

3

Jesus and the Disciples

THE WAY was prepared for Jesus by John the Baptist, in the thought of the early Christians the "forerunner" of the Messiah. Ascetic in life, he preached in the region of the Jordan that the day of judgment upon Israel was at hand, that the Messiah was about to come; and despising all formalism in religion, and all dependence on Abrahamic descent, he proclaimed in the spirit of the ancient prophets their message: "repent, do justice." His directions to the various classes of his hearers were simple and utterly non-legalistic.[1] He baptized his disciples in token of the washing away of their sins (the act perhaps symbolising submission to the coming river of fire by which God would purge and redeem the world); and he taught them a special prayer. Jesus classed him as the last and among the greatest of the prophets. Though many of his followers became those of Jesus, some persisted independently and were to be found as late as Paul's ministry in Ephesus.[2]

The materials are lacking for any adequate biography of Jesus such as would be available in the case of one living in modern times. The Gospel record is primarily a witness to the divine event of Jesus, the Christ; and its details have doubtless been colored by the experiences and situations of the early Church. Scholars are sharply divided concerning the historical accuracy of many incidents narrated in the Gospels. Yet the character and teaching of Jesus stand forth from the Gospel pages in their essential outlines. He was brought up in Nazareth of Galilee, in the simple surroundings of a carpenter's home. The land, though despised by the more purely Jewish inhabitants of Judæa on account of a considerable admixture of races, was loyal to the Hebrew religion and traditions, the home of a hardy, self-respecting population, and particularly pervaded by the Messianic hope. Here Jesus grew to manhood through years of unrecorded experience, which, from His later ministry, must have been also of profound spiritual insight and "favor with God and man."

From this quiet life He was drawn by the preaching of John the Baptist. To him He went, and by him was baptized in the Jordan. In connection with this baptism there came to Him the conviction that He was appointed

[1] *Luke* 3:2–14; *Matt.* 3:1–12.   [2] *Acts* 19:1–4.

by God to fulfil a unique rôle in the rapidly approaching kingdom to be inaugurated by the heavenly figure of the Son of Man coming in the clouds of heaven. Whether Jesus actually viewed Himself as Messiah is a much contested question. In any case the story of the temptations suggests the rejection of Messiahship in terms of popular Jewish expectation, and the refusal of political and self-seeking methods. The kingdom is God's reign, initiated by *Him,* and not to be anticipated by the overthrow of Roman rule. It is a kingdom of the pure in heart who acknowledge their sinfulness, repent and accept the radical demand of love and the claims of their heavenly Father.

After His baptism Jesus began at once to preach the kingdom and to heal the afflicted in Galilee, and soon had great popular following. He gathered about Him a company of intimate associates—the Apostles—and a larger group of less closely attached disciples. How long His ministry continued is uncertain, from one to three years will cover its possible duration. Opposition was aroused as the spiritual nature of His message became evident and His hostility to the current Pharisaism was recognized. Many of His first followers fell away. He journeyed to the northward toward Tyre and Sidon, and then to the region of Cæsarea Philippi, where the Gospels record the recognition of His Messianic mission by His disciples. He felt, however, that at whatever peril He must bear witness in Jerusalem, and thither He went with heroic courage, in the face of growing hostility, there to be seized and crucified, certainly under Pontius Pilate (A. D. 26–36) and probably in the year 29. His disciples were scattered, but speedily gathered once more, with renewed courage, in the glad conviction that He still lived, having risen from the dead. Such, in barest outline, is the story of the most influential life ever lived.

The kingdom of God, in Jesus' teaching, involves the recognition of God's sovereignty and fatherhood. We are His children. Hence we should love Him and our neighbors.[3] All whom we can help are our neighbors.[4] We do not so love now. Hence we need to repent with sorrow for sin, and turn to God; and this attitude of sorrow and trust (repentance and faith) is followed by the divine forgiveness.[5] The ethical standard of the kingdom is the highest conceivable. "Be ye therefore perfect, even as your Father which is in heaven is perfect." [6] It involves the utmost strenuousness toward self,[7] and unlimited forgiveness toward others.[8] Forgiveness of others is a necessary condition of God's forgiving us.[9] There are two ways in life: one broad and easy, the other narrow and hard. A blessed future or destruction are the ends.[10] Jesus was, like His age, strongly eschatological in His outlook. Though He felt that the kingdom is begun now,[11] it is to be much more powerfully

[3] *Mark* 12:28–34.   [4] *Luke* 10:25–37.   [5] *Luke* 15:11–32.   [6] *Matt.* 5:48.
[7] *Mark* 9:43–50.   [8] *Matt.* 18:21, 22.   [9] *Mark* 11:25, 26.   [10] *Matt.* 7:13, 14.
[11] *Mark* 4:1–32; *Luke* 17:21.

manifested in the near future. The end of the present age seemed not far off.[12]

Most of these views and sayings can doubtless be paralleled in the religious thought of the age; but the total effect was revolutionary. "He taught them as one that had authority, and not as the scribes." [13] He could say that the least of His disciples is greater than John the Baptist; [14] and that heaven and earth should pass away before His words.[15] He called the heavy-laden to Him and offered them rest.[16] He promised to those who confessed Him before men that He would confess them before His Father.[17] He declared that none knew the Father but a Son, and he to whom the Son should reveal the Father.[18] He proclaimed Himself lord of the Sabbath,[19] than which, in popular estimate, there was no more sacred part of the God-given Jewish law. He affirmed that He had power to pronounce forgiveness of sins.[20] On the other hand, He felt His own humanity and its limitations no less clearly. He prayed, and taught His disciples to pray. He declared that He did not know the day or the hour of ending of the present world-age; that was known to the Father alone.[21] It was not His to determine who should sit on His right hand and His left in His exaltation.[22] He prayed that the Father's will, not His own, be done.[23] He cried in the agony of the cross: "My God, why hast Thou forsaken me?" [24] The mystery of His person is in these utterances. Its divinity is no less evident than its humanity. The *how* is beyond our experience, and therefore beyond our powers of comprehension; but the church has always busied itself with the problem, and has too often practically emphasized one side to the exclusion of the other.

Jesus substituted for the external, work-righteous, ceremonial religion of contemporary Judaism, the thought of piety as consisting in love to God and to one's neighbor—to a God who is a Father and a neighbor who is a brother—manifested primarily in an attitude of the heart and inward life, the fruit of which is external acts. The motive power of that life is personal allegiance to Himself as the revelation of the Father, the type of redeemed humanity.

What Jesus taught and was, gained immense significance from the conviction of His disciples that His death was not the end—from the resurrection faith. The *how* of this conviction is one of the most puzzling of historical problems. The fact of this conviction is unquestionable. It seems to have come first to Peter,[25] who was in that sense at least the "rock" Apostle on whom the church was founded. All the early disciples shared it. It was the turning-point in the conversion of Paul. It gave courage to the scattered disciples, brought them together again, and made them witnesses. Hence-

---

[12] *Matt.* 10:23, 19:28, 24:34; *Mark* 13:30.   [13] *Mark* 1:22.   [14] *Matt.* 11:11.
[15] *Mark* 13:31.   [16] *Matt.* 11:28.   [17] *Matt.* 10:32.   [18] *Matt.* 11:27; *Luke* 10:22.
[19] *Mark* 2:23–28.   [20] *Mark* 2:1–11.   [21] *Mark* 13:32.   [22] *Mark* 10:40.
[23] *Mark* 14:36.   [24] *Mark* 15:34.   [25] 1 *Cor.* 15:5.

forth they had a risen Lord, in the exaltation of glory, yet ever interested in them. The Messiah of Jewish hope, in a profounder spiritual reality than Judaism had ever imagined Him, had really lived, died, and risen again for their salvation.

These convictions were deepened by the experiences of the day of Pentecost. The exact nature of the pentecostal manifestation is, perhaps, impossible to recover. Certainly the conception of a proclamation of the Gospel in many foreign languages is inconsistent with what we know of speaking with tongues elsewhere [26] and with the criticism reported by the author of *Acts* that they were "full of new wine," [27] which Peter deemed worthy of a reply. But the point of significance is that these spiritual manifestations appeared the visible and audible evidence of the gift and power of Christ.[28] To these first Christians it was the triumphant inauguration of a relation to the living Lord, confidence in which controlled much of the thinking of the Apostolic Church. If the disciple visibly acknowledged his allegiance by faith, repentance, and baptism, the exalted Christ, it was believed, in turn no less evidently acknowledged the disciple by His gift of the Spirit. Pentecost was indeed a day of the Lord; and though hardly to be called the birthday of the church, for that had its beginnings in Jesus' association with the disciples, it marked an epoch in the proclamation of the Gospel, in the disciples' conviction of Christ's presence, and in the increase of adherents to the new faith.

4

The Palestinian Christian Communities

THE CHRISTIAN COMMUNITY in Jerusalem seems to have grown rapidly. It speedily included Jews who had lived in the dispersion as well as natives of Galilee and Judæa, and even some of the Hebrew priests. By the Christian body the name "church" was very early adopted. The word may originally have meant little more than "the meeting," to contrast the congregation of those who accepted Jesus as Messiah, from fellow Jews who did not. The term, however, bore overtones from its Old Testament usage. In the Septuagint translation it had been employed to indicate the

[26] See 1 *Cor.* 14:2–19.   [27] *Acts* 2:13.   [28] *Acts* 2:33.

whole people of Israel as a divinely called congregation. As such it was a fitting title for the true Israel, the real people of God, and such the early Christians felt themselves to be. The early Jerusalem company were faithful in attendance at the temple, and in obedience to the Jewish law, but, in addition, they had their own special services among themselves, with prayer, mutual exhortation, and "breaking of bread" daily in private houses.[1] This "breaking of bread" served a twofold purpose. It was a bond of fellowship and a means of support for the needy. The expectation of the speedy coming of the Lord made the company at Jerusalem a waiting congregation, in which the support of the less well-to-do was provided by the gifts of the better able, so that they "had all things common." [2] The act was much more than that, however. It was a continuation and a reminder of the Lord's Last Supper with His disciples before His crucifixion. It had, therefore, from the first, a sacramental significance.

Organization was very simple. The leadership of the Jerusalem congregation was at first that of Peter, and in a lesser degree of John. With them the whole apostolic company was associated in prominence, though whether they constituted so fully a governing board as tradition affirmed by the time that *Acts* was written may be doubted. Questions arising from the distribution of aid to the needy resulted in the appointment of a committee of seven.[3] This is often viewed as the origin of the diaconate; but it is more likely the beginning of a system of presbyters to care for the local needs of the churches. In any case we soon hear definitely of "presbyters" (or "elders") in the churches formed by Paul,[4] and there can be little doubt that this system of organization owed something both to the *Zekenim* of Judaism, who constituted a council to rule each local community, interpreting the law and dispensing charity, and to the "elders" of brotherhoods like Qumran.

The Jerusalem congregation was filled with the Messianic hope, it would seem at first in a cruder and less spiritual form than Jesus had taught.[5] It was devoted in its loyalty to the Christ, who would soon return, but "whom the heaven must receive until the times of restoration of all things." [6] Salvation it viewed as to be obtained by repentance, which included sorrow for the national sin of rejecting Jesus as the Messiah as well as for personal sins. This repentance and acknowledgment of loyalty was followed by baptism in the name of Christ, as a sign of cleansing and token by new relationship, and was sealed with the divine approval by the bestowment of spiritual gifts.[7] This preaching of Jesus as the true Messiah, and fear of a consequent disregard of the historic ritual, led to an attack by Pharisaic Hellenist Jews, which resulted in the death of tne first Christian martyr, Stephen, by stoning at the hands of a mob. The immediate consequence was a partial scattering of the Jerusalem congregation, so that the seeds of

[1] *Acts* 2:46.   [2] *Acts* 2:44.   [3] *Acts* 6:1–6.   [4] *Acts* 14:23.
[5] See *Acts* 1:6.   [6] *Acts* 3:21.   [7] *Acts* 2:37, 38.

Christianity were sown throughout Judæa, in Samaria, and even in as remote regions as Cæsarea, Damascus, Antioch, and the island of Cyprus. Of the original Apostles the only one who is certainly known to have exercised a considerable missionary activity was Peter, though tradition ascribes such labors to them all. John may have engaged, also, in such endeavor, though the later history of this Apostle is much in dispute.

The comparative peace which followed the martyrdom of Stephen was broken for the Jerusalem church by a much more severe persecution about A. D. 44, instigated by Herod Agrippa I, who from 41 to his death in 44, was vassal-king over the former territories of Herod the Great. Peter was imprisoned, but escaped death, and the Apostle James was beheaded. In connection with the scattering consequent upon this persecution is probably to be found whatever truth underlies the tradition that the Apostles left Jerusalem twelve years after the crucifixion. At all events, Peter seems to have been only occasionally there henceforth; and the leadership of the Jerusalem church fell to James, "the Lord's brother," who even earlier had become prominent in its affairs.[8] This position, which he held till his martyr's death about 63, has often been called a "bishopric," and undoubtedly it corresponded in many ways to the monarchical bishopric in the Gentile churches. There is no evidence, however, of the application to James of the term "bishop" in his lifetime. When the successions of religious leadership among Semitic peoples are remembered, especially the importance attached to relationship to the founder, it seems much more likely that there was here a rudimentary caliphate. This interpretation is rendered the more probable because James's successor in the leadership of the Jerusalem church, though not chosen till after the conquest of the city by Titus in 70, was Simeon, esteemed Jesus' kinsman.

Under the leadership of James the church in Jerusalem embraced two parties, both in agreement that the ancient law of Israel was binding on Christians of Jewish race, but differing as to whether it was similarly regulative for Christian converts from heathenism. One wing held it to be binding on all; the other, of which James was a representative, was willing to allow freedom from the law to Gentile Christians, though it viewed with disfavor such a mingling of Jews and Gentiles at a common table as Peter was disposed, for a time at least, to welcome.[9] The catastrophe which ended the Jewish rebellion in the year 70 was fateful, however, to all the Christian communities in Palestine, even though that of Jerusalem escaped the perils of the siege by flight to Pella. The yet greater overthrow of Jewish hopes under Hadrian, in the war of 132 to 135, left Palestinian Christianity a feeble remnant. Even before the first capture of the city, more influential *foci* of Christian influence were to be found in other portions of the empire. The Jerusalem church and its associated Palestinian communities were important

[8] *Gal.* 1:19, 2:9; *Acts* 21:18. [9] *Gal.* 2:12–16.

as the fountain from which Christianity first flowed forth, and as securing the preservation of many memorials of Jesus' life and words that would otherwise have been lost, rather than as influencing, by direct and permanent leadership, the development of Christianity as a whole.

5

Paul and Gentile Christianity

*A*S HAS ALREADY been mentioned, the persecution which brought about Stephen's martyrdom resulted in the planting of Christianity beyond the borders of Palestine. Missionaries, whose names have perished, preached Christ to fellow Jews. In Antioch a further extension of this propaganda took place. Antioch, the capital of Syria, was a city of the first rank, a remarkably cosmopolitan meeting-place of Greeks, Syrians, and Jews. There the new faith was preached to Greeks. The effect of this preaching was the spread of the Gospel among those of Gentile antecedents. By the populace they were nicknamed "Christians"—a title little used by the followers of Jesus themselves till well into the second century, though earlier prevalent among the heathen. Nor was Antioch the farthest goal of Christian effort. By 51 or 52, under Claudius, tumults among the Jews consequent upon Christian preaching by unknown missionaries attracted governmental attention in Rome itself. At this early period, however, Antioch was the center of development. The effect of this conversion of those whose antecedents had been heathen was inevitably to raise the question of the relation of these disciples to the Jewish law. Should that rule be imposed upon Gentiles, Christianity would be but a Jewish sect; should Gentiles be free from it, Christianity could become a universal religion, but at the cost of much Jewish sympathy. That this inevitable conflict was decided in favor of the larger doctrine was primarily the work of the Apostle Paul.

Paul, whose Hebrew name, Saul, was reminiscent of the hero of the tribe of Benjamin, of which he was a member, was born in the Cilician city of Tarsus, of Pharisaic parentage, but of a father possessed of Roman citizenship. Tarsus was eminent in the educational world, and at the time of Paul's birth was a seat of Stoic teaching. Brought up in a strict Jewish home, there is no reason to believe that Paul ever received a formal Hellenic education. He was never a Hellenizer in the sense of Philo of Alexandria. A wide-awake youth in such a city could not fail, however, to receive many Hellenic ideas, and to become familiar, in a measure at least, with the political and religious atmosphere of the larger world outside his orthodox Jewish home. Still, it was in the rabbinical tradition that he grew up, and it was as a future scribe that he went, at an age now unknown, to study under the famous Gamaliel the elder, in Jerusalem. How much, if anything, he knew of the ministry of Jesus other than by common report, it is impossible to determine. His devotion to the Pharisaic conception of a nation made holy by careful observance of the Jewish law was extreme, and his own conduct, as tried by that standard, was "blameless." Always a man of the keenest spiritual insight, however, he came, even while a Pharisee, to feel deep inward dissatisfaction with his own attainments in character. The law did not give a real inward righteousness. Such was his state of mind when brought into contact with Christianity. If Jesus was no true Messiah, He had justly suffered, and His disciples were justly objects of persecution. Could he be convinced that Jesus was the chosen of God, then He must be to him the first object of allegiance, and the law for opposition to the Pharisaic interpretation of which He died—and Paul recognized no other interpretation—must itself be abrogated by divine intervention.

Though the dates of Paul's history are conjectural, it may have been about the year 35 that the great change came—journeying to Damascus on an errand of persecution he beheld in vision the exalted Jesus, who called him to personal service. What may have been the nature of that experience can at best be merely conjectured; but of its reality to Paul and of its transforming power there can be no question. Henceforth he was convinced not only that Jesus was all that Christianity claimed Him to be, but he felt a personal devotion to his Master that involved nothing less than union of spirit. He could say: "I live, and yet no longer I, but Christ liveth in me." [1] The old legalism dropped away, and with it the value of the law. To Paul henceforth the new life was one of devoted service to the exalted Lord, who was also the indwelling Christ. With the risen Jesus he felt the closest intimacy. He now viewed man, God, sin and the world in a new light. To do Christ's will was his highest desire. All that Christ had won was his. "If any man is in Christ, he is a new creature: the old things are passed away; behold they are become new." [2]

With an ardent nature such as Paul's this transformation manifested itself at once in action. Of the story of the next few years little is known. He went at first into Arabia—a region in the designation of that age not necessarily far south of Damascus. He preached in that city. Three years after his conversion he made a flying visit to Jerusalem, where he sojourned with Peter and met James, "the Lord's brother." He worked in Syria and Cilicia for years, in danger, suffering, and bodily weakness.[3] Of the circum-

[1] *Gal.* 2:20.   [2] 2 *Cor.* 5:17.   [3] Some few incidents are enumerated in 2 *Cor.* 11 and 12.

stances of this ministry little is known. He can hardly have failed to preach to Gentiles; and, with the rise to importance of a mixed congregation at Antioch, he was naturally sought by Barnabas as one of judgment in the questions involved. Barnabas, who had been sent from Jerusalem, now brought Paul from Tarsus to Antioch, probably in the year 46 or 47. Antioch had become a great focal point of Christian activity; and from it in obedience, as the Antiochian congregation believed, to divine guidance, Paul and Barnabas set forth for a missionary journey that took them to Cyprus and thence to Perga, Antioch of Pisidia, Iconium, Lystra, and Derbe—the so-called first missionary journey described in *Acts* 13 and 14. Apparently the most fruitful evangelistic endeavor thus far in the history of the church, it resulted in the establishment of a group of congregations in southern Asia Minor, which Paul afterward addressed as those of Galatia, though many scholars would find the Galatian churches in more northern and central regions of Asia Minor, to which no visit of Paul is recorded.

The growth of the church in Antioch and the planting of mixed churches in Cyprus and Galatia now raised the question of Gentile relation to the law on a great scale. The congregation in Antioch was turmoiled by visitors from Jerusalem who asserted: "Except ye be circumcised after the custom of Moses ye cannot be saved." [4] Paul determined to make a test case. Taking with him Titus, an uncircumcised Gentile convert, as a concrete example of non-legalistic Christianity, he went with Barnabas to Jerusalem and met the leaders there privately. The result reached with James, Peter, and John was a cordial recognition of the genuineness of Paul's work among the Gentiles, and an agreement that the field should be divided, the Jerusalem leaders to continue the mission to Jews, of course with maintenance of the law, while Paul and Barnabas should go with their free message to the Gentiles.[5] It was a decision honorable to both sides; but it was impossible of full execution. What were to be the relations in a mixed church? Could law-keeping Jews and law-free Gentiles eat together? That further question was soon raised in connection with a visit of Peter to Antioch.[6] It led to a public discussion in the Jerusalem congregation, probably in the year 49—the so-called Council of Jerusalem—and the formulation of certain rules governing mixed eating.[7] To Paul, anything but the freest equality of Jew and Gentile seemed impossible. To Peter and Barnabas the question of terms of common eating seemed of prime importance. Paul withstood them both. He must fight the battle largely alone, for Antioch seems to have held with Jerusalem in this matter of intercourse at table.

Then followed the brief years of Paul's greatest missionary activity, and the period to which we owe all his epistles. Taking with him a Jerusalem Christian of Roman citizenship, Silas by name, he separated from Barnabas

[4] *Acts* 15:1.   [5] *Gal.* 2:1–10.   [6] *Gal.* 2:11–16.   [7] *Acts* 15:6–29.

by reason of disagreement regarding eating, and also by dissension regarding the conduct of Barnabas' cousin, Mark.[8] A journey through the region of Galatia brought him Timothy as an assistant. Unable to labor in western Asia Minor, Paul and his companions now entered Macedonia, founding churches in Philippi and Thessalonica, being coldly received in Athens, and spending eighteen months in successful work in Corinth (probably 51–53). Meanwhile the Judaizers had been undermining his apostolic authority in Galatia, and from Corinth he wrote to these churches his great epistle vindicating not merely his own ministry, but the freedom of Christianity from all obligation to the Jewish law. It was the charter of a universal Christianity. To the Thessalonians he also wrote, meeting their peculiar difficulties regarding persecution and the expected coming of Christ.

Taking Aquila and Priscilla, who had become his fellow laborers in Corinth, with him to Ephesus, Paul left them there and made a hurried visit to Jerusalem and Antioch. On his return to Ephesus, where Christianity had already been planted, he began a ministry there of three years' duration (53?–56?). Largely successful, it was also full of opposition and of such peril that Paul "despaired even of life" [9] and ultimately had to flee. The Apostles' burdens were but increased during this stay at Ephesus by moral delinquencies, party strife, and consequent rejection of his authority in Corinth. These led not merely to his significant letters to the *Corinthians,* but on departure from Ephesus, to a stay of three months in Corinth itself. His authority was restored. In this Corinthian sojourn he wrote the greatest of his epistles, that to the *Romans.*

Meanwhile Paul had never ceased to hope that the breach between him and his Gentile Christians and the rank and file of the Jerusalem church could be healed. As a thank-offering for what the Gentiles owed to the parent community, he had been collecting a contribution from his Gentile converts. This, in spite of obvious peril, he determined to take to Jerusalem. Of the reception of this gift and of the course of Paul's negotiations nothing is known; but the Apostle himself was speedily arrested in Jerusalem and sent a prisoner of the Roman Government to Cæsarea, doubtless as an inciter of rioting. Two years' imprisonment (57?–59?) led to no decisive result, since Paul exercised his right of appeal to the imperial tribunal at Rome, and were followed by his adventurous journey to the capital as a prisoner. At Rome he lived in custody, part of the time at least in his own hired lodging, for two years (60?–62?). Here he wrote to his beloved churches our *Colossians, Philippians,* and briefer letters to *Philemon* and to *Timothy* (the second epistle). Whether he was released from imprisonment and made further journeys is a problem which still divides the opinion of scholars, but the weight of such slight evidence as there is appears to be against it. There is no reason to doubt

[8] *Acts* 15:36–40.   [9] *2 Cor.* 1:8.

the tradition that he was beheaded on the Ostian way outside of Rome; but the year is uncertain. Tradition places his martyrdom in connection with the great Neronian persecution of 64. It was not conjoined in place with that savage attack, and may well have occurred a little earlier without being dissociated in later view from that event.

Paul's heroic battle for a universal, non-legalistic Christianity has been sufficiently indicated. His Christology will be considered in another connection.[10] Was he the founder or the remaker of Christian theology? He would himself earnestly have repudiated these imputations. Yet an interpretation by a trained mind was sure to present the simple faith of primitive Christianity in somewhat altered form. Though Paul wrought into Christian theology much that came from his own rabbinic learning and Hellenic experience, his profound Christian feeling led him into a deeper insight into the mind of Christ than was possessed by any other of the early disciples. Paul the theologian is often at variance with the picture of Christ presented by the Gospels. Paul the Christian is profoundly at one.

Paul's conception of freedom from the Jewish law was as far as possible from any antinomian undervaluation of morality. If the old law had passed away, the Christian is under "the law of the Spirit of life." He who has the Spirit dwelling in him will mind "the things of the Spirit," and will "mortify the deeds of the body." [11] Paul evidently devoted much of his training of converts to moral instruction. He has a distinct theory of the process of salvation. By nature men are children of the first Adam, and share his inheritance of sin; [12] by adoption (a Roman idea) we are children of God and partakers of the blessings of the second Adam, Christ.[13] These blessings have special connection with Christ's death and resurrection. To Paul, these two events stand forth as transactions of transcendent significance. His attitude is well expressed in *Gal.* 6:14: "Far be it from me to glory save in the cross of our Lord Jesus Christ"; and the reason for this glorying is twofold, that sin is thereby forgiven and redemption wrought,[14] and that it is the source and motive of the new life of faith and love.[15] This degree of emphasis on Christ's death was certainly new. To Paul the resurrection was no less important. It was the evidence that Jesus is the Son of God,[16] the promise of our own resurrection,[17] and the guarantee of men's renewed spiritual life.[18] Hence Paul preached "Jesus Christ and Him crucified," [19] or "Jesus and the resurrection." [20]

The power by which men become children of the second Adam is a free gift of God through Christ. It is wholly undeserved grace.[21] This God sends to whom He will, and withholds from whom He will.[22] The condition

[10] Pp. 33–34.   [11] Romans 8:2, 5, 13.   [12] Romans 5:12–19.
[13] Romans 8:15–17; I Cor. 15:45.   [14] Romans 3:24–26.   [15] Gal. 2:20.
[16] Romans 1:4.   [17] I Cor. 15:12–19.   [18] Romans 6:4–11.   [19] I Cor. 2:2.
[20] Acts 17:18.   [21] Romans 3:24.   [22] Romans 9:10–24.

of the reception of grace on man's part is faith.[23] "If thou shalt confess with thy mouth Jesus as Lord, and shalt believe in thy heart that God raised Him from the dead, thou shalt be saved." [24] This doctrine is of great importance, for it makes the essence of the Christian life not any mere belief about Christ, nor any purely forensic justification, as Protestants have often interpreted Paul, but a vital, personal relationship. The designation of Jesus as "Lord" was one, as Bousset has pointed out,[25] which had its rise in the Gentile churches of Syria, not impossibly in Antioch, and was the natural expression of those who had long been accustomed to employ it regarding their highest objects of veneration for their devotion to their new Master. To Paul, it is an epitome of his faith. Christ is the "Lord," himself the "slave." Nor is confidence in the resurrection less necessary, as the crowning proof of Christ's divine Sonship.[26]

The Christian life is one filled with the Spirit. All graces are from Him, all gifts and guidance. Man having the Spirit is a new creature. Living the life of the Spirit, he no longer lives that of the "flesh." But that all-transforming and indwelling Spirit is from Christ Himself. If Christ thus stands in such relation to the individual disciple that union with Him is necessary for all true Christian life, He is in no less vital association with the whole body of believers—the church. Paul uses the word church in two senses, as designating the local congregation, Philippi, Corinth, Rome, "the church that is in their house," and as indicating the whole body of believers, the true Israel. In the latter sense it is the body of Christ, of which each local congregation is a part.[27] From Christ come all officers and helpers, all spiritual gifts.[28] He is the source of the life of the church, and these gifts are evidence of His glorified lordship.[29]

Like the early disciples generally, Paul thought the coming of Christ and the end of the existing world-order near; though his views underwent some modification. In his earlier epistles he evidently believed it would happen in his lifetime.[30] As he came toward the close of his work he felt it likely that he would die before the Lord's coming.[31] Regarding the resurrection, Paul had the greatest confidence. Here, however, Hebrew and Greek ideas were at variance. The Hebrew conception was a living again of the flesh. The Greek, the immortality of the soul. Paul does not always make his position clear. *Romans* 8:11 looks like the Hebrew thought; but the great passage in 1 *Cor.* 15:35–54 points to the Greek. A judgment is for all,[32] and even among the saved there will be great differences.[33] The end of all things is the subjection of all, even Christ, to God the Father.[34]

---

[23] *Romans* 3:25–28.   [24] *Romans* 10:9.   [25] *Kyrios Christos,* Göttingen, 1913.
[26] *Romans* 1:4.   [27] *Eph.* 1:22, 23; *Col.* 1:18.   [28] *Eph.* 4:11; 1 *Cor.* 12:4–11.
[29] *Eph.* 4:7–10.   [30] 1 *Thess.* 4:13–18.   [31] *Philippians* 1:23, 24; 2 *Tim.* 4:6–8.
[32] 2 *Cor.* 5:10.   [33] 1 *Cor.* 3:10–15.   [34] 1 *Cor.* 15:20–28.

6

The Close of the Apostolic Age

THE HISTORY and fate of most of the Apostles is unknown. Though Peter cannot have been in Rome while Paul was writing his epistles thence, the cumulative force of such intimations as have survived make the conclusion probable that he was in Rome for a short time at least, and that his stay ended in martyrdom by crucifixion in the Neronian persecutions.[1] Such a stay, and especially such a death, would link him permanently with the Roman Church. On the other hand, a residence of John in Ephesus is much less assured.

The persecution under Nero was as fierce as it was local. A great fire in Rome, in July, 64, was followed by charges unjustly involving the Christians, probably at Nero's instigation, to turn popular rumor from himself. Numbers suffered death by horrible torture in the Vatican gardens, where Nero made their martyrdom a spectacle.[2] Thenceforth he lived in Christian tradition as a type of antichrist; but the Roman Church survived in strength. The destruction of Jerusalem at the close of the Jewish rebellion, in 70, was an event of more permanent significance. It almost ended the already waning influence of the Palestinian congregations in the larger concerns of the church. This collapse and the rapid influx of converts from heathen antecedents soon made Paul's battle for freedom from law no longer a living question. Antioch, Rome, and before the end of the century, Ephesus, were now the chief centers of Christian development. The converts were mostly from the lower social classes,[3] though some of better position, notably women, were to be found among them. Such were Lydia of Philippi,[4] and, in much higher station, probably the consul, Flavius Clemens, and his wife, Flavia Domitilla, who suffered the one death and the other sentence of banishment in Rome under Domitian, in 95. To Domitilla, the Roman Church owed one of its oldest catacombs. Of this persecution under Domitian (81–96) few details are known, but it must have been of severity in Rome and in Asia Minor.[5]

Yet though some gleanings can be recovered from this period, the forty

---

[1] I *Peter* 5:13; *John* 21:18, 19; I *Clement*, 5:6; Ignatius, *Romans*, 4:3; Irenæus, *Against Heresies*, 3.1.1; Caius of Rome in Eusebius, *Church History*, 2.25.5–7.
[2] Tacitus, *Annals* 15:44; Ayer, *A Source Book for Ancient Church History*, p. 6.
[3] I *Cor.* 1:26–28.   [4] *Acts* 16:14.   [5] I *Clement*, I; *Rev.* 2:10, 13; 7:13, 14.

years from 70 to 110 remain one of the obscurest portions of church history. This is the more to be regretted because they were an epoch of rapid change in the church itself. When the characteristics of the church can once more be clearly traced its general conception of Christianity shows surprisingly little of the distinctive stamp of Paul. Not only must many now unknown missionaries have labored in addition to the great Apostle, but an inrush of ideas from other than Christian sources, brought undoubtedly by converts of heathen antecedents, modified Christian beliefs and practices, especially regarding the sacraments, fastings, and the rise of liturgical forms. The old conviction of the immediacy of the guidance of the Spirit faded, without becoming wholly extinguished. The constitution of the church itself underwent, in this period, a far-reaching development, of which some account will be given (pp. 39ff.).

An illustration of this non-Pauline Christianity, though without evidence of the infiltration of heathen ideas, is to be seen in the Epistle of James. Written late in the first century or early in the second, it is singularly poor in theological content. Its directions are largely ethical. Christianity, in the conception of the writer, is a body of right principles duly practised. Faith is not, as with Paul, a new, vital, personal relationship. It is intellectual conviction which must be supplemented by appropriate action. It is a new and simple moral law.[6]

To this obscure period is due the composition of the Gospels. No subject in church history is more difficult. It would appear, however, that at an early period, not now definitely to be fixed, a collection of the sayings of Christ was in circulation. Probably not far from 75–80, and according to early and credible tradition at Rome, *Mark's* Gospel came into existence. Its arrangement was not purely historic, the selection of the materials being determined evidently by the importance attached to the doctrines and ecclesiastical usages which they illustrated. With large use of the collection of sayings and of *Mark, Matthew* and *Luke's* Gospels came into being, probably between 80 and 95; the former probably having Syria as its place of writing, and the latter coming, there is some reason to believe, from Rome or Antioch. The Johannine Gospel is distinctly individual, and may not unfairly be ascribed to Ephesus, and to the period 95–110. Other gospels were in circulation, of which fragments survive, but none which compare in value with the four which the church came to regard as canonical. There seems to have been little of recollections of Jesus extant at the close of the first century which was not gathered into the familiar Gospels. That this was the case may be ascribed to the great Jewish war and the decline of the Palestinian Hebrew congregations. To the Gospels the church owes the priceless heritage of its knowledge of the life of its Master, and a perpetual corrective to the one-sidedness of an interpretation, which, like even the great message of Paul, pays little attention to His earthly ministry.

[6] *James* 1:25; 2:14–26.

7

The Interpretation of Jesus

*A*N INEVITABLE QUESTION of the highest importance which arose with the proclamation of Chistianity, and must always demand consideration in every age of the church, is: What is to be thought of the Founder? The earliest Christology, as has been pointed out, was Messianic. Jesus was the Messiah of Jewish hope, only in a vastly more spiritual sense than that hope commonly implied. He had gone, but only for a brief time.[1] He was now in exaltation, yet what must be thought of His earthly life, that had so little of "glory" in it, as men use that term? That life of humiliation, ending in a slave's death, was but the fulfilment of prophecy. God had foreshadowed the things that "His Christ should suffer."[2] Early Jewish Christian thought recurred to the suffering servant of Isaiah, who was "wounded for our transgressions."[3] Christ is the "servant" or "child" ($\pi\alpha\hat{\imath}\varsigma$ $\Theta\epsilon o\hat{\upsilon}$), in the early Petrine addresses.[4] The glorification was at the resurrection. He is now "by the right hand of God exalted."[5] This primitive conception of the suffering servant exalted, persisted. It is that, in spite of a good deal of Pauline admixture, of the epistle known as 1 *Peter* (3:18–22). Clement, writing from Rome to the Corinthians, 93–97, also shares it.[6] It does not necessarily imply pre-existence. It does not make clear the relationship of Christ to God. It had not thought that problem out.

An obvious distinction soon was apparent. The disciples had known Christ in His life on earth. They now knew Him by His gifts in His exaltation. They had known Him after the flesh; they now knew Him after the spirit,[7] that is, as the Jesus of history and the Christ of faith. To superficial consideration at least, these two aspects were not easy of adjustment. The Jesus of history lived in a definite land, under human conditions of space and time. The Christ of faith is Lord of all His servants, is manifested as the Spirit at the same moment in places the most diverse, is omnipresent and omniscient. Paul regards it as a mark of Christianity that men call upon Him everywhere.[8] He prays to Him himself.[9] In his most solemn asseveration that his apostleship is not of any human origin, Paul classes God and Christ to-

[1] *Acts* 3:21.   [2] *Acts* 3:18.   [3] *Isaiah* 53:5.   [4] *Acts* 3:13, 26; 4:27, 30.
[5] *Acts* 2:32, 33; 4:10, 12.   [6] 1 *Clem.*, 16.   [7] *Romans* 1:3, 4.   [8] 1 *Cor.* 1:2.
[9] 2 *Cor.* 12:8, 9.

gether as its source.[10] These attributes and powers of the Christ of faith are very like divine, it is evident; and they inevitably raised the question of Christ's relation to the Father as it had not been raised thus far, and in a mind of far subtler powers and greater training and education than that of any of the earlier disciples, that of Paul.

Paul knew Hebrew theology well, with its conception of the divine "wisdom" as present with God before the foundation of the world.[11] He also knew something of Stoicism, with its doctrine of the universal, omnipresent, fashioning divine intelligence, the Logos, that in many ways resembled the Hebrew wisdom. He knew the Isaian conception of the suffering servant. To Paul, therefore, the identification of the exalted Christ with the divine wisdom—Logos—was not only easy, but natural; and that wisdom—Logos—must be pre-existent and always with God. He is "the Spirit of God," [12] the "wisdom of God." [13] "In Him dwelleth all the fulness of the Godhead bodily." [14] Even more, as in the Stoic conception of the Logos, He is the divine agent in creation; "all things have been created through Him and unto Him." [15] Though Paul probably never in set terms called Christ God,[16] he taught Christ's unity in character with God. He "knew no sin"; [17] He is the full manifestation of the love of God, which is greater than any human love, and the motive spring of the Christian life in us.[18] It is plain, therefore, that though Paul often calls Christ man, he gives Him an absolutely unique position, and classes Him with God.

If the Christ of faith was thus pre-existent and post-existent in glory for Paul, how explain the Jesus of history? He was the suffering servant.[19] His humble obedience was followed, as in the earlier Petrine conception, by the great reward. "Wherefore also God highly exalted Him and gave unto Him the name which is above every name . . . that every tongue should confess that Jesus Christ is Lord." Paul looks upon the whole earthly life of Jesus as one of humiliation. It was indeed significant. "God was in Christ reconciling the world unto Himself." [20] Yet it was only "by the resurrection" that He was "declared to be the Son of God with power." [21] Paul's Christology combines, therefore, in a remarkable manner, Hebrew and Gentile conceptions. In it appear the suffering and exalted servant, the pre-existent divine wisdom, the divine agent in creation, and the redeemer power who for man's sake came down from heaven, died, and rose again.

Within half a generation of Paul's death, however, a differing interpretation appeared, probably representing an independent line of thought. It was that of the Gospel of Mark. The writer knew nothing of Paul's view of

[10] *Gal.* 1:1.   [11] *Prov.* 8:22, 23.   [12] I *Cor.* 2:10, 11.   [13] *Ibid.*, 1:24.
[14] *Col.* 2:9.   [15] *Col.* 1:16.
[16] The translation, which implies that in *Romans* 9:5, is for various reasons to be rejected as Pauline.
[17] 2 *Cor.* 5:21.   [18] *Romans* 8:39, 5:7, 8; *Gal.* 2:20.   [19] *Philippians* 2:6–11.
[20] 2 *Cor.* 5:19.   [21] *Romans* 1:4.

Christ's pre-existence. In his thought, Christ was from His baptism the Son of God by adoption.[22] That He was the Son of God thenceforth, in all His earthly lot, is the evangelist's endeavor to show. There was humiliation, indeed, but there was a glory also in His earthly life, of which Paul gives no hint. He had not to wait for the demonstration of the resurrection. The voice from heaven declared Him the Son of baptism. The man with an unclean spirit saluted Him at His first preaching as "the Holy One of God" (1:24). The spirits of those possessed cried, "Thou art the Son of God" (3:12). He was transfigured before Peter, James, and John, while a heavenly voice proclaims: "This is my beloved Son" (9:2–8). The evangelist can only explain the lack of universal recognition in Christ's lifetime on earth by the declaration that He charged spirits and disciples not to make Him known (e. g., 1:34, 3:12, 5:43, 9:9). It is evident that this is a very different interpretation from that of Paul.

Mark's view was evidently unsatisfactory to his own age. It had no real theory of the incarnation. It does not trace back the sonship far enough. If that sonship was manifested in a portion of Christ's life, why not in all His life? That impressed the writers of the next two Gospels, *Matthew* and *Luke*. Like *Mark*, they have no trace of Paul's doctrine of pre-existence— their authors did not move in Paul's theological or philosophical realm. But they make the manifestation of Christ's divine sonship date from the very inception of His earthly existence. He was of supernatural birth. Like Mark, both regard His life as other than one of humiliation only.

Yet for minds steeped in the thoughts of Paul even these could not be satisfying interpretations. A fourth Gospel appeared about 95–110, probably in Ephesus, which sprang into favor, not only on account of its profoundly spiritual interpretation of the meaning of Christ, but because it combined in one harmonious presentation the divided elements of the Christologies which had thus far been current. In the Gospel which bears the name of John, the pre-existence and creative activity of Christ is as fully taught as by Paul. Christ is the Logos, the Word who "was with God, and the Word was God"; "All things were made by Him" (1:1, 3). There is no hint of virgin birth, as in *Matthew* and *Luke,* but a real, though unexplained, incarnation is taught: "The Word became flesh and dwelt among us" (1:14). The tendency of the earlier Gospels to behold glory, as well as humiliation, in Christ's earthly life is carried much further. That life is one primarily in which He "manifested His glory" (2:11, see 1:14). He declares to the woman of Samaria that He is the Messiah (4:26). He is regarded as "making Himself equal with God" (518). He remembers the glory of His pre-existence (17:5). He walks through life triumphantly conscious of His high divine mission. In the account of the Garden of Gethsemane no note appears of the pathetic prayer

[22] *Mark* 1:9–11.

that this cup pass from Him.[23] In the story of the crucifixion there is no anguished cry: "My God, why hast thou forsaken me"; [24] rather, as with a sense of a predetermined work accomplished, He dies with the words: "It is finished." [25] Beyond question this Christology was eminently satisfactory to the second century. It gave an explanation, natural to the age, of that lordship which Christian feeling universally ascribed to Christ. It united the most valued portions of the older Christologies. Though much dissent from it was to appear, it was formative of what was to triumph as orthodoxy.

In spite of this Johannine Christology, traces of more naïve and less philosophic interpretations survived. Such were those of the obscure relics of extreme Judaizing Christianity, known in the second century as Ebionites. To them, Jesus was the son of Joseph and Mary, who so completely fulfilled the Jewish law that God chose Him to be the Messiah. He improved and added to the law, and would come again to found a Messianic kingdom for the Jews. Such, in a very different way, was Hermas of Rome (115–140), who strove to combine Paul's doctrine of "the holy pre-existent Spirit which created the whole creation" [26] with that of the suffering and exalted servant. The "servant," pictured as a slave in the vineyard of God, is the "flesh in which the holy Spirit dwelt . . . walking honorably in holiness and purity, without in any way defiling the Spirit." [27] As a reward, God chose the "flesh," i. e., Jesus, "as a partner with the holy Spirit"; but this recompense is not peculiar to Him. He is but a forerunner, "for all flesh, which is found undefiled and unspotted, wherein the holy Spirit dwelt, shall receive a reward." [28] This is, of course, in a sense adoptionist. It was not easy for unphilosophic minds to combine in one harmonious picture the Jesus of history and the Christ of faith; and even in philosophic interpretations this contrast had much to do with the rise and wide spread of Gnosticism in the second century.

The significance of the Gospel according to John in the development of Christology has been noted; its influence in the interpretation of salvation was no less important. With it are to be associated the Johannine Epistles. This literature probably had its rise in a region, Ephesus, where Paul long worked. Its position is Pauline, but developed in the direction of a much intenser mysticism. This mysticism centers about the thoughts of life and union with Christ, both of which are Pauline, and yet treated in a way unlike that of Paul. Life is the great word of the Johannine literature. He who knows the Christ of faith has life. "This is life eternal, that they should know Thee, the only true God, and Him whom Thou didst send, even Jesus Christ." [29] For the writer, the world is divisible into two simple classes: "He that hath the Son hath the life, he that hath not the Son of God hath not the life." [30] By

---

[23] 18:1–11; compare *Mark* 14:32–42.   [24] *Mark* 15:34.   [25] *John* 19:30.
[26] *Sim.*, 5:6.   [27] *Ibid.*   [28] *Ibid.*
[29] *John* 17:3; see also 3:16, 36; 6:47, 10:27, 28, etc.   [30] I *John* 5:12; compare *John* 3:36.

life, the author does not mean simple existence. To him it is blessed, purified immortality. "Now are we children of God, and it is not yet made manifest what we shall be. We know that if He shall be manifested we shall be like Him." [31] This life is based on union with Christ, and this union is a real sacramental participation. One can but feel that there is here the influence of ideas similar to those of the mystery religions. Paul had valued the Lord's Supper. To him it was a "communion" of the body and blood of Christ, a "remembrance" of Christ, through which: "Ye proclaim the Lord's death till He come." [32] The Johannine literature goes further: "Except ye eat the flesh of the Son of Man and drink His blood ye have not life in yourselves." [33] The Lord's Supper is already a mystical sacrament necessary for that union with Christ which is to procure a blessed immortality.

The Johannine literature stands on a spiritual plane of utmost loftiness. It is instructive to see how some of these problems looked to a contemporary of the same general school, an equally earnest Christian, but of far less spiritual elevation. Such a man is Ignatius of Antioch. Condemned as a Christian in his home city, in the last years of Trajan, 110–117, he was sent a prisoner to Rome to be thrown to the wild beasts. Of his history little is known, but from his pen seven brief letters exist, six of them written to the churches of Ephesus, Magnesia, Tralles, Rome, Philadelphia, and Smyrna; and one a personal note to Polycarp, bishop of Smyrna. They are full of gratitude for kindnesses shown on his journey, of warnings against spiritual perils, and of exhortations to unity. Their significance for the history of Christian institutions will be considered later. Ignatius has the same lofty Christology as the Johannine literature. Christ's sacrifice is "the blood of God." [34] He greets the Romans in "Jesus Christ our God." Yet he did not identify Christ wholly with the Father. "He is truly of the race of David according to the flesh, but Son of God by the divine will and power." [35] As in the Johannine literature, Ignatius held union with Christ necessary for life: "Christ Jesus, apart from whom we have not true life" [36] and that life is ministered through the Lord's Supper. He says of it: "Breaking one bread which is the medicine of immortality and the antidote that we should not die but live forever in Jesus Christ." [37] Ignatius' most original thought was that the incarnation was the manifestation of God for the revelation of a new humanity. Before Christ the world was under the devil and death. Christ brought life and immortality.[38]

In the Johannine and the Ignatian writings alike, salvation was life, in the sense of the transformation of sinful mortality into blessed immortality. This thought had roots in Paul's teaching. Through the school of Syria and Asia Minor this became, in the Greek-speaking church, the conception of salvation. It was one that lays necessary emphasis on the person of Christ and the incarnation. The Latin conception, as will be seen, was that salvation con-

---

[31] I John 3:2.   [32] I Cor. 10:16, 11:24, 26.   [33] John 6:53.   [34] Eph. 1.
[35] Smyrn., 1.   [36] Tral., 9.   [37] Eph. 20.   [35] Eph. 19, 20.

sists in the establishment of right relations with God and the forgiveness of sins. This, too, had its Pauline antecedents. It necessarily lays prime weight on divine grace, the death of Christ, and the atonement. These conceptions are not mutually exclusive; but to these differences of emphasis is ultimately due much of the contrast in the later theological development of East and West.

8

Gentile Christianity of the Second Century

*B*Y THE YEAR 100 Christianity was strongly represented in Asia Minor, Syria, Macedonia, Greece, and Rome, and probably also in Egypt, though regarding its introduction into that land there is no certain knowledge. It had extended very slightly, if at all, to the more western portion of the empire. Asia Minor was more extensively Christianized than any other land. About 111–113 Pliny, the governor of Bithynia, could report to Trajan that it was affecting the older temple worship.[1] It was strongly missionary in spirit, and constantly extending. Common Christianity, however, was far from representing, or even understanding, the lofty theology of Paul or of the Johannine literature. It moved in a much simpler range of thought. Profoundly loyal to Christ, it conceived of Him primarily as the divine revealer of the knowledge of the true God, and the proclaimer of a "new law" of simple, lofty, and strenuous morality. This is the attitude of the so-called "Apostolic Fathers," with the exception of Ignatius, whose thought has already been discussed.

These Christian writers were thus named because it was long, though erroneously, believed that they were personal disciples of the Apostles. They include Clement of Rome (*c.* 93–97); Ignatius of Antioch (*c.* 110–117); Polycarp of Smyrna (*c.* 110–117); Hermas of Rome (*c.* 100–140); the author who wrote under the name of Barnabas, possibly in Alexandria (c. 131); and the anonymous sermon called *Second Clement* (*c.* 160–170). To this literature should be added the *Teaching of the Twelve Apostles* (*c.* 130–160, but presenting a survival of very primitive conditions). The anonymous *Epistle to*

[1] *Letters,* 10:96; Ayer, p. 20.

Diognetus, often included among the writings of the Apostolic Fathers, is probably later than their period.

Christians looked upon themselves as a separated people, a new race, the true Israel, whose citizenship was no longer in the Roman Empire, though they prayed for its welfare and that of its ruler, but in the heavenly Jerusalem.[2] They are the church "which was created before the sun and moon," "and for her sake the world was framed."[3] The conception of the church was not primarily that of the aggregate of Christians on earth, but of a heavenly citizenship reaching down to earth, and gathering into its own embrace the scattered Christian communities.[4] To this church the disciple is admitted by baptism. It is "builded upon waters."[5] That baptism implied antecedent belief in the truth of the Christian message, engagement to live the Christian life, and repentance.[6] Services were held on Sunday, and probably on other days.[7] These had consisted from the Apostles' time of two kinds: meetings for reading the Scriptures, preaching, song and prayer;[8] and a common evening meal with which the Lord's Supper was conjoined. By the time Justin Martyr wrote his *Apology* in Rome (153), the common meal had disappeared, and the Supper was joined with the assembly for preaching, as a concluding sacrament.[9] The Supper was the occasion for offerings for the needy.[10] The beginnings of liturgical forms are to be found before the close of the first century.[11]

Christian life was ascetic and legalistic. Wednesday and Friday were fasts, which were called "stations," as of soldiers of Christ on guard.[12] The Lord's Prayer was repeated thrice daily.[13] "Fasting is better than prayer, but almsgiving than both."[14] Second marriage was discouraged.[15] Simple repentance is not sufficient for forgiveness, there must be satisfaction.[16] A Christian can even do more than God demands—works of supererogation—and will receive a corresponding reward.[17] Great generosity was exercised toward the poor, widows, and orphans, some going so far as to sell themselves into slavery to supply the needy.[18] The rich were felt to be rewarded and helped by the prayers of the poor.[19] Wealthy congregations redeemed prisoners and sent relief to a distance, and in these works none was more eminent than that of Rome. On the other hand, though slaves were regarded as Christian brethren, their manumission was discouraged lest, lacking support, they fall into evil ways.[20] There is evidence, also, that the more well-to-do and higher stationed found the ideal of brotherhood difficult to maintain in practice.[21]

[2] 1 *Clem.,* 61; Hermas, *Sim.,* 1.   [3] Hermas, *Vis.,* 2:4; 2 *Clem.,* 14.   [4] *Teaching,* 9.
[5] Hermas, *Vis.,* 3:3.   [6] Justin, *Apology,* 61; Ayer, p. 33.   [7] Justin, *ibid.,* 67; Ayer, p. 35.
[8] Justin, *ibid.,* 67; see also Pliny, *Letters,* 10:96; Ayer, pp. 21, 35.
[9] 65, 67; Ayer, pp. 33–35.   [10] Justin, *ibid.,* 67.
[11] 1 *Clem.,* 59–61, see also *Teaching,* 9, 10; Ayer, pp. 38, 39.
[12] *Teaching,* 8; Hermas, *Sim.,* 5:1; Ayer, p. 38.   [13] *Teaching,* 8; Ayer, p. 38.
[14] 2 *Clem.,* 16.   [15] Hermas, *Mand.,* 4:4.   [16] *Ibid., Sim.,* 7.
[17] *Ibid., Sim.,* 5:2, 3; Ayer, p. 48.   [18] 1 *Clem.,* 55.   [19] Hermas, *Sim.,* 2.
[20] *Ignatius to Polycarp,* 4.   [21] Hermas, *Sim.,* 9:20.

For Christians of heathen antecedents it was difficult to deny the existence of the old gods. They were very real to them, but were looked upon as demons, hostile to Christianity.[22] The Christians of the second century explained the resemblance between their own rites and those of the mystery religions, of which they were aware, as a parody by demons.[23] Fear, thus, of demon influence was characteristic, and led to much use of exorcism in the name of Christ.[24] For all men there is to be a resurrection of the flesh, and a final judgment.[25]

9

Christian Organization

NO QUESTION in church history has been more darkened by controversy than that of the origin and development of church officers, and none is more difficult, owing to the scantiness of the evidence that has survived. It is probable that the development was diverse in different localities. Not all early Christian congregations had identical institutions at the same time. Yet a substantial similarity was reached by the middle of the second century. Something has already been said of the constitution of the Jewish Christian congregations.[1] The present discussion has to do with those on Gentile soil.

The earliest Gentile churches had no officers in the strict sense. Paul's letters to the Galatians, Corinthians, and Romans make no mention of local officers. Those to the Corinthians could hardly have avoided some allusion, had such officers existed. Their nearest approach [2] is only an exhortation to be in subjection to such as Stephanas, and does not imply that he held office. The allusion in 1 *Thess.* 5:12 to those that "are over you in the Lord" is, at best, very obscure. Paul's earlier epistles show that all ministries in the church, of whatever sort, were looked upon as the direct gift of the Spirit, who inspires each severally for the service of the congregation.[3] It is fair to conclude that these bearers of the gifts of the Spirit might be different at different times, and many in the church might equally become vehicles of the charismatic inspiration. Paul, however, specifies three classes of leaders as in particular the gift of the Spirit—Apostles, prophets, teachers.[4] He himself regarded his

---

[22] Justin, *Apology*, 5. [23] *Ibid.*, 62. [24] *Ibid.*, *Dialogue*, 85. [25] 2 *Clem.*, 9, 16.
[1] *Ante*, p. 23. [2] 1 *Cor.* 16:15, 16. [3] 1 *Cor.* 12:4–11, 28–30, 14:26–33.
[4] 1 *Cor.* 12:28.

Apostolate as charismatic.[5] If the Apostles' work was primarily that of found-ing Christian churches, those of the prophet and teacher were the proclama-tion or interpretation of the divinely inspired message. The exact shade of difference between prophet and teacher is impossible to discover. All, how-ever, were charismatic men. The worst of sins was to refuse to hear the Spirit speaking through them.[6] Yet Paul undoubtedly exercised a real missionary superintendence over the churches founded by him, and employed his younger assistants in the work.[7] It is difficult to distinguish this from ordinary super-vision such as any founder might employ.

It was inevitable, however, that such unlimited confidence as the earliest congregations possessed in charismatic gifts should be abused. The *Teaching of the Twelve Apostles* shows that self-seeking and fraudulent claimants to divine guidance were soon preying on the churches.[8] Tests had to be found to discriminate the true from the false. In the *Teaching,* and in *Hermas* [9] the touchstone is character. In 1 *John* 4:1–4 it is orthodoxy of teaching. The prophets long continued. They are to be found in Rome as late as the time of Hermas (100–140), to say nothing of the claims of those whom the church judged heretical, like Montanus and his followers even later. Such uncertain leadership could not, in the nature of things, continue unmodified. For his farewell message Paul called to Miletus the "elders" ($\pi\rho\epsilon\sigma\beta\acute{v}\tau\epsilon\rho o\iota$) of the church of Ephesus, exhorting them to "take heed unto yourselves and to all the flock in which the Holy Ghost hath made you bishops"—$\acute{\epsilon}\pi\acute{\iota}\sigma\kappa o\pi o\iota$ —overseers.[10] These are in a certain sense charismatic men. They have been made bishops by the Holy Spirit. But they are recipients of a charism which makes them a definite group having particular duties to the congregation. In one of his latest letters Paul speaks of the "bishops and deacons" of the church in Philippi (1:1). Even if this be held to mean the discharge of functions only —"those who oversee and those who serve"—the advance beyond the con-ditions of the Corinthian epistles is apparent. The gifts may be charismatic, but the recipients are beginning to be holders of a permanent official relation. Why these local officers developed is unknown; but the interests of good order and worship, and the example of the synagogue, are probable sugges-tions. Absence of prophets and teachers by whom worship could be conducted and the congregation led was certainly a cause in some places. The *Teaching of the Twelve Apostles* directs: "Appoint for yourselves, therefore, bishops and deacons worthy of the Lord, men who are meek and not lovers of money, and true and approved; for unto you they also perform the service of the prophets and teachers. Therefore despise them not; for they are your honora-ble men along with the prophets and teachers" (15). At Philippi, Ephesus, and in the *Teaching,* these "bishops" are spoken of in the plural. This is also

---

[5] *Gal.* 1:1, 11–16; 1 *Cor.* 14:18.   [6] *Teaching,* 11; Ayer, p. 40.
[7] *E. g.,* Timothy in 1 *Cor.* 4:17, 16:10.
[8] 11; Ayer, p. 40.   [9] *Mand.,* 11.   [10] *Acts* 20:17–29.

true of Rome and of Corinth when Clement of Rome wrote in 93–97.[11] Clement speaks, also, of those against whom the church in Corinth had rebelled as its "appointed presbyters" (54); and of "those who have offered the gifts of the bishop's office" as presbyters (44). Polycarp of Smyrna, writing to Philippi in 110–117, mentions only presbyters and deacons and their duties. Hermas (100–140) would seem to imply that as late as his time there was this collegiate office at Rome. It is "the elders (presbyters) that preside over the church." [12] He speaks only of the duties of "deacons" and "bishops." [13]

Ancient interpretation, such as that of Jerome, saw in these collegiate bishops and presbyters the same persons, the names being used interchangeably. That is the opinion of most modern scholars, and seems the probable conclusion. The view of the late Edwin Hatch, as developed by Harnack, holds, however, that presbyters were the older brethren in the congregation, from whom the collegiate bishops were taken. A bishop would be a presbyter, but a presbyter not necessarily a bishop. The subject is one of difficulty, the more so as the word "presbyter," like the English "elder" is used in early Christian literature both as a general designation of the aged, and as a technical expression. Its particular meaning is hard always to distinguish. It is evident, however, that till some time after the year 100, Rome, Greece, and Macedonia had at the head of each congregation a group of collegiate bishops, or presbyter-bishops, with a number of deacons as their helpers. These were chosen by the church,[14] or at least "with the consent of the whole church." [15]

Contemporary with the later portion of the literature just described, there is another body of writings which indicates the existence of a threefold ministry consisting of a single, monarchical bishop, presbyters, and deacons in each congregation of the region to which it applies. This would appear to be the intimations of 1 *Timothy* and *Titus,* though the treatment is obscure. Whatever Pauline elements these much disputed letters contain, their sections on church government betray a development very considerably beyond that of the other Pauline literature, and can scarcely be conceived as belonging to Paul's time. It is interesting to observe that the regions to which the letters are directed are Asia Minor and the adjacent island of Crete, the former being one of the territories in which the monarchical bishopric is earliest evident in other sources.

What is relatively obscure in these epistles is abundantly clear in those of Ignatius (110–117). Himself the monarchical bishop of Antioch,[16] he exalts in every way the authority of the local monarchical bishop in the churches of Ephesus, Magnesia, Tralles, Philadelphia, and Smyrna. In four of these churches he mentions the bishop by name. Only when writing to the Romans he speaks of no bishop, probably for the sufficient reason that

---

[11] 1 *Clem.,* 42, 44.   [12] *Vis.,* 2:4.   [13] *Sim.,* 9:26, 27.
[14] *Teaching,* 15; Ayer, p. 41.   [15] 1 *Chem.,* 44; Ayer, p. 37.   [16] *Romans* 2.

there was as yet no monarchical bishop at Rome. The great value to Ignatius of the monarchical bishop is as a rallying-point of unity, and as the best opponent of heresy. "Shun divisions as the beginning of evils. Do ye all follow your bishop, as Jesus Christ followed the Father, and the presbytery as the Apostles, and to the deacons pay respect." [17] The monarchical bishopric is not yet diocesan, it is the headship of the local church, or at most of the congregations of a single city; but Ignatius does not treat it as a new institution. He accepts it as established, though it evidently did not always command the obedience which he desired.[18] It is evident, however, that the monarchical bishopric must have come into being between the time when Paul summoned the presbyter-bishops to Miletus [19] and that at which Ignatius wrote.

How the monarchical bishopric arose is a matter of conjecture. Reasons that have been advanced by modern scholars are leadership in worship and the financial oversight of the congregation in the care of the poor and other obligations of charity. These are probable, the first-named perhaps the more probable. We may note, furthermore, the importance attached by the *Teaching* to the settling prophet, who is supported by the tithes of the congregation.[20] Leadership, in any case, by a committee of equals is unworkable for any protracted time, and small congregations were doubtless unable to provide for more than one full-time official. Naturally he became the undisputed leader of the church.

One further observation of great importance is to be made. Clement of Rome (93–97), writing when Rome had as yet no monarchical bishop, traces the existence of church officers to apostolic succession.[21] It is no impeachment of the firmness of his conviction, though it militates against the historic accuracy of his view, that he apparently bases it on a misunderstanding of Paul's statement in 1 *Cor.* 16:15, 16. On the other hand, Ignatius, though urging in the strongest terms the value of the monarchical episcopate as the bond of unity, knows nothing of an apostolical succession. It was the union of these two principles, a monarchical bishop in apostolical succession, which occurred before the middle of the second century, that immensely enhanced the dignity and power of the bishopric. By the sixth decade of the second century monarchical bishops had become well-nigh universal. The institution was to gain further strength in the Gnostic and Montanist struggles; but it may be doubted whether anything less rigid could have carried the church through the crises of the second century.

---

[17] *Smyrn.*, 8.
[18] See *Phila.*, 7, where Ignatius declares it is by charismatic inspiration, and not by knowledge of divisions, that he exhorted: "Do nothing without the bishop."
[19] *Acts* 20:17–25.   [20] *Teaching* 13.   [21] 1 *Cor.* 42, 44; Ayer, pp. 36, 37.

10

Relations of Christianity to the Roman Government

CHRISTIANITY was at first regarded by the Roman authorities as a branch of Judaism, which stood under legal protection.[1] The hostility of the Jews themselves must have made a distinction soon evident, and by the time of the Neronian persecution in Rome (64) it was plainly drawn. The Roman victims were not then charged, however, primarily with Christianity, but with arson—though their unpopularity with the multitude made them ready objects of suspicion. By the time that 1 *Peter* was written (*c.* 90), the mere fact of a Christian profession had become a cause for punishment (4:16). How much earlier "the name" had become a sufficient criminal charge it is impossible to say. Trajan's reply to Pliny, the governor of Bithynia (111–113), presupposes that Christianity was already viewed as criminal. That already recognized, the Emperor orders what must be deemed mild procedure from his point of view. Christians are not to be hunted out, and, if willing to abjure by sacrifice, are to be acquitted. Only in case of persistence are they to be punished.[2] From the standpoint of a faithful Christian profession this was a test which could only be met by martyrdom. Trajan's immediate successors, Hadrian (117–138) and Antoninus Pius (138–161), pursued the same general policy, though discouraging mob accusations. Marcus Aurelius (161–180) gave renewed force to the law against strange religions (176), and initiated a sharper period of persecution which extended into the beginning of the reign of Commodus (180–192). Commodus, however, treated Christianity, on the whole, with the toleration of indifference. Always illegal, and with extreme penalties hanging over it, the Christian profession involved constant peril for its adherents; yet the number of actual martyrs in this period appears to have been relatively small compared with those of the third and fourth centuries. No general persecution occurred before 250.

The charges brought against the Christians were atheism and anarchy.[3] Their rejection of the old gods seemed atheism; their refusal to join in emperor-worship appeared treasonable.[4] Popular credulity, made possible by the degree to which the Christians held aloof from ordinary civil society,

[1] *Acts* 18:14–16. [2] Pliny's *Letters* 10:97; Ayer, p. 22.
[3] Justin, *Apology*, 5, 6; 11, 12. [4] *Martyrdom of Polycarp*, 3, 8–10.

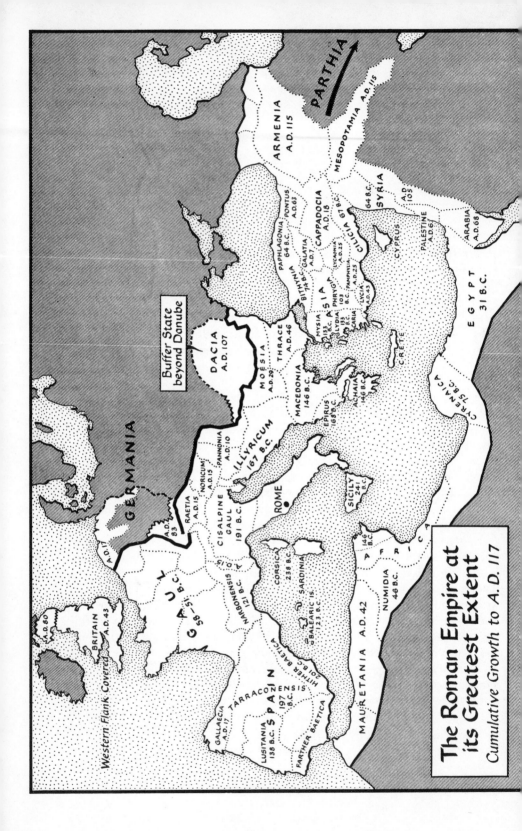

The Roman Empire at its Greatest Extent

Cumulative Growth to A.D. 117

charged them with crimes as revolting as they were preposterous. A misunderstanding of the Christian doctrine of Christ's presence in the Supper must be deemed the occasion of the common accusation of cannibalism; and its celebration secretly in the evening of that of gross licentiousness.[5] Much of the governmental persecution of Christianity in this period had its incitement in mob attacks upon Christians. That was the case at Smyrna when Polycarp suffered martyrdom in 156; while a boycott, on the basis of charges of immoral actions, was the immediate occasion of the fierce persecution in Lyons and Vienne in 177.[6] It is not surprising, therefore, that the majority of judicial proceedings against Christians in this period seem rather to have been under the general police power of magistrates to repress disturbance than by formal trial on the specific criminal charge of Christianity. Both procedures are to be found. To all these accusations the best answer of the Christians was their heroic constancy in loyalty to Christ, and their superior morality as judged by the standards of society about them.

11

The Apologists

THESE CHARGES against Christians, and the hostile attitude of the Roman government, aroused a number of literary defenders, who are known as the Apologists. Their appearance shows that Christianity was making some conquest of the more intellectual elements of society. Their appeal is distinctly to intelligence. Of these Apologists the first was Quadratus, probably of Athens, who about 125 presented a defense of Christianity, now preserved only in fragments, to the Emperor Hadrian. Aristides, an Athenian Christian philosopher, made a similar appeal, about 140, to Antoninus Pius. Justin wrote the most famous of these defenses, probably in Rome, about 153. His disciple, Tatian, who combined the four Gospels into his famous *Diatessaron,* also belonged to the Apologists. With them are to be reckoned Melito, bishop of Sardis, who wrote between 169 and 180; and Athenagoras, of whom little is known personally, whose defense, which survives, was made about the

[5] Justin, *Dialogue,* 10.   [6] Eusebius, *Church History,* 5:1.

year 177. Here also belongs the *Epistle to Diognetus,* often reckoned among the writings of the Apostolic Fathers.

There is no evidence that any of these Apologists greatly influenced heathen opinion, or that their appeal was seriously considered by the rulers whom it was their desire to persuade. Their work was deservedly valued in Christian circles, however, and undoubtedly strengthened Christian conviction of the nobility of the cause so earnestly defended. Several of the Apologists were from the ranks of the philosophers, and their philosophical interpretation aided in the development of theology. The most significant was Justin, and he may well stand as typical of the whole movement.

Justin, called the Martyr, from his heroic witness unto death in Rome under the prefect Rusticus, about 165, was born in Shechem, in the ancient Samaria, of heathen ancestry. He lived, for a time at least, in Ephesus, and it was in its vicinity probably that the conversion of which he gives a vivid account took place.[1] An eager student of philosophy, he accepted successively Stoicism, Aristotelianism, Pythagoreanism, and Platonism. While a Platonist his attention was directed to the Hebrew prophets, "men more ancient than all those who are esteemed philosophers." Theirs is the oldest and truest explanation "of the beginning and end of things and of those matters which the philosopher ought to know," since they were "filled with the holy Spirit." "They glorified the Creator, the God and Father of all things, and proclaimed His Son, the Christ." By his newly acquired conviction of the truth of their ancient prophetic message, Justin says: "straightway a flame was kindled in my soul; and a love of the prophets and of those men who are friends of Christ. . . . I found this philosophy alone to be safe and profitable." These quotations show the character of Justin's religious experience. It was not a profound and mystical union with a risen Lord, as with Paul. It was not a sense of forgiveness of sin. It was a conviction that in Christianity is the oldest, truest, and most divine of philosophies. Justin continued to look upon himself as a philosopher. He made his home in Rome and there wrote, about 153, his *Apology,* addressed to the Emperor Antoninus Pius and that sovereign's adopted sons, defending Christianity from governmental antagonism and heathen criticisms. A little later, perhaps on a visit to Ephesus, he composed his *Dialogue with Trypho,* similarly presenting the Christian case against Jewish objections. A second sojourn in Rome brought him to a martyr's death.

Justin's *Apology* (often called two Apologies, though the "second" is only an appendix) is a manly, dignified, and effective defense. Christians, if condemned at all, should be punished for definite proved crimes, not for the mere name without investigation of their real character. They are atheists only in that they count the popular gods demons unworthy of worship, not in respect to the true God. They are anarchists only to those who

[1] *Dialogue,* 2–8.

do not understand the nature of the kingdom that they seek. Justin then argues the truth of Christianity, especially from the fulfilment of Old Testament prophecy, and briefly explains Christian sacraments and worship.

Justin's central belief was that Christianity was the truest of philosophies, because taught by the prophets of the Old Testament, and by the divine Logos "our Teacher . . . who is both Son and Apostle of God the Father."[2] This divine Logos he conceives, in true Stoic fashion, as everywhere and always at work, teaching the Greeks, of whom he cites Socrates and Heraclitus, and the "barbarians," such as Abraham, so that these, and all who at any time obeyed the same guidance were really Christians.[3] His great advance on Stoicism is his conviction that this all-illuminating divine Logos became definitely incarnate in Christ, so that in Him is the full revelation of that which elsewhere is less distinctly seen. The content of the Christian message Justin conceives in terms very similar to those of the best contemporary heathen philosophy—knowledge of God, morality, the hope of immortality, and future rewards and punishments. Like common non-Pauline Christianity, he views the Gospel as a new law, teaching a somewhat ascetic moral life. Justin's emphasis is on the divine Logos, subordinate to God the Father, yet His Son, His agent, and one with Him in some true, though rather indefinite, sense. This emphasis is really at the expense of the historic Jesus, for though both are identified, the earthly life of Jesus is little stressed save as the great historic instance of the incarnation of the Logos, and therefore the occasion on which the divine philosophy was most fully revealed. He does, indeed, speak of Christ's "cleansing by His blood those who believe on Him";[4] but such thoughts are not primary. Hence the theology of Justin, faithful martyr though he was, betrayed little of the profoundly religious content so conspicuous in Paul, the Johannine literature, or even in Ignatius. It marks, however, a conscious union of Christian thought with the Gentile philosophy, and therefore the beginnings of a "scientific" theology. Moreover, it must be recognised that the aim of Justin and other Apologists was to write a brief for Christianity, claiming for it the same tolerance permitted to other religious philosophies. Hence they strove to show the similarities between Christianity and the best in pagan thought; and we should not necessarily imagine that their apologetic works reflect the whole of the faith they espoused.

[2] *Apology*, 12.   [3] *Ibid.*, 46; Ayer, p. 72.   [4] *Ibid.*, 32.

Period Two

FROM THE GNOSTIC CRISIS TO CONSTANTINE

1

Gnosticism

T HE LATER New Testament literature, and at least one of the Apostolic
Fathers, strongly combat conceptions of Christ which it is evident must
have been widely prevalent, especially in Asia Minor, in the opening years
of the second century. These views denied His real humanity and His
actual death. He had not come "in the flesh," but in ghost-like, Docetic appearance.[1] These opinions have sometimes been regarded as the beginnings
of Gnosticism. It is true that this Docetic conception of Christ was a feature
of much Gnostic teaching. It is more probable, however, that these early
teachings were more largely based on an attempt to explain a seeming
contradiction between the Jesus of history and the Christ of faith, than
on purely Gnostic speculations. That earthly life of humiliation was so contrasted with His pre-existent and post-existent glory, that the simplest solution of the Christological problem may well have seemed to some the
denial of the reality of His earthly life altogether. Christ did, indeed, appear.
He taught His disciples; but all the time as a heavenly being, not one of
flesh and blood.

Gnosticism, properly speaking, was something much more far-reaching.
The height of its influence was from about 135 to 160, though it continued
a force long after the latter date. It threatened to overwhelm the historic
Christian faith, and by so doing brought upon the Christian Church its
gravest crisis since the Pauline battle for freedom from law. Its spread and
consequent peril were made possible by the relatively weakly organized, and
doctrinally undefined state of the church at its beginning. The church overcame the danger; and in so doing developed a closely knit organization and
a clearly defined creed, which contrasted with the more spontaneous and
charismatic nature of primitive Christianity.

Gnosticism [2] professed to be based on "knowledge" ($\gamma\nu\tilde{\omega}\sigma\iota\varsigma$), but not
as that word is now commonly understood. Its knowledge was always a
mystical, supernatural wisdom, by which the initiates were brought to a

---

[1] I *John* 1:1–3, 2:22, 4:2, 3; Ignatius, *Trallians,* 9–11; *Smyrn.,* 1–6.
[2] Useful selections regarding Gnosticism may be found in Ayer, pp. 76–102. Our knowledge of this
movement will be greatly increased as the discoveries at Chenoboskion are published.

true understanding of the universe, and were saved from this evil world of matter. It had a fundamental doctrine of salvation. In these respects it was akin to the mystery religions. Its most prominent characteristic, however, was its syncretism. It took unto itself many elements from many sources, and assumed many forms. It is, therefore, impossible to speak of a single type of Gnosticism. It was prevailingly mystical, magical, or philosophical according to the dominant admixture in its syncretism. Gnosticism was pre-Christian in its origin, and was in existence before Christianity came into the world. There were Jewish and heathen types. It is represented in the Hermetic literature of Egypt. It had astral elements which may be traced back to Babylonian religious conceptions, a dualistic view of the universe, Persian in origin, and a doctrine of emanations from God in the "pleroma" or realm of spirit, which was probably Egyptian. Perhaps its most fundamental conception, the wholly evil character of the phenomenal world, was due to a combination of the Platonic theory of the contrast between the real spiritual sphere of "ideas," and this visible world of phenomena, interpreted in terms of Persian dualism—the one good and that to which man strives to return, the other wholly bad and the place of his imprisonment. The world of matter is evil. Its creator and ruler is not, therefore, the high, good God, but an inferior and imperfect being, the demiurge. Man, to be saved, must be freed from this bondage to the visible world, and its rulers, the planetary spirits; and the means of his freedom is "knowledge" ($\gamma\nu\hat{\omega}\sigma\iota\varsigma$), a mystical, spiritual enlightenment for the initiated which brings him into communion with the true realm of spiritual realities.

Strongly syncretistic already, Gnosticism found much in Christianity which it could use. In particular, the figure of Christ was especially adapted to give a definite and concrete center to its theory of a higher saving knowledge. He was the revealer of the hitherto unknown high and all-perfect God to men. By that illumination all "spiritual" men, who were capable of receiving it, would be led back to the realm of the good God. Since the material world is evil, Christ could not have had a real incarnation, and the Gnostics explained His appearance either as Docetic and ghostly, or as a temporary indwelling of the man Jesus, or as an apparent birth from a virgin mother without partaking of material nature. The God of the Old Testament, as the creator of this visible world, cannot be the high God whom Christ revealed, but the inferior demiurge. That all Christians did not possess the saving "knowledge," the Gnostics explained by holding it to be a secret teaching imparted by the Apostles to their more intimate disciples, a speaking "wisdom among the perfect." [3] It is true that while Paul was in no sense a Gnostic, there were many things in Paul's teachings of which Gnostics availed themselves. His sharp contrast between flesh and spirit; [4] his conception of Christ as victor over those "principalities and powers" which are the

[3] *I Cor.* 2:6.   [4] *Romans* 8:22–25; I *Cor.* 15:50.

"world rulers of this darkness," [5] and his thought of Christ as the Man from Heaven,[6] were all ideas which the Gnostics could employ. Paul was always to them the chief Apostle.

Gnosticism was divided into many sects and presented a great variety of forms. In all of them the high, good God is the head of the spiritual world of light, often called the "pleroma." From that world fragments have become imprisoned in this visible world of darkness and evil. In later Gnosticism this fallen element from the pleroma is represented as the lowest of a series of æons, or spiritual beings, emanating from the high God. To rescue this fallen portion, the seeds of light in the visible evil world, Christ came, bringing the true "knowledge." By His teaching those capable of receiving it are restored to the pleroma. They are at best few. Most Gnostics divided mankind into "spiritual," capable of salvation, and "material" who could not receive the message. Later Gnosticism, especially the school of Valentinus, taught a threefold division, "spiritual," who alone could attain "knowledge"; "psychical," capable of faith, and of a certain degree of salvation; and "material," who were hopeless.

Christian tradition represented the founder of Christian Gnosticism to be Simon Magus,[7] but of his real relations to it little is known. More clearly defined leaders are Satornilus of Antioch, who labored before 150; Basilides, who taught in Alexandria about 130; and, above all, Valentinus, who was active in Rome from about 135 to 165, and who must be regarded as one of the most gifted thinkers of the age.

Gnosticism was an immense peril for the church. It cut out the historic foundations of Christianity. Its God is not the God of the Old Testament, which is the work of an inferior or even evil being. Its Christ had no real incarnation, death, or resurrection. Its salvation is for the few capable of spiritual enlightenment. The peril was the greater because Gnosticism was represented by some of the keenest minds in the church of the second century. The age was syncretistic, and in some respects Gnosticism was but the fullest accomplishment of that amalgamation of Hellenic and Oriental philosophical speculation with primitive Christian beliefs which was in greater or less degree in process in all Christian thinking.

[5] *Col.* 2:15; *Eph.* 6:12.   [6] *1 Cor.* 15:47.
[7] *Acts* 8:9-24; Irenæus, *Heresies,* 1:23; Ayer, p. 79.

2

Marcion

A SPECIAL INTEREST attaches to Marcion as one who was the first church reformer.[1] Born in Sinope, in Asia Minor, where he was a wealthy ship-owner, he came to Rome about 139, and joined the Roman congregation, making it a gift for its benevolent work equivalent to ten thousand dollars. Haunted by the problem of evil and suffering, he came to espouse a sharp dualism which contrasted the god of this world with the God of mercy revealed in Jesus. Under the influence of the Gnostic, Cerdo, in Rome, he seems to have modified his position by regarding the creator-god of the Old Testament as weak rather than as wholly evil. In any case he sharply attacked all forms of legalism and Judaism, contending that Paul was the only Apostle who had faithfully understood the Gospel. All others had fallen into the errors of Judaism. The God of the Old Testament is a just God, in the sense of "an eye for an eye, and a tooth for a tooth." He created the world and gave the Jewish law. Christ, who was a Docetic manifestation, revealed the heretofore unknown good God of mercy. The God of the Old Testament opposed Him; but in Christ the authority of the Jewish law was done away, and the "just God" became unjust because of this unwarranted hostility to the revealer of the "good God." The Old Testament and its God are therefore to be rejected by Christians. Christ proclaimed a Gospel of love and mercy, and the only knowledge of God is that gained from Him. In his conception of the Christian life Marcion followed out the consequences of his Gnostic view. Since the material world is evil, the ascetic life is to be embraced. Meat-eating and sexual intercourse only play into the hands of the creator-god.

Marcion's endeavor to call the Roman Church back to what he deemed the Gospel of Christ and of Paul resulted in his own excommunication about 144. He now gathered followers into a separated church. For their use he compiled a canon of sacred books, composed of ten epistles of Paul (omitting the Pastorals), and the Gospel of Luke. He expurgated them of all passages which implied that Christ regarded the God of the Old Testament as His

[1] See selections, Ayer, pp. 102–105.

Father, or was in any way related to Him. As far as is known, this was the first attempt to form an authoritative collection of New Testament writings.

Marcion's movement was probably the most dangerous of those associated with Gnosticism. He sundered Christianity from its historic background as completely as had the more speculative Gnostic theories. He denied a real incarnation, and condemned the Old Testament and its God. All this was the more plausible because done in the name of a protest against growing legalism. For such a protest there was much justification. His churches spread extensively, in the Orient especially, and survived into the fifth century. His own later history is wholly unknown.

3

Montanism

UNLIKE GNOSTICISM, MONTANISM was a movement distinctly of Christian origin. In most of the churches of the second century the early hope of the speedy return of Christ was growing dim. The consciousness of the constant inspiration of the Spirit, characteristic of the Apostolic Churches, had also largely faded. With this declining sense of the immediacy of the Spirit's present work came an increasing emphasis on His significance as the agent of revelation. The Spirit had been the inspiration of prophecy in the Old Testament.[1] He guided the New Testament writers.[2] To Christian thought at the beginning of the second century the Holy Spirit was differentiated from Christ, but was classed, like Him, with God. This appears in the Trinitarian baptismal formula,[3] which was displacing the older baptism in the name of Christ.[4] Trinitarian formulæ were frequently in use by the close of the first and beginning of the second century.[5] The Johannine Gospel represented Christ as promising the coming of the Holy Spirit to the disciples: "When the Comforter is come, whom I will send unto you from the Father, even the Spirit of Truth, which proceedeth from the Father, He shall bear Witness of Me" (15:26). The second century was convinced, therefore, not only that the Holy Spirit was in peculiar association with God the Father

---

[1] E. g., 1 *Clem.* 8, 13, 16; "the prophetic Spirit," Justin, *Apology*, 13.   [2] 1 *Clem.*, 47.
[3] *Matt.* 28:19.   [4] *Acts* 2:38.   [5] E. g., 1 *Clem.* 46, 58; Ignatius, *Eph.*, 9.

and Christ; but that Christ had promised the Spirit's coming in more abundant measure in the future.

It was this thought of the special dispensation of the Holy Spirit, combined with a fresh outburst of the early prophetic enthusiasm, and a belief that the end of the world-age was close at hand, that were represented in Montanism. To a considerable extent Montanism was, also, a reaction from the secular tendencies already at work in the church. Montanus, from whom the movement was named, was of Ardabau, near the region of Asia Minor known as Phrygia—long noted for its ecstatic type of religion.[6] A tradition, recorded by Jerome, affirmed that, before conversion, he had been a priest of Cybele. About 156 Montanus proclaimed himself the passive instrument through whom the Holy Spirit spoke. In this new revelation Montanus declared the promise of Christ fulfilled, and the dispensation of the Holy Spirit begun. To him were soon joined two prophetesses, Prisca and Maximilla. They now affirmed, as mouthpieces of the Spirit, that the end of the world was at hand, and that the heavenly Jerusalem was about to be established in Phrygia, whither believers should betake themselves. In preparation for the fast-approaching consummation the most strenuous asceticism should be practised, celibacy, fastings, and abstinence from meat. This vigorous attitude won response as a protest against the growing worldliness of the church at large, and to many was the most attractive feature of Montanism.

The movement speedily attained considerable proportions. By the bishops of Asia Minor, who felt their authority threatened, one or more synods were held soon after 160, which have the distinction of being the earliest synods of church history, and in which Montanism was condemned. Its progress was not easily checked, even by the death of the last of its original prophets, Maximilla, in 179. Soon after 170 it was represented in Rome, and for years the Roman church was more or less turmoiled by it. In Carthage it won Tertullian, about 200, attracted chiefly by its ascetic demands, who thenceforth was the most eminent Montanist. Though gradually driven out of the dominant church, Montanism continued to be represented in the Orient till long after the acceptance of Christianity by the imperial government. In Carthage the followers of Tertullian persisted till the time of Augustine. In its ascetic demands Montanism represented a wide-spread tendency, and an asceticism as strict as anything Montanism taught was later to find a place in the great church in monasticism.

[6] See selections, Ayer, pp. 106–109.

4

The Catholic Church

NEITHER GNOSTICISM NOR MONTANISM, though extremely perilous, were ever embraced by a majority of Christians. The large church remained faithful to historic Christianity. By the latter third of the second century it was calling itself the "Catholic" Church. The word "Catholic" is first used of the church by Ignatius,[1] who employed it in the Platonic sense of "universal" as opposed to particular. It is next to be found in the letter of the Church of Smyrna, describing the martyrdom of Polycarp (156). Its employment as a technically descriptive adjective, almost the equivalent of "orthodox," gradually became common, so that the strongly consolidated church that came out of the Gnostic and Montanist crises is now usually described as the "Catholic." This Catholic Church developed its distinguishing characteristics between 160 and 190. The hitherto relatively independent congregations were now knit into an effective union. The power of the bishops was greatly strengthened, a collection of authoritative New Testament Scripture recognized, and a creed formulated. Comparatively loosely organized Christianity now became a closely knit corporate body, having recognized official leaders and capable not merely of defining its faith, but of shutting out from its communion all who did not accept its creed or its officers. As a recent German writer has epitomized the change: "About 50, he was of the church who had received baptism and the Holy Spirit and called Jesus, Lord; about 180, he who acknowledged the rule of faith (creed), the New Testament canon, and the authority of the bishops." [2]

In a measure, the beginnings of this great change may be seen before the Gnostic and Montanist crises; but it was those struggles that brought it effectively into being. The characteristic answer of the Catholic Church to the Gnostics may be seen in the argument of Irenæus of Lyons.[3] Against Gnostic claims Irenæus, writing about 185, held that the Apostles did not preach before they had "perfect knowledge" of the Gospel. That preaching they recorded in the Gospels—*Matthew and John* were written by Apostles themselves; while *Mark* reproduced the message of Peter and *Luke* that of

[1] *Smyrn.*, 8; Ayer, p. 42.   [2] Heussi, *Kompendium der Kirchengeschichte*, p. 44.
[3] *Heresies*, 3:1–4; Ayer, pp. 112–114.

Paul. Nothing Gnostic, Irenæus declares, is found in any of them. But the Gnostic may object that, besides this public apostolic teaching in the Gospels, there was a *viva voce* instruction, a speaking "wisdom among the perfect," [4] of which Gnosticism was the heir. This Irenæus denied. He argued that, had there been such private teaching, the Apostles would have intrusted it to those, above all others, whom they selected as their successors in the government of the churches. In these churches of apostolic foundation the apostolic teaching had been fully preserved, and its transmission had been guaranteed by the orderly succession of their bishops. Go therefore to Rome, or to Smyrna, or Ephesus, and learn what is there taught, and nothing Gnostic will be found. Every church must agree with that of Rome, for there apostolical tradition has been faithfully preserved as in other Apostolic Churches.

It is difficult to see what more effective argument Irenæus could have advanced in the peculiar situation which confronted him; but it was an answer which greatly increased the significance of the churches of real or reputed apostolical foundation, and of their heads, the bishops. Irenæus went further. The church itself is the depository of Christian teaching: "Since the Apostles, like a rich man in a bank, lodged in her hands most copiously all things pertaining to the truth." [5] This deposit is especially intrusted to "those who, together with the succession of the episcopate, have received the certain gift of truth," [6] *i. e.* to the heads of the churches. To agree with the bishops is therefore a necessity. This argument was not peculiar to Irenæus, it was that of the leaders of Catholic teaching generally.

While the power of the episcopate and the significance of churches of apostolical foundation was thus greatly enhanced, the Gnostic crisis saw a corresponding development of creed, especially in the West. From the very beginning Christian writers had produced succinct statements of the faith.[7] Furthermore, many liturgical occasions, such as the eucharistic prayer, exorcism and baptism, demanded them. Hence there arose a great variety of such summaries of the faith; but it is particularly in connection with baptism that the creed developed its official character. While the earliest baptismal confessions had been very simple, such as "Jesus is Lord," [8] by the time of Hippolytus (170?–235) in Rome the creed had grown to involve three questions which were posed to the candidate, and on the affirmation of which he was dipped in the water. It ran like this:

"Do you believe in God the Father Almighty?"
"I believe."
"Do you believe in Jesus Christ the Son of God, who was born of Holy Spirit and the Virgin Mary, who was crucified under Pontius Pilate and died, and rose the third day living from the dead, and ascended into heaven, and sat down at

[4] 1 *Cor.* 2:6.   [5] *Heresies*, 3.4.1.   [6] *Ibid.* 4.26.2
[7] E. g., 1 *Cor.* 15:3ff.; *Rom.* 1:3f.; 2 *Tim.* 2:8; 1 *Pet.* 3:18ff.; and many examples in Ignatius' letters.
[8] 1 *Cor.* 12:3.

the right hand of the Father, and will come to judge the living and the dead?"
"I believe."
"Do you believe in the Holy Spirit, and the Holy Church, and the resurrection
of the flesh?"
"I believe." [9]

From time to time additional phrases were added to these questions to
guard against current heresies. Gradually these interrogatory creeds gave
way to declaratory ones, starting with the familiar "I believe." The latter
have their origin in prebaptismal instruction where the creed was learned by
heart. With the decline of adult baptism from the fifth century onwards,
the catechetical ceremonies came to be merged with the actual baptism, and
declaratory creeds eventually supplanted interrogatory ones. Furthermore, the
use of creeds as tests of orthodoxy by the councils, such as Nicæa in 325,
gave added prominence to the declaratory type. The Apostles' Creed with
which we are familiar goes back to the old Roman interrogatory form, but
it had developed something of its present shape by 400 A. D.; though its
final phrasing is not attested until the eighth century.

The development of a canon of New Testament books was, also, the
work of the later second century. By the church from the beginning the Old
Testament was reckoned as Scripture. The Gospels and the letters of Paul
were doubtless highly valued, but they did not, at first, have Scriptural
authority. Clement of Rome (93–97), though constantly quoting the Old
Testament as the utterance of God, was very free in his use of the words
of the New Testament, and nowhere styled them divine. The earliest designation of a passage from the Gospels as "Scripture" was about 131, by the
so-called Barnabas [10] and of a quotation from Paul about 110–117, by Polycarp.[11] It is possible, however, that these authors imagine they are citing the
Old Testament. The first clear instance of apostolic writings being elevated
to the status of "Scripture" beside the Septuagint is in the second century
sermon we call *II Clement*.[12] By the time of Justin (153), the Gospels were
read in the services in Rome, together with the Old Testament prophets.[13]
The process by which the New Testament writings came to Scriptural authority seems to have been one of analogy. The Old Testament was everywhere regarded as divinely authoritative. Christians could think no less of their
own fundamental books. The question was an open one, however, as to which
were the canonical writings. Works like Hermas and Barnabas were read
in churches. An authoritative list was desirable. Marcion had prepared such
a canon for his followers. A similar enumeration was gradually formed,
probably in Rome, by the Catholic party. Apparently the Gospels were the
first to gain complete recognition, then the letters of Paul. By about 200,
according to the witness of the Muratorian fragment, Western Christendom

[9] *Apostolic Tradition*, 21:12ff.   [10] *Barn.*, 4.   [11] *Phil.* 12.   [12] 11 *Clem.* 2:4.
[13] *Apology*, 66, 67.

had a New Testament canon embracing *Matthew, Mark, Luke, John, Acts,*
1 and 2 Corinthians, Ephesians, Philippians, Colossians, Galatians, 1 and 2
Thessalonians, Romans, Philemon, Titus, 1 and 2 *Timothy, Jude,* 1 and 2
John, Revelation, and the so-called *Apocalypse of Peter.*[14] In the Orient the
development of a canon was not quite so rapid. Certain books, like *Hebrews*
and *Revelation,* were disputed. The whole process of canonical development
into its precise present form was not completed in the West till 400, and
in the East till even later.

By the year 200 the church of the western portion of the empire had,
therefore, an authoritative collection of New Testament books, in the main
like our own, to which to appeal. The East was not much behind. The formation of the canon was essentially a process of selection from the whole mass
of Christian literature, made originally by no council, but by the force of
Christian opinion—the criterion being that the books accepted were believed
to be either the work of an Apostle or of the immediate disciple of an
Apostle, and thus to represent apostolic teaching.

Thus out of the struggle with Gnosticism and Montanism came the
Catholic Church, with its strong episcopal organization, credal standard, and
authoritative canon. It differed much from the Apostolic Church; but it had
preserved historic Christianity and carried it through a tremendous crisis.
It may be doubted whether a less tightly knit organization than that developed
in this momentous second half of the second century could have achieved
as much.

5

The Growing Importance of Rome

THE ROMAN CHURCH had been of prominence since the time of Paul. To
it that Apostle wrote his most noteworthy letter. At Rome Paul and
Peter died. The church endured the severest of early persecutions under Nero,
and survived in vigor. Situated in the capital of the empire, it early developed a consciousness of strength and authority, which was doubtless increased
by the fact that, by 100, it was, it would appear, the largest single congregation in Christendom. Even before the close of the first century Clement,
writing anonymously to the Corinthians in the name of the whole Roman

[14] Ayer, pp. 117–120.

congregation (93–97), spoke as for those who expected to be obeyed.[1] The tone, if brotherly, was big-brotherly. This influence was increased by the well-known generosity of the Roman congregation.[2] Ignatius addressed it as "having the presidency of love." [3] The destruction of Jerusalem in the second Jewish war (135) ended any possible leadership of Christianity that might there have been asserted. The successful resistance to Gnosticism and Montanism strengthened it; and it reaped in abundance the fruits of that struggle. There the creed was formulated, there the canon formed. Above all, it was advantaged by the appeal of the opponents of Gnosticism to the tradition of the Apostolic churches, for Rome was the only church in the western half of the empire with which Apostles had had anything to do. Irenæus of Lyons, writing about 185, represented the general Western feeling of his time, when he not only pictures the Roman Church as founded by Peter and Paul, but declares "it is a matter of necessity that every church should agree with this church." [4] It was leadership in the preservation of the apostolic faith, not judicial supremacy, that Irenæus had in mind; but with such estimates wide-spread, the door was open for a larger assertion of Roman authority. Rather late in developing the monarchical episcopate, though it is foreshadowed in the unique place of Clement as a sort of foreign secretary of that church,[5] the prominence of its bishop grew rapidly in the Gnostic struggle, and with this growth came the first extensive assertion of the authority of the Roman bishop in the affairs of the church at large.

While Rome was thus gaining in strength Asia Minor was relatively declining. At the beginning of the second century Asia Minor and the adjacent portion of Syria had been the most extensively Christianized sections of the empire. That was probably also true at the century's close. Ephesus and Antioch had been, and were still, great Christian centers. Asia Minor had resisted Gnosticism, but it had been torn by Montanism and other sources of controversy, though the Montanists had been rejected. There is reason to think, however, that these disputes had borne hard on the united strength of its Christianity. The quarrel between Asia Minor and Rome arose over the time of the observance of Easter. While there is reason to suppose that Easter had been honored from early in Christian history, the first definite record of its celebration is in connection with a visit of Polycarp, bishop of Smyrna, to Anicetus, bishop of Rome, in 154 or 155. At that time the practice of Asia Minor, probably the more ancient, was to observe Easter with a vigil, terminating in the Lord's Supper, through the night of the fourteenth of the month Nisan, like the Jewish Passover, regardless of the day of the week on which it might fall. The Roman custom, and that of some parts of the East, was to hold the Easter feast always on Sunday. The

[1] 1 Clem., 59, 63.   [2] Eusebius, Church History, 4.23.10; Ayer, p. 24.   [3] Romans.
[4] Heresies, 3.3.2; Ayer, p. 113.   [5] See Hermas, Vis., 2.4.3.

question was, therefore, should the day of the week or that of the month be the norm. Polycarp and Anicetus could not agree, but parted with mutual good-will, each adhering to his own practice.[6] The problem was further complicated by a dispute, about 167, in Laodicea, in Asia Minor itself, as to the nature of the celebration on the fourteenth of Nisan, some holding that Christ died on the fourteenth, as the fourth Gospel intimates, and others placing His death, as do the other Gospels, on the fifteenth. The latter treated the commemoration of the fourteenth of Nisan, therefore, as a Christian continuation of the Hebrew Passover.

About 190 the problem became so acute that synods were held in Rome, Palestine, and elsewhere which decided in favor of the Roman practice. The churches of Asia Minor, led by Polycrates, bishop of Ephesus, refused conformity. Thereupon Victor, bishop of Rome (189–198), excommunicated the recalcitrant congregations. This high-handed action met with much protest, notably from Irenæus of Lyons, but it was a marked assertion of Roman authority.[7]

These embittered controversies were costly to Asia Minor, and any possible rivalry on equal terms of Ephesus and Rome was out of the question. The collapse of Jewish Christian leadership, the apparent lack at Antioch of men of eminence in the second century, and the decline of the influence of Asia Minor left Rome, by 200, the most eminent and influential center of Christianity—a position of which the Roman bishops had the will and the ability to make full use. The rise of Alexandria and of Carthage to importance in the Christian thought and life of the third century could not rob Rome of its leadership. Their attainment of Christian significance was far younger than that of the capital of the empire.

6

Irenæus

THE EARLIEST theological leader of distinction in the rising Catholic Church was Irenæus. His argument in defense of traditional Christianity against Gnosticism has already been outlined.[1] Born in Asia Minor, he was brought up in Smyrna, where he saw and heard Polycarp. The date of his

[6] Eusebius, *Church History*, 5.24.16, 17; Ayer, p. 164.
[7] Eusebius, *Church History*, 5.23.24; Ayer, pp. 161–165.   [1] See pp. 57–58.

birth has been most variously placed by modern scholars from about 115 to about 142, chiefly in the light of its possible bearing on traditions as to the authorship of the fourth Gospel. The later part of the period indicated has more probability than the earlier. From Asia Minor he removed to Lyons in what is now France, where he became a presbyter. The great persecution of 177, at Lyons, found him, fortunately, on an honorable mission to Rome; and, on his return, he was chosen bishop of Lyons, in succession to the martyred Pothinus. That post he continued to hold till his death (c. 200). Not far from 185 he wrote his chief work, *Against Heresies,* primarily to refute the various Gnostic schools, but incidentally revealing his own theology.

Brought up in the tradition of Asia Minor and spending his later life in Gaul, Irenæus was a connecting-link not merely between distant portions of the empire, but between the older theology of the Johannine and Ignatian literature and the newer presentations which the Apologists and the "Catholic" movement of his own day were introducing. A man of deeply religious spirit, his interest was in salvation. In its explication he developed the Pauline and Ignatian conceptions of Christ as the new man, the renewer of humanity, the second Adam. Affirming the goodness of creation, Irenæus contends that God created the first Adam with the capacity for immortality, the gift being dependent upon his obedience. But both goodness and immortality were lost by Adam's sin. What man lost in Adam is restored in Christ, the incarnate Logos, who now completes the interrupted work. He "recapitulates" in Himself the stages of Adam's fall, reversing the process, and going up step by step, as it were, the ladder which Adam descended. "I have shown that the Son of God did not then begin to exist [*i. e.* at Jesus' birth], being with the Father from the beginning; but when He became incarnate and was made man, He commenced afresh the long line of human beings, and furnished us, in a brief, comprehensive manner, with salvation; so that what we had lost in Adam—namely to be according to the image and likeness of God—that we might recover in Christ Jesus." [2] The work of Christ, thus described, Irenæus characterizes in a noble phrase. We follow "the only true and steadfast Teacher, the Word of God, our Lord Jesus Christ, who did through His transcendent love become what we are, that He might bring us to be even what He is Himself." [3] Christ is also the full revelation of God.[4] Our union with Him, following the teaching of Asia Minor and of Justin, Irenæus views as in some sense physical, through the Supper.[5] Irenæus' theory of Christ's new headship of humanity had added to it a suggestion of His mother as the second Eve. "The knot of Eve's disobedience was loosened by the obedience of Mary. For what the Virgin Eve had bound fast through unbelief, this did the Virgin Mary set free

---

[2] *Heresies,* 3.18.1; Ayer, pp. 137, 138.   [3] *Heresies,* 5; Preface.   [4] *Ibid.,* 4.20.7.
[5] *Ibid.,* 4.18.5; Ayer, p. 138.

through faith." [6] In this curious ascription is one of the earliest evidences of that exaltation of the Virgin which was to play so large a part in Christian history. In some ways, even for his time, Irenæus was an old-fashioned man. The belief in Christ's speedy second coming had been growing faint, and the contest with Montanism was to extinguish it almost entirely. With Irenæus it still burned brightly, and he looked eagerly for the time when the earth would be marvellously renewed.[7] For Irenæus the New Testament is as fully sacred Scripture as the Old.

7

Tertullian and Cyprian

TERTULLIAN was one of the most individual and remarkable personalities of the ancient church. Born (c. 150–155) of well-to-do heathen parentage in Carthage, he studied law and practised his profession in Rome. He was exceedingly well read in philosophy and history. Greek he had thoroughly mastered. About 190 to 195, he was converted to Christianity, probably in Rome, and now devoted himself with equal eagerness to the study of Christian literature, orthodox and heretical. Shortly after, he returned to Carthage where he became a presbyter, and remained till his death (c. 222–225). At first in fellowship with the Roman Church, a wave of persecution that broke over North Africa in 202 under the Emperor Septimius Severus (193–211), strengthened his native Puritanism and brought him into sympathy with Montanism. Its ascetic and unworldly aspects most appealed to him. About 200 he broke with the "Catholic" Church, which he thenceforth bitterly criticised, and died in continuing protest, apparently, as the founder of a little sect of his own.

In 197 Tertullian began a career of literary activity in defense and explication of Christianity which lasted till 220. He was the first ecclesiastical writer of prominence to use Latin. Even the leaders of the Roman Church wrote in Greek till after his time. His style was vivid, satirical, readable. His method was often that of an advocate in the court-room. He was frequently unfair to opponents. He was not always consistent with himself. But he was of a fiery earnestness of spirit that makes what he wrote always impressive. He well deserves the title of father of Latin theology.

[6] *Ibid.*, 3.22.4.   [7] *Ibid.*, 5.33.3; Ayer, p. 26.

Tertullian was, primarily, no speculative theologian. His own thought was based on that of the Apologists, Irenæus, and to some extent on other bearers of the tradition of Asia Minor, and quite as much on Stoic teaching and legal conceptions. He had the Roman sense of order and authority. All that he touched, however, he formulated with the clearness of definition of a trained judicial mind, and hence he gave precision, as none had before him, to many theological conceptions that had heretofore been vaguely apprehended.

For Tertullian Christianity was a great divine foolishness, wiser than the highest philosophical wisdom of men, and in no way to be squared with existing philosophical systems.[1] In reality he looked upon it largely through Stoic spectacles. Christianity is primarily knowledge of God. It is based on reason—"the soul by nature Christian"[2]—and authority. That authority is seated in the church, and only in the orthodox church, which alone has the truth, expressed in the creed, and alone has a right to use the Scriptures.[3] As with Irenæus, these valid churches are those that agree in faith with those founded by the Apostles, wherein the apostolic tradition has been maintained by the succession of bishops.[4] These are utterances of the still "Catholic" Tertullian. As with Justin and common Gentile Christianity of the second century, Christianity for Tertullian is a new law. "Jesus Christ . . . preached the new law and the new promises of the kingdom of heaven."[5] Admission to the church is by baptism, by which previous sins are removed. It is "our sacrament of water, in that by washing away the sins of our early blindness we are set free into eternal life."[6] Those who have received it are thenceforth "competitors for salvation in earning the favor of God."[7]

Tertullian had a deeper sense of sin than any Christian writer since Paul, and his teachings greatly aided the development of the Latin conceptions of sin and grace. Though not clearly worked out, and inconsistent with occasional expressions, Tertullian possessed a doctrine of original sin. "There is, then, besides the evil which supervenes on the soul from the intervention of the evil spirit, an antecedent, and in a certain sense natural evil, which arises from its corrupt origin."[8] But "the power of the grace of God is more potent indeed than nature."[9] The nature of grace he nowhere fully explains. It evidently included, however, not only "forgiveness of sins,"[10] but also "the grace of divine inspiration," by which power to do right is infused to give force to man's feeble, but free, will.[11] Loofs has shown that this latter conception, of the utmost significance for the theology of Western Christendom, is of Stoic origin.[12] But though salvation is thus based on grace, man has much to do. Though God forgives previous sins at baptism, satisfaction

---

[1] *Prescription*, 7. [2] *Apology*, 17. [3] *Prescription*, 13–19. [4] *Ibid.*, 32.
[5] *Ibid.*, 13. [6] *Baptism*, 1. [7] *Repentance*, 6. [8] *Anima*, 41. [9] *Ibid.*, 21.
[10] *Baptism*, 10. [11] *Patience*, 1.
[12] *Leitfaden zum Studium der Dogmengeschichte*, p. 164.

must be made for those committed thereafter by voluntary sacrifices, chiefly ascetic. The more a man punishes himself, the less God will punish him.[13]

Tertullian's most influential work was the definition of the Logos Christology, though he preferred to use the designation Son rather than Logos. If he advanced its content little beyond what had already been presented by the theologians of Asia Minor, and especially by the Apologists, his legal mind gave a clearness to its explanation such as had not before existed. Here his chief work was one written in his Montanist period—*Against Praxeas*. He defines the Godhead in terms which almost anticipate the Nicene result of more than a century later. "All are of one, by unity of substance; while the mystery of the dispensation is still guarded which distributes the unity into a Trinity, placing in their order the three, the Father, the Son, and the Holy Spirit; three, however . . . not in substance but in form; not in power but in appearance, for they are of one substance and one essence and one power, inasmuch as He is one God from whom these degrees and forms and aspects are reckoned under the name of the Father, and of the Son, and of the Holy Spirit." [14] He describes these distinctions of the Godhead as "persons," [15] meaning by the word not our usage in the sense of personalities, but objective modes of being. This unity of substance in Tertullian's thought is material, for he was sufficiently a Stoic to hold that "God is a body . . . for spirit has a bodily substance of its own kind." [16] With a similar precision, Tertullian distinguished between the human and divine in Christ. "We see His double state, not intermixed but conjoined in one person, Jesus, God and man." [17] Since both Son and Spirit are derived from the Father by emanation, both are subordinate to Him.[18] This doctrine of subordination, already taught in the Apologists, was to remain characteristic of the Logos Christology till the time of Augustine. These definitions were far more the work of a lawyer-like, judicial interpretation, than of philosophical consideration. As the first, also, to give technical usage to such expressions as *trinitas, substantia, sacramentum, satisfacere, meritum,* Tertullian left his permanent impress on Latin theology.

Cyprian was, in many ways, the intellectual heir of Tertullian, whom he called master. Born probably in Carthage, about 200, he spent all his life in that city. A man of wealth and education, he won distinction as a teacher of rhetoric. About 246 he was converted to the Christian faith, and two or three years later was chosen to the bishopric of Carthage. Here he showed high executive ability, and much practical good sense and kindliness of spirit without the touch of genius that characterized Tertullian. The persecution of 250 he escaped by flight; but in that of 258 he stood boldly forth and suffered as a martyr by beheading. Few leaders of the ancient church have been more highly regarded by subsequent ages.

In Cyprian's teaching the tendencies illustrated in the development of

[13] *Repentance*, 2, 9.   [14] *Praxeas*, 2.   [15] *Ibid.*, 12.   [16] *Ibid.*, 7.
[17] *Ibid.*, 27.   [18] *Praxeas*, 7, 9.

the "Catholic" Church received their full expression. The church is the one visible orthodox community of Christians. "There is one God, and Christ is one, and there is one church, and one chair (episcopate) founded upon the rock by the word of the Lord." [19] "Whoever he may be and whatever he may be, he who is not in the church of Christ is not a Christian." [20] "He can no longer have God for his Father, who has not the church for his mother." [21] "There is no salvation out of the church." [22] The church is based on the unity of its bishops, "whence ye ought to know that the bishop is in the church and the church in the bishop; and if any one be not with the bishop, that he is not in the church." [23] "The episcopate is one, each part of which is held by each one in its entirety." [24] This last quotation has its bearing on a controversy still alive as to whether Cyprian regarded all bishops as equal sharers in a common episcopal authority, the possession of each and of all; or held to the superiority of the bishop of Rome. He certainly quoted *Matt.* 16:18, 19.[25] He looked upon Peter as the typical bishop. He referred to Rome as "the chief church whence priestly unity takes its source." [26] Rome was to him evidently the highest church in dignity; but Cyprian was not ready to admit a judicial authority over others in the Roman bishop, or to regard him as more than the first among equals.

Cyprian's significance as a witness to the full development of the doctrine that the Lord's Supper is a sacrifice offered by the priest to God will be considered later. His conception of the Christian life, like that of Tertullian, was ascetic. Martyrdom is bringing forth fruit an hundred-fold; voluntary celibacy, sixtyfold.[27]

8

The Triumph of the Logos Christology in the West

THOUGH the "Catholic" Church was combating successfully the Gnostics, and though the Logos Christology was that of such formative minds as those of the writer of the fourth Gospel, Justin, Irenæus, and Tertullian, that Christology was not wholly regarded with sympathy by the rank and file of believers. Hermas had taught an adoptionist Christology at Rome as late as 140. The Apostles' Creed has no reference to any Logos doctrine.

[19] *Letters,* 39–43:5.   [20] *Ibid.,* 51–55:24.   [21] *Unity of the Church,* 6.
[22] *Letters,* 72–73:21.   [23] *Ibid.,* 68–66:8.   [24] *Unity of the Church,* 5; Ayer, p. 242.
[25] *E.g., Unity of the Church,* 4.   [26] *Letters,* 54–59:14.   [27] *Ibid.,* 76:6.

Tertullian says significantly of his own time (213–218): "The simple—I will not call them unwise or unlearned—who always constitute the majority of believers, are startled at the dispensation of the three in one, on the ground that their very rule of faith withdraws them from the world's plurality of gods to the one only true God." [1] It was difficult for them to see in trinitarian conceptions aught else but an assertion of tritheism. The last decade of the second and the first two of the third centuries were an important epoch, therefore, in Christological discussion, especially in Rome, where the question was in the balance.

To some extent this new Christological discussion seems to have been the indirect result of Montanism. That movement had made much of the fourth Gospel, proclaiming itself the inauguration of the dispensation of the Spirit, therein promised. Some opponents of Montanism in Asia Minor, in their reaction from its teachings, went so far as to reject the fourth Gospel and its doctrine of the Logos. Of these "Alogoi," as Epiphanius (?–403), writing much later, nicknamed them, little is known in detail, but some of the critics of the Logos Christology who now came into prominence were apparently influenced by them. To these opponents in general the name Monarchians is usually given—a title coined by Tertullian [2] since they asserted the unity of God. The Monarchians fell into two very unlike classes, those who held that Jesus was the Son of God by adoption, the so-called Dynamic Monarchians; and those who held that Christ was but a temporary form of manifestation of the one God, the party known as the Modalistic Monarchians. Thus, with the supporters of the Logos view, three Christologies were contesting in Rome at the beginning of the third century.

The first Dynamic Monarchian of prominence was Theodotus, called the currier, or tanner, from Byzantium. He was a man of learning, and is said to have been a disciple of the Alogoi, though, unlike them, he accepted in some sense the fourth Gospel. About 190 he came to Rome, and there taught that Jesus was a man, born of the Virgin, of holy life, upon whom the divine Christ (or the Holy Spirit) descended at His baptism. Some of Theodotus' followers denied to Jesus any title to divinity; but others held that He became in some sense divine at His resurrection. [3] One is reminded of the Christology of Hermas (see p. 35). Theodotus was excommunicated by Bishop Victor of Rome (189–198); but his work there was continued by Theodotus, "the money-changer," and Asclepiodorus, like their master, probably from the Orient; but their effort to found a rival communion outside the "Catholic" Church amounted to little. The last attempt to present a similar theology in Rome was that of a certain Artemon (230-40-270), but Dynamic Monarchianism in the West was already moribund. Yet it undoubtedly represented a type of Christology that was one of the oldest in the Christian Church.

[1] *Praxeas*, 3.   [2] *Praxeas*, 3, 10.   [3] Hippolytus, *Refutation*, 7:23, 10:19; Ayer, p. 172.

The Dynamic Monarchian party was stronger and more persistent in the East. There it had its most famous representative in Paul of Samosata, the able and politically gifted bishop of Antioch from c. 260 to 272. He represented the Logos, which he also described as the Son of God, as an impersonal attribute of the Father. This Logos had inspired Moses and the prophets. Jesus was a man, unique in that He was born of the Virgin, who was filled with the power of God, i. e., by God's Logos. By this indwelling inspiration Jesus was united in will by love to God, but did not become in substance one with God. That union is moral, but inseparable. By reason of it Christ was raised from the dead, and given a kind of delegated divinity. Between 264 and 269 three synods considered Paul of Samosata's views, by the last of which he was excommunicated; but he kept his place till driven out by the Emperor Aurelian.

Much more numerous than the Dynamic Monarchians were the Modalistic Monarchians, who made an appeal to the many for the reason already quoted from Tertullian (see p. 68), that in the presence of heathen polytheism, the unity of God seemed a prime article of the Christian faith, and any Logos conception or Dynamic Monarchianism seemed to them a denial of that unity. Cyprian coined for these Modalistic Monarchians the nickname Patripassians.[4] The leader of Modalistic Monarchianism was, like that of Dynamic Monarchianism, an Oriental Christian, Noetus, probably of Smyrna. The same controversies in Asia Minor may well have called forth both interpretations. Of Noetus little is known save that he taught in his native region in the period 180 to 200, "that Christ was the Father Himself, and that the Father Himself was born and suffered and died." [5] These views were transplanted to Rome, about 190, by a certain Praxeas, a follower of Noetus and an opponent of the Montanists, regarding whom Tertullian, then a Montanist and always a defender of the Logos Christology, said: "Praxeas did two works of the devil in Rome. He drove out prophecy and introduced heresy. He put to flight the Holy Spirit and crucified the Father." [6] A little later two other disciples of Noetus, Epigonus and Cleomenes, came to Rome and won, in large measure, the sympathy of Bishop Zephyrinus (198–217) for the Modalistic Monarchian position.

The most noted leader of the Modalistic school, whose name became permanently associated with this Christology, was Sabellius, of whose early life little is known, but who was teaching in Rome about 215. His theology was essentially that of Noetus, but much more carefully wrought out, especially in that it gave a definite place to the Holy Spirit as well as to the Son. Father, Son, and Holy Spirit are all one and the same. They are three names of the one God who manifests Himself in different ways according to circumstances. As Father He is the lawgiver of the Old Testament, as Son He is incarnate,

[4] *Letters,* 72–73:4.   [5] Hippolytus, *Against Noetus,* 1; Ayer, p. 177.
[6] *Praxeas,* 1; Ayer, p. 179.

as Spirit He is inspirer of the Apostles. But it is the one and the same God who thus appears in these successive and transitory relations, just as a human individual may be called by different titles to denote his varied rôles. Sabellius, though soon excommunicated at Rome, found large following for his views in the East, especially in Egypt and Libya. Nor was he without considerable influence on the development of what became the orthodox Christology. His absolute identification of Father, Son, and Holy Spirit was rejected; but it implied an equality which ultimately, as in Augustine, triumphed over the subordination of Son and Spirit characteristic of the Logos Christology both of Tertullian and Athanasius.

The great advocate of the Logos Christology at this juncture in Rome was Hippolytus (170?–c. 235), the most learned Christian writer then in the city, and the last considerable theologian there to use Greek rather than Latin as his vehicle of expression. As a commentator, chronicler, calculator of Easter dates, Apologist, and opponent of heretics, he was held in such high repute that his followers erected after his death the earliest Christian portrait statue known. He opposed vigorously the Monarchians of both schools. The fight in Rome waxed hot. Bishop Zephyrinus (198–217) hardly knew what to do, though he leaned toward the Monarchian side. On his death he was succeeded by Kallistos (Calixtus, 217–222), the most energetic and assertive bishop that Rome had yet seen—a man who had been born a slave, had engaged unsuccessfully in banking, and had, for a time, been a sufferer for his Christian faith in the mines of Sardinia. Over Zephyrinus he acquired great influence, and on his own attainment of the bishopric, issued in his own name certain regulations as to the readmission to the church of those repentant of sins of licentiousness, which show higher ecclesiastical claims than any heretofore advanced by a Roman bishop (see p. 93). Kallistos saw that these disputes were hurting the Roman Church. He therefore excommunicated Sabellius (c. 217), and charged Hippolytus with being a worshipper of two gods.[7] Hippolytus now broke with Kallistos, on this ground and on questions regarding discipline, and became the head of a rival communion in Rome —one of the first "counter-popes"—a position which he maintained till his banishment in the persecution of 235.

Kallistos tried to find a compromise formula in this Christological confusion. Father, Son and Logos, he held, are all names of "one indivisible spirit." Yet Son is also the proper designation of that which was visible, Jesus; while the Father was the spirit in Him. This presence of the Father in Jesus is the Logos. Kallistos was positive that the Father did not suffer on the cross, but suffered with the sufferings of the Son, Jesus; yet the Father "after He had taken unto Himself our flesh, raised it to the nature of deity, by bringing it into union with Himself, and made it one, so that Father and Son must be styled one God."[8] This is, indeed, far from logical or clear. One cannot blame

[7] Hippolytus, *Refutation*, 9:11.   [8] *Ibid.*, 9:12.

Hippolytus or Sabellius for not liking it. Yet it was a compromise which recognized a pre-existent Logos in Christ, even if it identified that Logos with the Father; it insisted on the identity of that which indwelt Jesus with God; and it claimed a human Jesus, raised to divinity by the Father, and made one with Him, thus really showing a distinction between the Father and the Son, while denying in words that one exists. This compromise won the majority in Rome, and opened the door for the full victory of the Logos Christology there. That victory was determined by the able exposition of that Christology which came at the turning-point in this conflict (213–218) from the pen of Tertullian of Carthage—*Against Praxeas* (see p. 66), with its clear definitions of a Trinity in three persons and of a distinction between the divine and human in Christ.

How completely this Christology won its way in Western Christendom is shown by the treatise on the *Trinity*, written by the Roman presbyter, Novatian, between 240 and 250. That eminent scholar was the first in the local Roman communion to use Latin rather than Greek. His quarrel with the dominant party in the church will be described later (p. 93). Novatian did little more than reproduce and expand Tertullian's views. But it is important that he treated this exposition as the only normal and legitimate interpretation of the "rule of truth"—the "Apostles' Creed." That symbol had been silent regarding the Logos Christology. To Novatian the Logos Christology is its only proper meaning. Between Father and Son a "communion of substance" exists.[9] The Latin equivalent of the later famous Nicene Homoousion—ὁμοούσιον—was therefore current in Rome before 250. Novatian has even a social Trinity. Commenting on *John* 10:30, "I and the Father are one," he declares that Christ "said one thing (*unum*). Let the heretics understand that He did not say one person. For one placed in the neuter intimates the social concord, not the personal unity."[10] The most valuable thing in Novatian is that he emphasized what was the heart of the conviction of the church in all this involved Christological controversy, that Christ was fully God and equally fully man.[11] Finally, about 262, the Roman bishop, Dionysius (259–268), writing against the Sabellians, expressed the Logos Christology in terms more nearly approximating to what was to be the Nicene decision of 325 than any other third-century theologian.[12] Thus the West had reached conclusions readily harmonizable with the result at Nicæa, more than sixty years before that great council. The East had attained no such uniformity.

[9] *Trinity*, 31.   [10] *Ibid.*, 27.   [11] *Ibid.*, 11, 24.
[12] In Athanasius, *De Decretis*, 26.

The Alexandrian School

ALEXANDRIA was, for more than six centuries, the second city of the ancient world, surpassed only by Rome, and later by Constantinople, in importance. Founded by Alexander the Great in B. C. 332, it was primarily a trading community, and as such, attracted numbers of Greeks and Jews. Its intellectual life was no less remarkable. Its library was the most famous in the empire. In its streets East and West met. There Greek philosophy entered into association, or competed in rivalry, with Judaism and many other Oriental cults, while the influence of ancient Egyptian thought persisted. It was the most cosmopolitan city of the ancient world. There the Old Testament was translated into Greek, and there Philo reinterpreted Judaism in terms of Hellenic philosophy. There Neo-Platonism was to arise in the third century of our era. Of the introduction of Christianity into Alexandria, or into Egypt generally, nothing is known, but it must have been early, since when the veil of silence was lifted Christianity was evidently strongly rooted there. The Gnostic, Basilides, taught in Alexandria in the reign of Hadrian (117–138). There the various philosophical systems had their "schools," where instruction could be obtained by all inquirers, and it was but natural that Christian teachers should imitate this good example, though it would appear that the beginnings of this work were independent of the Alexandrian Church authorities.

By about 185 a famous catechetical school existed in Alexandria, then under the leadership of a converted Stoic philosopher, Pantænus. Whether it originated with him, or what his own theological position may have been, it is impossible to determine. With Clement of Alexandria (?–c. 215), Pantænus's pupil and successor, it comes into the light. The course of religious development in Alexandria had evidently differed from that in Asia Minor and the West. In the latter regions the contest with Gnosticism had bred a distrust of philosophy such that Tertullian could declare that there was no possible connection between it and Christianity. That contest had, also, immensely strengthened the appeal to apostolical tradition and consolidated organization. In Alexandria these characteristics of the "Catholic" Church had not so fully developed, while philosophy was regarded not as inconsistent with Christianity, but as its handmaid. Here a union of what was best in ancient philosophy, chiefly Platonism and Stoicism, was effected to a degree nowhere else realized in orthodox circles, and the result was a Christian Gnosticism. Clement of Alexandria was typical of this movement. At the same time he was a presbyter in the Alexandrian Church, thus serving as a connecting link between the church and the school.

The more important of the works of Clement which have survived are three: his *Exhortation to the Heathen,* an apologetic treatise, giving incidentally no little information as to the mystery religions; his *Instructor,* the first treatise on Christian conduct, and an invaluable mine of information as to the customs of the age; and his *Stromata,* or *Miscellanies,* a collection of profound thoughts on religion and theology, arranged without much regard to system. Throughout he shows the mind of a highly trained and widely read thinker. Clement would interpret Christianity as Philo did Judaism, by philosophy, into scientific dogmatics. To him, as to Justin, whom he far surpassed in clearness of intellectual grasp, the divine Logos has always been the source of all the intelligence and morality of the human race—the teacher of mankind everywhere. "Our instructor is the holy God, Jesus, the Word who is the guide of all humanity." [1] He was the source of all true philosophy. "God is the cause of all good things; but of some primarily, as of the Old and the New Testament; and of others by consequence, as of philosophy. Perchance, too, philosophy was given to the Greeks directly and primarily, till the Lord should call the Greeks. For this was a schoolmaster to bring the Hellenic mind, as the law the Hebrews, to Christ." [2]

This training of humanity by the Logos has been, therefore, a progressive education. So it is, also, in the church. "Faith," that is simple, traditional Christianity, is enough for salvation; but the man who adds to his faith "knowledge," has a higher possession.[3] He is the true, Christian Gnostic. "To him that hath shall be given; to faith, knowledge; to knowledge, love; and to love, the inheritance." [4] The highest good to which knowledge leads— a good even greater than the salvation which it necessarily involves—is the knowledge of God. "Could we then suppose any one proposing to the Gnostic whether he would choose the knowledge of God or everlasting salvation; and if these, which are entirely identical, were separable, he would without the least hesitation choose the knowledge of God." [5] That highest good brings with it an almost Stoic absence of feeling, either of pleasure or of pain—a condition of blessedness in which Clement believes Christ stood, and to which the Apostles attained through His teaching.[6] One can readily comprehend that Clement, like Justin, had no real interest in the earthly life of Jesus. The Logos then became incarnate, indeed, but Clement's view of Christ's life is almost Docetic, certainly more so than that of any teacher of orthodox standing in the church of his own day.

[1] *Instructor*, 1:7.   [2] *Stromata*, 1:5; Ayer, p. 190.   [3] *Ibid.*, 1:6.   [4] *Ibid.*, 7:10.
[5] *Ibid.*, 4:22.   [6] *Ibid.*, 6:9.

Clement wrought out no complete theological system. That was to be the task of his even more celebrated pupil and successor in the headship of the Alexandrian catechetical school—Origen. Born of Christian parentage, probably in Alexandria, between 182 and 185, Origen grew up there into a familiarity with the Scriptures that was to render him the most fully acquainted with the Bible of any of the writers in the early church. His study of philosophy must also have been early begun. A youth of intense feeling and eager mental curiosity, he was as remarkable for his precocity as for the later ripeness of his scholarship. The persecution under Septimius Severus, in 202, cost the life of Origen's father, and he would have shared the same fate had not his mother frustrated his wishes by a stratagem. This persecution had driven Origen's teacher, Clement, from the city; and now, in 203, in spite of his youth, he gathered round himself inquirers with whom he reconstituted the catechetical school. This position he held with great success and with the approval of Bishop Demetrius, till 215, when the Emperor Caracalla drove all teachers of philosophy from Alexandria. His instruction had before been interrupted by visits to Rome (c. 211–212), where he met Hippolytus, and to Arabia (c. 213–214). His manner of life was ascetic in the extreme, and to avoid slander arising out of his relations with his numerous inquirers he emasculated himself, taking *Matt.* 19:12 as a counsel of perfection. The year 215 saw Origen in Cæsarea in Palestine, where he made friends of permanent value. Permitted to return to Alexandria, probably in 216, he resumed his instruction, and began a period of scholarly productivity the results of which were little short of marvellous.

Origen's labors in Alexandria were broken by a journey to Greece and Palestine in 230 or 231. He was still a layman; but by friendly Palestinian bishops he was ordained a presbyter in Cæsarea, probably that he might be free to preach. This ordination of an Alexandrian layman, Bishop Demetrius of Alexandria not unnaturally viewed as an intrusion on his jurisdiction, and jealousy of the successful teacher may have added to his resentment. At all events, Demetrius held synods by which Origen was banished from Alexandria, and as far as was in their power, deposed from the ministry. He now found a congenial home in friendly Cæsarea. Here he continued his indefatigable studies, his teaching, and to them he added frequent preaching. He made occasional journeys. He was surrounded by friends who held him in the highest esteem. With the great Decian persecution (see p. 80) of 250, this period of peace ended. He was imprisoned and tortured, and died either in Cæsarea or Tyre, probably in 251 (254?) as a consequence of the cruelties he had undergone. No man of purer spirit or nobler aims ornaments the history of the ancient church.

Origen was a man of many-sided scholarship. The field to which he devoted most attention was that of Biblical text-criticism and exegesis. Here his chief productions were his monumental *Hexapla,* giving the Hebrew and four parallel Greek translations of the Old Testament; and a long series of commentaries and briefer notes treating nearly the entire range of Scripture. It was the most valuable work that had yet been done by any Christian scholar. In the field of theology his *De Principiis,* written before 231, was not merely the first great systematic presentation of Christianity, but its thoughts and methods thenceforth controlled Greek dogmatic development. His *Against Celsus,* written between 246 and 248, in reply to the ablest criticism of Christianity that heathenism had produced—that of the Platonist Celsus (*c.* 177)—was the keenest and most convincing defense of the Christian faith that the ancient world brought forth, and one fully worthy of the greatness of the controversy. Besides these monumental undertakings he found time for the discussion of practical Christian themes, such as prayer and martyrdom, and for the preparation of many sermons. His was indeed a life of unwearied industry.

In Origen the process was complete which had long been interpreting Christian truths in terms of Hellenic thinking. He gave to the Christian system the fullest scientific standing, as tested by the science of that age, which was almost entirely comprised in philosophy and ethics. His philosophic standpoint was essentially Platonic and Stoic, with a decided leaning toward positions similar to those of the rising Neo-Platonism, the lectures of whose founder, Ammonius Saccas, he is said to have heard.[7] These philosophic principles he sought to bring into harmony with the Scriptures, as his great Hebrew fellow townsman, Philo, had done, by allegorical interpretation of the Bible. All normal Scripture, he held, has a threefold meaning. "The simple man may be edified by the 'flesh' as it were of the Scriptures, for so we name the obvious sense; while he who has ascended a certain way may be edified by the 'soul' as it were; the perfect man . . . may receive edification from the spiritual law, which has a shadow of good things to come. For as man consists of body and soul and spirit, so in the same way does Scripture." [8] This allegorical system enabled Origen to read practically what he wished into the Scriptures.

As a necessary foundation for his theological system, Origen posited that "which differs in no respect from ecclesiastical and apostolical tradition." [9] These fundamentals of traditional Christianity include belief (1) "in one God . . . the Father of our Lord Jesus Christ, [who] Himself gave the law and the prophets and the Gospels, being also the God of the Apostles and of the Old and New Testaments"; (2) "that Jesus Christ Himself . . . was born of the Father before all creatures . . . became a man, and was incarnate although God, and while made a man remained the God which He was . . . was born of a Virgin . . . was truly born and did truly suffer and . . . did truly die . . . did truly rise from the dead"; (3) "that the Holy Spirit was

[7] Eusebius, *Church History,* 6.19.6.   [8] *De Principiis,* 4.11.11; Ayer, pp. 200, 201.
[9] *De Principiis,* Preface.

associated in honor and dignity with the Father and the Son"; (4) in the resurrection and in future rewards and punishments; (5) in free will; (6) in the existence and opposition of the devil and his angels; (7) that the world was made in time and will "be destroyed on account of its wickedness"; (8) "that the Scriptures were written by the Spirit of God"; (9) "that there are certain angels of God, and certain good influences which are His servants in accomplishing the salvation of men." [10] These are essential beliefs for all Christians, learned and unlearned, as taught by the church; and on them Origen proceeded to erect his mighty fabric of systematic theology—that explanation of Christianity for him who would add to his faith knowledge.

Origen's conception of the universe was strongly Platonic. The real world is the spiritual reality behind this temporary, phenomenal, visible world. In that world great transactions have had their place. There, as with Plato, our spirits existed. There sin first entered. There we fell, and thither the redeemed will return. God, the uncreated, perfect Spirit, is the source of all. From Him the Son is eternally generated. "His generation is as eternal and everlasting as the brilliancy which is produced from the sun." [11] Yet Christ is "a second God," [12] a "creature." Christ's position, as Loofs has pointed out, was viewed by Origen as the same as that of the *nous*—mind, thought—in the Neo-Platonic system. He is the "mediator" between God and His world of creatures, the being through whom they were made. Highest of these creatures is the Holy Spirit, whom Origen reckons to the Godhead, by reason of churchly tradition, but for whom he has no real necessity in his system.

All spiritual beings, including the spirits of men, were made by God, through the Son, in the true spiritual world. "He had no other reason for creating them than on account of Himself, *i. e.,* His own goodness." [13] All were good, though their goodness, unlike that of God, was "an accidental and perishable quality." [14] All had free will. Hence some fell by sin in the invisible spiritual world. It was as a place of punishment and of reform that God created this visible universe, placing fallen spirits therein in proportion to the heinousness of their sins. The least sinful are angels and have as bodies the stars. Those of greater sinfulness are on the face of the earth, with animal souls, also, and mortal bodies. They constitute mankind. The worst are the demons, led by the devil himself.

Salvation was wrought by the Logos-Son becoming man, by uniting with a human soul that had not sinned in its previous existence and a pure body. While here Christ was God and man; but at the resurrection and ascension Christ's humanity was given the glory of His divinity, and is no longer human but divine. [15] That transformation Christ effects for all His disciples. "From Him there began the union of the divine with the human nature, in

[10] All *ibid.*   [11] *De Principiis*, 1.2.4.   [12] *Celsus*, 5:39.   [13] *De Principiis*, 2.9.6.
[14] *Ibid.*, 1.6.2.   [15] *Celsus*, 3:41.

order that the human, by communion with the divine, might rise to be divine, not in Jesus alone, but in all those who not only believe but enter upon the life which Jesus taught." [16] Origen, more than any theologian since Paul, emphasized the sacrificial character of Christ's death; but he interpreted it in many ways, some of which were not very consistent with others. Christ suffered what was "for the good of the human race" as a representative and an example.[17] He was in some sense a propitiatory offering to God. He was a ransom paid to the powers of evil.[18] He conquered the demons.[19] He frustrated their expectation that they could hold Him by the bonds of death and brought their kingdom to an end.[20] Those of mankind who are His disciples are received at death into Paradise; the evil find their place in hell. Yet, ultimately, not only all men, but even the devil and all spirits with him will be saved.[21] This will be the restoration of all things, when God will be all in all.

Origen's theological structure is the greatest intellectual achievement of the ante-Nicene Church. It influenced profoundly all after-thinking in the Orient. Yet it is easy to see how he could be quoted on either side in the later Christological controversies, and to understand, in the light of a later rigid orthodoxy, how he came to be regarded as a heretic, whose views were condemned by a synod in his native Alexandria in 399 or 400, by the Emperor Justinian in 543, and by the Fifth General Council in 553. His work was professedly for the learned, not for the common Christian. Because its science is not our science it seems strange to us. But it gave to Christianity full scientific standing in that age. In particular, the teachings of Clement and Origen greatly advanced the dominance of the Logos Christology in the Orient, though Sabellianism was still wide-spread there, and an adoptionist Christology had an eminent representative in the bishop of Antioch, Paul of Samosata, as late as 272.

Yet Origen was not without serious critics in the century in which he lived. Of these the most important, theologically, was Methodius, bishop of Olympus, in Lycia, who died about 311. Taking his stand on the tradition of Asia Minor, Methodius denied Origen's doctrines of the soul's pre-existence and imprisonment in this world, and affirmed the resurrection of the body. In ability he was not to be compared with Origen.

---

[16] Ibid., 3:28.   [17] Ibid., 7:17; Ayer, p. 197.
[18] Com. on Matt., 12:28, 16:8; Ayer, p. 197.   [19] Com. on John, 6:37.
[20] Com. on Matt., 13:9.   [21] De Principiis, 1.6.1–4; Ayer, p. 198.

10

Church and State from 180 to 260

*T*HE VISIBLE DECLINE of the Roman Empire is usually reckoned from the death of Marcus Aurelius (180), though its causes go back much further. Population was diminishing. Trade and industry were fettered by heavy taxation. The leadership passed more and more from the hands of the cultivated classes. The army was largely recruited from the outlying provinces of the empire, and even from tribes beyond its borders. From the death of Commodus (192), it dictated the choice of Emperors, who, in general, were very far from representing the higher type of Græco-Roman culture, as had the Antonines. The whole administrative machinery of the empire was increasingly inefficient, and the defense of its borders inadequate. From a military point of view, conditions grew steadily worse till the time of Aurelian (270–275), and were hardly securely bettered till that of Diocletian (284–305). In other respects no considerable pause was achieved in the decline. Yet this period was also one of increasing feeling of popular unity in the empire. The lines of distinction between the races were breaking down. In 212 the Roman citizenship was extended by Caracalla, not wholly from disinterested motives, to all free inhabitants of the empire. Above all, from a religious point of view, the close of the second and the whole of the third centuries were an age of syncretism, a period of deepening religious feeling, in which the mystery religions of the Orient—and Christianity also—made exceedingly rapid increase in the number of their adherents.

This growth of the church was extensive as well as intensive. To near the close of the second century it had penetrated little beyond those whose ordinary tongue was Greek. By the dawn of the third century the church was rapidly advancing in Latin-speaking North Africa and, though more slowly, in Spain and Gaul, and reaching toward, if it had not already arrived in, Britain. In Egypt Christianity was now penetrating the native population, while by 190 it was well represented in Syriac-speaking Edessa. The church was also reaching more extensively than earlier into the higher classes of society. It was being better understood; and though Tertullian shows that the old popular slanders of cannibalism and gross immorality were still prevalent in 197,[1] as the third century went on they seem to have much decreased, doubtless through growing acquaintance with the real significance of Christianity.

[1] *Apology,* 7.

The relations of the state to the church during the period from 180 to 260 were most various, depending on the will of the several Emperors, but, on the whole, such as to aid rather than to hinder its growth till the last decade of this period. Legally, Christianity was condemned. It had no right to exist.[2] Practically, it enjoyed a considerable degree of toleration during most of this epoch. The persecution which had been begun under Marcus Aurelius continued into the reign of Commodus, but he soon neglected the church as he did about everything else not connected with his own pleasures. This rest continued till well into the reign of Septimius Severus (193–211); but was broken in 202 by a persecution of considerable severity, especially in Carthage and Egypt. Under Caracalla (211–217), persecution again raged in North Africa. Elagabalus (218–222), though an ardent supporter of sun-worship, was disposed to a syncretism which was not openly hostile to Christianity. Alexander Severus (222–235) was distinctly favorable. A syncretist who would unite many religions, he placed a bust of Christ in his private chapel along with images of leaders of other faiths; while his mother, Julia Mamæa, under whose influence he stood, heard lectures by Origen. He even decided a dispute as to whether a piece of property in Rome should be used by its Christian claimants, doubtless as a place of worship, or by their opponents as a cook-shop, in favor of the Christians. A change of policy came under Maximinus (235–238), by whom an edict against the Christians was issued, which, though not extensively enforced, thrust both the "Catholic" bishop, Pontianus, and his schismatic rival Hippolytus from Rome into the cruel slavery of the mines, where they soon lost their lives. In eastern Asia Minor and Palestine this persecution made itself felt. Under Gordian (238–244) and till near the end of the reign of Philip the Arabian (244–249) the church had rest. For that new outbreak Philip was in no way responsible. Indeed, an erroneous rumor declared him to be secretly a Christian. The number of martyrs in these persecutions was not large, as Origen testified, writing between 246 and 248,[3] and these outbreaks were local, if at times of considerable extent. Though Christians were deprived of all legal protection, the average believer must have thought that the condition of the church was approaching practical safety.

This growing feeling of security was rudely dispelled. The year 248 saw the celebration of the thousandth anniversary of the founding of Rome. It was a time of revival of ancient traditions and of the memories of former splendors. The empire was never more threatened by barbarian attack or torn by internal disputes. The populace attributed these troubles to the cessation of persecution.[4] A fierce mob attack broke out in Alexandria before the death of Philip the Arabian. To the more observant heathens the growth of a rigidly organized church might well seem that of a state within the state, the more dangerous that Christians still largely refused army service or the duties of

[2] Tertullian, *Apology*, 4.   [3] *Celsus*, 3:8.   [4] Origen, *Celsus*, 3:15; Ayer, p. 206.

public office.[5] Nearer at hand lay the plausible, though fallacious, argument that as Rome had grown great when the old gods were worshipped by all, so now their rejection by a portion of the population had cost Rome their aid, and had caused the calamities evident on every hand. This was apparently the feeling of the new Emperor, Decius (249–251), and of a conservative Roman noble, Valerian, with whom Decius was intimately associated. The result was the edict of 250, which initiated the first universal and systematic persecution of Christianity.

The Decian persecution was by far the worst trial that the church as a whole had undergone—the more severe because it had principle and determination behind it. The aim was not primarily to take life, though there were numerous and cruel martyrdoms, but rather to compel Christians by torture, imprisonment, or fear to sacrifice to the old gods. Bishops Fabian of Rome and Babylas of Antioch died as martyrs. Origen and hosts of others were tortured. The number of these "confessors" was very great. So, also, was the number of the "lapsed"—that is, of those who, through fear or torture, sacrificed, burned incense, or procured certificates from friendly or venal officials that they had duly worshipped in the form prescribed by the state.[6] Many of these lapsed, when the persecution was over, returned to seek in bitter penitence readmission to the church. The question of their treatment caused a long, enduring schism in Rome, and much trouble elsewhere (see p. 93). Fierce as it was, the persecution under Decius and Valerian was soon over; but only to be renewed in somewhat milder form by Decius's successor, Gallus (251–253). In 253 Decius's old associate in persecution, Valerian, obtained possession of the empire (253–260). Though he at first left the Christians undisturbed, in 257 and 258 he renewed the attack with greater ferocity. Christian assemblies were forbidden; Christian churches and cemeteries confiscated; bishops, priests, and deacons ordered to be executed, and lay Christians in high places disgraced, banished, and their goods held forfeited. Under this persecution Cyprian died in Carthage, Bishop Sixtus II and the Deacon Laurentius in Rome, and Bishop Fructuosus in Tarragona in Spain. It was a fearful period of trial, lasting, with intermissions indeed, from 250 to 259.

In 260 Valerian became a prisoner in the hands of the victorious Persians. His son, associate Emperor and successor, Gallienus (260–268), a thoroughly weak and incompetent ruler, promptly gave up the struggle with Christianity. Church property was returned, and a degree of favor shown that has sometimes, though erroneously, been interpreted as a legal toleration. That the act of Gallienus was not. The old laws against Christianity were unrepealed. Practically, however, a peace began which was to last till the outbreak of the persecution under Diocletian, in 303, though probably threatened by Aurelian just before his death in 275. The church had come out of the struggle stronger than ever before.

[5] Origen, Celsus, 8:73, 75.   [6] Ayer, p. 210, for specimens.

11

The Constitutional Development of the Church

THE EFFECT of the struggle with Gnosticism and Montanism upon the development of the bishoprics as centers of unity, witnesses to apostolical tradition, and bearers of an apostolical succession, has already been seen (pp. 57 ff.). The tendencies then developed continued to work in increasing power, with the result that, between 200 and 260, the church as an organization took on most of the constitutional features which were to characterize it throughout the period of the dominance of Græco-Roman culture. Above all, this development was manifested in the increase of the power of the bishops. The circumstances of the time, the contests with Gnostics and Montanists, the leadership of increasing masses of ignorant recent converts from heathenism, the necessities of uniformity in worship and discipline, all tended to centralize in the bishop the rights and authority which in an earlier period had been more widely shared. The "gifts of the Spirit," which had been very real to the thought of Christians of the apostolic and subapostolic ages, and which might be possessed by any one, were now a tradition rather than a vital reality. The contest with Montanism, among other causes, had led such claims to be regarded with suspicion. The tradition, however, remained, but it was rapidly changing into a theory of official endowment. These "gifts" were now the official possession of the clergy, especially of the bishops. The bishops were the divinely appointed guardians of the deposit of the faith, and therefore those who could determine what was heresy. They were the leaders of worship—a matter of constantly increasing importance with the growing conviction, wide-spread by the beginning of the third century, that the ministry is a priesthood. They were the disciplinary officers of the congregation—though their authority in this respect was not firmly fixed—able to say when the sinner needed excommunication and when he showed sufficient repentance for restoration. As given full expression by Cyprian of Carthage, about 250 (see pp. 66–67), the foundation of the church is the unity of the bishops.

The Christians of a particular city had been regarded, certainly from the beginning of the second century, as constituting a single community, whether meeting in one congregation or many. As such they were under the guidance of a single bishop. Ancient civilization was strongly urban in its political constitution. The adjacent country district looked to its neighboring city. Christianity had been planted in the cities. By efforts going out from them, congregations were formed in the surrounding villages, which came at first into the city for their worship,[1] but as they grew larger must increasingly have met by themselves. Planted by Christians from the cities, they were under the oversight of the city bishop, whose immediate field of superintendence was thus growing, by the third century, into a diocese. In some rural portions of the East, notably Syria and Asia Minor, where city influence was relatively weak, country groups of congregations developed before the end of the third century, headed by a rural bishop, a *chorepiskopos*—χωρεπίσκοπος—but this system was not of large growth, nor were these country bishops deemed the equals in dignity of their city brethren. The system did not spread to the West at this time, though introduced there in the Middle Ages, only to prove unsatisfactory.

To Cyprian, the episcopate was a unit, and each bishop a representative of all its powers, on an equality with all other bishops. Yet even in his time this theory was becoming impracticable. The bishops of the great, politically influential cities of the empire were attaining a superiority in dignity over others, which those of Rome even more than the rest were striving to translate into a superiority of jurisdiction. Rome, Alexandria, Antioch, Carthage, and Ephesus, by reason of religious sentiment, had an outstanding eminence, and Rome most of all. Besides these greater posts, the bishop of the capital city of each province was beginning to be looked upon as having a certain superiority to those of lesser towns in his region; but the full development of the metropolitan dignity was not to come till the fourth century, and earlier in the East than in the West.

By the beginning of the third century clergy were sharply distinguished from laity. The technical use of the words *laikos*—λαικός—and *kleros*—κλῆρος—was a gradual development, as was the distinction which they implied. The earliest Christian employment of the former was by Clement of Rome.[2] The latter occurs in 1 *Peter* 5:3, in wholly untechnical usage. But κλῆρος and its Latin equivalent, *ordo,* were the common expressions for the "orders" of magistrates and dignitaries of the Roman Empire. It is probably from such popular usage that they come into Christian employment. The letter of the churches of Lyons and Vienne, giving a description of the persecution of 177, spoke of the "order" of the martyrs—κλῆρον.[3] Tertullian wrote of "clerical order" and "ecclesiastical orders."[4] By his time the distinction had become practically fixed; even if Tertullian himself could recall, for purposes of argument as a Montanist, the early doctrine of the priesthood of all believers,[5] "are not even we laics priests?"[6]

Admission to clerical office was by ordination, a rite which certainly goes

---

[1] Justin, *Apology,* 67; Ayer, p. 35.   [2] 93–97; in 1 *Clem.,* 40.
[3] Eusebius, *Church History,* 5.1.10.   [4] *Monogamy,* 12.   [5] *Chastity,* 7.
[6] Compare 1 *Peter* 2:5; *Rev.* 1:6.

back to the earliest days of the church, at least as a sign of the bestowal of charismatic gifts, or separation for a special duty.[7] The ordinary process of the choice of a bishop by the middle of the third century was a nomination by the other clergy, especially the presbyters, of the city; the approval of neighboring bishops, and ratification or election by the congregation.[8] Ordination followed at the hands of at least one already a bishop—a number of episcopal ordainers which had become fixed at a normal minimum of three by the end of the third century. The control of the choice of the presbyters, deacons, and lower clergy lay in the hand of their local bishop, by whom they were ordained.[9] The presbyters were the bishop's advisers. With his consent they administered the sacraments.[10] They preached. As congregations grew more numerous in a city, a presbyter would be placed in immediate charge of each, and their importance thereby enhanced, from its relative depression, immediately after the rise of the monarchical episcopate. There was no fixed limit to their number. The deacons were immediately responsible to the bishop, and were his assistants in the care of the poor and other financial concerns, in aiding in the worship and discipline. They often stood in closer practical relations to him than the presbyters. At Rome, the number of the deacons was seven, in remembrance of *Acts* 6:5. When Bishop Fabian (236–250) adopted the civil division of the city as its fourteen charity districts, he appointed seven sub-deacons in addition to the seven deacons, that the primitive number might not be surpassed. Sub-deacons also existed in Carthage in the time of Cyprian, and quite generally at a little later period. In many parts of the church there was no fixed rule as to the number of deacons.

Bishops, presbyters, and deacons constituted the major orders. Below them there stood, in the first half of the third century, the minor orders. In the general absence of all statistical information as to the early church, a letter of Bishop Cornelius of Rome, written about 251, is of high value as showing conditions in that important church. Under the single bishop in Rome there were forty-six presbyters and seven deacons. Below them, constituting what were soon to be known as the minor orders, were seven sub-deacons, forty-two acolytes, and fifty-two exorcists, readers, and janitors.[11] More than fifteen hundred dependents were supported by the church, which may have included thirty thousand adherents. Some of these offices were of very ancient origin. Those of readers and exorcists had originally been regarded as charismatic. Exorcists continued to be so viewed in the Orient, and were not there properly officers. By the time of Cyprian the reader's office was thought a preparatory step toward that of presbyter.[12] The exorcist's task was to drive out evil spirits, in whose prevalent working the age firmly believed. Of the duties of acolytes little is known save that they were assistants in service and aid. They

---

[7] *Acts* 6:6, 13:3; also 1 *Tim.* 4:14, 5:20; 2 *Tim.* 1:6.
[8] Cyprian, *Letters,* 51–55:8, 66–68:2, 67:4,5.   [9] *Ibid.,* 23–29, 33–39:5, 34–40.
[10] Tertullian, *Baptism,* 17; Ayer, p. 167.   [11] Eusebius, *Church History,* 6.43.11.
[12] *Letters,* 33:5.

were not to be found in the Orient. The janitors were especially important when it became the custom to admit none but the baptized to the more sacred parts of the service. In the East, though not in the West, deaconesses were to be found who were reckoned in a certain sense as of the clergy. Their origin was probably charismatic and was of high antiquity.[13] Their tasks were those of care for women, especially the ill. Besides these deaconesses there were to be found in the churches, both East and West, a class known as "widows," whose origin was likewise ancient.[14] Their duties were prayer and aid to the sick, especially of their own sex. They were held in high honor, though hardly to be reckoned properly as of the "clergy." All these were supported, in whole or in part, by the gifts of the congregation, which were of large amount, both of eatables and of money.[15] These gifts were looked upon, by the time of Cyprian, as "tithes," and were all at the disposal of the bishop.[16] By the middle of the third century the higher clergy were expected to give their whole time to the work of the ministry; [17] yet even bishops sometimes shared in secular business, not always of a commendable character. The lower clergy could still engage in trade. It is evident, however, that though the ancient doctrine of the priesthood of all believers might still occasionally be remembered, it had a purely theoretical value. In practical Christian life the clergy, by the middle of the third century, were a distinct, close-knit spiritual rank, on whom the laity were religiously dependent, and who were in turn supported by laymen's gifts.

12

Public Worship and Sacred Seasons

ALREADY, by the time of Justin (153), the primitive division of worship into two assemblies, one for prayer and instruction and the other for the Lord's Supper in connection with a common meal had ceased. The Lord's Supper was now the crowning act of the service of worship and edification.[1] Its separation from the common meal was now complete. The course of development during the succeeding century was determined by the prevalence of ideas drawn from the mystery religions. There is no adequate ground to believe that there was intentional imitation. Christians of the last half of

---

[13] *Romans* 16:1. [14] 1 *Tim.* 5:9, 10.
[15] *Teaching*, 13; Justin, *Apology*, 67; Tertullian, *Apology*, 39; Ayer, pp. 35, 41.
[16] *Letters*, 65–1:1. [17] Cyprian, *Lapsed*, 6. [1] Justin, *Apology*, 67; Ayer, p. 35.

the second and the third centuries lived in an atmosphere highly charged with influences sprung from these faiths. It was but natural that they should look upon their own worship from the same point of view. It is probable that already existing tendencies in this direction were strongly reinforced by the great growth of the church by conversion from heathenism in the first half of the third century.

The church came to be more and more regarded as possessed of life-giving mysteries, under the superintendence and dispensation of the clergy. Inquirers were prepared for initiation by instruction—the catechumens. Such preparation, in some degree, had existed from the apostolic days. It was now systematized. Origen taught in an already celebrated school in Alexandria in 203. Cyprian shows that in Carthage, by about 250, such instruction was in charge of an officer designated by the bishop.[2] Instruction was followed by the great initiatory rite of baptism (see pp. 86 ff.), which granted admission to the propitiatory sacrifice of the life-giving mystery of the Lord's Supper (see pp. 89 ff.). As in the time of Justin, the other elements of worship consisted of Scripture reading, preaching, prayers, and hymns. These were open to all honest inquirers. The analogy of the mystery religions barred all but those initiate or about to be initiated from presence at baptism or the Lord's Supper, and led to a constant augmentation of the valuation placed on these rites as the most sacred elements of worship. Whether the custom had arisen by the third century of regarding these sacraments as a secret discipline, in which the exact words of the Creed and of the Lord's Prayer were for the first time imparted to the baptized, and of which no mention was to be made to the profane, is uncertain. Such usages were wide-spread in the fourth and fifth centuries. Already in the third the forces were at work which were to lead to the practices.

Sunday was the chief occasion of worship, yet services were beginning to be held on week-days as well. Wednesday and Friday, as earlier (see p. 38), were days of fasting. The great event of the year was the Easter season. The period immediately before was one of fasting in commemoration of Christ's sufferings. Customs differed in various parts of the empire. In Rome a forty hours' fast and vigil was held in remembrance of Christ's rest in the grave. This was extended, by the time of the Council of Nicæa (325) to a forty days' Lent. All fasting ended with the dawn of Easter morning, and the Pentecostal period of rejoicing then began. In that time there was no fasting, or kneeling in prayer in public worship.[3] Easter eve was the favorite season for baptism, that the newly initiate might participate in the Easter joy. Beside these fixed seasons, the martyrs were commemorated with celebration of the Lord's Supper annually on the days of their deaths.[4] Prayers for the dead in general, and their remembrance by offerings on the anniversaries of

[2] *Letters*, 23–29.   [3] Tertullian, *Corona*, 3.
[4] *Letter of the Church of Smyrna on Martyrdom of Polycarp*, 18; Cyprian, *Letters*, 33–39:3; 36–12:2.

their decease, were in use by the early part of the third century.[5] Relics of martyrs had been held in high veneration since the middle of the second century.[6] The full development of saint-worship had not yet come; but the church was honoring with peculiar devotion the memory of the athletes of the Christian race who had not counted their lives dear unto themselves.

13

Baptism

BAPTISM is older than Christianity. The rite gave to John, the "Forerunner," his name. He baptized Jesus. His disciples and those of Jesus baptized, though Jesus Himself did not.[1] The origin of the rite is uncertain; but it was probably a spiritualization of the old Levitical washings. Jewish teaching, traceable probably to a period as early as the time of Christ, required proselytes to the Hebrew faith not merely to be circumcised, but to be baptized.[2] Furthermore, various lustrations were observed by brotherhoods like the Essenes and that at Qumran. Influenced, perhaps, by these, and understanding the need even for the Jew, no less than the proselyte, to be purified in view of the impending judgment, it seems probable that John derived his rite from contemporary practice, but gave it a special meaning as symbolising submission to the river of fire by which God would purge and redeem the world. It was a fitting token, moreover, of the spiritual purification that followed the repentance that he preached. The mystery religions had equivalent rites (see p. 11); but so purely Jewish was that primitive Christianity to which baptism belongs, that it is inconceivable that they should have had any effect on the origin of the practice, though they were profoundly to influence its development on Gentile soil. Peter represents baptism as the rite of admission to the church, and to the reception of the Holy Spirit.[3] As the sacrament of admission baptism always stood till the religious divisions of post-Reformation days. It so stands for the vast majority of Christians at present.

With Paul, baptism was not merely the symbol of cleansing from sin,[4] it involved a new relation to Christ,[5] and a participation in His death and resurrection.[6] Though Paul apparently did not think baptism essential to

---

[5] Tertullian, *Corona*, 3; *Monogamy*, 10.   [6] *Letter of Smyrna*, as cited, 18.
[1] *John* 3:22, 4:1, 2.   [2] See Schürer, *Geschichte des Jüdischen Volkes*, 2:569–573.
[3] *Acts* 2:38; see also 2:41; 1 *Cor.* 12:13.   [4] 1 *Cor.* 6:11.   [5] *Gal.* 3:26, 27.
[6] *Romans* 6:4; *Col.* 2:12.

salvation [7] his view approached that of the initiations of the mystery religions and his converts in Corinth, at least, held an almost magical conception of the rite, being baptized in behalf of their dead friends, that the departed might be benefited thereby.[8] Baptism soon came to be regarded as indispensable. The writer of the fourth Gospel represented Christ as declaring: "Verily, I say unto thee, except a man be born of water and the Spirit, he cannot enter the Kingdom of God." [9] The appendix to *Mark* pictured the risen Christ as saying: "He that believeth and is baptized shall be saved." [10] This conviction but deepened. To Hermas (100–140), baptism was the very foundation of the church, which "is builded upon waters." [11] Even to the philosophical Justin (153) baptism effected "regeneration" and "illumination." [12] In Tertullian's estimate it conveyed eternal life itself.[13]

By the time of Hermas [14] and of Justin [15] the view was general that baptism washed away all previous sins. As in the mystery religions it had become the great rite of purification, initiation, and rebirth into the eternal life. Hence it could be received but once. The only substitute was martyrdom, "which stands in lieu of the fontal bathing, when that has not been received, and restores it when lost." [16] With the early disciples generally baptism was "in the name of Jesus Christ." [17] There is no mention of baptism in the name of the Trinity in the New Testament, except in the command attributed to Christ in *Matt.* 28:19. That text is early, however. It underlies the Apostles' Creed, and the practice recorded in the *Teaching*,[18] and by Justin.[19] The Christian leaders of the third century retained the recognition of the earlier form, and, in Rome at least, baptism in the name of Christ was deemed valid, if irregular, certainly from the time of Bishop Stephen (254–257).[20]

Regarding persons baptized, the strong probability is that, till past the middle of the second century, they were those only of years of discretion. The first mention of infant baptism, and an obscure one, was about 185, by Irenæus.[21] Tertullian spoke distinctly of the practice, but discouraged it as so serious a step that delay of baptism was desirable till character was formed. Hence he doubted its wisdom for the unmarried.[22] Less earnest men than Tertullian felt that it was unwise to use so great an agency of pardon till one's record of sins was practically made up. A conspicuous instance, by no means solitary, was the Emperor Constantine, who postponed his baptism till his death-bed. To Origen infant baptism was an apostolic custom.[23] Cyprian favored its earliest possible reception.[24] Why infant baptism arose there is no certain evidence. Cyprian, in the letter just cited, argued in its

[7] *1 Cor.* 1:14–17.   [8] *1 Cor.* 15:29.   [9] *John* 3:5.   [10] *Mark* 16:16.
[11] *Vis.*, 3:33.   [12] *Apology*, 61; Ayer, p. 33.   [13] *Baptism*, 1.   [14] *Man.*, 4:3.
[15] *Apology*, 61.   [16] Tertullian, *Baptism*, 16.
[17] *Acts* 2:38; see also 8:16, 10:48, 19:5; *Romans* 6:3; *Gal.* 3:27.
[18] *Teaching*, 7; Ayer, p. 38.   [19] *Apology*, 61; Ayer, p. 33.
[20] Cyprian, *Letters*, 73–74:5.   [21] *Heresies*, 2.22.4.   [22] *Baptism*, 18.
[23] *Com. on Romans*, 5.   [24] *Letters*, 58–64:5.

favor from the doctrine of original sin. Yet the older general opinion seems to have held to the innocency of childhood.[25] More probable explanations are the feeling that outside the church there is no salvation, and the words attributed to Christ in *John* 3:5. Christian parents would not have their children fail of entering the Kingdom of God. Infant baptism did not, however, become universal till the sixth century, largely through the feeling already noted in Tertullian, that so cleansing a sacrament should not be lightly used.

As to the method of baptism, it is probable that the original form was by immersion, complete or partial. That is implied in *Romans* 6:4 and *Colossians* 2:12. Pictures in the catacombs would seem to indicate that the submersion was not always complete. The fullest early evidence is that of the *Teaching:* "Baptize in the name of the Father and of the Son and of the Holy Spirit in living [running] water. But if thou hast not living water, then baptize in other water; and if thou art not able in cold, then in warm. But if thou hast neither, then pour water upon the head thrice in the name of the Father and of the Son and of the Holy Spirit." [26] Affusion was, therefore, a recognized form of baptism. Cyprian cordially upheld it.[27] Immersion continued the prevailing practice till the late Middle Ages in the West; in the East it so remains. The *Teaching* and Justin show that fasting and an expression of belief, together with an agreement to live the Christian life, were necessary prerequisites. By the time of Tertullian an elaborate ritual had developed. The ceremony began with the formal renunciation by the candidate of the devil and all his works. Then followed the threefold immersion. On coming from the fount the newly baptized tasted a mixture of milk and honey, in symbolism of his condition as a new-born babe in Christ. To that succeeded anointing with oil and the laying on of the hands of the baptizer in token of the reception of the Holy Spirit.[28] Baptism and what was later known as confirmation were thus combined. Tertullian also shows the earliest now known existence of Christian sponsors, *i. e.,* godparents.[29] The same customs of fasting and sponsors characterized the worship of Isis.

In the apostolic age baptism was administered doubtless not only by Apostles and other leaders, but widely by those charismatically eminent in the church. By 110–117 Ignatius, in the interest of unity, was urging, "it is not lawful apart from the bishop either to baptize or to hold a love-feast." [30] In Tertullian's time, "of giving it, the chief priest, who is the bishop, has the right; in the next place the presbyters and deacons . . . besides these even laymen have the right, for what is equally received can be equally given." [31] In the Greek and Roman Churches baptism still continues the only sacra-

---

[25] Tertullian, *Baptism,* 18.   [26] Ayer, p. 38.   [27] *Letters,* 75–69:12.
[28] Tertullian, *Baptism,* 6–8; *Corona,* 3. For the very similar Roman rite see Hippolytus, *Apostolic Tradition,* 21–23.
[29] *Baptism,* 18.   [30] *Smyrna,* 8; Ayer, p. 42.   [31] *Baptism,* 17; Ayer, p. 167.

ment which any Christian, or indeed any seriously intending person, can administer in case of necessity.

The middle of the third century saw a heated discussion over the validity of heretical baptism. Tertullian had regarded it as worthless; [32] and his was undoubtedly the prevalent opinion of his time. After the Novatian schism (see p. 93) Bishop Stephen of Rome (254–257) advanced the claim that baptism, even by heretics, was effectual if done in proper form. His motives seem to have been partly the growing feeling that sacraments are of value in themselves, irrespective of the character of the administrant, and partly a desire to facilitate the return of the followers of Novatian. This interpretation was energetically resisted by Cyprian of Carthage, and Firmilian of Cæsarea in Cappadocia, [33] and led to certain important assertions of the authority of the Roman bishop. The deaths of Stephen and Cyprian gave a pause to the dispute; but the Roman view grew into general acceptance in the West. The East reached no such unanimity of judgment.

14

The Lord's Supper

SOME ACCOUNT has been given of the early development of the doctrine of the Lord's Supper (see pp. 22, 36). It has been seen that "breaking of bread," in connection with a common meal, was a Christian practice from the beginning. From the time of Paul, certainly, it was believed to be by command of Christ Himself, and in peculiar remembrance of Him and of His death. Outside the New Testament three writers refer to the Lord's Supper before the age of Irenæus. Of these the account in the *Teaching*,[1] reflects the most primitive Christian conditions. It provides a simple liturgy of gratitude. Thou "didst bestow upon us spiritual food and drink and eternal life through Thy Son." From Christ come "life and knowledge." A more mystical explanation of the Supper, however, began early. *John* 6:47–58 teaches the necessity of eating the flesh and drinking the blood of Christ to have "life." To Ignatius the Supper "is the medicine of immortality, and the antidote that we should not die but live forever." [2] Justin affirmed, "for not as common bread and common drink do we receive these; but in like manner as Jesus Christ our Saviour, having been made flesh by the Word

[32] *Baptism*, 15.   [33] Cyprian, *Letters*, 69–76.   [1] 9–11; Ayer, p. 38.   [2] *Eph.*, 20.

of God, had both flesh and blood for our salvation, so likewise have we been taught that the food which is blessed by the prayer of His Word, and from which our blood and flesh by transmutation are nourished, is the flesh and blood of that Jesus who was made flesh." [3] By Justin's time (153) the Lord's Supper was already separated from the common meal. It was held early on Sunday morning and comprised the following items: scripture readings interspersed with psalmody, common prayers with the congregational "Amen," the kiss of peace, the consecration of the bread and wine (the earliest such prayer being preserved for us in Hippolytus [4]), and the communion. The prayers were offered extemporaneously by the bishop, though their themes followed a general pattern, and it is probable that the intercessions were cast in the form of preface, silence and concluding collect.

Irenæus continued and developed the thought of the fourth Gospel and of Ignatius that the Supper confers "life." "For as the bread, which is produced from the earth, when it receives the invocation of God, is no longer common bread but the Eucharist, consisting of two realities, earthly and heavenly; so also our bodies, when they receive the Eucharist, are no longer corruptible, having the hope of the resurrection to eternity." [5] In how far these conceptions were due to the mystery religions, with their teaching that sharing a meal with the god is to become a partaker of the divine nature, is difficult to decide; but they undoubtedly grew out of the same habit of thought. It may be said that, by the middle of the second century, the conception of a real presence of Christ in the Supper was wide-spread.

In early Christian thought not only were believers themselves "a living sacrifice, holy, acceptable to God," [6] but all actions of worship were sacrificial. The leaders of the church "offered the gifts of the bishop's office." [7] The eucharistic gifts of bread and wine presented to God were viewed as the "pure sacrifice" foretold by Malachi [8] and as the Christian form of the Old Testament offerings of fine flour and firstfruits. [9] The development of a realistic view of the Lord's Supper as a sacrifice was determined by many factors. It was the occasion of the offering of gifts in kind as well as in money for the clergy and needy. [10] Again, the struggle with Docetism meant an increasing emphasis on the reality of Christ's passion as presented in the Supper, while the ancient sense of a vital and mystical relation between a sacramental likeness and its inner reality naturally furthered this way of thinking. Moreover, the ever present fact of Christian martyrdom could not fail to intensify the sacrificial meaning of the Eucharist. Christianity, too, was born into a world where sacrificial conceptions were familiar in the

[3] *Apology*, 66; Ayer, p. 34.   [4] *Apostolic Tradition*, 4.
[5] *Heresies*, 4.18.5; Ayer, pp. 138, 139.   [6] *Romans* 12:1.   [7] 1 *Clem.*, 44; Ayer, p. 37.
[8] *Mal.* 1:11; see *Teaching*, 14.   [9] Justin, *Trypho*, 41; Irenæus, *Heresies*, 4.17.5.
[10] Justin, *Apology*, 67; Ayer, p. 35; Hippolytus, *Apostolic Tradition*, 28.

religions on every hand. Sacrifice demands a priest. With Tertullian the term *sacerdos* first comes into full use.[11]

With Cyprian the developed doctrine of the Lord's Supper as a sacrifice offered to God by a priest has been fully reached. "For if Jesus Christ, our Lord and God, is Himself the chief priest of God the Father, and has first offered Himself a sacrifice to the Father, and has commanded this to be done in commemoration of Himself, certainly that priest truly discharges the office of Christ, who imitates that which Christ did; and he then offers a true and full sacrifice in the church when he proceeds to offer it according to what he sees Christ Himself to have offered." [12] The business of the Christian priest is "to serve the altar and to celebrate the divine sacrifices." [13] Already by Tertullian's time the Lord's Supper was held in commemoration of the dead.[14] Cyprian shows such "sacrifices" for martyrs.[15] The sense of the life-giving quality of the Supper led, also, to the custom of infant communion, of which Cyprian is a witness.[16] The "Catholic" conception of the Supper was thus developed as (*a*) a sacrament in which Christ is really present (the *how* of that presence was not to be much discussed till the Middle Ages), and in which the believer partakes of Christ, being thereby brought into union with Him and built up to the immortal life; and (*b*) a sacrifice offered to God by a priest and inclining God to be gracious to the living and the dead. Much was still left obscure, but the essentials of the "Catholic" view were already at hand by 253.

15

Forgiveness of Sins

THE GENERAL VIEW of early Christianity was that "if we confess our sins, He is faithful and righteous to forgive us our sins." [1] But there were sins so bad that they could not be forgiven, they were "unto death." [2] Just what this unforgivable sin was, is not altogether clear, but the Gospels indicate it meant, in the first place, to attribute to Satan and not to God's Spirit the mighty works of Jesus.[3] In the second place it meant the refusal to confess Jesus during persecution and the unwillingness to follow the

---

[11] *Baptism*, 17; Ayer, p. 167.   [12] *Letters*, 62–63:14.   [13] *Ibid.*, 67:1.
[14] *Chastity*, 11.   [15] *Letters*, 33–39:3.   [16] *Lapsed*, 25.   [1] I *John* 1:9.
[2] *Ibid.*, 5:16.   [3] *Mark* 3:28–9.

Spirit's prompting when one was brought before tribunals.[4] The meaning was further extended by the *Teaching* which held that "any prophet speaking in the Spirit, ye shall not try neither discern; for every sin shall be forgiven, but this sin shall not be forgiven." [5] Eventually the general feeling emerged that the unforgivable sins were idolatry or denial of the faith, murder, and gross licentiousness. The first-named was specially hopeless. No severer denunciations can be found in the New Testament than those directed by the writer of *Hebrews* toward such as "crucify to themselves the Son of God· afresh" (6:4–8, 10:26–31). To Tertullian the "deadly sins" were seven, "idolatry, blasphemy, murder, adultery, fornication, false-witness and fraud." [6]

While, by the time of Hermas (100–140), baptism was regarded as cleansing all previous sins, those committed after it, of the class just described, were "deadly." But the tendency was toward some modification of this strictness. The burden of Hermas' special revelation was that, by exception, in view of the near end of the world, one further repentance had been granted after baptism.[7] This extended to adultery and some forms of apostasy.[8] Similarly Irenæus gives an account of the reclaiming of an adulteress, who "spent her whole time in the exercise of public confession." [9] In Tertullian great stress is laid upon the one repentance after baptism,[10] but he seems to apply it *not* to the deadly sins of apostasy, adultery and murder, but to less serious sins such as ambiguous denial, blasphemy and attendance at gladiatorial games. In any case in his tract on *Modesty* (19) he is very clear that the three cardinal sins are not, and never have been, subject to the remedy of second repentance. However, there are sufficient instances elsewhere to show that a variety of serious sins was being forgiven in the Church, and particularly on the question of adultery there was no unanimity of opinion.

The second repentance involved a humiliating public confession, an "exomologesis," "to feed prayers on fastings, to groan, to weep and make outcries unto the Lord your God; to bow before the feet of the presbyters, and kneel to God's dear ones." [11] Yet practice was perhaps not always as rigorous as Tertullian would imply.

The question inevitably arose as to when a sinner had done enough to be restored. The feeling appeared early that the absolving power was divinely lodged in the congregation.[12] This authority was also regarded as directly committed to Peter, and, by implication, to church officers, when such developed.[13] But, curiously, a double practice prevailed. About to be martyrs and confessors, *i. e.*, those who endured tortures or imprisonment for their faith, were deemed also able to absolve because filled with the Spirit.[14] This

---

[4] *Luke* 12:10.   [5] 11; Ayer, p. 40.   [6] *Against Marcion*, 4:9.
[7] *Man.*, 4:3; Ayer, pp. 43, 44.   [8] *Sim.* 6:5; 9:6.   [9] *Heresies*, 1.13.5.
[10] *Repentance*, 7.   [11] *Repentance*, 9.   [12] *Matt.* 8:15–18.   [13] *Ibid.*, 16:18, 19.
[14] Tertullian, *Modesty*, 22.

twofold authority led to abuse. Many of the confessors were lax. Cyprian, in particular, had trouble on this score.[15] Naturally bishops tried to repress this right of confessors; but it remained a popular opinion till the cessation of persecution. Absolution ultimately raised the question of a scale of penance, a standard as to when enough had been done to justify forgiveness, but that development is beyond the limits of the present period. It is not to be found till about 300.

These restorations, which were particularly of the licentious,[16] were deemed exceptional, however common; and it came as a shock, at least to a rigid Montanist ascetic like Tertullian, when the aggressive Roman bishop, Kallistos (217–222), (see p. 70), who had himself been a confessor, issued a declaration in his own name, which is a landmark in the development of papal authority, that he would absolve sins of the flesh on a proper repentance.[17] This was an *official* breach in the popular list of "sins unto death," whatever actual breach earlier practice may have made.

In common judgment, denial of the faith was the worst of these offenses, and not even Kallistos had promised pardon for that. The question was raised on a tremendous scale by the Decian persecution. Thousands lapsed and sought restoration after the storm was over. The policy which finally came to prevail was largely worked out by Cyprian, the bishop of Carthage, whose moderate position, steering between the undue laxity of the confessors and the equally undue rigor of the traditionalists, commended itself to the Church's conscience. In Rome, after the martyrdom of Bishop Fabian in 250, the church was rent on the question of the lapsed. A dispute beginning in personal antipathies, not at first involving this issue, resulted in the choice by the majority of Cornelius, a comparative nobody, as bishop over Novatian, the most distinguished theologian in Rome (see p. 71). The minority supported Novatian. The majority soon advocated the milder treatment of the lapsed, while Novatian advanced to the rigorist position. Novatian began a schism that lasted till the seventh century, and founded protesting churches wide-spread in the empire. He renewed the older practice and denied restoration to all guilty of "sins unto death." His was a lost cause. Synods in Rome and Carthage in 251 and 252, representative of the majority, permitted the restoration of the lapsed, under strict conditions of penance. Though the question was to rise again in the persecution under Diocletian, which began in 303,[18] and though varied practice long continued in different parts of the church, the decision in Rome in 251 was ultimately regulative. All sins were thereby forgivable. The old distinction continued in name, but it was henceforth only between great sins and small.

[15] *Letters*, 17–26, 20–21, 21–22, 22–27.   [16] Tertullian, *Modesty*, 22.
[17] Tertullian, *Modesty*, 1.   [18] The Melitian schism, Donatists.

16

The Composition of the Church
and the Higher and Lower Morality

*I*N APOSTOLIC TIMES the church was undoubtedly conceived as composed
exclusively of experiential Christians.[1] There were bad men who needed
discipline in it,[2] but the church could be described ideally as "not having spot
or wrinkle or any such thing."[3] It was natural that this should be so. Christianity came as a new faith. Those who embraced it did so as a result of
personal conviction, and at the cost of no little sacrifice. It was long the
feeling that the church is a community of saved men and women. Even
then, it was true that many were unworthy. This is Hermas' complaint. The
oldest sermon outside the New Testament has a modern sound. "For the
Gentiles when they hear from our mouth the oracles of God, marvel at them
for their beauty and greatness; then, when they discover that our works
are not worthy of the words which we speak, forthwith they betake themselves to blasphemy, saying that it is an idle story and a delusion."[4] Yet,
in spite of the recognition of these facts the theory continued. But the increasing age of Christianity forced a change of view. By the beginning of
the third century there were many whose parents, possibly remoter ancestors,
had been experiential Christians, but who, though they attended public
worship, were Christians in little more than in name. What were they?
They did not worship with the heathen. The public regarded them as Christians. Some of them had been baptized in infancy. Had the church a place
for them? Their numbers were such that the church was compelled to
feel that it had. Its own conception of itself was altering from that of a
communion of saints to that of an agency for salvation. This change was
evident in the teaching of Bishop Kallistos of Rome (217–222). He cited
the parable of the tares and the wheat,[5] and compared the church to the
ark of Noah in which were "things clean and unclean."[6] The earlier and
later theories thus indicated divide the allegiance of modern Christendom
to this day.

The rejection of the Montanists and the decay of the expectation of

[1] *Romans* 1:7; 1 *Cor.* 1:2; 2 *Cor.* 1:1; Col. 1:2.   [2] *E. g.,* 1 *Cor.* 5:1–13.
[3] *Eph.* 5:27.   [4] *2 Clem.,* 13.   [5] *Matt.* 13:24–30.
[6] Hippolytus, *Refutation,* 9:12.

the speedy end of the world undoubtedly greatly favored the spread of worldliness in the church—a tendency much increased by its rapid growth from heathen converts between 202 and 250. As common Christian practice became less strenuous, however, asceticism grew as the ideal of the more serious. Too much must not be expected of common Christians. The *Teaching,* in the first half of the second century, had exhorted: "If thou art able to bear the whole yoke of the Lord, thou shalt be perfect; but if thou art not able, do that which thou art able" (6). Hermas (100–140) had taught that a man could do more than God commanded, and would receive a proportionate reward.[7] These tendencies but increased. They were, however, greatly furthered by a distinction between the "advice" and the requirements of the Gospel, which was clearly drawn by Tertullian [8] and Origen.[9]

While the requirements of Christianity are binding on all Christians, the advice is for those who would live the holier life. On two main phases of conduct the Gospel was thought to give such counsels of perfection. Christ said to the rich young man: "If thou wouldest be perfect, go, sell that thou hast, and give to the poor, and thou shalt have treasure in heaven." [10] He also declared that some are "eunuchs for the kingdom of heaven's sake," and that, "in the resurrection they neither marry nor are given in marriage, but are as angels." [11] Paul said "to the unmarried and to widows, it is good for them if they abide even as I." [12] Voluntary poverty and voluntary celibacy were, therefore, deemed advice impossible of fulfilment by all Christians, indeed, but conferring special merit on those who practised them. About these two conceptions all early Christian asceticism centered, and they were to be the foundation stones of monasticism when that system arose at the close of the third century. As the clergy should set a specially good example, not only was second marriage discouraged from the sub-apostolic age; [13] but, by the beginning of the third century, marriage after entering on office was deemed unallowable.[14] The life of celibacy, poverty, and contemplative retirement from the activities of the world was admired as the Christian ideal, and was widely practised, though as yet without separation from society. The road to full monasticism had been fairly entered. Probably the most unfortunate aspect of this double ideal was that it tended to discourage the efforts of the ordinary Christian.

[7] *Sim.,* 5:2, 3.   [8] *To his Wife,* 2:1.   [9] *Com. on Romans,* 3:3.   [10] *Matt.* 19:21.
[11] *Matt.* 19:12, 22:30.   [12] I *Cor.* 7:8.
[13] I *Tim.* 3:2, see also Hermas, *Man.,* 4:4, against second marriage of Christians in general.
[14] Hippolytus, *Refutation,* 9:12.

17

Rest and Growth, 260–303

THE END of the period of persecution affected by the edict of Gallienus, in 260, was followed by more than forty years of practical peace. Legally, the church had no more protection than before, and the able Emperor Aurelian (270–275) is said to have intended a renewal of persecution when prevented by death. Even with him it apparently did not come to the proclamation of a new hostile edict. The chief feature of this epoch was the rapid growth of Christianity. By 300 Christianity was effectively represented in all parts of the empire. Its distribution was very unequal, but it was influential in the central provinces of political importance, in Asia Minor, Macedonia, Syria, Egypt, northern Africa, central Italy, southern Gaul and Spain. Nor was its upward progress in the social scale less significant. During this period it won many officers of government and imperial servants. Most important of all, it began now to penetrate the army on a considerable scale. As late as 246–248 the best that Origen could say in reply to Celsus's criticism that Christians failed of their duty to the state by refusal of army service, was that Christians did a better thing by praying for the success of the Emperor.[1] Origen also expresses and defends Christian unwillingness to assume the burdens of governmental office.[2] Even then Christians had long been found in the Roman armies;[3] but Origen undoubtedly voiced prevalent Christian feeling in the middle of the third century. By its end both Christian feeling and practice had largely changed.

This period of rapid growth was one of greatly increasing conformity to worldly influences also. How far this sometimes went a single illustration may show. The Council of Elvira, now Granada, in Spain (*c.* 313), provided that Christians who as magistrates wore the garments of heathen priesthood could be restored after two years' penance, provided they had not actually sacrificed or paid for sacrifice.[4]

As compared with the first half of the third century, its latter portion was a period of little literary productivity or theologic originality in Christian circles. No names of the first rank appeared. The most eminent was that of Dionysius, who held the bishopric of Alexandria (247–264), a pupil of

[1] *Celsus*, 8:73.   [2] *Ibid.*, 8:75.   [3] *E. g.*, Tertullian, *Corona*, 1.   [4] *Canon*, 55.

Origen and like him for a time head of the famous catechetical school. Through his writings the influence of Origen was extended, and the great theologian's thoughts were in general dominant in that period in the East. Dionysius combated the wide-spread Eastern Sabellianism. He also began the practice of sending letters to his clergy, notifying them of the date of Easter—a custom soon largely developed by the greater bishoprics, and made the vehicle of admonition, doctrinal definition, and controversy. Beside the Sabellianism, which Dionysius combated, Dynamic Monarchianism was vigorously represented in Antioch by Paul of Samosata till 272 (see p. 69). This administratively gifted bishop held a high executive position under Zenobia, Queen of Palmyra, to whom Antioch belonged for a period before her overthrow by the Emperor Aurelian. Paul's opponents, being unable to deprive him of possession of the church building, appealed to Aurelian, who decided that it rightfully belonged to "those to whom the bishops of Italy and of the city of Rome should adjudge it." [5] Doubtless Aurelian was moved by political considerations in this adjudication, but this Christian reference to imperial authority, and the Emperor's deference to the judgment of Rome were significant.

With Antioch of this period is to be associated the foundation of a school of theology by Lucian, of whom little is known of biographical detail, save that he was a presbyter, held aloof from the party in Antioch which opposed and overcame Paul of Samosata, taught there from c. 275 to c. 303, and died a martyr's death in 312. Arius and Eusebius of Nicomedia were his pupils, and the supposition is probable that his views were largely reproduced in them. Like Origen, he busied himself with textual and exegetical labors on the Scriptures, but had little liking for the allegorizing methods of the great Alexandrian. A simpler, more grammatical and historical method of treatment both of text and doctrine characterized his teaching.

18

Rival Religious Forces

THE LATTER HALF of the third century was the period of the greatest influence of Mithraism in the empire. As the *Sol Invictus*, Mithras was widely worshipped, and this cult was popular in the army and favored by

[5] Eusebius, *Church History*, 7.30.19.

the Emperors who rose from its ranks. Two other forces of importance arose in the religious world. The first was Neo-Platonism. Founded in Alexandria by Ammonius Saccas (?–c. 245), its real developer was Plotinus (205–270), who settled in Rome about 244. From him, the leadership passed to Porphyry (233–304). Neo-Platonism was a pantheistic, mystical interpretation of Platonic thoughts. God is simple, absolute existence, all perfect, from whom the lower existences come. He is the One, above the duality implied in thought, and from Him the Nous ($\nu o\hat{\upsilon}\varsigma$) emanates like the Logos in the theology of Origen. From the Nous the world-soul derives being, and from that individual souls. From the world-soul the realm of matter comes. Yet each stage is inferior in the amount of being it possesses to the one above— has less of reality—reaching in gradations from God, who is all-perfect, to matter which, compared with Him, is negative. The morals of Neo-Platonism, like those of later Greek philosophy generally, were ascetic, and its conception of salvation was that of a rising of the soul to God in mystic contemplation, the end of which was union with the divine. Neo-Platonism was much to influence Christian theology, notably that of Augustine. Its founders were not conspicuously organizers, however, and it remained a way of thinking for the relatively few rather than an inclusive association of the many.

Far otherwise was it with a second movement, that of Manichæism. Its founder, Mani, was born in Persia in 216, began his preaching in Babylon in 242, and was martyred in 277. Strongly based on the old Persian dualism, Manichæism was also exceedingly syncretistic; indeed, Mani's aim was the foundation of a world religion and community, which would overcome the spacial limitations of previous religious traditions. He incorporated elements from Zoroastrianism, Buddhism, Judaism and Christianity, recognising each as a preparatory step in the universal message he proclaimed. Light and darkness, good and evil are eternally at war. Mani's conception of the relations of spirit and matter, and of salvation, in many ways resembled those of Gnosticism. Man is essentially a material prison house of the realm of evil, in which some portion of the realm of light is confined. The "Father of Goodness" has sent various messengers, including Jesus and Mani himself, to liberate man from this bondage. Salvation is based on right knowledge of man's true nature, and desire to return to the realm of light, coupled with extreme ascetic rejection of all that belongs to the sphere of darkness, especially the physical appetites and desires. Manichæan worship was as simple as its asceticism was strict. Its membership was in two classes, the perfect, always relatively few, who practised its full austerities; and the hearers, who accepted its teachings, but with much less strictness of practice—a distinction not unlike that between monks and ordinary Christians in the church. Its organization was fairly centralized and rigid. In Manichæism Christianity had a real rival. Its spread was rapid in the empire, and it absorbed not only many of the followers of Mithraism, but the remnants of Christian-Gnostic sects, and other early heresies. Its great growth was to be in the fourth and fifth centuries, and its influence was to be felt till the late Middle Ages through sects which were heirs of its teachings, like the Cathari.

19

The Final Struggle

*I*N 284 Diocletian became Roman Emperor. A man of the humblest origin, probably of slave parentage, he had a distinguished career in the army, and was raised to the imperial dignity by his fellow soldiers. Though a soldier-emperor, he was possessed of great abilities as a civil administrator, and determined to reorganize the empire so as to provide more adequate military defense, prevent army conspiracies aiming at a change of Emperors, and render the internal administration more efficient. To these ends he appointed an old companion-in-arms, Maximian, regent of the West, in 285, with the title of Augustus, which Diocletian himself bore. In further aid of military efficiency he designated, in 293, two "Cæsars"—one, Constantius Chlorus, on the Rhine frontier, and the other, Galerius, on that of the Danube. Each was to succeed ultimately to the higher post of "Augustus." All was held in harmonious working by the firm hand of Diocletian.

In internal affairs the changes of Diocletian were no less sweeping. The surviving relics of the old republican empire, and of senatorial influence, were now set aside. The Emperor became an autocrat in the later Byzantine sense. A new division of provinces was effected; and Rome was practically abandoned as the capital, Diocletian making the more conveniently situated Nicomedia, in Asia Minor, his customary residence. In character Diocletian was a rude but firm supporter of heathenism of the cruder camp type.

To such a man of organizing abilities, the closely knit, hierarchically ordered church presented a serious political problem. It must have seemed a state within the state over which he had no control. Though there had never been a Christian uprising against the empire, and Christianity had held aloof from politics to a remarkable degree, the church was rapidly growing in numbers and strength. Two courses lay open for a vigorous ruler, either to force it into submission and break its power, or to enter into alliance with it and thus secure political control of the growing organism. The latter was to be the method of Constantine; the former the attempt of Diocletian.

No other course could be expected from a man of his religious outlook. The Eastern Cæsar, Galerius, was even more hostile to Christianity, and had much influence over Diocletian. To him the suggestions of persecution may have been due. The growth of Christianity, moreover, was uniting all the forces of threatened heathenism against it; while Diocletian and Galerius were disposed to emphasize emperor-worship and the service of the old gods.

Diocletian moved slowly, however. A cautious effort to rid the army and the imperial palace service of Christians was followed, beginning in February, 303, by three great edicts of persecution in rapid succession. Churches were ordered destroyed, sacred books confiscated, clergy imprisoned and forced to sacrifice by torture. In 304 a fourth edict required all Christians to offer sacrifices. It was a time of fearful persecution. As in the days of Decius there were many martyrs, and many who "lapsed." Popular feeling was, however, far less hostile than in previous persecutions. The Christians had become better known. The severity of the persecution varied with the attitude of the magistrates by whom its penalties were enforced. Cruel in Italy, North Africa, and the Orient, the friendly "Cæsar," Constantius Chlorus, made apparent compliance in Gaul and Britain by destroying church edifices, but left the Christians themselves unharmed. He thereby gained a popularity with those thus spared that was to redound to the advantage of his son.

The voluntary retirement of Diocletian, and the enforced abdication of his colleague, Maximian, in 305, removed the strong hand of the only man able to master the complex governmental situation. Constantius Chlorus and Galerius now became "Augusti," but in the appointment of "Cæsars," the claims of the sons of Constantius Chlorus and Maximian were passed over in favor of two protégés of Galerius, Severus and Maximinus Daia. Persecution had now practically ceased in the West. It continued in increased severity in the East. Constantius Chlorus died in 306, and the garrison in York acclaimed his son Constantine as Emperor. On the strength of this army support, Constantine forced from Galerius his own recognition as "Cæsar," with charge of Gaul, Spain, and Britain. Soon after Maximian's son, Maxentius, defeated Severus and made himself master of Italy and North Africa. The next trial of strength in the struggle for the empire to which Constantine had set himself must be with Maxentius. Its outcome would determine the mastery of the whole West. Licinius, a protégé of Galerius, succeeded to a portion of the former possessions of Severus.

Before the decisive contest for the West took place, however, Galerius, in conjunction with Constantine and Licinius, issued in April, 311, an edict of toleration to Christians "on condition that nothing is done by them contrary to discipline." [1] This was, at best, a grudging concession, though why it was granted at all by the persecuting Galerius, who was its main source, is not wholly evident. Perhaps he had become convinced of the

[1] Eusebius, *Church History*, 8.17.9; Ayer, p. 262.

futility of persecution. Perhaps the long and severe illness which was to cost him his life a few days later may have led him to believe that some help might come from the Christians' God. The latter supposition is given added probability because the edict exhorts Christians to pray for its authors.

The death of Galerius in May, 311, left four contestants for the empire. Constantine and Licinius drew together by mutual interest; while Maximinus Daia and Maxentius were united by similar bonds. Daia promptly renewed persecution in Asia and Egypt. Maxentius, while not a persecutor, was a pronounced partisan of heathenism. Christian sympathy naturally flowed toward Constantine and Licinius. Constantine availed himself to the full of its advantages. To what extent he was now a personal Christian it is impossible to say. He had inherited a kindly feeling toward Christians. He had joined in the edict of 311. His forces seemed scarcely adequate for the great struggle with Maxentius. He doubtless desired the aid of the Christians' God in the none too equal conflict—though it is quite probable that he may not then have thought of Him as the only God. A brilliant march and several successful battles in northern Italy brought him face to face with Maxentius at Saxa Rubra, a little to the north of Rome, with the Mulvian bridge across the Tiber between his foes and the city. There, it would seem, in a dream the night before the battle, he saw the initial letters of the name of Christ with the words, "By this sign you will conquer." [2] Taking this as an omen, he had the monogram ☧ hastily painted on his helmet and on the shields of his soldiers, and so in some sense he entered the conflict as a Christian. On October 28, 312, occurred one of the decisive struggles of history, in which Maxentius lost the battle and his life. The West was Constantine's. The Christian God, he believed, had given him the victory, and every Christian impulse was confirmed. He was, thenceforth, in all practical respects a Christian, even though heathen emblems still appeared on coins, and he retained the title of Pontifex Maximus.

Probably early in 313 Constantine and Licinius met at Milan and came to some mutual agreement permitting full freedom to Christianity. This has generally been known as the "Edict of Milan," [3] though we have no evidence of the publication of an actual edict. What we do have, however, is the rescript of Licinius, defining for the guidance of officials in Nicomedia the new regulations regarding Christianity. It would appear that local rescripts gave substance to revolutionary decisions reached by the two Emperors at their meeting in Milan. The new policy was no longer, as in 311, one merely of toleration; nor did it make Christianity the religion of the empire. It proclaimed absolute freedom of conscience, placed Christianity on a full legal equality with any religion of the Roman world, and ordered the restoration of all church property confiscated in the recent persecution.

---

[2] Lactantius, *Deaths of Persecutors*, 44.   [3] Eusebius, *Church History*, 10:5; Ayer, p. 263.

A few months after the edict was issued, in April, 313, Licinius decisively defeated the persecutor, Maximinus Daia, in a battle not far from Adrianople, which seemed to the Christians a second Mulvian bridge. Two Emperors were, however, one too many. Licinius, defeated by Constantine in 314, held scarcely more than a quarter of the empire. Estranged from Constantine, Licinius increasingly resented the favor shown by the latter to Christianity. His hostility grew to persecution. It was, therefore, with immense satisfaction that the Christians witnessed his final defeat in 323. Constantine was at last sole ruler of the Roman world. The church was everywhere free from persecution. Its steadfastness, its faith, and its organization had carried it through its perils. But, in winning its freedom from its enemies, it had come largely under the control of the occupant of the Roman imperial throne. A fateful union with the state had begun.

Period Three

✻

THE IMPERIAL STATE CHURCH

1

The Changed Situation

To CONSTANTINE'S essentially political mind Christianity was the completion of the process of unification which had long been in progress in the empire. It had one Emperor, one law, and one citizenship for all free men. It should have one religion. Constantine moved slowly, however. Though the Christians were very unequally distributed and were much more numerous in the East than in the West, they were but a fraction of the population when the agreements at Milan granted them equal rights. The church had grown with great rapidity during the peace in the last half of the third century. Under imperial favor its increase was by leaps and bounds. That favor Constantine promptly showed. By a law of 319 the clergy were exempted from the public obligations that weighed so heavily on the well-to-do portion of the population.[1] In 321 the right to receive legacies was granted, and thereby the privileges of the church as a corporation acknowledged.[2] The same year Sunday work was forbidden to the people of the cities.[3] In 319 private heathen sacrifices were prohibited.[4] Gifts were made to clergy, and great churches erected in Rome, Jerusalem, Bethlehem, and elsewhere under imperial auspices. Above all, Constantine's formal transference of the capital to the rebuilt Byzantium, which he called New Rome, but which the world has named in his honor, Constantinople, was of high significance. Undoubtedly political and defensive in its motives, its religious consequences were far-reaching. From its official foundation, in 330, it established the seat of empire in a city of few heathen traditions or influences, situated in the most strongly Christianized portion of the world. It left the bishop of Rome, moreover, the most conspicuous man in the ancient capital, to which the Latin-speaking West still looked with reverence—in a conspicuity which was the more possible of future importance because it was wholly unintended by Constantine, and was spiritual rather than political. Great as were the favors which Constantine showed to the church, they were only for that strong, close-knit, hierarchically organized portion that called itself the "Catholic." The various "heretical" sects, and they were still many, could look for no bounty from his hands.

[1] *Codex Theodosianus*, 16.2.2; Ayer, *Source Book*, p. 283. [2] *Ibid.*, 16.2.4; Ayer, p. 283.
[3] *Codex Justinianus*, 3.12.3; Ayer, p. 284. [4] *Codex Theodosianus*, 9.16.2; Ayer, p. 286.

If Christianity was to be a uniting factor in the empire, the church must be one. Constantine found that unity seriously threatened. In North Africa the persecution under Diocletian had led to a schism, somewhat complicated and personal in its causes, but resembling that of Novatian in Rome, half a century earlier (see p. 93). The church there was divided. The strict party charged that the new bishop of Carthage, Cæcilian, had received ordination in 311, from the hands of one in mortal sin, who had surrendered copies of the Scriptures in the recent persecution. That ordination it held invalid, and chose a counter-bishop, Majorinus. His successor, in 316, was the able Donatus the Great, from whom the schismatics received the name Donatists. In 313 Constantine made grants of money to the "Catholic" clergy of North Africa.[5] In these the Donatists did not share, and appealed to the Emperor. A synod held in Rome the same year decided against them, but the quarrel was only the more embittered. Constantine thereupon mapped out what was to be henceforth the imperial policy in ecclesiastical questions. He summoned a synod of his portion of the empire to meet, at public expense, in Arles, in southern Gaul. The church itself should decide the controversy, but under imperial control. Here a large council assembled in 314. The Donatist contentions were condemned. Ordination was declared valid even at the hands of a personally unworthy cleric. Heretical baptism was recognized, and the Roman date of Easter approved.[6] The Donatists appealed to the Emperor, who once more decided against them, in 316, and as they refused to yield, now proceeded to close their churches and banish their bishops. The unenviable spectacle of the persecution of Christians by Christians was exhibited. North Africa was in turmoil. Constantine was, however, dissatisfied with the results, and in 321 abandoned the use of force against these schismatics. They grew rapidly, claiming to be the only true church possessed of a clergy free from "deadly sins" and of the only valid sacraments. Not till the Mohammedan conquest did the Donatists disappear.

2

The Arian Controversy to the Death of Constantine

A MUCH MORE serious danger to the unity of the church than the Donatist schism which Constantine encountered was the great Arian controversy. It has already been pointed out that while the West, thanks to

[5] Eusebius, *Church History*, 10:6; Ayer, p. 281.   [6] See Ayer, p. 291.

the work of Tertullian and Novatian, had reached practical unanimity regarding the unity of substance between Christ and the Father (see pp. 66–71), the East was divided. Origen, still its most dominating theological influence, could be quoted in opposing senses. If he had taught the eternal generation of the Son, he had also held Him to be a second God and a creature (see p. 76). Adoptionist tendencies persisted, also, about Antioch; while Sabellianism was to be found in Egypt. The East, moreover, was vastly more interested in speculative theology than the West, and therefore more prone to discussion; nor can there be any doubt that, in the fourth century, much more of intellectual ability was to be found in the Greek-speaking than in the Latin-speaking portion of the empire.

The real cause of the struggle was these varying interpretations; but the actual controversy began in Alexandria, about 320, in a dispute between Arius and his bishop, Alexander (312?–328). Arius, a pupil of Lucian of Antioch (see p. 97), was presbyter in charge of the church known as Baucalis. He was advanced in years and held in high repute as a preacher of learning, ability, and piety. Monarchian influences imbibed in Antioch led him to emphasize the unity and self-contained existence of God. In so far as he was a follower of Origen, he represented the great Alexandrian's teaching that Christ was a created being. As such He was not of the substance of God, but was made like other creatures of "nothing." Though the first-born of creatures, and the agent in fashioning the world, He was not eternal. "The Son has a beginning, but . . . God is without beginning." [1] Christ was, indeed, God in a certain sense to Arius, but a lower God, in no way one with the Father in essence or eternity. In the incarnation, this Logos entered a human body, taking the place of the human reasoning spirit. To Arius's thinking, Christ was neither fully God nor fully man, but a *tertium quid* between. This is what makes his view wholly unsatisfactory.

Bishop Alexander was influenced by the other side of Origen's teaching. To him the Son was eternal, like in essence to the Father, and wholly uncreated.[2] His view was, perhaps, not perfectly clear, but its unlikeness to that of Arius is apparent. Controversy arose between Arius and Alexander, apparently on Arius's initiative. It soon grew bitter, and about 320 or 321 Alexander held a synod in Alexandria by which Arius and a number of his sympathizers were condemned. Arius appealed for help to his fellow pupil of the school of Lucian, the powerful bishop, Eusebius of Nicomedia, and soon found a refuge with him. Alexander wrote widely to fellow bishops, and Arius defended his own position, aided by Eusebius. The Eastern ecclesiastical world was widely turmoiled.

Such was the situation when Constantine's victory over Licinius made him master of the East as well as of the West. The quarrel threatened the unity

[1] Arius to Eusebius, Theodoret, *Church History*, 1:4; Ayer, p. 302.
[2] Letter of Alexander in Socrates, *Church History*, 1:6.

of the church which he deemed essential. Constantine therefore sent his chief ecclesiastical adviser, Bishop Hosius of Cordova, in Spain, to Alexandria with an imperial letter, counselling peace and describing the issue involved as "an unprofitable question." [3] The well-meant, but bungling effort was in vain. Constantine, therefore, proceeded to employ the same device he had already made use of at Arles in the Donatist dispute. He called a council of the entire church. That of Arles had been representative of all the portion of the empire then ruled by Constantine. Constantine was now master of all the empire, and therefore bishops of all the empire were summoned. The principle was the same, but the extent of Constantine's enlarged jurisdiction made the gathering in Nicæa the First General Council of the church.

The council, which assembled in Nicæa in May, 325, has always lived in Christian tradition as the most important in the history of the church. To it the bishops were summoned at government expense, accompanied by lower clergy, who did not, however, have votes in its decisions. The East had the vast preponderance. Of about three hundred bishops present only six were from the West. It included three parties. A small section, led by Eusebius of Nicomedia, were thoroughgoing Arians. Another small group were equally strenuous supporters of Alexander. The large majority, of whom the church historian, Eusebius of Cæsarea, was a leader, were not deeply versed in the question at issue. Indeed, the majority, as a whole, were described by an unsympathetic writer as "simpletons." [4] As far as they had any opinion, they stood on the general basis of the teachings of Origen. Conspicuous in the assembly was the Emperor himself, who, though not baptized, and therefore not technically a full member of the church, was far too eminent a personage not to be welcomed enthusiastically.

Almost at the beginning of the council a creed presented by the Arians was rejected. Eusebius of Cæsarea then offered the creed of his own church. It was a sweet-sounding confession, dating from before the controversy, and was, therefore, wholly indefinite as to the particular problems involved. This Cæsarean creed was now amended most significantly by the insertion of the expressions, "begotten, not made," "of one essence (*homoousion, ὁμοούσιον*) with the Father"; and by the specific rejection of Arian formulæ such as "there was when He was not" and "He was made of things that were not." The later technically unlike words "essence," "substance" (*οὐσία*), and "hypostasis" (*ὑπόστασις*) were here used as equivalent expressions. Loofs has attempted to show [5] that the influences which secured these changes were Western, doubtless above all that of Hosius of Cordova, supported by the Emperor. In particular, the test word, *homoousion,* had long been orthodox in its Latin equivalent, and had been in philosophic usage in the second century, though rejected by a synod in Antioch in the proceedings

---

[3] Letter in Eusebius, *Life of Constantine,* 2:64–72.   [4] Socrates, *Church History,* 1:8.
[5] *Realencyklopädie für prot. Theol. u. Kirche,* 2:14, 15.

against Paul of Samosata (see p. 69). Indeed, it was used very sparingly by Athanasius himself in his earlier defense of the Nicene faith. It is easy to understand Constantine's attitude. Essentially a politician, he naturally thought a formula that would find no opposition in the Western half of the empire, and would receive the support of a portion of the East, more acceptable than one which, while having only a part of the East in its favor, would be rejected by the whole West. To Constantine's influence the adoption of the Nicene definition was due. That he ever understood its shades of meaning is more than doubtful; but he wanted a united expression of the faith of the church on the question in dispute, and believed that he had found it. Under his supervision, all but two of the bishops present signed it. These, and Arius, Constantine sent into banishment. The imperial politics had apparently secured the unity of the church, and had given it what it had never before possessed, a statement which might be assumed to be a universally recognized creed.

Besides this action in thus formulating the creed, the Council of Nicæa issued a number of important canons regulating church discipline, paved the way for the return of those in Egypt who had joined the Melitian schism over the treatment of the lapsed, made easy the readmission of Novatians, and ordered a uniform date in the observation of Easter.

It is not strange, in view of the manner in which the Nicene creed was adopted, that soon after the council ended great opposition to its test word, *homoousion,* was manifested in the East. To the defeated Arians it was, of course, obnoxious. They were few. To the large middle party of disciples of Origen it was scarcely less satisfactory, for to them it seemed Sabellian. Though Eusebius of Nicomedia and his Arian sympathizer, Theognis of Nicæa, had signed, their evident hostility was such that Constantine sent both bishops into exile. By 328, however, they were home again, possibly through the favor of the Emperor's sister, Constantia. Eusebius soon acquired a greater influence over Constantine than any other ecclesiastic of the East, and used it to favor the cause of Arius. With such elements of opposition to the Nicene result, the real battle was not in the council but in the more than half a century which followed its conclusion.

Meanwhile the great defender of the Nicene faith had come fully on the scene. Athanasius was born in Alexandria about 295. In the early stages of the Arian controversy he was a deacon, and served as private secretary to Bishop Alexander. As such he accompanied his bishop to Nicæa, and on Alexander's death, in 328, was chosen in turn to the Alexandrian bishopric—a post which he was to hold, in spite of attack and five banishments, till his own demise in 373. Not a great speculative theologian, Athanasius was a great character. In an age when court favor counted for much, he stood like a rock for his convictions, and that the Nicene theology ultimately conquered was primarily due to him, for the Nicene West possessed no able theologian.

To him, the question at issue was one of salvation, and that he made men feel it to be so was a main source of his power. The Greek conception of salvation had been, since the beginnings of the tradition of Asia Minor, the transformation of sinful mortality into divine and blessed immortality—the impartation of "life" (see p. 36). Only by real Godhead coming into union with full manhood in Christ could the transformation of the human into the divine be accomplished in Him, or be mediated by Him to His disciples. As Athanasius said: "He [Christ] was made man that we might be made divine." [6] To his thinking the great error of Arianism was that it gave no basis for a real salvation. Well was it for the Nicene party that so moderate, yet determined, a champion stood for it, since the two other prominent defenders of the Nicene faith, Bishops Marcellus of Ancyra and Eustathius of Antioch, were certainly far from theologically impeccable, and were accused, not wholly rightly, of opinions decidedly Sabellian.

Eusebius of Nicomedia soon saw in Athanasius the real enemy. Constantine would not desert the Nicene decision, but the same practical result could be achieved, Eusebius thought, by striking its defenders. Political and theological differences were cleverly used to secure the condemnation of Eustathius in 330. The Eusebians determined to secure the discomfiture of Athanasius and the restoration of Arius. The latter, who had returned from banishment even before Eusebius, now presented to Constantine a creed carefully indefinite on the question at issue.[7] To Constantine's untheological mind this seemed a satisfactory retraction, and an expression of willingness to make his peace. He directed Athanasius to restore Arius to his place in Alexandria. Athanasius refused. Charges of overbearing and disloyal conduct were brought against Athanasius. Constantine was finally persuaded that the main obstacle in the path of peace was Athanasius's stubbornness. The bishops assembled for the dedication of Constantine's just completed church in Jerusalem, met in Tyre, and then in Jerusalem, under Eusebian influences, and decided in favor of Arius's restoration in 335, and near the end of the year Constantine banished Athanasius to Gaul. Shortly after the same forces procured the deposition of Marcellus of Ancyra for heresy. The leading defenders of the Nicene creed being thus struck down, the Eusebians planned the restoration of Arius himself to church fellowship; but on the evening before the formal ceremony was to take place Arius suddenly died (336). He was an aged man, and the excitement may well have been fatal.

The Nicene faith seemed thus not officially overthrown, but practically undermined, when Constantine died on May 22, 337. Shortly before his demise he was baptized at the hands of Eusebius of Nicomedia. The changes which his life had witnessed, and he had largely wrought, in the status of the church were enormous; but they were not by any means wholly advantageous. If persecution had ceased, and numbers were rapidly growing under

---

[6] *Incarnation,* 54:3.   [7] Socrates, *Church History,* 1:26; Ayer, p. 307.

imperial favor, doctrinal discussions that earlier would have run their course were now political questions of the first magnitude, and the Emperor had assumed a power in ecclesiastical affairs which was ominous for the future of the church. Yet in the existing constitution of the Roman Empire such results were probably inevitable, once the Emperor himself should become, like Constantine, an adherent of the Christian faith.

3

Controversy under Constantine's Sons

THE DEATH of Constantine was succeeded by the division of the empire among his three sons, with some intended provisions for other relatives that were frustrated by a palace intrigue and massacre. Constantine II, the eldest, received Britain, Gaul, and Spain; Constantius, Asia Minor, Syria, and Egypt; while the intermediate portion came to the youngest, Constans. Constantine II died in 340, so that the empire was speedily divided between Constans in the West, and Constantius in the East. Both Emperors showed themselves, from the first, more partisan in religious questions than their father had been. A joint edict of 346 ordered temples closed, and forbade sacrifice on pain of death.[1] The law was, however, but slightly enforced. The Donatist controversy in North Africa had greatly extended, and that land, in consequence, was the scene of much agrarian and social agitation. The Donatists were, therefore, attacked in force by Constans, and though not wholly crushed, were largely rooted out.

The most important relationship of the sons of Constantine to the religious questions of the age was to the continuing Nicene controversy. Under their rule it extended from a dispute practically involving only the East, as under Constantine, to an empire-wide contest. At the beginning of their joint reigns the Emperors permitted the exiled bishops to return. Athanasius was, therefore, once more in Alexandria before the close of 337. Eusebius was, however, still the most influential party leader in the East, and his authority was but strengthened when he was promoted, in 339, from the bishopric of Nicomedia to that of Constantinople, where he died about 341. Through the influence of Eusebius Athanasius was forcibly driven from Alexandria in the spring of 339, and an Arian bishop, Gregory of Cappadocia, put in his place

[1] *Codex Theodosianus,* 16.10.4; Ayer, p. 323.

by military power. Athanasius fled to Rome, where Marcellus of Ancyra soon joined him.

East and West were now under different Emperors, and Constans held to the Nicene sympathies of his subjects. Not merely was the empire divided, but Bishop Julius of Rome could now interfere from beyond the reach of Constantius. He welcomed the fugitives and summoned their opponents to a synod in Rome, in 340, though the Eusebians did not appear. The synod declared Athanasius and Marcellus unjustly deposed. The Eastern leaders replied not merely with protests against the Roman action, but with an attempt to do away with the Nicene formula itself, in which they had the support of Constantius. Two synods in Antioch, in 341, adopted creeds, far, indeed, from positively Arian in expression, but from which all that was definitely Nicene was omitted. In some respects they represented a pre-Nicene orthodoxy. The death of Eusebius, now of Constantinople, at this juncture cost the opponents of the Nicene decision his able leadership. The two brother Emperors thought that the bitter quarrel could best be adjusted by a new General Council, and accordingly such a body gathered in Sardica, the modern Sofia, in the autumn of 343. General Council it was not to be. The Eastern bishops, finding themselves outnumbered by those of the West, and seeing Athanasius and Marcellus in company with them, withdrew. By the Westerners Athanasius and Marcellus were once more approved, though the latter was a considerable burden to their cause by reason of his dubious orthodoxy. East and West seemed on the point of ecclesiastical separation.

The Council of Sardica had completely failed in its object of healing the quarrel, but the Westerners there assembled passed several canons, under the leadership of Hosius of Cordova, that are of great importance in the development of the judicial authority of the bishop of Rome. What they did was to enact the actual recent course of proceedings regarding Athanasius and Marcellus into a general rule. It was decided that in case a bishop was deposed, as these had been, he might appeal to Bishop Julius of Rome, who could cause the case to be retried by new judges, and no successor should be appointed till the decision of Rome was known.[2] They were purely Western rules and seem to have aroused little attention, even in Rome, at the time, but were important for the future.

The two imperial brothers were convinced that the controversy was assuming too serious aspects. At all events, Constans favored Athanasius, and the rival bishop, Gregory, having died, Constantius permitted Athanasius to return to Alexandria in October, 347, where he was most cordially welcomed by the overwhelming majority of the population, which had always heartily supported him. The situation seemed favorable for Athanasius, but political events suddenly made it worse than it had ever been. A rival Emperor arose

[2] See Ayer, pp. 364–366.

in the West in the person of Magnentius, and in 350 Constans was murdered. Three years of struggle brought victory over the usurper to Constantius, and left him sole ruler of the empire (353).

Constantius, at last in full control, determined to end the controversy. To his thinking Athanasius was the chief enemy. The leadership against Athanasius was now in the hands of Bishops Ursacius of Singidunum, and Valens of Mursa. At synods held in Arles in 353, and in Milan in 355, Constantius forced the Western bishops to abandon Athanasius, and to resume communion with his Eastern opponents. For resistance to these demands Liberius, bishop of Rome, Hilary of Poitiers, the most learned bishop of Gaul, and the aged Hosius of Cordova were sent into banishment. Athanasius, driven from Alexandria by military force in February, 356, began his third exile, finding refuge for the next six years largely among the Egyptian monks. At a synod held in Sirmium, the Emperor's residence, in 357, *ousia* (substance) in any of its combinations was forbidden as unscriptural.[3] This, so far as the influence of the synod went, was an abolition of the Nicene formula. Hosius signed it, though he absolutely refused to condemn Athanasius. The declaration of Sirmium was strengthened by an agreement secured by Constantius at the little Thracian town of Nice, in 359, in which it was affirmed "we call the Son like the Father, as the holy scriptures call Him and teach." [4] The Emperor and his episcopal favorites, notably Valens of Mursa, now secured its acceptance by synods purporting to represent East and West, held in Rimini, Seleucia, and Constantinople. The Old-Nicene formula was set aside, and the whole church had, theoretically, accepted the new result. The proper term, the only one allowed in court circles, was "the Son is like the Father"— *homoios*—hence those who supported its use were known as the Homoion ("like") party. Apparently colorless, the history of its adoption made it a rejection of the Nicene faith, and opened the door to Arian assertions. The Arians had triumphed for the time being, and that success was largely aided by the fact that its Homoion formula appealed to many who were heartily tired of the long controversy.

Really, however, the Arian victory had prepared the way for the ruin of Arianism, though that result was not immediately apparent. The opposition to the Nicene formula had always been composed of two elements: a small Arian section, and a much larger conservative body, which stood mainly on positions reached by Origen, to which Arianism was obnoxious, but which looked upon *homoousios,* the Nicene phrase, as an unwarranted expression already condemned in Antioch, and of Sabellian ill-repute. Both elements had worked together to resist the Nicene formula, but their agreement went no further. Extreme Arians were raising their heads in Alexandria and elsewhere. The conservatives were even more hostile to them than to the

[3] Hilary of Poitiers, *De Synodis,* 11; Ayer, p. 317.   [4] Ayer, p. 319.

Nicene party. They would not say *homoousios*—of one substance—but they were willing to say *homoiousios*—not in the sense of like substance, as the natural translation would be, but of equality of attributes. They were also beginning to draw a distinction between *ousia*—substance, essence—and *hypostasis*—now using the latter in the sense of "subsistence," instead of making them equivalent, as in the Nicene symbol. This enabled them to preserve the Origenistic teaching of "three hypostases," while insisting on the community of attributes. The newly formed middle party came first into evidence with a synod at Ancyra, in 358, and its chief early leaders were Bishops Basil of Ancyra, and George of Laodicea. They have usually been called the Semi-Arians, but the term is a misnomer. They are better referred to as the "Conservatives." They rejected Arianism energetically. They really stood near to Athanasius. He recognized this approach, and Hilary of Poitiers furthered union by urging that the conservatives meant by *homoiousios* what the Nicene party understood by *homoousios*.[5] The ultimate Nicene victory was to come about through the fusion of the Nicene and the "Semi-Arian" or "Conservative" parties. In that union the tradition of Asia Minor, and the interpretations of Origen were to combine with those of Alexandria. It was a slow process, however, and in its development the earlier Nicene views were to be somewhat modified into the New-Nicene theology.

4

The Later Nicene Struggle

CONSTANTIUS died in 361 as he was preparing to resist his cousin, Julian, whom the soldiers in Paris had declared Emperor. His death left the Roman world to Julian. Spared on account of his youth at the massacre of his father and other relatives on the death of Constantine, he looked upon Constantius as his father's murderer. Brought up in peril of his life, and forced to strict outward churchly observance, he came to hate everything which Constantius represented, and was filled with admiration for the literature, life, and philosophy of the older Hellenism. He was not an "apostate," in the sense of a turncoat. Though necessarily concealed from the public, his heathenism had long been real, when his campaign against Constantius enabled him pub-

[5] *De Synodis*, 88; Ayer, p. 319.

licly to declare it. It was heathenism of a mystical, philosophical character. On his accession he attempted a heathen revival. Christianity was everywhere discouraged, and Christians removed from office. Bishops banished under Constantius were recalled, that the quarrels of Christians might aid in the heathen reaction. Athanasius was thus once more in Alexandria in 362, but before the year was out was exiled for the fourth time by Julian, who was angered by his success in making converts from heathenism. Julian's reign was soon over. In 363 he lost his life in a campaign against the Persians. In him Rome had its last heathen Emperor.

The reign of Julian showed the real weakness of the Arianizing elements which Constantius had supported. Athanasians and the Conservatives drew together. Furthermore, the Nicene debate was broadening out to include a discussion of the relations of the Holy Spirit to the Godhead. Since the time of Tertullian, in the West, Father, Son, and Holy Spirit had been regarded as three "persons," of one substance (see p. 66). The East had reached no such unanimity. Even Origen had been uncertain whether the Spirit was "created or uncreated," or "a son of God or not." [1] There had not been much discussion of the theme. Now that it had come forward, the *homoousia* of the Holy Spirit with the Father, seemed to Athanasius and his friends a corollary from the *homoousia* of the Son. At a synod held in Alexandria in 362, by the just returned Athanasius, terms of union were drawn up for rival parties in Antioch. It would be sufficient "to anathematize the Arian heresy and confess the faith confessed by the holy Fathers of Nicæa, and to anathematize also those who say that the Holy Ghost is a creature and separate from the essence of Christ." [2] The employment of the terms "three hypostases" and "one hypostasis" the synod regarded as indifferent, provided "three" was not used in the sense of "alien in essence," and "one" in that of Sabellian unity. The door was thus opened by Athanasius himself not only for the full definition of the doctrine of the Trinity, but for the New-Nicene orthodoxy, with its Godhead in one essence (substance) and three hypostases.

The death of Julian was succeeded by the brief reign of Jovian. The empire had once more a Christian ruler, and happily, one who interfered little in ecclesiastical politics. Athanasius promptly returned from his fourth exile. Jovian's rule ended in 364, and he was succeeded by Valentinian I (364–375), who, finding the imperial defense too great a task, took charge of the West, giving to his brother, Valens (364–378) the sovereignty of the East. Valentian interfered little with churchly affairs. Valens came under the influence of the Arian clergy of Constantinople, and both Homoousian and Homoiousian sympathizers shared his dislike—a situation which helped to bring these parties nearer together. He condemned Athanasius to a fifth and final exile, in 365; but it was brief, and the aged bishop did not have to go far from the city. Valens was, however, no such vigorous supporter of Arianism

---

[1] *De Principiis*, Preface.   [2] *Tomus ad Antiochenos*, 3; Ayer, p. 350.

as Constantius had been. Athanasius died in Alexandria, in 373, full of years and honors.

At the death of Athanasius the leadership in the struggle was passing into the hands of new men, of the New-Nicene party. Chief of these were the three great Cappadocians, Basil of Cæsarea in Cappadocia, Gregory of Nazianzus, and Gregory of Nyssa. Born of a prominent Cappadocian family about 330, Basil received the best training that Constantinople and Athens could yield, in student association with his life-long friend Gregory of Nazianzus. About 357 he yielded to the ascetic Christian tendencies of the age, and gave up any idea of a career of worldly advancement, living practically as a monk. He visited Egypt, then the home of the rising monastic movement, and became the great propagator of monasticism in Asia Minor. He was, however, made for affairs and not for the cloister. Deeply versed in Origen, and in sympathy with the Homoiousian party, he belonged to the section which gradually came into fellowship with Athanasius, and like Athanasius he supported the full consubstantiality of the Holy Spirit. To the wing of the Homoiousian party which refused to regard the Spirit as fully God—the so-called Macedonians—he offered strenuous opposition. It was a far-reaching victory for his cause when Basil became bishop of the Cappadocian Cæsarea, in 370. The post gave him ecclesiastical authority over a large section of eastern Asia Minor, which he used to the full till his early death, in 379, to advance the New-Nicene cause. He sought also to promote a good understanding between the opponents of Arianism in the East and the leaders of the West.

Gregory of Nyssa was Basil's younger brother. An orator of ability, and a writer of even greater skill and theological penetration than Basil, he had not Basil's organizing and administrative gifts. Rather did he significantly develop the mystical theology of the Eastern Church; and more successfully than his great "master" Origen, he brought Hellenistic philosophy to the support of Christian truth. His title was derived from the little Cappadocian town—Nyssa—of which he became bishop in 371 or 372. He lived till after 394, and ranks among the four great Fathers of the Oriental Church.

Gregory of Nazianzus (329?–389?) had his title from the town of his birth, where his father was bishop. Warmly befriended with Basil from student days, like Basil he felt strongly the monastic attraction. His ability as a preacher was greater than that of either of his associates, but was exercised in most varying stations. As a priest he aided his father, from about 361. By Basil he was made bishop of the village of Sasima. About 378 he went to Constantinople to oppose the Arianism which was the faith of the vast majority of its inhabitants. The accession of the zealously Nicene Emperor, Theodosius, in 379, gave him the needed support, and he preached with such success that he gained the repute of having turned the city to the Nicene faith. By Theodosius he was made bishop of Constantinople in 381. But the frictions of party strife and the inclination to ascetic retirement which had several times before driven him from the world, caused him speedily to relinquish this most exalted ecclesiastical post. As a writer he ranked with Gregory of Nyssa, though he was more of a rhetorician and preacher, and less of a profound thinker than his namesake. Like him he is reckoned one of the Eastern Fathers, and the later Orient has given him the title, the "Theologian."

To the three Cappadocians, more than to any others, the intellectual victory of the New-Nicene faith was due. To the men of that age their work seemed the triumph of the Nicene viewpoint, but the extent to which this is true is still a matter of dispute. There are those who claim the Nicene orthodoxy was severely modified by the Cappadocians. A German writer expresses it thus: [3]

> Athanasius (and Marcellus) taught the one God, leading a threefold personal life, who reveals Himself as such. The Cappadocians think of three divine hypostases, which, as they manifest the same activity, are recognized as possessing one nature and the same dignity. The mystery for the former lay in the trinity; for the latter, in the unity. . . . The Cappadocians interpreted the doctrine of Athanasius in accordance with the conceptions and underlying principles of the Logos-Christology of Origen. They paid, however, for their achievement a high price, the magnitude of which they did not realize—the idea of the personal God. Three personalities and an abstract, impersonal essence, are the resultant.

On the other hand the Cappadocians can be understood in a rather different sense. The three of the Godhead are not three "personalities" (in our sense), but three "modes of being" of an *identical* (not a common) essence. Thus there is not an "impersonal essence" behind three "persons" (in the current sense), but one personal God who exists in three modes which interpenetrate each other and are not subject to the circumscription we apply to individuals.[4]

The original Nicene success and the temporary triumph of Arianism had been made possible by imperial interference. The same force was to give victory to the New-Nicene orthodoxy. The death of Valens in the great Roman defeat by the West Goths, near Adrianople, in 378, left his nephew, Gratian, the sole surviving ruler. Gratian preferred the care of the West, and wisely appointed as Emperor for the East an able general and administrator, Theodosius, who became ultimately, for a brief period, the last sole ruler of the Roman Empire. Born in Spain, he grew up in full sympathy with the theology of the West, and shared to the utmost its devotion to the Nicene faith. In 380, in conjunction with Gratian, he issued an edict that all should "hold the faith which the holy Apostle Peter gave to the Romans," which he defined more particularly as that taught by the existing bishops, Damasus of Rome,

[3] Seeberg, *Text-Book of the History of Doctrines*, Eng. tr., 1:232.
[4] See *Christology of the Later Fathers*, ed. by E. R. Hardy and C. C. Richardson, pp. 241ff.

and Peter of Alexandria.[5] This edict constitutes a reckoning point in imperial politics and ecclesiastical development. Henceforth there was to be but one religion in the empire, and that the Christian. Moreover, only that form of Christianity was to exist which taught one divine essence in three hypostases, or, as the West would express it in supposedly similar terms, one substance in three persons.

In 381 Theodosius held an Eastern synod in Constantinople, which ultimately gained repute as the Second General Council, and obtained an undeserved credit as the supposed author of the creed which passed into general use as "Nicene." Of its work little is known. It undoubtedly rejected, however, that wing of the Homoiousian party—the Macedonian—which refused to accept the consubstantiality of the Holy Spirit, and approved the original Nicene creed. Personal differences continued between East and West, and between Eastern parties; but the forcible way in which the Emperor now drove out the Arians decided the fate of Arianism in the empire, in spite of a brief toleration of Arianism in northern Italy by Gratian's successor, Valentinian II, influenced by his mother, against which Ambrose of Milan had to strive. Here, too, the authority of Theodosius was potent after her death, about 388. Arianism in the empire was a lost cause, though it was to continue for several centuries among the Germanic invaders, thanks to the missionary work of Ulfila (see p. 120).

Yet even when the synod of 381 met, the Nicene creed, as adopted in 325, failed to satisfy the requirements of theologic development in the victorious party. It said nothing regarding the consubstantiality of the Holy Spirit, for instance. A creed more fully meeting the state of discussion was desirable, and actually such a creed came into use, and by 451 was regarded as adopted by the General Council of 381. It ultimately took the place of the genuine Nicene creed, and is that known as the "Nicene" to this day. Its exact origin is uncertain, but it is closely related to the baptismal creed of Jerusalem, as reconstructible from the teaching of Cyril, afterward bishop of that city, about 348; and also to that of Epiphanius of Salamis, about 374.[6] Perhaps it was the local creed, current in the Church of Constantinople at the time.

On reviewing this long controversy, it may be said that it was a misfortune that a less disputed phrase was not adopted at Nicæa, and doubly a misfortune that imperial interference played so large a part in the ensuing discussions. In the struggle the imperial church came into existence, and a policy of imperial interference was fully developed. Departure from official orthodoxy had become a crime.

Theodosius' attitude was no less strenuous toward remaining heathenism than in regard to heretical Christian parties. In 392 he forbade heathen worship under penalties similar to those for lese-majesty and sacrilege.[7] It was the

[5] *Codex Theodosianus*, 16:1; Ayer, p. 367.   [6] Ayer, *Source Book*, pp. 354–356.
[7] *Codex Theodosianus*, 16:10, 12; Ayer, p. 347.

old weapon of heathenism against Christianity now used by Christian hands against heathenism. Constantine's toleration had fully disappeared. Nevertheless, heathen worship persisted, and only slowly died out.

5

Arian Missions and the Germanic Invasions

THROUGHOUT THE HISTORY of the empire the defense of the frontiers of the Rhine and the Danube against the Teutonic peoples beyond had been an important military problem. Under Marcus Aurelius a desperate, but ultimately successful war had been waged by the Romans on the upper Danube (167–180). Considerable shifting of tribes and formations of confederacies took place behind the screen of the Roman frontier; but by the beginning of the third century the group known as the Alemans had formed across the upper Rhine, and half a century later, that of the Franks on the lower right side of that river. Between these two developments, about 230–240, the Goths completed their settlement in what is now southern Russia. In 250 and 251 the Roman hold in the Balkans was seriously threatened by a Gothic invasion, in which the persecuting Emperor, Decius, lost his life. The Goths effected a settlement in the region north of the lower Danube. They invaded the empire, and the peril was not stayed till the victories of Claudius (269), from which he derived his title, "Gothicus." The stronger Emperors, Aurelian, Diocletian, and Constantine, held the frontiers of the Rhine and the Danube effectively; but the danger of invasion was always present. By the fourth century the Goths north of the Danube, who were most in contact with Roman civilization of any of the Germanic tribes, were known as the Visigoths, while their kinsmen in southern Russia were called Ostrogoths. The exact meaning of these names is uncertain, though they are generally regarded as signifying West and East Goths.

There was, indeed, much interchange between Romans and Germans, especially from the time of Aurelian onward. Germans served, in increasing numbers, in the Roman armies. Roman traders penetrated far beyond the borders of the empire. Germans settled in the border provinces and adopted Roman ways. Prisoners of war, taken probably in the raid of 264, from Cappadocia, had introduced the germs of Christianity among the Visigoths before the close of the third century, and even a rudimentary church organization in certain places. The Visigoths, as a nation, had not been converted. To that work Ulfila was to contribute. Born about 310, of parentage sprung, in part at least, from the captives just mentioned, he was of Christian origin, and became a "reader" in the services of the little Christian Gothic circle. In 341 he accompanied a Gothic embassy, and was ordained bishop by the Arian Eusebius of Nicomedia, then bishop of Constantinople, whether in the latter city, or in Antioch where the synod (see p. 112) was then sitting, is uncertain. His theology, which seems to have been very simple, was thenceforth anti-Nicene, and after the formation of the new Homoion party he was to be reckoned one of its adherents. For the next seven years he labored in his native land, till persecution compelled him and his fellow Christians to seek refuge on Roman soil, living and laboring for many years near the modern Plevna, in Bulgaria. His great work was the translation of the Scriptures, or at least of the New Testament, into the Gothic tongue. In 383 he died on a visit to Constantinople. Unfortunately, the complete oblivion into which these Arian labors fell, owing to their unorthodox character in the view of the following age, allows no knowledge of Ulfila's associates, nor a judgment as to how far the credit of turning the Visigoths to Christianity belonged to him, or to the Gothic chieftain Fritigern, about 370.

But, however brought about, the Visigoths, in spite of heathen persecution, rapidly accepted Arian Christianity. Not only they, but their neighbors the Ostrogoths, the Vandals in part, and remoter Germanic tribes, such as the Burgundians and Lombards, had embraced the Arian faith before invading the empire. Indeed, so widely had Christianity penetrated that it seems not improbable that, had the invasions been a couple of generations delayed, all might have entered the empire as Christians. As it was, those tribes only which were the farthest removed from the influences going out from the Visigoths— those of northwestern Germany, of whom the chief were the Franks and the Saxons—remained overwhelmingly heathen at the time of the invasions. Such rapid extension of Christianity shows that the hold of native paganism must have been slight, and that many, whose names have utterly perished, shared in the work of conversion. It was of the utmost significance that when the walls of the empire were broken the Germans came, for the most part, not as enemies of Christianity. Had the Western empire fallen, as well it might, a century before, the story of Christianity might have been vastly different.

Pressed by an invasion of Huns from western Central Asia, the Visigoths sought shelter across the frontier of the lower Danube in 376. Angered by ill-treatment from Roman officials, they crossed the Balkans and annihilated the Roman army near Adrianople, in 378, in a battle in which the Emperor Valens lost his life. The strong hand of Theodosius (379–395) restrained their further attacks; but on his death the empire, divided between his son of eighteen, Arcadius, in the East, and his eleven-year-old son, Honorius, in the West, was no longer able to resist the attack. Under Alaric, the Visigoths plundered almost to the walls of Constantinople, and thence moved into Greece, penetrating as far as Sparta. By 401 the Visigoths were pressing into northern Italy, but were resisted for the next few years by Theodosius' able Vandal general, Stilicho, whom he had left as guardian for the young Honorius. Stilicho's murder, in 408, opened the road to Rome, and Alaric promptly marched thither. It was not till 410, however, that the Visigothic chieftain actually captured the city. The popular impression of this event was profound. The old mistress of the world had fallen before the barbarians. Alaric, desirous of establishing a kingdom for himself and of securing Roman Africa, the granary of Italy, marched at once for southern Italy, and there died before the close of 410. Under Ataulf the Visigothic host marched northward, invading southern Gaul in 412. Here the Goths settled by 419, developing ultimately a kingdom that included half of modern France, to which they added most of Spain by conquest during the course of the century. The Roman inhabitants were not driven out, but they were subjected to their Germanic conquerors, who appropriated much of the land, and placed its older occupants in a distinctly inferior position. Commerce was hampered, the life of the cities largely broken down, and civilization crippled.

While these events were in progress, the tribes across the Rhine had seen their opportunity. The Arian Vandals and heathen Alans and Suevi invaded Gaul at the close of 406, ultimately pushing their way into Spain, where they arrived before the Visigoths. The Franks had pressed into northern Gaul and the Burgundians conquered the region around Strassburg, and thence gradually the territory of eastern Gaul which still bears their name. Britain, involved in this collapse of Roman authority, was increasingly invaded by the Saxons, Angles, and Jutes, who had been attacking its coasts since the middle of the fourth century. There Roman civilization had a weaker grasp than on the continent, and as Germanic conquest slowly advanced, it drove the Celtic element largely westward, and made much of Britain a heathen land. The Vandals from Spain, having entered Africa by 425, invaded it in full force in 429, under Gaiseric. They soon established there the most powerful of the early Germanic kingdoms, whose piratical ships speedily dominated the western Mediterranean. A Vandal raid sacked Rome in 455. A fearful invasion of Gaul in 451, by the Huns under Attila, was checked in battle near Troyes by the combined forces of the Romans and Visigoths. The next year Attila carried his devastations into Italy, and was barely prevented from taking Rome by causes which are now obscure, but among which the efforts of its bishop, Leo I, were believed to have been determinative.

Though the rule of the Emperors was nominally maintained in the West, and even the Germanic conquerors, who established kingdoms in Gaul, Spain, and Africa were professedly their dependents, the Emperors became the tools of the chiefs of the army. On the death of Honorius, in 423, the empire passed to Valentinian III. His long reign, till 455, was marked by the quarrels of Boniface, count of Africa, and Aetius, the count of Italy, which permitted the Vandal conquest of North Africa. Aetius won, indeed, about the last victory of the empire when, with the Visigoths, he defeated Attila in 451. Between 455 and 476 no less than nine Emperors were set up and deposed in the West. The real ruler of Italy was the head of the army. From 456 to 472 this post was held by Ricimer, of Suevic and Visigothic descent. After his death the command was taken by a certain Orestes, who conferred the imperial title on his son, Romulus, nicknamed Augustulus. The army in Italy was recruited chiefly from smaller Germanic tribes, among them the Rugii and Heruli. It now demanded a third of the land. Orestes refused, and the army rose in mutiny in 476 under the Germanic general Odovakar, whom it made King. This date has usually been taken as that of the close of the Roman Empire. In reality it was without special significance. Romulus Augustulus was deposed. There was no further Emperor in the West till Charlemagne. But Odovakar and his contemporaries had no thought that the Roman Empire was at an end. He ruled in Italy as the Visigoths ruled in southern France and Spain, a nominal subject of the Roman Emperor, who sat on the throne in Constantinople.

Odovakar's sovereignty in Italy was ended in 493 in the struggle against new Germanic invaders of Italy, the Ostrogoths, led by Theodoric. Under that successful conqueror a really remarkable amalgamation of Roman and Germanic institutions was attempted. His capital was Ravenna, whence he ruled till his death in 526. The Ostrogothic kingdom in Italy was brought to an end by the long wars under the Emperor Justinian, which were fought, from 535 to 555, by Belisarius and Narses, who restored a ravaged Italy to the empire. Contemporaneously (534) the imperial authority was re-established in North Africa and the Vandal kingdom brought to an end. Italy was not long at peace. Between 568 and 572 a new Germanic invasion, that of the Lombards, founded a kingdom that was to last for two centuries. Masters of northern Italy, to which region they gave their name, the Lombards did not, however, win Rome and the southern part of the peninsula, nor did they gain Ravenna, the seat of the imperial exarch, till the eighth century. Rome remained, therefore, connected with the empire which had its seat in Constantinople, but so distant and so close to the Lombard frontier that effective control from Constantinople was impossible—a condition extremely favorable for the growth of the political power of its bishop.

Contemporaneously with the earlier of the events just described, changes of the utmost significance were in process in Gaul. The Franks, of whom mention has been made, had long been pressing into the northern part of the ancient provinces. Divided into several tribes, the King of the Salic Franks, from about 481, was Clovis. A chieftain of great energy, he soon extended his sovereignty as far as the Loire. He and his people were still heathen, though he treated the church with respect. In 493 he married Clotilda, a Burgundian, but, unlike most of her fellow countrymen, a "Catholic," not an Arian. After a great victory over the Alemans, in 496, he declared for Christianity, and was baptized with three thousand of his followers in Rheims, on Christmas of that year. His was the first Germanic tribe, therefore, to be converted to the ortho-dox faith. Visigoths, Ostrogoths, Vandals, Burgundians, and Lombards were Arians. This agreement in belief won for Clovis not only the good-will of the old Roman population and the support of the bishops whom he, in turn, favored but, added to his own abilities, enabled him before his death, in 511, to take from the Visigoths most of their possessions north of the Pyrenees and to become so extensive a ruler that he may well be called the founder of France, his territories stretching even beyond the Rhine. That the Franks were "Catholic" was ultimately, though not immediately, to bring connections be-tween them and the papacy of most far-reaching consequences.

The conversion of the Franks had also much influence on the other Germanic invaders, though the example of the native population among whom they were settled worked even more powerfully. The Burgundians abandoned Arianism in 517, and in 532 became part of the Frankish kingdom. The imperial conquests of Justinian ended the Arian kingdoms of the Vandals and Ostrogoths. The rivalry of the creeds was terminated in Spain by the renun-ciation of Arianism by the Visigothic King, Recared, in 587, and confirmed at the Third Council of Toledo, in 589. About 590 the gradual conversion of the Lombards to Catholicism began—a process not completed till about 660. Thus all Arianism ultimately disappeared.

6

The Growth of the Papacy

TO THE DISTINCTION already attaching to the Roman Church and its bishop the period of the invasions brought new eminence. Believed to be founded by Peter, situated in the ancient capital, the guardian of apostolical tradition, the largest and most generous church of the West, it had stood orthodox in the Arian controversy, and in the ruin of the Germanic invasions it seemed the great surviving institution of the ancient world which they were unable to overthrow. While most of the bishops of Rome in this period were men of moderate abilities, several were the strongest leaders of the West, and to them great advancement in the authority of the Roman bishop—the development

of a real papacy—was due. Such a leader of force was Innocent I (402–417).
He claimed for the Roman Church not only custody of apostolical tradition
and the foundation of all Western Christianity, but ascribed the decisions of
Sardica (see p. 112) to the Council of Nicæa, and based on them a universal jurisdiction of the Roman bishop.[1] Leo I (440–461) greatly served
Rome, in the judgment of the time, during the invasions of the Huns and
Vandals, and largely influenced the result of the Council of Chalcedon (pp.
138–9). He emphasized the primacy of Peter among the Apostles, both in faith
and government, and taught that what Peter possessed had passed to Peter's
successors.[2] These claims Leo largely made good. He ended the attempt to
create an independent Gallic see in Arles; he exercised authority in Spain and
North Africa. In 445 he procured an edict from the Western Emperor,
Valentinian III, ordering all to obey the Roman bishop, as having the "primacy
of Saint Peter." [3] On the other hand, the Council of Chalcedon, in 451, by
its twenty-eighth canon placed Constantinople on a practical equality with
Rome.[4] Against this action Leo at once protested; but it foreshadowed the
ultimate separation, far more political than religious, between the churches of
East and West.

In the struggle with Monophysitism (pp. 140 ff.), the bishops of Rome
resisted the efforts of the Emperor Zeno (474–491) and the Patriarch Acacius
of Constantinople to modify the results of Chalcedon by the so-called *Henoticon*,[5] with the result that Pope Felix III (483–492) excommunicated Acacius, and a schism began between East and West which ended in 519 in a
papal triumph. During this controversy Pope Gelasius (492–496) wrote a
letter to Zeno's successor, the Eastern Emperor Anastasius, in which he declared "there are . . . two by whom principally this world is ruled: the sacred
authority of the pontiffs and the royal power. Of these the importance of the
priests is so much the greater, as even for Kings of men they will have to give
an account in the divine judgment." [6] In 502 Bishop Ennodius of Pavia urged
that the Pope can be judged by God alone.[7] The later claims of the mediæval
papacy were, therefore, sketched by the beginning of the sixth century. Circumstances prevented their development in full practice in the period immediately following. The rise of the Ostrogothic kingdom in Italy and the reconquest of Italy by the Eastern empire, diminished the independence of the
papacy. Outside of Italy the growth of a new Catholic power, the Franks,
and the gradual conversion of Arian Germanic rulers, brought about a harmony between the new sovereigns and their bishops that gave to the latter
extensive independence of Roman claims, though accompanied by great dependence on the Germanic sovereigns. The full realization of the papal ideal,
thus early established, was to be a task of centuries, and was to encounter
many vicissitudes.

---

[1] *Letters,* 2, 25; Mirbt, *Quellen zur Geschichte des Papsttums,* 54, 55.
[2] *Sermons,* 3:2, 3; Ayer, p. 477.   [3] Mirbt, p. 65.   [4] Ayer, p. 521.
[5] Ayer, p. 527.   [6] Ayer, p. 531.   [7] Mirbt, p. 70.

7

Monasticism

*I*T HAS BEEN pointed out that ascetic ideals and a double standard of Christian morality had long been growing in the church before the time of Constantine (see pp. 94 ff.). Their progress was aided by the ascetic tendencies inherent in the better philosophies of the ancient world. Origen, for instance, who was permeated with the Hellenistic spirit, was distinguished for his asceticism. Long before the close of the third century the holy virgins were a conspicuous element in the church, and men and women, without leaving their homes, were practising asceticism. Nor is asceticism, or even monasticism, peculiar to Christianity. Its representatives are to be found in the religions of India and among Jews, Greeks, and Egyptians.

Certain causes led to its increased development contemporary with the recognition of Christianity by the state. The low condition of the church, emphasized by the influx of vast numbers in the peace from 260 to 303, and after the conversion of Constantine, led to enlarged valuation of the ascetic life by serious-minded Christians. The cessation of martyrdoms left asceticism the highest Christian achievement attainable. The world was filled with sights that offended Christian morality, from which it seemed well to flee. The mind of antiquity regarded the practice of contemplation as more estimable than the active virtues. Above all, the increasing formalism of public worship, as developed by the close of the third century, led to a desire for a freer and more individual approach to God. Monasticism was soon to become formal enough; but in its initiation it was a breach with the limitations of conventional Christian worship and service. It was in origin a layman's movement.

Anthony, the founder of Christian monasticism, was born in Koma, in central Egypt, about 250, of native (Coptic) stock. Impressed with Christ's words to the rich young man,[1] he gave up his possessions, and about 270 took up the ascetic life in his native village. Some fifteen years later he went into the solitude, becoming a hermit. Here he is said to have lived till 356 (?). He believed himself tormented by demons in every imaginable form. He fasted. He practised the strictest self-denial. He prayed constantly. He would draw near to God by overcoming the flesh. Anthony soon had many imitators, some of whom lived absolutely alone, others in groups, of which the largest were

[1] *Matt.* 19:21.

in the deserts of Nitria and Scetis. Whether singly or in groups, these monks were as far as possible hermit-like. Their worship and their self-denials were largely of their own devising. Their ideal was that of the individual hero who had left all for Christ.

The first great improver of monasticism was Pachomius. Born about 292, he became a soldier, and was converted from heathenism to Christianity when perhaps twenty years old. At first he adopted the hermit life, but dissatisfied with its irregularities, he established the first Christian monastery in Tabennisi, in southern Egypt, about 315–320. Here all the inmates were knit into a single body, having assigned work, regular hours of worship, similar dress, and cells close to one another—in a word, a life in common under an abbot. This was a vastly more healthful type of monasticism. Here was born the conception of the ideal Christian society in contrast to that of the secular world and of the Church corrupted by compromise. It was also a way of life possible for women, for whom Pachomius established a convent. At his death, in 346, there were ten of his monasteries in Egypt.

The two types, the hermit form of Anthony and the cenobite organization of Pachomius, continued side by side in Egypt, and both were carried from that land to the rest of the empire. Syria saw a considerable development early in the fourth century. There the hermit form took extravagant expression, of which an example, a little later, is that of the famous Simeon Stylites, who dwelt for thirty years, till his death in 459, on the top of a pillar, situated east of Antioch. Monasticism in Asia Minor, on the other hand, continued the tradition of Pachomius, chiefly owing to the efforts of its great popularizer, Basil (see p. 116), who labored for its spread from about 360 to his death in 379. The Rule which bears his name, whether his actual composition or not, was even more that of a life in common than that of Pachomius. It emphasized work, prayer, and Bible reading. It taught that monks should aid those outside by the care of orphans, and similar good deeds. It discouraged extreme asceticism. Basil's Rule is, in a general way, a basis of the monasticism of the Greek and Russian Churches to the present day, though with much less weight laid than by him on work and helpfulness to others.

The introduction of monasticism into the West was the work of Athanasius. By the closing years of the fourth century the exhortations and examples of Jerome, Ambrose, and Augustine brought it much favor, though it also encountered no little opposition. In France its great advocate was Martin of Tours, who established a monastery near Poitiers about 362. Soon monasticism, both in its cenobite and in its hermit forms, was to be found throughout the West. The earliest monks, as in the East, were laymen; but Eusebius, bishop of Vercelli in Italy, who died in 371, began the practice of requiring the clergy of his cathedral to live the monastic life. Through the influence of this example the originally lay character of the movement was modified.

Western monasticism was long in a chaotic condition. Individual monasteries had their separate rules. Asceticism, always characteristic in high degree of Eastern monasticism, found many disciples. On the other hand, many monasteries were lax. The great reformer of Western monasticism was Benedict of Nursia. Born about 480, he studied for a brief time in Rome, but, oppressed by the evils of the city, he became a hermit (c. 500) in a cave of the mountains at Subiaco, east of Rome. The fame of his sanctity gathered disciples about him, and led to the offer of the headship of a neighboring monastery, which he accepted only to leave when he found its ill-regulated monks unwilling to submit to his discipline. At some uncertain date, traditionally 529, he now founded the mother monastery of the Benedictine order, on the hill of Monte Cassino, about half-way between Rome and Naples. To it he gave his Rule, and in it he died about 547, the last certain event of his life, his meeting with the Ostrogothic King, Totila, having taken place in 542.

Benedict's famous Rule [2] exhibited his profound knowledge of human nature and his Roman genius for organization. His conception of a monastery was that of a permanent, self-contained and self-supporting garrison of Christ's soldiers. At its head was an abbot, who must be implicitly obeyed, yet who was bound in grave matters of common concern to consult all the brethren, and in minor questions the elder monks. None was to become a monk without having tried the life of the monastery for a year; but, once admitted, his vows were irrevocable. To Benedict's thinking, worship was undoubtedly the prime duty of a monk. Its daily common observance occupied at least four hours, divided into seven periods. Almost as much emphasis was laid on work. "Idleness is the enemy of the soul." Hence Benedict prescribed manual labor in the fields and reading. Some fixed time must be spent in reading each day, varying with the seasons of the year; and in Lent books must be assigned, with provision to insure their being read. These injunctions made every Benedictine monastery, at all true to the founder's ideal, a center of industry, and the possessor of a library. The value of these provisions in the training of the Germanic nations and the preservation of literature was inestimable. Yet they were but secondary to Benedict's main purpose, that of worship. In general, Benedict's Rule was characterized by great moderation and good sense in its requirements as to food, labor, and discipline. It was a strict life, but one not at all impossible for the average earnest man.

In the Benedictine system early Western monasticism is to be seen at its best. His Rule spread slowly. It was carried by Roman missionaries to England and Germany. It did not penetrate France till the seventh century; but by the time of Charlemagne it had become well-nigh universal. With the Rule of Benedict the adjustment between monasticism and the church was complete. The services of its monks as missionaries and pioneers were of in-

[2] Extracts in Ayer, pp. 631–641; practically in full in Henderson, *Select Historical Documents of the Middle Ages*, pp. 274–314.

estimable value. In troubled times the monastery afforded the only refuge for peace-loving souls. The highest proof of its adaption to the later Roman Empire and the Middle Ages was that not only the best men supported the institution; they were to be found in it.

In sharp contrast to the stable and moderating ideals of Benedictine monasticism stands the Celtic type with its mystical spirit, its undisciplined restlessness and its ascetic rigor. Derived originally from the East by way of South Gaul, it flourished from the fifth to the seventh centuries in Ireland, Scotland, and England, its unique contributions lying in its fervent missionary activity and in its devotion to learning. The great monastic schools of Ireland in the fifth and sixth centuries were widely renowned. There the study of Greek was preserved and the Celtic Christian art was developed. Eventually with the triumph of Roman Christianity in Britain, the Celtic monastery yielded to the Benedictine rule; but it infused its missionary spirit into later British monks like Willibrord and Boniface (p. 184), who did so much to convert Northern Europe. A distinctive feature of the Celtic monasticism was its adaptation to the clan system and the consequent hereditary position of the abbot. Moreover, the basis of church organization in Celtic Christianity was monastic rather than diocesan, the bishop being inferior to the abbot and even the abbess. Hence, for instance, the see of Kildare in Ireland, where St. Bridget was abbess in the early sixth century, could be referred to as "a see at once episcopal and virginal." The great names in Celtic monasticism such as Finian of Clonard, Columba and Columbanus will be treated later (pp. 180 ff.).

8

Ambrose and Chrysostom

THE CONTRAST between East and West is in many ways illustrated by the unlike qualities and experiences of Chrysostom and Ambrose. Ambrose was born in Trier, now in western Germany, where his father held the high civil office of prætorian prefect of Gaul, about 337–340. Educated in Rome for a civil career, his talents, integrity, and likableness led to his appointment, about 374, as governor of a considerable part of northern Italy, with his residence in Milan, then practically an imperial capital. The death of the Arian bishop, Auxentius, in 374, left the Milanese see vacant. The two factions were soon in bitter struggle as to the theological complexion of his successor. The young governor entered the church to quiet the throng, when the cry was raised, "Ambrose Bishop!" and he found himself, though unbaptized, elected bishop of Milan. To Ambrose, this was a call of God. He gave up his wealth to the poor and the church. He studied theology. He became a most acceptable preacher. Above all, he possessed to the full the Roman talent for administration, and he soon became the first ecclesiastic of the West. Strongly attached to the Nicene faith, Ambrose would make no compromise with the Arians, and resisted all their attempts to secure places of worship in Milan—an effort in which they were aided by the Empress Justina, mother of the youthful Valentinian II. In the same spirit he opposed successfully the efforts of the heathen party in Rome to obtain from Valentinian II the restoration of the Altar of Victory in the Senate chamber, and other privileges for the older worship. His greatest triumph was in the case of the Emperor Theodosius. That quick-tempered ruler, angered by the murder of the governor of Thessalonica, in 390, caused a punitive massacre of its inhabitants. Ambrose, with rare moral courage, called on the Emperor to manifest his public repentance.[1] It throws a pleasing light on the character of Theodosius that he obeyed the admonition.

Ambrose was a theological writer of such reputation that the Roman Church reckons him as one of its "Doctors"—or authoritative teachers. His work, however, in this field was largely a reproduction of the thoughts of Greek theologians, though with a deeper sense of sin and grace than they. "I will not glory because I am righteous, but I will glory because I am redeemed. I will not glory because I am free from sin, but because my sins are forgiven." [2] Ambrose's bent was practical. He wrote on Christian ethics, in full sympathy with the ascetic movement of the time. He contributed much to the development of Christian hymnology in the West. Forceful and sometimes overbearing, he was a man of the highest personal character and of indefatigable zeal—a true prince of the church. Such men were needed in the shock of the collapsing empire if the church was to survive in power. He died in 397.

Very different was the life of Chrysostom. John, to whom the name Chrysostom, "golden-mouthed," was given long after his death, was born of noble and well-to-do parents in Antioch about 345–347. Losing his father shortly after his birth, he was brought up by his religious-minded mother, Anthusa, and early distinguished himself in scholarship and eloquence. About 370, he was baptized and probably ordained a "reader." He now practised extreme asceticism, and pursued theological studies under Diodorus of Tarsus, one of the leaders of the later Antiochian school. Not satisfied with his austerities, he became a hermit (c. 375), and so remained till ill health com-

[1] Ayer, pp. 390, 391.   [2] *De Jacob et vita beata*, 1.6.21.

pelled his return to Antioch, where he was ordained a deacon (*c.* 381). In 386 he was advanced to the priesthood. Then followed the happiest and most useful period of his life. For twelve years he was the great preacher of Antioch —the ablest that the Oriental Church probably ever possessed. His sermons were exegetical and eminently practical. The simple, grammatical understanding of the Scriptures, always preferred in Antioch to the allegorical interpretation beloved in Alexandria, appealed to him. His themes were eminently social—the Christian conduct of life. He soon had an enormous following.

Such was Chrysostom's fame that, on the see of Constantinople falling vacant, he was practically forced by Eutropius, the favorite of the Emperor Arcadius, to accept the bishopric of the capital in 398. Here he soon won a popular hearing like that of Antioch. From the first, however, his way in Constantinople was beset with foes. The unscrupulous patriarch of Alexandria, Theophilus, desired to bring Constantinople into practical subjection. Himself the opponent of Origen's teaching, he charged Chrysostom with too great partiality for that master. Chrysostom's strict discipline, for which there was ample justification, was disliked by the loose-living clergy of Constantinople. Worst of all, he won the hostility of the vigorous Empress Eudoxia, by reasons of denunciations of feminine extravagance in dress, which she thought aimed at herself. Chrysostom was certainly as tactless as he was fearless in denouncing offenses in high places. All the forces against him gathered together. A pretext for attack soon arose. In his opposition to Origen, Theophilus had disciplined certain monks of Egypt. Four of these, known as the "tall brothers," fled to Chrysostom, by whom they were well received. Theophilus and Chrysostom's other enemies now secured a synod, at an imperial estate near Constantinople known as "The Oak," which, under the leadership of Theophilus, condemned and deposed Chrysostom in 403. The Empress was as superstitious as she was enraged, and an accident in the palace—later tradition pictured it probably mistakenly as an earthquake—led to Chrysostom's recall shortly after he had left the capital. Peace was of brief duration. A silver statue of the Empress, erected hard by his cathedral, led to denunciations by Chrysostom of the ceremonies of its dedication. The Empress saw in him more than ever a personal enemy. This time, in spite of warm popular support, he was banished to the miserable town of Cucusus, on the edge of Armenia. Pope Innocent I protested, but in vain. Yet from this exile Chrysostom continued so to influence his friends by letter that his opponents determined to place him in deeper obscurity. In 407 he was ordered to Pityus, but he never reached there, dying on the journey.

The fate of this most deserving, if not most judicious, preacher of righteousness illustrates the seamy side of imperial interference in ecclesiastical affairs, and the rising jealousies of the great sees of the East, from whose mutual hostility the church and the empire were greatly to suffer.

9

The Christological Controversies

THE NICENE result determined that Christ is fully God, and "was made man." On the common basis of Nicene orthodoxy, however, the further question arose as to the relations of the divine and human in Him. Regarding that problem the Nicene creed was silent, and even the great Nicene champion, Athanasius, had not paid much attention to it. Only in the West had a general formula come into extensive use. As the Nicene decision had been largely anticipated by Tertullian, with the result that the West had been united when the East was divided, so thanks to the clear definitions of that great African writer, the West had a conception of full deity and full manhood existing in Christ, without confusion, and without diminution of the qualities appropriate to each. In the new struggle, as in that of Nicæa, the Western view was to triumph. Yet neither in its conception of "one substance in three persons," nor in that of "one person, Jesus, God, and man" (see p. 66), had the West any wrought-out philosophical theory. What Tertullian had given it were clear-cut judicial definitions of traditional beliefs rather than philosophically thought-out theology. It was the advantage of the West once more, as in the Nicene struggle, that it was now united, even if its thought was not so profound as that of the divided East, when the East fairly began to wrestle with the intellectual problems involved.

It was possible to approach the Christological problem from two angles. The unity of Christ might be so emphasized as to involve a practical absorption of His humanity into divinity; or the integrity of each element, the divine and the human, maintained in such fashion as to give color to the interpretation that in Him were two separate beings. Both tendencies were manifested in the controversy—the first being that toward which the theological leaders of Alexandria leaned, and the latter being derivable from the teachings of the school of Antioch.

The first and one of the ablest of those who undertook a really profound discussion of the relation of the human and the divine in Christ was Apollinaris, bishop of Laodicea in Syria (?–*c.* 390). A hearty supporter of the Nicene decision, he enjoyed for a considerable time at least the friendship of Athanasius. His intellectual gifts were such as to command respect even from his opponents. Moreover, as with Athanasius, Apollinaris' interest was primarily religious. To both, Christ's work for men was the transformation of our sinful mortality into divine and blessed immortality. This salvation, Apollinaris thought with Athanasius, could be achieved only if Christ was completely and perfectly divine. But how, Apollinaris argued, could Christ be made up of a perfect man united with complete God? Was that not to assert two Sons, one eternal, and the other by adoption? [1] Nor could Apollinaris explain Christ's sinlessness or the harmony of His wills, if Christ was complete man joined with full God.[2] To him, the best solution seemed akin to that of Arius, whom he otherwise opposed, that in Jesus the place of the soul was taken by the Logos, and only the body was human. That view having been condemned, though without mention of his name, by a synod in Alexandria in 362,[3] Apollinaris apparently altered his theory so as to hold that Jesus had the body and animal soul of a man, but that the reasoning spirit in Him was the Logos.[4] By this he meant that the highest directing principle of His existence could not be a human mind, but must be divine. For Apollinaris the human mind is corrupt and in the service of the flesh. In consequence it must have been replaced in Jesus by the Logos, the archetype of all minds (*logoi*), which are made in His image but which are fallen. In this way he sought to find the unity of Jesus Christ and to avoid a duality of Sons. Hence he held that the divine so made the human one with it, that "God has in His own flesh suffered our sorrows." [5] These opinions seemed to do special honor to Christ's divinity, and were destined to be widely and permanently influential in Oriental Christian thinking, but they really denied Christ's true humanity, and as such speedily called down condemnation on their author. Rome decided against him in 377 and 382, Antioch in 379, and finally the so-called Second Ecumenical Council—that of Constantinople —in 381.[6] Yet it will be seen later that an element of Apollinaris' view did finally triumph in orthodoxy. What he had expressed more crudely was eventually accepted, when put in a more guarded and refined way. While it was acknowledged, against Apollinaris, that Jesus had a human mind, it was held that the center, the subject of Jesus was not that of a man but was the Logos Himself.

Apollinaris was strongly opposed by Gregory of Nazianzus and by the school of Antioch. The founder of the latter, in its later stage, was Diodorus (?–394), long a presbyter of Antioch, and from 378 to his death bishop of Tarsus. Its roots, indeed, ran back into the earlier teaching of Paul of Samosata (see p. 69) and Lucian (see p. 97); but the extreme positions which they represented, and their leadership, were rejected, and the school stood on the basis of the Nicene orthodoxy. It was marked by a degree

---

[1] Ayer, p. 495.   [2] *Ibid.*   [3] Athanasius, *Tomus ad Antiochenos*, 7.
[4] Ayer, p. 495.   [5] *Ibid.*, p. 496.   [6] *Canon*, 1.

of literalism in its exegesis of Scripture quite in contrast to the excessive use of allegory by the Alexandrians. Its philosophy showed the influence of Aristotle as theirs that of Plato. Its thought of Christ was more influenced by the tradition of Asia Minor, of the "second Adam," and by the reality of the human experiences of temptation and suffering, than was Alexandria. Antioch, therefore, laid more weight of teaching on the earthly life and human nature of Jesus than was the tendency in Alexandria. In this attempt to give true value to Christ's humanity, Diodorus approached the view that in Christ were two persons in moral rather than essential union. Since the Logos is eternal and like can only bear like, that which was born of Mary was the human only. The incarnation was the indwelling of the Logos in a perfect man, as of God in a temple. The union of human and divine resembled that of body and soul, or even of man and wife. These views are reminiscent of the adoptionist Christology, which had found one of its latest avowed defenders in Paul of Samosata in Antioch a century earlier. They were out of touch with the Greek conception of salvation—the making divine of the human.

Among the disciples of Diodorus were Chrysostom (see p. 129), Theodore of Mopsuestia, and Nestorius. Theodore, a native of Antioch, who held the bishopric for which he is named for thirty-six years, till his death in 428, was the ablest exegete and theologian of the Antiochian school. Though he maintained that God and man in Christ constituted one person—*prosopon, πρόσωπον*—he had difficulty in making that contention real, and held theories largely influenced by those of Diodorus.[7] The union of the human and the divine in Jesus Christ he understood in terms of God's "good will" or "good pleasure." There was a conjunction of will between the Logos and the man Jesus.

Nestorius, a presbyter and monk of Antioch, held in high repute there as a preacher, was made patriarch of Constantinople in 428. Recent discoveries, especially of his own autobiographical work, *The Treatise of Heraclides of Damascus,* have immensely broadened knowledge of his real theological position, as well as of the facts of his later life. His dogmatic standpoint was essentially that of the school of Antioch; yet he would not admit that there were in Christ two persons—the doctrine with which he was charged. "With the one name Christ we designate at the same time two natures. . . . The essential characteristics in the nature of the divinity and in the humanity are from all eternity distinguished."[8] Perhaps his furthest departure from the current Greek conception of salvation is to be seen in such an expression as: "God the Word is also named Christ because He has always conjunction with Christ. And it is impossible for God the Word to do anything without the humanity, for all is planned upon an intimate conjunction, not on the

[7] Ayer, pp. 498–501.   [8] *Ibid.,* p. 502.

deification of the humanity." [9] Nestorius would emphasize the reality and completeness of the human and the divine in the Christian's Lord, and the conjunction of will between them.

Opposed to Nestorius, and to be his bitterest enemy, was Cyril, the patriarch of Alexandria (412–444), the nephew and successor of the patriarch who had had so unworthy a part in the downfall of Chrysostom. In him unscrupulous ambition combined with the jealousy of Constantinople long entertained in Alexandria—and it must be admitted, reciprocated—and with the hostility of the rival schools of Alexandria and Antioch. Yet it is but just to Cyril to note that there was more in his opposition to Nestorius than mere jealousy and rivalry, however prominent those unlovely traits may have been. Cyril, following the Alexandrian tradition, and in consonance with the Greek conception of salvation, saw in Christ the full making divine of the human. Though he rejected the view of Apollinaris and held that Christ's humanity was complete in that it possessed body, soul, and mind, he really stood very near to Apollinaris. His emphasis on the divine in Christ was such that, though he described the union in Him as that out of "two natures," the center or subject of His Person was the Logos. His watchword was, "One *physis* (nature) of the Word, and it made flesh," by which he meant one unified Being, one concrete existence centered in the Word. A tragic feature of the whole controversy was the ambiguity of the word "nature." By it Cyril intended a concrete existence, the unified and living individual. By others it was used in a more abstract sense for the totality of human or divine properties (as it came to be used at Chalcedon). Hence untold confusion could and did arise in the course of the debate, with neither side fully understanding the other. For Cyril the Logos "took flesh," He clothed Himself with humanity. The human element had no center apart from the Logos. Jesus was not an individual man. Yet while Cyril held to an interchange of qualities between the divine and the human, each is a complete nature. "From two natures, one"; and that one is the Logos united with humanity. For Cyril it was, therefore, God made flesh, who was born, who died, of whom we partake in the Supper, and whose making divine of humanity is the proof and means that we, too, shall be made partakers of the divine nature.[10] If the school of Antioch came near such a separation of the divine and the human as to leave Christ only the Son of God by adoption, that of Cyril allowed Him little more than an impersonal humanity centered in the divinity.

An ancient designation of the Mother of Jesus was "Mother of God"— *Theotokos,* Θεοτόκος, literally "Bearer of God." It had been used by Alexander of Alexandria, Athanasius, Apollinaris, and Gregory of Nazianzus. To Cyril it was, of course, a natural expression. Everywhere in the East it may

[9] Ayer, p. 502.   [10] See Ayer, pp. 505–507.

be said to have been in good usage, save where the school of Antioch had influence, and even Theodore of Mopsuestia of that school was willing to employ the expression, if carefully guarded.[11] Nestorius found it current coin in Constantinople. To his thinking it did not sufficiently distinguish the human from the divine in Christ. He therefore preached against it, at the beginning of his bishopric, declaring the proper form to be "Mother of Christ"—"for that which is born of flesh is flesh." [12] Yet even he expressed himself a little later as willing to say *Theotokos,* in the guarded way in which Theodore would employ it. "It can be endured in consideration of the fact that the temple, which is inseparably united with God the Word, comes of her." [13] In preaching against this expression Nestorius had touched popular piety and the rising religious reverence for the Virgin on the quick. Cyril saw his opportunity to humiliate the rival see of Constantinople and the school of Antioch at one blow, while advancing his own Christology. Cyril promptly wrote to the Egyptian monks defending the disputed phrase, and there soon followed an exchange of critical letters between Cyril and Nestorius. It speedily came to an open attack on the patriarch of Constantinople.

Cyril now brought every influence at his command to his aid in one of the most tragic contests in church history. He appealed to the Emperor and Empress, Theodosius II and Eudocia, and to the Emperor's sister, Pulcheria, representing that Nestorius's doctrines destroyed all basis of salvation. He presented his case to Pope Celestine I (422–432). Nestorius, in his turn, also wrote to the Pope. Celestine promptly found in favor of Cyril, and ordered, through a Roman synod in 430, that Nestorius recant or be excommunicated. The action of the Pope is hard to understand. The letter of Nestorius agreed more nearly in its definition of the question at issue with the Western view than did the theory of Cyril. Nestorius declared his faith in "both natures which by the highest and unmixed union are adored in the one person of the Only Begotten." [14] Politics were probably the determining factor. Rome and Alexandria had long worked together against the rising claims of Constantinople. Nestorius was less respectful in his address to the Pope than Cyril. Moreover, without being a Pelagian, Nestorius had given some degree of favor to the Pelagians whom the Pope opposed (see p. 170). Nestorius' attack on the much-prized *Theotokos* was also displeasing to Celestine.

The empire being now widely involved in the dispute, the two Emperors, Theodosius II of the East, and Valentinian III in the West, called a general council to meet in Ephesus in 431. Cyril and his followers were early on hand, as was Nestorius, but the friends of Nestorius were slow in arriving. Cyril and Memnon, bishop of Ephesus, promptly organized such

[11] Ayer, p. 500.   [12] *Ibid.,* p. 501.   [13] *Ibid.*   [14] In Loofs, *Nestoriana,* p. 171.

of the council as were present and they could secure. Nestorius was condemned and deposed in a single day's session.[15] A few days later Nestorius' friends, led by John, the patriarch of Antioch, arrived. They organized and, in turn, condemned and deposed Cyril and Memnon.[16] Cyril's council, meanwhile, had been joined by the papal delegates, and added John to its list of deposed, at the same time condemning Pelagianism (see p. 168), doubtless to please the West. The Emperor Theodosius II was at a loss as to what course to pursue. He at first imprisoned Nestorius, Cyril and Memnon as troublemakers; but politics inclined to Cyril's side, and he and Memnon were soon allowed to return to their sees. The real victim was Nestorius, who was deposed and retired to a monastery.

Antioch and Alexandria were now in hostility more than ever, but both, under imperial pressure, were made willing to compromise. Antioch would sacrifice Nestorius, and Cyril concede something to Antioch in creedal formula. Accordingly, in 433, John of Antioch sent to Cyril a creed composed, it is probable, by Theodoret of Cyrus, then the leading theologian of the school of Antioch. This creed was more Antiochian than Alexandrian, though it could be interpreted in either direction. "We therefore acknowledge our Lord Jesus Christ . . . complete God and complete man. . . . A union of the two natures has been made, therefore we confess one Christ. . . . The holy Virgin is *Theotokos,* because God the Word was made flesh and became man, and from her conception united with Himself the temple received from her." [17] Cyril now signed this creed, though without retracting any of his former utterances. By so doing he made irrevocable the overthrow of Nestorius. Yet Nestorius could have signed it, perhaps, even more willingly than he. This agreement enabled Cyril to secure general recognition in the East for his council of 431, in Ephesus—in the West the participation of papal representatives had always accredited it as the Third General Council.

Nestorius himself was finally banished to upper Egypt. There he lived a miserable existence, and there he wrote, certainly as late as the autumn of 450, his remarkable *Treatise of Heraclides of Damascus.* Whether he survived the Council of Chalcedon is uncertain. There is some reason to think that he did. At all events he rejoiced in the steps which led to it, and felt himself in sympathy with the views which were then proclaimed orthodox.

Not all of Nestorius's sympathizers shared in his desertion. Ibas, the leading theologian of the Syrian school of Edessa, supported his teaching. Persecuted in the empire, Nestorianism found much following even in Syria, and protection in Persia. There it developed a wide missionary activity. In the seventh century it entered China, and about the same time southern India. Nestorian churches still exist in the region where Turkey and Persia divide the territory between Lake Urumia and the upper Tigris, and also in India.

[15] Ayer, p. 507.　　[16] *Ibid.,* 509.　　[17] *Ibid.,* pp. 510, 511.

The agreement of 433 between Antioch and Alexandria was, in reality, but a truce. The division of the two parties but increased. Cyril undoubtedly represented the majority of the Eastern Church, with his emphasis on the divine in the person of Christ, at the expense of reducing the human to an impersonal humanity. Though he vigorously rejected Apollinarianism, his tendency was that of Apollinaris. It had the sympathy of the great party of monks; and many, especially in Egypt, went further than Cyril, and viewed Christ's humanity as practically absorbed in His divinity. Cyril died in 444, and was succeeded as patriarch of Alexandria by Dioscurus, a man of far less intellectual acumen and religious motive, but even more ambitious, if possible, to advance the authority of the Alexandrian see. Two years later, 446, a new patriarch, Flavian, took the bishop's throne in Constantinople. Though little is known of his early history, it seems probable that his sympathies were with the school of Antioch. From the first, Flavian's course promised to be stormy. He had the opposition not only of Dioscurus, but of the imperial favorite minister, Chrysaphius, who had supplanted Pulcheria in the counsels of Theodosius II. Chrysaphius was a supporter of the Alexandrians.

Occasion for quarrel soon arose. Dioscurus planned an attack on the remaining representatives of the Antiochian school as Nestorian heretics. In sympathy with this effort, and as a leader of the monastic party, on the help of which Dioscurus counted, stood the aged abbot or "archimandrite," Eutyches of Constantinople, a man of little theological ability, a partisan of the late Cyril, and influential not only by reason of his popularity, but by the friendship of Chrysaphius. Eutyches was now charged with heresy by Bishop Eusebius of Dorylæum. Flavian took up the case with reluctance, evidently knowing its possibilities of mischief; but at a local synod in Constantinople, late in 448, Eutyches was examined and condemned. His heresy was that he affirmed: "I confess that our Lord was of two natures before the union [*i. e.,* the incarnation], but after the union one nature." [18] Precisely what Eutyches meant is not altogether clear. His words could be taken in the sense that the two natures were so fused together as to result in a confused, divine-human being. This confusion of the natures is what "Eutychianism" has come to stand for. Yet some of Eutyches's words can also be read in Cyril's sense and be given an orthodox meaning. Perhaps Eutyches was himself more confused in some of his statements than he actually confused the natures.

However that may be, Rome had now one of the ablest of its Popes in the person of Leo I (440–461) (see p. 124), and to Leo both Eutyches and Flavian speedily presented the case. [19] To Flavian, whom he heartily supported, Leo wrote his famous letter of June, 449, usually called the *Tome,*[20] in which the great Pope set forth the view which the West had entertained

---

[18] Ayer, pp. 513, 514.   [19] *Letters of Leo,* 20–28.   [20] *Ibid.,* 28; extracts, Ayer, p. 515.

since the time of Tertullian, that in Christ were two full and complete natures, which, "without detracting from the properties of either nature and substance, came together in one person." What may be said chiefly in criticism of Leo's letter is that, while representing clearly and truly the Western tradition, it did not touch the intellectual depths to which the subtler Greek mind had carried its speculations. Probably it was well that it did not.

Meanwhile Dioscurus was moving actively in Eutyches' defense and the extension of his own claims. At his instance the Emperor called a general council to meet in Ephesus in August, 449. At Ephesus Dioscurus was supreme. Eutyches was rehabilitated, Flavian and Eusebius of Dorylæum condemned. Leo's *Tome* was denied a reading. It was a stormy meeting, but probably not more so than that of Ephesus, in 431, or Chalcedon, in 451. Flavian died shortly after, and rumor had it in consequence of physical violence at the council. The report seems unfounded. Dioscurus had achieved a great victory, but at the fatal cost of a rupture of the ancient alliance between Alexandria and Rome. Leo promptly denounced the council as a "synod of robbers"; but the Emperor, Theodosius II, gave it his hearty support and a sympathizer with Dioscurus became patriarch of Constantinople.

Leo had no success with Theodosius II, but much with the Emperor's sister, Pulcheria; and the situation was profoundly altered when the accidental death of Theodosius in July, 450, put Pulcheria and her husband, Marcian, on the throne. The new sovereigns entered at once into relations with Leo. The Pope wished a new council in Italy, where his influence would have been potent, but this did not satisfy imperial politics. The new General Council was called to meet in Nicæa, in the autumn of 451. Imperial convenience led to the change of place to Chalcedon, opposite Constantinople, and there some six hundred bishops, all but the papal delegates and two others from the Orient, assembled in what has ever since been known as the Fourth Ecumenical Council (that of Ephesus, in 449, being rejected).

The council proceeded rapidly with its work. Dioscurus was deposed and sent into exile by imperial authority, where he died three years later. After imperial pressure had been exerted, a commission was appointed, of which the papal delegates were members, to draw up a creed. Its production was promptly ratified by the council. The result was, indeed, a Western triumph. Rome had given the decision to the question at issue, and in so doing had made a compromise between the positions of Antioch and Alexandria that was wholly satisfactory to neither. The result was a lengthy document, reciting the so-called Nicæno-Constantinopolitan creed (see p. 118), approving Leo's *Tome,* and condemning previous heresies.[21] Its essential part—the creed of Chalcedon—is as follows:

[21] Ayer, pp. 517–521.

We, then, following the holy Fathers, all with one consent, teach men to confess one and the same Son, our Lord Jesus Christ, the same perfect in Godhead and also perfect in manhood; truly God and truly man, of a reasonable soul and body; consubstantial (όμοούσιον) with the Father according to the Godhead, and consubstantial with us according to the manhood, in all things like unto us, without sin; begotten before all ages of the Father according to the Godhead, and in these latter days, for us and for our salvation, born of the Virgin Mary, the Mother of God (*Theotokos*), according to the manhood; one and the same Christ, Son, Lord, Only-begotten, in two natures, inconfusedly, unchangeably, indivisibly, inseparably, the distinction of natures being by no means taken away by the union, but rather the property of each nature being preserved, and concurring in one person (*prosopon*) and one subsistence (*hypostasis*), not parted or divided into two persons, but one and the same Son and Only-begotten, God the Word, the Lord Jesus Christ; as the prophets from the beginning have declared concerning Him, and the Lord Jesus Christ Himself has taught us, and the creed of the holy Fathers has handed down to us.

Such is the creed that has ever since been regarded in the Greek, Latin, and most Protestant Churches as the "orthodox" solution of the Christological problem. It is easy to criticise it. Its adoption was greatly involved in ecclesiastical politics. It solved few of the intellectual difficulties regarding Christology which had been raised in the East. It did not even heal the Christological quarrels. But, when all is admitted, it must be said that its formulation was fortunate and its consequences useful. It established a norm of doctrine in a field in which there had been great confusion. More important than that, it was true to the fundamental conviction of the church that in Christ a complete revelation of God is made in terms of a genuine human life.

If a coincidence of imperial and Roman interests had secured a great dogmatic victory for Rome, the imperial authority was determined that the victory should not be one of Roman jurisdiction. By a canon, against which Leo protested, the council exalted the claims of Constantinople to a dignity like that of Rome (see p. 124). Nor was the downfall of Alexandria less damaging. Alexandrian rivalry of Constantinople had been Rome's advantage in the East. Now successful rivalry was at an end, for the consequences of the Chalcedonian decision crippled Alexandria permanently. By the council the historic distribution of the Orient was completed, Jerusalem being given the patriarchal standing which it had long claimed, side by side with the three older patriarchates, Constantinople, Alexandria, and Antioch.

10

The East Divided

THE CREED OF CHALCEDON was now the official standard of the empire. Its Western origin and spirit made it unacceptable, however, to a large portion of the East. To many Orientals it seemed "Nestorian." This was especially true in those regions which shared most strongly in the Alexandrian tendency to emphasize the divine in Christ, and these elements of opposition included most of the monks, the old native stock of Egypt generally, and a large portion of the population of Syria and Armenia. Undoubtedly the tendencies which the "orthodox" Cyril and his heretical successor, Dioscurus, had represented were consonant with the Greek conception of salvation, and seemed to do special honor to Christ. These rejecters of the creed of Chalcedon included many shades of opinion, but as a whole they showed little departure from Cyril. Their chief difference from Chalcedon and the West was one of emphasis. They found Chalcedon primarily at fault for "hypostatizing" the natures, giving each, that is, an independent existence and so endangering the unity of Christ's Person. Since they thought of "nature," as Cyril did, in concrete rather than abstract terms, they could not accept Chalcedon's definition of *"in* two natures." This, to them, implied a duality of Christs. He could be said to be *"out of* two natures," in the sense that there was the Logos on the one hand and the humanity to which He was united on the other. But after the union there could only be *one* Jesus Christ, the humanity gaining its center and concrete existence from its union with the Word, and never really existing previously or independently. This stress upon the unity of Christ, together with their way of expressing it as "one nature (*i. e.,* one concrete, living existence) after the union," led to their being dubbed "Monophysites," believers in one nature. But it must be emphasized that, apart from some extreme writers who used excessive language, their position faithfully followed that of Cyril. They altogether rejected Eutyches and the confusion of natures, which rightly or wrongly was attributed to him.

Immediately after the Council of Chalcedon Palestine and, next, Egypt were in practical revolution, which the government was able only slowly to master. By 457 the see of Alexandria was in possession of a Monophysite,

Timothy, called by his enemies the Cat; by 461, Peter the Fuller, of the same faith, held that of Antioch. These captures were not to be permanent, but the native populations of Egypt and Syria were throwing off the dominance of Constantinople and largely sympathized with the Monophysite protest. In Antioch Peter the Fuller caused fresh commotion by adding to the *Trisagion,* so that the ascription ran: "Holy God, holy Strong, holy Immortal, *who was crucified for us."*

The empire found itself grievously threatened, politically no less than religiously, by these disaffections; and much of the imperial policy for more than two centuries was devoted to their adjustment, with slight permanent success. In the contest between Zeno and Basilicus for the imperial throne, the latter made a direct bid for Monophysite support by issuing, in 476, an *Encyclion,* in which he anathematized "the so-called *Tome* of Leo, and all things done at Chalcedon" in modification of the Nicene creed.[1] For such a reversal the East was not yet ready, and this action of Basilicus was one of the causes that led to his overthrow by Zeno. Zeno, however, probably induced by the patriarch Acacius of Constantinople, made a new attempt to heal the schism. In 482 he published his famous *Henoticon.*[2] In it the results of the Councils of Nicæa and Constantinople were confirmed, Nestorius and Eutyches condemned, and Cyril's "twelve chapters"[3] approved. It gave a brief Christological statement, the exact relationship of which to that of Chalcedon was not, and was not intended to be, clear. Its chief significance was in the declaration: "These things we write, not as making an innovation upon the faith, but to satisfy you; and every one who has held or holds any other opinion, either at the present or at another time, whether at Chalcedon or in any synod whatever, we anathematize." This left it free to hold the Chalcedonian creed to be erroneous. The consequence was not peace but confusion. While many Monophysites accepted it, the Monophysite extremists would have nothing to do with the *Henoticon.* On the other hand, the Roman see, feeling its honor and its orthodoxy attacked by this practical rejection of Chalcedon, excommunicated Acacius and broke off relations with the East, the schism continuing till 519, when the Emperor Justin renewed the authority of Chalcedon, under circumstances that increased the prestige of the papacy,[4] but only alienated Egypt and Syria the more.

Justin's successor, the great Justinian (527–565), more fully than any other of the Eastern Emperors, succeeded in making himself master of the church. His conspicuous military successes restored to the empire for a time control of Italy and North Africa. The church was now practically a department of the state. Heathenism was suppressed and persecuted as never before. While Justinian himself was, at first, strongly Chalcedonian in his sympathies, his Empress, Theodora, leaned to the Monophysite side. He

[1] Ayer, pp. 523–526. [2] *Ibid.,* pp. 527–529. [3] *Ibid.,* pp. 505–507.
[4] P. 124; see Ayer, p. 536.

soon gave up the persecution of Monophysites with which his reign began. Himself one of the ablest theological minds of the age, he sought to develop an ecclesiastical policy that would so interpret the creed of Chalcedon that, while leaving it technically untouched, would exclude any possible Antiochian or "Nestorian" construction, thus bringing its significance fully into accord with the theology of Cyril of Alexandria. By this means he hoped to placate the Monophysites, and also to satisfy the wishes of the East generally, whether "orthodox" or Monophysite, without offending Rome and the West too deeply by an actual rejection of the Chalcedonian decision. Hence the establishment of a Cyrillic-Chalcedonian orthodoxy was Justinian's aim. It was a difficult task. As far as concerned a satisfaction of the Monophysites in general it failed. In its effort to render the Cyrillic interpretation of the creed of Chalcedon the only "orthodox" view it succeeded. Any form of Antiochianism was permanently discredited. By this result Justinian undoubtedly satisfied the wishes of the overwhelming majority of the "orthodox" East.

Justinian was greatly aided in his task by the rise of a fresh interpretation of the Chalcedonian creed, in the teaching of a monastic theologian, Leontius of Byzantium (c. 485–543). The age was witnessing a revival of the Aristotelian philosophy, and Leontius applied Aristotelian distinctions to the Christological problems. The feeling of much of the East, both "orthodox" and Monophysite, was that the affirmation of two natures in Christ could not be interpreted without involving two hypostases—subsistences—and therefore being "Nestorian." An explanation without these "Nestorian" consequences was what Leontius now gave. He viewed the human nature neither as having its own *hypostasis* (center of being), nor as being abstract and impersonal, but as ever united with the Word (ἐνυπόστατος). It gained its existence from having the Word as its subject, and never existed as an entity independently of Him. Thus Leontius would interpret the creed of Chalcedon in terms wholly consonant with the aim, if not with the exact language, of Cyril. The human in Christ is real, but its center or subject is the Logos. This, indeed, expressed by Leontius in Aristotelian terms, is the position which the moderate Monophysite, Severus, Patriarch of Antioch (512–518), had foreshadowed some years earlier. "We call the union 'hypostatic' because the flesh gained subsistence in that very union with the Word who was prior to the ages, and it came into existence in the very course of that event and obtained union with existence itself." [5]

Such an interpretation seemed, at the time, a quite possible basis of reunion with the more moderate Monophysites, who constituted their majority. The large section led by Severus, Monophysite patriarch of Antioch (512–518), who, till his death in 538, found a refuge in Egypt, held essentially the same position as Leontius. Their chief difference was that they regarded the Chalcedonian Council and its creed with greater suspicion. With the more

[5] *Contra Gramm.* 3.1.4.

radical Monophysites, led by Julian of Halicarnassus (*d.* after 518), the prospect of union was less auspicious. They went so far as to hold that Christ's body was incorruptible from the beginning of the incarnation, and incapable of suffering save so far as Christ Himself permitted it. Its enemies charged the theory of Julian with Docetic significance, but they undoubtedly misconstrued his somewhat extreme language. What he meant by "incorruptible" was "free from sin," not free from blameless passion.

To meet this situation by establishing an anti-Antiochian, Cyrillic interpretation of the creed of Chalcedon, and winning, if possible, the moderate Monophysites, was the aim of Justinian. He came to favor the so-called "Theopaschite" (*i. e.,* "suffering God") formula of the Scythian monks, "one of the Trinity suffered in the flesh," after a controversy lasting from 519 to 533. Because of monastic quarrels in Palestine, and also because the Emperor's theological sympathies, like those of his age, were exceedingly intolerant, Justinian condemned the memory and teachings of Origen in 543.[6]

Justinian's great effort to further his theological policy was the occasion of the discussion known as that of the "Three Chapters." In 544 Justinian, defining the issue by his own imperial authority, condemned the person and writings of Theodore of Mopsuestia, now more than a century dead, but once the revered leader of the school of Antioch (see p. 133), the writings of Theodoret of Cyrus in criticism of Cyril (see p. 136), and a letter of Ibas of Edessa to Maris the Persian (see p. 136). Theodoret and Ibas had been approved by the Council of Chalcedon. The action of the Emperor nominally left the creed of Chalcedon untouched, but made it impossible of interpretation in any but a Cyrillic sense, condemned the school of Antioch, and greatly disparaged the authority of the Council of Chalcedon. The edict aroused not a little opposition. Pope Vigilius (537–555) disliked it, but the imperial reconquest of Italy had placed the Popes largely in the power of the Emperor. Between his knowledge of the feeling of the West and his fear of Justinian, Vigilius's attitude was vacillating and unheroic.[7] To carry out his will, Justinian now convened the Fifth General Council, which met in Constantinople in 553. By it the "Three Chapters," *i. e.,* Theodore and the writings just described, were condemned, the "Theopaschite" formula approved, and Origen once more reckoned a heretic.[8] Pope Vigilius, though in Constantinople, refused to share in these proceedings, but such was the imperial pressure that within less than a year he acceded to the decision of the council. The Cyrillic interpretation of the creed of Chalcedon was now the only "orthodox" understanding. The action of the council was resisted for a few years in North Africa; and the yielding attitude of the Pope led to a schismatic separation of northern Italy from Rome which lasted till the time of Gregory the Great, and in the neighboring Illyricum and Istria even

[6] Ayer, pp. 542, 543.   [7] See Ayer, pp. 544–551.   [8] Ayer, pp. 551, 552.

longer. One main purpose of the condemnation of the "Three Chapters"—the reconciliation of the Monophysites—failed. In Egypt and Syria Monophysitism remained the dominant force, these provinces developing a native national consciousness which was antagonistic to the empire, and which was fortified by theological differences.

Under Justinian's successors, Justin II (565–578), and Tiberius II (578–582), alternate severe persecution of the Monophysites and vain attempts to win them occurred. These efforts were now of less significance as the Monophysite groups were now practically separated national churches. The native Monophysite body of Egypt can hardly be given a fixed date for its origin. From the Council of Chalcedon the land was increasingly in religious rebellion. That church, the Coptic, is still the main Christian body of Egypt, numbering more than six hundred and fifty thousand adherents, strongly Monophysite to this day in doctrine, under the rule of a patriarch who still takes his title from Alexandria, though his seat has long been in Cairo. Its services are still chiefly in the ancient Coptic, though Arabic has to some extent replaced it. The most conspicuous daughter of the Coptic Church is the Abyssinian. When Christianity was introduced into "Ethiopia" is uncertain. There is some reason to think that its first missionary was Frumentius, ordained a bishop by Athanasius, about 330. The effective spread of Christianity there seems to have been by Egyptian monks, about 480. The Abyssinian Church stands to the present day in dependent relations to that of Egypt, its head, the *Abuna,* being appointed by the Coptic patriarch of Alexandria. It is Monophysite, and differs little from that of Egypt, save in the backwardness of its culture, and the great extent to which fasting is carried.

While Egypt presented the spectacle of a united Monophysite population, Syria was deeply divided. Part of its inhabitants inclined to Nestorianism (see p. 136). Some were orthodox, and many Monophysite. The great organizer of Syrian Monophysitism, after its persecution in the early part of the reign of Justinian, was Jacob, nicknamed Baradæus (?–578). Born near Edessa, he became a monk and enjoyed the support of Justinian's Monophysite-disposed Empress, Theodora. In 541 or 543 he was ordained bishop of Edessa, and for the rest of his life served as a Monophysite missionary, ordaining, it is said, eighty thousand clergy. To him Syrian Monophysitism owed its great growth, and from him the Syrian Monophysite Church, which exists to the present day, derives the name given by its opponents, Jacobite. Its head calls himself patriarch of Antioch, though his seat has for centuries been in the Tigris Valley, where most of his flock are to be found. They number about eighty thousand.

Armenia during the first four centuries of the Roman Empire was a vassal kingdom, never thoroughly Romanized, maintaining its own language and peculiarities under its own sovereigns. Christian beginnings are obscure;

but the great propagator of Christianity in the land was Gregory, called the Illuminator, who labored in the closing years of the third century. By him King Tiridates (*c.* 238–314) was converted and baptized—Armenia thus becoming the first country to have a Christian ruler, since this event antedated the Christian profession of Constantine. Armenian Christianity grew vigorously. Never very closely bound to the Roman world, Armenia was in part conquered by Persia in 387. In the struggles of the next century hatred of Persia seems to have turned Armenia in the Monophysite direction, since Persia favored Nestorianism (see p. 136). By an Armenian council, held in Etchmiadzin (Valarshabad), in 491, the Council of Chalcedon and the *Tome* of Leo were condemned, and the Armenian or Gregorian Church— so named from its founder—has been ever since Monophysite.

The effect of the Christological controversies was disastrous to church and state. By the close of the sixth century the Roman state church of the East had been rent, and separated churches, Nestorian and Monophysite had been torn from it. Egypt and Syria were profoundly disaffected toward the government and religion of Constantinople—a fact that largely accounts for the rapid conquest of those lands by Mohammedanism in the seventh century.

11

Catastrophes and Further Controversies in the East

JUSTINIAN'S BRILLIANT RESTORATION of the Roman power was but of brief duration. From 568, the Lombards were pressing into Italy. Without conquering it wholly, they occupied the north and a large portion of the center. The last Roman garrisons were driven out of Spain by the Visigoths in 624. The Persians gained temporary control of Syria, Palestine, and Egypt between 613 and 629, and overran Asia Minor to the Bosphorus. On the European side the Avars, and the Slavic Croats and Serbs, conquered the Danube lands and most of the Balkan provinces, largely annihilating Christianity there, penetrating in 623 and 626 to the defenses of Constantinople itself. That the empire did not then perish was due to the military genius of the Emperor Heraclius (610–642), by whom the Persians were brilliantly defeated, and the lost eastern provinces restored. Before his death, however, a new power, that of Mohammedanism, had arisen. Its prophet died in

Medina in 632, but the conquest which he had planned was carried out by the Caliphs Omar and Othman. Damascus fell in 635, Jerusalem and Antioch in 638, Alexandria in 641. In 651, the Persian kingdom was brought to an end. By 711, the Mohammedan flood crossed the Strait of Gibraltar into Spain, bringing the Visigothic monarchy to a close, and swept forward into France, where its progress was permanently checked by the Franks, under Charles Martel, in the great battle of 732, between Tours and Poitiers. In the East, Constantinople successfully resisted it, in 672–678, and again in 717–718. Syria, Egypt, and North Africa were permanently taken by the Mohammedans.

Under such circumstances, before the final catastrophe, efforts were naturally made to secure unity in the threatened portions of the empire. After negotiations lasting several years, in which the patriarch Sergius of Constantinople was the leader, a union policy was inaugurated by the Emperor Heraclius, on the basis of a declaration that in all that He did Christ acted by "one divine-human energy." Cyrus, the "orthodox" patriarch of Alexandria, set up a formula of union, of which this was the substance, in Egypt, in 633, with much apparent success in conciliating Monophysite opinion.[1] Opposition arose, led by a Palestinian monk, Sophronius, soon to be patriarch of Jerusalem. Sergius was alarmed and now tried to stop any discussion of the question. He now wrote, in that sense, to Pope Honorius (625–638), who advised against the expression "energy" as unscriptural, and said, rather incidentally, that Christ had one will. Heraclius now, in 638, issued his *Ekthesis,* composed by Sergius, in which he forbade discussion of the question of one or two energies and affirmed that Christ had one will.

It was easier to start a theological controversy than to end it. Pope John IV (640–642) condemned the doctrine of one will in Christ—or Monothelite heresy as it was called—in 641. Heraclius died that year, and was succeeded by Constans II (642–668), who issued, in 648, a *Typos,* in which he forbade discussion of the question of Christ's will or wills.[2] The holder of the papacy was the ambitious Martin I (649–655), who saw in the situation an opportunity not only to further an interpretation of the theological problem consonant with the views of the West, which had always held that Christ's natures were each perfect and entire, but also to assert papal authority in the Orient. He therefore assembled a great synod in Rome in 649, which proclaimed the existence of two wills in Christ—human and divine—and not only condemned Sergius and other patriarchs of Constantinople, but the *Ekthesis* and the *Typos.*[3] This was flat defiance of the Emperor. Constans had Pope Martin arrested and brought a prisoner to Constantinople in 653, where he was treated with great brutality. Martin had the courage of his convictions. He was exiled to the Crimea, where he died. Strained relations between Rome and Constantinople followed. Constans II was succeeded by Constantine IV (668–685). By that time, the Mo-

[1] Ayer, pp. 661, 662.   [2] *Ibid.,* pp. 662–664.   [3] Extracts, Ayer, pp. 664, 665.

nophysite provinces, the retention of which had been the source of the discussion, had been taken by the Mohammedans. It was more important to placate Italy than to favor them. The Emperor entered into negotiations with Pope Agatho (678–681), who issued a long letter of definition as Leo I had once set forth his *Tome*. Under imperial auspices a council, the Sixth General Council, was held in Constantinople in 680 and 681. By it Christ was declared to have "two natural wills or willings . . . not contrary one to the other . . . but His human will follows, not as resisting or reluctant, but rather as subject to His divine and omnipotent will." It also condemned Sergius and other of his successors in the patriarchate of Constantinople, Cyrus of Alexandria and Pope Honorius.[4] For the third time Rome had triumphed over the divided East in theological definition. Nicæa, Chalcedon, and Constantinople had all been Roman victories. It must be said, also, that a human will was necessary for that complete and perfect humanity of Christ as well as perfect divinity, for which the West had always stood. The significance of the Monothelite controversy involved a question of spirituality. Will or "energy" was regarded as an attribute of nature, and the affirmation of the human will of Christ meant that the humanity of the Saviour had a freedom of its own. This stood in contrast to the Monophysite or Monothelite position, which, intent upon stressing the unity of Christ's existence, looked upon the humanity as merely a *passive* instrument of the Logos. The question reaches far into the Christian life. Does the divine work *through* the human will or override it? The doctrine as defined at Constantinople was the logical completion of that of Chalcedon. With its definition, the Christological controversies were ended in so far as doctrinal determination was concerned.

While the Sixth General Council was thus a Western success, it had a sort of appendix which was, in a sense, a Western defeat. Like the council of the "Three Chapters" (553), it had formulated no disciplinary canons. A council to do this work was summoned by Justinian II (685–695, 704–711), to meet in Constantinople in 692, and is called from the domed room in which it assembled—which was that in which the council of 680 and 681 had met—the Second Trullan Council, or *Concilium Quini-sextum,* as completing the Fifth and Sixth General Councils. It was entirely Eastern in its composition, and is looked upon by the Oriental Church as the completion of the council of 680 and 681, though its validity is not accepted by that of Rome. Many ancient canons were renewed; but several of the new enactments directly contradicted Western practice. It enacted, in agreement with Chalcedon, that "the see of Constantinople shall enjoy equal privilege with the see of Old Rome." It permitted marriage to deacons and presbyters, and condemned the Roman prohibition of such marriages. The Greek Church still maintains this permission. It forbade the Roman custom of fasting on Saturdays in Lent. It prohibited the favorite Western representation of Christ

[4] Ayer, pp. 665–672.

under the symbol of a lamb, ordering instead the depiction of a human figure to emphasize the reality of the incarnation.[5] Though not very important in themselves, these enactments are significant of the growing estrangement in feeling and practice between East and West.

The apparent collapse of the Eastern empire in the seventh century was followed by a very considerable renewal of its strength under the able Leo III, the Isaurian (717–740), to whose military and administrative talents its new lease of life was due. A forceful sovereign, he would rule the church in the spirit of Justinian. To accomplish this he championed and enforced a movement which sought to purify the church from superstition by banning the veneration of religious pictures. Protests against the use of icons in worship did not begin with Leo; but he used the movement to further his purposes of centralizing the Empire. His aim was to make himself master of the church which enjoyed many immunities, especially through its monasteries, and cut off from the State taxes, soldiers and public servants. The significance of the "Iconoclastic Controversy," as it was called, lay, however, deeper than this. In parts of Asia Minor, including that from which Leo came, there were oriental influences abroad, which led to despising the material world and to the demand for a spiritualistic religion. In some sects as the Manichaeans (p. 98) and the Paulicians (p. 213) this attitude was rooted in a clear-cut oriental dualism. To Jews and Moslems, on the other hand, the veneration of icons appeared as idolatry. Since Leo's armies had recruits from some of these sources, he hoped, perhaps, to win them for the Church. But he hoped, too, to destroy the power of the monks who were the champions of the icons. Moreover, he had an ally in the extreme Monophysites whose views led logically to the rejection of images. Since the divine cannot be circumscribed and since the human in Christ is only the passive instrument of the Logos and is ultimately absorbed by Him, the true reality of Jesus Christ cannot be depicted by the icon.

The abolition of the icons led to an increasing stress on the imperial portrait, and here Leo's ideal of the unification of the Empire found expression. The church was to be concerned with the abstract; the Empire and the Emperor were to be viewed as the material embodiment of Christendom. Behind this conception lay the ever-present influences of extreme Origenism with its concern for the intellectual and heavenly world of pure spirit as the proper province of the church. The image stands in the way of, rather than being a ladder to, the noetic world.

Thus it was that in 725 Leo forbade the use of the icons in worship. The result was religious revolt. The monks and common people resisted in defense both of the veneration of images and of the freedom of the Church. Leo enforced his decree by the army. In most of the empire he had his will. Italy was too remote, and there Popes and people resisted him. Under Pope Greg-

[5] Ayer, pp. 673–679.

ory III (731–741), a Roman synod of 731 excommunicated the opponents of pictures. The Emperor answered by removing all of Sicily and such portions of Italy as he could from the Pope's jurisdiction. Leo's able and tyrannous son, Constantine V (740–775), pursued the same policy even more relentlessly. A synod assembled by him in Constantinople in 754 condemned pictures and approved his authority over the church. Pictures, it was contended, "draw down the spirit of man from the lofty adoration of God to the low and material adoration of the creature." In this struggle the papacy sought the help of the Franks and tore itself permanently from dependence on the Eastern Emperors. A change of imperial policy came, however, with the accession of Constantine VI (780–797), under the dominance of his mother, Irene, a partisan of pictures. By imperial authority, and with the presence of papal delegates, the Seventh and, in the estimate of the Greek Church, the last, General Council now assembled in Nicæa in 787. By its decree pictures, the cross, and the Gospels "should be given due salutation and honorable reverence, not indeed that true worship, which pertains alone to the divine nature. . . . For the honor which is paid to the image passes on to that which the image represents, and he who shows reverence to the image shows reverence to the subject represented in it." [6] In the Council's letter to the Emperor the justification of the icon was based upon the fact that Christ was "very man" and the Gospel events were truly historical. Hence there triumphed the principle that the divine is not remote from the material world; but, as in the incarnation, the latter can be the medium of access to God.

Among the vigorous supporters of image-reverence was John of Damascus (700?–753?), the most honored of the later theologians of the Eastern portion of the ancient church. Born in the city from which he took his name, the son of a Christian high-placed in the civil service of the Mohammedan Caliph, he succeeded to his father's position, only to abandon it and become a monk of the cloister of St. Sabas near Jerusalem. His chief work, *The Fountain of Knowledge,* is a complete, systematic presentation of the theology of the church of the East. With little of originality, and much use of extracts from earlier writers, he presented the whole in clear and logical form, so that he became the great theological instructor of the Greek Church, and, thanks to a Latin translation of the twelfth century, influenced the scholasticism of the West. His philosophical basis is an Aristotelianism largely influenced by Neo-Platonism. In the Christological discussion he followed Leontius (see p. 142), in an interpretation of the Chalcedonian symbol consonant with the views of Cyril. To him the death of Christ is a sacrifice offered to God, not a ransom to the devil. The Lord's Supper is fully the body and blood of Christ, not by transubstantiation, but by a miraculous transformation wrought by the Holy Spirit.

John of Damascus summed up the theological development of the Ori-

[6] Ayer, pp. 694–697.

ent, and beyond the positions which he represented the East made little progress until more modern times. Eastern Orthodoxy has held resolutely to the "Holy Tradition" of the patristic period, and in its thinking and worship has been dominated by the spirit of the ancient Fathers. If, however, it did not advance theologically, its religious vitality was evident in other ways. In the realm of Christian mysticism it struck out on new and creative lines with Hesychasm (p. 213), but perhaps its most notable later achievement was the formation of Russian spirituality with its profound understanding of suffering and humility.

12

The Constitutional Development of the Church

THE ACCEPTANCE of Christianity as the religion of the empire gave to the Emperors a practical authority over the church. By the time of Justinian, the Emperor declared, on his own initiative, what was sound doctrine, and to a considerable extent regulated churchly administration.[1] The Emperors largely controlled appointment to high ecclesiastical office, especially in the East. This imperial power was limited, however, by the necessity, which even Emperors as powerful as Justinian felt, of securing the approval of the church through general councils for statements of faith and canons of administration. The imperial support of these edicts and decisions of general councils made heresy a crime, and must seriously have limited freedom of Christian thought. It was a very narrow path both in doctrinal opinion and in administration, that a bishop of Constantinople, for instance, had to walk. If conditions were more favorable for the papacy (see pp. 123–124), it was largely a consequence of the general ineffectiveness of imperial control in Italy, though cases were not lacking where the Popes felt the heavy hands of the Emperors.

As in the third century, the bishops continued to be the centers of local ecclesiastical administration, and their power tended to increase. By them the other clergy were not merely ordained, but the pay of those below them was in their hands. The First Council of Nicæa provided that other clergy should not remove from a diocese without the bishop's consent.[2] In each of the provinces the bishop of the capital city was the metropolitan, who, according to the synod of Antioch (341), should "have precedence in rank . . . that the other bishops do nothing extraordinary without him." [3] The ancient custom

[1] E. g., Ayer, pp. 542, 555.   [2] Ayer, p. 361.   [3] *Ibid.*, p. 363.

of local synods, for the consideration of provincial questions was extended, the First Council of Nicæa requiring them to be held twice a year.[4] This metropolitan arrangement was fully introduced into the East by the middle of the fourth century. In the West it was about half a century later in development, and was limited in Italy by the dominance of the papacy. Nevertheless it won its way in northern Italy, Spain, and Gaul. Above the metropolitans stood the bishops of the great capitals of the empire, the patriarchs, whose prominence antedated the rise of the metropolitan system. These were the bishops, or patriarchs, of Rome, Constantinople (by 381), Alexandria, Antioch, and, by 451, Jerusalem.

By Constantine, the clergy were made a privileged class and exempted from the public burdens of taxation (319).[5] The government, anxious not to lose its revenues through the entrance into clerical office of the well-to-do, ordered that only those "of small fortune" should be ordained (326).[6] The result of this policy was that, though the ordination of slaves was everywhere discouraged, and was forbidden in the East by the Emperor Zeno in 484, the clergy were prevailingly recruited from classes of little property or education. The brilliant careers of some men of talent and means, of whom Ambrose is an example, show the possibilities then before those of high ability who passed these barriers. The feeling, which had long existed, that the higher clergy, at least, should not engage in any worldly or gainful occupation, grew, and such works were expressly forbidden by the Emperor Valentinian III in 452. Such exclusive devotion to the clerical calling demanded an enlarged support. The church now received not merely the gifts of the faithful, as of old; but the income of a rapidly increasing body of landed estates presented or bequeathed to it by wealthy Christians, the control of which was in the hands of the bishops. An arrangement of Pope Simplicius (468–483) provided that ecclesiastical income should be divided into quarters, one each for the bishop, the other clergy, the up-keep of the services and edifices, and for the poor.

The feeling was natural that the clergy should be moral examples of their flocks. Celibacy had long been prized as belonging to the holier Christian life. In this respect the West was stricter than the East. Pope Leo I (440–461) held that even sub-deacons should refrain from marriage,[7] though it was to be centuries before this rule was universally enforced in the Western Church. In the East, the practice which still continues was established by the time of Justinian, that only celibates could be bishops, while clergy below that rank could marry before ordination. This rule, though not without advantages, has had the great disadvantage of blocking promotion in the Eastern Church, and leading to the choice of bishops prevailingly from the ranks of the monks.

While the bishop's power was thus extensive, the growth of the church into the rural districts about the cities, and of many congregations in the cities themselves, led to the formation of congregations in charge of presbyters,

[4] *Ibid.*, p. 360.   [5] *Ibid.*, p. 283.   [6] *Ibid.*, p. 280.   [7] *Letters*, 14:5.

and thus to a certain increase in the importance of the presbyterial office. These congregations still belonged, in most regions, to the undivided city church, ruled by the bishop; but by the sixth century the parish system made its appearance in France. There the priest (presbyter) in charge received two-thirds of the local income, paying the rest to the bishop.

The incoming of masses from heathenism into the church led, at first, to an emphasis on the catechumenate. Reception to it, with the sign of the cross and laying on of hands, was popularly regarded as conferring membership in the church, and actual baptism was frequently long delayed. The growth of generations of exclusively Christian ancestry, and, in the West, the spread of Augustinian doctrines of baptismal grace, brought this half-way attitude to an end. The catechumenate lost its significance when the whole population had become supposedly Christian.

In one important respect East and West fell asunder in this period regarding rites connected with baptism. As already described, by the time of Tertullian (see p. 88), baptism proper was followed by anointing and laying on of hands in token of the reception of the Holy Spirit. In Tertullian's age both baptism and laying on of hands were acts of the bishop, save in case of necessity, when baptism could be administered by any Christian (see p. 88). With the growth of the church, presbyters came to baptize regularly in East and West. With regard to the further rite the two regions differed. The East saw its chief significance in the anointing, and allowed that to be performed, as it does to-day, by the presbyter with oil consecrated by the bishop. The West viewed the laying on of hands as the all-important matter, and held that that could be done by the bishop alone [8] as successor to the Apostles. The rites therefore became separated in the West. "Confirmation" took place often a considerable time after baptism, when the presence of the bishop could be secured, though it was long before the age of the candidate was fixed in the Western Church.

13

Public Worship and Sacred Seasons

PUBLIC WORSHIP in the fourth and fifth centuries stood wholly under the influence of the conception of secret discipline, the so-called *disciplina arcani,* derived, it is probable, from conceptions akin to or borrowed from

[8] *Acts* 8:14-17.

the mystery religions. Its roots run back apparently into the third century. Under these impulses the services were divided into two parts. The first was open to catechumens and the general public, and included Bible reading, singing, the sermon, and prayer. To the second, the true Christian mystery, none but the baptized were admitted. It had its crown in the Lord's Supper, but the creed and the Lord's Prayer were also objects of reserve from those uninitiated by baptism. With the disappearance of the catechumenate in the sixth century, under the impression that the population was all now Christian, the secret discipline came to an end.

The public portion of Sunday worship began with Scripture reading, interspersed with the singing of psalms. These selections presented three passages, the prophets, *i. e.,* Old Testament, the epistles, the Gospels, and were so read as to cover the Bible in the course of successive Sundays. The desirability of reading appropriate selections at special seasons, and of some abbreviation led, by the close of the fourth century, to the preparation of lectionaries. In the Arian struggle the use of hymns other than psalms grew common, and was furthered in the West with great success by Ambrose of Milan.

The latter part of the fourth and the first half of the fifth centuries was above all others an age of great preachers in the ancient church. Among the most eminent were Gregory of Nazianzus, Chrysostom, and Cyril of Alexandria in the East, and Ambrose, Augustine, and Leo I in the West. This preaching was largely expository, though with plain application to the problems of daily life. In form it was often highly rhetorical, and the hearers manifested their approval by applause. Yet, while this preaching was probably never excelled, preaching was by no means general, and in many country districts, or even considerable cities, few sermons were to be heard. Prayer was offered before and after the sermon in liturgical form. The benediction was given by the bishop, when present, to the various classes for whom prayer was made, and the non-baptized then dismissed.

The most sacred part of the service—the Lord's Supper—followed. Both East and West held that, by divine power, Christ was made present in the sacramental elements. They differed, however, on the moment at which this took place. In the judgment of the East it was during the prayer known as the invocation, *epiklesis,* wherein the descent of the Holy Spirit was prayed for, to effect the change in the consecrated elements. The general Western view was different. There emphasis was placed upon the historic words of Christ whose sacramental presence in the bread and wine was attested and effected by the words of institution, "This is My Body . . . this is the new covenant in My blood." To Gregory of Nyssa and Cyril of Alexandria the Supper is the repetition of the incarnation, wherein Christ takes the elements into union with Himself as once He did human flesh. The Lord's Supper was at once a sacrifice and a communion. It was possible to emphasize one aspect or the other. The East put that of communion in the foreground. Consonant with its theory of salvation, the Supper was viewed as primarily a great, life-giving mystery, wherein the partaker received the transforming body and blood of his Lord, and thereby became, in a measure at least, a partaker of the divine nature, built up to the immortal and sinless life. This view was far from denied in the West. It was held to be true. But the Western conception of salvation as coming into right relations with God, led the West to emphasize the aspect of sacrifice, as inclining God to be gracious to those in whose behalf the Divine Victim was offered. The Western mind did not lend itself so readily as the Eastern to mysticism. In general, the Oriental administration of the Lord's Supper tended to become a mystery-drama, in which the divine and eternal manifested itself in life-giving energy. The sense of mystery connected with the consecration expressed itself by the fifth century in the development of veils which hid the altar during the most solemn part of the liturgy. These eventually gave way, in the eighth century, to the distinctive feature of the Byzantine church—the iconostasis, the screen, that is, which conceals the sanctuary and on which the icons are hung. Behind the screen the priest celebrated the "awe-inspiring mysteries," while the deacon standing outside it led the congregation in various devotions and litanies.

Beside the Sunday worship, daily services of a briefer character were now very common, and had widely developed into morning and evening worship.

The older festivals of the Christian year, Easter and Pentecost, were, as earlier, great periods of religious observance. Easter was preceded by a forty days' fast, though the method of reckoning this lenten period varied. The Roman system became ultimately that of the whole West, and continues to the present. The whole of Holy Week was now a time of special penitential observance, passing over to the Easter rejoicing. By the fourth century the observance of Ascension was general. The chief additions to the festivals of the church which belong to this period are those of Epiphany and Christmas, though their history is still very unclear. There is some slight evidence that the earliest feast of the nativity was in May, but by the early fourth century there had developed in the East a festival on January 6, which celebrated both the baptism and the birth of Jesus. The date is not unconnected with a pagan water festival in Alexandria in relation to the winter solstice (hence the liturgical stress on the blessing of waters and baptism), and with another pagan feast where the birth of the new Aeon was celebrated in the temple of Kore. We know, furthermore, that some Gnostic Basilidians in Alexandria kept January 6 as the date of Christ's baptism, as early as the second century. With their "adoptionist" Christology the baptism was, of course, also the divine birth of the redeemer. In any case, January 6 came to be widely observed by the orthodox in the East as the birth and baptism of Jesus, "Epiphany" referring to God's "manifesting" Himself in these events. Among the Armenians, till the present day, this is the only "Christmas."

About the same time, the early fourth century, there developed in the West a distinctive nativity festival on December 25. The date was partly determined by the idea that the birth of the world occurred on the vernal equinox (March 25) and correspondingly its new birth in the Saviour would have been at the same moment. This was understood as the conception by the Virgin, and hence the actual birth would be nine months later, December 25. But perhaps even more the date was influenced by the fact that December 25 was a great pagan festival, that of *Sol Invictus,* which celebrated the victory of light over darkness and the lengthening of the sun's rays at the winter solstice. The assimilation of Christ to the Sun god, as Sun of Righteousness, was widespread in the fouth century and was furthered by Constantine's legislation on Sunday (p. 105), which is not unrelated to the fact that the sun god was the titular divinity of his family. In any case these two celebrations of Epiphany and Christmas arose independently of each other in the early fourth century, the one in the East and the other in the West. Eventually (4th–5th centuries) both parts of the church adopted each other's celebration. Christmas became everywhere (except in Armenia) the feast of the nativity, while Epiphany was stressed in the East as the celebration of the baptism, though in the West it was especially connected with the manifestation of Christ to the Magi. The gift-giving we associate with Christmas has its origin partly in the similar custom at the Roman Saturnalia (December 17–24), and partly in observances which were associated with the feast of St. Nicholas of Myra (the prototype of Santa Claus) on December 6.

14

Popular Christianity

*T*HE BEGINNINGS of veneration of martyrs and of their relics run back to the middle of the second century. Their deaths were regularly commemorated with public services (see p. 85). With the conversion of Constantine, however, and the accession to the church of masses fresh from heathenism, this reverence largely increased. Constantine himself built a great church in honor of Peter in Rome. His mother, Helena, made a pilgrimage to Jerusalem, where the true cross was thought to be discovered. Men looked back on the time of persecution with much reason, as a heroic age, and upon its martyrs as the athletes of the Christian race. Popular opinion, which had long sanctioned the remembrance of the martyrs in prayer and worship, had passed over, before the close of the fourth century, to the feeling that they were to be prayed to as intercessors with God,[1] and as able to protect, heal, and

[1] Augustine, *Sermons,* 159:1.

aid those who honored them. There arose thus a popular Christianity of the second rank, as Harnack has called it. The martyrs, for the masses, took the place of the old gods and heroes. To the martyrs, popular feeling added distinguished ascetics, church leaders, and opponents of heresy. There was, as yet, no regular process of weighing claims to sainthood. Inclusion in its ranks was a matter of common opinion. They were guardians of cities, patrons of trades, curers of disease. They are omnipresent. As Jerome expressed it: "They follow the Lamb, whithersoever He goeth. If the Lamb is present everywhere, the same must be believed respecting those who are with the Lamb." [2] They were honored with burning tapers. [3]

Chief of all these sacred personages was the Virgin Mary. Pious fancy busied itself with her early. To Irenæus she was the second Eve (see pp. 63–64). Yet, curiously enough, she did not stand out pre-eminent till well into the fourth century, at least in the teaching of the intellectual circles in the church though popular legend, as reflected for instance in the apocryphal *Protevangelium of James,* had made much of her. Ascetic feelings, as illustrated in Tertullian and Clement of Alexandria, asserted her perpetual virginity. With the rise of monasticism, the Virgin became a monastic ideal. The full elevation of Mary to the first among created beings came with the Christological controversies, and the complete sanction of the description "Mother of God," in the condemnation of Nestorius and the decision of the Councils of Ephesus and Chalcedon. Thenceforth the Virgin was foremost among all saints in popular and official reverence alike. To her went out much of that feeling which had found expression in the worship of the mother goddesses of Egypt, Syria, and Asia Minor, though in a far nobler form. Above that was the reverence rightfully her due as the chosen vehicle of the incarnation. All that martyr or Apostle could do for the faithful as intercessor or protector, she, as blessed above them, could dispense in yet more abundant measure. In proportion, also, as the Cyrillic interpretation of the Chalcedonian creed and Monophysitism tended to emphasize the divine in Christ at the expense of the human, and therefore, however unintentionally, put Him afar from men, she appeared a winsome sympathizer with our humanity. In a measure, she took the place of her Son, as mediator between God and man.

The roots of angel-worship are to be found in apostolic times, [4] yet though made much of in certain Gnostic systems, and playing a great rôle, for instance, in the speculations of an Origen, angels were not conspicuously objects of Christian reverence till late in the fourth century. They were always far less definite and graspable by the common mind than the martyrs. Reverence for angels was given great furtherance by the Neo-Platonic Christian mystic work composed in the last quarter of the fifth century in the name of Dionysius the Areopagite, [5] and called that of Pseudo-Dionysius. Of all angelic beings, the Archangel Michael was the most honored. A church in commemoration of him was built a few miles from Constantinople by Con-

[2] *Against Vigilantius,* 6.   [3] *Ibid.,* 7.   [4] *Col.* 2:18.   [5] *Acts* 17:34.

stantine, and one existed in Rome early in the fifth century. When the celebration of his festival on Michaelmas, September 29—one of the most popular of mediæval feast-days in the West—was instituted, is uncertain.

It has already been pointed out that reverence for relics began early. By the fourth century it was being developed to an enormous extent, and included not merely the mortal remains of martyrs and saints, but all manner of articles associated, it was believed, with Christ, the Apostles, and the heroes of the church. Their wide-spread use is illustrated by the statute of the Seventh General Council (787): "If any bishop from this time forward is found consecrating a temple without holy relics, he shall be deposed as a transgressor of the ecclesiastical traditions." [6] Closely connected with this reverence for relics was the valuation placed on pilgrimages to places where they were preserved, and above all to the Holy Land, or to Rome.

Reverence for pictures had begun by the third century, and protests against it had quickly followed.[7] Yet their veneration gained increasing headway and was furthered after the peace of the church by the assimilation of features of the imperial cult by Christian worship. It was believed that the icon participated in that which it portrayed, and as St. Basil the Great said in reference to the imperial portrait itself, "The honor paid to the image passes on to the prototype." [8] The struggles ending in the full authorization of pictures by the Seventh General Council have already been narrated (see p. 149). Christian feeling was that representation on a flat surface only, paintings, and mosaics, not statues, should be allowed, at least in the interior of churches, and this remains the custom of the Greek Church to the present, though this restriction was not a matter of church law.

This popular Christianity profoundly affected the life of the people, but it had also its heartiest supporters in the monks, and it was furthered rather than resisted by the great leaders of the church, certainly after the middle of the fifth century. To some extent it made the way from heathenism to Christianity easier for thousands, but it even stood in danger of heathenizing the church itself.

15

Some Western Characteristics

WHILE EAST AND WEST shared in the theological development already outlined, and Western influences contributed much to the official decisions in the Arian and Christological controversies, there was a very appreciable difference in the weight of theological interest in the two por-

[6] *Canon 7.*   [7] *E. g.,* Synod of Elvira, Canon 36., A. D. 305.   [8] *De Spiritu Sancto,* 45.

tions of the empire. The West produced no really conspicuous theological leader between Cyprian (*d.* 258) and Ambrose (340?–397). Even Hilary of Poitiers (300?–367) was not sufficiently eminent as an original thinker to make a real exception. Both Hilary and Ambrose were devoted students of the Greek Fathers—the latter especially of the great Cappadocians. Though Tertullian was personally discredited by his Montanism, his influence lived on in the greatly valued Cyprian. While, therefore, Greek elements entered largely into Western thinking, it developed its own peculiarities.

The western part of the empire was disposed, like Tertullian, to view Christianity under judicial rather than, like the East, under philosophical aspects. Its thought of the Gospel was that primarily of a new law. While the West did not deny the Eastern conception that salvation is a making divine and immortal of our sinful mortality, that conception was too abstract for it readily to grasp. Its own thought was that salvation is getting right with God. Hence, in Tertullian, Cyprian, and Ambrose there is a deeper sense of sin, and a clearer conception of grace than in the East. Religion in the West had a closer relation to the acts of every-day life than in the East. It was more a forgiveness of definitely recognized evil acts, and less an abstract transformation of nature, than in the East—more an overcoming of sin, and less a rescue from earthiness and death. In the West, through the teaching of Tertullian, Cyprian, and Ambrose, sin was traced to an inherited vitiation of human nature in a way that was not so strikingly developed in the East. There can be no doubt, also, that this Western estimate of sin and grace, imperfectly worked out though it yet was, combined with the firmer ecclesiastical organization of the West, gave the Western Church a stronger control of the daily life of the people than was achieved by that of the East. All these Western peculiarities were to come to their full fruition in the work of Augustine.

16

Jerome

J EROME was the ablest scholar that the ancient Western Church could boast. Born about 340 in Strido in Dalmatia, he studied in Rome, where he was baptized by Pope Liberius in 360. Aquileia he made his headquarters for a while, where he became the friend of Rufinus (?–410), the translator of Origen, like Jerome to be a supporter of monasticism and a monk in Palestine, but with whom he was to quarrel over Origen's orthodoxy. Jerome had a restless desire to know the scholarly and religious world. From 366 to 370 he visited the cities of Gaul. The next three years saw him again in Aquileia. Then came a journey through the Orient to Antioch, where he was overtaken with a severe illness in which he believed Christ Himself appeared and reproached him for devotion to the classics. He now turned to the Scriptures, studying Hebrew, and living as a hermit from 373 to 379, not far from Antioch. Ordained a presbyter in Antioch, in 379, he studied in Constantinople under Gregory Nazianzus. The year 382 saw him in Rome, where he won the hearty support of Pope Damasus (366–384), and preached in season and out of season the merits of the monastic life. Soon he had a large following, especially among Roman women of position; but also much enmity, even among the clergy, for monasticism was not as yet popular in the West, and Jerome himself was one of the most vindictive of disputants. The death of Damasus made Jerome's position so uncomfortable in Rome that he retired, in 385, to Antioch, whither a number of his Roman converts to monastic celibacy, led by Paula and her daughter, Eustochium, soon followed him. With them he journeyed through Palestine and to the chief monastic establishments of Egypt, returning to Bethlehem in 386, where Paula built nunneries and a monastery for men. Here, as head of the monastery, Jerome made his headquarters till his death, in 420.

Jerome's best use of his unquestionable learning was as a translator of the Scriptures. The older Latin versions were crude, and had fallen into much corruption. Pope Damasus proposed to Jerome a revision. That he completed for the New Testament about 388. The Old Testament he then translated in Bethlehem, with the aid of Jewish friends. It is a proof of Jerome's soundness of scholarship that, in spite even of the wishes of Augustine, he went back of the Septuagint to the Hebrew. The result of Jerome's work was the *Vulgate,* still in use in the Roman Church. It is his best monument. Jerome had, also, no small deserts as a historian. He continued the *Chronicle* of Eusebius. His *De Viris Inlustribus* is a biographical dictionary of Christian writers to and including himself. He was an abundant commentator on the Scriptures. He urged by treatise and by letter the advantages of celibacy and of the monastic life. As a theologian he had little that was original to offer. He was an impassioned defender of tradition and of Western popular usage. A controversialist who loved disputation, he attacked opponents of asceticism like Jovinianus, critics of relic-reverence like Vigilantius, and those who, like Helvidius, held that Mary had other children than our Lord. He condemned Origen, whom he had once admired. He wrote in support of Augustine against the Pelagians. In these controversial writings Jerome's littleness of spirit is often painfully manifest. Though deserving to be reckoned, as he is by the Roman Church, one of its "Doctors," by reason of the greatness of his learning and the use which he made of it, the title "saint" seems more a tribute to the scholar than to the man.

17

Augustine

*I*N AUGUSTINE the ancient church reached its highest religious attainment since apostolic times. Though his influence in the East was to be relatively slight, owing to the nature of the questions with which he was primarily concerned, all Western Christianity was to become his debtor. Such superiority as Western religious life came to possess over that of the East was primarily his bequest to it. He was to be the father of much that was most characteristic in mediæval Roman Catholicism. He was to be the spiritual ancestor, no less, of much in the Reformation. His theology, though buttressed by the Scriptures, philosophy, and ecclesiastical tradition, was so largely rooted in his own experience as to render his story more than usually the interpretation of the man.

Africa gave three great leaders to Latin Christianity, Tertullian, Cyprian, and Augustine. Augustine was born in Tagaste, in Numidia, now Suk Ahras in the Department of Constantine in Algeria, on November 13, 354. His father, Patricius, was a heathen of good position but of small property, an easy-going, worldly character, who did not embrace Christianity till near the end of life. His mother, Monnica, was a Christian woman of high worth, eagerly ambitious for her son, though the full radiance of her Christian life was to be manifested in her later years, developed through Ambrose and Augustine himself. In Augustine there were two natures, one passionate and sensuous, the other eagerly high-minded and truth-seeking. It may not be wrong to say that father and mother were reflected in him. From Tagaste he was sent for the sake of schooling to the neighboring Madaura, and thence to Carthage, where he pursued the study of rhetoric. Here, when about seventeen, he took a concubine, to whom he was to hold for at least fourteen years, and to them a son, Adeodatus, whom he dearly loved, was born in 372. If the sensuous Augustine was thus early aroused, the truth-seeking Augustine was speedily awakened. When nineteen, the study of Cicero's now almost completely lost *Hortensius* "changed my affections, and turned my prayers to Thyself, O Lord." [1] This imperfect conversion caused Augustine to desire to seek truth as that alone of value. He began to study the

[1] *Confessions,* 3:4.

Scriptures, "but they appeared to me unworthy to be compared with the dignity of Cicero." [2] He now turned for spiritual and intellectual comfort to the syncretistic, dualistic system known as Manichæism (see p. 98). He was willing to pray "Grant me chastity and continence, but not yet." [3]

For nine years Augustine remained a Manichæan, living partly in Carthage and partly in Tagaste, engaged in study and teaching. He was crowned at Carthage for a theatrical poem.[4] He gathered friends about him, of whom Alypius was to prove the closest. As he went on he began to doubt the intellectual and moral adequacy of Manichæism. His associates urged him to meet the highly respected Manichæan leader, Faustus. The inadequacy of Faustus' expositions completed his mental disillusion. Though he remained outwardly a Manichæan, Augustine was now inwardly a sceptic. By the advice of Manichæan friends Augustine removed to Rome in 383, and by their aid, in 384, he obtained from the prefect, Symmachus, a government appointment as teacher of rhetoric in Milan—then the Western capital of the empire.

Here in Milan, Augustine came under the powerful preaching of Ambrose, whom he heard as an illustration of pulpit eloquence rather than with approval of the message, since he was now under the sway of the sceptical philosophy of the New Academy. Here Monnica and Alypius joined him. At his mother's wish he now became betrothed as befitted his station in life, though marriage was postponed on account of the youth of the woman. He dismissed regretfully his faithful concubine and entered on an even less creditable relation with another.[5] It was the lowest point of his moral life. At this juncture Augustine came in contact with Neo-Platonism, (see p. 98), through the translations of Victorinus. It was almost a revelation to him. Instead of the materialism and dualism of Manichæism, he now saw in the spiritual world the only real world, and in God the source not only of all good, but of all reality. Evil was no positive existence, as with the Manichæans. It was negative, a lack of good, an alienation of the will from God. To know God is the highest of blessings. This new philosophy, which always colored Augustine's teachings, made it possible for him to accept Christianity. He was impressed by the authority of the church, as a hearer of Ambrose might well have been. As he said later, "I should not believe the Gospel except as moved by the authority of the Catholic Church." [6]

A crisis in Augustine's experience was now at hand. He had never felt more painfully the cleft between his ideals and his conduct. He was impressed by learning of the Christian profession made in old age, some years before, by the Neo-Platonist Victorinus, whose writings had so recently influenced him.[7] A travelled African, Pontitianus, told him and Alypius of the monastic life of Egypt. He was filled with shame that ignorant men like these monks could

[2] *Ibid.*, 3:5.   [3] *Ibid.*, 8:7.   [4] *Ibid.*, 4:2, 3.   [5] *Confessions*, 6:15.
[6] *Against the Epistle of Manichœus*, 5; Ayer, p. 455.   [7] *Confessions*, 8:2; Ayer, pp. 431–433.

put away temptations which he, a man of learning, felt powerless to resist.[8] Overcome with self-condemnation, he rushed into the garden and there heard the voice of a child from a neighboring house, saying: "Take up and read." He reached for a copy of the epistles that he had been reading, and his eyes fell on the words: "Not in rioting and drunkenness, not in chambering and wantonness, not in strife and envying; but put ye on the Lord Jesus Christ, and make not provision for the flesh to fulfil the lusts thereof." [9] From that moment Augustine had the peace of mind and the sense of divine power to overcome his sins which he had thus far sought in vain. It may be that it was, as it has been called, a conversion to monasticism. If so, that was but its outward form. In its essence it was a fundamental Christian transformation of nature.

Augustine's conversion occurred in the late summer of 386. He resigned his professorship partly on account of illness, and now retired with his friends to the estate named Cassisiacum, to await baptism. He was far from being the master in theology as yet. His most characteristic tenets were undeveloped. He was still primarily a Christianized Neo-Platonist; but the type of his piety was already determined. At Cassisiacum the friends engaged in philosophical discussion, and Augustine wrote some of the earliest of his treatises. At the Easter season of 387 he was baptized, with Adeodatus and Alypius, by Ambrose in Milan. Augustine now left Milan for his birthplace. On the journey Monnica died in Ostia. The story of her death, as told by Augustine, is one of the noblest monuments of ancient Christian literature.[10] His plans thus changed, he lived for some months in Rome, but by the autumn of 388 was once more in Tagaste. Here he dwelt with a group of friends, busied in studies much as at Cassisiacum. During this period in Tagaste his brilliant son, Adeodatus, died. Augustine thought to found a monastery, and to further this project went to Hippo, near the modern Bona, in Algeria, early in 391. There he was ordained to the priesthood, almost forcibly. Four years later he was ordained colleague-bishop of Hippo. When his aged associate, Valerius, died is unknown, but Augustine probably soon had full episcopal charge. In Hippo he founded the first monastery in that portion of Africa, and made it also a training-school for the clergy. He died on August 28, 430, during the siege of Hippo by the Vandals.

Almost from the time of his baptism Augustine wrote against the Manichæans. With his entrance on the ministry, and especially as bishop, he was brought into conflict with the Donatists (see p. 106), then widespread in northern Africa. This discussion led Augustine to a full consideration of the church, its nature and its authority. By the early years of his episcopate he had reached his characteristic opinions on sin and grace. They were not the product of the great Pelagian controversy which occupied much of his strength from 412 onward, though that struggle clarified their expression.

[8] *Confessions*, 8:8.   [9] *Romans* 13:13, 14; *Confessions*, 8:12; Ayer, pp. 435–437.
[10] *Confessions*, 9:10–12.

The secret of much of Augustine's influence lay in his mystical piety. Its fullest expression, though everywhere to be found in his works, is perhaps in the remarkable *Confessions,* written about 400, in which he gave an account of his experiences to his conversion. No other similar spiritual autobiography was written in the ancient church, and few at any period in church history. It has always stood a classic of religious experience. "Thou hast formed us for Thyself, and our hearts are restless till they find their rest in Thee" (1:1). "It is good, then, for me to cleave unto God, for if I remain not in Him, neither shall I in myself; but He, remaining in Himself, reneweth all things. And Thou art the Lord my God, since Thou standest not in need of my goodness" (7:11). "I sought a way of acquiring strength sufficient to enjoy Thee; but I found it not until I embraced that 'Mediator between God and man, the man Christ Jesus,' 'who is over all God blessed forever' calling me" (7:18). "My whole hope is only in Thy exceeding great mercy. Give what Thou commandest, and command what Thou wilt" (10:29). "I will love Thee, O Lord, and thank Thee, and confess unto Thy name, because Thou hast put away from me these so wicked and nefarious acts of mine. To Thy grace I attribute it, and to Thy mercy, that Thou hast melted away my sin as it were ice" (2:7). Here is a deeper note of personal devotion than the church had heard since Paul, and the conception of religion as a vital relationship to the living God was one the influence of which was to be permanent, even if often but partially comprehended.

Augustine's first thought of God was thus always one of personal connection with a being in whom man's only real satisfaction or good is to be found; but when he thought of God philosophically, it was in terms borrowed from Neo-Platonism. God is simple, absolute being, as distinguished from all created things which are manifold and variable. He is the basis and source of all that really exists. This conception led Augustine to emphasize the divine unity, even when treating of the Trinity. His doctrine he set forth in his great work *On the Trinity.* It became determinative henceforth of Western thinking. "Father, Son, and Holy Spirit, one God, alone, great, omnipotent, good, just, merciful, creator of all things visible and invisible." [11] "Father, Son, and Holy Spirit, of one and the same substance, God the creator, the omnipotent Trinity, work indivisibly" (4:21). "Neither three Gods, nor three goods, but one God, good, omnipotent, the Trinity itself." [12] Tertullian, Origen, and Athanasius had taught the subordination of the Son and Spirit to the Father. Augustine so emphasized the unity as to teach the full equality of the "persons." "There is so great an equality in that Trinity, that not only the Father is not greater than the Son, as regards divinity, but neither are the Father and the Son together greater than the Holy Spirit." [13] Augustine was not satisfied with the distinction "persons"; but it was consecrated by usage, and he could find nothing more fitting: "When it is asked, what are the three? human language labors under great poverty of speech.

[11] *Trinity,* 7.6.12.   [12] *Ibid.,* 8, Preface.   [13] *Ibid.*

Yet we say, three 'persons,' not in order to express it, but in order not to be silent." [14] It is evident that, though Augustine held firmly to the ecclesiastical tradition, his own inclinations, and his Neo-Platonic philosophy inclined toward the Modalistic Monarchian position. It would, however, be wholly unjust to call him a Modalist. He attempted to illustrate the Trinity by many comparisons, such as memory, understanding, will,[15] or the even more famous lover, loved, and love.[16]

This sense of unity and equality made Augustine hold that "God the Father alone is He from whom the Word is born, and from whom the Holy Spirit principally proceeds. And therefore I have added the word principally, because we find that the Holy Spirit proceeds from the Son also." [17] Eastern remains of subordinationism and feeling that the Father is the sole source of all, taught that the Holy Spirit proceeds from the Father alone, but Augustine had prepared the way for that *filioque*, which, acknowledged in Spain, at the Third Council of Toledo, in 589, as a part of the so-called Nicene creed, spread over the West, and remains to this day a dividing issue between the Greek and Latin Churches.

In the incarnation Augustine emphasized the human as strongly as the divine. "Christ Jesus, the Son of God, is both God and man; God before all worlds; man in our world. . . . Wherefore, so far as He is God, He and the Father are one; so far as He is man, the Father is greater than He." [18] He is the only mediator between God and man, through whom alone there is forgiveness of sins. "It [Adam's sin] cannot be pardoned and blotted out except through the one mediator between God and man, the man, Christ Jesus." [19] Christ's death is the basis of that remission. As to the exact significance of that death, Augustine had not thought to consistent clearness. He viewed it sometimes as a sacrifice to God, sometimes as an endurance of our punishment in our stead, and sometimes as a ransom by which men are freed from the power of the devil. To a degree not to be found in the Greek theologians, Augustine laid stress on the significance of the humble life of Jesus. That humility was in vivid contrast to the pride which was the characteristic note in the sin of Adam. It is an example to men. "The true mediator, whom in Thy secret mercy Thou hast pointed out to the humble, and didst send, that by His example also they might learn the same humility." [20]

Man, according to Augustine, was created good and upright, possessed of free will, endowed with the possibility of not sinning and of immortality.[21] There was no discord in his nature. He was happy and in communion with God.[22] From this state Adam fell by sin, the essence of which was pride.[23] Its consequence was the loss of good.[24] God's grace was forfeited, the soul died, since it was forsaken of God.[25] The body, no longer controlled by the soul,

---

[14] *Ibid.*, 5:9.   [15] *Ibid.*, 10:12.   [16] *Ibid.*, 9:2.   [17] *Ibid.*, 15:17.
[18] *Enchiridion*, 35.   [19] *Ibid.*, 48.   [20] *Confessions*, 10:43.
[21] *Rebuke and Grace*, 33.   [22] *City of God*, 14:26.   [23] *Nature and Grace*, 33.
[24] *Enchiridion*, 11.   [25] *City of God*, 13:2.

came under the dominion of "concupiscence," of which the worst and most characteristic manifestation is lust. Adam fell into a state of total and hopeless ruin, of which the proper ending is eternal death.[26] This sin and its consequences involved all the human race; "for we were all in that one man [Adam] when we were all that man who fell into sin." [27] "The Apostle, however, has declared concerning the first man that 'in him all have sinned.'" [28] Not only were all men sinners in Adam, but their sinful state is made worse since all are born of "concupiscence." [29] The result is that the whole human race, even to the youngest infant, is a "mass of perdition," [30] and as such deserves the wrath of God. From this hopeless state of original sin "no one, no, not one, has been delivered, or is being delivered, or ever will be delivered, except by the grace of the Redeemer." [31]

Salvation comes by God's grace, which is wholly undeserved, and wholly free. "Wages is paid as a recompense for military service. It is not a gift; wherefore he says 'the wages of sin is death,' to show that death was not inflicted undeservedly, but as the due recompense of sin. But a gift, unless it is wholly unearned, is not a gift at all. We are to understand, then, that man's good deserts are themselves the gift of God, so that when these obtain the recompense of eternal life, it is simply grace given for grace." [32] This grace comes to those to whom God chooses to send it. He therefore predestinates whom He will, "to punishment and to salvation." [33] The number of each class is fixed.[34] Augustine had held, in the period immediately following his conversion, that it is in man's power to accept or reject grace, but even before the Pelagian controversy, he had come to the conclusion that grace is irresistible. The effect of this saving grace is twofold. Faith is instilled, and sins, both original and personal, are forgiven at baptism: "The faith by which we are Christians is the gift of God." [35] As such it is immediate justification. But grace does much more. As with Tertullian (see p. 65), it is the infusion of love by the Holy Spirit. It frees the enslaved will to choose that which is pleasing to God, "not only in order that they may know, by the manifestation of that grace, what should be done, but moreover in order that, by its enabling, they may do with love what they know." [36] It is a gradual transformation of nature, a sanctification. Through us, God does good works, which He rewards as if they were men's own and to which He ascribes merit. No man can be sure of his salvation in this life. He may have grace now, but, unless God adds the gift of perseverance, he will not maintain it to the end.[37] It would seem that Augustine may have been led to this conclusion largely by the doctrine of baptismal regeneration. It is evident that if men receive grace at baptism, many do not keep it.

This doctrine of grace was coupled in Augustine with a high valuation

[26] Ibid., 14:15.   [27] Ibid., 13:14; Ayer, p. 439.
[28] Romans 5:12; Forgiveness of Sins, 1:11.   [29] Marriage, 1:27.   [30] Original Sin, 34.
[31] Ibid.   [32] Enchiridion, 107.   [33] Ibid., 100; Ayer, p. 442.   [34] Ayer, p. 442.
[35] Predestination, 3.   [36] Rebuke and Grace, 3.   [37] Gift of Perseverance, 1.

of the visible Catholic Church, as that only in which the true infusion of love by the Holy Spirit may be found. Replying to the Donatists, who were thoroughly "orthodox" in doctrine and organization, and yet rejected the Catholic Church as impure, because allowing the sacraments to be administered by men who may have been guilty of "deadly" sins, Augustine said: "Those are wanting in God's love who do not care for the unity of the Church; and consequently we are right in understanding that the Holy Spirit may be said not to be received except in the Catholic Church . . . whatever, therefore, may be received by heretics and schismatics, the charity which covereth the multitude of sins is the especial gift of Catholic unity." [38] Sacraments are the work of God, not of men. They do not, therefore, depend on the character of the administrator. Hence baptism or regular ordination need not be repeated on entering the Catholic Church. But while those outside have thus the true and valid form of the sacraments, it is only in the Catholic Church that the sacraments attain their appropriate fruition, for there only can that love be found to which they witness, and which is of the essence of the Christian life. Even in the Catholic Church, not all are in the way of salvation. That is a mixed company, of good and bad. "It is not by different baptisms, but by the same, that good Catholics are saved, and bad Catholics or heretics perish." [39]

To Augustine, sacraments include all the holy usages and rites of the church. They are the visible signs of the sacred things which they signify. Thus, he names as sacraments, exorcism, ordination, marriage, and even the salt given to catechumens. Baptism and the Lord's Supper are pre-eminently sacraments. By the sacraments the church is knit together. "There can be no religious society, whether the religion be true or false, without some sacrament or visible symbol to serve as a bond of union." [40] Furthermore, the sacraments are necessary for salvation. "The churches of Christ maintain it to be an inherent principle, that without baptism and partaking of the Supper of the Lord it is impossible for any man to attain either to the kingdom of God or to salvation and everlasting life." [41] Yet, by reason of his doctrines of grace and predestination, the sacraments for Augustine are signs of spiritual realities, rather than those realities themselves. They are essential; but the verities to which they witness are, whenever received, the work of divine grace. He who does not "obstruct faith" may expect, however, to receive the benefit of the sacrament.[42] The problem was not yet wrought out as it was to be in the Middle Ages; but Augustine may be called the father of the doctrine of the sacraments in the Western Church.

Augustine's greatest treatise was his *City of God,* begun in 412, in the dark days after the capture of Rome by Alaric, and finished about 426. It was his philosophy of history, and his defense of Christianity against the heathen

---

[38] *Baptism,* 3:16, 21.   [39] *Ibid.,* 5:28, 39.   [40] *Reply to Faustus,* 19:1.
[41] *Forgiveness of Sins,* 1:34.   [42] *Letters,* 98:10; Ayer, p. 450.

charge that neglect of the old gods under whom Rome had grown great was the cause of its downfall. He showed that the worship of the old gods had neither given Rome strength, virtue, nor assurance of a happy future life. The loss of the old gods, that the worship of the one true God should come, was not a loss, but a great gain. Augustine then discusses the creation and the origin and consequences of evil. That brings him to his great theory of history. Since the first rebellion against God "two cities have been formed by two loves: the earthly by love of self, even to the contempt of God; the heavenly by the love of God, even to the contempt of self." [43] These had their representatives in Cain and Abel. Of the City of God, all have been members who have confessed themselves strangers and pilgrims on the earth. The Earthly City, with its God-defying spirit, has as its highest representatives heathen Babylon and Rome, but all other civil states are to some extent its embodiment. Yet it is a relative good. To it peace and civil order are due. In a world of sin, though having love of self as its principle, it represses disorder and secures to each his own. But it must pass away as the City of God grows. Those who make up the City of God are the elect whom God has chosen to salvation. These are now in the visible church, though not all in that church are elect. "Therefore the church even now is the kingdom of Christ, and the kingdom of heaven. Accordingly, even now His saints reign with Him, though otherwise than as they shall reign hereafter; and yet, though the tares grow in the church along with the wheat, they do not reign with Him." [44] It is, therefore, the visible, hierarchically organized church, that is the City of God and must more and more rule the world. This it does, in Augustine's view, by its close relation with the Christian state. The latter exists not only to preserve peace but to act as a "pious father" toward its citizens. Hence it must promote the true worship of God; and between the church and the ideal state there will exist relations of mutual dependence and reciprocal obligation. Here is foreshadowed the mediæval idea of the theocratic state.

It is evident that, clear as was the system of Augustine in many respects, it contained profound contradictions, due to the intermingling of deep religious and Neo-Platonic thoughts and popular ecclesiastical traditionalism. Thus, he taught a predestination in which God sends grace to whom He will, yet he sometimes tended to confine salvation to the visible church endowed with a sacramental ecclesiasticism. [45] He approached the distinction made at the Reformation between the visible and the invisible church, without clearly reaching it. His heart piety, also, saw the Christian life as one of personal relation to God in faith and love, yet he taught no less positively a legalistic and monastic asceticism. The Middle Ages did not advance in

[43] *City of God*, 14:28.   [44] *Ibid.*, 20:2.
[45] But in *De Baptismo* 5:28 he is very clear that "many who seem to be without [the Church] are in reality within."

these respects beyond Augustine. It did not reconcile his contradictions. It is by reason of them that most various later movements could draw inspiration from him.

18

The Pelagian Controversy

AUGUSTINE'S most famous controversy, and that in which his teachings on sin and grace came to clearest expression, was with Pelagius and that teacher's disciples. Pelagius was a British, or perhaps an Irish monk, of excellent repute, much learning, and great moral earnestness, who had settled in Rome about the year 400, when probably well on in years. He seems to have been shocked at the low tone of Roman morals and to have labored earnestly to secure more strenuous ethical standards. Instead of being an innovator, his teaching in many ways represented older views than those of Augustine. With the East generally, and in agreement with many in the West, he held to the freedom of the human will. "If I ought, I can," well expresses his position. His attitude was that of the popular Stoic ethics. "As often as I have to speak of the principles of virtue and a holy life, I am accustomed first of all to call attention to the capacity and character of human nature and to show what it is able to accomplish; then from this to arouse the feelings of the hearer, that he may strive after different kinds of virtue." [1] He, therefore, denied any original sin inherited from Adam, and affirmed that all men now have the power not to sin. Like the Stoics generally, he recognized that the mass of men are bad. Adam's sin set them an ill example, which they have been quick to follow. Hence they almost all need to be set right. This is accomplished by justification by faith alone, through baptism, by reason of the work of Christ. No man between Paul and Luther so emphasized justification by faith alone. After baptism, man has full power and duty to keep the divine law.

Pelagius won a vigorous follower in the much younger Cœlestius, a lawyer, and possibly a Roman though he has been claimed as an Irishman. About 410, the two went to North Africa and called on Augustine in Hippo, without finding him. Pelagius then journeyed to the East, while Cœlestius remained in Carthage and sought to be ordained a presbyter by Bishop

[1] Ayer, pp. 458, 459.

Aurelius. That bishop now received from Paulinus, a deacon of Milan, a letter charging Cœlestius with six errors. (1) "Adam was made mortal and would have died whether he had sinned or had not sinned. (2) The sin of Adam injured himself alone, and not the human race. (3) New-born children are in that state in which Adam was before his fall. (4) Neither by the death and sin of Adam does the whole race die, nor by the resurrection of Christ does the whole race rise. (5) The law leads to the kingdom of heaven as well as the Gospel. (6) Even before the coming of the Lord there were men without sin." [2] This was an unfriendly statement, but Cœlestius did not reject it; and it probably represents his views, which may have been somewhat more radical than those of Pelagius. An advisory synod in Carthage, in 411, decided against his ordination. Cœlestius then journeyed to Ephesus, where he apparently received the desired consecration.

Augustine had not been present in Carthage, but he soon heard of the matter, and at once began his long-continued literary polemic against Pelagianism, which he found had many supporters. Augustine's own religious experience was deeply wounded. He believed that he had been saved by irresistible divine grace from sins which he could never have overcome by his own strength. He held Pelagius in error as denying original sin, rejecting salvation by infused grace, and affirming human power to live without sin. Pelagius did not reject grace, but to him grace was remission of sins in baptism and general divine teaching. To Augustine the main work of grace was that infusion of love by which character is gradually transformed. Pelagius found support in the East. Early in 415, Augustine sent Orosius to Jerome, then in Palestine, to interest him for the Augustinian cause. By Jerome, Pelagius was accused before Bishop John of Jerusalem, but was approved by the bishop; and before the year was out, a synod held in Diospolis (Lydda in Palestine) declared Pelagius orthodox.

In this situation Augustine and his friends caused two North African synods to be held in 416, one for its local district in Carthage and the other for Numidia in Mileve. These condemned the Pelagian opinions and appealed to Pope Innocent I (402–417) for confirmation. Innocent was undoubtedly pleased at this recognition of papal authority, and did as the African synods wished. Innocent died shortly after, and was succeeded by Zosimus (417–418), a Greek, and therefore naturally no special sympathizer with the distinctive Augustinian positions. To Zosimus, Cœlestius now appealed in person. The new Pope declared that the African synods had been too hasty, and seems to have regarded Cœlestius as orthodox. A new synod met in Carthage early in 418, but the Africans made a more effective move. In April, 418, at their instance the Western Emperor, Honorius, issued a rescript condemning Pelagianism and ordering the exile of its adherents. In May a large council was held in Carthage, which held that Adam became mortal

[2] Ayer, p. 461.

by sin, that children should be baptized for the remission of original sin, that grace was necessary for right living, and that sinlessness is impossible in this life. Moved by these actions, Zosimus now issued a circular letter condemning Pelagius and Cœlestius.

Pelagius now disappears. He probably died before 420. A new and able champion of his opinions now appeared in the person of Bishop Julian of Eclanum, in southern Italy. An edict of the Emperor Honorius, in 419, required the bishops of the West to subscribe a condemnation of Pelagius and Cœlestius. Julian and eighteen others in Italy refused. Several of them were driven into exile and sought refuge in the East. In Julian, Augustine found an able opponent, and Pelagianism its chief systematizer; but a defender who was much more of a rationalist than Pelagius. About 429 Julian and Cœlestius found some support from Nestorius in Constantinople, though Nestorius was not a Pelagian. This favor worked to Nestorius' disadvantage in his own troubles, and together with the wish of the Pope led to the condemnation of Pelagianism by the so-called Third General Council in Ephesus in 431 (see pp. 135–136). Pelagianism, thus officially rejected in the West and East, nevertheless lived on in less extreme forms, and has always represented a tendency in the thinking of the church.

19

Semi-Pelagianism

A UGUSTINE'S FAME as the great teacher of the Western Church was secure even before his death in 430. By no means all accepted, however, the more peculiar portions of his theology, even where Pelagianism was definitely rejected. Thus, Jerome ascribed to the human will a share in conversion, and had no thought of an irresistible divine grace, though deeming grace essential to salvation. Northern Africa, which had led the Western Church intellectually since the time of Tertullian, was now devastated by the Vandals. Its pre-eminence in leadership now passed to southern France, and it was there that the chief controversy over Augustinian principles arose. John Cassianus, probably from Gaul, but who had journeyed to the East, visited Egypt, and had served as deacon under Chrysostom, founded a monastery and a nunnery in Marseilles about 415, and died there about 435. Around 429 he wrote his *Collationes,* in the form of conversations with Egyptian monks.

In his opinion "the will always remains free in man, and it can either neglect or delight in the grace of God." [1]

In 434 Vincent, a monk of Lérins, wrote a *Commonitorium,* in which, without attacking Augustine by name, his design was to do so really, by representing Augustine's teachings on grace and predestination as novelties without support in Catholic tradition. "Moreover, in the Catholic Church itself all possible care should be taken that we hold that faith which has been believed everywhere, always and by all." [2] These men and their associates were called in the sixteenth century "Semi-Pelagians," though Semi-Augustinians would be more correct, since they agreed in most points with Augustine, though rejecting his essential doctrines of predestination and irresistible grace. These were earnest men who sincerely feared that Augustine's doctrines would cut the nerve of all human effort after righteousness of life, especially that righteousness as sought in monasticism. Predestination and irresistible grace seemed to deny human responsibility.

This dissent from Augustine appeared in still more positive form in the writings of Faustus, abbot of Lérins, and afterward bishop of Riez. In his treatise on *Grace,* of about 474, he recognized original sin, but held that men still have "the possibility of striving for salvation." Grace is the divine promise and warning which inclines the weakened but still free will to choose the right rather than, as with Augustine, an inward transforming power. God foresees what men will do with the invitations of the Gospel. He does not predestinate them. Though Faustus rejected Pelagius, he really stood closer to him than to Augustine.

A more Augustinian direction was given to the thought of southern France by the able and devoted Cæsarius (469?–542), for a time a monk of Lérins, and from 502 onward bishop of Arles. In 529 he held a little synod in Orange, the canons of which received a much larger significance because approved by Pope Boniface II (530–532). They practically ended the Semi-Pelagian controversy, though Semi-Pelagian positions have always largely been maintained in the church.[3] It was affirmed by this synod that man is not only under original sin, but has lost all power to turn to God, so that "it is brought about by the infusion of the Holy Spirit and His operation in us that we wish to be set free." It is "by the free gift of grace, that is, by the inspiration of the Holy Spirit," that we have "the desire of believing" and "come to the birth of holy baptism." All good in man is the work of God. Thus many of the main thoughts of Augustine were approved; but with a decided weakening of emphasis. The irresistibility of grace is nowhere affirmed. On the contrary, those in error are said to "resist that same Holy Spirit." Predestination to evil is condemned. But, most marked of all, the reception of grace is so bound to baptism that the sacramental quality of grace and the merit of

---

[1] *Collationes,* 12; Ayer, p. 469.
[2] *Quod ubique, quod semper, quod ab omnibus,* 2:4; Ayer, p. 471.   [3] Ayer, pp. 472–476.

good works are put in the foreground. "We also believe this to be according to the Catholic faith, that grace having been received in baptism, all who have been baptized, can and ought, by the aid and support of Christ, to perform those things which belong to the salvation of the soul, if they labor faithfully." [4] Augustinianism was approved, but with undoubted modification in the direction of popular "Catholic" religious conceptions. Its sharp points were blunted.

20

Gregory the Great

THE TENDENCIES toward a modified, ecclesiastically and sacramentally emphasized presentation of Augustinianism, which have already been noted, characterized the thinking of Gregory the Great, the interpreter of Augustine to the Middle Ages. A teacher of little originality, he presented the theological system already developed in the West, in essential harmony with the popular Christianity of his age. His influence was thus far-reaching. He is reckoned with Ambrose, Augustine, and Jerome one of the Doctors of the Latin Church. In administrative abilities and achievements Gregory was one of the greatest of the Popes, and Latin Christianity generally had in him a leader of broad vision and permanent accomplishment.

Gregory was born in Rome of a senatorial Christian family about 540. Before 573 he was made prefect, or governor, of the city by the Emperor Justin II. The monastic life attracted him from civil distinctions, and by 574 he had devoted his wealth to the founding of monasteries and to the poor, and become a member of the monastery of St. Andrew in what had formerly been his own home on the Cælian hill. Gregory always retained his interest in monasticism, and did much for the regulation and extension of the monastic life. His own temperament was too active for the cloister, and in 579 Pope Pelagius II (579–590) sent him as papal ambassador to the court of Constantinople, where he served with ability, though, curiously, without acquiring a knowledge of Greek. About 586 he was once more in Rome as the abbot of St. Andrew. In 590 he was chosen Pope, being the first monk to attain that office. He died on March 12, 604.

The time of Gregory's papacy was propitious for an able Pope. The papacy, which had risen high under Innocent I (402–417) and Leo I (440–

[4] Ayer, p. 475.

461), had sunk in power after Justinian had conquered the Ostrogoths and restored the imperial authority in Italy. Since 568, however, the control of the Emperors in Italy had more and more waned before the Lombards, who threatened Rome itself. Though nominally subject to the Emperor, Gregory was the real leader against Lombard aggression. He raised troops, defended Rome by force and by tribute, even made a peace with the Lombards on his own authority, and succeeded, after infinite effort and confused struggles both with the Lombards and the imperial representatives, in keeping Rome unconquered throughout his pontificate. He was the strongest man in Italy, and must have seemed to the Romans and to the Lombards alike far more a real sovereign than the distant and feeble Emperor.

The support of the papacy as well as the source of much of the food of Rome was in its large estates, the Patrimony of Peter, in Sicily, Italy, and even in southern France and northern Africa. Of these Gregory showed himself an energetic but kindly landlord. Their management took much of his attention. Their revenues increased, and Gregory employed this income liberally not only in the maintenance of the clergy and public worship, and in the defense of Rome, but in charitable foundations and good works of all kinds.

Gregory was convinced that "to all who know the Gospel it is apparent that by the Lord's voice the care of the whole church was committed to the holy Apostle and prince of all the Apostles, Peter." [1] He would exercise a jurisdiction over the church as Peter's successor. As such, he protested against certain acts of ecclesiastical discipline inflicted by the patriarch of Constantinople, John the Faster; and announced that he would receive an appeal. In the acts sent for his inspection Gregory found John described as "universal bishop." Against this claim for Constantinople he raised vigorous protest.[2] His own practice was the employment of the title still borne by the Roman bishops, "servant of the servants of God." He exercised judicial authority with greater or less success in the affairs of the churches of Ravenna and Illyria. He attempted to interfere in the almost independent life of the church of France, re-establishing the papal vicariate in Arles, in 595, coming into friendly relations with the Frankish court, and attempting to remove abuses in French ecclesiastical administration.[3] Here his success was small. With some good fortune he asserted the papal authority in Spain, where the Visigothic sovereign, Recared, had renounced Arianism in 587.

Even more significant for the future was Gregory's far-reaching missionary campaign for the conversion of England, inaugurated in 596, of which some account will be given (p. 181). It not only advanced markedly the cause of Christianity, but was the initiation of a closer relationship of England, and ultimately of Germany, with the papacy than had yet been achieved elsewhere. Nearer home, among the Arian Lombards, Gregory inaugurated ultimately successful efforts to turn them to the Catholic faith, especially through

[2] Ayer, pp. 592–595.   [3] *Ibid.*, pp. 591–592.   [1] *Letters*, 5:20.

the aid of Theodelinda, who was successively the Queen of Kings Authari (584–591) and Agilulf (592–615).

Tradition has ascribed to Gregory a great work in the reformation of church music—the "Gregorian chants"—and in the development of the Roman liturgy; but the absence of contemporary reference makes it probable that his services in both these respects were relatively inconspicious. On the other hand, his abilities as a preacher were undoubted. As a writer three of his works maintained high popularity throughout the Middle Ages—his exposition of Job, or *Moralia,* his treatise on the character and duties of the pastoral office, the *Regula Pastoralis,* and his credulous *Dialogues on the Life and Miracles of the Italian Fathers.*

Gregory's theology is Augustinian, but with another emphasis than that of Augustine. He developed all of Augustine's ecclesiastical tendencies, and that mass of material from popular Christianity which Augustine took up into his system. Miracles, angels, and the devil have an even greater part in Gregory's system than in that of Augustine. While Gregory held that the number of the elect is fixed, and depends upon God, he had no such interest in predestination as had Augustine. He often speaks as if predestination is simply divine foreknowledge. His interests were practical. Man is fettered in original sin, the evidence of which is his birth through lust. From this condition he is rescued by the work of Christ, received in baptism; but sins committed after baptism must be satisfied. Works of merit wrought by God's assisting grace make satisfaction. "The good that we do is both of God and of ourselves; of God by prevenient grace, our own by good will following." [4] Penance is the proper reparation for sins after baptism. It involves recognition of the evil of the sin, contrition, and satisfaction. The church has many helps for him who would seek merit or exercise penance. Of these the greatest is the Lord's Supper, which Gregory viewed as a repetition of the sacrifice of Christ, available for the living and the dead. There is also the aid of the saints. "Those who trust in no work of their own should run to the protection of the holy martyrs." [5] For those who, while really disciples of Christ, make an insufficient use of these opportunities to achieve works of merit, fail to do penance, or avail themselves inadequately of the helps offered in the church, there remain the purifying fires of purgatory.

The thought of purgatory was not new with Gregory. The first faint intimation may be found in Hermas of Rome.[6] With Cyprian it is more evident, and he cites in this connection *Matt.* 5:26.[7] Augustine, on the basis of 1 *Cor.* 3:11–15, argued that purgatory was not improbable, though he felt no absolute certainty regarding it.[8] Cæsarius of Arles held more definitely to the conception. To him it was a fact. Gregory now taught purgatory as a matter essential to the faith. "It is to be believed that there is a purgatorial fire

---

[4] *Moralia,* 33:21.   [5] *Moralia,* 16:51.   [6] *Vis.,* 3:7.   [7] *Letters,* 51–55:20.
[8] *Enchiridion,* 69; *City of God,* 21:26.

before the judgment for certain light sins." [9] Though the Eastern Church held that an intermediate state exists between death and the judgment, and souls can be helped therein by prayer and sacrifice, its conception of purgatory has always been vague compared with that of the West.

Thus, in all departments of ecclesiastical activity Gregory stood forth the most conspicuous leader of his time. In him the Western Church of the Middle Ages already exhibited its characteristic traits, whether of doctrine, life, worship, or organization. Its growth was to be in the directions in which Gregory had moved.

Contemporary with Gregory in part, and of significance as the transmitter of much of the theological learning of the ancient church to the Middle Ages, was Isidore, the head of the Spanish church from about 600 to 636, as bishop of Seville. His *Book of Sentences*—brief statements of doctrine—was to be the theological text-book of the Western Church till the twelfth century. His *Origins or Etymologies* embraced well-nigh the round of learning of his age, ecclesiastical and secular, and was a main source of knowledge in the Middle Ages of the thought of antiquity. His value as a historian of the Goths and Vandals was great. In him, as the most learned man of his age, all the earlier Middle Ages were to find a teacher of little originality but of remarkable breadth of learning.

[9] *Dialogues,* 4:30.

Period Four

THE MIDDLE AGES TO THE CLOSE OF THE INVESTITURE CONTROVERSY

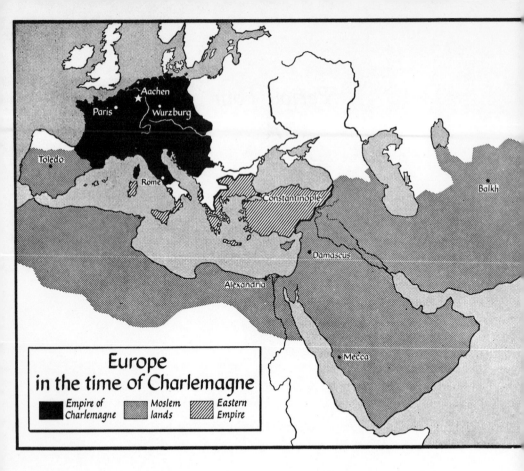

Europe
in the time of Charlemagne

Empire of Charlemagne | Moslem lands | Eastern Empire

1

Missions in the British Islands

THE SPREAD of Arianism among the Germanic tribes, the conversion of the Franks to the Roman faith, and the gradual acceptance of Catholic orthodoxy by the Germanic invaders have already been noted (see pp. 119–123). Much, however, remained to be done. There is no more striking proof of the vitality of the church in the collapsing empire and the opening Middle Ages than the vigor and success with which it undertook the extension of Christianity.

Christianity had some foothold in the British Isles before the conversion of Constantine. Bishops of York, London, and probably Lincoln, were present at the Council of Arles in 314. Yet it survived the downfall of the Roman Empire but feebly among the Celtic population, while much of the soil of southern and eastern England was won for heathenism by the Anglo-Saxon invaders. Some slight Christian beginnings were to be found chiefly in the south of Ireland before the time of Patrick; but he so advanced the cause of the Gospel in that island and so organized its Christian institutions, that he deserves the title of the Apostle of Ireland.

Born about 389, possibly in southern Wales, Patrick was the son of a deacon and the grandson of a priest. His training was therefore Christian. Seized in a raid about 405, he was for six years a slave in Ireland. Escaped to the Continent, Patrick was for a considerable time an inmate of the monastery of Lérins, off the southern coast of France. In 432 he was ordained a missionary bishop by Bishop Germanus of Auxerre, and began the work in Ireland which ended with his death in 461. Most of Patrick's missionary labors were in northeastern Ireland, though not without some efforts in the south and wilder west. Few facts survive; but of his zeal there can be no question, and as little of his conspicuous abilities as an organizer under whom the hitherto scattered Christianity of Ireland was systematized and made great advance. He brought the island in some measure into association with the Continent and with Rome.

It seems certain that Patrick introduced the diocesan episcopate into Ireland; but that institution was soon modified by the clan system of the island, so that there were, instead, many monastic and tribal bishops. Monasticism was favored by Patrick; but the great developer of the peculiar Irish monasticism was Finian of Clonard (470?–548), under whose leadership a strongly missionary and, for the time, a notably learned group of Irish monasteries came into being. The monastic schools of Ireland were justly famous in the sixth and seventh centuries. The glory of this Irish monasticism was its missionary achievement.

The beginnings of Christianity in Scotland are very obscure. Ninian is said to have labored there in the fourth century and the early years of the fifth, but of his date and real work little can be said. Kentigern, or Mungo (527?–612?), who spread Christianity in the neighborhood of Glasgow, is almost as dim a figure. It would seem probable that the northern Irish settlers who founded, about 490, the kingdom of Dalriada, embracing the modern Argyleshire, came as Christians. The great missionary to Scotland was Columba (521–597), a man closely related with some of the most powerful tribal families of Ireland, and a pupil of Finian of Clonard. Distinguished already as a monk and a founder of monasteries in Ireland, he transferred his labors, in 563, to Scotland, establishing himself with twelve companions on the island of Iona or Hy, under the protection of his fellow countryman and relative, the King of Dalriada. There Columba developed a most flourishing monastery, and thence he went forth for missionary labors among the Picts, who occupied the northern two-thirds of Scotland. By Columba and his associates the kingdom of the Picts was won for the Gospel. As in Ireland, Christian institutions were largely monastic. There were no dioceses, and even the bishops were under the authority, save in ordination, of Columba, who was a presbyter, and of his successors as abbots of Iona.

These Irish missionary efforts were carried to northern England, among the Anglo-Saxons of Northumbria. There, on the island of Lindisfarne, off the extreme northeastern coast of England, a new Iona was established by Aidan, a monk from Iona, in 634. Thence Christianity was widely spread in the region by him till his death in 651, and afterward by his associates. Nor was the missionary zeal of these Celtic monks by any means confined to the British Islands. Columbanus, or Columba the Younger (543?–615), became a monk of the celebrated Irish monastery of Bangor, which was founded in 558 by Comgall, a leader in learning and missionary zeal. From Bangor, Columbanus set forth, about 585, with twelve monastic companions, and settled in Anegray, in Burgundy, near which he planted the monastery of Luxeuil. Driven forth about 610, in consequence of his prophet-like rebuke of King Theuderich II and the King's grandmother, Brunhilda, Columbanus worked for a brief time in northern Switzerland, where his Irish companion and disciple, Gallus, was to live as an anchorite, and to give his name to, rather than to found, the later monastery of St. Gall. Columbanus made his way to northern Italy, and there established in 614, in the Appenines, the monastery of Bobbio, in which he died a year later.

Columbanus was only one of the earlier of a number of Irish monks who labored on the Continent—many of them in what is now central and southern Germany. Thus, Kilian wrought in Würzburg and Virgil in Salzburg. One modification of Christian practice, of great later importance, was introduced on the Continent by these Irish monks, notably by Columbanus. The entrance of thousands into the church when Christianity was accepted by the state had largely broken down the old public discipline. There had grown up the custom of private confession among the monks of East and West. Basil had strongly favored it in the East. Nowhere had it more hearty support than among the Irish monks, and by them it was extended to the laity, as was indeed the case, to some extent, by the monks of the East. The Irish on the Continent were the introducers of private lay confession. In Ireland, also, grew up the first extensive penitential books, in which appropriate satisfactions were assessed for specific sins—though these books had their antecedents in earlier canons of councils. These penitential treatises the Irish monks made familiar on the Continent.

Meanwhile, a work of the utmost significance for the religious history of Britain and the papacy had been undertaken by Pope Gregory the Great. Moved by a missionary impulse which he had long felt, and taking advantage of the favorable situation afforded by the marriage of Æthelberht, "King" of Kent and overlord of much of southeastern England, to a Frankish Christian princess, Bertha, Gregory sent a Roman friend, Augustine, the prior of his beloved monastery on the Cælian hill, with a number of monastic companions, to attempt the conversion of the Anglo-Saxons. The expedition left Rome in 596, but its courage was small, and all the persuasive power of Gregory was required to induce it to proceed. It was not till the spring of 597 that the party, reinforced by Frankish assistants, reached Canterbury. Æthelberht and many of his followers soon accepted Christianity. Gregory looked upon the struggle as already won. Augustine received episcopal consecration from Vergilius of Arles in November, 597, and, by 601, Gregory appointed Augustine metropolitan with authority to establish twelve bishops under his jurisdiction. When northern England should be converted a similar metropolitanate was to be established in York. London and York were to be the ecclesiastical capitals. The British bishops, over whom Gregory had no recognized jurisdiction, the Pope committed to the superintendency of Augustine.[1] The task in reality was to prove much more arduous than it seemed to Gregory's sanguine vision, and the greater part of a century was to pass before Christianity was to be dominant in England. Yet the movement, thus inaugurated, was vastly to strengthen the papacy. The Anglo-Saxons owed their conversion chiefly to the direct efforts of Rome, and they in turn displayed a devotion to the papacy not characteristic of the older lands, like France and Spain, where Christianity had been otherwise introduced. Anglo-Saxon Chris-

[1] Gee and Hardy, *Documents Illustrative of English Church History,* pp. 9, 10.

tianity was to produce, moreover, some of the most energetic of missionaries by whom the Gospel and papal obedience were alike to be advanced on the Continent.

England was not brought to the acceptance of Christianity without much vicissitude. The hegemony of Kent was waning before the death of Æthelberht, and with it the first Christian triumphs were eclipsed. Northumbria gradually gained leadership. It was a success when Edwin, King of Northumbria, was converted through the work of Paulinus, soon to be bishop of York, in 627. The heathen King, Penda of Mercia, however, defeated and slew Edwin in 633, and a heathen reaction followed in Northumbria. Under King Oswald, who had become a Christian when an exile in Iona, Christianity was re-established in Northumbria, chiefly through the aid of Aidan (see p. 180). It was of the Irish, or as it is often called, the "Old British" type. Penda once more attacked, and in 642 Oswald was killed in battle. Oswald's brother, Oswy, like him a convert of Iona, after much struggle secured all of Northumbria by 651, and a widely recognized overlordship besides. English Christianity was becoming firmly established.

From the first coming of the Roman missionaries there had been controversy between them and their Irish or Old British fellow Christians. The points of difference seem of minor importance. An older system of reckoning, discarded in Rome, resulted in diversity as to the date of Easter. The forms of tonsure were unlike. Some variations, not now recoverable, existed in the administration of baptism. Furthermore, as has been pointed out, Roman Christianity was firmly organized and diocesan, while that of the Old British Church was monastic and tribal. While the Old British missionaries looked upon the Pope as the highest dignitary in Christendom, the Roman representatives ascribed to him a judicial authority which the Old British did not fully admit. Southern Ireland accepted the Roman authority about 630. In England the decision came at a synod held under King Oswy at Whitby in 663. There Bishop Colman of Lindisfarne defended the Old British usages, while Wilfrid, once of Lindisfarne, but won for Rome on a pilgrimage, and soon to be bishop of York, opposed. The Roman custom regarding Easter was approved, and with it the Roman cause in England won the day. By 703 northern Ireland had followed the same path, and by 718, Scotland. In Wales the process of accommodation was much slower, and was not completed till the twelfth century. In England this strengthening of the Roman connection was much furthered by the appointment, in 668, by Pope Vitalian, of a Roman monk, Theodore, a native of Tarsus in Cilicia, as archbishop of Canterbury. An organizer of ability, he did much to make permanent the work begun by his predecessors.

The two streams of missionary effort combined to the advantage of English Christianity. If that from Rome contributed order, the Old British gave missionary zeal and love of learning. The scholarship of the Irish monasteries was transplanted to England, and was there strengthened by frequent Anglo-

Saxon pilgrimages to Rome. Of this intellectual movement a conspicuous illustration was Bede, generally called the "Venerable" (672?–735). An almost life-long member of the joint monastery of Wearmouth and Jarrow in Northumbria, his learning, like that of Isidore of Seville, a century earlier, embraced the full round of knowledge of his age, and made him a teacher of generations to come. He wrote on chronology, natural phenomena, the Scriptures, and theology. Above all, he is remembered for his *Ecclesiastical History of the English Nation,* a work of great merit and the chief source of information regarding the Christianization of the British Islands.

2

Continental Missions and Papal Growth

WITH THE CONVERSION of Clovis to orthodox Christianity (496) (see p. 122), a close relationship of church and state began in the Frankish dominions. To a large extent it was true that Frankish conquest and Christianization were two sides of the same shield. Under the descendants of Clovis—the Merovingian Kings—the internal condition of the Frankish church sank, however, to a low ebb. Bishops and abbots were appointed for political considerations, much church land was confiscated or put in secular hands. Even the efforts of Gregory I to gain more effective papal control in France and to effect reform had little lasting result.

The political collapse of the Merovingians, led to the rise to power of the Carolingian house, originally "mayors of the palace," which was accomplished when Pippin, called, not wholly correctly, of Heristal, won the battle of Tertry in 687. The Merovingian Kings continued in name, but the real authority was exercised by Pippin as "duke of the Franks." After his death in 714, his illegitimate son Charles Martel (715–741) exercised all the powers of a King. By him the Mohammedan advance in western Europe was permanently stayed, by the great battle between Tours and Poitiers in 732. He saw the advantage of churchly aid, and supported missionary effort in western Germany and the Netherlands, where he wished to extend his political control. Yet neither Pippin "of Heristal" nor Charles Martel were more helpful to the church of their own territories than the Merovingians. They exploited it for political reasons, confiscated its lands, and did little to check its disorders. Nevertheless, under Charles Martel a great missionary and reformatory work was initiated that was to Christianize large sections of western Germany, reform the Frankish church, and bring the papacy and the Franks into relations of the utmost consequence to both.

Willibrord (657?–739), a Northumbrian, began missionary work in Frisia with the support of Pippin of Heristal, and, in 695, was consecrated a missionary bishop by Pope Sergius I—an action which resulted in the establishment of the see of Utrecht. His work had scanty success, and was taken up by one of the ablest and most remarkable men of the period—Winfrid or Boniface (680?–754). An Anglo-Saxon of Devonshire by birth, Winfrid became a monk of Nutcell near Winchester. In 716, he began missionary labors in Frisia, but with such ill success that he returned to England. In 718 and 719, he was in Rome, where he received from Pope Gregory II (715–731) appointment to labor in Germany. From 719 to 722, he worked in Frisia and Hesse, going once more to Rome in the year last named, and receiving consecration as a missionary bishop, swearing allegiance to the Pope.[1] The next ten years witnessed a great success in Hesse and Thuringia. Not only were heathens converted, but the Irish monks were brought largely into obedience to Rome. Gregory III (731–741) made Boniface an archbishop in 732, with authority to found new sees. After a third journey to Rome, in 738, he thus organized the church of Bavaria, and a little later that of Thuringia. In 744, he aided his disciple, Sturm, in the foundation of the great Benedictine monastery of Fulda. destined to be a center of learning and priestly education for all western-central Germany. Between 746 and 748, Boniface was made archbishop of Mainz, which thus became the leading German see. In all this Boniface strengthened the causes of order and discipline and increased papal authority. His work was greatly aided by the considerable numbers of men and women who came as fellow workers from his native England, and for whom he found place in monastic and other Christian service.

The death of Charles Martel in 741 saw his authority divided between his sons Carloman (741–747), and Pippin the Short (741–768). Both were far more churchly than their father, and Carloman ultimately retired from power to become a monk. While neither would abandon authority over the Frankish church, both supported Boniface in the abolition of its worst irregularities and abuses, and in a closer connection with Rome. In a series of synods held under Boniface's leadership, beginning in 742, the worldliness of the clergy was attacked, wandering bishops censured, priestly marriage condemned, and stricter clerical discipline enforced. At a synod held in 747 the bishops assembled recognized the jurisdiction of the papacy, though, as the civil rulers were not present, these conclusions lacked the force of Frankish law. The Frankish church, thanks to the work of Boniface, was vastly bettered in organization, character, and discipline, while, what was equally valued by him, the authority of the papacy therein was very decidedly increased, even though that of the mayor of the palace continued the more potent.

[1] Robinson, *Readings in European History,* 1: 105–111.

As Boniface drew toward old age his thoughts turned toward the mission work in Frisia, with which he had begun. He secured the appointment of his Anglo-Saxon disciple, Lull, as his successor in the see of Mainz. In 754 he went to Frisia, and there was murdered by the heathen, thus crowning his active and widely influential life with a death of witness to his faith. His work had been one for order, discipline, and consolidation, as well as Christian advancement, and these were the chief needs of the age.

3

The Franks and the Papacy

I T HAS ALREADY been pointed out (p. 149) that the papacy, and Italy generally, opposed the iconoclastic efforts of the Emperor Leo III, going so far as to excommunicate the opponents of pictures in a Roman synod held under Gregory III, in 731. The Emperor answered by removing southern Italy and Sicily from papal jurisdiction, and placing these regions under the see of Constantinople—a matter long a thorn in the side of the papacy. In Rome and northern Italy the imperial power exercised from Constantinople was too feeble to control papal action. The imperial representative was the exarch of Ravenna, under whom stood a duke of Rome for military affairs, though the Pope was in many respects the Emperor's representative in the civil concerns for the city. The papacy was now in practical rebellion against the rulers who had their seat in Constantinople. It was, however, in a most dangerous position. The Lombards were pressing, and were threatening the capture of Rome. The disunion consequent on the iconoclastic dispute made it necessary, if the papacy was to maintain any considerable independence in Rome, to find other protection against the Lombards than that of the Emperor. This the Popes sought, and at last obtained, from the Franks.

In 739 Gregory III appealed to Charles Martel for aid against the Lombards, but in vain. With Pippin the Short it was otherwise. He was more ecclesiastically minded, and greater plans than even his father had entertained now moved him. Pippin and the papacy could be of mutual assistance each to the other. The new Lombard King, Aistulf (749–756), conquered Ravenna from the Emperor in 751 and was grievously pressing Rome itself. Pippin desired the kingly title as well as the kingly power in France. He had determined upon a revolution which should relegate the last of the feeble Merovingians, Childeric III, to a monastery, and place Pippin himself on the throne. For this change he desired not only the approval of the Frankish nobility, but the moral sanction of the church. He appealed to Pope Zacharias (741–752). The Pope's approval was promptly granted, and before the close of 751, Pippin was formally in the kingly office. To this he was anointed and crowned, but whether by Boniface, as has usually been supposed, is uncertain.

This transaction, which seems to have been simple at the time, was fraught with the most far-reaching consequences. From it might be drawn the conclusion that it was within the Pope's power to give and withhold kingdoms. All unseen in it, were wrapped up the re-establishment of the empire in the West, the Holy Roman Empire, and that interplay of papacy and empire which forms so large a part of the history of the Middle Ages. From this point of view it was the most important event of mediæval history.

If the Pope could thus help Pippin, the latter could be no less serviceable to the Pope. Aistulf and his Lombards continued to press Rome. Stephen II, therefore, went to Pippin himself, crowning and anointing Pippin and his sons afresh in the church of St. Denis near Paris, in 754, and confirming to them the indefinite title of "Patricians of the Romans"—all the more useful, perhaps, because implying a relation to Rome that was wholly undefined. It had been borne by the imperial exarch in Ravenna. Soon after this crowning, Pippin fulfilled his reciprocal obligation. At the head of a Frankish army, late in 754, or early in 755, he invaded Italy and compelled Aistulf to agree to surrender to the Pope Ravenna and the other recent Lombard conquests. A second campaign, in 756, was necessary before the Lombard King made good his promise. The Exarchate of which Ravenna was the capital and the Pentapolis were now the possessions of the Pope. The "States of the Church" were begun—that temporal sovereignty of the papacy which was to last till 1870. Yet, as far as can now be judged, in thus granting the Exarchate to Pope Stephen, Pippin regarded himself as overlord. Rome itself, Pippin did not give to the Pope. It was not his to give. Legally, the status of Rome would have been hard to define. Though the Popes had practically broken with the Emperor at Constantinople, Rome had not been conquered from him. Indeed the papacy recognized the sovereignty of the Eastern Emperor in the style of its public documents till 772. Pippin had the wholly nebulous rights that might be included in the title "Patrician of the Romans." Actually, Rome was in the possession of the Pope.

Though the Pope was thus now a territorial ruler, the extent of his possessions was far from satisfying papal ambition, if one may judge by a curious forgery, the authorship of which is unknown, but which seems to date from this period—the so-called "Donation of Constantine." [1] In charter form, and with an expression of a creed, and a fabulous account of his conversion and baptism, Constantine ordered all ecclesiastics to be subject to Pope Sylvester and successive occupants of the Roman see, and transferred to them "the city of Rome and all the provinces, districts, and cities of Italy or of the Western

[1] Henderson, *Select Historical Documents*, pp. 319–329.

regions." This meant a sovereignty over the Western half of the empire—at least an overlordship. Discredited by a few of the wiser men of the Middle Ages, the "Donation" was generally believed, till its falsity was demonstrated by Nicholas of Cues in 1433 and Lorenzo Valla in 1440.

4

Charlemagne

PIPPIN THE SHORT died in 768. A strong ruler, his fame has been unduly eclipsed by that of his greater son, who, in general, simply carried further what the father had begun. Pippin had divided his kingdom between his two sons, Charles and Carloman. Ill will existed between the brothers, but the situation was relieved by the death of Carloman in 771. With that event the real reign of Charles, to whom the world has so ascribed the title "Great" as to weave it indissolubly with his name—Charlemagne—began.

Charlemagne, perhaps more than any other sovereign in history, was head over all things to his age. A warrior of great gifts, he more than doubled his father's possessions. When he died his sway ruled all of modern France, Belgium, and Holland, nearly half of modern Germany and Austria-Hungary, more than half of Italy, and a bit of northeastern Spain. It was nearer imperial size than anything that had been seen since the downfall of the Western Roman Empire. Conquest was but part of his work. His armies, by extending the frontier, gave rest and time for consolidation to the central portion of his territories. He was the patron of learning, the kindly master of the church, the preserver of order, to whom nothing seemed too small for attention or too great for execution.

A quarrel with Desiderius, King of the Lombards, resulted in the conquest and extinction of that kingdom by Charlemagne in two campaigns in the years 774 to 777. Pippin's grants to the papacy were renewed, but the situation was practically altered. The papacy was no longer separated as it had been from the main Frankish territories by the intervening Lombard kingdom. Charlemagne's connection with Rome was a much more effective overlordship than that of his father, and he thenceforth treated the Pope as the chief prelate of his realm, rather than as an independent power, though he did not go so far as to dictate the choice of the Popes, as he did that of the bishops of his kingdom.

Highly important for the extension of Christianity was Charlemagne's conquest of the Saxons, then occupying what is now northwestern Germany —a result achieved only after a series of campaigns lasting from 772 to 804.

His forcible imposition of Christianity was made permanent by the more peaceful means of planting bishoprics and monasteries throughout the Saxon land. By this conversion the last considerable Germanic tribe, and one of the most gifted and energetic, was brought into the Christian family of Europe to its permanent advantage. Frisia, also, now became a wholly Christian land. Charlemagne's contests with the rebellious duke, Tassilo, of already Christianized Bavaria, led not only to the full absorption of the Bavarian bishoprics in the Frankish ecclesiastical system, but to successful wars against the Avars and the extension of Christianity into much of what is now Austria.

Such a ruler, devoted equally to the extension of political power and of Christianity, and controlling the greater part of Western Christendom, was, indeed, a figure of imperial proportions. It was not surprising, therefore, that Pope Leo III (795–816), who was greatly indebted to Charlemagne for protection from disaffected Roman nobles, placed on the head of the Frankish King the Roman imperial crown as the latter knelt in St. Peter's Church on Christmas day, 800. To the thinking of the Roman populace who applauded, as to the West generally, it was the restoration of the empire to the West, that had for centuries been held by the ruler in Constantinople. It placed Charlemagne in the great succession from Augustus. It gave a theocratic stamp to that empire. Unexpected, and not wholly welcome at the time to Charlemagne, it was the visible embodiment of a great ideal. The Roman Empire, men thought, had never died, and now God's consecration had been given to a Western Emperor by the hands of His representative. It was not, necessarily, a rejection of the imperial title of the ruler in Constantinople. The later empire had frequently seen two Emperors, East and West. Leo V (813–820), the Emperor in Constantinople, later, formally recognized the imperial title of his Western colleague. For the West and for the papacy the coronation was of the utmost consequence. It raised questions of imperial power and of papal authority that were to be controverted throughout the Middle Ages. It emphasized the feeling that church and state were but two sides of the same shield, the one leading man to temporal happiness, the other to eternal blessedness, and both closely related and owing mutual helpfulness. It made more evident than ever the deep-seated religious and political cleavage between East and West. To the great Emperor himself it seemed the fulfilment of the dream of Augustine's *City of God* (see p. 166)—the union of Christendom in a kingdom of God, of which he was the earthly head. His power was never greater than when he died, in 814.

At Charlemagne's accession no schools were so flourishing in Western Europe as those to be found in connection with the monasteries of the British Islands. It was from England that this many-sided monarch procured his chief intellectual and literary assistant. Alcuin (735?–804) was probably a native, and certainly a student of York. From 781 to his death, with some interruptions, he was Charlemagne's main aid in a real renaissance of classical and Biblical learning, that rendered the reign bright compared with the years before, and raised the intellectual life of the Frankish state. Charlemagne himself, though without becoming much of a scholar, set the example as an occasional pupil in this "school of the palace." In 796 Charlemagne made Alcuin the head of the monastery of St. Martin in Tours, which now became under his leadership a center of learning for the whole Frankish realm. Others helped in this intellectual revival, like the Lombard, Paul the Deacon (720?–795), the Frank, Einhard (770?–840), or the Visigoth, Theodulf (760?–821). The mere mention of these various national relationships shows the care which Charlemagne exhibited to secure from any portion of Western Europe those who could raise the intellectual standards of his empire.

With this growth of learning came theological discussion. The Spanish bishops, Elipandus of Toledo and Felix of Urgel, taught an adoptionist Christology—that Christ, though in His divine nature the Son of God, was in His human nature only a son by adoption. Under Charlemagne's leadership these opinions were condemned in synods held in Regensburg (792) and Frankfort (794). In this work Charlemagne regarded himself as the theological guide no less than the protector of the church. In similar fashion, at the synod of Frankfort just mentioned, Charlemagne had the conclusions of the General Council of 787, in Nicæa (see p. 149), condemned, rejected its approval of picture reverence, and caused the *Libri Carolini,* defending his position, to be issued. Behind this action we can detect two factors. For one thing the decisions of II Nicæa and the distinctions between "reverence" due to icons and "true worship" due only to God (p. 149) were not understood. Only a garbled account had reached the West. For another thing Charlemagne's idea of the Old Testament theocratic king stood (as it did in Leo the Isaurian) in conflict with the spiritual independence of the Church, represented by the icon. In 809, at a synod in Aachen, Charlemagne approved the Spanish addition *filioque* (see p. 164) to the so-called Nicene-Constantinopolitan creed. All these acts were in consultation with the bishops and theologians of his realm, but with no special deference to the Pope or reference of the matters to papal judgment.

5

Ecclesiastical Institutions

ROMAN POLITICAL INSTITUTIONS were based on the cities, on which the surrounding country was dependent, and Christian organization followed the same rule. The country districts were dependent upon and were cared for by the city bishops and their appointees, save where, in the East, there were "country bishops." The Germanic invasions altered this situation.

By the sixth century the beginnings of the parish system were to be found in France (see p. 152). There it rapidly grew, and it was stimulated by the custom of the foundation of churches by large landowners. The founders and their heirs retained the right of nominating the incumbent. This situation left episcopal control uncertain. Charlemagne, therefore, provided that besides the right of ordination of all parish priests, the bishop should have visitorial and disciplinary power throughout his diocese. The churchly status was further strengthened by the full legal establishment of tithes. Long favored by the clergy through Old Testament example, they were demanded by a Frankish synod in Macon, in 585. By Pippin they were treated as a legal charge, and full legal sanction was given them by Charlemagne. They were to be collected not only by bishops, but by and for the use of the incumbent of each parish. Moreover, constant gifts of lands to the church had raised ecclesiastical possessions, by the time of the early Carolingians, to a third of the soil of France. The great holdings were a constant temptation in the financial need of a Charles Martel, who appropriated much, but under the friendly government of Charlemagne they were respected, if earlier confiscations were not restored.

Under Charlemagne, preaching was encouraged and books of sermons prepared. Confession was favored, though not yet obligatory. Every Christian was expected to be able to repeat the Lord's Prayer and the Apostles' Creed.

Charlemagne renewed and extended the metropolitan system which had fallen into abeyance. At the beginning of his reign there was but one metropolitan in the Frankish kingdom. At its end there were twenty-two. These were now generally known as archbishops—a title which goes back to the time of Athanasius, though long loosely used. In Carolingian theory the archbishop was the judge and disciplinary officer of the bishops of his province, possessed of powers which the growth of papal jurisdiction was soon to curtail. It was also his duty to call frequent synods to consider the religious problems of the archdiocese, or as it was usually styled, the province.

For the better regulation of his immediate clerical assistants, Bishop Chrodegang of Metz introduced, about 760, a semimonastic life in common, which was favored and spread by Charlemagne. From the designation of this life as the *vita canonica,* the name "canons" for the clergy attached to a cathedral or collegiate church arose. Their place of meeting was called the *capitulum,* or chapter—a title soon applied to the canons themselves. By this means the life and work of the bishop and his immediately associated clergy was largely regulated. Charlemagne himself designated the bishops of his realm.

In all these changes, save that of personal authority over episcopal appointments, Charlemagne was but carrying further the reforms begun by Boniface. Much that he completed his father, Pippin, had commenced. At Charlemagne's death, the Frankish church was in a far better state of education, discipline, and efficiency than it had been under the later Merovingians and early Carolingians.

6

Collapsing Empire and Rising Papacy

*C*HARLEMAGNE'S GREAT POWER was personal. Scarcely had he died when the rapid decline of his empire began. His son and successor, Louis the Pious (814–840), was of excellent personal character, but wholly unequal to the task left by Charlemagne, or even to the control of his own sons, who plotted against him and quarrelled with one another. After his death they divided the empire between them by the Treaty of Verdun in 843. To Lothair (843–855) came Frankish Italy and a strip of territory including the valley of the Rhone and the region lying immediately west of the Rhine, together with the imperial title. To Louis (843–875) was given the region east of the Rhine, whence he acquired the nickname, "the German." To Charles the Bald (843–877) came most of modern France and ultimately the imperial crown. This Treaty of Verdun is usually regarded as the point whence France and Germany go their separate ways.

These rulers proved utterly inadequate for unity or defense. France suffered grievously from attacks by the Scandinavian Normans, who pushed up its rivers and burned its towns, ultimately (911) establishing themselves permanently in Normandy. Italy was a prey to Saracen raids, in one of which (841) St. Peter's itself, in Rome, was plundered. A little later, with the beginning of the tenth century, the raids of the Hungarians brought devastation to Germany and Italy. Under these circumstances, when national unity or defense was impossible, feudalism developed with great rapidity. Its roots run back to the declining days of the Roman Empire, but with the death of Charlemagne it was given great impetus. It was based on the principle of tenure of land in return for military service, and was the only practical means of securing local defense during the collapse of central authority and the barbarian invasions. Between the tenant and his lord there was a peculiar personal relation, resting upon a religious sanction. In its ideal form the lord was as obligated to give his vassal protection as his vassal was to yield him obedience. With the lack of a strong, central government feudalism naturally proved divisive, and issued in constant local struggles for power. Churches and monasteries became largely the prey of local nobles, or defended their rights with difficulty as parts of the feudal system with armies of their own. Abbeys and bishoprics no less than local parish churches came under secular control, and lay investiture became common.

The impulse given to learning by Charlemagne did not immediately die. At the court of Charles the Bald, John Scotus (?–877?), to whom the name Erigena was much later added, held somewhat the same position that Alcuin had occupied under Charlemagne. He translated the much admired writings of the Pseudo-Dionysius (see p. 156), and developed his own Neo-Platonic philosophy, which his age was too ignorant to judge heretical or orthodox. In Germany, Hrabanus Maurus (776?–856), abbot of Fulda and archbishop of Mainz, a pupil of Alcuin, attained a deserved reputation as a teacher, commentator on the Scriptures, furtherer of clerical education and author of what was well-nigh an encyclopædia. In Hincmar (805?–882), archbishop of Rheims, France possessed not only a prelate of great assertiveness and influence, but a theological controversialist of decided gift.

The renewed study of Augustine which this intellectual revival effected led to two doctrinal controversies. The first was regarding the nature of Christ's presence in the Supper. About 831 Paschasius Radbertus, a monk of the monastery of Corbie, near Amiens, of remarkable learning in Greek as well as in Latin theology, set forth the first thoroughgoing treatise on the Lord's Supper, *De corpore et sanguine Domini*. In it he taught with Augustine, that only those who partake in faith eat and drink the body and blood of Christ, and with the Greeks that it is the food of immortality; and also that by divine miracle the substance of the elements is made the very body and blood of Christ. That was in effect transubstantiation, though the word was not to be coined before the eleventh century. To Radbertus, Hrabanus Maurus replied; but a more elaborate answer was that of a fellow monk of Corbie, Ratramnus, about 844. He rejected the idea of a realistic change in the elements. Regarding their substance "they are after the consecration what they were before." But it is "according to their power" that they become the body and blood of Christ. Invisibly and by faith the gift of the sacrament is received. Moreover, what is received and really present in the consecrated elements is not the actual body born of the Virgin, crucified and risen (as it was for Paschasius), but something else—the "Spirit" of Christ, the "power of the divine Word," a mysterious "spiritual" body appropriate to the sacrament. The controversy was not decided at the time, but the future, in the Roman Church, was with Radbertus.

The second controversy was aroused by Gottschalk (808?–868?). A monk of Fulda, made so by parental dedication, his efforts for release from his bonds were frustrated by Hrabanus Maurus. He then turned to the study of Augustine, and his hard fate, perhaps, led him to emphasize a double divine predestination—to life or to death. He was attacked by Hrabanus Maurus and Hincmar, but found vigorous defenders. Condemned as a heretic at a synod in Mainz in 848, he spent the next twenty years in monastic imprisonment, persecuted by Hincmar, and refusing to retract. The controversy was a fresh flaring up of the old dispute between thoroughgoing Augustinianism and the modified type which was the actual theory of a large portion of the church.

As the collapse of Charlemagne's empire grew more complete, however, these controversies and the intellectual life out of which they sprang faded. By 900 a renewed barbarism had largely extinguished the light which had shone brightly a century before. One great exception to this general condition existed. In England, Alfred the Great (871–901?), distinguished as the successful opponent of the Danish conquerors, in a spirit like that of Charlemagne gathered learned men about him, and encouraged the education of the clergy.

The collapsing empire of Charlemagne led to the rise of a churchly party in France, which, despairing of help from the state, looked toward the papacy as the source of unity and hope. This party regarded with suspicion also any control of the church by the sovereigns or nobility, and it represented the jealousy of the ordinary bishops and lower clergy toward the great archbishops with their often arbitrary assertions of authority, of whom Hincmar was a conspicuous example. The aim of the movement was not the exaltation of the papacy for its own sake; rather its exaltation as a means of checking secular control and that of the archbishops, and of maintaining ecclesiastical unity. From this circle, between 847 and 852, and probably from Hincmar's own region of Rheims, came one of the most remarkable of forgeries—the so-called Pseudo-Isidorian Decretals—purporting to be collected by a certain Isidore Mercator, by whom Isidore of Seville (see p. 175) and Marius Mercator were doubtless intended. It consisted of decisions of Popes and councils from Clement of Rome in the first century to Gregory II in the eighth, part genuine and part forged. The "Donation of Constantine" (see p. 186) is included. The early Popes therein claim for themselves supreme jurisdiction. All bishops may appeal directly to papal authority. Intervening archiepiscopal rights are limited, and neither papacy nor bishops are subject to secular control. With its origin the papacy had nothing to do; but it was to be used mightily to the furtherance of papal claims. The age was uncritical. It passed immediately as genuine, and was not exposed till the Reformation had awakened historical study.

With the decline of imperial power, the independence of the papacy rapidly rose. The Popes showed themselves the strongest men in Italy. Leo IV (847–855), aided by south Italian cities, defeated the Saracens and surrounded the quarter of St. Peter's in Rome with a wall—the "Leonine City." In Nicholas I (858–867) the Roman see had its ablest and most assertive occupant between Gregory the Great and Hildebrand. He sketched out a program of papal claims, hardly surpassed later, but which the papacy was to be centuries in achieving. Nicholas attempted to realize the ideals of Augustine's *City of God*. In his thought, the church is superior to all earthly powers, the ruler of the whole church is the Pope, and the bishops are his agents. These conceptions he was able to make effective in two notable cases, in which he had also the advantage of choosing the side on which right lay. The first was that of Thietberga, the injured wife of Lothair II of Lorraine. Divorced that that sovereign might marry his concubine, Waldrada, she appealed to Nicholas, who declared void the sanctioning decision of a synod held in Metz, in 863, and excommunicated the archbishops of Trier and Cologne who had supported Lothair. The Pope had defended helpless womanhood. He none the less humbled two of the most powerful German prelates and thwarted a German ruler. In the second case, Nicholas received the appeal of the deposed Bishop Rothad of Soissons, who had been removed by the overbearing Archbishop Hincmar of Rheims, and forced his restoration. Here Nicholas appeared as the protector of the bishops against their metropolitans and the defender of their right to appeal to the Pope as the final judge. In this quarrel the Pseudo-Isidorian Decretals were first employed in Rome.

In a third case, Nicholas, though having right on his side, was less successful. The Emperor in Constantinople, Michael III, "the Drunkard," was ruled by his uncle, Bardas, a man of unsavory reputation. The patriarch, Ignatius, refused Bardas the sacrament, and was deposed. In his place, Bardas procured the appointment of one of the most learned men of the later Greek world, Photius (patriarch 858–867, 878–886), then a layman. Ignatius, thus injured, appealed to Nicholas, who sent legates to Constantinople. They joined in approval of Photius. The Pope repudiated their action, and, in 863, declared Photius deposed. Photius now accused the Western Church of heresy for admitting the *filioque* clause to the creed, fasting on Saturdays, using milk, butter, and cheese in Lent, demanding priestly celibacy, and confining confirmation to the bishops. At a synod under his leadership in Constantinople, in 867, the Pope was condemned. Nicholas failed in his attempt to exercise his authority over the Eastern Church. The ill feeling between East and West was but augmented, which was to lead, in 1054, to the complete separation of the churches.

During this period following the death of Charlemagne important missionary efforts were begun. Ansgar (801?–865), a monk of Corbie, entered Denmark in 826, but was driven out the next year. In 829 and 830 he labored in Sweden. In 831 he was appointed archbishop of the newly constituted see of Hamburg, with prospective missionary jurisdiction over Denmark, Norway, and Sweden. The destruction of Hamburg by the Danes, in 845, resulted in Ansgar's removal to Bremen, which was united ecclesiastically with Hamburg. Ansgar's efforts were backed by no Frankish military force, and his patient labors accomplished little. The full Christianization of Scandinavia was yet in the future.

Larger success attended missions in the East. The Bulgars, originally a Turanian people from eastern Russia, had conquered a large territory in the

Balkan region in the seventh century, and, in turn, had adopted the manners and speech of their Slavic subjects. Under their King, Boris (852–884), Christianity was introduced, Boris being baptized in 864. For some time un-decided between Constantinople and Rome, Boris finally chose spiritual al-legiance to the former, since the patriarch of Constantinople was willing to recognize a self-governing Bulgarian church. This adhesion was of immense consequence in determining the future growth of the Greek Church in Eastern Europe. The most celebrated missionaries among the Slavs were, however, the brothers Cyril (?–869) and Methodius (?–885). Natives of Thessalonica, they had attained high position in the Eastern empire. On the request of Rostislav, duke of Moravia, the Eastern Emperor, Michael III, sent the brothers thither in 864. In preparation for the mission Cyril invented a Slavic script which became the foundation of the Russian alphabet, and began a translation of the Gospels. The brothers labored in Moravia with great success and introduced a Slavic version of the liturgy. A struggle of several years between the papacy and Constantinople for possession of this new-won territory resulted in the ultimate victory of Rome. The use of a Slavic liturgy was permitted by Pope John VIII (872–882), though soon withdrawn. From Moravia, Christianity in its Roman form came to Bohemia about the close of the ninth century.

7

Papal Decline and Renewal by the Revived Empire

IT MAY SEEM STRANGE that the papacy which showed such power under Nicholas I should within twenty-five years of his death have fallen into its lowest degradation. The explanation is the growing anarchy of the times. Up to a certain point the collapse of the empire aided the development of papal authority; that passed, the papacy became the sport of the Italian nobles and ultimately of whatever faction was in control of Rome, since the Pope was chosen by the clergy and people of the city. The papacy could now appeal for aid to no strong outside political power as Zacharias had to Pippin against the Lombards.

At the close of the ninth century the papacy was involved in the quarrels for the possession of Italy. Stephen V (885–891) was overborne by Guido, duke of Spoleto, and compelled to grant him the empty imperial title. Formosus (891–896) was similarly dependent, and crowned Guido's son,

Lambert, Emperor in 892. From this situation Formosus sought relief in 893 by calling in the aid of Arnulf, whom the Germans had chosen King in 887. In 895 Arnulf captured Rome, and was crowned Emperor by Formosus the next year. A few months later Lambert was in turn master of Rome, and his partisan, Stephen VI (896–897), had the remains of the lately deceased Formosus disinterred, condemned in a synod, and treated with extreme indignity. A riot, however, thrust Stephen VI into prison, where he was strangled.

Popes now followed one another in rapid succession, as the various factions controlled Rome. Between the death of Stephen VI (897) and the accession of John XII (955) no less than seventeen occupied the papal throne. The controlling influences in the opening years of the tenth century were those of the Roman noble Theophylact, and his notorious daughters, Marozia and Theodora. The Popes were their creatures. From 932 to his death in 954 Rome was controlled by Marozia's son Alberic, a man of strength, ability, and character, who did much for churchly reforms in Rome, but nevertheless secured the appointment of his partisans as Popes. On his death he was succeeded as temporal ruler of Rome by his son Octavian, who had few of the father's rough virtues. Though without moral fitness for the office, Octavian secured his own election as Pope in 955, choosing as his name in this capacity John XII (955–964), being one of the earliest Popes to take a new name on election. He altered the whole Roman situation and introduced a new chapter in the history of the papacy, by calling for aid upon the able German sovereign, Otto I, against the threatening power of Berengar II, who had gained control of a large part of Italy.

The line of Charlemagne came to an end in Germany, in 911, with the death of Louis the Child. With the disintegration of the Carolingian empire and the growth of feudalism, Germany threatened to fall into its tribal divisions, Bavaria, Swabia, Saxony, Franconia, and Lorraine. The most powerful men were the tribal dukes. The necessities of defense from the Northmen and Hungarians forced a degree of unity, which was aided by the jealousy felt by the bishops of the growing power of the secular nobility. In 911 the German nobles and great clergy, therefore, chose Conrad, duke of Franconia, as King (911–918). He proved inadequate, and in 919 Henry the Fowler, duke of Saxony, was elected his successor (919–936). His ability was equal to the situation. Though having little power, save in Saxony, he secured peace from the other dukes, fortified his own territories, drove back the Danes, subdued the Slavs east of the Elbe, and finally, in 933, defeated the Hungarian invaders. The worst perils of Germany had been removed, and the foundations of a strong monarchy laid, when he was succeeded as King by his even abler son, Otto I (936–973).

Otto's first work was the consolidation of his kingdom. He made the semi-independent dukes effectively his vassals. In this work he used above all the aid of the bishops and great abbots. They controlled large territories of

Germany, and by filling these posts with his adherents, their forces, coupled with his own, were sufficient to enable Otto to control any hostile combination of lay nobles. He named the bishops and abbots, and under him they became, as they were to continue to the Napoleonic wars, lay rulers as well as spiritual prelates. The peculiar constitution of Germany thus arose, by which the imperial power was based on control of ecclesiastical appointments—a situation which was to lead to the investiture struggle with the papacy in the next century. As Otto extended his power he founded new bishoprics on the borders of his kingdom, partly political and partly missionary in aim, as Brandenburg and Havelberg among the Slavs, and Schleswig, Ripen, and Aarhus for the Danes. He also established the archbishopric of Magdeburg.

Had Otto confined his work to Germany it would have been for the advantage of that land, and for the permanent upbuilding of a strong central monarchy. He was, however, attracted by Italy, and established relations there of the utmost historic importance, but which were destined to dissipate the strength of Germany for centuries. A first invasion in 951 made him master of northern Italy. Rebellion at home (953) and a great campaign against the Hungarians (955) interrupted his Italian enterprise; but in 961 he once more invaded Italy, invited by Pope John XII, then hard pressed by Berengar II (see p. 196). On February 2, 962, Otto was crowned in Rome by John XII as Emperor—an event which, though in theory continuing the succession of the Roman Emperors from Augustus and Charlemagne, was the inauguration of the Holy Roman Empire, which was to continue in name till 1806. Theoretically, the Emperor was the head of secular Christendom, so constituted with the approval of the church expressed by coronation by the papacy. Practically, he was a more or less powerful German ruler, with Italian possessions, on varying terms with the Popes.

John XII soon tired of Otto's practical control, and plotted against him. Otto, of strong religious feeling, to whom such a Pope was an offense, doubtless was also moved by a desire to strengthen his hold on the German bishops by securing a more worthy and compliant head of the church. In 963 Otto compelled the Roman people to swear to choose no Pope without his consent, caused John XII to be deposed, and brought about the choice of Leo VIII (963–965). The new Pope stood solely by imperial support. On Otto's departure John XII resumed his papacy, and on John's death the Roman factions chose Benedict V. Once more Otto returned, forced Benedict into exile, restored Leo VIII, and after Leo's speedy demise, caused the choice of John XIII (965–972). Otto had rescued the papacy, for the time being, from the Roman nobles, but at the cost of subserviency to himself.

Otto's son and successor, Otto II (973–983), pursued substantially the same policy at home, and regarding the papacy, as his father, though with a weaker hand. His son, Otto III (983–1002), went further. The Roman nobles had once more controlled the papacy in his minority, but in 996 he entered Rome, put them down, and caused his cousin Bruno to be made

Pope as Gregory V (996–999)—the first German to hold the papal office. After Gregory's decease Otto III placed on the papal throne his tutor, Gerbert, archbishop of Rheims, as Silvester II (999–1003)—the first French Pope, and the most learned man of the age.

The death of Otto III ended the direct line of Otto I, and the throne was secured by Henry II (1002–1024), duke of Bavaria and great-grandson of Henry the Fowler. A man filled with sincere desire to improve the state of the church, he yet felt himself forced by the difficulties in securing and maintaining his position to exercise strict control over ecclesiastical appointments. His hands were too fully tied by German affairs to interfere effectually in Rome. There the counts of Tusculum gained control of the papacy, and secured the appointment of Benedict VIII (1012–1024), with whom Henry stood on good terms, and by whom he was crowned. Henry even persuaded the unspiritual Benedict VIII at a synod in Pavia in 1022, at which both Pope and Emperor were present, to renew the prohibition of priestly marriage and favor other measures which the age regarded as reforms.

With the death of Henry II the direct line was once more extinct, and the imperial throne was secured by a Franconian count, Conrad II (1024–1039), one of the ablest of German rulers, under whom the empire gained great strength. His thoughts were political, however, and political considerations determined his ecclesiastical appointments. With Rome he did not interfere. There the Tusculan party secured the papacy for Benedict VIII's brother, John XIX (1024–1032), and on his death for his twelve-year-old nephew, Benedict IX (1033–1048), both unworthy, and the latter one of the worst occupants of the papal throne. An intolerable situation arose at Rome, which was ended (see p. 200) by Conrad's able and far more religious son, Henry III, Emperor from 1039 to 1056.

8

Reform Movements

CHARLEMAGNE himself valued monasticism more for its educational and cultural work than for its ascetic ideals. Those ideals appealed, however, in Charlemagne's reign to a soldier-nobleman of southern France, Witiza, or as he was soon known, Benedict (750?–821) called of Aniane, from the monastery founded by him in 779. Benedict's aim was to secure everywhere the full ascetic observation of the "Rule" of Benedict of Nursia (see p. 127).

The educational or industrial side of monasticism appealed little to him. He would raise monasticism to greater activity in worship, contemplation, and self-denial. Under Louis the Pious, Benedict became that Emperor's chief monastic adviser, and by imperial order, in 816 and 817, Benedict of Aniane's interpretation of the elder Benedict's Rule was made binding on all monasteries of the empire. Undoubtedly a very considerable improvement in their condition resulted. Most of these benefits were lost, however, in the collapse of the empire, in which monasticism shared in the common fall.

The misery of the times itself had the effect of turning men's minds from the world, and of magnifying the ascetic ideal. By the early years of the tenth century a real ascetic revival of religion was beginning that was to grow in strength for more than two centuries. Its first conspicuous illustration was the foundation in 910 by Duke William the Pious, of Aquitaine, of the monastery of Cluny, not far from Macon in eastern France.[1] Cluny was to be free from all episcopal or worldly jurisdiction, self-governing, but under the protection of the Pope. Its lands were to be secure from all invasion or secularization, and its rule that of Benedict, interpreted with great ascetic strictness. Cluny was governed by a series of abbots of remarkable character and ability. Under the first and second of these, Berno (910–927) and Odo (927–942), it had many imitators, through their energetic work. Even the mother Benedictine monastery of Monte Cassino, in Italy, was reformed on Cluny lines, and, favored by Alberic, a monastery, St. Mary on the Aventine hill, was founded which represented Cluny ideas in Rome. By the death of Odo the Cluny movement was wide-spread in France and Italy.

It was no part of the original purpose of Cluny to bring other monasteries into dependence on it, or to develop far-reaching churchly political plans. Its aim was a monastic reformation by example and influence. Yet even at the death of the first abbot five or six monasteries were under the control of the abbot of Cluny. Under the fifth abbot, Odilo (994–1048), however, Cluny became the head of a "congregation," since he brought all monasteries founded or reformed by Cluny into dependence on the mother house, their heads being appointed by and responsible to the abbot of Cluny himself. This was new in monasticism, and it made Cluny practically an order, under a single head, with all the strength and influence that such a constitution implies. It now came to have a force comparable with that of the Dominicans or Jesuits of later times. With this growth came an enlargement of the reformatory aims of the Cluny movement. An illustration is the "Truce of God." Though not originated by Cluny, it was taken up and greatly furthered by Abbot Odilo from 1040 onward. Its aim was to limit the constant petty wars between nobles by prescribing a closed season in memory of Christ's passion, from Wednesday evening till Monday morning, during which acts of violence should be visited with severe ecclesiastical punishments. Its purpose was excellent; its success but partial.

[1] Henderson, *Select Historical Documents*, pp. 329–333.

As the Cluny movement grew it won the support of the clergy, and became an effort, not for the reform of monasticism, as at first, but for a wide-reaching betterment of clerical life. By the first half of the eleventh century the Cluny party, as a whole, stood in opposition to "Simony" [2] and "Nicolaitanism." [3] By the former was understood any giving or reception of a clerical office for money payment or other sordid consideration. By the latter, any breach of clerical celibacy, whether by marriage or concubinage. These reformers desired a worthy clergy, appointed for spiritual reasons, as the age understood worthiness. While many of the Cluny party, and even abbots of Cluny itself, had apparently no criticism of royal ecclesiastical appointments, if made from spiritual motives, by the middle of the eleventh century a large section was viewing any investiture by a layman as simony, and had as its reformatory ideal a papacy strong enough to take from the Kings and princes what it deemed their usurped powers of clerical designation. This was the section that was to support Hildebrand in his great contest.

Elsewhere than in the Cluny movement ascetic reform was characteristic of the tenth and eleventh centuries. In Lorraine and Flanders a monastic revival of large proportions was instituted by Gerhard, abbot of Brogne (?–959). In Italy, Romuald of Ravenna (950?–1027) organized settlements of hermits, called "deserts," in which the strictest asceticism was practised, and from which missionaries and preachers went forth. The most famous "desert," which still exists and gave its name to the movement, is that of Camaldoli, near Arezzo. Even more famous was Peter Damiani (1007?–1072), likewise of Ravenna, a fiery supporter of monastic reform, and opponent of simony and clerical marriage, who was, for a time, cardinal bishop of Ostia, and a leading ecclesiastical figure in Italy in the advancement of Hildebrandian ideas, preceding Hildebrand's papacy.

It is evident that before the middle of the eleventh century a strong movement for churchly reform was making itself felt. Henry II had, in large measure, sympathized with it (see p. 198). Henry III (1039–1056) was even more under its influence. Abbot Hugh of Cluny (1049–1109) was a close friend of that Emperor, while the Empress, Agnes, from Aquitaine, had been brought up in heartiest sympathy with the Cluny party, of which her father had been a devoted adherent. Henry III was personally of a religious nature, and though he had no hesitation in controlling ecclesiastical appointments for political reasons as fully as his father, Conrad II, he would take no money for so doing, denounced simony, and appointed bishops of high character and reformatory zeal.

The situation in Rome demanded Henry III's interference, for it had now become an intolerable scandal. Benedict IX, placed on the throne by the Tuscan party, had proved so unworthy that its rivals, the nobles of the Crescenzio faction, were able to drive him out of Rome, in 1044, and

[2] *Acts* 8:18–24.   [3] *Rev.* 2:6, 14, 15.

install their representative as Silvester III in his stead. Benedict, however, was soon back in partial possession of the city, and now, tiring temporarily of his high office, and probably planning marriage, he sold it in 1045 for a price variously stated as one or two thousand pounds of silver. The purchaser was a Roman archpriest of good repute for piety, John Gratian, who took the name Gregory VI. Apparently the purchase was known to few. Gregory was welcomed at first by reformers like Peter Damiani. The scandal soon became public property. Benedict IX refused to lay down the papacy, and there were now three Popes in Rome, each in possession of one of the principal churches, and each denouncing the other two. Henry III now interfered. At a synod held by him in Sutri in December, 1046, Silvester III was deposed, and Gregory VI compelled to resign and banished to Germany. A few days later, a synod in Rome, under imperial supervision, deposed Benedict IX. Henry III immediately nominated and the overawed clergy and people of the city elected a German, Suidger, bishop of Bamberg, as Clement II (1046–1047). Henry III had reached the highwater mark of imperial control over the papacy. So grateful did its rescue from previous degradation appear that the reform party did not at first seriously criticise this imperial domination; but it could not long go on without raising the question of the independence of the church. The very thoroughness of Henry's work soon roused opposition.

Henry III had repeated occasion to show his control of the papal office. Clement II soon died, and Henry caused another bishop of his empire to be placed on the papal throne as Damasus II. The new Pope survived but a few months. Henry now appointed to the vacant see his cousin Bruno, bishop of Toul, a thoroughgoing reformer, in full sympathy with Cluny, who now journeyed to Rome as a pilgrim, and after merely formal canonical election by the clergy and people of the city—for the Emperor's act was determinative —took the title of Leo IX (1049–1054).

9

The Reform Party Secures the Papacy

LEO IX set himself vigorously to the task of reform. His most effective measure was a great alteration wrought in the composition of the Pope's immediate advisers—the cardinals. The name, cardinal, had originally been employed to indicate a clergyman permanently attached to an ecclesiastical position. By the time of Gregory I (590–604), its use in Rome was, however, becoming technical. From an uncertain epoch, but earlier than the conversion of Constantine, in each district of Rome a particular church was deemed, or designated, the most important, originally as the exclusive place for baptisms probably. These churches were known as "title" churches, and their presbyters or head presbyters were the "cardinal" or leading priests of Rome. In a similar way, the heads of the charity districts into which Rome was divided in the third century were known as the "cardinal" or leading deacons. At a later period, but certainly by the eighth century, the bishops in the immediate vicinity of Rome, the "suburbicarian" or suburban bishops, were called the "cardinal bishops." This division of the college of cardinals into "cardinal bishops," "cardinal priests," and "cardinal deacons" persists to the present day. As the leading clergy of Rome and vicinity, they were, long before the name "cardinal" became exclusively or even primarily attached to them, the Pope's chief aids and advisers.

On attaining the papacy Leo IX found the cardinalate filled with Romans, and so far as they were representative of the noble factions which had long controlled the papacy before Henry III's intervention, with men unsympathetic with reform. Leo IX appointed to several of these high places men of reformatory zeal from other parts of Western Christendom. He thus largely changed the sympathies of the cardinalate, surrounded himself with trusted assistants, and in considerable measure rendered the cardinalate thenceforth representative of the Western Church as a whole and not simply of the local Roman community. It was a step of far-reaching consequence. Three of these appointments were of special significance. Humbert, a monk of Lorraine, was made cardinal bishop, and to his death in 1061 was to be a leading opponent of lay investiture and a force in papal politics. Hugh the White, a monk from the vicinity of Toul, who was to live till after 1098, became a cardinal priest, was long to be a supporter of reform, only to become for the last twenty years of his life the most embittered of opponents of Hildebrand and his successors. Finally, Hildebrand himself, who had accompanied Leo IX from Germany, was made a sub-deacon, charged with the financial administration, in some considerable measure, of the Roman see. Leo IX appointed other men of power and reformatory zeal to important, if less prominent, posts in Rome and its vicinity.

Hildebrand, who now came into association with the cardinalate, is the most remarkable personality in mediæval papal history. A man of diminutive stature and unimpressive appearance, his power of intellect, firmness of will, and limitlessness of design made him the outstanding figure of his age. Born in humble circumstances in Tuscany, not far from the year 1020, he was educated in the Cluny monastery of St. Mary on the Aventine in Rome, and early inspired with the most radical of reformatory ideals. He accompanied Gregory VI to Germany on that unlucky Pope's banishment (see p. 201), and thence returned to Rome with Leo IX. Probably he was already a monk, but whether he was ever in Cluny itself is doubtful. He was, however, still a young man, and to ascribe to him the leading influence under the vigorous Leo IX is an error. Leo was rather his teacher.

Leo IX entered vigorously on the work of reform. He stood in cordial relations with its chief leaders, Hugo, abbot of Cluny, Peter Damiani, and Frederick of Lorraine. He made extensive journeys to Germany and France, holding synods and enforcing papal authority. At his first Easter synod in Rome, in 1049, he condemned simony and priestly marriage in the severest terms. A synod held under his presidency in Rheims the same year affirmed the principle of canonical election, "no one shall be promoted to ecclesiastical rulership without the choice of the clergy and people." By these journeys and assemblies the influence of the papacy was greatly raised.

In his relations with southern Italy and with Constantinople Leo IX was less fortunate. The advancing claims of the Normans, who since 1016 had been gradually conquering the lower part of the peninsula, were opposed by the Pope, who asserted possession for the papacy. Papal interference with the churches, especially of Sicily, which still paid allegiance to Constantinople, aroused the assertive patriarch of that city, Michael Cerularius (1043–1058), who now, in conjunction with Leo, the metropolitan of Bulgaria, closed the churches of the Latin rite in their regions and attacked the Latin Church in a letter written by the latter urging the old charges of Photius (see p. 194), and adding a condemnation of the use of unleavened bread in the Lord's Supper—a custom which had become common in the West in the ninth century. Leo IX replied by sending Cardinal Humbert and Frederick of Lorraine, the papal chancellor, to Constantinople in 1054, by whom an excommunication of Michael Cerularius and all his followers was laid on the high altar of St. Sofia. This act has been usually regarded as the formal separation of the Greek and Latin Churches. In 1053 Leo's forces were defeated and he himself captured by the Normans. He did not long survive this catastrophe, dying in 1054.

On the death of Leo IX, Henry III appointed another German, Bishop Gebhard of Eichstädt, as Pope. He took the title of Victor II (1055–1057). Though friendly to the reform party, Victor II was a devoted admirer of his imperial patron, and on the unexpected death of the great Emperor in 1056, did much to secure the quiet succession of Henry III's son Henry IV, then a boy of six, under the regency of the Empress Mother, Agnes. Less than a year later Victor II died.

10

The Papacy Breaks with the Empire

*H*ENRY III'S DOMINANCE was undoubtedly displeasing to the more radical reformers, who had endured it partly of necessity, since it was not apparent how the papacy could otherwise be freed from the control of the Roman nobles, and partly because of Henry's sympathy with many features of the reform movement. Henry himself had been so firmly intrenched in his control of the German church, and of the papacy itself, that the logical consequences of the reform movement appear not to have been clear to him. Now he was gone. A weak regency had taken his place. The time seemed ripe to the reformers for an advance which should lessen imperial control, or, if possible, end it altogether.

The investiture struggle, in which this reform issued, was outwardly a conflict about the way in which the clergy were to be inducted into office. Who was to elect? Who had the privilege to grant the ecclesiastical and secular powers which clerical benefices involved in the feudal system? With the barbarian invasions and the increasing decline of central authority, the church had more and more come under the control of the local nobility, who exercised religious as well as secular rights, in a way similar to that of the Germanic "house-father." The private oratory, for instance, became the village church, and the right of presentation was vested in the secular patron. Bishoprics, on the other hand, had grown to be vast domains, and as royal authority increased in Germany and other lands, the bishop became the direct vassal of the king.

The outward conflict about investiture involved a fundamental struggle between two ideas of authority. On the one hand, there was the priestly idea of the sacramental hierarchy, which claimed for itself independence of all secular control. Fully to assert this right was impossible for the church under the feudal system. Hence the reform movement of the earlier eleventh century satisfied itself with attacking the royal investiture with staff and ring (the symbols of spiritual authority), and did not question the secular right of granting temporal authority over estates. By the end of the century, however, a revolutionary advance had been made in the church's claims, even to the denial of feudal subordination altogether. Thus Urban II, for instance, at the Council of Clermont (1095) forbade ecclesiastics to do fealty as vassals to kings or other laymen. As we shall see later, the church was never able to enforce this, and had to be content with a practical division of the spiritual and temporal powers.

Over against the church's view was that of the royal hierarchy. The king claimed to exercise his power by divine right and to be much more than a mere layman. As the anointed of God he was mystically elevated above the laity and enjoyed a priestly office. Indeed, he stood at the apex of society, symbolizing Christ the King, and by his consecration representing both the heavenly and earthly natures of Christ in himself. Thus he ruled in things spiritual as well as in things temporal by the ecclesiastics and nobility under him. In the course of the controversy this theory of the royal hierarchy was sharply attacked by the reform leaders. The king, they held, was a mere layman, and hence subject to the church. Eventually the king had to bow to the spiritual authority no less than the church to the temporal, and to abandon the extreme claims in this royal theory.

On Victor II's death the Romans, led by the reform clergy, chose Frederick of Lorraine Pope as Stephen IX (1057–1058) without consulting the German regent. A thoroughgoing reformer, the new Pope was the brother of Duke Godfrey of Lorraine, an enemy of the German imperial house, who by his marriage with the Countess Beatrice of Tuscany had become the strongest noble in northern Italy. Under Stephen, Cardinal Humbert now issued a program for the reform party in his *Three Books Against the Simoniacs,* in which he declared all lay appointment invalid and, in especial, attacked lay investiture, that is the gift by the Emperor of a ring and a staff to the elected bishop in token of his induction into office. The victory of these principles would undermine the foundations of the imperial power in Germany. Their strenuous assertion could but lead to a struggle of gigantic proportions. Nevertheless, Stephen did not dare push matters too far. He, therefore, sent Hildebrand and Bishop Anselm of Lucca, who secured the approval of the Empress Agnes for his papacy. Scarcely had this been obtained when Stephen died in Florence.

Stephen's death provoked a crisis. The Roman nobles reasserted their old authority over the papacy and chose their own partisan, Benedict X, only a week later. The reform cardinals had to flee. Their cause seemed for the moment lost. The situation was saved by the firmness and political skill of Hildebrand. He secured the approval of Godfrey of Tuscany and of a part of the people of Rome for the candidacy of Gerhard, bishop of Florence, a reformer and, like Godfrey, a native of Lorraine. A representative of this Roman minority obtained the consent of the regent, Agnes. Hildebrand now gathered the reform cardinals in Siena, and Gerhard was there chosen as Nicholas II (1058–1061). The military aid of Godfrey of Tuscany soon made the new Pope master of Rome. Under Nicholas II the real power was that of Hildebrand, and in lesser degree of the cardinals Humbert and Peter Damiani.

The problem was to free the papacy from the control of the Roman nobles without coming under the overlordship of the Emperor. Some physical support for the papacy must be found. The aid of Tuscany could be counted as assured. Beatrice and her daughter, Matilda, were to be indefatigable in assistance. Yet Tuscany was not sufficient. Under the skilful guidance of Hildebrand, Nicholas II entered into cordial relations with the Normans, who had caused Leo IX so much trouble, recognized their conquests, and received them as vassals of the papacy. With like ability, intimate connections were now established, largely through the agency of Peter Damiani and Bishop Anselm of Lucca, with the democratic party in Lombardy known as the Pataria, opposed to the antireformatory and imperialistic higher clergy of that region. Strengthened by these new alliances, Nicholas II at the Roman synod of 1059 expressly forbad lay investiture under any circumstances.

The most significant event of the papacy of Nicholas II was the decree of this Roman synod of 1059 regulating choice to the papacy—the oldest written constitution now in force, since, in spite of considerable modification, it governs the selection of Popes to this day. In theory, the choice of the Pope had been, like that of other bishops, by the clergy and people of the city of his see. This was termed a canonical election. In practice, such election had meant control by whatever political power was dominant in Rome. The design of the new constitution was to remove that danger. In form, it put into law the circumstances of Nicholas' own election.[1] Its chief author seems to have been Cardinal Humbert. It provided that, on the death of a Pope, the cardinal bishops shall first consider as to his successor and then advise with the other cardinals. Only after their selection has been made should the suffrages of the other clergy and people be sought. In studiously vague language, the document guards "the honor and reverence due to our beloved son Henry"—that is the youthful Henry IV—but does not in the least define the Emperor's share in the choice. The evident purpose was to put the election into the hands of the cardinals, primarily of the cardinal bishops. It was, furthermore, provided that the Pope might come from anywhere in the church, that the election could be held elsewhere than in Rome in case of necessity, and that the Pope chosen should possess the powers of his office immediately on election wherever he might be. This was, indeed, a revolution in the method of choice of the Pope, and would give to the office an independence of political control not heretofore possessed.

Scarcely had these new political and constitutional results been achieved than they were imperilled by the death of Nicholas II in 1061. That of the energetic Cardinal Humbert also occurred the same year. Hildebrand became more than ever the ruling force in the reform party. Within less than three months of Nicholas's death, Hildebrand had secured the election of

[1] Text in Henderson, *Select Historical Documents*, pp. 361–365. The so-called "Papal Version" is in all probability the original.

his friend Anselm, bishop of Lucca, as Alexander II (1061–1073). The German bishops were hostile, however, to the new method to papal election, the Lombard prelates disliked the papal support of the Pataria, and the Roman nobles resented their loss of control over the papacy. These hostile elements now united, and at a German assembly held in Basel in 1061 procured from the Empress-regent the appointment as Pope of Cadalus, bishop of Parma, who took the name of Honorius II. In the struggle that followed, Honorius nearly won; but a revolution in Germany in 1062 placed the chief power in that realm and the guardianship of the young Henry IV in the hands of the ambitious Anno, archbishop of Cologne. Anno wished to stand well with the reform party, and threw his influence on the side of Alexander, who was declared the rightful Pope at a synod of German and Italian prelates held in Mantua in 1064. Thus Hildebrand's bold policy triumphed over a divided Germany.

Alexander II, with Hildebrand's guidance, advanced the papal authority markedly. Anno of Cologne and Siegfried of Mainz, two of the most powerful prelates of Germany, were compelled to do penance for simony. He prevented Henry IV from securing a divorce from Queen Bertha. He lent his approval to William the Conqueror's piratical expedition which resulted in the Norman conquest of England in 1066, and further aided William's plans by the establishment of Norman bishops in the principal English sees. He gave his sanction to the efforts of the Normans of southern Italy which were to result in the conquest of Sicily. Meanwhile Henry IV came of age in 1065. Far from being a weak King, he soon showed himself one of the most resourceful of German rulers. It was inevitable that the papal policy regarding ecclesiastical appointments should clash with that historic control by German sovereigns on which their power in the empire so largely rested. The actual dispute came over the archbishopric of Milan—a post of the first importance for the control of northern Italy. Henry had appointed Godfrey of Castiglione, whom Alexander had charged with simony. The Pataria of Milan chose a certain Atto, whom Alexander recognized as rightful archbishop. In spite of that act, Henry now secured Godfrey's consecration, in 1073, to the disputed post. The struggle was fully on. The contest involved the power of the imperial government and the claims of the radical papal reform party. Alexander looked upon Henry as a well-intentioned young man, misled by bad advice, and he therefore excommunicated not Henry himself, but Henry's immediate counsellors as guilty of simony. Within a few days thereafter Alexander II died, leaving the great dispute to his successor.

11

Hildebrand and Henry IV

H ILDEBRAND'S ELECTION came about in curious disregard of the new constitution established under Nicholas II. During the funeral of Alexander II, in St. John Lateran, the crowd acclaimed Hildebrand Pope, and carried him, almost in a riot, to the church of St. Peter in Chains, where he was enthroned. He took the name of Gregory VII (1073–1085). In his accession the extremest interpretation of the principles of Augustine's *City of God* had reached the papal throne. The papacy he viewed as a divinely appointed universal sovereignty, which all must obey, and to which all earthly sovereigns are responsible, not only for their spiritual welfare, but for their temporal good government. Though Cardinal Deusdedit, rather than Hildebrand, was probably the author of the famous *Dictatus,* it well expresses Hildebrand's principles: "That the Roman Church was founded by God alone." "That the Roman pontiff alone can with right be called universal." "That he alone can depose or reinstate bishops." "That he alone may use [*i. e.,* dispose of] the imperial insignia." "That it may be permitted him to depose Emperors." "That he himself may be judged of no one." "That he may absolve subjects from their fealty to wicked men." [1] It was nothing less than an ideal of world-rulership. In view of later experience it may be called impracticable and even unchristian; but neither Hildebrand nor his age had had that experience. It was a great ideal of a possible regenerated human society, effected by obedience to commanding spiritual power, and as such was deserving of respect in those who held it, and worthy of that trial which alone could reveal its value or worthlessness.

The opening years of Hildebrand's pontificate were favorable for the papacy. A rebellion against Henry IV by his Saxon subjects, who had many grievances, and the discontent of the nobles of other regions kept Henry fully occupied. In 1074 he did penance in Nuremberg before the papal legates, and promised obedience. At the Easter synod in Rome in 1075, Hildebrand renewed the decree against lay investiture, denying to Henry any share in creating bishops. A few months later Henry's fortunes changed. In June, 1075, his defeat of the Saxons made him apparently master of Germany, and

[1] Henderson, *Select Historical Documents,* pp. 366, 367; extracts in Robinson, *Readings in European History,* 1:274.

his attitude toward the papacy speedily altered. Henry once more made an appointment to the archbishopric of Milan. Hildebrand replied, in December, 1075, with a letter calling Henry to severe account.[2] On January 24, 1076, Henry, with his nobles and bishops, held a council in Worms, at which the turncoat cardinal, Hugh the White, was forward with personal charges against Hildebrand. There a large portion of the German bishops joined in a fierce denunciation of Hildebrand and a rejection of his authority as Pope[3]—an action for which the approval of the Lombard prelates was speedily secured.

Hildebrand's reply was the most famous of mediæval papal decrees. At the Roman synod of February 22, 1076, he excommunicated Henry, forbad him authority over Germany and Italy, and released all Henry's subjects from their oaths of allegiance.[4] It was the boldest assertion of papal authority that had ever been made. To it Henry replied by a fiery letter addressed to Hildebrand, "now no pope, but a false monk," in which he called on Hildebrand to "come down, to be damned throughout all eternity." [5]

Had Henry IV had a united Germany behind him the result might easily have been Hildebrand's overthrow. Germany was not united. The Saxons and Henry's other political enemies used the opportunity to make him trouble. Even the bishops had regard for the authority of a Pope they had nominally rejected. Henry was unable to meet the rising opposition. An assembly of nobles in Tribur, in October, 1076, declared that unless released from excommunication within a year he would be deposed, and the Pope was invited to a new assembly to meet in Augsburg, in February, 1077, at which the whole German political and religious situation should be considered. Henry was in great danger of losing his throne. It became a matter of vital importance to free himself from excommunication. Hildebrand refused all appeals; he would settle the questions at Augsburg.

Henry IV now resolved on a step of the utmost dramatic and political significance. He would meet Hildebrand before the Pope could reach the assembly in Augsburg and wring from him the desired absolution. He crossed the Alps in the winter and sought Hildebrand in northern Italy, through which the Pope was passing on his way to Germany. In doubt whether Henry came in peace or war, Hildebrand sought refuge in the strong castle of Canossa, belonging to his ardent supporter, the Countess Matilda of Tuscany, the daughter of Beatrice (see p. 206). Thither Henry went, and there presented himself before the castle gate on three successive days, barefooted as a penitent. The Pope's companions pleaded for him, and on January 28, 1077, Henry IV was released from excommunication. In many ways it was a political triumph for the King. He had thrown his German

[2] Henderson, pp. 367–371; Robinson, 1:276–279.   [3] Henderson, pp. 373–376.
[4] Henderson, pp. 376, 377; Robinson, 1:281, 282.
[5] Henderson, pp. 372, 373; Robinson, 1:279–281. The letter seems to belong here, rather than to January, 1076, to which it is often assigned.

opponents into confusion. He had prevented a successful assembly in Augsburg under papal leadership. The Pope's plans had been disappointed. Yet the event has always remained in men's recollection as the deepest humiliation of the mediæval empire before the power of the church.[6]

In March, 1077, Henry's German enemies, without Hildebrand's instigation, chose Rudolf, duke of Swabia, as counter-King. Civil war ensued, while the Pope balanced one claimant against the other, hoping to gain for himself the ultimate decision. Forced at last to take sides, Hildebrand, at the Roman synod in March, 1080, a second time excommunicated and deposed Henry.[7] The same political weapons can seldom be used twice effectively. Sentiment had crystallized in Germany, and this time the Pope's action had little effect. Henry answered by a synod in Brixen in June, 1080, deposing Hildebrand,[8] and choosing one of Hildebrand's bitterest opponents, Archbishop Wibert of Ravenna, as Pope in his place. Wibert called himself Clement III (1080–1100). The death of Rudolf in battle, in October following, left Henry stronger in Germany than ever before. He determined to be rid of Hildebrand. In 1081 Henry invaded Italy, but it was three years before he gained possession of Rome. Pressed upon by the overwhelming German and Lombard forces, Hildebrand's political supporters proved too weak to offer permanently effective resistance. The Roman people, and no less than thirteen of the cardinals, turned to the victorious German ruler and his Pope. In March, 1084, Wibert was enthroned, and crowned Henry Emperor. Hildebrand, apparently a beaten man, still held the castle of San Angelo, and absolutely refused any compromise. In May a Norman army came to Hildebrand's relief, but these rough supporters so burned and plundered Rome, that he had to withdraw with them, and after nearly a year of this painful exile, he died in Salerno, on May 25, 1085.

Hildebrand's relations to other countries have been passed by in the account of his great struggle with Germany. It may be sufficient to say that his aims were similar, though so engrossed was he in the conflict with Henry IV that he never pushed matters to such an extreme with the Kings of England and France. He attempted to bring the high clergy everywhere under his control. He caused extensive codification of church law to be made. He enforced clerical celibacy as not only the theoretical but the practical rule of the Roman Church. If his methods were worldly and unscrupulous, as they undoubtedly were, no misfortune ever caused him to abate his claims, and even in apparent defeat he won a moral victory. The ideals that he had established for the papacy were to live long after him.

---

[6] The best account is that of Hildebrand himself. Henderson, pp. 385–387; Robinson, 1:282–283.
[7] Henderson, pp. 388–391.   [8] *Ibid.*, pp. 391–394.

12

The Struggle Ends in Compromise

O N THE DEATH of Hildebrand, the cardinals faithful to him chose as his successor Desiderius, the able and scholarly abbot of Monte Cassino, who took the name of Victor III (1086–1087). So discouraging was the outlook that he long refused the doubtful honor. When at last he accepted it, he quietly dropped Hildebrand's extremer efforts at world-rulership, though renewing the prohibition of lay investiture with utmost vigor. He was, however, able to be in Rome but a few days. That city remained in the hands of Wibert, and before the end of 1087 Victor III was no more. The situation of the party of Hildebrand seemed well-nigh hopeless. After much hesitation, a few of the reform cardinals met in Terracina, and chose a French Cluny monk, who had been appointed a cardinal bishop by Hildebrand, Odo of Lagary, as Pope Urban II (1088–1099). A man of Hildebrandian convictions, without Hildebrand's genius, Urban was far more conciliatory and politically skilful. He sought with great success to create a friendly party among the German clergy, aided thereto by the monks of the influential monastery of Hirschau. He stirred up disaffection for Henry IV, often by no worthy means. Yet it was not till the close of 1093 that Urban was able to take effective possession of Rome and drive out Wibert. His rise in power was thence rapid. At a great synod held in Piacenza in March, 1095, he sounded the note of a crusade. At Clermont in November of the same year he brought the Crusade into being (p. 220). On the flood of the crusading movement Urban rose at once to a position of European leadership. Henry IV and Wibert might oppose him, but the papacy had achieved a popular significance compared with which they had nothing to offer.

Though men were weary of the long strife, the next Pope, Paschal II (1099–1118), made matters worse rather than better. Henry IV's last days were disastrous. A successful rebellion, headed by his son, Henry V (1106–1125), forced his abdication in 1105. His death followed the next year. Henry V's position in Germany was stronger than his father's ever had been, and he was more unscrupulous. His assertion of his rights of investiture was as insistent as that of his father. In 1110 Henry V marched on Rome in force. Paschal II was powerless and without the courage of a Hildebrand. The

Pope and Henry now agreed (1111) that the King should resign his right of investiture, provided the bishops of Germany should relinquish to him all temporal lordships.[1] That would have been a revolution that would have reduced the German church to poverty, and the protest raised on its promulgation in Rome, in February, 1111, showed it impossible of accomplishment. Henry V then took the Pope and the cardinals prisoners. Paschal weakened. In April, 1111, he resigned to Henry investiture with ring and staff, and crowned him Emperor.[2] The Hildebrandian party stormed in protest. At the Roman synod of March, 1112, Paschal withdrew his agreement, which he could well hold was wrung from him by force. A synod in Vienne in September excommunicated Henry and forbad lay investiture, and this action the Pope approved.

Yet the basis of a compromise was already in sight. Two French church leaders, Ivo, bishop of Chartres, and Hugo of Fleury, in writings between 1099 and 1106, had argued that church and state each had their rights of investiture, the one with spiritual, the other with temporal authority. Anselm, the famous archbishop of Canterbury, a firm supporter of reform principles (1093–1109), had refused investiture from Henry I of England (1100–1135). This led to a contest which ended in the resignation by the King of investiture with ring and staff, while retaining to the crown investiture with temporal possession by the reception of an oath of fealty. These principles and precedents influenced the further course of the controversy. The compromise came in 1122, in the Concordat of Worms, arranged between Henry V and Pope Calixtus II (1119–1124). By mutual agreement, elections of bishops and abbots in Germany were to be free and in canonical form, yet the presence of the Emperor at the choice was allowed, and in case of disputed election he should consult with the metropolitan and other bishops of the province. In other parts of the empire, Burgundy and Italy, no mention was made of the imperial presence. The Emperor renounced investiture with ring and staff, *i. e.,* with the symbols of spiritual authority. In turn, the Pope granted him the right of investiture with the temporal possessions of the office by the touch of the royal sceptre, without demand of payment from the candidate. This imperial recognition was to take place in Germany before consecration, and in the other parts of the empire within six months thereafter.[3] The effect was that in Germany at least a bishop or abbot must be acceptable both to the church and to the Emperor. In Italy the imperial power, which had rested on control of churchly appointments, was greatly broken. It was an outcome of the struggle which would but partially have satisfied Hildebrand. Yet the church had won much. If not superior to the state, it had vindicated its equality with the temporal power.

[1] Henderson, pp 405–407; Robinson, 1:290–292.   [2] Henderson, pp. 407, 408.
[3] Henderson, pp. 408, 409; Robinson, 1:292, 293.

13

The Greek Church after the Picture Controversy

THE ISAURIAN DYNASTY in Constantinople (717–802), witnessed the severe internal conflicts caused by the picture-worshipping controversy, which was in a measure a struggle for the freedom of the church from imperial control (see p. 148). It beheld the loss of Rome and of the Exarchate, and the rise of the renewed Western empire under Charlemagne. The periods of the Phrygian (820–867) and Macedonian dynasties (867–1057) were marked by a notable revival of learning, so that, intellectually, the East was decidedly superior to the West. The patriarch, Photius, whose quarrel with Nicholas I has already been noted, was of eminent scholarship. His *Myriobiblon* is of permanent worth, as preserving much of ancient classical authors otherwise lost. Symeon "Metaphrastes" compiled his famous collection of the lives of the Eastern saints in the tenth century. In Symeon, "the New Theologian" (?–1040?), the Greek Church had its noblest mystic, who believed that the revelation of the divine light—the very vision of God—is possible of attainment. From him the mystical tradition of "Hesychasm" (or "quietude") was developed in the Eastern Church. It was believed that the monastic visionary in his wrapt contemplation partook of the very substance of God Himself and was surrounded by the uncreated light which was revealed on Mount Tabor at the transfiguration. The ablest champion of this mysticism, which was practiced especially in the monastery on Mount Athos, was the monk, St. Gregory Palamas (1292–1359), who later became Archbishop of Thessalonika and who was involved in the civil wars of the time of John Palaeologos.

The chief religious controversy in the East of this epoch was that caused by the Paulicians. The origin and history of the movement is obscure. They called themselves Christians simply, their nickname being apparently due to their reverence for Paul the Apostle, rather than as sometimes claimed to any real connection with Paul of Samosata. The movement appears to have begun with a Constantine-Silvanus, of Mananalis, near Samosata, about 650–660. In it ancient heretical beliefs, akin to and perhaps derived from the Marcionites and Gnostics, reappeared. Though the Paulicians repudiated Manichæism, they were dualists, holding that this world is the creation of an evil power, while souls are from the kingdom of the good God. They accepted the New Testament, with the possible exception of the writings ascribed to Peter, as the message of the righteous God. They viewed Christ as an angel sent by the good God, and hence Son of God by adoption. His work was primarily that of instruction. They rejected monasticism, the external sacraments, the cross, images, and relics. Their ministry was that of wandering preachers and "copyists." The Catholic hierarchy they repudiated. They opposed the externalism of current orthodox religious life.

The Paulicians seem to have spread rapidly in the Eastern empire, and to have taken strong root in Armenia. Persecuted by the orthodox, their military powers procured them considerable respect. Constantine V transplanted colonies of them to the Balkan peninsula in 752, as a defense against the Bulgarians—a process which was repeated on a larger scale by the Emperor, John Tzimiskes, in 969. There they seem to have given origin to the very similar Bogomiles, who in turn were to be influential in the development of the Cathari of southern France (p. 228). Driven to seek refuge among the Saracens, some sections of the Paulicians harassed the borders of the empire in the ninth century, and even penetrated deeply into it, till their military success, though not their religious activity, was permanently checked by the Emperor, Basil I, in 871.

The latter half of the ninth and the tenth centuries was a period of revived military power for the Eastern empire, especially under John Tzimiskes (969–976) and Basil II (976–1025). By the latter, Bulgaria and Armenia were conquered. Internal dissensions and a fear of usurping militarism weakened the empire in the eleventh century, so that the rise of the Seljuk Turks found it unprepared. In 1071 the Turks conquered a large part of Asia Minor, and in 1080 established themselves in Nicæa, less than a hundred miles from Constantinople. This great loss to Christianity was to be one of the causes leading to the Crusades.

14

The Spread of the Church

THE TENTH and eleventh centuries were an epoch of large extension of Christianity. Ansgar's work in the Scandinavian lands (see p. 194) had left few results. Scandinavian Christianization was a slow and gradual process. Unni, archbishop of Hamburg (918–936), imitated Ansgar, but without great success. The work was carried forward by Archbishop Adaldag (937–988). Under his influence, King Harold Bluetooth of Denmark accepted Christianity, and Danish bishoprics were established. Under Harold's son, Sweyn, heathenism was again in power; but he was brought to favor the church in 995, and the work was completed in Denmark by King Canute the Great (1015–1035), who also ruled England and, for a time, Norway.

The story of Norway is similar. Some Christian beginnings were made under Hakon I (935–961), and missionaries were sent by Harold Bluetooth of Denmark. Christianity in Norway was not permanently established till the time of Olaf I (995–1000), who brought in English preachers. The work was now extended to the Orkneys, Shetland, Hebrides, Faroe, Iceland, and Greenland, then in Scandinavian possession. Olaf II (1015–1028) enforced Christianity in Norway with such extreme measures that he was deposed and Canute gained control; yet he lives in tradition as St. Olaf. Magnus I (1035–1047) completed the work.

In Sweden, after many beginnings from the time of Ansgar, Christianity was effectively established by King Olaf Sköttkonung (994–1024), who was baptized in 1008. Yet the work was slow, and heathenism was not fully overthrown till about 1100. Finland and Lapland were not reached till two centuries later.

After various efforts in the tenth century, Christianity was effectively established in Hungary by King Stephen I (997–1038), the organizer of the Hungarian monarchy, who lives in history as St. Stephen. The Polish duke, Mieczyslaw, accepted Christianity in 967, and in 1000 King Boleslaus I (992–1025) organized the Polish church with an archbishopric in Gnesen. Pomerania was not Christianized till 1124–1128.

The movements just considered were the work of the Latin Church. The great extension of the Greek Church lies in this period and was accomplished by the conversion of Russia. Its beginnings are obscure. Efforts for the spread of Christianity in Russia seem to have been made as early as the time of the patriarch of Constantinople Photius (866). The Russian Queen, Olga, received baptism on a visit to Constantinople in 957. The work was at last definitely established by Grandduke Vladimir I (980–1015), who received baptism in 988, and compelled his subjects to follow his example. A metropolitan, nominated by the patriarch of Constantinople, was placed at the head of the Russian church, with his see in Kiev, from which it was transferred in 1299 to the city of Vladimir, and in 1325 to Moscow.

Period Five

THE LATER MIDDLE AGES

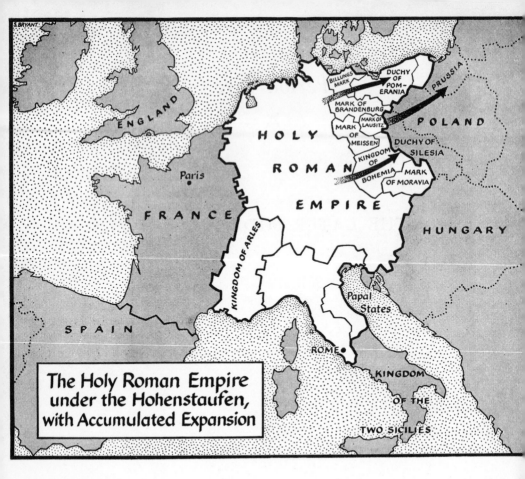

The Holy Roman Empire under the Hohenstaufen, with Accumulated Expansion

1

The Crusades

*T*HE CRUSADES are in many ways the most remarkable of the phenomena of the Middle Ages. Their causes were many. The historian who emphasizes economic influences may well claim the unusually trying conditions of the eleventh century as a main source. Between 970 and 1040 forty-eight famine years were counted. From 1085 to 1095 conditions were even worse. Misery and unrest prevailed widely. The more settled conditions of the age made impossible such migrations of nations as had been exhibited in the Germanic invasions at the downfall of the Western empire. The same desire to change environment was, however, felt.

Stimulated by these economic conditions, the whole eleventh century was a period of deepening religious feeling. Its manifestations took monastic and ascetic forms. It was characterized by a strong sense of "other-worldliness," of the misery of earth and the blessedness of heaven. This increasing religious zeal had been the force which had reformed the papacy, and had supported antagonism to simony and Nicolaitanism, and nerved the long struggle with the empire. Those regions where the reform movement had shone brightest, or which had come into closest relations with the reforming papacy, France, Lorraine, and southern Italy, were the recruiting-grounds of the chief crusading armies. The piety of the time placed great value on relics and pilgrimages, and what more precious relic could there be, or what nobler pilgrimage shrine, than the land hallowed by the life, death, and resurrection of Christ? That land had been an object of pilgrimage since the days of Constantine. Though Jerusalem had been in Moslem possession since 638, pilgrimages had been, save for brief intervals, practically uninterrupted. They had never been more numerous than in the eleventh century, till the conquest of much of Asia Minor, from 1071 onward, and the capture of Jerusalem, by the Seljuk Turks, made pilgrimages almost impossible and desecrated the holy places.

It was to an age profoundly impressed with the spiritual advantage of pilgrimages that the news of these things came. The time, moreover, was witnessing successful contests with Mohammedanism. Between 1060 and 1090 the Normans of southern Italy had wrested Sicily from the Moslems. Under Ferdinand I of Castile (1028–1065) the effective Christian reconquest of Spain from the Mohammedans had begun. The feeling was wide-spread that Christianity could dispossess Mohammedanism. Love of adventure, hopes for plunder, desire for territorial advancement and religious hatred, undoubtedly moved the Crusaders with very earthly impulses. We should wrong them, however, if we did not recognize with equal clearness that they thought they were doing something of the highest importance for their souls and for Christ.

The first impulse to the Crusades came from an appeal of the Eastern Emperor, Michael VII (1067–1078), to Hildebrand for aid against the Seljuks. That great Pope, to whom this seemed to promise the reunion of Greek and Latin Christendom, took the matter up in 1074, and was able to report to Henry IV of Germany that fifty thousand men were ready to go under the proper leadership. The speedy outbreak of the investiture struggle frustrated the plan. It was effectively to be revived by Urban II, the heir in so many directions of Hildebrand.

Alexius I (1081–1118), a stronger ruler than his immediate predecessors in Constantinople, felt unable to cope with the perils which threatened the empire. He, therefore, appealed to Urban II for assistance. Urban received the imperial messengers at the synod in Piacenza, in northern Italy, in March, 1095, and promised his help. At the synod held in Clermont, in eastern France, in the following November, Urban now proclaimed the Crusade in an appeal of almost unexampled consequence. The enterprise had magnified in his conception from that of aid to the hard-pressed Alexius to a general rescue of the holy places from Moslem hands. He called on all Christendom to take part in the work, promising plenary indulgence to all who would participate in the enterprise. The message found immediate and enthusiastic response. Among the popular preachers who took it up none was more famous than Peter the Hermit, a monk from Amiens or its vicinity. Early legend attributed to him the origin of the Crusade itself, of which he was unquestionably one of the most effective proclaimers. He does not deserve the distinction thus attributed to him, nor was his conduct on the Crusade, once it had started, such as to do credit to his leadership or even to his courage.

Such was the enthusiasm engendered, especially in France, that large groups of peasants, with some knights among them, set forth in the spring of 1096, under the lead of Walter the Penniless; a priest, Gottschalk, and Peter the Hermit himself. By some of these wild companies many Jews were massacred in the Rhine cities. Their own disorderly pillage led to savage reprisals in Hungary and the Balkans. That under Peter reached Constantinople, but was almost entirely destroyed by the Turks in an attempt to reach Nicæa. Peter himself did not share this catastrophe, joined the main crusading force, and survived the perils of the expedition.

The real work of the First Crusade was accomplished by the feudal nobility of Europe. Three great armies were raised. That from Lorraine and Flanders included Godfrey of Bouillon, the moral hero of the Crusade, since he commanded the respect due to his single-minded and unselfish devotion to its aims, though not its ablest general. With Godfrey were his brothers, Baldwin and Eustace. Other armies from northern France were led by Hugh of Vermandois and Robert of Normandy. From southern France came a large force under Count Raimond of Toulouse, and from Norman Italy a well-equipped army led by Bohemund of Taranto and his nephew Tancred. The earliest of these forces started in August, 1096. No single commander led the hosts. Urban II had appointed Bishop Ademar of Puy his legate; and Ademar designated Constantinople as the gathering place. Thither each army made its way as best it could, arriving there in the winter and spring of 1096–1097, and causing Alexius no little difficulty by their disorder and demands.

In May, 1097, the crusading army began the siege of Nicæa. Its surrender followed in June. On July 1 a great victory over the Turks near Dorylæum opened the route across Asia Minor, so that Iconium was reached, after severe losses through hunger and thirst, by the middle of August. By October the crusading host was before the walls of Antioch. That city it captured only after a difficult siege, on June 3, 1098. Three days later the Crusaders were besieged in the city by the Turkish ruler Kerbogha of Mosul. The crisis of the Crusade was this time of peril and despair; but on June 28 Kerbogha was completely defeated. Yet it was not till June, 1099, that Jerusalem was reached, and not till July 15 that it was captured and its inhabitants put to the sword. The complete defeat of an Egyptian relieving army near Ascalon on August 12, 1099, crowned the success of the Crusade.

On the completion of the work, Godfrey of Bouillon was chosen Protector of the Holy Sepulchre. He died in July, 1100, and was succeeded by his abler brother, who had established a Latin county in Edessa, and now took the title of King Baldwin I (1100–1118). The Crusaders were from the feudal West, and the country was divided and organized in full feudal fashion. It included, besides the Holy Land, the principality of Antioch, and the counties of Tripoli and Edessa, which were practically independent of the King of Jerusalem. In the towns important Italian business settlements sprang up; but most of the knights were French. Under a patriarch of the Latin rite in Jerusalem, the country was divided into four archbishoprics and ten bishoprics, and numerous monasteries were established.

The greatest support of the kingdom soon came to be the military orders. Of these, that of the Templars was founded by Hugo de Payens in 1119, and granted quarters near the site of the temple—hence their name—by King Baldwin II (1118–1131). Through the hearty support of Bernard of Clairvaux the order received papal approval in 1128, and soon won wide popularity in the West. Its members took the usual monastic vows and pledged themselves, in addition, to fight against infidels, to defend the Holy Land and to protect pilgrims. They were not clergy, but laymen. In some respects the order was like a modern missionary society. Those who sympathized with the

Crusade, but were debarred by age or sex from a personal share in the work, gave largely that they might be represented by others through the order. Since property was mostly in land, the Templars soon became great landholders in the West. Their independence and wealth made them objects of royal jealousy, especially after their original purpose had been frustrated by the end of the Crusades, and led to their brutal suppression in France in 1307 by King Philip IV (1285–1314). While the Crusades lasted they were a main bulwark of the kingdom of Jerusalem.

Much the same thing may be said of the great rivals of the Templars, the Hospitallers or Knights of St. John. Charlemagne had founded a hospital in Jerusalem, which was destroyed in 1010. Refounded by citizens of Amalfi, in Italy, it was in existence before the First Crusade, and was named for the church of St. John the Baptist, near which it stood. This foundation was made into a military order by its grand master, Raymond du Puy (1120–1160?), though without neglecting its duties to the sick. After the crusading epoch it maintained a struggle with the Turks from its seat in Rhodes (1310–1523), and then from Malta (1530–1798). A third and later order was that of the Teutonic Knights, founded by Germans in 1190. Its chief work, however, was not to be in Palestine but, from 1229 onward, in Prussia, or as it is now known, East Prussia, where it was a pioneer in civilization and Christianization.

In spite of feudal disorganization the kingdom of Jerusalem was fairly successful till the capture of Edessa by the Mohammedans in 1144 robbed it of its northeastern bulwark. Bernard of Clairvaux, now at the height of his fame, proclaimed a new Crusade and enlisted Louis VII of France (1137–1180) and the Emperor Conrad III (1138–1152) from Germany in 1146. In 1147 the Second Crusade set forth; but it showed little of the fiery enthusiasm of its predecessor, its forces largely perished in Asia Minor, and such as reached Palestine were badly defeated in an attempt to take Damascus, in 1148. It was a disastrous failure, and its collapse left a bitter feeling in the West toward the Eastern empire, to whose princes that failure, rightly or wrongly, was charged.

One reason of the success of the Latin kingdom had been the quarrels of the Mohammedans. In 1171 the Kurdish general, Saladin, made himself master of Egypt; by 1174 he had secured Damascus, and by 1183 Saladin's territories surrounded the Latin kingdom on the north, east, and south. A united Mohammedanism had now to be met. Results soon followed. At Hattin the Latin army was defeated in July, 1187. The loss of Jerusalem and of most of the Holy Land speedily followed. The news of this catastrophe roused Europe to the Third Crusade (1189–1192). None of the Crusades were more elaborately equipped. Three great armies were led by the Emperor Frederick Barbarossa (1152–1190), the first soldier of his age, by King Philip Augustus of France (1179–1223), and by King Richard "Cœur de Lion" of England (1189–1199). Frederick was accidentally drowned in Cilicia. His army, deprived of his vigorous leadership, was utterly ineffective. The quarrels between the Kings of France and England, and Philip's speedy return to France to push his own political schemes, rendered the whole expedition almost abortive. Acre was recovered, but Jerusalem remained in Moslem possession.

The Fourth Crusade (1202–1204) was a small affair as far as numbers engaged, but of important political and religious consequences. Its forces were from the districts of northern France known as Champagne and Blois, and from Flanders. Men had become convinced that the true route to the recovery of Jerusalem was the preliminary conquest of Egypt. The Crusaders therefore bargained with the Venetians for transportation thither. Unable to raise the full cost, they accepted the proposition of the Venetians that, in lieu of the balance due, they stop on their way and conquer Zara from Hungary for Venice. This they did. A much greater proposal was now made to them. They should stop at Constantinople, and assist in dethroning the imperial usurper, Alexius III (1195–1203). Alexius, son of the deposed Isaac II, promised the Crusaders large payment and help on their expedition provided they would overthrow the usurper, and crafty Venice saw bright prospects of increased trade. Western hatred of the Greeks contributed. Though Pope Innocent III forbad this division of purpose, the Crusaders were persuaded. Alexius III was easily driven from his throne; but the other Alexius was unable to keep his promises to the Crusaders, who now with the Venetians, in 1204, captured Constantinople, and plundered its treasures. No booty was more eagerly sought than the relics in the churches, which now went to enrich the places of worship of the West. Baldwin of Flanders was made Emperor, and a large portion of the Eastern empire was divided, feudal fashion, among Western knights. Venice obtained a considerable part and a monopoly of trade. A Latin patriarch of Constantinople was appointed, and the Greek Church made subject to the Pope. The Eastern empire still continued, though it was not to regain Constantinople till 1261. This Latin conquest was disastrous. It greatly weakened the Eastern empire, and augmented the hatred between Greek and Latin Christianity.

A melancholy episode was the so-called "Children's Crusade" of 1212. A shepherd boy, Stephen, in France, and a boy of Cologne, in Germany, Nicholas, gathered thousands of children. Straggling to Italy, they were largely sold into slavery in Egypt. Other crusading attempts were made. An expedition against Egypt, in 1218–1221, had some initial success, but ended in failure. It is usually called the Fifth Crusade. The most curious was the Sixth (1228–1229). The free-thinking Emperor Frederick II (1212–1250), had taken the cross in 1215, but showed no haste to fulfill his vows. At last, in 1227, he started, but soon put back. He seems to have been really ill, but Pope Gregory IX (1227–1241), believing him a deserter, and having other grounds of hostility, excommunicated him. In spite of the ban, Frederick went forward in 1228, and the next year secured, by treaty with the Sultan of Egypt, possession of Jerusalem, Bethlehem, Nazareth and a path to the coast. Jerusalem was once more in Christian keeping till 1244, when it was permanently lost. The crusading spirit was now well-nigh spent, though Louis IX of France (St. Louis, 1226–1270) led a disastrous expedition against Egypt in 1248–1250, in which he was taken prisoner, and an attack on Tunis in 1270, in which he lost his life. The last considerable expedition was that of Prince Edward, soon to be Edward I of England (1272–1307), in 1271 and 1272. In 1291, the last of the Latin holdings in Palestine was lost. The Crusades were over, though men continued to talk of new expeditions for nearly two centuries more.

Viewed from the aspect of their purpose the Crusades were failures. They made no permanent conquest of the Holy Land. It may be doubted whether they greatly retarded the advance of Mohammedanism. Their cost in lives and treasure was enormous. Though initiated in a high spirit of devotion, their conduct was disgraced throughout by quarrels, divided motives, and low standards of personal conduct. When their indirect results are examined, however, a very different estimate is to be made of their worth. Civilization is the result of so complex factors that it is hard to assign precise values to single causes. Europe would have made progress during this period had there been no Crusades. But the changes wrought are so remarkable that the conclusion is unavoidable that the largest single influence was that of the Crusades.

By the commerce which the Crusades stimulated the cities of northern Italy and of the great trade route over the Alps and down the Rhine rose to importance. By the sacrifices of feudal lands and property which they involved, a new political element, that of the towns—a "third estate"—was greatly stimulated, especially in France. The mental horizon of the Western world was immeasurably extended. Thousands who had grown up in the densest ignorance and narrow-mindedness were brought into contact with the splendid cities and ancient civilization of the East. Everywhere there was intellectual awakening. The period witnessed the highest theological development of the Middle Ages—that of Scholasticism. It beheld great popular religious movements, in and outside of the church. It saw the development of the universities. Modern vernacular literature began to flourish. A great artistic development, the national architecture of northern France, misnamed the Gothic, now ran its glorious career. The Europe of the period of the Crusades was awake and enlightened compared with the centuries which had gone before. Admitting that the Crusades were but one factor in this result, they were worth all their cost.

2

New Religious Movements

THE EPOCH of the First Crusade was one of increasing religious earnestness, manifesting itself in other-worldliness, asceticism, mystical piety, and emphasis on the monastic life. The long battle against simony and Nicolaitanism had turned popular sympathies from the often criticised "secular," or ordinary clergy, to the monks as the true representatives of the religious ideal. Cluny had, in a measure, spent its force. Its very success had led to luxury of living. New religious associations were arising, of which the most important was that of the Cistercians—an order which dominated the twelfth century as Cluny had the eleventh.

Like Cluny, the Cistercians were of French origin. A Benedictine monk, Robert, of the monastery of Montier, impressed with the ill discipline of contemporary monasticism, founded a monastery of great strictness in Citeaux, not far from Dijon, in 1098. From the first, the purpose of the foundation of Citeaux was to cultivate a strenuous, self-denying life. Its buildings, utensils, even the surroundings of worship, were of the plainest character. In food and clothing it exercised great austerity. Its rule was that of Benedict, but its self-denial was far beyond that of Benedictines generally. Under its third abbot, Stephen Harding (1109–1134), an Englishman, the significance of Citeaux rapidly grew. Four affiliated monasteries were founded by 1115, under his leadership. Thenceforth its progress was rapid throughout all the West. By 1130, the Cistercian houses numbered thirty; by 1168, two hundred and eighty-eight, and a century later six hundred and seventy-one. Over all these the abbot of Citeaux had authority, assisted by a yearly assembly of the heads of the affiliated monasteries. Much attention was devoted to agriculture, relatively little to teaching or pastoral work. The ideals were withdrawal from the world, contemplation, and imitation of "apostolic poverty."

Not a little of the early success of the Cistercians was due to the influence of Bernard (1090–1153), the greatest religious force of his age, and, by common consent, deemed one of the chief of mediæval saints. Born of knightly ancestry in Fontaines, near Dijon, he inherited from his mother a deeply religious nature. With some thirty companions, the fruit of his powers of persuasion, he entered the monastery of Citeaux, probably in 1112. Thence he went forth in 1115 to found the Cistercian monastery of Clairvaux, abbot of which he remained, in spite of splendid offers of ecclesiastical preferment, till his death. A man of the utmost self-consecration, his prime motive was a love to Christ, which in spite of extreme monastic self-mortification, found so evangelical an expression as to win the hearty approval of Luther and Calvin. The mystic contemplation of Christ was his highest spiritual joy. It determined not merely his own type of piety, but very largely that of the age in its nobler expressions. Above all, men admired in Bernard a moral force, a consistency of character, which added weight to all that he said and did.

Bernard was far too much a man of action to be confined to the monastery. The first preacher of his age, and one of the greatest of all ages, he moved his fellows profoundly, from whatever social class they might come. He conducted a vast correspondence on the problems of the time. The interests of the church, of which he was regarded as the most eminent ornament, led to wide journeyings. In particular, the healing of the papal schism which resulted in the double choice by the cardinals in 1130 of Innocent II (1130–1143) and Anacletus II (1130–1138) was Bernard's work. His dominating part in organizing the unfortunate Second Crusade has already been considered (see p. 222). His influence with the papacy seemed but confirmed when a former monk of Clairvaux was chosen as Eugene III (1145–1153), though many things that Eugene did proved not to Bernard's liking. To him he addressed his chief literary work *"De consideratione,"* an ecclesiological treatise, critical of the political ambitions of the Papacy. Acting in defense of orthodoxy, he persuaded others, also, and secured the condemnation of Abelard (p. 241) by the synod of Sens in 1140, and its approval by the Pope. In 1145 Bernard preached, with some temporary success, to the heretics of southern France. In 1153 he died, the best-known and the most widely mourned man of his age.

Bernard's ascetic and other-worldly principles were represented, curiously, in a man whom he bitterly opposed—Arnold of Brescia (?–1155). With all his devotion to "apostolic poverty," Bernard had no essential quarrel with the hierarchical organization of his day, or hostility to its exercise of power in worldly matters. Arnold was much more radical. Born in Brescia, a student in France, he became a clergyman in his native city. Of severe austerity, he advanced the opinion that the clergy should abandon all property and worldly power. So only could they be Christ's true disciples. In the struggle between Innocent II and Anacletus II he won a large following in Brescia, but was compelled to seek refuge in France, where he became intimate with Abelard, and was joined with him in condemnation, at Bernard's instigation, by the synod of Sens (1140). Bernard secured Arnold's expulsion from France. In 1143 the Roman nobles had thrown off the temporal control of the papacy and established what they believed to be a revival of the Senate. To Rome Arnold went. He was not a political leader so much as a preacher of "apostolic poverty." In 1145 Eugene III restored Arnold to church fellowship, but by 1147, Arnold and the Romans had driven Eugene out of the city. There Arnold remained influential till the accession of the vigorous Hadrian IV

(1154–1159)—the only Englishman who has ever occupied the papal throne. Hadrian, in 1155, compelled the Romans to expel Arnold by proclaiming an interdict forbidding religious services in the city; and bargained with the new German sovereign, Frederick Barbarossa (1152–1190), for the destruction of Arnold as the price of imperial coronation. In 1155 Arnold was hanged and his body burned. Though charged with heresy, these accusations are vague and seem to have had little substance. Arnold's real offense was his attack upon the riches and temporal power of the church.

Far more radical had been a preacher in southern France, in the opening years of the twelfth century—Peter of Bruys, of whose origin or early life little is known. With a strict asceticism he combined the denial of infant baptism, the rejection of the Lord's Supper in any form, the repudiation of all ceremonies and even of church buildings, and the rejection of the cross, which should be condemned rather than honored as the instrument through which Christ had suffered. Peter also opposed prayers for the dead. Having burned crosses in St. Gilles, he was himself burned by the mob at an uncertain date, probably between 1130 and 1135. Reputed to be Peter's disciple, but hardly so to be regarded, was Henry, called "of Lausanne," once a Benedictine monk, who preached, with large following, from 1101 till his death after 1145, in western and especially southern France. Above all, a preacher of ascetic righteousness, he denied in ancient Donatist spirit the validity of sacraments administered by unworthy priests. His test of worthiness was ascetic life and apostolic poverty. By this standard he condemned the wealthy and power-seeking clergy. Arnold, Peter, and Henry have been proclaimed Protestants before the Reformation. To do so is to misunderstand them. Their conception of salvation was essentially mediæval. They carried to a radical extreme a criticism of the worldly aspects of clerical life which was widely shared and had its more conservative manifestation in the life and teachings of Bernard.

3

Antichurchly Sects. Cathari and Waldenses. The Inquisition

THE MANICHÆISM of the later Roman Empire, of which Augustine was once an adherent (see pp. 98, 161), seems never absolutely to have died out in the West. It was stimulated by the accession of Paulicians and Bogomiles (see p. 213) whom the persecuting policy of the Eastern Emperors drove from Bulgaria, and by the new intercourse with the East fostered by the Crusades. The result was a new Manichæism. Its adherents were called Cathari, as the "Pure," or Albigenses, from Albi, one of their chief seats in southern France. With the ascetic and enthusiastic impulse which caused and accompanied the Crusades, the Cathari rose to great activity. Though to be found in many parts of Europe, their chief regions were southern France, northern Italy, and northern Spain. In southern France, Bernard himself labored in vain for their conversion. With the criticism of existing churchly conditions consequent upon the disastrous failure of the Second Crusade (see p. 222), they multiplied with great rapidity. In 1167 they were able to hold a widely attended council in St. Felix de Caraman, near Toulouse; and before the end of the century they had won the support of a large section, possibly a majority, of the population of southern France and the protection of its princes. In northern Italy they were very numerous. The Cathari in Florence alone in 1228 counted nearly one-third of the inhabitants. By the year 1200 they were an exceeding peril for the Roman Church. In the movement the ascetic spirit of the age found full expression, and criticism of the wealth and power of the church saw satisfaction in complete rejection of its clergy and claims.

Like the ancient Manichæs, the Cathari were dualists. The Bogomiles and many of the Cathari of Italy held that the good God had two sons, Satanel and Christ—of whom the elder rebelled and became the leader of evil. The Cathari of France generally asserted two eternal powers, the one good, the other malign. All agreed that this visible world is the work of the evil power, in which souls, taken prisoners from the realm of the good God, are held in bondage. The greatest of sins, the original sin of Adam and Eve, is human reproduction, whereby the number of prison-houses is increased. Salvation is by repentance, asceticism, and the "consolation." This rite, like baptism in the church, works forgiveness of sins and restoration to the kingdom of the good God. It is conferred by laying on of hands by one who has received it, together with placing the Gospel of John on the head of the candidate. It is the true apostolical succession. One who has received the "consolation" becomes perfect, a *perfectus;* but lest he lose the grace, he must henceforth eschew marriage, avoid oaths, war, possession of property, and the eating of meat, milk, or eggs, since they are the product of the sin of reproduction. The "perfect," or, as they were called in France, the *bons hommes*—good men—were the real clergy of the Cathari, and there are notices of "bishops" and even of a "Pope" among them, though exactly what the gradations in authority were it is impossible to say. By a convenient belief the majority of adherents, the *credentes* or "believers," were allowed to marry, hold property, and enjoy the good things of this world, even outwardly to conform to the Roman Church, assured that, should they receive the "consolation" before death, they would be saved. Those who died unconsoled would, in the opinion of most of the Cathari, be reincarnated in human, or even animal, bodies till at last they, too, should be brought to salvation. The "believers" seem not always to have been fully initiated into the tenets of the system.

The Cathari made great use of Scripture, which they translated and in which they claimed to find their teachings. Some rejected the Old Testament entirely as the work of the evil power, others accepted the Psalms and the prophets. All believed the New Testament to come from the good God. Since all things material are of evil, Christ could not have had a real body or died a real death. They therefore rejected the cross. The sacraments, with their material elements, were evil. The good God is dishonored by the erection of churches built and ornamented with material creations of the evil power. The services of the Cathari were simple. The Scriptures were read, especially the Gospel of John, as the most spiritual of all. A sermon was preached. The "believers" then knelt and adored the "perfect" as those indwelt with the divine Spirit. The "perfect," in turn, gave their blessing. Only the Lord's Prayer was used in the service. A common meal, at which the bread was consecrated, was held in many places once a month, as a kind of Lord's Supper. The student of the movement will find in it extremely interesting survivals of ancient Christian rites and ceremonies, orthodox and heretical. In general, the "perfect" seem to have been men and women of uprightness, moral earnestness, and courageous steadfastness in persecution. Of their effectiveness in gaining the allegiance of thousands, especially from the humbler walks of life, there can be no question.

Unlike the Cathari, the Waldenses originated in no conscious hostility to the church and, had they been treated with skill, would probably never have separated from it. In 1176 Valdez, or Waldo, a rich merchant of Lyons, impressed by the song of a wandering minstrel recounting the sacrifices of St. Alexis, asked a master of theology "the best way to God." The clergyman quoted that golden text of monasticism: "If thou wouldst be perfect, go, sell that thou hast, and give to the poor, and thou shalt have treasure in heaven; and come, follow Me." [1] Valdez put this counsel literally into practice. Providing modestly for his wife and daughters, he gave the rest of his means to the poor. He determined to fulfil the directions of Christ to the Apostles [2] absolutely. He would wear the raiment there designated. He would live by what was given him. To know his duty better he procured a translation of the New Testament. His action made a deep impression on his friends. Here, they thought, was true "apostolic poverty." By 1177 he was joined by others, men and women, and the little company undertook to carry further Christ's directions by preaching repentance. They called themselves the "Poor in Spirit." [3] They now appealed to the Third Lateran Council, in 1179, for permission to preach. The council did not deem them heretical. It thought them ignorant laymen, and Pope Alexander III (1159–1181) refused consent. This led to

[1] *Matt.* 19:21.   [2] *Matt.* 10.   [3] Probably from *Matt.* 5:3.

decisive action. Valdez, who appears in what is known of his later history as determined, not to say obstinate, felt that this refusal was the voice of man against that of God. He and his associates continued preaching. As disobedient, they were, therefore, excommunicated, in 1184, by Pope Lucius III (1181–1185).

These unwise acts of the papacy not only forced the Waldenses out of the church against their will, they brought to them a considerable accession. The Humiliati were a company of lowly folk who had associated themselves for a common life of penance in and about Milan. These, too, were forbidden to hold separate meetings, or to preach, by Alexander III, and were excommunicated in 1184 for disobedience. A very considerable part of these Lombard Humiliati now joined the Waldenses, and came under the control of Valdez. The early characteristics of the Waldenses now rapidly developed. Chief of all was the principle that the Bible, and especially the New Testament, is the sole rule of belief and life. Yet they read it through thoroughly mediæval spectacles. It was to them a book of law—of minute prescriptions, to be followed to the letter. Large portions were learned by heart. In accordance with what they believed to be its teachings they went about, two by two, preaching, clad in a simple woollen robe, barefooted or wearing sandals, living wholly on the gifts of their hearers, fasting on Mondays, Wednesdays, and Fridays, rejecting oaths and all shedding of blood, and using no prayers but the Lord's and a form of grace at table. They heard confessions, observed the Lord's Supper together, and ordained their members as a ministry. Unbiblical, they rejected masses and prayers for the dead, and denied purgatory. They held the sacraments invalid if dispensed by unworthy priests. They believed prayer in secret more effective than in church. They defended lay preaching by men and women. They had bishops, priests, and deacons, and a head, or rector, of the society. The first was Valdez himself; later appointment was by election. Besides this inner circle, the society proper, they soon developed a body of sympathizers, "friends" or "believers," from whom the society was recruited, but who remained outwardly in communion with the Roman Church. Most of this development seems to have been immediately subsequent to their excommunication in 1184. Much of it was due to Catharite example, yet they opposed the Cathari and justly regarded themselves as widely different.

Certain conflicts of opinion, and a feeling that the government of Valdez was arbitrary, led to the secession of the Lombard branch by 1210—a breach that attempts at reunion in 1218, after Valdez's death, failed to heal. The two bodies remained estranged. The able Pope, Innocent III (1198–1216), improved these disputes by countenancing in 1208 the organization of *pauperes catholici,* which allowed many of the practices of the Waldenses under strict churchly oversight. Considerable numbers were thus won back to the church. Nevertheless, the Waldensian body spread. Waldenses were to be found in northern Spain, in Austria and Germany, as well as in their original homes. They were gradually repressed, till their chief seat came to be the Alpine valleys southwest of Turin, where they are still to be found. At the Reformation they readily accepted its principles, and became fully Protestant. Under modern religious freedom they are laboring with success in many parts of Italy. Their story is one of heroic endurance of persecution—a most honorable history—and they are the only mediæval sect which still survives, though with wide modification of their original ideals and methods.

By the opening of the thirteenth century the situation of the Roman Church in southern France, northern Italy, and northern Spain was dubious. Missionary efforts to convert Cathari and Waldenses had largely failed. It was felt that sharper measures were needed. A crusade was ordered as early as 1181 by Pope Alexander III (1159–1181), against the viscount of Béziers as a supporter of the Cathari, but it accomplished little. Under Innocent III (1198–1216) the storm broke. After having vainly tried missionary efforts, the murder of the papal legate, Peter of Castelnau, in 1208, induced Innocent to proclaim a crusade against the heretics of southern France. The attack was agreeable to the French monarchy, which had found the nobles of the region too independent vassals. These combined interests of Pope and King led to twenty years of destructive warfare (1209–1229), in which the power of the southern nobles was shattered and cities and provinces devastated. The defenders of the Cathari were rendered impotent or compelled to join in their extermination.

The termination of the struggle was followed by a synod of great importance held in Toulouse in 1229. The Cathari and Waldenses had made much use of the Bible. The synod, therefore, forbad the laity to possess the Scriptures, except the psalter and such portions as are contained in the breviary, and especially denounced all translations. The decree was, indeed, local, but similar considerations led to like prohibitions in Spain and elsewhere. No universal denial of Bible reading by the laity was issued during the Middle Ages.

A second act of significance which marked the synod of Toulouse was the beginning of a systematic inquisition. The question of the punishment of heretics had been undetermined in the earlier Middle Ages. There had been a good many instances of death, generally by fire, at the hands of rulers, churchmen, or the mob, but ecclesiastics of high standing had opposed this. The identification of the Cathari with the Manichæans, against whom the later Roman Emperors had denounced the death penalty, gave such punishment the sanction of Roman law. Peter II of Aragon, in 1197, ordered the execution of heretics by fire. Pope Innocent III (1198–1216) held that heresy, as treason against God, was of even greater heinousness than treason against a King. The investigation of heresy was not as yet systematized. That task the synod of Toulouse undertook. Its work was speedily perfected by Pope Gregory IX

(1227–1241), who intrusted the discovery of heresy to inquisitors chosen chiefly from the Dominican order—a body formed with very different aims. As speedily developed, the inquisition became a most formidable organ. Its proceedings were secret, the names of his accusers were not given to the prisoner, who, by a bull of Innocent IV, in 1252, was liable to torture. The confiscation of the convict's property was one of its most odious and economically destructive features, and, as these spoils were shared by the lay authorities, this feature undoubtedly kept the fires of persecution burning where otherwise they would have died out. Yet, thanks to the inquisition, and other more praiseworthy means shortly to be described, the Cathari were utterly rooted out in the course of a little more than a century, and the Waldenses greatly repressed. This earlier success accounts, in large measure, for the tenacity with which the Roman Church clung to the inquisition in the Reformation age.

4

The Dominicans and Franciscans

THE CATHARI AND WALDENSES profoundly affected the mediæval church. Out of an attempt to meet them by preachers of equal devotion, asceticism, and zeal, and of greater learning, grew the order of the Dominicans. In the same atmosphere of "apostolic poverty" and literal fulfilment of the commands of Christ in which the Waldenses flourished, the Franciscans had their birth. In these two orders mediæval monasticism had its noblest exemplification. In Francis of Assisi mediæval piety had its highest and most inspiring representative.

Dominic was a native of Calaroga, in Castile, and was born in 1170. A brilliant student in Palencia, and a youth of deep religious spirit, he became a canon of Osma, about ninety miles northeast of Madrid. From 1201 he enjoyed the friendship of a kindred spirit, Diego of Acevedo, the bishop of Osma. The two journeyed on political business in 1203 through southern France, where the Cathari were then in the height of their power. There they found the Roman missionaries treated with contempt. At a meeting with these missionary leaders in Montpellier, in 1204, Diego urged a thorough reform of method. Only by missionaries as self-denying, as studious of "apostolic poverty," and as eager to preach as the "perfect" of the Cathari, could these wanderers be won back to the Roman fold. Moved by the bishop's exhortation, the missionaries endeavored to put his advice into practice. A nunnery, chiefly for converted Catharite women, was established in 1206, in Prouille, not far from Toulouse. Thus far Diego seems to have been the leader, but he had to return to his diocese, and died in 1206. Thenceforward Dominic carried on the work. The storm of the great anti-Cathari war made it most discouraging. Dominic was tempted by the offer of bishoprics to leave so thankless a task, but he persisted. He would take the Apostle Paul as his model. He would win the people by preaching. Gradually he gathered like-minded men about him. In 1215 friends presented them a house in Toulouse. The same year Dominic visited the Fourth Lateran Council in Rome, seeking papal approval for a new order. It was refused, though his efforts were commended, and he now adopted the so-called "Rule" of St. Augustine. Recognition amounting to the practical establishment of the order was, however, obtained from Pope Honorius III (1216–1227) in 1216.

Even in 1217, when the new association numbered but a few, Dominic determined to send his preachers widely. With a view to influencing future leaders, he directed them first to the great centers of education, Paris, Rome, and Bologna. The order grew with amazing rapidity. Its first general chapter was held in Bologna in 1220. Here, under the influence of Franciscan example, it adopted the principle of mendicancy—the members should beg even their daily food. By this chapter, or that of the following year, the constitution of the "Order of Preachers," or Dominicans, as they were popularly called, was developed. At the head was a "master-general," chosen by the general chapter, originally for life. The field was divided into "provinces," each in charge of a "provincial prior," elected for a four-year term by the provincial chapter. Each monastery chose a "prior," also for four years. The general chapter included the "master-general," the "provincial priors," and an elected delegate from each province. The system was one, therefore, that combined ingeniously authority and representative government. It embraced monasteries for men, and nunneries for women, though the latter were not to preach, but ultimately developed large teaching activities.

Dominic died in 1221. The order then numbered sixty houses, divided among the eight provinces of Provence, Toulouse, France, Lombardy, Rome, Spain, Germany, and England, and for years thereafter it increased rapidly. Always zealous for learning, it emphasized preaching and teaching, sought work especially in university towns, and soon became widely represented on the university faculties. Albertus Magnus and Thomas Aquinas, the theologians; Eckhart and Tauler, the mystics; Savonarola, the reformer, are but a few of the great names that adorn the catalogue of Dominicans. Their learning led to their employment as inquisitors—a use that formed no part of Dominic's ideal. The legends which represent him as an inquisitor are baseless. He would win men, as did his example, Paul, by preaching. To achieve that result he would undergo whatever sacrifice or asceticism that would make his preachers acceptable to those whom they sought. Yet it is evident that lowly and self-sacrificing as were Dominic's aims, the high intellectualism of his order tended to give it a relatively aristocratic flavor. It represented, however, an emphasis on work for others, such as had appeared in the Waldenses. Its ideal was not contemplation apart from the world, but access to men in their needs.

Great as was the honor paid to Dominic and the Dominicans, it was exceeded by the popular homage given to the Franciscans, and especially to their founder. The austere preacher, of blameless youth, planning how he may best reach men, and adopting poverty as a means to that end, is not so winsome a figure as that of the gay, careless young man who sacrifices all for Christ and his fellows, and adopts poverty not as a recommendation of his message, but as the only means of being like his Master. In Francis of Assisi is to be seen not merely the greatest of mediæval saints, but one who, through his absolute sincerity of desire to imitate Christ in all things humanly possible, belongs to all ages and to the church universal.

Giovanni Bernadone was born in 1182, the son of a cloth merchant of Assisi, in central Italy. To the boy the nickname Francesco—Francis—was given, and soon supplanted that bestowed on him in baptism. His father, a serious man of business, was little pleased to see the son leading in the mischief and revelry of his young companions. A year's experiences as a prisoner of war in Perugia, following a defeat in which he had fought on the side of the common people of Assisi, against the nobles, wrought no change in his life. A serious illness began to develop another side of his character. He joined a military expedition to Apulia, but withdrew, for what reason is not evident. His conversion was a gradual process. "When I was yet in my sins it did seem to me too bitter to look upon the lepers, but the Lord Himself did lead me among them, and I had compassion upon them. When I left them, that which had seemed to me bitter had become sweet and easy." [1] This note of Christlike compassion was that to which Francis's renewed nature first responded. On a pilgrimage to Rome he thought he heard the divine command to restore the fallen house of God. Taking it literally, he sold cloth from his father's warehouse to rebuild the ruined church of St. Damian, near Assisi. Francis's father, thoroughly disgusted with his unbusinesslike ways, now took him before the bishop to be disinherited; but Francis declared that he had henceforth no father but the Father in heaven. This event was probably in 1206 or 1207.

For the next two years Francis wandered in and about Assisi, aiding the unfortunate, and restoring churches, of which his favorite was the Portiuncula, in the plain outside the town. There, on February 24, 1208, the

---

[1] *Testament of Francis.* Highly illuminative as to his spirit and purposes. Robinson, *Readings* 1:392–395.

words of Christ to the Apostles,[2] read in the service, came to him, as they had to Valdez, as a trumpet-call to action. He would preach repentance and the kingdom of God, without money, in the plainest of garments, eating what might be set before him. He would imitate Christ and obey Christ's commands, in absolute poverty, in Christ-like love, and in humbled deference to the priests as His representatives. "The Most High Himself revealed to me that I ought to live according to the model of the holy Gospel." Like-minded associates gathered about him. For them he drafted a "Rule," composed of little besides selections from Christ's commands, and with it, accompanied by eleven or twelve companions, he applied to Pope Innocent III for approval. It was practically the same request that Valdez had preferred in vain in 1179. But Innocent was now trying to win some of the Waldenses for the church, and Francis was not refused. The associates now called themselves the Penitents of Assisi, a name for which, by 1216, Francis had substituted that of the Minor, or Humbler, Brethren, by which they were henceforth to be known.

Francis' association was a union of imitators of Christ, bound together by love and practising the utmost poverty, since only thus, he believed, could the world be denied and Christ really followed. Two by two, they went about preaching repentance, singing much, aiding the peasants in their work, caring for the lepers and outcasts. "Let those who know no trade learn one, but not for the purpose of receiving the price of their toil, but for their good example and to flee idleness. And when we are not given the price of our work, let us resort to the table of the Lord, begging our bread from door to door."[3] Soon wide-reaching missionary plans were formed, which the rapid growth of the association made possible of attempting. Francis himself, prevented by illness from reaching the Mohammedans through Spain, went to Egypt in 1219, in the wake of a crusading expedition, and actually preached before the Sultan.

Francis himself was little of an organizer. The free association was increasing enormously. What were adequate rules for a handful of like-minded brethren were soon insufficient for a body numbering several thousands. Change would have come in any event. It was hastened, however, by the organizing talents of Cardinal Ugolino of Ostia, the later Pope Gregory IX (1227–1241), who had befriended Francis, and whose appointment Francis secured as "protector" of the society. Under Ugolino's influence, and that of Brother Elias of Cortona, the transformation of the association into a full monastic order went rapidly forward. From the time of Francis' absence in Egypt and Syria in 1219 and 1220, his real leadership ceased. A new rule was adopted in 1221, and a third in 1223. In the latter, emphasis was no longer laid on preaching, and begging was established as the normal, not the ex-

[2] *Matt.* 10:7–14.   [3] *Testament.*

ceptional, practice. Already, in 1219, provinces had been established, each in charge of a "minister." Papal directions, in 1220, had prescribed obedience to the order's officers, established a novitiate, a fixed costume, and irrevocable vows.

Probably most of these changes were inevitable. They were unquestionably a grief to Francis, though whether so deeply as has often been contended is doubtful. He was always deferential to ecclesiastical authority, and seems to have regarded these modifications more with regret than with actual opposition. He withdrew increasingly from the world. He was much in prayer and singing. His love of nature, in which he was far in advance of his age, was never more manifest. Feeble in body, he longed to be present with Christ. He bore what men believed to be the reproduction of Christ's wounds. How they may have been received is an unsolved, and perhaps insoluble, problem. On October 3, 1226, he died in the church of Portiuncula. Two years later he was proclaimed a saint by Pope Gregory IX. Few men in Christian history have more richly deserved the title.

In organization, by Francis' death, the Franciscans were like the Dominicans. At the head stood a "minister general" chosen for twelve years. Over each "province" was a "provincial minister," and over each group a "custos," for, unlike the Dominicans, the Franciscans did not at first possess houses. As with the Dominicans, provincial and general chapters were held by which officers were chosen and legislation achieved. Like the Dominicans, also, the Franciscans had almost from the first, their feminine branch —the so-called "second order." That of the Franciscans was instituted by Francis himself, in 1212, through his friend and disciple, Clara Sciffi of Assisi (1194–1253). The growth of the Franciscans was extremely rapid, and though they soon counted many distinguished scholars, they were always more the order of the poor than the Dominicans.

The Dominicans and Franciscans, known respectively as Black Friars and Gray Friars in England, soon exercised an almost unbounded popular influence. Unlike the older orders, they labored primarily in the cities, chiefly because it was only there that mendicancy proved practicable. There can be no doubt that their work resulted in a great strengthening of religion among the laity. At the same time they lessened the influence of the bishops and ordinary clergy, since they were privileged to preach and absolve anywhere. They thus strengthened the power of the papacy by diminishing that of the ordinary clergy. One chief influence upon the laity was the development of the "Tertiaries" or "third orders"—a phenomenon which first appeared in connection with the Franciscans, though the tradition which connects it with Francis himself is probably baseless. The "third order" permitted men and women, still engaged in ordinary occupations, to live a semi-monastic life of fasting, prayer, worship, and benevolence. A conspicuous illustration is St. Elizabeth of Thuringia (1207–1231). Ultimately all the mendicant orders developed Tertiaries. As time went on the system tended to become an almost complete monasticism, from which the married were excluded. It must be regarded as a very successful attempt to meet the religious ideals of an age which regarded the monastic as the true Christian life.

The piety of the twelfth and thirteenth centuries found many expressions other than through the Dominicans and Franciscans. One important manifestation, especially in the Netherlands, Germany, and France, was through the Beguines—associations of women living in semi-monastic fashion, but not bound by irrevocable vows. They seem to have received their name from those hostile to them in memory of the preacher of Liège, Lambert le Bègue, who was regarded as having been a heretic; and the Beguine movement undoubtedly often sheltered antichurchly sympathizers. It was in the main orthodox, however, and spread widely, existing in the Netherlands to the present. Its loose organization made effective discipline difficult, and, in general, its course was one of deterioration. A parallel, though less popular, system of men's associations was that of the Beghards.

The divisions in the Franciscan order, which had appeared in Francis's lifetime between those who would emphasize a simple life of Christ-like poverty and those who valued numbers, power, and influence, were but intensified with his death. The stricter party found a leader in Brother Leo, the looser in Elias of Cortona. The papal policy favored the looser, since ecclesiastical politics would be advanced by the growth and consolidation of the order along the lines of earlier monasticism. The quarrel became increasingly embittered. The use of gifts and buildings was secured by the laxer party on the claim that they were held not by the order itself but by "friends." Pope Innocent IV (1243–1254), in 1245, allowed such use, with the reservation that it was the property of the Roman Church, not of the order. These tendencies the stricter party vigorously opposed. But that party itself fell into dubious orthodoxy. Joachim of Floris, in extreme southern Italy (1145?–1202), a Cistercian abbot who had been reputed a prophet, had divided the history of the world into three ages, those of the Father, the Son, and the Holy Spirit. That of the Spirit was to come in full power in 1260. It was to be an age of men who understood "the eternal Gospel" [4]— not a new Gospel, but the old, spiritually interpreted. Its form of life was to be monastic. In the sixth decade of the thirteenth century many of the stricter Franciscans adopted these views and were persecuted not merely by the laxer element, but by the moderates, who obtained leadership when Bonaventura was chosen general minister in 1257. These stricter friars of prophetic faith were nicknamed "Spirituals." Under Pope John XXII (1316–1334) some of the party were burned by the inquisition in 1318. During his papacy a further quarrel arose as to whether the poverty of Christ and the Apostles was complete. John XXII decided in 1322 in favor of the laxer view, and imprisoned the great English schoolman, William of Occam, and other asserters of Christ's absolute poverty. The quarrel was irreconcilable,

[4] Rev. 14:6.

and finally Pope Leo X (1513–1521) formally recognized the division of the Franciscans in 1517 into "Observant," or strict, and "Conventual," or loose sections, each with its distinct officers and general chapters.

5

Early Scholasticism

*T*HE EDUCATIONAL WORK of cathedral and monastic schools has already been noted in connection with Bede, Alcuin, and Hrabanus Maurus (see pp. 183, 188, 192). It was long simply imitative and reproductive of the teaching of the Church Fathers, especially of Augustine and Gregory the Great. Save in the case of John Scotus Erigena (see p. 192), it showed little that was original. Schools, however, increased, especially in France in the eleventh century, and with their multiplication came an application of the methods of logic, or of dialectics, to the discussion of theological problems which resulted in fresh and fertile intellectual development. Since it originated in the schools, the movement was known as "Scholasticism." Most of the knowledge of dialectic method was at first derived from scanty translations of portions of Aristotle's writings and of Porphyry's *Isagoge,* both the work of Boethius (480?–524).

The development of Scholasticism was inaugurated and accompanied by a discussion as to the nature of "universals"—that is as to the existence of genera and species—a debate occasioned by Porphyry's *Isagoge.* Three positions might be taken. The extreme "realists," following Platonic influences (see p. 5), asserted that universals existed apart from and antecedent to the individual objects—*ante rem, i. e.,* the genus man was anterior to and determinative of the individual man. The moderate "realists," under the guidance of Aristotle (see p. 5), taught that universals existed only in connection with individual objects—*in re.* The "nominalists," following Stoic precedent, held that universals were only abstract names for the resemblances of individuals, and had no other existence than in thought—*post rem.* The only real existence for them was the individual object. This quarrel between "realism" and "nominalism" continued throughout the scholastic period and profoundly influenced its theological conclusions.

The first considerable scholastic controversy was a renewal of the dispute once held between Paschasius Radbertus and Ratramnus as to the nature of Christ's presence in the Lord's Supper (see p. 192). Berengar

(?–1088), head of the cathedral school in Tours about 1049, attacked the prevalent conception that the elements are changed as to substance into the actual body and blood of Christ. His position was similar to that of Ratramnus. He denied a change of the substances of bread and wine, but argued that by the consecration something invisible but real is added to the natural elements, namely the whole heavenly Christ. Only believers receive him at communion. Berengar was immediately opposed by Lanfranc (?–1089), then prior of the monastery of Bec in Normandy, and to be William the Conqueror's celebrated archbishop of Canterbury. Synods at Rome (1050) and Tours (1054) condemned Berengar's views. In 1059, Cardinal Humbert compelled him to sign a statement to the effect that at the communion service the priest touches the body and blood of Christ and that the communicants bite into the Lord's body with their teeth. About ten years later he reasserted his opinions, but once more withdrew them in 1079. The discussion showed that the view soon to be known as "transubstantiation" had become the dominant opinion in Latin Christendom. It was to have full approval at the Fourth Lateran Council in 1215, where it was proclaimed a dogma.

Berengar's dialectic methods were employed, with very dissimilar results, by Anselm, who has often been called the Father of the Schoolmen. Born in Aosta in northern Italy about 1033, Anselm became a monk under Lanfranc in Bec, whom he succeeded as prior. Under him the school of Bec attained great distinction. In 1093 he became archbishop of Canterbury—having a stormy episcopate by reason of his Hildebrandian principles. He died in office in 1109. As a theologian, Anselm was an extreme realist, and was moreover convinced of the full capacity of a proper dialectic to prove the truths of theology. His famous ontological demonstration of the existence of God is at once "realistic" and Neo-Platonic. As set forth in his *Proslogium,* God is the greatest of all beings. He must exist in reality as well as in thought, for if He existed in thought only, a yet greater being, existing in reality as well as in thought, could be conceived; which is impossible. This proof, which aroused the opposition of Gaunilo, a monk of Marmoutiers, in Anselm's lifetime, seems to most a play on words, though its permanent validity has not lacked defenders.

Anselm next directed his attention to Roscelin, a canon of Compiègne, who, under nominalistic influence, had asserted that either the Father, Son, and Spirit are identical or are three Gods. At a synod held in Soissons in 1092 Roscelin was compelled to abjure tritheism. Anselm now declared that nominalism was essentially heretical, and that view was the prevalent one for the next two centuries.

Anselm's most influential contribution to theology was his discussion of the atonement in his *Cur Deus homo,* the ablest treatment that had yet appeared. Anselm totally rejected any thought, such as the early church had entertained, of a ransom paid to the devil. Man, by sin, has done dishonor to

God. His debt is to God alone. God's nature demands "satisfaction." Man, who owes obedience at all times, has nothing wherewith to make good past disobedience. Yet, if satisfaction is to be made at all, it can be rendered only by one who shares human nature, who is Himself man, and yet as God has something of infinite value to offer. Such a being is the God-man. Not only is His sacrifice a satisfaction, it deserves a reward. That reward is the eternal blessedness of His brethren. Anselm's widely influential theory rests ultimately on the "realistic" conviction that there is such an objective existence as humanity which Christ could assume.

Anselm was of devout spirit, fully convinced that dialectic explanation could but buttress the doctrines of the church. "I believe, that I may understand," is a motto that expresses his attitude. The same high realist position was maintained by William of Champeaux (1070?–1121), who brought the school of St. Victor, near Paris, into great repute, and died as bishop of Chalons.

The ablest use of the dialectic method in the twelfth century was made by Abelard (1079–1142), a man of irritating method, vanity, and critical spirit, but by no means of irreligion. Born in Pallet, in Brittany, he studied under Roscelin and William of Champeaux, both of whom he opposed and undoubtedly far surpassed in ability. On the vexed question of the universals he took a position intermediate between the nominalism of one teacher and the realism of the other. Only individuals exist, but genera and species are more than names. Hence he is usually called a "conceptualist," though he gave universals greater value than mere mental conceptions. His view is well summarized in the formula: *universale est in intellectu cum fundamento in re.*

Abelard's life was stormy. By the age of twenty-two he was teaching with great following in Melun, near Paris. By 1115 he was a canon of Notre Dame, with a following in Paris such as no lecturer had yet enjoyed. He fell in love with Heloise—the niece of his fellow canon, Fulbert—a woman of singular devotion of nature. With her he entered into a secret marriage. The enraged uncle, believing his niece deceived, revenged himself by having Abelard emasculated, and thus barred from clerical advancement. Abelard now became a monk. To teach was his breath of life, however, and he soon resumed lecturing. A reply to Roscelin's tritheism leaned so far in the other direction that his enemies charged him with Sabellianism, and his views were condemned at a synod in Soissons in 1121. His criticisms of the traditional career of St. Denis (Dionysius) made the monastery of St. Denis an uncomfortable place of abode, and he now sought a hermit's life. Students gathered about him and founded a little settlement which he called the Paraclete. His criticisms had aroused, however, the hostility of that most powerful religious leader of the age, the orthodox traditionalist Bernard, and he now sought refuge as abbot of the rough monastery in Rhuys, in remote Brittany. Yet he left this retreat to lecture for a while in Paris, and engaged in a correspondence with Heloise, who had become the head of a little nunnery at the Paraclete, which is the most interesting record of affection—especially on the part of Heloise—which the Middle Ages has preserved. Bernard procured his condemnation at the synod of Sens in 1140, and the rejection of his appeal by Pope Innocent II. Abelard was now a broken man. He made submission and found a friend in Peter, the abbot of Cluny. In 1142 he died in one of the monasteries under Cluny jurisdiction.

Abelard's spirit was essentially critical. Without rejecting the Fathers or the creeds, he held that all should be subjected to philosophical examination, and not lightly believed. His work, *Sic et non*—*Yes and No*—setting against each other contrary passages from the Fathers on the great doctrines, without attempt at harmony or explanation, might well arouse a feeling that he was a sower of doubts. His doctrine of the Trinity was almost Sabellian. His teaching that man has inherited not guilt but punishment from Adam was contrary to the Augustinian tradition. His ethical theory that good and evil inhere in the intention rather than in the act, disagreed with current feeling. His belief that the philosophers of antiquity were sharers of divine revelation, however consonant with ancient Christian opinion, was not that of his age. Nor was Abelard less individual, though decidedly modern, in his conception of the atonement. Like Anselm, he rejected all ransom to the devil; but he repudiated Anselm's doctrine of satisfaction no less energetically. In Abelard's view the incarnation and death of Christ are the highest expression of God's love to men, the effect of which is to awaken love in us. Abelard, though open to much criticism from the standpoint of his age, was a profoundly stimulating spirit. His direct followers were few, but his indirect influence was great, and the impulse given by him to the dialectic method of theological inquiry far-reaching.

A combination of a moderate use of the dialectic method with intense Neo-Platonic mysticism is to be seen in the work of Hugo of St. Victor (1097–1141). A German by birth, his life was uneventful. About 1115 he entered the monastery of St. Victor, near Paris, where he rose to be head of its school. A quiet, modest man, of profound learning and piety, his influence was remarkable. He enjoyed the intimate friendship of Bernard. Probably his most significant works were his commentary on the *Celestial Hierarchy* of Pseudo-Dionysius the Areopagite (see p. 156) and his treatise *On the Mysteries of the Faith* (*De sacramentis Christianae fidei*). In true mystic fashion he pictured spiritual progress as in three stages—cogitation, the formation of sense-concepts; meditation, their intellectual investigation; contemplation, the intuitive penetration into their inner meaning. This last attainment is the true mystical vision of God, and the comprehension of all things in Him.

No original genius, like Abelard and Hugo, but a man of great intellectual service to his own age, and held in honor till the Reformation, was Peter Lombard, "the Master of the Sentences" (?–1160). Born in humble circumstances in northern Italy, Peter studied in Bologna and Paris, in part at least aided by the generosity of Bernard. In Paris he became ultimately teacher of theology in the school of Notre Dame, and near the close of his life, in 1159, bishop of the Parisian see. Whether he was ever a pupil of Abelard is uncertain; but he was evidently greatly influenced by Abelard's works. Under Hugo of St. Victor he certainly studied, and owed that teacher much. Between 1147 and 1150 he wrote the work on which his fame rests —the *Four Books of Sentences.* After the well-accustomed fashion, he gathered citations from the creeds and the Fathers on the several Christian doctrines. What was fresh was that he proceeded to explain and interpret them by the dialectic method, with great moderation and good sense, and with constant reference to the opinions of his contemporaries. He showed the influence of Abelard constantly, though critical of that thinker's extremer positions. He was even more indebted to Hugo of St. Victor. Under the four divisions, God, Created Beings, Salvation, Sacraments and the Last Things, he discussed the whole round of theology. The result was a handbook which so fully met the needs of the age that it remained till the Reformation the main basis of theological instruction.

With the middle of the twelfth century the first period of Scholasticism was over. The schools continued in increasing activity, but no creative geniuses appeared. The last half of the century was distinguished, however, by the introduction to the West, which had thus far had little of Aristotle, of the greater part of his works and of much Greek philosophy besides, by the Jews of Spain and southern France, who, in turn, derived them from the Arabs. The Latin conquest of Constantinople, in 1204 (see p. 223), led ultimately to direct translations from the originals. The result was to be a new and greater outburst of scholastic activity in the thirteenth century.

6

The Universities

CATHEDRAL and monastic schools were never more flourishing than in the twelfth century. Teachers were multiplying and gathering about them students. Anselm, Abelard, William of Champeaux, Hugo of St. Victor, and Peter Lombard were simply the most eminent of a host. Students flocked to them in large numbers from all parts of Europe. Paris and Oxford were famed for theology, Bologna for church and civil law, Salerno for medicine.

Under these circumstances the universities developed in a manner which it is difficult exactly to date. The change which they implied was not the establishment of teaching where none had been before, but the association of students and teachers into a collective body, after the fashion of a trade guild, primarily for protection and good order, but also for more efficient management and the regulation of admission to the teaching profession. Hence the name "universitas scholarium," *i. e.,* university of scholars, both students and teachers. The beginnings of university organization—which must be distinguished from the commencement of teaching—may be placed about the year 1200.

By the close of the twelfth century there were in Bologna two "universities," or mutual protective associations of students. The organization in Paris became normal, however, for northern Europe. Its earliest rules date from about 1208, and its recognition as a legal corporation from a letter of Pope Innocent III of about 1211. In Paris there was a single "university," originally formed by the union of the cathedral school and the more private schools of the city, and divided for instruction into four faculties—one preparatory, that of the "arts," in which the *trivium* (grammar, rhetoric, and dialectics or logic) and the *quadrivium* (astronomy, arithmetic, geometry, and music) were taught; and the three higher faculties of theology, canon law, and medicine. Over each faculty a dean presided. Besides this educational organization students and professors were also grouped, for mutual aid, in "nations," each headed by a proctor. These varied in number in the several institutions. In Paris they were four—the French, the Picards, the Normans, and the English.

Teaching was principally by lecture (*lectura*) and by constant debate (*disputatio*), a method which, whatever its shortcomings, rendered the student ready master of his knowledge, and brought talent to light. The first degree, that of bachelor, was similar to an admission to apprenticeship in a guild. The second degree, that of master or doctor, resembling the master workman in a guild, carried with it full authority to teach in the institution where it was conferred, and soon, for the graduates of the larger universities, to teach anywhere. The use of Latin as the sole language of the classroom made possible the assembly of students from all parts of Europe, and they flocked to the more famous universities in immense numbers.

The needs of these students, many of whom were of extreme poverty, early aroused the interest of benefactors. One of the most influential and oldest foundations thus established was that formed in Paris by Robert de Sorbon (1201–1274) in 1252. It provided a home and special teaching for poor students, under the guidance of "fellows" of the house. Such establishments, soon known as "colleges," rapidly multiplied, and gave shelter to the great majority of students, rich and poor. The system still survives in the English universities. So prominently was the Sorbonne identified with theological instruction that its name came to be popularly, though erroneously, attached to the faculty of theology in Paris. That university ranked till the Reformation as the leader of Europe, especially in the theological studies.

Universities, many of which were short-lived, sprang up with great rapidity. In general, they were regarded as ecclesiastical—authorization by the Pope being almost essential. The most conspicuous early lay approval was that of Naples, in 1225, by the Emperor Frederick II.

7

High Scholasticism and Its Theology

THE RECOVERY of the whole of Aristotle, the rise of the universities, and the devotion of the mendicant orders to learning, ushered in a new period of Scholasticism in the thirteenth century, and marked the highest intellectual achievement of the Middle Ages. The movement toward this "modern theology" was not without much opposition, especially from traditionalists and adherents to the Augustinian Neo-Platonic development. Aristotle met much hostility. A series of great thinkers, all from the mendicant orders, made his victory secure. Yet even they, while relying primarily on Aristotle, made much use of Plato as reflected in Augustine and the Pseudo-Dionysius (see pp. 156, 163).

To Alexander of Hales (?–1245), an Englishman and ultimately a Franciscan, who taught in Paris, was due the treatment of theology in the light of the whole of Aristotle. Yet to him the Scripture is the only final truth. With this new period of Scholasticism a broader range of intellectual interest is apparent than in the earlier, though the old problem between realism and nominalism continued its pre-eminence. Alexander was a moderate realist. Universals exist *ante rem* in the mind of God, *in re* in the things themselves, and *post rem* in our understanding. In this he was followed by Albertus Magnus and Aquinas.

Albertus Magnus (1193?–1280), a German and a Dominican, studied in Padua, and taught in many places in Germany, but principally in Cologne. He served as provincial prior for his order, and was, for a few years, bishop of Regensburg. The most learned man of his age, his knowledge of science was really remarkable. His acquaintance not merely with Aristotle, but with the comments of Arabian scholars, was profounder than that of Alexander of

Hales. He was, however, a great compiler and commentator rather than an original theological genius. That which he taught was brought to far clearer expression by his pupil, Thomas Aquinas.

Thomas Aquinas (1225–1274) was a son of Landulf, count of Aquino, a small town about half-way between Rome and Naples. Connected with the German imperial house of Hohenstaufen and with that of Tancred, the Norman Crusader, it was against the wishes of his parents that Thomas entered the Dominican order in 1243. His spiritual superiors were aware of his promise, and sent him to Cologne to study under Albertus Magnus, who soon took his pupil to Paris. On receiving the degree of bachelor of divinity, Thomas returned to Cologne in 1248, and now taught as subordinate to Albertus Magnus. These were years of rapid intellectual growth. Entrance into the Paris faculty was long refused him on account of jealousy of the mendicant orders, but in 1257 he was given full standing there. From 1261 for some years he taught in Italy, then once more in Paris, and finally, from 1272, in Naples. He died, on his way to the Council of Lyons, in 1274 in the Cistercian monastery Fossanuova near Terracina. In these crowded years of teaching Thomas was constantly consulted on important civil and ecclesiastical questions, and was active in preaching; yet his pen was busy with results as voluminous as they were important. His great *Summa Theologiæ* was begun about 1265, and not fully completed at his death. Personally he was a simple, deeply religious, prayerful man. Intellectually his work was marked by a clarity, a logical consistency, and a breadth of presentation that places him among the few great teachers of the church. In the Roman communion his influence has never ceased. By declaration of Pope Leo XIII (1878–1903), in 1879, his work is the basis of present theological instruction.

Closely associated with Aquinas in friendship and for a time in teaching activities in the University of Paris, was John Fidanza (1221–1274), generally known as Bonaventura. Born in Bagnorea, in the States of the Church, he entered the Franciscan order in 1238, rising to become its "general" in 1257. A year before his death he was made a cardinal. Famed as a teacher in Paris, he was even more distinguished for his administration of the Franciscan order and for his high character. Much less an Aristotelian than Aquinas, he was especially influenced by the Neo-Platonic teachings of Augustine and Pseudo-Dionysius. He was essentially a mystic. By meditation and prayer one may rise into that union with God which brings the highest knowledge of divine truth. Yet, though a mystic, Bonaventura was a theologian of dialectic ability whose work, more conservative and less original than that of Aquinas, nevertheless commanded high respect.

According to Aquinas, in whom Scholasticism attained its noblest development, the aim of all theological investigation is to give knowledge of God and of man's origin and destiny. Such knowledge comes in part by reason—natural theology—but the attainments of reason are inadequate. They must be augmented by revelation. That revelation is contained in the Scriptures, which are the only final authority; but they are to be understood in the light of the interpretations of the councils and the Fathers—in a word, as comprehended by the church. The truths of revelation cannot be attained by reason, but they are not contrary to reason, and reason can show the inadequacy of objections to them. Aquinas is thus far from sharing Anselm's conviction that all truths of Christianity are philosophically demonstrable; but he holds that there can be no contradiction between philosophy and theology, since both are from God.

In treating of God Aquinas combined Aristotelian and Neo-Platonic conceptions. He is the first cause. He is pure act (*actus purus*). He is also the most real and perfect being. He is the absolute substance, the source and end of all things. As perfect goodness, God does always that which He sees to be right. Regarding the Trinity and the person of Christ, Aquinas stood essentially on the basis of Augustine and the Chalcedonian formula (see p. 139).

God needs nothing, and therefore the creation of the world was an expression of the divine love which He bestows on the existences He thus called into being. God's providence extends to all events, and is manifested in the predestination of some to everlasting life, and in leaving others to the consequences of sin in eternal condemnation. Aquinas's position is largely determinist. Man has, indeed, freedom. He is autonomous; but that does not preclude the determining or permissive providence of God. The divine permission of evil results in the higher good of the whole.

Aquinas abandoned the ancient distinction between "soul" and "spirit." The soul of man is a unit, possessing intellect and will. It is immaterial. Man's highest good is the vision and enjoyment of God. As originally created man had, in addition to his natural powers, a superadded gift which enabled him to seek that highest good and practise the three Christian virtues—faith, hope, and love. This Adam lost by sin, which also corrupted his natural powers, so that his state became not merely a lack of original righteousness, but a positive turning toward lower aims. Sin is, therefore, more than merely negative. In this fallen state it was impossible for Adam to please God, and this corruption was transmitted to all his posterity. Man still has the power to attain the four natural virtues, prudence, justice, courage, and self-control; but these, though bringing a certain measure of temporal honor and happiness, are not sufficient to enable their possessor to attain the vision of God.

Man's restoration is possible only through the free and unmerited grace of God, by which the super-added gift is restored to man's nature, his sins forgiven, and power to practise the three Christian virtues infused. No act of his can win this grace. While God could conceivably have forgiven man's sins and granted grace without the sacrifice of Christ—here Aquinas differed from Anselm—the work of Christ was the wisest and most efficient method God could choose, and man's whole redemption is based on it. That work involved satisfaction for man's sin, and Christ won a merit which deserves a reward. It also moves men to love. Aquinas thus developed and combined views presented by Anselm and Abelard. Christ's satisfaction superabounds man's sin, and the reward which Christ cannot personally receive, since as God He needs nothing, comes to the advantage of His human brethren. Christ does for men what they cannot do for themselves.

Once redeemed, however, the good works that God's grace now enables man to do deserve and receive a reward. Man now has power to fulfil not only the precepts but the counsels of the Gospel (see p. 95). He can do works of supererogation, of which the chief would be the faithful fulfilment of the monastic life. He cannot merely fit himself for heaven; he can add his mite to the treasury of the superabundant merits of Christ and the saints. Yet all this is made possible only by the grace of God. Aquinas thus finds full room for the two dominating conceptions of mediæval piety—grace and merit.

Grace does not come to men indiscriminately. It has its definite channels and these are the sacraments, and the sacraments alone. Here Scholasticism attained far greater clearness of definition than had previously existed. The ancient feeling that all sacred actions were sacraments was still alive in the twelfth century, but Hugo of St. Victor and Abelard clearly placed five in a more conspicuously sacramental category than others, and Peter Lombard defined the sacraments as seven. Whether this reckoning was original with him is still an unsolved problem; nor was it at once universally accepted. The influence of his *Sentences* ultimately won the day. As enumerated by Peter Lombard, the sacraments are baptism, confirmation, the Lord's Supper, penance, extreme unction, ordination, and matrimony. All were instituted by Christ, directly or through the Apostles, and all convey grace from Christ the head to the members of His mystical body, the church. Without them there is no true union with Christ.

Every sacrament consists of two elements which are defined in Aristotelian terms of form and matter (see p. 4)—a material portion (water, bread, and wine, etc.); and a formula conveying its sacred use ("I baptize thee," etc.). The administrant must have the intention of doing what Christ and the church appointed, and the recipient must have, at least in the case of those of years of discretion, a sincere desire to receive the benefit of the sacrament. These conditions fulfilled, the sacrament conveys grace by the fact of its reception—that is *ex opere operato*. Of this grace God is the principal cause; the sacrament itself is the instrumental cause. It is the means by which the virtue of Christ's passion is conveyed to His members.

By baptism the recipient is regenerated, and original and previous personal sins are pardoned, though the tendency to sin is not obliterated. Man is now given the grace, if he will use it, to resist sin, and the lost power to attain the Christian virtues.

The sole recognized theory regarding Christ's presence in the Supper was that which had been taught by Paschasius Radbertus (see p. 192) and Lanfranc (see p. 239), and had been known since the first half of the twelfth century as transubstantiation. It had been given full dogmatic authority by the Fourth Lateran Council in 1215. Aquinas but added clearness of definition. At the words of consecration by the priest the miracle is wrought by the power of God, so that while the "accidents" of bread and wine (shape, taste, and the like) remain unaltered, their "substance" is transformed into the very body and blood of Christ.

Aquinas also accepted and developed the view that the whole body and blood of Christ is present in either element. It was far from original with him, but had grown with the increasing custom of the laity to partake of the bread only. A withdrawal of the cup instigated by the clergy did not take place. The abandonment of the cup was rather a layman's practice due to fear of dishonoring the sacrament by misuse of the wine. Such anxiety had manifested itself as early as the seventh century in the adoption of the Greek custom of dipping the bread in the wine—a practice repeatedly disapproved by ecclesiastical authority, but supported by lay sentiment. By the twelfth century the laity were avoiding the use of the wine altogether, apparently first of all in England. By the time of Aquinas lay communion in the bread alone had become prevalent. Similar considerations led to the general abandonment by the Western Church, in the twelfth and thirteenth centuries, of the practice of infant communion, which had been universal, and which continues in the Greek Church to the present.

Mediæval piety and worship reach their highest point in the Lord's Supper. It is the continuation of the incarnation, the repetition of the passion, the source of spiritual upbuilding to the recipient, the evidence of his union with Christ, and a sacrifice well pleasing to God, inclining Him to be gracious to those in need on earth and in purgatory.

Penance, though not reckoned a sacrament of equal dignity with baptism or the Lord's Supper, was really of great, if not prime, importance in mediæval practice. Mediæval thought regarding the personal religious life centered about the two conceptions of grace and merit. Baptism effected the forgiveness of previous sins; but for those committed after baptism penance was necessary. The Latin mind has always been inclined to view sin and righteousness in terms of definite acts rather than as states, and therefore to look upon man's relations to God under the aspects of debt and credit— though holding that the only basis of credit is the effect of God's grace. These tendencies were never more marked than in the scholastic period. They represented wide-spread popular views which the schoolmen explained theologically, rather than originated.

According to Aquinas, penance involves the act of penance: contrition, confession, satisfaction, and absolution. Contrition is sincere sorrow for the offense against God and a determination not to repeat it. Yet Aquinas holds that, as all sacraments convey grace, a penance begun in "attrition," that is, in fear of punishment, may by infused grace become a real contrition.

Private confession to the priest had made gradual progress since its advocacy of the old British missionaries (see p. 181). Abelard and Peter Lombard were of opinion that a true contrition was followed by divine forgiveness, even without priestly confession, though they thought such confession desirable. The Fourth Lateran Council, in 1215, required confession to the priest at least once a year of all laymen of age of discretion. Such confession thereby became church law. Alexander of Hales argued its necessity, and Aquinas gave it more logical exposition. It must be made to the priest as the physician of the soul, and include all "deadly" sins—the catalogue of which was now much larger than in the early church (see p. 92).

Though God forgives the eternal punishment of the penitent, certain temporal penalties remain as a consequence of sin. This distinction was clearly made by Abelard and became the current property of the schoolmen. These temporal penalties satisfy the sinner's offense against God so far as it is in his power to do so. They also enable him to avoid sin in the future. They are the "fruits of repentance." It is the business of the priest to impose these satisfactions, which, if not adequate in this life, will be completed in purgatory.

On evidence thus of sorrow for sin, confession, and a willingness to give satisfaction, the priest, as God's minister or agent, pronounces absolution. Here, then, was the great control of the priesthood over the laity till the Reformation, and in the Roman Church to the present. Without priestly pardon no one guilty after baptism of a "deadly" sin has assurance of salvation.

A great modification of these satisfactions was, however, rapidly growing in the century and a half before Aquinas. A remission of a portion or of all of these "temporal" penalties could be obtained. Such remission was called an "indulgence." Bishops had long exercised the right to abridge satisfactions in cases where circumstances indicated unusual contrition. Great services to the church were held to deserve such consideration. Peter Damiani (1007?–1072) regarded gifts of land for a monastery or a church as affording such occasions. These did not constitute the full indulgence system, however. That seems to have originated in southern France, and the earliest, though not undisputed, instance is about the year 1016. Their first conspicuous employment was by a French Pope, Urban II (1088–1099), who promised full indulgence to all who engaged in the First Crusade, though Pope Alexander II had given similar privileges on a smaller scale for battle against the Saracens in Spain about 1063. Once begun, the system spread with great rapidity. Not only Popes but bishops gave indulgences, and on constantly easier terms. Pilgrimages to sacred places or at special times, contributions to a good work, such as building a church or even a bridge or a road, were deemed deserving of such reward. The financial possibilities of the system were soon perceived and exploited. Since "temporal" penalties included those of purgatory, the value of an indulgence was enormous, though undefined, and the tendency to substitute it for a real penance was one to which human nature readily responded.

Such was the practice to which Aquinas now gave the classic interpretation. Following Alexander of Hales, he taught that the superabundant merits of Christ and of the saints form a treasury of good works from which a portion may be transferred by the authority of the church, acting through its officers, to the needy sinner. It can, indeed, avail only for those who are really contrite, but for such it removes, in whole or in part, the "temporal" penalties here and in purgatory. Indulgences were never a license to commit sin. They were an amelioration of penalties justly due to sins already committed and regretted. But, however interpreted, there can be no doubt as to the moral harmfulness of the system, or that it grew worse till the Reformation, of which it was an immediately inducing cause.

At their deaths, according to Aquinas, the wicked pass immediately to hell, which is endless, and from which there is no release. Those who have made full use of the grace offered in the church go at once to heaven. The mass of Christians who have but imperfectly availed themselves of the means of grace must undergo a longer or shorter purification in purgatory.

The church is one, whether in heaven, on earth, or in purgatory. When one member suffers, all suffer; when one does well, all share in his good work. On this unity of the church Aquinas bases prayers to the saints and for those in purgatory. The visible church requires a visible head. To be subject to the Roman Pontiff is necessary for salvation. To the Pope, also, belongs the right to issue new definitions of faith, and Aquinas implies the doctrine of papal infallibility.

It was Aquinas' good fortune that his philosophy and his theology alike found a hearty disciple in the greatest of mediæval poets, Dante Alighieri (1265–1321), whose *Divina Commedia* moves, in theological respects, almost wholly in Aquinas' realm of thought.

Aquinas was a Dominican, and their natural rivalry soon drew upon his system the criticism of Franciscan scholars, many of whom were of English birth. Such a critic was Richard of Middletown (?–1300?); but the most famous of all, and one of the greatest of the schoolmen, was John Duns Scotus (1265?–1308). In spite of his name he appears to have been an Englishman. Educated in Oxford, where he became its most famous teacher, he removed to Paris in 1304. Four years later the general of the order sent him to Cologne, where he died just as his work there had begun. The keenest critic and the ablest dialectician of all the schoolmen, he critically analysed certain doctrines of Aquinas with the utmost acumen. He attained a position as authoritative teacher in the Franciscan order similar to that of Aquinas in the Dominican, and the theological rivalries of the Thomists and Scotists continued to rage till the Reformation.

Aquinas had held that the essence of God is being. To Scotus, it is supreme will. The will in God and man is free. Aquinas held that God did what He saw to be right. To Scotus what God wills is right by the mere fact of willing. Though, like Aquinas, Scotus was an Aristotelian and as such a modified realist, he laid emphasis on the individual rather than on the universal. To him the individual is the more perfect form.

Since God is absolute will, the sacrifice of Christ has the value which God puts upon it. Any other act would have been sufficient for salvation had God seen fit so to regard it. Nor can we say, with Aquinas, that Christ's death was the wisest way of salvation. That would be to limit God's will. All we can affirm is that it was the way chosen by God. Similarly, Scotus minimized the repentance necessary for salvation. Aquinas had demanded contrition or an "attrition"—fear of punishment—that by the infusion of grace became contrition. Scotus held that "attrition" is sufficient by divine appointment to secure fitness for pardon. It is followed by forgiveness, and that by the infusion of grace by which a man is enabled to do certain acts to which God has been pleased to attach merit. The sacraments do not of themselves convey grace, but are the conditions appointed by God upon which, if fulfilled, grace is bestowed.

The most fundamental difference between Aquinas and Scotus is one of attitude. To Aquinas there could be no real disagreement between theology and philosophy, however inadequate the latter to reach all the truths of the former. To Duns much in theology is philosophically improbable, yet must be accepted on the authority of the church. The breakdown of Scholasticism had begun, for its purpose had been to show the reasonableness of Christian truth.

The dispute which roused the loudest controversy between Thomists and Scotists was regarding the "immaculate conception" of the Virgin Mary. Aquinas, concerned to maintain and underline the view that Jesus Christ was the Saviour of *all* men, had taught that she shared in the original sin of the race. Scotus held that she was free from it—a doctrine that was to be declared that of the church by Pope Pius IX (1846–1878) in 1854.

Yet more radical in his divorce of philosophy from theology was Scotus' pupil, William of Occam (?–1349?). An English Franciscan of the most earnest type, he studied in Oxford, taught in Paris, defended the complete poverty of Christ and the Apostles against Pope John XXII (see p. 263), suffered imprisonment, only to escape in 1328 and find refuge with Louis of Bavaria, then in quarrel with the Pope. For the rest of his life he defended the independence of the state from ecclesiastical authority with the utmost steadfastness.

Occam attacked any form of "realism" fiercely. Only individual objects exist. Any association in genera or species is purely mental, having no objective reality. It is simply a use of symbolic "terms." Hence, Occam was called a "terminist." His system was a far more vigorous and destructive nominalism than that of Roscelin (see p. 239). Yet actual knowledge of things in themselves men do not have, only of mental concepts. This denial led him to the conclusion that no theological doctrines are philosophically provable. They are to be accepted—and he accepted them— simply on authority. That authority he made in practice that of the church; though in his contest with what he deemed a derelict papacy he taught that Scripture, and not the decisions of councils and Popes, is alone binding on the Christian. No wonder that Luther, in this respect, could call him "dear master."

Occam's philosophical views gained increasing sway after his death. From thence onward till just before the Reformation nominalism was the dominant theological position. It was known as the *via moderna* in contrast to Thomism and Scotism which were called the *via antiqua*. It was the bankruptcy of Scholasticism. While it undoubtedly aided investigation by permitting the freest (philosophical) criticism of existing dogma, it based all Christian belief on arbitrary authority. That was really to undermine theology, for men do not long hold as true what is intellectually indefensible. It robbed of interest the great speculative systems of the older Scholasticism. Men turned increasingly, in the fourteenth and fifteenth centuries, to mysticism, or returned to Augustine for the intellectual and religious comfort which Scholasticism was unable longer to afford.

8

The Mystics

BESIDES THE INTELLECTUAL, the mystical tendency was strongly represented in many of the schoolmen. Hugo of St. Victor and Bonaventura may as rightly be reckoned to the mystics as to the scholastics. Aquinas showed marked mystic leanings, derived from Augustine and the Pseudo-Dionysius. Aristotle never wholly conquered Neo-Platonic influences. Neo-Platonism itself enjoyed a measure of revival in the twelfth and thirteenth centuries, partly through the strongly Neo-Platonizing Arabian commentaries on Aristotle, but even more through the widely read *Liber de Causis,* falsely ascribed to Aristotle, but containing excerpts from the Neo-Platonic philosopher Proclus (410–485), and ultimately by translations directly from Proclus' accredited works.

An important representative of this mystical spirit was "Meister" Eckhart (1260–1327), a German Dominican who studied in Paris, served as provincial prior of the Saxon district, lived for a time in Strassburg, and taught in Cologne. At the close of his life Eckhart was under trial for heresy. He himself declared his readiness to submit his opinions to the judgment of the church, but two years after his death a number of his teachings were condemned by Pope John XXII. In true Neo-Platonic fashion Eckhart taught that that which is real in all things is the divine. In the soul of man is a spark of God. That is the true reality in all men. All individualizing qualities are essentially negative. Man should, therefore, lay them aside. His struggle is to have God born in his soul, that is to enter into full communion with and to come under the control of the indwelling God. In this effort Christ is the pattern and example, in whom Godhead dwelt in humanity in all fulness. With God dominant the soul is filled with love and righteousness. Churchly observances may be of some value, but the springs of the mystic life are far deeper and its union with God more direct. Good works do not make righteous. It is the soul already righteous that does good works. The all-important matter is that the soul enters into its full privilege of union with God.

Perhaps the most eminent of Eckhart's disciples was John Tauler (1300?–1361), a Dominican preacher who worked long in Strassburg, of which he was probably a native, in Cologne and in Basel. The times in Germany were peculiarly difficult. The long contest for the empire between Frederick of Austria and Louis of Bavaria, and papal interferences therein, wrought religious as well as political confusion. The bubonic plague of 1348–1349, known in England as the "black death," devastated the population. To his distressed age Tauler was a preacher of helpfulness, whose sermons have been widely read ever since. In them are many "evangelical" thoughts, which aroused the admiration of Luther, and have often led to the claim that he was a Protestant before Protestantism. He emphasized the inward and the vital in religion, and condemned dependence on external ceremonies and dead works. His real position was that of a follower of Eckhart, with similar mystic emphasis on union with the divine, on "God being born within," though he avoided the extreme statements (those tending toward Pantheism) which had led to churchly condemnation of Eckhart's opinions. A less practical but widely influential representative of the same tendencies was the ascetic Dominican, Henry Suso (1295?–1366), whose writings, especially the *Booklet on Eternal Wisdom,* did much to further this mystic point of view.

Through these influences a whole group of mystic sympathizers was raised up in southwestern Germany and Switzerland, who called themselves "Friends of God." [1] These included not only many of the clergy, but nuns and a considerable number of laity. Among the laymen, Ruleman Merswin, of Strassburg (1307–1382), was the most influential. Originally a banker and merchant, he was intimate with Tauler, whose views he shared, and devoted all the latter part of his life to religious labors. He mystified his contemporaries and posterity by letters and books which he set forth purporting to come from a "great Friend of God" in the Highlands (*i. e.*, Switzerland), whose existence was long believed real, but now is practically proved to have been a fiction of Merswin himself. The most important work of these Friends of God was the "German Theology," written late in the fourteenth century by an otherwise unknown and unnamed priest of the *Deutschherrn Haus* of Frankfurt, which was to influence Luther, and to be printed by him in 1516 and 1518.

These German mystics all leaned strongly toward pantheism. They all, however, represented a view of the Christian life which saw its essence in a transforming personal union of the soul with God, and they all laid little weight on the more external methods of ordinary churchly life.

This mystical movement was furthered in the Netherlands by John of Ruysbroeck (1293–1381), who was influenced by Eckhart's writings and enjoyed the personal friendship of Tauler and others of the Friends of God. Ruysbroeck's friend, in turn, was Gerhard Groot (1340–1384)—a brilliant scholar, who upon his conversion, about 1374, became the most influential popular preacher of the Netherlands. A more conservative churchly thinker than Ruysbroeck, Groot was much less radical in his mysticism. A man of great practical gifts, Groot's work led shortly after his death to the foundation by his disciple, Florentius Radewyn (1350–1400), of the Brethren of the Common Life. This association, of which the first house was established in Deventer, grew out of the union of Groot's converts for a warmer religious life. They grouped themselves in houses of brethren, who lived essentially a monastic life under common rules, but without permanent vows, engaged in religious exercises, copying books of edification, and especially in teaching. Work was required of all. These houses were wide-spread in the Netherlands and in Germany, and did much to promote popular piety in the fifteenth century.

The Brethren of the Common Life were non-monastic in the matter of vows. Groot's preaching led to an influential movement for those who preferred the monastic life, though it, also, did not take full form till shortly after his death. This was the foundation of the famous monastery of Windesheim, which soon gathered a number of affiliated convents about it, and became a reformatory influence of power in the monastic life of the

[1] *Cf.* John 15:14 f.

Netherlands and Germany. In both these movements the mystic influence was strongly present, though in a much more churchly form than among the immediate disciples of Eckhart.

The noblest product of this simple, mystical, churchly piety is the *Imitation of Christ*—a book the circulation of which has exceeded that of any other product of the Middle Ages. Though its authorship has been the theme of heated controversy, it was probably the work of Thomas à Kempis (1380?–1471). A pupil of the Brethren of the Common Life in Deventer, most of his long life was spent in the monastery of Mount St. Agnes, near Zwolle. This foundation was a member of the Windesheim congregation, of which Thomas's older brother, John, was one of the founders. Thomas's life was outwardly the most uneventful conceivable; but few have understood, as did he, the language of simple, mystical devotion to Christ.

The mystical movement had its reverse side in a pantheism which broke with all churchly and even all moral teaching. Such was that of Amalrich of Bena (?–1204), a teacher in Paris, who was led by the writings of John Scotus Erigena (see p. 192) and the extreme Neo-Platonic opinions of the Spanish Mohammedan expositor of Aristotle, Averroes (1126–1198), to the conclusions that God is all, that He is incarnate in the believer as in Christ, and that the believer cannot sin. He also held that as the Jewish law and ritual had been abolished by the coming of Christ, so that of earlier Christianity was now done away with by the coming of the Holy Spirit. Amalrich was compelled to recant by Pope Innocent III, but he left a number of followers.

Similar extravagances kept cropping out in the regions of Germany and the Netherlands, where the mysticism already described had its chief following. In many ways it was simply that mysticism carried to a pantheistic extreme. It was usually quietist, believing that the soul could become one with God by contemplation, and in consequence of that union its acts could no longer be sinful, since it is controlled by God. All sacraments and penances, even prayer, become superfluous. These views were not united into a compact system, nor did their holders constitute a sect, though they have often been so regarded and named the "Brethren and Sisters of the Free Spirit." Undoubtedly, however, such notions were rather frequently to be found in monasteries and nunneries, where mysticism was practised extravagantly, and among the Beguines, whom they brought into doubtful repute. They were not only repressed by the inquisition, but were opposed by the greater mystic leaders of whom an account has been given.

9

Missions and Defeats

THE PERIOD between the Crusades and the Reformation was one of gains and losses for Christendom. In Spain the Christian forces struggled with increasing success against the Mohammedans. Gradually, four Christian states dominated the peninsula. Castile conquered Toledo in 1085, defeated the Moslems at Las Navas de Tolosa in 1212, and united with Leon into a strong state in 1230. Little Navarre stretched on both sides of the Pyrenees. Meanwhile Aragon on the east and Portugal on the west were winning their independence, so that by 1250 Mohammedan power on the peninsula was confined to the kingdom of Granada, whence it was to be driven in 1492. The Spanish Christian kingdoms were weak. The real power of Spain was not to be manifest till the joint reign of Ferdinand and Isabella united Castile and Aragon in 1479.

In the East the great Mongol empire, which began with the conquest of northern China in 1208, stretched across northern Asia, conquering most of what is now European Russia between 1238 and 1241, and reaching the borders of Palestine in 1258. By this devastation the flourishing Nestorian Church in central Asia (see p. 136) was almost annihilated. Yet after the first rush of conquest was over, central Asia under Mongol control was accessible as it had never been before and was not to be till the nineteenth century. About 1260 two Venetian merchants, Nicolo and Maffeo Polo, made the long journey by land to Peking, where they were well received by the Mongol Khan, Kublai. Returning in 1269, they started again in 1271, taking Nicolo's more famous son, Marco, who entered the Khan's service. It was not till 1295 that the Polos were back in Venice. Even before their return an Italian Franciscan, John of Monte Corvino, had started in 1291 for Peking, where he established a church about 1300. Christianity flourished for a time. Pope Clement V (1305–1314) appointed John an archbishop with six bishops under him. The work came to an end, however, when the Mongols and other foreigners were expelled from China by the victorious native Ming dynasty in 1368.

Efforts were made to reach the Mohammedans, but with little success. Francis of Assisi himself preached to the Sultan in Egypt in 1219 (see p. 235). More famous as a missionary was Raimon Lull (1232?–1315), a native of the island of Majorca. From a wholly worldly life he was converted in 1266, and studied Arabic as a missionary preparation, writing also his *Ars Magna,* which he intended as an irrefutable demonstration of the truth of Christianity to philosophically trained Moslems. In 1291 he began missionary work in Tunis, only to be expelled at the end of a year. He labored to induce the Pope to establish schools for missionary training. He went once more to Africa and was again driven out. His eloquence persuaded the Council of Vienne in 1311 to order teaching in Greek, Hebrew, Chaldee, and Arabic, in Avignon, Paris, Salamanca, Bologna, and Oxford, though this remained a pious wish. Back to Tunis he went as a missionary in 1314, and met a martyr's death by stoning the next year. He had little to show of missionary achievement, but much of missionary inspiration.

The prevailing characteristic of this period was the loss of once Christian territories. The last of the conquests of the Crusaders in Palestine passed out of their hands in 1291. A new Mohammedan force was arising in the Ottoman Turks. Sprung from central Asia, they attained an independent position in Asia Minor in 1300. In 1354 they invaded the European portion of the Eastern empire, capturing Adrianople in 1361, and gradually spreading their rule over the Balkan lands. But a fragment of the empire remained till 1453, when Constantinople fell and the Byzantine empire was at an end. The victorious career of the Turks was to carry them, in the Reformation age, nearly half across Europe. Christians ruled by them were deprived of political rights, though Christian worship and organization continued, under conditions of much oppression. The Greek Church, which had stood higher in culture than the Latin, certainly till the thirteenth century, was now largely robbed of significance. Its daughter in Russia was not conquered, however, and was growing rapidly in strength and importance. With it lay the future of the Eastern Church.

10

The Papacy at Its Height and Its Decline

THE CONTEST between papacy and empire was by no means ended by the Concordat of Worms (see p. 212). The religious interest in the struggle was thereafter far less. Hildebrand's quarrel had involved a great question of church purification. The later disputes were plain contests for supremacy.

Frederick "Barbarossa" (1152–1190), of the house of Hohenstaufen, was one of the ablest of the Holy Roman Emperors. His model was Charlemagne, and he aspired to a similar control of churchly affairs. In spite of the Concordat of Worms he practically controlled the appointment of German bishops. On the other hand, his claims met with energetic resistance from the cities of northern Italy, which were growing strong on the commerce induced by the Crusades. This hostility he at first successfully overcame. With Alexander III (1159–1181) Frederick's most able enemy mounted the papal throne. The cardinals were divided in the choice, and an imperialistic minority elected a rival Pope, who called himself Victor IV, and whom Frederick and the German bishops promptly supported. Alexander's position was long difficult. In 1176, however, Frederick was defeated at Legnano by the Lombard league of Italian cities, and was forced to recognize Alexander. Frederick's attempt to control the papacy had been shattered, but his authority over the German bishops was scarcely diminished.[1] Frederick won a further success over the papacy, in 1186, by the marriage of his son Henry with the heiress of Sicily and southern Italy, thus threatening the papal states from north and south.

Alexander III also won at least an apparent success over Henry II (1154–1189), one of the ablest of English Kings. That monarch, in order to strengthen his hold over the English church, secured the election of his apparently complaisant chancellor, Thomas Becket, as archbishop of Canterbury in 1162. Once in office, Becket showed himself a determined upholder of ecclesiastical claims. Henry now, in 1164, secured the enactment of the Constitutions of Clarendon,[2] limiting the right of appeal to Rome in ecclesiastical cases, restricting the power of excommunication, subjecting the clergy to civil courts, and putting the election of bishops under the control of the King, to whom they must do homage. Becket now openly broke with the King. In 1170 a truce was brought about, but it was of short duration, and a hasty expression of anger on the part of Henry led to Becket's murder at the hands of Norman knights just at the close of the year. Alexander used the deed skilfully. In 1172 Becket was canonized, and continued till the Reformation one of the most popular of English saints. Henry was forced to abandon the Constitutions of Clarendon, and do penance at Becket's grave. Yet in spite of this apparent papal victory, Henry continued his control of English ecclesiastical affairs much as before.

Frederick "Barbarossa" died in 1190, on the Third Crusade. He was succeeded by his son, Henry VI (1190–1197), who, in 1194, obtained full possession of his wife's inheritance in Sicily and southern Italy and developed ambitious plans of greatly extending his imperial sway. The papacy, with both ends of Italy in the possession of the German sovereign, was in great political danger; but the situation was relieved by the early death of Henry VI in 1197, and the accession to the papacy in 1198 of one of its ablest mediæval representatives, Innocent III (1198–1216).

---

[1] See "Peace of Venice," Henderson, *Select Historical Documents*, pp. 425–430.
[2] Gee and Hardy, *Documents Illustrative of English Church History*, pp. 68–73.

Innocent III was unquestionably a man of personal humility and piety, but no Pope ever had higher conceptions of the papal office and under him the papacy reached its highest actual power. The death of Henry VI saw Germany divided. One party supported the claims of Henry's brother, Philip of Swabia, the other those of Otto of Brunswick, of the rival house of Welf (Guelph). Out of this confused situation Innocent strove with great skill to bring advantage to the papacy. He secured large concessions in Italy and Germany from Otto, yet when Philip gradually gained the upper hand, Innocent secured an agreement that the rival claims should be submitted to the judgment of a court controlled by the Pope. The murder of Philip in 1208 frustrated this plan, and put Otto IV once more to the fore. Innocent now obtained from Otto the desired guarantee of the extent of the papal states, and a promise to abandon control of German episcopal elections, and on the strength of these concessions crowned Otto Emperor in 1209. Otto promptly forgot all his promises. The angered Pope now put forward Frederick II (1212–1250), the young son of the late Emperor, Henry VI, who was chosen to the German throne by the elements opposed to Otto, in 1212, and renewed all Otto's broken promises. In 1214 Otto was wholly defeated by the French King, Philip II (1179–1223) on the field of Bouvines, and Frederick was assured of the empire. Thus, Innocent III seemed wholly to have defended papal claims and to have dictated the imperial succession. The supremacy of the papacy appeared realized.

Nor was Innocent III less successful in humbling the sovereigns of other lands. He compelled the powerful Philip II of France, by the prohibition of religious services—an interdict—to take back the Queen, Ingeborg, whom Philip had unjustly divorced. He separated King Alfonso IX of Leon from a wife too closely related. King Peter of Aragon received his kingdom as a fief from the Pope. Innocent's greatest apparent victory was, however, in the case of England. The cruel and unpopular King John (1199–1216), in a divided election tried to secure his candidate as archbishop of Canterbury. The dispute was appealed to Rome. The King's choice was set aside and Innocent's friend, Stephen Langton, received the prize. John resisted. Innocent laid England under an interdict. The King drove out his clerical opponents. The Pope now excommunicated him, declared his throne forfeited and proclaimed a crusade against him. The defeated King not merely made a humiliating submission to the Pope, in 1213, but acknowledged his kingdom a fief of the papacy, agreeing to pay a feudal tax to the Pope of a thousand marks annually.[3] Yet when the barons and clergy wrung *Magna Charta* from John in 1215, Innocent denounced it as an injury to his vassal.

In the internal affairs of the church Innocent's policy was strongly centralizing. He claimed for the papacy the right of decision in all disputed episcopal elections. He asserted sole authority to sanction the transfer of bishops

[3] Henderson, pp. 430–432.

from one see to another. His crusade against the Cathari has already been noted (see p. 231). The great Fourth Lateran Council of 1215, at which transubstantiation was declared an article of faith, and annual confession and communion required, was also a papal triumph. The conquest of Constantinople by the Fourth Crusade (see p. 223), though not approved by Innocent, seemed to promise the subjection of the Greek Church to papal authority.

In Innocent III the papacy reached the summit of its worldly power. The succeeding Popes continued the same struggle, but with decreasing success. The Emperor Frederick II, ruler of Germany, as well as of northern and southern Italy and Sicily, a man of much political ability and of anything but mediæval piety, though put in office largely by Innocent III, soon proved the chief opponent of the political pretensions of the papacy. Under Gregory IX (1227–1241), the organizer of the inquisition and the patron of the Franciscans (see pp. 231, 235), and Innocent IV (1243–1254) the papal contest was carried on against Frederick II, with the utmost bitterness and with very worldly weapons. Frederick was excommunicated, and rivals were raised up against him in Germany by papal influence. The papacy seemed convinced that only the destruction of the Hohenstaufen line, to which Frederick belonged, would assure its victory. On Frederick's death in 1250 it pursued his son, Conrad IV (1250–1254), with the same hostility, and gave his heritage in southern Italy and Sicily to Edmund of England, son of King Henry III. A new influence, that of France, was making itself felt in papal counsels. Urban IV (1261–1264) was a Frenchman and appointed French cardinals. He now gave, in 1263, southern Italy and Sicily to Charles of Anjou, brother of King Louis IX of France (1226–1270). This was a turning-point in papal politics, and with it the dependence of the papacy on France really began. The next Pope was also a Frenchman, Clement IV (1265–1268). During his papacy Conradin, the young son of Conrad IV, asserted his hereditary claims to southern Italy and Sicily by force of arms. He was excommunicated by Clement IV and defeated by Charles of Anjou, by whose orders he was beheaded in Naples, in 1268. With him ended the line of Hohenstaufen, which the Popes had so strenuously opposed, though there is no reason to think that the Pope was responsible in any way for Conradin's execution.

These long quarrels and the consequent confusion had greatly enfeebled the power of the Holy Roman Empire. Thenceforward, to the Reformation, it was far more a group of feeble states than an effective single sovereignty. It was able to offer little resistance to papal demands. Other forces were, however, arising that would inevitably make impossible such a sovereignty as Innocent III had exercised. One such force was the new sense of nationality, which caused men to feel that, as Frenchmen or Englishmen, they had common interests against all foreigners, even the Pope himself. Such a sense of unity had not existed in the earlier Middle Ages. It was rapidly developing, especially in France and England in the latter half of the thirteenth century. A second cause was the rise in intelligence, wealth, and political influence of the middle class, especially in the cities. These were restive under ecclesiastical interference in temporal affairs. Closely associated with this development was the growth of a body of lay lawyers and the renewed study of the Roman law. These men were gradually displacing ecclesiastics as royal advisers, and developing the effectiveness of the royal power by precedents from a body of law—the Roman—which knew nothing of mediæval ecclesiastical conditions. There was also a growing conviction among thoughtful and religious men that such worldly aims as the recent papacy had followed were inconsistent with the true interests of the church. These were growing forces with which the papacy must reckon. The weakness of the papacy, from a worldly point of view, was that it had no adequate physical forces at its disposal. It must balance off one competitor against another, and the wreck wrought in Germany left the door open to France without forces which could be matched against her.

Papal interference in Germany continued. Pope Gregory X (1271–1276) ordered the German electors, in 1273, to choose a King, under threat that the Pope himself would make the appointment if they failed. They chose Rudolf I, of Habsburg (1273–1291), who promptly renewed the concessions to the papacy which had been once made by Otto IV and Frederick II.

Quite otherwise was it speedily with France. The power of that monarchy had been rapidly growing and in Philip IV, "the Fair" (1285–1314), France had a King of unscrupulousness, obstinacy, and high conceptions of royal authority. In Boniface VIII (1294–1303) the papacy was held by a man of as lofty aspirations to world-rule as had ever there been represented. Neither participant in the struggle commands much sympathy. War had arisen between France, Scotland, and England which compelled the English King, Edward I (1272–1307), to rally the support of all his subjects by inviting the representatives of the Commons to take a place in Parliament, in 1295, thus giving them a permanent share in the English national councils. The struggle also induced the Kings of France and England to tax their clergy to meet its expenses. The clergy complained to Pope Boniface, who, in 1296, issued the bull *Clericis laicos*,[4] inflicting excommunication on all who demanded or paid such taxes on clerical property without papal permission. Philip replied by prohibiting the export of money from France, thus striking at the revenues of the Pope and of the Italian bankers. The latter moved Boniface to modify his attitude so that the clergy could make voluntary contributions. He even allowed that, in great necessities, the King could lay a tax. It was a royal victory.

Comparative peace prevailed between Philip and Boniface for a few years. In 1301 the struggle again began. Philip had Bernard Saisset, bishop of Pamiers, whom the Pope had recently sent to him as nuntius, arrested and charged with high treason. The Pope ordered Bernard's release and cited the French bishops, and ultimately King Philip himself, to Rome. In reply, Philip

[4] Henderson, pp. 432–434; Robinson, 1:488–490.

summoned the first French States-General, in which clergy, nobles, and commoners were represented. This body, in 1302, sustained the King in his attitude of resistance. The Pope answered with the famous bull *Unam sanctam,*[5] the high-water mark of papal claim to supremacy over civil powers. It affirmed that temporal powers are subject to the spiritual authority, which is judged in the person of the Pope by God alone. It declared, following the opinion of Aquinas (see p. 250), "that it is altogether necessary to salvation for every human being to be subject to the Roman pontiff"—an affirmation the exact scope of which has led to much subsequent discussion. Philip answered with a new assembly, where the Pope was charged with an absurd series of crimes, involving heresy and moral depravity, and appeal was issued for a general council of the church before which the Pope might be tried. Philip was determined that this should be no mere threat: He would force the Pope to consent. He therefore sent his able jurist vice-chancellor, William Nogaret, who joined to himself Boniface's ancient family enemy, Sciarra Colonna. Together they gathered a force and made Boniface a prisoner in Anagni, just as he was about to proclaim Philip's excommunication, in 1303. Boniface was courageous. He would make no concessions. His friends soon freed him, but a month later he died.

These events were a staggering blow to the temporal claims of the papacy. It was not primarily that Philip's representatives had held Boniface for a short time a prisoner. A new force had arisen, that of national sentiment, to which the King had appealed successfully, and against which the spiritual weapons of the papacy had been of little avail. The papal hope of rulership in temporal affairs had proved impossible of permanent realization.

Worse for the papacy was speedily to follow. After the death of Boniface's successor, the excellent Benedict XI (1303–1304), the cardinals chose a Frenchman, Bertrand de Gouth, who took the title of Clement V (1305–1314). A man of weakness of character and grave moral faults, he was fully under the influence of King Philip IV, of France. He declared Philip innocent of the attack on Boniface VIII, and cancelled Boniface's interdicts and excommunications, modifying the bull *Unam sanctam* to please the King. An evidence of French domination that was patent to all the world was the removal of the seat of the papacy, in 1309, to Avignon—on the river Rhone— a town not belonging indeed to the French kingdom, but in popular estimate amounting to the establishment of the papacy in France. Undoubtedly the troubled state of Italian politics had something to do with this removal. At Avignon the papacy was to have its seat till 1377—a period so nearly equal to the traditional exile of the Jews as to earn the name of the Babylonish Captivity. Nor was the cup of Clement's humiliation yet filled. The cold-blooded King compelled him to join in the cruel destruction of the Templars (see p. 222).

[5] Henderson, pp. 435–437; Robinson, 1:346–348.

Clement V's pontificate is interesting as marking the conclusion, to the present, of the official collections of church or "canon" law. That great body of authority was the product of the history of the church since the early councils, and embraced their decisions, the decrees of synods and of Popes. The Middle Ages had seen many collections, of which the most famous was the *Concordantia discordantium canonum,* commonly called *Decretum,* gathered, probably in 1148, by Gratian, a teacher of canon law in Bologna. Pope Gregory IX (1227–1241) caused an official collection to be formed, in 1234, including new decrees up to his time. Pope Boniface VIII (1294–1303) published a similar addition in 1298, and Clement V (1305–1314) enlarged it in 1314, though his work was not published till 1317, under his successor, John XXII (1316–1334). The great structure, thus laboriously erected through the centuries, is a mass of ecclesiastical jurisprudence embracing all domains of ecclesiastical life. Though official collections ceased from Clement V to the twentieth century, the creation of church law has continued in all ages. Finally, Pius X (1903–1914), in 1904 ordered the codification and simplification of the whole body of canon law by a special commission. In May 1917, his successor, Benedict XV (1914–1922), promulgated the *Codex juris canonici* (five "books" containing 2414 canons).

11

The Papacy in Avignon, Criticism. The Schism

THE POPES, while the papacy was in Avignon, were all Frenchmen. It seemed as if the papacy had become a French institution. This association caused greatly increased restlessness in view of papal claims, especially in nations which, like England, were at war with France during much of this period, or Germany on which the still continuing interference of the papacy bore hard. The ablest of the Avignon Popes was unquestionably John XXII (1316–1334). The double imperial election in Germany, in 1314, had divided that land between supporters of Louis the Bavarian (1314–1347) and Frederick of Austria. John XXII, supported by King Philip V of France (1316–1322), thought the occasion ripe to diminish German influence in Italy for the benefit of the States of the Church. He declined to recognize either claimant, and declared that the Pope had the right to administer the empire during vacancies. When Louis interfered in Italian affairs the Pope excommunicated

him, and a contest with the papacy ensued which lasted till Louis' death. In
its course the German electors issued the famous declaration of 1338, in Rense,
which was confirmed by the Reichstag in Frankfurt the same year, that the
chosen head of the empire needs no approval from the papacy whatever for
full entrance on or continuation in the duties of his office.

These attacks upon the state aroused literary defenders of considerable
significance. One of these was the great Italian poet, Dante Alighieri (1265–
1321). His Latin treatise, *On Monarchy,* is not surely dated, but was composed between 1311 and 1318. Dante holds that peace is the best condition of
mankind. It is most effectively secured by an Emperor. The power of empire
rightfully came to Rome. It is as necessary for man's temporal happiness as
the papacy is to guide men to eternal blessedness. Each is directly from God,
and neither should interfere in the province of the other. Dante carefully
controverts the papal interpretation of the Bible texts and historical instances
on which claims to control over the state were based. All this is the more impressive since Dante was no free-thinker but theologically of most impeccable
orthodoxy.

Much more radical than Dante, and vastly influential on later political
theories were several treatises produced in France. The Dominican, John of
Paris (1265?–1306), taught that both papal and royal powers are based on
the sovereignty of the people, and neither has a right to interfere with the
sphere of the other. The most important of these works was the *Defensor Pacis*
of Marsilius of Padua (?–1342?) and John of Jandun (?–1328). It is the
most startlingly modern treatise that the age produced. Its principal author,
Marsilius, was long a teacher in Paris, where he was rector of the university in
1313, and was regarded as learned in medicine. The *Defensor Pacis* was written in 1324, in the controversy between Pope John XXII and the Emperor
Louis the Bavarian. Its radical views caused its authors to seek protection from
the Emperor, which they enjoyed, though with some hesitation, for the rest
of their lives. They were excommunicated by John XXII in 1327, and Pope
Clement VI declared, in 1343, that he had never read a worse heretical book.

According to Marsilius, who was deeply versed in Aristotle, the basis
of all power is the people; in the state the whole body of citizens; in the
church the whole body of Christian believers. They are the legislative power;
by them rulers in church and state are appointed, and to them these executive
officers are responsible. The only final authority in the church is the New
Testament; but priests have no power of physical force to compel men to
obey it. Their sole duty is to teach, warn, and reprove. The New Testament
teaches that bishops and priests are equivalent designations, yet it is well, as a
purely human constitution, to appoint some clergy superintendents over
others. This appointment gives no superior spiritual power, nor has one
bishop spiritual authority over another, or the Pope over all. Peter had no
higher rank than the other Apostles. There is no New Testament evidence
that he was ever in Rome. The New Testament gives no countenance to the

possession of earthly lordships and estates by clergymen. No bishop or Pope has authority to define Christian truth as contained in the New Testament, or make binding laws. These acts can be done only by the legislative body of the church—the whole company of Christian believers, represented in a general council. Such a council is the supreme authority in the church. Since the Christian state and the Christian church are coterminous, the executive of the Christian state, as representing a body of believers, may call councils, appoint bishops, and control church property.[1] Here were ideas that were to bear fruit in the Reformation, and even in the French Revolution; but they were too radical greatly to impress their age. Their time was later, and something was lacking in Marsilius himself. He was a cool thinker rather than a man who could translate theory into action in such fashion as to create large leadership.

Because of a zeal which Marsilius lacked, and of ideas not too much in advance of the age, a greater authority was wielded by William of Occam, whose theological influence and energetic defense of the extremer Franciscan doctrine of the absolute poverty of Christ and the Apostles have been noted (see pp. 237, 251). Occam, like Marsilius, found a refuge with Louis the Bavarian. To him, as to Dante, papacy and empire are both founded by God, and neither is superior to the other. Each has its own sphere. The church has purely religious functions. Its final authority is the New Testament.

Voices were raised in defense of papal claims. One of the most celebrated, though typical rather than original, was that of the Italian Augustinian monk, Augustinus Triumphus (1243–1328). In his *Summa de potestate ecclesiastica,* written about 1322, he holds that all princes rule as subject to the Pope, who can remove them at pleasure. No civil law is binding if disapproved by him. The Pope can be judged by none; nor can one even appeal from the Pope to God, "since the decision and court of God and the Pope are one." Yet should the Pope fall into heresy, his office is forfeited.

These opinions of the papal supporters were far from being shared by Germans engaged in a struggle against the papacy for the political autonomy of the empire, or by Englishmen at war with France, who believed the Avignon papacy the tool of the French sovereign. Pope Clement V (1305–1314) had asserted the right of the papacy to appoint to all ecclesiastical office. Such appointees were called "provisors," and the intrusion of papal favorites in England aroused King and Parliament in 1351 to enact the Statute of Provisors. Elections to bishoprics and other ecclesiastical posts should be free from papal interference. In case appointment was made by the regular authorities, and also by the Pope, the provisor was to be imprisoned till he resigned his claim. This law inevitably led to disputes between papal and royal authority, and a further statute of 1353, known as that of *Præmunire* forbad appeals outside of the kingdom under penalty of outlawry.[2] In enforcement these statutes

[1] See, for some extracts, Robinson, 1:491–497.
[2] Gee and Hardy, *Documents,* pp. 103, 104, 113–119.

were largely dead letters, but they show the growth of a spirit in England which was further illustrated when Parliament, in 1366, refused longer to recognize the right of King John to subject his kingdom, in 1213, to the Pope as a fief (see p. 259).

No feature of the Avignon papacy contributed to its criticism so largely as its offensive taxation of church life. The Crusades had been accompanied by a much readier circulation of money, and a great increase in commerce. Europe was passing rapidly from barter to money payments. Money taxes, rather than receipts in kind, were everywhere increasing. It was natural that this change should take place in church administration also; but the extent to which taxation was pushed by the Popes of the thirteenth and fourteenth centuries was a scandal, and it was much aggravated when the removal of the papacy to Avignon largely cut off the revenues from the papal estates in Italy without diminishing the luxury or expensiveness of the papal court. This period saw the extensive development, in imitation of secular feudal practice, of the annates, that is a tax of one year's income, more or less, from each new appointment. Since the reservation of posts to exclusive papal appointment was at the same time immensely extended, this became a large source of revenue. The income of vacant benefices, also, became a significant source of papal receipts. Taxes for bulls and other papal documents also rose rapidly in amount and productivity. These were but a portion of the papal exactions, and the total effect was the impression that the papal administration was heavily and increasingly burdensome on the clergy, and through them on the people. This feeling was augmented by the ruthless manner in which churchly censures, such as excommunication, were imposed on delinquent taxpayers. The papacy seemed extravagant in expenditure and offensive in taxation, and its repute in both respects was to grow worse till the Reformation.

The collapse of the imperial power in Italy, for which the papacy was largely responsible, and the transfer to Avignon left Italy to the wildest political confusion. Nowhere was the situation worse than in Rome. In 1347 Cola di Rienzi headed a popular revolution against the nobles and established a parody of the ancient republic. He was soon driven out, but in 1354 was in power again, only to be murdered in the partisan struggles. Innocent VI (1352–1362) sent the Spanish cardinal Albornoz (?–1367) as his legate to Italy. By Albornoz' military and diplomatic abilities the papal interests in Rome and Italy generally were much improved, so that Urban V (1362–1370) actually returned to the Eternal City in 1367. The death of Albornoz deprived him of his chief support, and in 1370 the papacy was once more in Avignon. Urban V was succeeded by Gregory XI (1370–1378), whom St. Catherine of Siena (1347–1380) urged in the name of God to return to Rome. The distracted state of the city also counselled his presence if papal interests were to be preserved. Accordingly he transferred the papacy to Rome in 1377, and there died the next year.

The sudden death of Gregory XI found the cardinals in Rome. A majority were French, and would gladly have returned to Avignon. The Roman people were determined to keep the papacy in Rome, and to that end to have an Italian Pope. Under conditions of tumult the cardinals chose Bartolommeo Prignano, the archbishop of Bari, who took the name Urban VI (1378–1389). A tactless man, who desired to terminate French influence over the papacy, and effect some reforms in the papal court, he soon had the hostility of all the cardinals. They now got together, four months after his election, declared their choice void since dictated by mob violence, and elected Cardinal Robert of Geneva as Pope Clement VII (1378–1394). A few months later Clement VII and his cardinals were settled in Avignon. There had been many rival Popes before, but they had been chosen by different elements. Here were two Popes, each duly elected by the same body of cardinals. The objection that Urban VI had been chosen out of fear had little force, since the cardinals had recognized him without protest for several months; but they had done all they could to undo the choice. Europe saw two Popes, each condemning the other. There was no power that could decide between them, and the several countries followed the one or the other as their political affinities dictated. The Roman Pope was acknowledged by northern and central Italy, the greater part of Germany, Scandinavia, and England. To the Pope in Avignon, France, Spain, Scotland, Naples, Sicily, and some parts of Germany adhered. It was a fairly equal division. The great schism had begun. Europe was pained and scandalized, while the papal abuses, especially of taxation, were augmented, and two courts must now be maintained. Above all, the profound feeling that the church must be visibly one was offended. The papacy sank enormously in popular regard.

In Rome Urban VI was succeeded by Boniface IX (1389–1404), and he by Innocent VII (1404–1406), who was followed by Gregory XII (1406–1415). In Avignon Clement VII was followed by a Spaniard, Peter de Luna, who took the name Benedict XIII (1394–1417).

12

Wyclif and Huss

THE ENGLISH OPPOSITION to the encroachments of the Avignon papacy has already been noted (see p. 265). Other forces were also working in the island. Of these that of Thomas Bradwardine (?–1349) was one of the most potent in the intellectual realm. Bradwardine, who was long an eminent theologian in Oxford, and died archbishop of Canterbury, was a leader in the revival of the study of Augustine, which marked the decline of Scholasticism, and was to grow in influence till it profoundly affected the Reformation. He taught predestination in most positive form; like Augustine, he conceived religion as primarily a personal relationship of God and the soul, and emphasized grace in contrast to merit. There were now, therefore, other intellectual traditions besides those of later nominalistic Scholasticism in the Oxford of Wyclif's student days.

John Wyclif (1328?–1384) was born in Hipswell in Yorkshire. Few details of his early life are known. He entered Balliol College, Oxford, of which he became ultimately for a short time "master." In Oxford he rose to great scholarly distinction, lecturing to large classes, and esteemed the ablest theologian of its faculty. Philosophically he was a realist, in contrast to the prevailing nominalism of his age. He was deeply influenced by Augustine, and through Augustine by Platonic conceptions. Wyclif gradually became known outside of Oxford. In 1374 he was presented, by royal appointment, to the rectory of Lutterworth, and the same year was one of the King's commissioners—probably theological adviser—to attempt in Bruges with the representatives of Pope Gregory XI an adjustment of the dispute regarding "provisors" (see p. 265). In how far these appointments were due to the powerful son of King Edward III, John of Gaunt, Duke of Lancaster, is uncertain, though he probably regarded Wyclif as likely to be useful in his designs on church property; but Wyclif's opinions cannot then have been widely known. There is no evidence that the Pope yet looked on him with distrust, and recent investigation has shown that his reformatory work did not begin in 1366, as formerly supposed.

By 1376, however, it was the wealth of the church and clerical interference, especially that of the Popes, in political life, that aroused his opposition. He lectured that year in Oxford *On Civil Lordship*. Wyclif's view of ecclesiastical office and privilege was curiously feudal. God is the great overlord. He gives all positions, civil and spiritual, as fiefs, to be held on condition of faithful service. They are stewardships, not property. God gives the use but not the ownership. If the user abuses his trust he forfeits his tenure. Hence a bad ecclesiastic loses all claim to office, and the temporal possessions of unworthy clergy may well be taken from them by the civil rulers, to whom God has given the lordship of temporal things, as He has that of things spiritual to the church. This doctrine, advanced in all simplicity and sincerity, was undoubtedly pleasing to John of Gaunt and his hungry crew of nobles who hoped for enrichment from church spoliation. It was no less satisfactory to many commoners, who had long been critical of the wealth, pretensions, and too often lack of character of the clergy. It was not displeasing to the mendicant orders, who had always, in theory at least, advocated "apostolic poverty."

Wyclif's teaching aroused the opposition of the high clergy, the property-holding orders, and of the papacy. In 1377 he was summoned to answer before the bishop of London, William Courtenay. The protection of John of Gaunt and other nobles rendered the proceeding abortive. The same year Pope Gregory XI issued five bulls ordering Wyclif's arrest and examination.[1] Yet Wyclif enjoyed the protection of a strong party at court and much popular favor, so that further proceedings against him by the archbishop of Canterbury and the bishop of London were frustrated in 1378.

Wyclif was now rapidly developing his reforming activities in a flood of treatises in Latin and English. The Scriptures, he taught, are the only law of the church. The church itself is not, as the common man imagined, centered in the Pope and the cardinals. It is the whole company of the elect. Its only certain head is Christ, since the Pope may not be one of the elect. Wyclif did not reject the papacy. The church may well have an earthly leader, if such a one is like Peter, and strives for the simple conditions of early Christianity. Such a Pope would be presumably one of the elect. But a Pope who grasps worldly power and is eager for taxes is presumptively non-elect, and therefore antichrist. With his deeper knowledge of the Bible, Wyclif now attacked the mendicant orders, which had supported him in his assertion of apostolic poverty, regarding them as without Scriptural warrant and the main pillars of the existing papacy. He was now fighting current churchly conditions all along the line.

Wyclif proceeded to more constructive efforts. Convinced that the Bible is the law of God, Wyclif determined to give it to the people in the English tongue. Between 1382 and 1384 the Scriptures were translated from the Vulgate. What share Wyclif had in the actual work is impossible to say. It has been usually thought that the New Testament was from his pen, and the Old from that of Nicholas of Hereford. At all events, the New Testament translation was vivid, readable, and forceful, and did a service of fundamental importance for the English language—to say nothing of English piety. The whole was revised about 1388, possibly by Wyclif's disciple, John Purvey. Its circulation was large. In spite of severe repression in the next century, at least one hundred and fifty manuscripts survive.

To bring the Gospel to the people Wyclif began sending out his "poor priests." In apostolic poverty, barefoot, clad in long robes, and with staff in the hand, they wandered two by two, as had the early Waldensian or Franciscan preachers. Unlike the latter, they were bound by no permanent vows. Their success was great.

But events soon lamed the Lollard movement, as the following of Wyclif was popularly called. Convinced that the elect are a true priesthood, and that all episcopal claims are unscriptural, Wyclif saw in the priestly power of exclusive human agency in the miracle of transubstantiation a main buttress of what he deemed erroneous priestly claim. He therefore attacked this doctrine in 1379. His own view of Christ's presence seems to have been essentially that later known as consubstantiation. It was not his positive assertions, but his

[1] Gee and Hardy, pp. 105–108.

attack that aroused resentment, for to oppose transubstantiation was to touch one of the most popularly cherished beliefs of the later Middle Ages. That attack cost Wyclif many followers and roused the churchly authorities to renewed action. This tide of opposition was strengthened by events in 1381, for which Wyclif was in no way responsible. The unrest of the lower orders, which had been growing since the dislocation of the labor market by the "black death" of 1348–1350, culminated in 1381 in a great peasant revolt, which was with difficulty put down. This bloody episode strengthened the party of conservatism. In 1382 the archbishop of Canterbury held a synod in London by which twenty-four Wyclifite opinions were condemned.[2] Wyclif was no longer able to lecture in Oxford. His "poor priests" were arrested. He was too strong in popular and courtly support, however, to be attacked personally, and he died still possessed of his pastorate in Lutterworth on the last day of 1384.

No small element in Wyclif's power was that he was thought to have no scholastic equal in contemporary England. Men hesitated to cross intellectual swords with him. Equally conspicuous were his intense patriotism and his deep piety. He voiced the popular resentment of foreign papal taxation and greed, and the popular longing for a simpler, more Biblical faith. It was his misfortune that he left no follower of conspicuous ability to carry on his work in England. Yet throughout the reign of Richard II (1377–1399) the Lollard movement continued to grow. With the accession of the usurping house of Lancaster in the person of Henry IV (1399–1413), the King, anxious to placate the church, was persuaded to secure the passage in 1401 of the statute *De haeretico comburendo*,[3] under which a number of Lollards were burned. Henry IV spared Lollards in high lay station. Not so his son, Henry V (1413–1422). Under him their most conspicuous leader, Sir John Oldcastle, Lord Cobham, a man of the sternest religious principles, whom tradition and dramatic license transformed into the figure of Falstaff, was condemned, driven into rebellion, and executed in 1417. With his death the political significance of Lollardy in England was at an end, though adherents continued in secret till the Reformation. Wyclif's chief influence was to be in Bohemia rather than in the land of his birth.

Bohemia had undergone a remarkable intellectual and political development in the fourteenth century. The Holy Roman Emperor, Charles IV (1346–1378), was also King of Bohemia, and did much for that land. In 1344 he secured the establishment of Prague as an archbishopric, releasing Bohemia from ecclesiastical dependence on Mainz. Four years later he procured the foundation of a university in Prague. In no country of Europe was the church more largely a landholder, or the clergy more worldly than in Bohemia. Charles IV was not unfriendly to moral reform. During and following his reign a series of preachers of power stirred Bohemia, attacking the seculariza-

[2] Gee and Hardy, pp. 108–110.   [3] *Ibid.*, pp. 133–135.

tion of the church. Such were Conrad of Waldhausen (?–1369), Milicz of Kremsier (?–1374), Matthias of Janov (?–1394), and Thomas of Stitny (1331–1401). These all opposed clerical corruption, emphasized the Scriptures as the rule of life, and sought a more frequent participation in the Lord's Supper. Milicz and Matthias taught that antichrist was at hand, and was manifest in an unworthy clergy. These men had little direct influence on Huss, but they stirred Bohemia to a readiness to accept his teachings.

Bohemia was torn, furthermore, by intense rivalry between the Germanic and the Slavonic (Czech) elements of the population. The latter was marked by a strong desire for racial supremacy and Bohemian autonomy.

Curiously, also, Bohemia, hitherto so little associated with England, was brought into connection with that country by the marriage of the Bohemian princess, Anna, to King Richard II, in 1383. Bohemian students were attracted to Oxford, and thence brought Wyclif's doctrines and writings into their native land, especially to the University of Prague. The great propagator of Bohemian Wyclifism was to be John Huss, in whom, also, all Czech national aspirations were to have an ardent advocate. It was this combination of religious and patriotic zeal that gave Huss his remarkable power of leadership.

John Huss was born, of peasant parentage, in Husinecz, whence he derived his name by abbreviation, about the year 1373. His studies were completed in the University of Prague, where he became Bachelor of Theology in 1394, and Master of Arts two years later. In 1401 he was ordained to the priesthood, still maintaining a teaching connection with the university, of which he was "rector" in 1402. Meanwhile Huss had become intimately acquainted with Wyclif's philosophical treatises, with the "realism" of which he sympathized. Wyclif's religious works, known by Huss certainly from 1402, won his approbation, and henceforth Huss was, theologically, a disciple of Wyclif. More conservative than his master, he did not deny transubstantiation; but like him he held the church to consist of the predestinate only, of whom the true head is not the Pope, but Christ, and of which the law is the New Testament, and its life that of Christ-like poverty. Though the publication of Huss's commentary on the *Sentences* of Peter Lombard has led to a higher estimate of his scholarly gifts than formerly prevailed, it is certain that in his sermons and treatises Huss usually reproduced not only the thoughts but the language of Wyclif.

In 1402 Huss became preacher at the Bethlehem chapel, in Prague, and soon gained immense popular following through his fiery sermons in the Bohemian language. Though Wyclifite views were condemned by the majority of the university in 1403 Huss's preaching had, at first, the support of the archbishop, Zbynek (1403–1411); but his criticisms of the clergy gradually turned this favor into opposition, which was increased as Huss's essential agreement with Wyclif constantly became more evident. New causes of dissent speedily arose. In the schism Bohemia had held to the Roman Pope, Gregory XII (1406–1415). As a step toward the healing of the breach King Wenzel of Bohemia now favored a policy of neutrality between the rival Popes. Huss and the Bohemian element in the university supported Wenzel. Archbishop Zbynek, the German clergy, and the German portion of the university clung to Gregory XII. Wenzel therefore, in 1409, arbitrarily changed the constitution of the university, giving the foreign majority one vote in its decisions and the Bohemians three, thus completely reversing the previous proportion. The immediate result was the secession of the foreign elements and the foundation, in 1409, of the University of Leipzig. This Bohemian nationalist victory, of doubtful permanent worth or right, Huss fully shared. Its immediate consequences were that he became the first "rector" of the newly regulated university, and enjoyed a high degree of courtly favor. His views were now spreading widely in Bohemia.

Meanwhile the luckless Council of Pisa had run its course (1409) (see p. 275). Zbynek now supported its Pope, Alexander V (1409–1410), to whom he complained of the spread of Wyclifite opinions in Bohemia, and by whom he was commissioned to root them out. Huss protested, and was excommunicated by Zbynek in 1410. The result was great popular tumult in Prague, where Huss was more than ever a national hero. King Wenzel supported him. In 1412 Alexander V's successor, Pope John XXIII (1410–1415), promised indulgence to all who should take part in a crusade against King Ladislaus of Naples. Huss opposed, holding that the Pope had no right to use physical force, that money payments effected no true forgiveness, and, unless of the predestinate, the indulgence could be of no value to a man. The result was an uproar. The Pope's bull was burned by the populace. Huss, however, lost many strong supporters in the university and elsewhere, and was once more excommunicated, while Prague was placed under papal interdict. Wenzel now persuaded Huss, late in 1412, to go into exile from Prague. To this period of retirement is due the composition of his chief work—essentially a reproduction of Wyclif—the De Ecclesia (On the Church). In 1413 a synod in Rome formally condemned Wyclif's writings.

The great Council of Constance (see p. 276) was approaching, and the confusion in Bohemia was certain to demand its consideration. Huss was asked to present himself before it, and promised a "safe-conduct," afterward received, by the Holy Roman Emperor, Sigismund. Huss, though he felt his life in grave peril, determined to go, partly believing it his duty to bear witness to what he deemed the truth, and partly convinced that he could bring the council to his way of thinking. Shortly after his arrival in Constance he was imprisoned. Sigismund disregarded his promised safe-conduct. His Bohemian enemies laid bitter charges against him. On May 4, 1415, the council condemned Wyclif, and ordered his long-buried body burned. Huss could hope for no favorable hearing. Yet, in the end, the struggle resolved itself into a contest of principles. The council maintained that every Christian was bound to submit to its decisions. Only by so holding could it hope to end the papal schism which was the scandal of Christendom. It insisted on Huss's complete submission. The Bohemian reformer was of heroic mould. He would play no tricks with his conscience. Some of the accusations he declared false charges. Other positions he could not modify unless convinced of their error. He would not submit his conscience to the overruling judgment of the council. On July 6, 1415, he was condemned and burned, meeting his death with the most steadfast courage.

While Huss was a prisoner in Constance his followers in Prague began administering the cup to the laity in the Lord's Supper—an action which Huss approved and which soon became the badge of the Hussite movement. The news of Huss's death aroused the utmost resentment in Bohemia, to which fuel was added when the Council of Constance forbad the use of the cup by laymen, and caused Huss's disciple, Jerome of Prague, to be burned on May 30, 1416. Bohemia was in revolution. Two parties speedily developed there —an aristocratic, having its principal seat in Prague, and known as the Utraquists (communion in both bread and wine), and a radical, democratic, called from its fortress "Tabor" the Taborites.

The Utraquists would forbid only those practices which they deemed prohibited by the "law of God," i. e., the Bible. They demanded free preaching of the Gospel, the cup for the laity, apostolic poverty, and strict clerical life. The Taborites repudiated all practices for which express warrant could not be found in the "law of God." Fierce quarrel existed between these factions, but both united to resist repeated crusades directed against Bohemia. Under the leadership of the blind Taborite general, John Zizka, all attempts to crush the Hussites were bloodily defeated. Church property was largely confiscated. Nor were the opponents of the Hussites more successful after Zizka's death in 1424. Under Prokop the Great the Hussites carried the war beyond the borders of Bohemia. Some compromise seemed unavoidable. The Council of Basel (see p. 277), after long negotiation, therefore, met the wishes of the Utraquists part way in 1433, granting the use of the cup, and in a measure the other demands outlined above. The Taborites resisted and were almost swept away by the Utraquists, in 1434, at the battle of Lipan, in which Prokop was killed. The triumphant Utraquists now came to an agreement with the Council of Basel, in 1436, and on these terms were nominally given place in the Roman communion. Yet, in 1462, Pope Pius II (1458–1464) declared this agreement void. The Utraquists, nevertheless, held their own, and the Bohemian Parliament, in 1485 and 1512, declared their full equality with the Catholics. At the Reformation a considerable portion welcomed the newer ideas; others then returned to the Roman Church.

The real representatives of Wyclifite principles were the Taborites rather than the Utraquists. Out of the general Hussite movement, with elements drawn from Taborites, Utraquists, and Waldenses, rather than exclusively from the Taborites, there grew, from about 1453, the *Unitas Fratrum,* which absorbed much that was most vital in the Hussite movement, and became the spiritual ancestor of the later Moravians (see pp. 450–452).

Wyclif and Huss have often been styled forerunners of the Reformation. The designation is true if regard is had to their protest against the corruption of the church, their exaltation of the Bible, and their contribution to the sum total of agitation that ultimately resulted in reform. When their doctrines are examined, however, they appear to belong rather to the Middle Ages. Their conception of the Gospel was that of a "law." Their place for faith was no greater than in the Roman communion. Their thought of the church was a one-sided development of Augustinianism. Their conception of the relation of the clergy to property is that common to the Waldenses and the founders of the great mendicant orders. Their religious earnestness commands deep admiration, but in spite of Luther's recognition of many points of agreement with Huss, the Reformation owed little to their efforts.

13

The Reforming Councils

THE PAPAL SCHISM was the scandal of Christendom, but its termination was not easy. The logic of mediæval development was that no power exists on earth to which the papacy is answerable. Yet good men everywhere felt that the schism must be ended, and that the church must be reformed "in head and members"—that is, in the papacy and clergy. The reforms desired were moral and administrative. Doctrinal modifications were as yet unwished by Christendom as a whole. A Wyclif might proclaim them in England, but he was generally esteemed a heretic. Foremost among those who set themselves seriously to the task of healing the schism were the teachers of the age, especially those of the University of Paris. Marsilius of Padua had there proclaimed the supremacy of a general council in his *Defensor Pacis* of 1324. The necessities of the situation rather than his arguments were rapidly leading to the same conclusion. It was presented first with clearness by a doctor of canon law, then in Paris, Conrad of Gelnhausen (1320?–1390), who advised King Charles V of France (1364–1380), in written treatises of 1379 and 1380, to unite with other princes in calling a council, if necessary, without the consent of the rival Popes. Conrad went no further than to hold that such a council was justified by the necessities of an anomalous situation. Conrad's proposal was reinforced, in such fashion as to rob him of the popular credit of its origination, by the treatise of another German scholar at the University of Paris, Heinrich of Langenstein (1340?–1397), set forth in 1381.

The thought of a general council as the best means of healing the schism, thus launched, made speedy converts, not only in the University of Paris, but in the great school of canon law in Bologna, and even among the cardinals. To call a council presented many difficulties, however, and the leaders at Paris, Peter of Ailli (Pierre d'Ailli) (1350–1420) and John Gerson (Jean Charlier de Gerson) (1363–1429), famed for their mastery of nominalistic theology, and the latter eminent among Christian mystics, were slow to adopt the conciliar plan. Efforts were vainly made for years to induce the rival Popes to resign. France withdrew from the Avignon Pope, without recognizing the Roman, from 1398 to 1403, and again in 1408; but its example found slight following elsewhere. By 1408 d'Ailli and Gerson had come to see in a council the only hope, and were supported by Nicholas of Clémanges (1367–1437), a former teacher of the Parisian university who had been papal secretary in Avignon from 1397 to 1405, to whom one great source of evil in the church seemed the general neglect of the Scriptures.

The cardinals of both Popes were now convinced of the necessity of a council. Meeting together in Leghorn, in 1408, they issued a call in their own names for such an assembly in Pisa, to gather on March 25, 1409. There it met with an attendance not only of cardinals, bishops, the heads of the great orders, and leading abbots, but also of doctors of theology and canon law, and the representatives of lay sovereigns. Neither Pope was present or acknowledged its rightfulness. Both were declared deposed. This was a practical assertion that the council was superior to the papacy. Its action, however, was too hasty, for instead of ascertaining, as d'Ailli advised, whether the person of the proposed new Pope would be generally acceptable, the cardinals now elected Peter Philargès, archbishop of Milan, who took the name Alexander V (1409–1410). The council then dissolved, leaving the question of reform to a future council.

In some respects the situation was worse than before the Council of Pisa met. Rome, Naples, and considerable sections of Germany clung to Gregory XII. Spain, Portugal, and Scotland supported Benedict XIII. England, France, and some portions of Germany acknowledged Alexander V. There were three Popes where before there had been two. Yet, though mismanaged, the Council of Pisa was a mark of progress. It had shown that the church was one, and it increased the hope that a better council could end the schism. This assembly had been called by the cardinals. For such invitation history had no precedent. A summons by the Emperor, if possible with the consent of one or more of the Popes, would be consonant with the practice of the early church. To that end those supporting the council idea now labored.

The new Holy Roman Emperor-elect, Sigismund (1410–1437), was convinced of the necessity of a council. He recognized as Pope John XXIII (1410–1415), one of the least worthy of occupants of that office, who had been chosen successor to Alexander V in the Pisan line. Sigismund used John's difficulties with King Ladislaus of Naples, to secure from him joint action by which Emperor-elect and Pope called a council to meet in Constance on November 1, 1414. There the most brilliant and largely attended gathering of the Middle Ages assembled. As in Pisa, it included not only cardinals and bishops, but doctors of theology and representatives of monarchs, though the lay delegates were without votes. Sigismund was present in person, and also John XXIII.

John XXIII hoped to secure the indorsement of the council. To this end he had brought with him many Italian bishops. To neutralize their votes the council organized by "nations," the English, German, and French, to which the Italians were forced to join as a fourth. Each "nation" had one vote, and one was assigned also to the cardinals. Despairing of the council's approval, John XXIII attempted to disrupt its session by flight, in March, 1415. Under Gerson's vigorous leadership the council, however, declared on April 6, 1415, that as "representing the Catholic Church militant [it] has its power immediately from Christ, and every one, whatever his position or rank, even if it be the papal dignity itself, is bound to obey it in all those things which pertain to the faith, to the healing of the schism, and to the general reformation of the Church of God." [1] On May 29 the council declared John XXIII deposed. On July 4 Gregory XII resigned. The council had rid the church of two Popes by its successful assertion of its supreme authority over all in the church. It is easy to see why its leaders insisted on a full submission from Huss, whose trials and martyrdom were contemporary with these events (see p. 273).

Benedict XIII proved more difficult. Sigismund himself, therefore, journeyed to Spain. Benedict he could not persuade to resign, and that obstinate pontiff asserted himself till death, in 1424, as the only legitimate Pope. What Sigismund was unable to effect with Benedict he accomplished with the Spanish kingdoms. They and Scotland repudiated Benedict. The Spaniards joined the council as a fifth "nation," and, on July 26, 1417, Benedict, or Peter de Luna, as he was once more called, was formally deposed. The careful action of the council, in contrast to the haste in Pisa, had made it certain that no considerable section of Christendom would support the former Popes.

[1] Robinson, 1:511.

One main purpose of the council had been moral and administrative reform. Here the jealousies of the several interests prevented achievement of real importance. The cardinals desired no changes that would materially lessen their revenue. Italy, on the whole, profited by the existing situation. England had relative self-government already in ecclesiastical affairs, thanks to its Kings. France was at war with England, and indisposed to unite with that land. So it went, with the result that the council finally referred the question of reforms to the next Pope "in conjunction with this holy council or with the deputies of the several nations"—that is, each nation was left to make the best bargain it could. The council enumerated a list of subjects for reform discussion, which relate almost entirely to questions of appointment, taxation, or administration.[2] As a reformatory instrument the Council of Constance was a bitter disappointment. Its one great achievement was that it ended the schism. In November, 1417, the cardinals, with six representatives from each nation, elected a Roman cardinal, Otto Colonna, as Pope. He took the name Martin V (1417–1431). Roman Christendom had once more a single head. In April, 1418, the council ended, the new Pope promising to call another in five years, in compliance with the decree of the council.[3]

The Council of Constance was a most interesting ecclesiastical experiment. It secured the transformation of the papacy from an absolute into a constitutional monarchy. The Pope was to remain the executive of the church, but was to be regulated by a legislative body, meeting at frequent intervals and representing all interests in Christendom.

It seemed that this great constitutional change had really been accomplished. Martin V called the new council to meet in Pavia in 1423. The plague prevented any considerable attendance. The Pope would gladly have had no more of councils. The Hussite wars distressed Europe, however (see p. 273), and such pressure was brought to bear on him that in January, 1431, Martin V summoned a council to meet in Basel, and appointed Cardinal Giuliano Cesarini his legate to conduct it. Less than two months later Martin V was dead and Eugene IV (1431–1447) was Pope. The council opened in July, 1431, but in December Eugene ordered it adjourned, to meet in Bologna in 1433. The council refused, and re-enacted the declaration of Constance that it was superior to the Pope. Thus, almost from the first, bad feeling existed between the Council of Basel and the papacy. Mindful that jealousies between "nations" had frustrated the reform plans in Constance, the council rejected such groupings, and instead organized four large committees, on reform, doctrine, public peace, and general questions. It began its work with great vigor and promise of success. It made an apparent reconciliation with the moderate Hussites in 1433 (see p. 273). Roman unity seemed restored. The Pope found little support and, before the close of 1433, formally recognized the council. Its future seemed assured.

[2] *Ibid.*, 1:513.   [3] Robinson, 1:512.

The Council of Basel now proceeded to those administrative and moral reforms which had failed of achievement at Constance. It ordered the holding of a synod in each diocese annually, and in each archbishopric every two years, in which abuses should be examined and corrected. It provided for a general council every ten years. It reasserted the ancient rights of canonical election against papal appointments. It limited appeals to Rome. It fixed the cardinals at twenty-four in number, and ordered that no nation should be represented by more than a third of the college. It cut off the annates and the other more oppressive papal taxes entirely. All this was good, but the spirit in which it was done was increasingly a vindictive attitude toward Pope Eugene. The taxes by which the papacy had heretofore been maintained were largely abolished, but no honorable support of the papacy was provided in their stead. This failure not only increased the anger of the papacy but caused division in the council itself. At this point a great opportunity presented itself, of which Eugene IV made full use, and regarding which the council so put itself in the wrong as to ruin its prospects.

The Eastern empire was now hard pressed in its final struggles with the conquering Turks. In the hope of gaining help from the West the Emperor, John VIII (1425–1448), with the patriarch of Constantinople, Joseph II (1416–1439), and Bessarion (1395–1472), the gifted archbishop of Nicæa, were ready to enter into negotiation for the union of the Greek and Latin Churches. Both Pope and council were disposed to use this approach for their several advantage. The majority of the council would have the Greeks come to Avignon. The Pope offered an Italian city, which the Greeks naturally preferred. The council divided on the issue in 1437, the minority seceding, including Cesarini. The Pope now announced the transferrence of the council to Ferrara to meet the Greeks. Thither the minority went, and there in March, 1438, the Eastern Emperor, with many Oriental prelates, arrived. The Pope had practically won. An event so full of promise as the reunion of Christendom robbed the still continuing Council of Basel of much of its interest.

The Council of Ferrara, which was transferred to Florence in 1439, witnessed protracted discussion between Greeks and Latins, in which as a final result the primacy of the Pope was accepted in vague terms. This seemed to preserve the rights of the Eastern patriarchs, the Greeks retained their peculiarities of worship and priestly marriage, while the disputed *filioque* clause of the creed was acknowledged by the Greeks, though with the understanding that they would not add it to the ancient symbol. Mark, the vigorous archbishop of Ephesus, refused agreement, but the Emperor and most of his ecclesiastical following approved, and the reunion of the two churches was joyfully proclaimed in July, 1439. An event so happy greatly increased the prestige of Pope Eugene IV. The hollowness of the achievement was not at once apparent. Reunions with the Armenians, and with certain groups of

Monophysites and Nestorians, were also announced in Florence or speedily after the council. The reconciliation of the Armenians in 1439 was the occasion of a famous papal bull defining the mediæval doctrine of the sacraments. Yet from the first the Oriental monks were opposed. On the Greeks' return Mark of Ephesus became the hero of the hour. Bessarion, whom Eugene had made a cardinal, had to fly to Italy, where he was to have a distinguished career of literary and ecclesiastical service. No efficient military help came to the Greeks from the West, and the capture of Constantinople by the Turks in 1453 permanently frustrated those political hopes which had inspired the union efforts of 1439.

Meanwhile the majority in Basel proceeded to more radical action under the leadership of its only remaining cardinal, the able and excellent but dictatorial Louis d'Allemand (1380?–1450). In 1439 it voted Eugene IV deposed, and chose as his successor a half-monastic layman, Duke Amadeus of Savoy, who took the name Felix V. By this time, however, the Council of Basel was fast losing its remaining influence. Eugene IV had won, and was succeeded in Rome by Nicholas V (1447–1455). Felix V laid down his impossible papacy in 1449. The council put the best face on its defeat by choosing Nicholas V his successor, and ended its troubled career. Though the council idea still lived and was to be powerful in the Reformation age, the fiasco in Basel had really ruined the hope of transforming the papacy into a constitutional monarchy or of effecting needed reform through conciliar action.

Yet if the council thus failed, individual nations profited by its quarrel with the papacy, notably France, where the monarchy was coming into new power through effective resistance to England under impulses initiated by Joan of Arc (1410?–1431). In 1438 King Charles VII (1422–1461), with the clergy and nobles, adopted the "Pragmatic Sanction" of Bourges, by which the greater part of the reforms attempted in Basel were enacted into law for France. France therefore secured relief from the most pressing papal taxes and interferences, and this freedom had not a little to do with the attitude of the land previous to the Reformation age.

Not so fortunate was Germany. There the nobles in the Reichstag in Mainz of 1439 adopted an "acceptation" much resembling the French "pragmatic sanction"; but the divisions and weakness of the country gave room to papal intrigue, so that its provisions were practically limited by the Concordat of Aschaffenburg of 1448. Certain privileges were granted to particular princes; but Germany, as a whole, remained under the weight of the papal taxation.

Throughout the period of the councils a new force was manifesting itself—that of nationality. The Council of Constance had authorized the nations to make terms with the papacy. Bohemia had dealt with its religious situation as a nation. France had asserted its national rights. Germany had tried to do so. With the failure of the councils to effect administrative reform, men began asking whether what they had sought might not be secured by national action. It was a feeling that was to increase till the Reformation, and greatly to influence the course of that struggle.

14

The Italian Renaissance and Its Popes

THE MOST REMARKABLE intellectual event contemporary with the story of the papacy in Avignon and the schism was the beginning of the Renaissance. That great alteration in mental outlook has been treated too often as without mediæval antecedents. It is coming to be recognized that the Middle Ages were not uncharacterized by individual initiative, that the control of the church was never such as to make other-worldliness wholly dominant, and that the literary monuments of Latin antiquity, at least, were widely known. The revival of Roman law had begun contemporaneously with the Crusades, and had attracted increasing attention to that normative feature of ancient thought, first in Italy and later in France and Germany. Yet when all these elements are recognized, it remains true that the Renaissance involved an essentially new outlook on the world, in which emphasis was laid on its present life, beauty, and satisfaction—on man as man—rather than on a future heaven and hell, and on man as an object of salvation or of loss. The means by which this transformation was wrought was a reappreciation of the spirit of classical antiquity, especially as manifested in its great literary monuments.

The Renaissance first found place in Italy. Its rise was favored by many influences, among which three, at least, were conspicuous. The two great dominating powers of the Middle Ages, the papacy and empire, were suddenly lamed, as far as Italy was concerned, by the collapse of the imperial power in the latter part of the thirteenth century and the removal of the papacy to Avignon early in the fourteenth. The commerce of Italy, fostered by the Crusades and continuing after their close, had led to a higher cultural development in the peninsula than elsewhere in Europe. The intense division of Italian politics gave to the cities a quality of life not elsewhere existent, rendering local recognition of talent easy, and tending to emphasize individualism.

The earliest Italian in whom the Renaissance spirit was a dominating force was Petrarch (1304–1374). Brought up in Avignon, and in clerical orders, his real interest was in the revival of Latin literature, especially the writings of Cicero. A diligent student, and above all a man of letters, he was the friend of princes, and a figure of international influence. Scholasticism he despised. Aristotle he condemned. Though really religious in feeling, however lacking in practice, his point of view was very unlike the mediæval. He had, moreover, that lack of profound seriousness, that egotistical vanity and that worship of form rather than of substance which were to be characteristic of much of Italian humanism; but he aroused men to a new interest in antiquity and a new world-outlook. Petrarch's friend and admirer was Boccaccio (1313–1375), now chiefly remembered for his *Decameron,* but greatly influential in his own age in promoting the study of Greek, in unlocking the mysteries of classical mythology, and in furthering humanistic studies in Florence and Naples.

Greek may never have died out in southern Italy, but its humanistic cultivation began when, in 1360, Boccaccio brought Leontius Pilatus to Florence. About 1397 Greek was taught, under the auspices of the government of the same city, by Manuel Chrysoloras (1355?–1415), who translated Homer and Plato. The Council of Ferrara and Florence (1438–1439) (see p. 278) greatly fostered this desire to master the treasures of the East by bringing Greeks and Latins together. Bessarion (see p. 278) thenceforth aided the work. To the influence of Gemistos Plethon (1355–1450), another Greek attendant on this reunion council, was due the founding of the Platonic Academy, about 1442, by Cosimo de' Medici (1389–1464), the real ruler of Florence. There the study of Plato was pursued ardently, later, under the leadership of Marsilio Ficino (1433–1499). Ficino, who became a priest, combined an earnest Christianity with his platonic enthusiasm. He believed a return to the Christian sources the chief need of the time—a feeling not shared by the majority of Italian humanists, but to be profoundly influential beyond the Alps, as propagated by his admirers, Jacques Le Fèvre in France and John Colet in England. Colet, in turn, transmitted it to Erasmus. Almost as influential was Pico della Mirandola (1463–1494), whose zeal for Hebrew and knowledge of the Kabala were to influence Reuchlin.

Historical criticism was developed by Lorenzo Valla (1405–1457), who exposed the falsity of the Donation of Constantine (see p. 204) about 1440, and denied the composition of the Apostles' Creed by the Apostles. He criticised the rightfulness of monastic vows, and laid the foundation of New Testament studies, in 1444, by a comparison of the Vulgate with the Greek.

An examination of the dates just given will show that the Renaissance movement in Italy was in full development before the fall of Constantinople, in 1453. By the middle of the fifteenth century it was dominating the educated class in Italy. In general, its attitude toward the church was one of indifference. It revived widely a pagan point of view, and sought to reproduce the life of antiquity in its vices as well as its virtues. Few periods in the world's history have been so boastfully corrupt as that of the Italian Renaissance.

The Renaissance movement was given wings by a great invention by Johannes Gutenberg of Mainz, about 1450—that of printing from movable type. The art spread with rapidity, and not only made available to the many the books which had heretofore been the property of the few, but, from the multiplication of copies, rendered the results of learning practically indestructible. More than thirty thousand publications were issued before 1500.

No mention of the Renaissance could fail to note its services to art. Beginnings of better things had been made, indeed, in Italy before its influence was felt. Cimabue (1240?–1302?), Giotto (1267?–1337), and Fra Angelico (1387–1455) belong to the pre-Renaissance epoch, remarkable as is their work. With Masaccio (1402–1429), Filippo Lippi (1406–1469), Botticelli (1444–1510), and Ghirlandajo (1449–1494), painting advanced through truer knowledge of perspective, greater anatomical accuracy, and more effective grouping to the full noonday of a Leonardo da Vinci (1452–1519), a Raphael Sanzio (1483–1520), a Michelangelo Buonarroti (1475–1564), and their mighty associates. Sculpture received a similar impulse in the work of Ghiberti (1378–1455), and Donatello (1386–1466); while architecture was transformed by Brunelleschi (1379–1446), Bramante (1444?–1514), and Michelangelo. Most of the work of these great artists, however classical in motive, was wrought in the service of the church.

The most conspicuous early seat of the Italian Renaissance was Florence, though it was influential in many cities. With the papacy of Nicholas V (1447–1455), it found, for the first time, a mighty patron in the head of the church, and Rome became its chief home. To him the foundation of the Vatican library was due. The next Pope, Alfonso Borgia, a Spaniard, who took the name Calixtus III (1455–1458), was no friend of humanism, and was earnestly though fruitlessly, intent on a crusade that should drive the Turks from the recently conquered Constantinople. In Enea Silvio Piccolomini, who ruled as Pius II (1458–1464), the papacy had a remarkable occupant. In early life a supporter of the conciliar movement, and active at the Council of Basel, he had won distinction as a humanistic writer of decidedly unclerical tone. Reconciled to Eugene IV, he became a cardinal, and ultimately Pope, now opposing all the conciliar views that he had once supported, and forbidding future appeals to a general council. His efforts to stir Europe against the Turks were unavailing. Yet, in spite of his changing and self-seeking attitude, he had the most worthy conception of the duties of the papal office of any Pope of the latter half of the fifteenth century. The succeeding Popes, till after the dawn of the Reformation, were patrons of letters and artists, great builders who adorned Rome and felt the full impulse of the Renaissance.

Meanwhile a change had come over the ideals and ambitions of the papacy. The stay in Avignon and the schism had rendered effective control in the States of the Church impossible. They were distracted by the contests of the people of Rome, and especially by the rivalries of the noble houses, notably those of the Colonna and the Orsini. Italy had gradually consolidated into five large states, Venice, Milan, Florence, Naples, or the Kingdom of the Two Sicilies, as it was called, and the States of the Church, though many smaller territories remained outside these larger groups, and were objects of contest. The politics of Italy became a kaleidoscopic effort to extend the possessions of the larger powers, and to match one against the other, in which intrigue, murder, and duplicity were employed to an almost un-exampled extent.

Into this game of Italian politics the papacy now fully plunged. Its desire was to consolidate and increase the States of the Church and maintain political independence. Its ambitions and its aims were like those of other Italian rulers. The papacy became secularized as at no other period in its history, save possibly the tenth century. Martin V (1417–1431), the Pope chosen at the Council of Constance, himself a Colonna, succeeded, in a measure, in restoring papal authority in Rome. His successor, Eugene IV (1431–1447), was not so fortunate, and spent a large part of his pontificate in Florence. Nicholas V (1447–1455), the humanist, effectively controlled Rome and strengthened the papal authority—a policy which was continued by Calixtus III (1455–1458), Pius II (1458–1464), and Paul II (1464–1471). With Sixtus IV (1471–1484) political ambition took almost complete con-trol of the papacy. He warred with Florence, he sought to enrich and ad-vance his relatives, he aimed to extend the States of the Church. A patron of learning, he built extensively. The Sistine Chapel preserves his name. All these endeavors required money, and he increased papal taxation and the financial abuses of the curia. He made into an article of faith the wide-spread belief that indulgences are available for souls in purgatory by a bull of 1476.[1]

The next Pope, Innocent VIII (1484–1492), was of weak and pliant nature, notorious through the open manner in which he sought to advance the fortunes of his children, his extravagant expenditures, and his sale of offices. He even received a pension from Sultan Bayazid II for keeping the latter's brother and rival, Djem, a prisoner. Innocent's successor, Alexander VI (1492–1503), a nephew of Calixtus III, and a Spaniard (Rodrigo Borgia), obtained the papacy not without bribery, and was a man of unbridled im-morality, though of considerable political insight. His great effort was to advance his bastard children, especially his daughter, Lucrezia Borgia, by advantageous marriages, and his unscrupulous and murderous son, Cesare

[1] Kidd, *Documents Illustrative of the Continental Reformation*, p. 3.

Borgia, by aiding him to carve a principality out of the States of the Church. His reign saw the beginning of the collapse of Italian independence through the invasion of Charles VIII of France (1483–1498), in 1494, in an attempt to assert the French King's claim to the throne of Naples. In 1499 Louis XII of France (1498–1515) conquered Milan, and in 1503 Ferdinand the Catholic, of Spain (1479–1516), secured Naples. Italy became the wretched battleground of French and Spanish rivalries.

Under such circumstances to increase the temporal power of the papacy was not easy; but the task was achieved by the most warlike of the Popes, Julius II (1503–1513), nephew of Sixtus IV. The Orsini and Colonna were reconciled, Cesare Borgia driven from Italy, the cities of Romagna freed from their Venetian conquerors, the various nations in Europe grouped in leagues, with the result that the French were, for the time, expelled from Italy. In this contest Louis XII secured a parody of a general council in Pisa, which Pope Julius answered by calling the Fifth Lateran Council in Rome. It met from 1512 to 1517, and though reforms were ordered it accomplished nothing of importance. Julius II was undoubtedly a ruler of great talents, who led his soldiers personally, and was animated by a desire to strengthen the temporal power of the papacy, rather than to enrich his relatives. As a patron of art and a builder he was among the most eminent of the Popes.

Julius II was succeeded by Giovanni de' Medici, who took the name Leo X (1513–1521). With all the artistic and literary tastes of the great Florentine family of which he was a member, he combined a love of display and extravagant expenditure. Far less warlike than Julius II, and free from the personal vices of some of his predecessors, he nevertheless made his prime interests the enlargement of the States of the Church, and the balancing of the various factions of Italy, domestic and foreign, for the political advantage of the papacy. He strove to advance his relatives. In 1516 he secured by a "concordat" with Francis I of France (1515–1547) the abolition of the "Pragmatic Sanction" (see p. 279) on terms which left to the King the nomination of all high French ecclesiastics and the right to tax the clergy, while the annates and other similar taxes went to the Pope. The next year a revolt began in Germany, the gravity of which Leo never really comprehended, which was to tear half of Europe from the Roman obedience.

Such Popes represented the Italian Renaissance, but they in no sense embodied the real spirit of a church which was to millions the source of comfort in this life and of hope for that to come. A revolution was inevitable. Nor did such a papacy represent the real religious life of Italy. The Renaissance affected only the educated and the upper classes. The people responded to appeals of preachers and the example of those they believed to be saints, though unfortunately seldom with lasting results save on individual lives.

Such a religious leader, when the Renaissance was young, was St. Catherine (1347–1380), the daughter of a dyer of Siena. A mystic, the recipient as she believed of divinely sent visions, she was a practical leader of affairs, a healer of family quarrels, a main cause in persuading the papacy to return from Avignon to Rome, a fearless denouncer of clerical evils, and an ambassador to whom Popes and cities listened with respect. Her correspondence involved counsel of almost as much political as religious value to many of the leaders of the age in church and state alike.

Even more famous in the later period of the Renaissance was Girolamo Savonarola of Florence (1452–1498). A native of Ferrara, intended for the medical profession, a refusal of marriage turned his thoughts to a monastic life. In 1474 he became a Dominican in Bologna. Eight years later his work in Florence began. At first little successful as a preacher, he came to speak with immense popular effectiveness, that was heightened by the general conviction which he himself shared that he was a divinely inspired prophet. He was in no sense a Protestant. His religious outlook was thoroughly mediæval. The French invasion of 1494 led to a popular revolution against the Medici, and Savonarola now became the real ruler of Florence, which he sought to transform into a penitential city. A semi-monastic life was adopted by many of the inhabitants. At the carnival seasons of 1496 and 1497, masks, indecent books and pictures were burned. For the time being the life of Florence was radically changed. But Savonarola aroused enemies. The adherents of the deposed Medici hated him, and above all, Pope Alexander VI, whose evil character and misrule Savonarola denounced. The Pope excommunicated him and demanded his punishment. Friends sustained him for a while, but the fickle populace turned against him. In April, 1498, he was arrested, cruelly tortured, and on May 23 hanged and his body burned by the city government. Not the least of Alexander VI's crimes was his persecution of this preacher of righteousness, though Savonarola's death was due quite as much to Florentine reaction against him as to the hostility of the Pope.

15

The New National Powers

THE HALF-CENTURY from 1450 to 1500 saw a remarkable growth in royal authority and national consciousness in the western kingdoms of Europe. France, which had seemed well-nigh ruined by the long wars with England, from 1339 to 1453, came out of them with the monarchy greatly strengthened, since these struggles had been immensely destructive to the feudal nobility. Louis XI (1461–1483), by intrigue, arms, and tyranny, with the aid of commoners, broke the power of the feudal nobility and secured for the crown an authority it had not hitherto possessed. His son, Charles VIII (1483–1498), was able to lead the now centralized state into a career of foreign conquest in Italy that was to open a new epoch in European politics and give rise to rivalries that were to determine the political background of the whole Reformation age. What these Kings had attempted in centralization at home, and in conquest abroad, was carried yet further by Louis XII (1498–1515), and by the brilliant and ambitious Francis I (1515–1547). France was now a strong, centralized monarchy. Its church was largely under royal control, and to a considerable degree relieved of the worst papal abuses, thanks to the "Pragmatic Sanction" of 1438 (see p. 279), and the custom which grew up with the strengthening of the monarchy in the fifteenth century that appeals could be taken from church courts to those of the King. The control of the monarchy over clerical appointments, clerical taxation, and clerical courts was increased by the "concordat" of 1516 (see p. 284), which gave to the Pope in turn desired taxes. By the dawn of the Reformation the church of France was, in many respects, a state church.

In England the Wars of the Roses, between Yorkists and Lancastrians, from 1455 to 1485, resulted in the destruction of the power of the high nobility to the advantage of the crown. Parliament survived. The King must rule in legal form; but the power of a Henry VII (1485–1509), the first of the house of Tudor, was greater than that of any English sovereign had been for a century, and was exercised with almost unlimited absolutism, though in parliamentary form, by his even abler son, Henry VIII (1509–1547). The English sovereigns had attained, even before the Reformation, a large degree of authority in ecclesiastical affairs, and, as in France, the church in England was largely national at the close of the fifteenth century.

This nationalizing process was nowhere in so full development as in Spain, where it was taking on the character of a religious awakening, which was to make that land a pattern for the conception of reform, often, though not very correctly, called the Counter-Reformation—a conception that was ultimately able to hold the allegiance of half of Europe to a purified Roman Church. The rise of Spain was the political wonder of the latter part of the fifteenth century. Aside from the main currents of mediæval European life, the history of the peninsula had been a long crusade to throw off the Mohammedan yoke, which had been imposed in 711. Nowhere in Europe were patriotism and Catholic orthodoxy so interwoven. The struggle had resulted, by the thirteenth century, in the restriction of the Moors to the kingdom of Granada, and in the formation of four Christian kingdoms, Castile, Aragon, Portugal, and Navarre. These states were weak, and the royal power limited by the feudal nobility. A radical change came when the prospective rulership of the larger part of the peninsula was united, in 1469, by the marriage of Ferdinand, heir of Aragon (King, 1479–1516) with Isabella, heiress of Castile (Queen, 1474–1504). Under their joint sovereignty Spain took a new place in European life. The disorderly nobles were repressed. The royal authority was asserted. In 1492 Granada was conquered and Mohammedanism overcome. The same year witnessed the discovery of a new world by Columbus, under Spanish auspices, which speedily became a source of very considerable revenue to the royal treasury. The French invasions of Italy led to Spanish interference, which lodged Spain firmly in Naples by 1503, and soon rendered Spanish influence predominant throughout Italy. On Ferdinand's death, in 1516, these great possessions passed to his grandson, already heir of Austria and the Netherlands, and to wear the imperial title as Charles V. Spain had suddenly become the first power in Europe.

The joint sovereigns, Ferdinand and Isabella, devoted themselves no less energetically to the control of the church than to the extension of their temporal authority. The "Spanish awakening" was in no sense unique. It did not differ in principle from much that had been attempted elsewhere in the later Middle Ages. No nation with a history like that of Spain could desire doctrinal change. It was intensely devoted to the system of which the papacy was the spiritual head. But it believed that papal aggressions in administrative affairs should be limited by royal authority, and that an educated, moral, and zealous clergy could, by the same power, be encouraged and maintained. It was by reason of the success with which these results were accomplished that the Spanish awakening became the model of the "Counter-Reformation."

No more conscientious or religiously minded sovereign ever ruled than Isabella, and if Ferdinand was primarily a politician, he was quick to see the political advantages of a policy that would place the Spanish church in subjection to the crown. In 1482 the joint sovereigns forced Pope Sixtus IV to agree to a concordat placing nomination to the higher ecclesiastical posts in the royal control. The policy thus begun was speedily extended by the energetic sovereigns. Papal bulls now required royal approval for promulgation. Church courts were supervised. The clergy were taxed for the benefit of the state.

Ferdinand and Isabella now proceeded to fill the important stations in the Spanish church not only with men devoted to the royal interests, but of strenuous piety and disciplinary zeal. In this effort they had the aid of many men of ability, but chief among them stood Gonzalez (or Francisco) Ximenes de Cisneros (1436–1517), in whom the Spanish awakening had its typical representative.

Born of a family of the lower nobility, Ximenes went to Rome after studies in Alcalá and Salamanca. On his return, in 1465, after six years in the seat of the papacy, he showed great ability in church business and much talent as a preacher. About 1480 he was appointed vicar-general of the diocese by Mendoza, then bishop of Siguenza. In the full tide of success Ximenes now renounced all his honors and became a Franciscan monk of the strictest observance. Not content with these austerities, he adopted the hermit's life. In 1492, however, on recommendation of Mendoza, now become archbishop of Toledo, Queen Isabella appointed Ximenes her confessor, and consulted him in affairs of state as well as questions of conscience. Queen and confessor worked in harmony, and under their vigorous action a thoroughgoing reform of discipline was undertaken in the disorderly monasteries of the land. Ximenes' influence was but increased when, in 1495, on Isabella's insistence, and against his own protests, he became Mendoza's successor in the archbishopric of Toledo, not only the highest ecclesiastical post in Spain, but one with which the grand-chancellorship of Castile was united. Here he maintained his ascetic life. Supported by the Queen, he turned all the powers of his high office to rid Spain of unworthy clergy and monks. No opposition could thwart him, and more than a thousand monks are said to have left the peninsula rather than submit to his discipline. The moral character and zeal of the Spanish clergy were greatly improved.

Ximenes, though no great scholar, saw the need of an educated clergy. He had encountered Renaissance influences in Rome, and would turn them wholly to the service of the church. In 1498 he founded the University of Alcalá de Henares, to which he devoted a large part of his episcopal revenues, and where he gathered learned men, among them four professors of Greek and Hebrew. A quarter of a century later Alcalá counted seven thousand students. Though opposed to general reading of the Bible by the laity, Ximenes believed that the Scriptures should be the principal study of the clergy. The noblest monument of this conviction is the Complutensian Polyglot (Alcalá = Complutum), on which he directed the labor from 1502 to 1517. The Old Testament was presented in Hebrew, Greek, and Latin, with the Targum on the Pentateuch; the New Testament in Greek and Latin. The New Testament was in print by 1515. To Ximenes belongs the honor, therefore, of first printing the New Testament in Greek, though as papal permission for publication could not be obtained till 1520, the Greek Testament, issued in 1516 by Erasmus, was earlier on the market.

The less attractive side of Ximenes's character is to be seen in his willingness to use force for the conversion of the Mohammedans. In affairs of state his firmness and wisdom were of vast service to Isabella, Ferdinand, and Charles V, till his death in 1517.

The intellectual impulse thus inaugurated by Ximenes led ultimately to a revival of the theology of Aquinas, begun by Francisco de Vittoria (?–1546) in Salamanca, and continued by Vittoria's disciples, the great Roman theologians of the early struggle with Protestantism, Domingo de Soto (1494–1560) and Melchior Cano (1525–1560).

Characteristic of the Spanish awakening was the reorganization of the inquisition. The Spanish temper viewed orthodoxy and patriotism as essentially one, and regarded the maintenance of their religions by Jews and Mohammedans, or relapse by such of those dissenters as had embraced Christianity, as perils to church and state alike. Accordingly, in 1480, Ferdinand and Isabella established the inquisition entirely under royal authority, and with inquisitors appointed by the sovereign. It was this national character that was the distinguishing feature of the Spanish inquisition, and led to protests by Pope Sixtus IV, to which the sovereigns turned deaf ears. Supported by the crown, it speedily became a fearful instrument, under the leadership of Tomas Torquemada (1420–1498). Undoubtedly its value in breaking the independence of the nobles and replenishing the treasury by confiscation commended it to the sovereigns, but its chief claim to popular favor was its repression of heresy and dissent.

Spain had, therefore, at the close of the fifteenth century, the most independent national church of any nation in Europe, in which a moral and intellectual renewal—not destined to be permanent—was in more vigorous progress than elsewhere; yet a church intensely mediæval in doctrine and practice, and fiercely intolerant of all heresy.

In Germany the situation was very different. The empire lacked all real unity. The imperial crown, in theory elective, was worn by members of the Austrian house of Habsburg from 1438 to 1740, but the Emperors had power as possessors of their hereditary lands, rather than as holders of imperial authority. Under Frederick III (1440–1493) wars between the princes and cities and the disorder of the lower nobility, who lived too often by what was really highway robbery, kept the land in a turmoil which the Emperor was powerless to suppress. Matters were somewhat better under Maximilian I (1493–1519), and an attempt was made to give stronger central authority to the empire by frequent meetings of the old feudal Reichstag, the establishment of an imperial supreme court (1495), and the division of the empire into districts for the better preservation of public peace (1512). Efforts were made to form an imperial army and collect imperial taxes. These reforms had little vitality. The decisions of the court could not be enforced nor the taxes collected. The Reichstag was, indeed, to play a great rôle in the Reformation days, but it was a clumsy parliament, meeting in three houses, one of the imperial electors, the second of lay and spiritual princes, and the third of delegates from the free imperial cities. The lower nobles and the common people had no share in it.

The imperial cities were an important element in German life, owning no superior but the feeble rule of the Emperor. They were industrious and wealthy and were thoroughly self-seeking as far as the larger interests of Germany were concerned. Their commercial spirit led them to resist the exactions of clergy and princes alike.

In no country of Europe was the peasantry in a state of greater unrest, especially in southwestern Germany, where insurrections occurred in 1476, 1492, 1512, and 1513. The peasants were serfs—a condition that had passed away in England, and largely in France. Their state had been made rapidly worse by the substitution of the Roman law—a law made largely for slaves —for the old feudal customs, and by the close of the fifteenth century they were profoundly disaffected.

Yet if German national life as a whole was thus disordered and dissatisfied, the larger territories of Germany were growing stronger, and developing a kind of semi-independent local national life in themselves. This was notably true of Austria, electoral and ducal Saxony, Bavaria, Brandenburg, and Hesse. The power of their rulers was increasing, and they were beginning to exercise a local authority in churchly affairs, controlling the nomination of bishops and abbots, taxing the clergy, and limiting to some extent ecclesiastical jurisdiction. This local territorial churchmanship had not gone far, but that it existed was of the utmost importance in giving a framework which the Reformation was rapidly to develop when Roman obedience was rejected.

The years preceding the Reformation witnessed two marriages by the Habsburg rulers of Austria of the utmost importance for the political background of the Reformation age. In 1477 the death of Charles the Bold, the ambitious duke of Burgundy, left the heirship of his Burgundian territories and the Netherlands to his daughter, Mary. Her marriage that year, with Maximilian I, to the dissatisfaction of Louis XI of France, who seized upper Burgundy, sowed the seeds of quarrel between the Kings of France and the Habsburg line which were largely to determine the politics of Europe till 1756. Philip, the son of Maximilian and Mary, in turn married Juana, heiress of Ferdinand and Isabella of Spain. So it came about that Philip and Juana's son, Charles, became possessor of Austria, the Netherlands, and the wide-extended Spanish territories in Europe and the New World—a larger sovereignty than had been held by a single ruler since Charlemagne—to which the imperial title was added in 1519. Charles V became heir also to the rivalry between the Habsburg line to which he belonged and the Kings of France. That rivalry and the struggle for religious reform were to interplay throughout the Reformation age, constantly modifying each other.

16

Renaissance and Other Influences North of the Alps

THOUGH THE FIFTEENTH CENTURY was a notable period of university
foundation in Germany—no less than twelve coming into existence
between 1409 and 1506—these new creations did not owe their existence
to the Renaissance. They grew partly out of a strong desire for learning, but
even more from the ambition of the larger territorial rulers to possess such
schools in their own lands. An influence favorable to the ultimate triumph
of humanism was the revival of the older "realistic" mediæval theology, and a
tendency to go back of even the earlier schoolmen to Augustine, and to
Neo-Platonic rather then Aristotelian conceptions. These revivals were strongly
represented in the University of Paris by the last quarter of the fifteenth
century, and spread thence to German universities with considerable following. They made for many the bridge to humanism, and they rendered
possible that dominance of Augustinian conceptions which was to be characteristic of the Reformation age.

The Renaissance beyond the Alps was inaugurated by contact with
Italian humanists at the Councils of Constance and Basel, but it did not
become a powerful influence till near the close of the fifteenth century. Its
conquests were earlier in Germany than in France, England, or Spain. Some
considerable impulse was given by the learned philosopher, Nicholas of Cues
(1401–1464), who died a cardinal and bishop of Brixen. He can hardly be
considered a humanist, but in his writings he expressed a way of thinking
which transcended that of Scholasticism. His works were first printed at
Strassburg in 1490 and again in 1505 at Milan, and the most important
edition of them was prepared by the leading French humanist Jacques
LeFèvre (in three volumes, Paris 1514). He stood in the tradition of Neo-
platonic mysticism and developed a highly original cosmology and philosophical theology, the full importance of which was made plain only in
modern times, in connection with the views of Giordano Bruno, Leibniz
and the German Idealists. The basic idea of Cusa was that of the *"coincidentia
oppositorum"* which he had conceived in ecstasy in view of the infinity of
the sea and which he expounded in his first philosophical treatise, entitled
De docta ignorantia (1440). He saw God as the infinite unity of all finite
contrasts of the universe and he conceived of the universe as an infinite

process. *Deus ergo est omnia complicans, in hoc quod omnia in eo; et omnia explicans, in hoc qui ipse in omnibus.* His philosophical universalism led him to inquire for the unity of faith in the diversity of religions. In 1453, he wrote a treatise, in the form of a Platonic dialogue, under the title *De pace seu concordantia fidei.* In it he compared Christianity with Judaism and Mohammedanism. He was able to arrive at the remarkable conclusion: *Una religio in rituum diversitate, una veritas in varietate resplendet.*

In the light of later developments, the thought of Nicholas of Cusa can be interpreted as one of the first expressions of modern universalism and individualism. In his own time, however, his genius was not recognized. Nobody then associated him with humanism. Many of its earlier representatives in Germany were little fitted, however, to commend it to the serious-minded. German students brought home from Italy the love of the classics, and also the loose living too often characteristic of the Italian Renaissance. Such were men like the vagabond poet, Peter Luder, who passed from university to university, a disreputable exponent of the new learning, from 1456 to 1474. A very different teacher, who had studied in Italy, was Rudolf Agricola (1443–1485), who closed his life as professor in Heidelberg. A man of worth and influence, he did much to further classical education in the fitting schools. Through Agricola's disciple, Alexander Hegius, who dominated the school in Deventer from 1483 to 1498, that foundation became a center of classical instruction, of which Erasmus was to be the most famous pupil. By the close of the fifteenth century a great improvement in the teaching of Latin had taken place in the secondary schools of Germany.

Humanism found footing in the universities, not without severe struggle. Its earliest conquest was the University of Vienna, where the semi-pagan Latin poet, Conrad Celtes (1459–1508), enjoyed the patronage of the humanistically inclined Emperor, Maximilian I. By the first decade of the sixteenth century, humanism was pressing into the Universities of Basel, Tübingen, Ingolstadt, Heidelberg, and Erfurt. It also found many patrons in the wealthy commercial cities, notably in Nürnberg, Strassburg, and Augsburg. So numerous were its sympathizers by the close of the fifteenth century that learned circles were being formed, like the Rhenish Literary Association, organized by Celtes in Mainz, in 1491, the members of which corresponded, circulated each other's works, and afforded mutual assistance. By 1500 humanism was becoming a vital factor in Germany.

German humanism presented many types, but was, in general, far less pagan and more serious-minded than that of Italy. Many of its leaders were sincere churchmen, anxious to reform and purify religious life. It is to be seen at its best in its two most famous representatives, Reuchlin and Erasmus.

Born in humble circumstances, in Pforzheim, in 1455, Johann Reuchlin early gained local reputation as a Latinist, and was sent as companion to the young son of the margrave of Baden to the University of Paris, about 1472. Here, in Paris, he began the study of Greek, instruction in which had been offered there since 1470. In 1477 he received the master's degree in Basel, and there taught Greek. Even before his graduation he published a Latin dictionary (1475–1476). He studied law in Orléans and Poitiers, and in later life was much employed in judicial positions; but his interests were always primarily scholarly. The service of the count of Württemberg took him to Florence and Rome in 1482—cities which he visited again in 1490 and 1498. At Florence, even on his first visit, his acquaintance with Greek commanded admiration. There he met and was influenced by the scholars of the Platonic Academy (see p. 281), and from Pico della Mirandola (see p. 281) he acquired that strange interest in Kabalistic doctrines that added much to his fame in Germany. Reuchlin was regarded as the ablest Greek scholar of the closing years of the fifteenth century in Germany, and his influence in promotion of Greek studies was most fruitful.

Reuchlin had the Renaissance desire to return to the sources, and this led him, first of non-Jewish scholars in Germany, to make a profound study of Hebrew that he might the better understand the Old Testament. The fruit of twenty years of this labor was the publication in 1506 of a Hebrew grammar and lexicon—*De Rudimentis Hebraicis*—which unlocked the treasures of that speech to Christian students. The bitter quarrel into which the peace-loving scholar was drawn by reason of these Hebrew studies, and with him all educated Germany, will be described in treating of the immediate antecedents of the Lutheran revolt. Reuchlin was no Protestant. He refused approval to the rising Reformation, which he witnessed till his death in 1522. But he did a service of immense importance to Biblical scholarship, and his intellectual heir was to be his grandnephew, that scholar among the reformers, Philip Melanchthon.

Desiderius Erasmus was born out of wedlock in Rotterdam or Gouda, in 1466 or 1469. The school of Deventer awakened his love of letters and probably also turned his mind toward the piety of the Brethren of the Common Life. His poverty caused him to enter the monastery of the Augustinian Canons at Steyn, but he had no taste for the monastic life, nor for that of the priesthood for which he was ordained in 1492 when he left the cloister in order to become secretary of the Bishop of Cambrai. By 1495 he was studying in Paris. Though he obtained the degree of B.D. in 1498, he had no love for scholastic theology. The year 1499 saw him in England where he became acquainted with John Colet and Thomas More, both of whom were to be his close friends. They excited his interest in Cicero, Socrates and Paul. Colet in particular directed him to the Bible and urged him to study Greek. A few years of studious labors with classical literature laid the basis of his literary, historical and philological scholarship. He began a wide correspondence with the leading minds of his age. From 1506–1509 he was in Italy gathering knowledge by the study of the primary sources of ancient literature and deepening his conception of a Christian humanism. In 1509 he again returned to England in order to teach Greek at the University of Cambridge, meanwhile enjoying the friendship of many of the most distinguished men of the Kingdom. The years 1515–1521 were spent for the most part in the Netherlands, particularly in Brussels and Louvain. By this time he was regarded as the prince of humanistic scholars. From 1521, he made his home in Basel, whose famous publisher Froben printed his books, particularly the Greek edition of the New Testament and the editions of the works of the Fathers. When the Reformation was introduced in this city (1529), he moved to Freiburg. He died during a visit to Basel in 1536.

Erasmus was, above all, a man of letters, who touched the issues of his time with consummate wit and brilliancy of expression, set forth daring criticism of clergy and civil rulers, and withal was moved by deep sincerity of purpose. Convinced that the church of his day was overlaid with super-stition, corruption, and error, and that the monastic life was too often ignorant and unworthy, he had yet no wish to break with the church that he so freely criticised. He was too primarily intellectual to have sympathy with the Lutheran revolution, the "tumults" of which repelled him. He was too clear-sighted not to see the evils of the Roman Church. Hence neither side in the struggle that opened in the latter part of his life understood him, and his memory has been condemned by polemic writers, Protestant and Catholic. His own thought was that education, return to the sources of Christian truth, and flagellation of ignorance and immorality by merciless satire would bring the church to purity. To this end he labored. His *Handbook of the Christian Soldier* of 1502, which made him famous, was a simple, earnest presentation of an unecclesiastical Christianity, largely Stoic in char-acter. His *Praise of Folly* of 1509 was a biting satire on the evils of his age in church and state. His *Familiar Colloquies* of 1518 were witty dis-cussions in which fastings, pilgrimages, and similar external observances were the butts of his brilliant pen. His constructive work was of the highest im-portance. In 1516 came the first edition of his Greek Testament, the pioneer publication of the Greek text, for that of Ximenes was still inaccessible (see p. 288). This was followed by a series of the Fathers—Jerome, Origen, Basil, Cyril, Chrysostom, Irenæus, Ambrose, and Augustine, not all wholly from his pen, but all from his impulse, which placed scholarly knowledge of early Christianity on a new plane, and profoundly aided the Reformation, the deeper religious springs of which Erasmus never understood. Erasmus rendered a service for the Christian classics, much like that of the Italian humanists for the pagan writers of Greece and Rome.

Yet Erasmus did something more than revive a knowledge of Christian sources. In a measure, he had a positive theology. To him Christianity was but the fullest expression through Christ, primarily in the Sermon on the

Mount, of universal, essentially ethical religion, of which the philosophers of antiquity had also been bearers. He had little feeling for the sacramental or for the deeply personal elements in religion. A universal ethical theism, having its highest illustration in the *"philosophia Christi,"* was his idea. His way of thinking was to have little influence on the Reformation as a whole, though much on Socinianism, and is that represented in a great deal of modern theology, of which he was thus the spiritual ancestor.

Though Germany was more largely influenced by the Renaissance at the beginning of the sixteenth century than any other land beyond the Alps, the same impulses were stirring elsewhere. The efforts of Ximenes in Spain have already been noted (see p. 288). In England John Colet (1467?–1519) was introducing educational reforms and lecturing on the epistles of Paul in Oxford and London. His influence in turning Erasmus to Biblical studies was considerable (see p. 293). He rejected all allegorical interpretation of the Scriptures, criticised clerical celibacy and auricular confession, and desired to better the education and morals of the clergy. As the sixteenth century dawned, humanism was gaining constantly increasing following in England, and King Henry VIII (1509–1547) was deemed its patron.

The situation in France was similar. The chief representative of a Christian humanism was Jacques LeFèvre, of Etaples (1455–1536), most of whose active years were spent in or near Paris. A modest, kindly man, he developed a Christian humanism nourished not only by the new Platonism of Nicholas of Cusa (whose works he published) and Marsilio Ficino (with whom he had become personally acquainted during one of his three trips to Italy), but also by his broad acquaintance with areopagitic mysticism and his enthusiasm for the philosophy of Raimond Lull and the Cabala. He rediscovered the Bible and proceeded to interpret it by means of the grammatical method, breaking radically with the spiritual-allegorical exegesis of the mediæval schoolmen. In 1509, he published the *Psalterium Quincuplex,* a critical exposition of the Psalms based on a philological comparison of five different Latin versions. Three years later (1512), there appeared his translation and commentary of the Pauline epistles which denied the justifying merits of good works and held salvation a free gift of God. Later he wrote commentaries on the four Gospels (1522) and on the Catholic Epistles (1525). At the same time (1523–1525), he published French translations of the Vulgate versions of the New Testament and of the Psalter. Without intending to break with the Roman Church, he hoped for a religious reform, chiefly on the basis of the Bible. He gathered round himself a body of devoted pupils, destined to most unlike participation in the Reformation struggle, Guillaume Briçonnet, to be bishop of Meaux; Guillaume Budé, eminent in Greek and to be instrumental in founding the Collège de France; Louis de Berquin, to die a Protestant martyr; and Guillaume Farel, to be the fiery reformer of French-speaking Switzerland.

To all these religious-minded humanists the path of reform seemed similar. Sound learning, the study and preaching of the Bible and the Fathers, and the correction of ignorance, immorality, and glaring administrative abuses would make the church what it should be. This solution did not meet the deep needs of the situation; but the humanists rendered an indispensable preparation for the Reformation. They led men to study Christian sources afresh. They discredited the later scholastic theology. They brought in new and more natural methods of exegesis. To a large degree they looked on life from another standpoint than the mediæval. They represented a release of the mind, in some considerable measure, from mediæval traditionalism.

Partly as a result of the Renaissance emphasis on the sources, but even more in consequence of the invention of printing, the latter half of the fifteenth century witnessed a wide distribution of the Bible in the Vulgate and in translation. No less than ninety-two editions of the Vulgate were put forth before 1500. Eighteen editions of a German version were printed before 1521. The New Testament was printed in French in 1477; the whole Bible ten years later; 1478 saw the publication of a Spanish translation; 1471 the printing of two independent versions in Italian. In the Netherlands one of the best of all translations was printed in 1477 and the *Psalms* were seven times published between 1480 and 1507. The Scriptures were printed in Bohemian in 1488. If England had no printed Bible before the Reformation, many manuscripts of Wyclif's translation were in circulation.

Efforts were made to restrict the reading of the Bible by the laity, since its use seemed the source of mediæval heresies; but there can be no doubt that familiarity with it much increased among the less educated priesthood and among laymen. Yet the real question of the influence of this Bible reading is the problem of Biblical interpretation. The Middle Ages never denied the final authority of the Bible. Augustine and Aquinas so regarded it. It was the Bible interpreted, however, by the Fathers, the teachers, and the councils of the church. Should that churchly right to interpret be denied, there remained only the right of private interpretation; but the voices from Bohemia and the mediæval sects which denied the interpreting authority of the church, found no general response as yet. The commanding word had yet to be spoken. The mere reading of the Bible involved no denial of mediæval ideals. Only when those ideals were rejected could the interpreting authority which supported them be denied and the Bible become the support of the newer conceptions of salvation and of the church. The Bible was not so much the cause of Protestantism as was Protestantism a new interpretation of the Scriptures.

The closing years of the fifteenth century were, as has been seen, a period of religious betterment in Spain. No such corresponding revival of interest in religion is to be traced in France or England; but Germany was undergoing a real and pervasive religious quickening in the decades immediately preceding the Reformation. Its fundamental motive seems to have been fear.

Much in the popular life of Germany tended to increase the sense of apprehension. The witchcraft delusion, though by no means new, was rapidly spreading. A bull of Pope Innocent VIII in 1484 declared Germany full of witches, and the German inquisitors, Jakob Sprenger and Heinrich Krämer, published their painfully celebrated *Malleus Maleficarum* in 1489. It was a superstition that added terror to popular life, and was to be shared by the reformers no less than by their Roman opponents. The years from 1490 to 1503 were a period of famine in Germany. The Turkish peril was becoming threatening. The general social unrest has already been noted (see p. 290). All these elements contributed to the development of a sense of the reality and nearness of divine judgments, and the need of propitiating an angry God.

The religious spirit of Germany at the close of the fifteenth century found expression in pilgrimages. A few of the more wealthy journeyed to the Holy Land, more went to Rome, but the most popular foreign pilgrimage shrine was that of St. James at Compostella in Spain. German pilgrim shrines were thronged, and great collections of relics were made, notably by the Saxon Elector, Frederick the Wise (1486–1525), to be Luther's protector, who placed them in the castle church, to the door of which Luther was to nail his famous Theses. The intercession of Mary was never more sought, and Mary's mother, St. Anna, was but little less valued. Christ was popularly regarded as a strict judge, to be placated with satisfactions or absolutions.

Yet side by side with this external and work-trusting religious spirit, Germany had not a little of mystic piety, that saw the essence of religion in the relation of the individual soul to God; and a good deal of what has been called "non-ecclesiastical religion," which showed itself not only in simple, serious lives, like that of Luther's father, but in increasing attempts of lay princes to improve the quality of the clergy, of towns to regulate beggary, to control charitable foundations, which had been in exclusive ecclesiastical hands, and in various ways to vindicate for laymen, as such, a larger share in the religious life of the community. The active life was asserting its claims against the contemplative. Theology, as such, had largely lost its hold on popular thought, discredited by nominalism, despised by humanism, and supplanted by mysticism.

It was no dead age to which Luther was to speak, but one seething with unrest, vexed with multitudinous unsolved problems and unfulfilled longings.

Period Six

THE REFORMATION

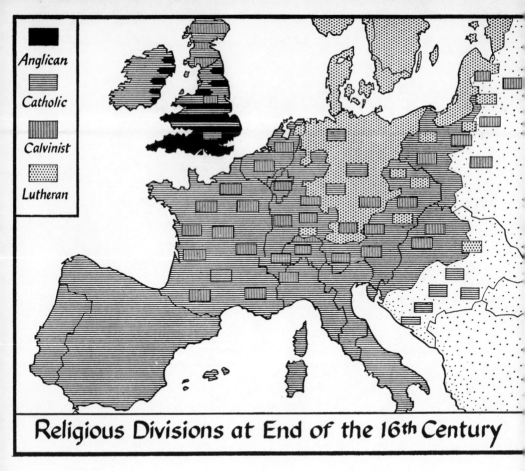

Religious Divisions at End of the 16th Century

1

Luther's Development and the Beginnings of the Reformation

THE RELIGIOUS and economic situation of Germany at the beginning of the sixteenth century was in many respects critical. Papal taxation and papal interference with churchly appointments were generally deemed oppressive. The expedition of clerical business by the papal curia was deemed expensive and corrupt. The clergy at home were much criticised for the unworthy examples of many of their number in high station and low. The trading cities were restive under clerical exemptions from taxation, the prohibition of interest, the many holidays, and the churchly countenance of beggars. Monasteries were in many places in sore need of reform, and their large landed possessions were viewed with ill favor, both by the nobles who would gladly possess them, and the peasantry who labored on them. The peasantry in general were in a state of economic unrest, not the least of their grievances being the tithes and fees collected by the local clergy. Added to these causes of restlessness were the intellectual ferment of rising German humanism and the stirrings of popular religious awakening, manifested in a deepening sense of terror and concern for salvation. It is evident that, could these various grievances find bold expression in a determined leader, his voice would find wide hearing.

In the intellectual world of Germany, moreover, division was being greatly intensified by a quarrel involving one of the most peace-loving and respected of humanists, Reuchlin (see p. 293), and uniting in his support the advocates of the new learning. Johann Pfefferkorn (1469–1522), a convert from Judaism, procured an order from the Emperor, Maximilian, in 1509, confiscating Jewish books as doing dishonor to Christianity. The archbishop of Mainz, to whom the task of inquiry was intrusted, consulted Reuchlin and Jakob Hochstraten (1460–1527), the Dominican inquisitor in Cologne. They took opposite sides. Hochstraten supported Pfefferkorn, while Reuchlin defended Jewish literature as with slight exceptions desirable, urged a fuller knowledge of Hebrew, and the substitution of friendly discussion with the Jews for the confiscation of their books. A storm of controversy was the result. Reuchlin was accused of heresy and put on trial by Hochstraten. The case was appealed to Rome, and dragged till 1520, when it was decided against Reuchlin. The advocates of the new learning, however, looked upon the whole proceeding as an ignorant and unwarranted attack on scholarship, and rallied to Reuchlin's support.

From this humanistic circle came, in 1514 and 1517, one of the most successful satires ever issued—the *Letters of Obscure Men*. Purporting to be written by opponents of Reuchlin and the new learning, they aroused widespread ridicule by their barbarous Latinity, their triviality, and their ignorance, and undoubtedly created the impression that the party opposed to Reuchlin was hostile to learning and progress. Their authorship is still uncertain, but Crotus Rubeanus (1480?–1539?) of Dornheim and Ulrich von Hutten (1488–1523) certainly had parts in it. Hutten, vain, immoral, and quarrelsome, but brilliantly gifted as a writer of prose and verse, and undoubtedly patriotic, was to give support of dubious worth to Luther in the early years of the Reformation movement. The effect of the storm raised over Reuchlin was to unite German humanists, and to draw a line of cleavage between them and the conservatives, of whom the Dominicans were the most conspicuous.

It was while this contest was at its height that a protest against an ecclesiastical abuse, made, in no unusual or spectacular fashion, by a monastic professor in a recently founded and relatively inconspicuous German university, on October 31, 1517, found immediate response and launched the most gigantic revolution in the history of the Christian Church.

Martin Luther, from whom this protest came, is one of the few men of whom it may be said that the history of the world was profoundly altered by his work. Not an organizer or a politician, he moved men by the power of a profound religious faith, resulting in unshakable trust in God, and in direct, immediate and personal relations to Him, which brought a confident salvation that left no room for the elaborate hierarchical and sacramental structures of the Middle Ages. He spoke to his countrymen as one profoundly of them in aspirations and sympathies, yet above them by virtue of a vivid and compelling faith, and a courage, physical and spiritual, of the most heroic mould. Yet so largely was he of his race, in his virtues and limitations, that he is understood with difficulty, to this day, by a Frenchman or an Italian, and even Anglo-Saxons have seldom appreciated that fulness of sympathetic admiration with which a German Protestant speaks his name. But whether honored or opposed, none can deny his pre-eminent place in the history of the church.

Luther was born on November 10, 1483, in Eisleben, where his father was a peasant miner. His father and mother were of simple, unecclesiastical piety. The father, more energetic and ambitious than most peasants, removed to Mansfeld a few months after Martin's birth, where he won respect and a modest competence, and was fired with ambition to give his son an education fitting to a career in the law. After preparatory schooling in Mansfeld, Magdeburg, and Eisenach, Martin Luther entered the University of Erfurt in 1501, where he was known as an earnest, companionable, and music-loving student. The humanistic movement beginning to be felt in Erfurt had little influence upon him, though he read fairly widely in the Latin classics.

Luther felt strongly that deep sense of sinfulness which was the ground note of the religious revival of the age in Germany. His graduation as master of arts in 1505, made it necessary then to begin his special preparation in law. He was profoundly moved, however, by the sudden death of a friend and by a narrow escape from lightning, and he therefore broke off his career, and, in deep anxiety for his soul's salvation, entered the monastery of Augustinian hermits in Erfurt, on July 17, 1505. The "German congregation" of Augustinians, recently reformed by Andreas Proles (1429–1503), and now under the supervision of Johann von Staupitz (?–1524), enjoyed deserved popular respect and represented mediæval monasticism at its best. Thoroughly mediæval, in general, in its theological position, it made much of preaching, and included some men who were disposed to mystical piety and sympathetic with the deeper religious apprehensions of Augustine and Bernard. To Staupitz, Luther was to owe much. In the monastic life Luther won speedy recognition. In 1507 he was ordained to the priesthood. The next year saw him in Wittenberg, at the command of his superiors, preparing for a future professorship in the university which had been there established by the Saxon Elector, Frederick III, "the Wise" (1486–1525), in 1502. There he graduated bachelor of theology in 1509, but was sent back the same year to Erfurt, possibly to study for the degree of sententiarius, or licensed expounder of that great mediæval text-book of theology, the "Sentences" of Peter Lombard (see p. 242). On business of his order he made a memorable journey to Rome, November 1510 till April 1511. Back once more in Wittenberg, which was thenceforth to be his home, he became a doctor of theology in 1512 and began at once to lecture on the Bible, treating the *Psalms* from 1513 to 1515, then *Romans* till late in 1516, and thereupon *Galatians, Hebrews,* and *Titus.* His practical abilities were recognized by his appointment, in 1515, as director of studies in his own cloister and as district vicar in charge of eleven monasteries of his order, and he began, even earlier, the practice of preaching in which, from the first, he displayed remarkable gifts. In his order he bore the repute of a man of singular piety, devotion, and monastic zeal.

Yet, in spite of all monastic strenuousness, Luther found no peace of soul. His sense of sinfulness overwhelmed him. Staupitz helped him by pointing out that true penitence began not with fear of a punishing God, but with love to God. But if Luther could say that Staupitz first opened his eyes to the Gospel, the clarifying of his vision was a slow and gradual process. Till 1509 Luther devoted himself to the later scholastics, Occam, d'Ailli, and Biel. To them he owed permanently his disposition to emphasize the objective facts of revelation, and his distrust of reason. Augustine, however, was opening new visions to him by the close of 1509, and leading him to a rapidly growing hostility toward the dominance of Aristotle in theology. Augustine's mysticism and emphasis on the salvatory significance of the human life and death of Christ fascinated him. Anselm and Bernard helped him. By the time that Luther lectured on the *Psalms* (1513–1515), he had become convinced that salvation is a new relation to God, based not on any work of merit on man's part, but on absolute trust in the divine promises, so that the redeemed man, while not ceasing to be a sinner, yet is freely and fully forgiven, and from the new and joyous relationship to God in Christ, the new life of willing conformity to God's will flows. It was a re-emphasis of a most important side of the Pauline teaching. Yet it was not wholly Pauline. To Paul the Christian is primarily a renewed moral being. To Luther he is first of all a forgiven sinner; but Luther, like Paul, made salvation in essence a right personal relationship to God. The ground and the pledge of this right relationship is the mercy of God displayed in the sufferings of Christ in man's behalf. Christ has borne our sins. We, in turn, have imputed to us His righteousness. The German mystics, especially Tauler, now helped Luther to the conclusion that this transforming trust was not, as he had supposed, a work in which a man had a part, but wholly the gift of God. The work preparatory to his lectures on *Romans* (1515–1516) but intensified these convictions. He now declared that the common opinion that God would infallibly infuse grace into those who did what was in their power was absurd and Pelagian. The basis of any work-righteousness had been overthrown for Luther.

While thus convinced as to the nature and method of salvation, Luther's own peace of soul was not yet secured. He needed the further conviction of certainty of his own personal justification. That certainly he had, with Augustine, denied. Yet as he labored on the latter part of his lectures on *Romans,* and even more clearly in the closing months of 1516, his confidence that the God-given nature of faith involved personal assurance became conviction. Thenceforth, in his own personal experience the sum of the Gospel was the forgiveness of sins. It was "good news," filling the soul with peace, joy, and absolute trust in God. It was absolute dependence on the divine promises, on God's "word."

By 1516 Luther did not stand alone. In the University of Wittenberg his opposition to Aristotelianism and Scholasticism and his Biblical theology found much sympathy. His colleagues, Andreas Bodenstein of Karlstadt (1480–1541), who, unlike Luther, had represented the older Scholasticism of Aquinas, and Nikolaus von Amsdorf (1483–1565), now became his hearty supporters.

In 1517 Luther felt compelled to speak up against a crying abuse. Pope Leo X had decided in favor of the claims of Albrecht of Brandenburg to hold at the same time the archbishopric of Mainz, the archbishopric of Magdeburg, and the administration of the bishopric of Halberstadt, an argument moving thereto being a large financial payment. To indemnify himself, Albrecht secured as his share half the proceeds in his district of the indulgences that the papacy had been issuing, since 1506, for building that new church of St. Peter which is still one of the ornaments of Rome. A commissioner for this collection was Johann Tetzel (1470–1519), a Dominican monk of eloquence, who, intent on the largest possible returns, painted the benefits of indulgences in the crassest terms.[1] To Luther, convinced that only a right personal relation with God would bring salvation, such teaching seemed destructive of real religion. As Tetzel approached—he was not allowed to enter electoral Saxony —Luther preached against the abuse of indulgences and, on October 31, 1517, posted on the door of the castle church, in Wittenberg, which served as the university bulletin board, his ever memorable Ninety-five Theses.[2]

Viewed in themselves, it may well be wondered why the Ninety-five Theses proved the spark which kindled the explosion. They were intended for academic debate. They do not deny the right of the Pope to grant indulgences. They question the extension of indulgences to purgatory, and make evident the abuses of current teaching—abuses which they imply the Pope will repudiate when informed. Yet though they are far from expressing the full round of Luther's thought, certain principles are evident in them which, if developed, would be revolutionary of the churchly practice of the day. Repentance is not an act, but a life-long habit of mind. The true treasury of the church is God's forgiving grace. The Christian seeks rather than avoids divine discipline. "Every Christian who feels true compunction has of right plenary remission of pain and guilt, even without letters of pardon." In the restless condition of Germany it was an event of the utmost significance that a respected, if humble, religious leader had spoken boldly against a great abuse, and the Theses ran the length and breadth of the empire.

Luther had not anticipated the excitement. Tetzel answered at once,[3] and stirred Konrad Wimpina (?–1531) to make reply. A more formidable opponent was the able and disputatious Johann Maier of Eck (1486–1543), professor of theology in the University of Ingolstadt, who answered with a tract circulated in manuscript and entitled *Obelisci*. Luther was charged with heresy. He defended his position in a sermon on "Indulgence and Grace"; [4] he replied to Eck. By the beginning of 1518, complaints against Luther had been lodged in Rome by Archbishop Albrecht of Mainz and the Dominicans. The result was that the general of the Augustinians was ordered to end the dispute and Luther was summoned before the general chapter of the order met in Heidelberg, in April. There Luther argued against free will and the control of Aristotle in theology and won new adherents, of whom one of the most important was Martin Butzer (Bucer). At about the same time Luther

[1] See extracts in Kidd, *Documents Illustrative of the Continental Reformation*, pp. 12–20.
[2] Kidd, pp. 21–26; English tr. Wace and Buchheim, *Luther's Primary Works*, pp. 6–14.
[3] Kidd, pp. 30, 31.   [4] *Ibid.*, p. 29.

put forth a more elaborate defense of his position on indulgences, the *Resolutiones*.

Luther had desired no quarrel with the papacy. He seems to have believed that the Pope might see the abuses of indulgences as he did, but the course of events was leading to no choice save the sturdy maintenance of his views or submission. In June, 1518, Pope Leo X issued a citation to Luther to appear in Rome, and commissioned his censor of books, the Dominican Silvestro Mazzolini of Prierio, to draw up an opinion on Luther's position. The summons and the opinion reached Luther early in August. Prierio asserted that "the Roman Church is representatively the college of cardinals, and moreover is virtually the supreme pontiff," and that "He who says that the Roman Church cannot do what it actually does regarding indulgences is a heretic." [5] Luther's case would apparently have speedily ended in his condemnation had he not had the powerful protection of his prince, the Elector Frederick "the Wise." In how far Frederick sympathized with Luther's religious beliefs at any time is a matter of controversy; but, at all events he was proud of his Wittenberg professor, and averse to an almost certain condemnation in Rome. His political skill effected a change of hearing from the Roman court to the papal legate at the Reichstag in Augsburg, the learned commentator on Aquinas, Cardinal Thomas Vio (1469–1534), known from his birthplace (Gaeta) as Cajetanus. Cajetanus was a theologian of European repute and seems to have thought the matter rather beneath his dignity. He ordered Luther to retract, especially criticisms of the completeness of papal power of indulgence. Luther refused,[6] and, on October 20, fled from Augsburg, having appealed to the Pope "to be better informed." [7] Not satisfied with this, Luther appealed from Wittenberg, in November, 1518, to a future general council.[8] How little chance of a favorable hearing he had in Rome is shown by the bull issued the same month by Leo X defining indulgences in the sense which Luther had criticised.[9] Luther had no real hope of safety. If his courage was great, his danger was no less so; but he was rescued from immediate condemnation by the favorable turn of political events.

Meanwhile the summer of 1518 had seen the installation as professor of Greek in Wittenberg of a young scholar, a native of Bretten and grandnephew of Reuchlin, Philip Melanchthon (1497–1560), who was to be singularly united with Luther in the years to come. Never was there a greater contrast. Melanchthon was timid and retiring; but he was without a superior in scholarship, and under the strong impress of Luther's personality, he devoted his remarkable abilities, almost from his arrival in Wittenberg, to the furtherance of the Lutheran cause.

The Emperor, Maximilian, was now visibly nearing the end of his life, which was to come in January, 1519, and the turmoil of a disputed election

[5] Kidd, pp. 31, 32.   [6] *Ibid.*, pp. 33–37.   [7] *Ibid.*, pp. 37–39.   [8] *Ibid.*, p. 40.
[9] *Ibid.*, p. 39.

was impending. Pope Leo X, as an Italian prince, looked with disfavor on the candidacy of Charles of Spain, or Francis of France, as increasing foreign influence in Italy, and sought the good-will of the Elector Frederick, whom he would gladly have seen chosen. It was no time to proceed against Frederick's favored professor. Leo, therefore, sent his chamberlain, the Saxon Karl von Miltitz, as his nuncio, with a golden rose, a present expressive of high papal favor, to the Elector. Miltitz flattered himself that he could heal the ecclesiastical quarrel and went far beyond his instructions. On his own motion he disowned Tetzel, and held an interview with Luther, whom he persuaded to agree to keep silent on the questions in dispute, to submit the case, if possible, to learned German bishops, and to write a humble letter to the Pope.[10]

Any real agreement was impossible. Luther's Wittenberg colleague, Andreas Bodenstein of Karlstadt (1480–1541), had argued in 1518, in opposition to Eck, that the text of the Bible is to be preferred even to the authority of the whole church. Eck demanded a public debate, to which Karlstadt agreed, and Luther soon found himself drawn into the combat, proposing to contend that the supremacy of the Roman Church is unsupported by history or Scripture. In June and July, 1519, the great debate was held in Leipzig. Karlstadt, who was an unready disputant, succeeded but moderately in holding his own against the nimble-witted Eck. Luther's earnestness acquitted itself much better; but Eck's skill drove Luther to the admission that his positions were in some respects those of Huss, and that in condemning Huss the revered Council of Constance had erred. To Eck this seemed a forensic triumph, and he believed victory to be his, declaring that one who could deny the infallibility of a general council was a heathen and a publican.[11] It was, indeed, a momentous declaration into which Luther had been led. He had already rejected the final authority of the Pope, he now admitted the fallibility of councils. Those steps implied a break with the whole authoritative system of the Middle Ages, and allowed final appeal only to the Scriptures. Eck felt that the whole controversy might now be speedily ended by a papal bull of condemnation, which he now set himself to secure and which was issued on June 15, 1520.[12]

Luther was now, indeed, in the thick of the battle. His own ideas were rapidly crystallizing. Humanistic supporters, like Ulrich von Hutten, were now rallying to him as one who could lead in a national conflict with Rome. Luther himself was beginning to see his task as a national redemption of Germany from a papacy which, rather than the individual Pope, he was coming to regard as antichrist. His doctrine of salvation was bearing larger fruitage. In his little tract, *On Good Works,* of May, 1520, after defining "the noblest of all good works" to be "to believe in Christ," he affirmed the essential goodness of the normal trades and occupations of life, and denounced those who "limit good works so narrowly that they must consist in praying in church,

[10] Kidd, pp. 41–44.   [11] *Ibid.,* pp. 44–51.   [12] Kidd, pp. 74–79.

fasting or giving alms." [13] This vindication of the natural human life as the best field for the service of God, rather than the unnatural limitations of asceticism, was to be one of Luther's most important contributions to Protestant thought, as well as one of his most significant departures from ancient and mediæval Christian conceptions.

Luther's great accomplishment of the year 1520 and his completion of his title to leadership were the preparation of three epoch-making works. The first of these treatises was published in August, entitled *To the Christian Nobility of the German Nation*.[14] Written with burning conviction, by a master of the German tongue, it soon ran the breadth of the empire. It declared that three Roman walls were overthrown by which the papacy had buttressed its power. The pretended superiority of the spiritual to the temporal estate is baseless, since all believers are priests. That truth of universal priesthood casts down the second wall, that of exclusive papal right to interpret the Scriptures; and the third wall, also, that a reformatory council can be called by none but the Pope. "A true, free council" for the reform of the church should be summoned by the temporal authorities. Luther then proceeded to lay down a program for reformation, his suggestions being practical rather than theological. Papal misgovernment, appointments, and taxation are to be curbed; burdensome offices abolished; German ecclesiastical interests should be placed under a "Primate of Germany"; clerical marriage permitted; the far too numerous holy days reduced in the interest of industry and sobriety; beggary, including that of the mendicant orders, forbidden; brothels closed; luxury curbed; and theological education in the universities reformed. No wonder the effect of Luther's work was profound. He had voiced what earnest men had long been thinking.

Two months later Luther put forth in Latin his *Babylonish Captivity of the Church*,[15] in which questions of the highest theological import, namely, the sacraments, were handled and the teaching of the Roman Church unsparingly attacked. The sole value of a sacrament, Luther taught, is its witness to the divine promise. It seals or attests the God-given pledge of union with Christ and forgiveness of sins. It strengthens faith. Tried by the Scripture standard, there are only two sacraments, baptism and the Lord's Supper, though penance has a certain sacramental value as a return to baptism. Monastic vows, pilgrimages, works of merit, are a man-made substitute for the forgiveness of sins freely promised to faith in baptism. Luther criticised the denial of the cup to the laity, doubted transubstantiation, and especially rejected the doctrine that the Supper is a sacrifice to God. The other Roman sacraments, confirmation, matrimony, orders, and extreme unction, have no sacramental standing in Scripture.

[13] Robinson, *Readings*, 2:66–68.
[14] Translated in full in Wace and Buchheim's, *Luther's Primary Works*, pp. 17–92.
[15] *Luther's Primary Works*, pp. 141–245.

It is one of the marvels of Luther's stormy career that he was able to compose and issue, contemporaneously with these intensely polemic treatises, and while the papal bull was being published in Germany, his third great tractate of 1520, that *On Christian Liberty*.[16] In calm confidence he presented the paradox of Christian experience: "A Christian man is the most free lord of all, and subject to none; a Christian man is the most dutiful servant of all, and subject to every one." He is free, since justified by faith, no longer under the law of works and in new personal relationship with Christ. He is a servant because bound by love to bring his life into conformity to the will of God and to be helpful to his neighbor. In this tract, in an elsewhere unmatched measure, the power and the limitations of Lutheranism are evident. To Luther the essence of the Gospel is the forgiveness of sins, wrought through a faith, which, as with Paul, is nothing less than a vital, personal transforming relationship of the soul with Christ. To this tract Luther prefaced a letter to Pope Leo X, which is a most curious document, breathing good-will to the Pontiff personally, but full of denunciation of the papal court and its claims for the papacy, in which the Pope is represented as "sitting like a lamb in the midst of wolves." Though Luther's vision was to clarify hereafter regarding many details, his theological conception of the Christian gospel was thus practically complete in its main outlines by 1520.

Meanwhile Eck and Girolamo Aleander (1480–1542) had come with the papal bull, as nuncios, to Germany. In Wittenberg its publication was refused, and its reception in large parts of Germany was lukewarm or hostile, but Aleander secured its publication in the Netherlands, and procured the burning of Luther's books in Louvain, Liège, Antwerp, and Cologne. On December 10, 1520, Luther answered by burning the papal bull and the canon law, with the approving presence of students and citizens of Wittenberg, and without opposition from the civil authorities. It was evident that a considerable section of Germany was in ecclesiastical rebellion, and the situation demanded the cognizance of the highest authorities of the empire.

On June 28, 1519, while the Leipzig disputation was in progress, the imperial election had resulted in the choice of Maximilian's grandson Charles V (1500–1558). Heir of Spain, the Netherlands, the Austrian territories of the house of Habsburg, master of a considerable portion of Italy, and of newly discovered territories across the Atlantic, his election as Holy Roman Emperor made him the head of a territory vaster than that of any single ruler since Charlemagne. It was an authority greatly limited, however, in Germany by the territorial powers of the local princes. As yet Charles was young and unknown, and both sides in the religious struggles of the day had strong hope of his support. In reality he was an earnest Roman Catholic, of the type of his grandmother, Isabella of Castile, sharing her reformatory views, desirous of improvement in clerical morals, education, and administration, but wholly

[16] *Ibid.*, pp. 95–137.

unsympathetic with any departure from the doctrinal or hierarchical system of the Middle Ages. He had at last come to Germany, and partly to regulate his government in that land, partly to prepare for the war about to break out over the rival claims of France and Spain in Italy, had called a Reichstag to meet in Worms in November, 1520. Though there was much other business, all felt the determination of Luther's case of high importance. The papal nuncio, Aleander, pressed for a prompt condemnation, especially after the final papal bull against Luther was issued on January 2, 1521. Since Luther was already condemned by the Pope, the Reichstag had no duty, Aleander urged, but to make that condemnation effective. On the other hand, Luther had wide popular support, and his ruler, the Elector Frederick the Wise, a master of diplomatic intrigue, was, fortunately for Luther, of the opinion that the condemned monk had never had an adequate hearing. Frederick, and other nobles, believed that he should be heard before the Reichstag previous to action by that body. Between the two counsels the Emperor wavered, convinced that Luther was a damnable heretic, but politician enough not to oppose German sentiment too sharply, or to throw away the possible advantage of making the heretic's fate a lever in bringing the Pope to the imperial side in the struggle with France.

The result was that Luther was summoned to Worms under the protection of an imperial safe-conduct. His journey thither from Wittenberg was well-nigh a popular ovation. On April 17, 1521, Luther appeared before the Emperor and Reichstag. A row of his books was pointed out to him and he was asked whether he would recant them or not. Luther requested time for reflection. A day was given him, and on the next afternoon he was once more before the assembly. Here he acknowledged that, in the heat of controversy, he had expressed himself too strongly against persons, but the substance of what he had written he could not retract, unless convinced of its wrongfulness by Scripture or adequate argument. The Emperor, who could hardly believe that such temerity as to deny the infallibility of a general council was possible, cut the discussion short. That Luther cried out, "I cannot do otherwise. Here I stand. God help me, Amen," is not certain, but seems not improbable. The words at least expressed the substance of his unshaken determination. He had borne a great historic witness to the truth of his convictions before the highest tribunal of his nation. Of his dauntless courage he had given the complete proof. The judgment of his hearers was divided, but if he alienated the Emperor and the prelates by his strong and, as it seemed to them, self-willed assertion, he made a favorable impression on many of the German nobility and, fortunately, on the Elector Frederick. That prince, though he thought Luther too bold, was confirmed in his determination that no harm should come to the reformer. Yet the result seemed a defeat for Luther. A month after Luther had started on his homeward journey he was formally put under the ban of the empire, though not till after many of the members of the Reichstag had left. He was to be seized for punishment and his books burned.[17] This ban was never formally abrogated, and Luther remained the rest of his life under imperial condemnation.

Had Germany been controlled by a strong central authority Luther's career would soon have ended in martyrdom. Not even an imperial edict, however, could be executed against the will of a vigorous territorial ruler, and Frederick the Wise proved once more Luther's salvation. Unwilling to come out openly as his defender, perhaps somewhat afraid to do so, he had Luther seized by friendly hands, as the reformer journeyed homeward from Worms, and carried secretly to the Wartburg Castle, near Eisenach. For months Luther's hiding place was practically unknown; but that he lived and shared in the fortunes of the struggle his ready pen made speedily apparent. His attacks on the Roman practice grew more intense, but the most lasting fruit of this period of enforced retirement was his translation of the New Testament, begun in December, 1521, and published in September of the following year. Luther was by no means the first to translate the Scriptures into German, but the earliest versions had been made from the Vulgate, and were hard and awkward in expression. Luther's work was not merely from the Greek, for which the labors of Erasmus gave the basis, it was idiomatic and readable. It largely determined the form of speech that should mark future German literature—that of the Saxon chancery of the time—wrought and polished by a master of popular expression. Few services greater than this translation have ever been rendered to the development of the religious life of a nation. Nor, with all his deference to the Word of God, was Luther without his own canons of criticism. These were the relative clearness with which his interpretation of the work of Christ and the method of salvation by faith is taught. Judged by these standards, he felt that *Hebrews, James, Jude,* and *Revelation* were of inferior worth. Even in Scripture itself there were differences in value.

The month which saw the beginning of Luther's work as a translator—December, 1521—witnessed the publication in Wittenberg of a small volume by Melanchthon, the *Loci Communes,* meaning Cardinal Points of Theology. With it the systematic presentation of Lutheran theology may be said to have begun.[18] It was to be enlarged, developed, and modified in many later editions.

[17] Kidd, *Documents,* pp. 79–89.   [18] Extracts in Kidd, *Documents,* pp. 90–94.

2

Separations and Divisions

*L*UTHER'S SOJOURN in the Wartburg left Wittenberg without his powerful leadership; but there were not wanting many there to continue the ecclesiastical revolution. To his earlier associates in the university, Karlstadt, Melanchthon, and Nikolaus von Amsdorf (1483–1565), there had been added, in the first half of the year 1521, Johann Bugenhagen (1485–1558) and Justus Jonas (1493–1555). Of these, Karlstadt had unquestionably greatest natural leadership, but was rash, impulsive, and radical. Luther had as yet made no changes in public worship or in monastic life. Yet it was inevitable that demand for such changes should come. Luther's fiery fellow monk, Gabriel Zwilling (1487?–1558), by October, 1521, was denouncing the mass and urging the abandonment of clerical vows. He soon had a large following, especially in the Augustinian monastery of Wittenberg, many of the inmates of which now renounced their profession. With equal zeal Zwilling was soon attacking images. At Christmas, 1521, Karlstadt celebrated the Lord's Supper in the castle church, without priestly garb, sacrificial offering, elevation of the host, and with the cup offered to the laity. Auricular confession and fasts were abandoned. Karlstadt taught that all ministers should marry, and, in January, 1522, took to himself a wife. He was soon opposing the use of pictures, organs, and the Gregorian chanting in public worship. Under his leadership the Wittenberg city government broke up the ancient religious fraternities and confiscated their property, decreed that the services should be in German, condemned pictures in the churches, and forbad beggary, ordering that really needy cases be aided from the city treasury. The public commotion was augmented by the arrival, on December 27, 1521, of three radical preachers from Zwickau, chief of whom were Nikolaus Storch and Markus Thomä Stübner. These men claimed immediate divine inspiration, opposed infant baptism, and prophesied the speedy end of the world. Melanchthon was somewhat shaken by them at first, though their influence in general has been exaggerated. They undoubtedly added something to a state of turmoil.[1]

These rapid changes, followed by a popular attack on images, were highly displeasing to Elector Frederick the Wise, and they drew forth the

[1] Kidd, pp. 94–104.

warning protests of German princes and the imperial authorities. Though Luther was to further, within the next three or four years, most of the changes which Karlstadt and Zwilling had made, he now felt that his cause was in peril through a dangerous radicalism. The city government appealed to Luther to return. The Elector nominally forbade him, out of political considerations, but on March 6, 1522, Luther was once more in Wittenberg, which thenceforth was to be his home. Eight days of preaching showed his power. The Gospel, he declared, consists in the knowledge of sin, in forgiveness through Christ, and in love to one's neighbor. The alterations, which had raised the turmoil, had to do with externals. They should be effected only in a spirit of consideration of the weak. Luther was master of the situation. Karlstadt lost all influence and had to leave the city. Many of the changes were, for the moment, undone, and the old order of worship largely re-established. Luther thus showed a decidedly conservative attitude. He opposed not merely the Romanists, as heretofore, but those of the revolution who would move, as he believed, too rapidly. The separations in the reform party itself had begun. Yet there can be no doubt as to Luther's wisdom. His action caused many of the German rulers to look upon him with kindliness, as one who, though condemned at Worms, was really a force for order in troublous times, and continued especially that favor of his Elector without which his cause would even now have made speedy shipwreck.

Meanwhile the Emperor's hands were tied by the great war with France for the control of Italy, which was to keep him absent from Germany from 1521 to 1530. Effective interference on his part with the Reformation was impossible. Pope Leo X had closed his splendor-loving reign in December, 1521, and had been succeeded by Charles V's old Netherlandish tutor as Adrian VI—a man of strict mediæval orthodoxy, but fully conscious of the need of moral and administrative reform in the papal court, whose brief papacy of twenty months was to be a painfully fruitless effort to check the evils for which he believed Luther's heretical movement to be a divine punishment. Sympathy with Luther was rapidly spreading, not merely throughout Saxony, but in the cities of Germany. To the Reichstag, which met in Nürnberg in November, 1522, Adrian now sent a nuncio with a *Breve,* demanding the enforcement of the edict of Worms against Luther, while admitting that much was amiss in ecclesiastical administration. The Reichstag replied by declaring the edict impossible of enforcement, and by demanding a council for churchly reform, to meet within a year in Germany, while, pending its assembly, only the "true, pure, genuine, holy Gospel" was to be preached. The old complaints against papal misgovernment were renewed by the Reichstag. Though not in form, it was in reality a victory for Luther and his cause. It looked as if the Reformation might gain the support of the whole German nation.[2]

[2] Kidd, pp. 105–121.

Under these favorable circumstances Evangelical congregations were rapidly forming in many regions of Germany, as yet without any fixed constitution or order of service. Luther now was convinced that such associations of believers had full power to appoint and depose their pastors. He held, also, however, that the temporal rulers, as in the positions of chief power and responsibility in the Christian community, had a prime duty to further the Gospel. The experiences of the immediate future, and the necessities of actual church organization within extensive territories, were to turn Luther from whatever sympathy he now had with this free-churchism to a strict dependence on the state. To meet the demands of the new Evangelical worship, Luther issued, in 1523, his *Ordering of Worship,* in which he emphasized the central place of preaching; his *Formula of the Mass,* in which, though still using Latin, he did away with its sacrificial implications, recommended the cup for lay usage, and urged the employment of popular hymns by the worshippers; and his *Taufbüchlein,* in which he presented a baptismal service in German. The abandonment of private masses and masses for the dead, with their attendant fees, raised a serious problem of ministerial support, which Luther proposed to solve by salaries from a common chest maintained by the municipality. Luther held that great freedom was permissible in details of worship, as long as the "Word of God" was kept central. The various reformed congregations, therefore, soon exhibited considerable variety, and the tendency to the use of German rapidly increased, Luther himself issuing a *German Mass* in 1526. Confession Luther regarded as exceedingly desirable as preparing the undeveloped Christian for the Lord's Supper, but not as obligatory. Judged by the development of the Reformation elsewhere, Luther's attitude in matters of worship was strongly conservative, his principle being that "what is not contrary to Scripture is for Scripture and Scripture for it." He therefore retained much of Roman usage, such as the use of candles, the crucifix, and the illustrative employment of pictures.[3]

Thus far the tide had been running strongly in directions favorable to Luther, but with the years 1524 and 1525 separations began, the effects of which were to limit the Reformation movement, to make Luther a party rather than a national leader, to divide Germany, and to throw Luther into the arms of the temporal princes. The first of these separations was from the humanists. Their admired leader, Erasmus, had little sympathy with Luther's doctrine of justification by faith alone. To his thinking reform would come by education, the rejection of superstition and a return to the "sources" of Christian truth. The stormy writings of Luther and the popular tumult were becoming increasingly odious to him. In common with humanists generally, he was alarmed by the great decline in attendance on the German universities, which set in universally with the rise of the religious controversy, and the fading of interest in purely scholarly questions. Though frequently urged, he was

[3] Kidd, pp. 121–133.

long reluctant to attack Luther; but at last, in the autumn of 1524, he challenged Luther's denial of free will. In his carefully reasoned *"Diatribe de libero arbitrio,"* he argued, on the basis of an examination of the relevant passages of Scripture, for an ethical interpretation of religion. He concluded that the doctrine of the church asserting both man's freedom of decision for God and his need of grace was preferable to Luther's predestinarian extremism, because it avoided Manichaeism as well as Pelagianism. A year later Luther replied by his treatise *"De servo arbitrio"* (On the Bondage of the Will). He closely followed Erasmus' outline and attempted to refute it section by section. On the basis of the witness of the Bible, which he regarded as clear and unified, he argued for man's absolute dependence upon the all-ruling omnipotent God and his freely given gift of grace. He declared himself a predestinarian and did not hesitate to affirm doctrines which bordered on determinism. The breach between Luther and Erasmus was incurable. Most of the humanists deserted Luther, though among the disciples of Melanchthon a younger school of Lutheran humanists slowly developed.[4]

To some in Germany Luther seemed but a half-way reformer. Such a radical was his old associate Karlstadt, who, having lost all standing in Wittenberg, went on to yet more radical views and practices and, securing a large following in Orlamünde, practically defied Luther and the Saxon government. He denied the value of education, dressed and lived like the peasantry, destroyed images, and rejected the physical presence of Christ in the Supper. Even more radical was Thomas Münzer (1488?–1525), who asserted immediate revelation and attacked Romanists and Lutherans alike for their dependence on the letter of the Scripture. A former Roman Catholic priest, he had come under Luther's influence during a stay in Wittenberg (1519–1520). As an ardent evangelical preacher, he had worked in Zwickau and then in Bohemia, where he had hoped to build "the new church." As the minister in the Thuringian town of Allstedt (since 1522), he went far beyond Luther both in the interpretation of the gospel and in developing a program of reformation. Opposing Luther's reliance upon the Scripture and his teaching on justification by faith, he argued for a spiritualism that rendered the Bible subject to the test of religious experience and that resulted in rebirth under the sway of divine election. He was a man of great originality and obvious prophetic power. The order of worship he developed for Allstedt broke radically with all Roman Catholic tradition, including infant baptism. He believed that the Reformation should lead to the establishment of a church of the elect which would bring about a new social order of justice and love. Opposing the "easy-going flesh of Wittenberg," *i. e.,* Luther's refusal to derive from his rediscovery of the gospel a new law, either of morals or of social life, he advocated, if necessary, bloody revolution in order to put down priestly injustice. It was no wonder that, in due time, he assumed a position

[4] Kidd, pp. 171–174.

of leadership in the peasant revolt. These and men like them Luther strongly opposed, naming them Schwärmer, *i. e.,* fanatics; but their presence indicated a growing rift in the forces of reform.

Yet more serious was a third separation—that caused by the peasants' rebellion. The state of the German peasantry had long been one of increasing misery and consequent unrest, especially in southwestern Germany, where the example of better conditions in neighboring Switzerland fed the discontent. With the peasant revolt Lutheranism had little directly to do. Its strongest manifestations were in regions into which the reform movement had but slightly penetrated. Yet the religious excitement and radical popular preaching were undoubtedly contributing, though not primary, causes. Begun in extreme southwestern Germany in May and June, 1524, the insurrection was exceedingly formidable by the spring of the following year. In March, 1525, the peasants put forth twelve articles,[5] demanding the right of each community to choose and depose its pastor, that the great tithes (on grain) be used for the support of the pastor and other community expenses, and the small tithes abolished, that serfdom be done away, reservations for hunting restricted, the use of the forests allowed to the poor, forced labor be regulated and duly paid, just rents fixed, new laws no longer enacted, common lands restored to communities from which they had been taken, and payments for inheritance to their masters abolished.

Other groups of peasants, one of which had Thomas Münzer as a leader, were far more radical. Luther at first was disposed to find wrong on both sides; but as the ill-led rising fell into greater excesses and appeared to become anarchistic he turned on the peasants with his savage pamphlet, *Against the Murderous and Thieving Rabble of the Peasants,* demanding that the princes crush them with the sword. The great defeat of Francis I of France, near Pavia by the imperial army on February 24, 1525, had enabled the princes of Germany to master the rising. The peasant insurrection was stamped out in frightful bloodshed.

Of the separations, that occasioned by the peasants' war was undoubtedly the most disastrous. Luther felt that his Gospel could not be involved in the social and economic demands of the disorderly peasants. In his eyes, all revolution was rebellion against God. But the cost was great. Popular sympathy for his cause among the lower orders of Germany was largely forfeited, his own distrust of the common man was augmented, his feeling that the reform must be the work of the temporal princes greatly strengthened. His opponents, moreover, pointed to these risings as the natural fruitage of rebellion against the ancient church.

Meanwhile the mediæval, though in his way reformatory, Adrian VI had died, and had been succeeded in the papacy, in November, 1523, by Giulio de' Medici as Clement VII (1523–1534)—a man of respectable char-

[5] Kidd, pp. 174–179.

acter but with little sense of the importance of religious questions, and primarily in policy an Italian worldly prince. To the new Reichstag assembled in Nürnberg in the spring of 1524, Clement sent as his legate the skilful cardinal, Lorenzo Campeggio (1474–1539). With the Reichstag Campeggio could effect little. It promised to enforce the Edict of Worms against Luther "as far as possible," and demanded a "general assembly of the German nation" to meet in Speier, in the following autumn. This gathering the absent Emperor succeeded in frustrating. Campeggio's real success was, however, outside the Reichstag. Through his efforts a league to support the Roman cause was formed in Regensburg, on July 7, 1524, embracing the Emperor's brother, Ferdinand, the dukes of Bavaria, and a number of south German bishops. A fifth of the ecclesiastical revenues was assigned to the lay princes, regulations to secure a more worthy clergy enacted, clerical fees lightened, the number of saints' days to be observed as holidays diminished, and preaching to be in accordance with the Fathers of the ancient church rather than the schoolmen.[6] It was the beginning of a real Counter-Reformation; but its effect was to increase the separation of parties in Germany, and to strengthen the line of demarcation on the basis of the possessions of rival territorial princes. The nation was in hopeless division.

While Rome was thus strengthened in southern Germany Luther's cause received important accessions. Chief of these was the adhesion, in 1524, of the far-sighted landgrave Philip of Hesse (1518–1567), the ablest politician among the Lutheran princes. At the same time Albert of Prussia, grand master of the Teutonic Knights, George of Brandenburg, Henry of Mecklenburg, and Albert of Mansfeld were showing a decided interest in the Evangelical cause. The important cities, Magdeburg, Nürnberg, Strassburg, Augsburg, Esslingen, Ulm, and others of less moment had also been won by 1524.

It was in the dark days of the peasant revolt that Luther's cautious protector, Frederick the Wise, died (May 5, 1525), and was succeeded by his brother John "the Steadfast" (1525–1532). The change was favorable to Luther, for the new Elector was a declared and active Lutheran. In these months falls, also, Luther's marriage to Katherine von Bora (1499–1552), on June 13, 1525, a union which was to manifest some of the most winsome traits of the reformer's character. The marriage was rather suddenly arranged, and the charge sometimes made that desire for matrimony had any share in Luther's revolt from Rome is palpably absurd; but, though this repudiation of clerical celibacy was undoubtedly favorable in its ultimate results, it was, at the time, an added cause of division, and the union of an ex-monk and a former nun seemed to give point to the bitter jibe of Erasmus that the Reformation, which had appeared a tragedy, was really a comedy, the end of which was a wedding.[7]

[6] Kidd, pp. 133–151.   [7] Kidd, pp. 179, 180.

The suppression of the peasant revolt had left the princes and the cities the real ruling forces in Germany, and political combinations were now formed for or against the Reformation. Such a league of Catholics was instituted by Duke George of Saxony, and other Catholic princes met in Dessau in July, 1525; and as a reply Philip of Hesse and the new Elector John of Saxony organized a Lutheran league in Torgau. The great imperial victory of Pavia in the previous February had resulted in the captivity of the defeated King of France, Francis I. The war had gone decisively in favor of the Emperor, and its results seemed to be garnered by the Treaty of Madrid of January, 1526, by which Francis gained his release. Both monarchs pledged themselves to combined efforts to put down heresy.[8] The prospects of Lutheranism was indeed dark. From this peril the Lutheran cause owed its rescue primarily to the Pope. Clement VII, always more an Italian prince than a churchman, was thoroughly alarmed at the increase of imperial power in Italy. He formed an Italian league against the Emperor, which was joined by the French King in May, 1526. Francis I repudiated the Treaty of Madrid, and now the League of Cognac ranged France, the Pope, Florence, and Venice against the Emperor. The results of Pavia seemed lost. The war must be fought over again. The Emperor's hands were too full to interfere in the religious struggles of Germany.[9]

So it came about that when the new Reichstag met in Speier in the summer of 1526, though the imperial instructions forbade alterations in religion and ordered the execution of the Edict of Worms, the Lutherans were able to urge that the situation had changed from that contemplated by the Emperor when his commands were issued from Spain. The terrifying advance of the Turks, which was to result in the Hungarian disaster of Mohacz on August 29, 1526, also counselled military unity. The Reichstag, therefore, enacted that, pending a "council or a national assembly," each of the territorial rulers of the empire is "so to live, govern, and carry himself as he hopes and trusts to answer it to God and his imperial majesty." [10]

This was doubtless a mere *ad interim* compromise; but the Lutheran princes and cities speedily interpreted it as full legal authorization to order their ecclesiastical constitutions as they saw fit. Under its shelter the organization of Lutheran territorial churches was now rapidly accomplished. Some steps had been taken toward such territorial organization even before the Reichstag of 1526. Beyond the borders of the empire Albert of Brandenburg (1511–1568), the grand master of the Teutonic Knights in East Prussia, transformed his office into a hereditary dukedom under the overlordship of Poland, in 1525, and vigorously furthered the Lutheranization of the land.[11] In electoral Saxony itself, Elector John was planning a more active governmental control of ecclesiastical affairs, and Luther had issued his *German Mass and Order of Divine Service,* of 1526, before the Reichstag.[12] The decree of

[8] *Ibid.,* p. 180.   [9] *Ibid.,* p. 182.   [10] Kidd, pp. 183–185.   [11] *Ibid.,* pp. 185–193.   [12] *Ibid.,* pp. 193–202.

the Reichstag now greatly strengthened these tendencies. In Hesse, Landgrave Philip caused a synod to be held in Homberg, in October, 1526, where a constitution was adopted largely through the influence of Francis Lambert (1487–1530), a pupil of Luther. In each community the faithful communicants were to constitute the governing body by which pastor should be chosen and discipline administered. Representatives from these local bodies, a pastor and a lay brother from each, should constitute an annual synod for all Hesse, of which the landgrave and high nobles should also be members.[13] Here was an organization proposed which was consonant, in large measure, with Luther's earlier views. But Luther had changed. He had come to distrust the common man, and on his advice the landgrave rejected the proposals and adopted instead the procedure of electoral Saxony.

In Saxony, which became the norm in a general way for the creation of territorial churches, "visitors" were appointed by the Elector to inquire into clerical doctrine and conduct on the basis of articles drawn up by Melanchthon in 1527, and enlarged the following year.[14] The old jurisdiction of bishops was cast off, the land was divided into districts, each under a "superintendent" with spiritual, but not administrative superiority over the parish minister, and in turn responsible to the Elector. Unworthy or recalcitrant clergy were driven out, similarity of worship secured, and monastic property, altar endowment and similar foundations confiscated, in part for the benefit of parish churches and schools, but largely for that of the electoral treasury. In a word, a Lutheran state church, coterminous with the electoral territories, and having all baptized inhabitants as its members, was substituted for the old bishop-ruled church. Other territories of Evangelical Germany were similarly organized. To aid in popular religious instruction, which the confusion of a decade had reduced to a deplorable condition, Luther prepared two catechisms in 1529, of which the *Short Catechism* is one of the noblest monuments of the Reformation.[15]

That this development of territorial churches could take place was due to favoring political conditions. The Emperor had a tremendous war to wage with domination in Italy as its prize. His brother, Ferdinand, was crowned King of Hungary on November 3, 1527, and thenceforth was in struggle with the Turks. Effective interference in Germany was impossible. But fortune favored the Emperor. On May 6, 1527, an imperial army containing many German Landsknechts, captured Rome, shut up Pope Clement VII in the castle of San Angelo, and subjected the city to every barbarity. Though fortune seemed to turn toward the French in the early part of 1528, before the end of that year the imperial forces had asserted their mastery. The Pope was compelled to make his peace with the Emperor, at Barcelona, on June 29, 1529,[16] and France gave up the struggle by the Peace of Cambrai, on the 5th of the following August. The great war which had

[13] *Ibid.,* pp. 222–230.   [14] Kidd, pp. 202–205.   [15] *Ibid.,* pp. 205–222.
[16] *Ibid.,* p. 246.

raged since 1521 was over, and Charles V could now turn his attention to the suppression of the Lutheran revolt. Nor had the Lutheran leaders been wholly fortunate. Deceived by a forgery by Otto von Pack, an official of ducal Saxony, the Landgrave Philip of Hesse and the Elector John of Saxony had been convinced that the Catholics intended to attack them. Philip determined to anticipate the alleged plot, and was arming for that purpose in 1528, when the forgery was discovered. The effect of the incident was to embitter the relations of the two great ecclesiastical parties.

Under these circumstances it was inevitable that when the next Reichstag met in Speier, in February, 1529, the Catholic majority should be strongly hostile to the Lutheran innovators. That Reichstag now ordered, by a majority decision, that no further ecclesiastical changes should be made, that Roman worship should be permitted in Lutheran lands, and that all Roman authorities and orders should be allowed full enjoyment of their former rights, property, and incomes. This would have been the practical abolition of the Lutheran territorial churches. Unable to defeat this legislation, the Lutheran civil powers represented in the Reichstag, on April 19, 1529, entered a formal protest of great historic importance, the *Protestatio,* since it led to the designation of the party as "Protestant." It was supported by John of electoral Saxony, Philip of Hesse, Ernst of Lüneburg, George of Brandenburg-Ansbach, Wolfgang of Anhalt, and the cities Strassburg, Ulm, Constance, Nürnberg, Lindau, Kempten, Memmingen, Nördlingen, Heilbronn, Isny, St. Gallen, Reutlingen, Weissenburg, and Windsheim.[17]

The Protestant prospects were dark, and the situation demanded a defensive union, which Philip of Hesse undertook to secure. At this critical juncture the Reformation cause was threatened by division between the reformers of Saxony and Switzerland, and by the rapid spread of the Anabaptists.

3

The Swiss Reformation

SWITZERLAND, though nominally a part of the empire, had long been practically independent. Its thirteen cantons were united in a loose confederacy, each being a self-governing republic. The land, as a whole, was deemed the freest in Europe. Its sons were in great repute as soldiers and

[17] Kidd, pp. 239–245.

were eagerly sought as mercenaries, particularly by the Kings of France and the Popes. Though the general status of education was low, humanism had penetrated the larger towns, and in the early decades of the sixteenth century had notably its home in Basel. The Swiss reformation was to have its sources in humanism, in local self-government, in hatred of ecclesiastical restraint, and in resistance to monastic exactions, especially where the monasteries were large landowners.

Huldreich Zwingli, chief of the reformers of German-speaking Switzerland, was born on January 1, 1484, in Wildhaus, where his father was the bailiff of the village and in comfortable circumstances. An uncle, the dean of Wesen, started him on the road to an education, which was continued in Basel, and then in Bern under the humanist Heinrich Wölflin (Lupulus), from 1498 to 1500. For two years Zwingli was a student in the University of Vienna, where Conrad Celtes had great fame in the classics. From 1502 to 1506 he continued his studies in the University of Basel, graduating as bachelor of arts in 1504, and receiving the master's degree two years later. At Basel he enjoyed the instruction of the humanist Thomas Wyttenbach (1472–1526), whom he gratefully remembered as having taught him the sole authority of Scripture, the death of Christ as the only price of forgiveness, and the worthlessness of indulgences. Under such teaching Zwingli became naturally a humanist himself, eager to go back to the earlier sources of Christian belief, and critical of what the humanists generally deemed superstition. He never passed through the deep spiritual experience of sin and forgiveness that came to Luther. His religious attitude was always more intellectual and radical than that of the Saxon reformer.

The year of Zwingli's second graduation saw his appointment, apparently through the influence of his clerical uncle, as parish priest in Glarus. Here he studied Greek, became an influential preacher, opposed the employment of Swiss as mercenaries, save by the Pope, and in 1513 received a pension from the Pope, anxious to secure the continued military support of the Swiss. He accompanied the young men of his parish as chaplain in several Italian campaigns. He corresponded with Erasmus and other humanists. His knowledge of the world was increasing, and he touched life on many sides.[1]

Zwingli was patriotically convinced of the moral evil of mercenary service, but the French, eager to enlist Swiss soldiers, made so much trouble in his Glarus parish that, without resigning the post, he transferred his activities in 1516 to the still-famous pilgrim shrine of Einsiedeln. The change brought him enlarged reputation as a preacher and a student. To this Einsiedeln sojourn Zwingli, always jealous of admitting indebtedness to Luther, later ascribed his acceptance of the Evangelical position. The evidence that has survived points, however, to little then beyond the more advanced humanistic attitude. His own life at this time was, moreover, not free from reproach for breach of the vow of chastity.

[1] Kidd, pp. 374–380.

His opposition to foreign military service and reputation as a preacher and scholar led to Zwingli's election by the Minster chapter in Zürich as people's priest, an office on which he entered with the commencement of 1519. He began at once the orderly exposition of whole books of the Bible, commencing with Matthew's Gospel. He now became acquainted with Luther's writings. He was brought near to death by the plague. He preached faithfully against mercenary soldiering, so that Zürich ultimately (May, 1521) forbade the practice.[2] His own spiritual life deepened, through bereavement by the death of a beloved brother in 1520, and the same year he resigned his papal pension.

Though Zwingli had thus long been moving in the reformatory direction, it was with 1522 that his vigorous reforming work began. It is interesting to note that the question first at issue did not grow, as with Luther, out of a concern to become acceptable to God, but out of the conviction that only the Bible is binding on Christians. Certain of the citizens broke the lenten fast, citing Zwingli's assertion of the sole authority of Scripture in justification. Zwingli now preached and published in their defense. The bishop of Constance, in whose diocese Zürich lay, now sent a commission to repress the innovation. The cantonal civil government ruled that the New Testament imposed no fasts, but that they should be observed for the sake of good order. The importance of this compromise decision was that the cantonal civil authorities practically rejected the jurisdiction of the bishop and took the control of the Zürich churches into their own hands. In the August following the Zürich burgomaster laid down the rule that the pure Word of God was alone to be preached, and the road to reformation was thus fully open.[3]

Zwingli believed that the ultimate authority was the Christian community, and that the exercise of that authority was through the duly constituted organs of civil government acting in accordance with the Scriptures. Only that which the Bible commands, or for which distinct authorization can be found in its pages, is binding or allowable. Hence his attitude toward the ceremonies and order of the older worship was much more radical than that of Luther's. Really the situation in Zürich was one in which the cantonal government introduced the changes which Zwingli, as a trusted interpreter of Scripture and a natural popular leader, persuaded that government to sanction. Zwingli now began a process of governmental and popular education, which he employed with great success. Persuaded by Zwingli, the cantonal government ordered a public discussion, in January, 1523, in which the Bible only should be the touchstone. For this debate Zwingli prepared sixty-seven brief articles, affirming that the Gospel derives no authority from the church, that salvation is by faith, and denying the sacrificial character of the mass, the salvatory character of good works, the value of saintly intercessors, the binding

[2] Kidd, pp. 384–387.   [3] *Ibid.*, pp. 387–408.

character of monastic vows, or the existence of purgatory. He also declared Christ to be the sole head of the church, and advocated clerical marriage. In the resulting debate the government declared Zwingli the victor, in that it affirmed that he had not been convicted of heresy, and directed that he should continue his preaching. It was an indorsement of his teaching.[4]

Changes now went rapidly. Priests and nuns married. Fees for baptisms and burials were done away. In a second great debate, in October, 1523, Zwingli and his associate minister, Leo Jud (1482–1542), attacked the use of images and the sacrificial character of the mass. The government was with them, but moved cautiously.[5] January, 1524, saw a third great debate. The upholders of the old order were given choice of conformity or banishment. In June and July, 1524, images, relics, and organs were done away. December witnessed the confiscation of the monastic establishments, their property being wisely used, in large part, in the establishment of excellent schools. The mass continued till Holy Week of 1525, when it too was abolished. The transformation was complete. Episcopal jurisdiction had been thrown off, the services put into German, the sermon made central, the characteristic doctrines and ceremonies of the older worship done away.[6] Zwingli explained and justified these changes in his chief theological work: *The Commentary on True and False Religion*, 1525. Meanwhile, on April 2, 1524, Zwingli had publicly married Anna Reinhard, a widow, whom he and his friends, not without considerable unfriendly gossip, had treated as in some sense his wife since 1522. All this time the Popes had made no effective interference in Zürich affairs, largely by reason of the political value of Switzerland in the wars. The bishop of Constance had done what he could, but to no avail.

Naturally Zwingli followed with eagerness the fortunes of the ecclesiastical revolution in other parts of Switzerland and the adjacent regions of Germany, and aided it to the utmost of his ability. Basel, where the civil authority had gained large influence in churchly affairs before the revolt, was won gradually for the Evangelical cause, chiefly by Johann Œcolampadius (1482–1531), who labored there continuously from 1522. There the mass was abolished in 1529. Œcolampadius and Zwingli were warm friends. Bern, the greatest of the Swiss cantons, was won for the reform in 1528, after much preliminary Evangelical labor, by a public debate in which Zwingli took part.[7] St. Gallen, Schaffhausen, Glarus, and Mülhausen in Alsace were also won. Of even larger importance was the inclination of the great German city of Strassburg to the Zwinglian, rather than the Lutheran, point of view. In that city the Evangelical movement, begun in 1521 by Matthew Zell (1477–1548), had been carried forward vigorously from 1523 by Wolfgang Capito (1478–1541) and by the able and peace-loving Martin Butzer (1491–1551), though not wholly completed till 1529.

[4] Kidd, pp. 408–423.   [5] *Ibid.*, pp. 424–441.   [6] Kidd, pp. 441–450.
[7] *Ibid.*, pp. 459–464.

Zwingli and Luther were in many respects in substantial agreement, but they were temperamentally unlike, and their religious experiences had been very different. Luther had reached his goal by a profound religious struggle, involving a transforming sense of relationship between his soul and God. Zwingli had travelled the humanists' road, though going much farther than most humanists. His emphases were unlike Luther's. To Zwingli the will of God rather than the way of salvation was the central fact of theology. To Luther the Christian life was one of freedom in forgiven sonship. To Zwingli it was far more one of conformity to the will of God as set forth in the Bible.

Zwingli's nature was intellectual and critical. In no point of Christian doctrine was his diversity from Luther more apparent than in their unlike interpretation of the Lord's Supper, and here their disagreement unfortunately ultimately sundered the Evangelical ranks. To Luther Christ's words, "This is my body," were literally true. His deep religious feeling saw in an actual partaking of Christ the surest pledge of that union with Christ and forgiveness of sins of which the Supper was the divinely attested promise. But as early as 1521 a Dutch lawyer, Cornelius Hoen, had urged that the proper interpretation is "This signifies my body." Hoen's argument came to Zwingli's notice in 1523, and confirmed the symbolic understanding of the words to which he was already inclined. Henceforth he denied any physical presence of Christ in the Supper, and emphasized its memorial character and its significance as uniting a congregation of believers in a common attestation of loyalty to their Lord. By 1524 the rival interpretations had led to an embittered controversy of pamphlets in which Luther and Bugenhagen on the one side and Zwingli and Œcolampadius on the other, and their respective associates, took part. The most important work of Luther's was his [Great] Confession Concerning the Lord's Supper, of 1528. Little charity was shown on either side. To Zwingli Luther's assertion of the physical presence of Christ was an unreasoning remnant of Catholic superstition. A physical body could be only in one place. To Luther Zwingli's interpretation was a sinful exaltation of reason above Scripture, and he sought to explain the physical presence of Christ on ten thousand altars at once by a scholastic assertion, derived largely from Occam, that the qualities of Christ's divine nature, including ubiquity, were communicated to His human nature. Luther was anxious, also, to maintain that the believer partook of the whole divine-human Christ, and to avoid any dismemberment of His person. Luther declared Zwingli and his supporters to be no Christians, while Zwingli affirmed that Luther was worse than the Roman champion, Eck. Zwingli's views, however, met the approval not only of German-speaking Switzerland but of much of southwestern Germany. The Roman party rejoiced at this evident division of the Evangelical forces.

Zwingli was the most gifted of any of the reformers politically, and developed plans which were far-reaching, though in the end futile. The old rural cantons, Uri, Schwyz, Unterwalden, and Zug, were strongly conservative and opposed to the changes in Zürich, and with them stood Lucerne, the whole constituting a vigorous Roman party. By April, 1524, these had formed a league to resist heresy. To offset this effort and to carry Evangelical preaching into yet wider territories, Zwingli now proposed that Zürich enter into alliance with France and Savoy, and began negotiations with the dispossessed Duke Ulrich of Württemberg. Matters drifted along, but a more successful attempt was the organization of "The Christian Civic Alliance," late in 1527, between Zürich and Constance,[8] a league to which Bern and St. Gallen were added in 1528, and Biel, Mülhausen, Basel, and Schaffhausen in 1529. Though Strassburg joined early in 1530, the league was far less extensive than Zwingli planned. As it was it was divisive of Swiss unity, and the conservative Roman cantons formed a counter "Christian Union" and secured alliance with Austria in 1529. Hostilities were begun. But Austrian help for the Roman party was not forthcoming, and on June 25, 1529, peace was made between the two parties at Kappel, on terms very favorable to Zürich and the Zwinglians.[9] The league with Austria was abandoned.

Zürich was now at the height of its power, and was widely regarded as the political head of the Evangelical cause. Yet the peace had been but a truce, and when, in 1531, Zürich tried to force Evangelical preaching on the Roman cantons by an embargo on shipment of food to them, war was once more certain. Zürich, in spite of Zwingli's counsels, made no adequate preparation for the struggle. The Roman cantons moved rapidly. On October 11, 1531, they defeated the men of Zürich in battle at Kappel. Among the slain was Zwingli himself. In the peace that followed [10] Zürich was compelled to abandon its alliances, and each canton was given full right to regulate its internal religious affairs. The progress of the Reformation in German-speaking Switzerland was permanently halted, and the lines drawn substantially as they are to-day. In the leadership of the Zürich church, not in his political ambitions, Zwingli was succeeded by the able and conciliatory Heinrich Bullinger (1504–1575). The Swiss movement, as a whole, was to be modified and greatly developed by the genius of Calvin; and to the churches which trace their spiritual parentage to him, and thus in part to Zwingli, the name "Reformed," as distinguished from "Lutheran," was ultimately to be given.

[8] Kidd, p. 469.   [9] *Ibid.*, p. 470.   [10] *Ibid.*, pp. 475–476.

4

The Anabaptists

*I*T HAS BEEN SAID, in speaking of Karlstadt, that some who once worked with Luther came to feel that he was but a half-way reformer. Such was even more largely Zwingli's experience. Among those who had been most forward in favoring innovations in Zürich were Conrad Grebel and Felix Manz, both from prominent families of the city and humanistically trained. They and others soon came to feel that Zwingli's leadership in the application of the Biblical test to Zürich practices was far too conservative. This element first came into evidence at the second great debate, in October, 1523 (see p. 322), where it demanded the immediate abolition of images and of the mass—steps for which the cantonal authorities were not as yet fully ready. An abler participant in that debate was Balthasar Hubmaier (1480?–1528), once a pupil, then colleague and friend of Luther's opponent, Eck, but now preacher in Waldshut, on the northern edge of Switzerland. Led to Evangelical views by Luther's writings in 1522, he was successfully urging reform in his city. As early as May, 1523, he had come to doubt infant baptism, and had discussed it with Zwingli, who, according to his testimony, then sympathized with him. His criticisms were based on want of Scriptural warrant for administration to infants.[1] By 1524 Grebel and Manz had reached the same conclusion,[2] but it was not till early in 1525 that they or Hubmaier translated theory into practice.

Their criticisms led, on January 17, 1525, to a public debate with Zwingli, as a consequence of which the cantonal authorities of Zürich on January 18, ordered all children baptized—there had evidently been delay on the part of some parents—and in particular directed Grebel and Manz to cease from disputing, and banished the priest of Wytikon, Wilhelm Röubli, and other members of the group.[3] To these men this seemed a command by an earthly power to act counter to the Word of God. They and some of their friends gathered, probably at Zürich in the house of Felix Manz, in the evening of January 21, 1525. After prayer, George Blaurock rose to ask Conrad Grebel to baptize him. Grebel complied with this request and then Blaurock proceeded to baptize the rest.

[1] Kidd, p. 451.   [2] *Ibid.,* p. 452.   [3] *Ibid.,* pp. 453, 454.

In the following week, several members of the group held revival meetings in the village of Zollikon near Zürich. They led prayer meetings in private homes. Those who experienced regeneration were baptized by sprinkling. Having thus instituted believers' baptism, they proceeded to celebrate their membership in the fellowship of Christ by a simple observance of the Lord's Supper. A few weeks later a case of immersion occurred, and after Easter, Hubmaier was baptized in Waldshut by Röubli.[4]

These acts constituted the groups separate communions. By their opponents they were nicknamed "Anabaptists," or rebaptizers. Really, since they denied the validity of their baptism in infancy, the name was inappropriate, and "Baptists" would be the truer designation; but as a title consecrated by long usage to a remarkable movement of the Reformation age, the more common name is convenient. The Zürich government, in March, 1526, ordered Anabaptists drowned, in hideous parody of their belief, and on June 5, 1527, Manz thus suffered martyrdom.[5] Grebel escaped a similar fate only because he had died of the plague shortly before. Zwingli opposed them with much bitterness, but with little success in winning them from their position.[6]

Grebel and his friends differed from him not only in so far as they saw the test of Christian faith in discipleship of Christ that, they felt, must be experienced in a spiritual rebirth or awakening and expressed in a life of saintliness, but particularly on account of their opposition to the use of force in matters of faith and their abandonment of the age-old requirement of religious uniformity as the guarantee of public peace and order. They refused to have any part in state-churches of the kind that Zwingli built in Zürich and as they were to be established in other centers of the Reformation. They chose rather to set themselves apart in free communities and conventicles of their own. Thus they were the first to practice the separation of church and state. It was chiefly on account of this non-conformism that they were subjected to persecution. Their sectarianism was interpreted as an expression of hostility to ordered society.

In Waldshut Hubmaier soon gathered a large Anabaptist community, and was even more successful in propagating his opinions by his pen. In his view the Bible is the sole law of the church, and according to the Scriptural test the proper order of Christian development is, preaching the Word, hearing, belief, baptism, works—the latter indicating a life lived with the Bible as its law. Waldshut, however, was soon involved in the peasant revolt—in how far through Hubmaier is doubtful—and shared the collapse of that movement. Hubmaier had to fly, and the city was once more Catholic. Imprisoned and tortured in Zürich, he fled to Moravia, where he propagated the Anabaptist movement with much success.

These persecutions had the effect of spreading the Anabaptist propa-

[4] Kidd, pp. 454, 455.   [5] Ibid., p. 455.   [6] Ibid., pp. 456–458.

ganda throughout Germany, Switzerland and the Netherlands. The movement soon assumed great proportions, especially among the lower classes, when the miserable failure of the peasant revolt had caused deep distrust of the Lutheran cause, now wholly associated with territorial princes and aristocratic city magistrates. In the still Catholic parts of the empire the Anabaptist propaganda practically superseded the Lutheran. The territorial rulers at first tried to check the movement by issuing mandates against it, just as the Zürich authorities had done. Ferdinand of Austria was the first to do so and his brother, the Emperor Charles V, supported him (January 4, 1528). But despite the fact that many became victims of these prohibitions, the Anabaptists became more and more troublesome. Hence at the diets of Speier (1529) and of Augsburg (1530), the assembled German estates, both Roman Catholic and Protestant, applied the old Roman law against heresy to them. Henceforth membership in any Anabaptist group was punishable by death. In Roman Catholic territories, particularly Austria and Bavaria, this newly proclaimed law was executed with utmost severity. In Evangelical lands, Anabaptists were not treated as heretics but as seditionists. If they were unwilling to conform to the established ecclesiastical order, they were given the chance to emigrate. If they refused to do so and continued to profess their faith publicly, they were regarded as disturbers of the peace and punished by imprisonment or death. Only in Hesse, Württemberg and Strassburg "blood-judgments" were avoided.

The expansion of the Anabaptist movement issued from three centers: Switzerland, South Germany, and Moravia.

When Zürich began to suppress it, the earliest converts naturally carried their faith to other parts of Switzerland. Many Anabaptist congregations were soon established throughout the high valleys of the Alps. That they grew rapidly is indicated by the actions which the public authorities had to take against them. On December 29, 1529, the City Council of Basel arranged for a public discussion between the Evangelical preachers and spokesmen of the Anabaptists and then prohibited the movement. In 1530–31, three believers were executed, many others were exiled. In the Canton of Bern, a long disputation with twenty-three Anabaptists took place on July 1–9, 1532 at Zofingen. Here, too, the result was public condemnation. Between 1529 and 1571 forty public executions of Anabaptists took place. The situation was similar in the Cantons of Appenzell and Aargau. The chief center of Swiss Anabaptist propaganda became the Grisons and the region around Chur. There Blaurock was the main agent, until he was burned at the stake in Tyrol on September 6, 1529. For a long time, Anabaptist groups continued to be active there as is shown by the correspondence of Bullinger, Zwingli's successor, who was one of their most ardent literary antagonists. From the Grisons (Graubünden) the sectarians were in constant touch with friends and sympathizers in Moravia and upper Italy, especially Venice.

The chief German center was at first Augsburg. Here Hubmaier baptized Hans Denck (1495?–1527) in May, 1526. He, in turn, shortly thereafter, baptized Hans Hut who proceeded to organize a rapidly growing congregation, winning even members of patrician families (in February, 1527, he baptized Eitelhans Langenmantel). On August 20, 1527, a synod (later called the "Martyrs"-Synod) was held, chiefly in order to deal with Hut's apocalyptic ideas. He regarded himself a prophet, affirming that the persecution of the saints would be followed by the destruction of the Empire by the Turks. Thereafter the saints would be gathered and all priests and unworthy rulers would be destroyed by them, whereupon Christ would visibly rule on earth. The majority rejected these views and Hut promised to keep them to himself. The "synod" decided to send out evangelists to Austria, Salzburg, Bavaria, Worms, Basel and Zürich. Almost all who went out shortly thereafter suffered the death of martyrs. Hans Hut was imprisoned in Augsburg. He died from burns he suffered in an attempt to escape from the prison by setting it afire. His body was publicly burned on December 7, 1527. Denck made his way to Basel, where his career was ended by death from the plague. He was one of the most remarkable figures among the sectarians. Humanistically trained, he had become the rector of the famous school of St. Sebald in Nürnberg. He was widely respected but dismissed from his post in 1525, when he expressed sympathy with the mystical ideas of Münzer. Although he then joined the Anabaptists, probably attracted to them by their ideal of Christian discipleship and by their pacifism, his views really were those of a spiritualist mystic. Before his death, he seems to have severed all connection with the sectarians, because he rejected all visible organization of the Christian life. His faith rested on an inner light superior to all Scripture. In Christ he saw the highest example of love; and he held that the Christian may live without sin. His writings, marked by a beautiful Christian inwardness, show that his thinking was nourished by the traditions of Christian Platonism and mysticism, especially the "German Theology."

From 1528 until 1533, Strassburg was a main German center of Anabaptist activity. An Anabaptist congregation had existed there since 1526, founded probably by Röubli. It was led by Michael Sattler, a former monk of St. Peter in Freiburg, who was everywhere highly regarded because of his deep Christian piety. The Strassburg preachers, especially Capito and Zell and his wife, were friendly to him. Bucer, who saw in the Anabaptists a threat to the Christian community which he believed had to be one, felt that persuasion might convince them to give up their sectarianism. In the fall of 1526, Denck came to Strassburg and won a considerable following. On December 22, Bucer engaged him in a public discussion. As a result,

Denck was ordered from the city by the Council. Shortly thereafter Sattler left voluntarily. On February 24, 1527, he presided over the Anabaptist Council in Schlatt, convened for the purpose to unify the Swiss and Swabian groups. It adopted seven articles of faith, written by Sattler, a very characteristic formulation of Anabaptist convictions. In them believers' baptism is asserted. The church is regarded as composed only of local associations of baptized regenerated Christians, united as the body of Christ by the common observance of the Lord's Supper; its only weapon is excommunication. Absolute rejection of all "servitude to the flesh," such as the worship of the Roman, Lutheran, and Zwinglian churches, is demanded. Each congregation is to choose its own officers and administer through them its discipline. While civil government is held to be a necessity in this imperfect world, the Christian must have no share in it; he should not bear arms or use coercion, nor should he take any form of oath. These were ideas which were to be represented in varying proportions by later Baptists, Congregationalists, and Quakers, and through them to have a profound influence on the religious development of England and America. Shortly thereafter, Sattler was apprehended by Austrian authorities and put to the stake in Rottenburg (May 21, 1527). His wife was drowned. The Anabaptist community in Strassburg continued to flourish, chiefly because ever new leaders sought refuge in the city. For a time, the outstanding figure was Pilgram Marpeck, an engineer from Tyrol who built water-conduits for the city of Strassburg and occupied an honored position there. In 1531 and 1532, the Evangelical leaders engaged him in respectful discussions, until he was finally ordered from the city. He then made his way to Augsburg, where he continued to be intermittently active on behalf of his faith until his death in 1546. Marpeck defended his convictions in laborious writings, which only recently have again come to light. In them he tries to justify the Anabaptist doctrines on the basis of a strict Biblicism. In 1542, he wrote a kind of Catechism under the title *Vermahnung Oder Taufbüchlein* and during the last part of his life (1542–46) a very long "Reply" to Caspar Schwenckfeld (1489–1561), the chief spokesman of a spiritualist Pietism among the German Evangelicals.

From 1533 on, the Strassburg government took stricter measures against the sectarians (imprisonment), chiefly because Melchior Hoffmann instilled in them a fanatical apocalypticism. This strange man, born in Swabia and a tanner by profession, had come under the influence of Luther in Latvia in 1523. He then became a lay-preacher, expounding his confused evangelical ideas during his travels through the Baltics, Sweden, Denmark and Holstein, constantly in conflict with Roman Catholic priests and evangelical preachers. At the end of 1529, he came to Strassburg and there made contact with the Anabaptists. Their opposition to the churches caused him to develop an original form of Apocalypticism. He expounded it in connection with the book of Revelation. He now regarded Luther, "the apostle of the beginnings," as a Judas and proclaiming himself "apostle of the end" he predicted that the last judgment would come in 1533, spreading throughout the world from Strassburg. He was ordered from the city, and went to the Netherlands, where he succeeded in gathering the scattered followers of the Reformation, filling them with the expectation that they would triumph while all others would perish by violence. In 1532 he returned to Strassburg, the "new Jerusalem." Bucer was ordered to engage him in public discussion. This was held on July 11–15, 1532. Sure of himself, he dared the government to imprison him. His wish was granted, but not until May, 1533. He stayed in confinement until his death in 1543, adhering to the last to his convictions and his hope.

In Moravia, it was on the large estates of the Liechtensteins that the Anabaptists found a refuge. In 1526, Balthasar Hubmaier founded an Anabaptist congregation in Nikolsburg. Under his leadership it grew rapidly. Thousands of refugees from Germany and from Tirol settled there and formed several communities. Hubmaier, who produced more tracts (eighteen within one year!) than any other Anabaptist (practically all of them dealt with believers' baptism), was their chief leader, until, in July 1527, he was surrendered to the Austrian authorities. He was burned at the stake in Vienna, on March 10, 1528, and his wife was drowned in the Danube.

There were many divisions among the Moravian Baptists. At the end of 1526, a discussion took place in Nikolsburg between Hans Hut and Hubmaier. Hut expected the end of the world by 1528 and defended a radical pacifism. Hubmaier argued for the need of civil government and advocated submission under it, including the duty to render military service and to pay taxes. The Brethren who sided with Hut founded a community at Austerlitz, in 1528, which grew rapidly and soon comprised several thousand members. They developed a communist social order, the only ones among the Anabaptists to do so, although it was a common charge against them, wherever they were persecuted, that they all had abolished private property in order to be able to share all their goods with one another. The Austerlitz community suffered many divisions and separations, until Jacob Hutter firmly organized them, from 1529 until 1536, when he too suffered the martyr's death in Innsbruck. He left the "Hutterite Brethren" economically so well organized that they were able to maintain their communist order, until 1622 in Moravia and until 1685 in Hungary and, later, in the Ukraine and since 1874 in the United States of America, where groups of them exist to this day, especially in South Dakota. The successors of Hutter were a line of energetic bishops: Hans Amon (1536–42); Peter Riedemann (1542–56), who wrote a notable book entitled "Rechenschaft" which is one of the most impressive statements of Anabaptist faith; Peter Walpot (1556–78); and Claus Braidl (1585–1611).

At the end of the Reformation period, Anabaptist congregations existed, apart from Moravia, in Switzerland, the Palatinate, the Netherlands, and Friesland, in Prussia and Poland. In the thirties and forties, they had been active also in Hesse and Saxony, the chief Lutheran territories. Philip of Hesse sought to deal leniently with them. Those among them who were apprehended and refused to recant were banished. The severest penalty imposed upon them was imprisonment. The most radical leader among the Hessian Anabaptists was Melchior Rink, a former associate of Thomas Münzer. He spent the last ten years of his life in prison, where he died around 1540. One of the most remarkable events in Hessian Anabaptist history was a discussion (*Gespräch*) which Bucer held with some of them on the order of the Landgrave on October 30–November 2, 1538 in Marburg. This was one of the very rare occasions when Anabaptist believers felt compelled to yield to the arguments of their opponents and to give up their faith.

In Saxony and Thuringia, the Anabaptists were vigorously suppressed. Luther, who unjustly identified them with Karlstadt and Münzer, the *"Schwärmer,"* regarded them as perverters of the faith, because in his opinion they believed in salvation by works and by the law. The ordinarily peaceful Melanchthon was their fierce enemy. He believed them to be enemies of the social-political order. The chief Saxon literary opponent of the Anabaptists was Justus Menius. Between 1530 and 1544 he published several writings against them, the chief ones being "Doctrine and Secret of the Anabaptists, refuted from the Bible" and "Of the Spirit of the Anabaptists."

It is a most remarkable fact that all later works of the Reformers, for example Luther's "Commentary on the Epistle to the Galatians," first published in 1535, and Calvin's "Institutes," expounded the evangelical faith, on the one hand, in opposition to Roman Catholicism and, on the other, by way of a contrast to the Anabaptists.

5

German Protestantism Established

THE SUCCESSFUL CONCLUSION of the great war with France and reconciliation with Pope Clement VII had left the Emperor free, in 1529, to interfere at last effectively in German affairs. The Reichstag of Speier, of that year, alarmed at Lutheran progress and the spread of the Anabaptists, and conscious of the change in the Emperor's prospects, had forbidden further

Lutheran advance, and practically ordered the restoration of Roman episcopal authority. The Lutheran minority had protested. In this threatening situation Philip of Hesse had attempted to secure a defensive league of all German and Swiss Evangelical forces. The chief hindrances were the doctrinal differences between the two parties, but Philip hoped that they might be adjusted by a conference, and though Luther was opposed, consent was at last secured, and October 1, 1529, saw Luther and Melanchthon met face to face with Zwingli and Œcolampadius, in Philip's castle in Marburg. With them were a number of the lesser leaders of both parties. During the succeeding days the Marburg colloquy ran its course. Luther was somewhat suspicious of the soundness of the Swiss on the doctrines of the Trinity and original sin, but the real point of difference was the presence or absence of Christ's physical body in the Supper. Luther held firmly to the literal interpretation of the words: "This is My body." Zwingli urged the familiar argument that a physical body could not be in two places at the same time. Agreement was impossible. Zwingli urged that both parties were, after all, Christian brethren, but Luther declared himself unwilling to accept anyone as a brother in faith unless there was unanimity in all basic articles of faith. His famous remark: "You have a different spirit than we," [1] was not addressed to Zwingli, however, but to Butzer.

Yet Philip would not let the hope of a protective league thus vanish, and he persuaded the two parties to draw up fifteen articles of faith. On fourteen there was agreement. The fifteenth had to do with the Supper, and here there was unanimity on all save the one point as to the nature of Christ's presence, where the differences were stated. These Marburg Articles both sides now signed with the provision that "each should show Christian love to the other as far as the conscience of each may permit." [2] Luther and Zwingli each left Marburg with the conviction that he was the victor. The Lutherans now were resolved to enter any political confederation only on the basis of confessional agreement. The "Schwabach Articles," prepared by Luther and the Wittenbergers, probably in June, 1529, were to serve such a purpose.[3] Their greatest significance for the development of Lutheranism is, perhaps, the declaration that "the church is nothing else than believers in Christ who hold, believe, and teach the above enumerated articles." The original Lutheran conception of a church composed of those justified by their faith, had become transformed into that of those who not only have faith but accept a definite and exact doctrinal statement. These Schwabach Articles were now made by the Elector of Saxony and the margrave of Brandenburg-Ansbach the test of political confederacy. Only Nürnberg of the great south German cities would accept them. The defensive league of Evangelicals, which Philip had hoped, was impossible. The Lutherans and the Swiss each went their own way, for the division was permanent.

[1] Kidd, pp. 247–254.   [2] *Ibid.*, pp. 254, 255.   [3] Kidd, p. 255.

In January, 1530, the Emperor sent the call from Italy, where he was about to be crowned by the Pope, for a Reichstag to meet in Augsburg. With unexpected friendliness, while declaring the adjustment of religious differences to be a main object of its meeting, he promised a kindly hearing for all representations. That demanded of the Protestants a statement of their beliefs and of their criticisms of the older practice, and these they now set about to prepare.[4] Luther, Melanchthon, Bugenhagen, and Jonas drew up their criticisms of Roman practices, which, as worked over by Melanchthon, constitute the second, or negative, part of the *Augsburg Confession;* and a little later Melanchthon prepared its affirmative articles, which form the first part. On June 25, 1530, it was read to the Emperor in German. It bore the approving signatures of Elector John of Saxony, his heir, John Frederick, Margrave George of Brandenburg-Ansbach, Dukes Ernst and Franz of Brunswick-Lüneburg, Landgrave Philip of Hesse, Wolfgang of Anhalt, and of the representatives of Nürnberg and Reutlingen. Before the close of the Reichstag the cities of Heilbronn, Kempten, Weissenburg, and Windsheim also signified their approval of this *Augsburg Confession.*[5]

The *Augsburg Confession* was chiefly the work of the mild and con-ciliatory Melanchthon. Though kept informed of the course of events, Luther, as under imperial ban, could not come to Augsburg and remained in Coburg. Melanchthon modified his draft and made concessions, till checked by his fellow Protestants. Nor was it wholly conciliation that moved Melanch-thon. His purpose was to show that the Lutherans had departed in no vital and essential respect from the Catholic Church, or even from the Roman Church, as revealed in its earlier writers. That agreement is expressly affirmed, and many ancient heresies are carefully repudiated by name. On the other hand, Zwinglian and Anabaptist positions are energetically rejected. The sole authority of Scripture is nowhere expressly asserted. The papacy is no-where categorically condemned. The universal priesthood of believers is not mentioned. Yet Melanchthon gave a thoroughly Protestant tone to the confession as a whole. Justification by faith is admirably defined, the Protestant notes of the church made evident; invocation of saints, the mass, denial of the cup, monastic vows, and prescribed fasting rejected.

To the Emperor Zwingli sent a vigorous expression of his views, which received scanty attention. A more significant event was the presentation of a joint confession by the Zwinglian-inclined south German cities, Strassburg, Constance, Memmingen, and Lindau—the *Confessio Tetrapolitana*—largely from the pen of Butzer, in which a position intermediate between that of the Zwinglians and Lutherans was maintained.

The papal legate, Cardinal Campeggio, advised [6] that the confession

---

[4] *Ibid.,* pp. 257–259.
[5] *Ibid.,* pp. 259–289; in Eng. tr. Schaff, *Creeds of Christendom,* 3:3–73.
[6] Kidd, pp. 289–293.

be examined by Roman theologians present in Augsburg. This the Emperor approved, and chief among these experts was Luther's old opponent, Eck. Melanchthon was willing to make concessions that would have ruined the whole Lutheran cause,[7] but fortunately for it the Evangelical princes were of sterner stuff. The Catholic theologians prepared a confutation, which was sent back to them by the Emperor and Catholic princes as too polemic, and was at last presented to the Reichstag in much milder form on August 3.

The Emperor still hoped for reconciliation, and committees of conference were now appointed; but their work was vain—a result to which Luther's firmness largely contributed.[8] The Catholic majority voiced the decision of the Reichstag that the Lutherans had been duly confuted, that they be given till April 15, 1531, to conform; that combined action be had against Zwinglians and Anabaptists, and that a general council be sought within a year to heal abuses in the church. The reconstituted imperial law court should decide, in Catholic interest, cases of secularization.[9] The Lutherans protested, declared their confession not refuted, and called attention to Melanchthon's *Apology*, or defense of the confession, which he had hastily prepared when the vanity of concessions was at last becoming apparent even to him. That *Apology*, rewritten and published the next year (1531), was to be one of the classics of Lutheranism.

Such a situation demanded defensive union. Even Luther, who had held it a sin to oppose the Emperor by force, now was willing to leave the rightfulness of such resistance to the decision of the lawyers. At Christmas the Lutheran princes assembled in Schmalkalden and laid the foundations of a league. Butzer, whose union efforts were unremitting, persuaded Strassburg to accept the *Augsburg Confession*—an example which had great effect on other south German cities. Finally, on February 27, 1531, the Schmalkaldic league was completed. Electoral Saxony, Hesse, Brunswick, Anhalt, and Mansfeld stood in defensive agreement with the cities Strassburg, Constance, Ulm, Reutlingen, Memmingen, Lindau, Isny, Biberach, Magdeburg, Bremen, and Lübeck.[10]

Strong as the position of Charles V appeared on the surface it was not so in reality in the face of this united opposition. The Catholic princes were jealous of one another and of the Emperor. The Pope feared a general council. France was still to be reckoned with. The fatal day—April 15, 1531—therefore passed without the threatened result. In October, 1531, the death of Zwingli at Kappel (see p. 325) deprived Swiss Evangelicalism of its vigorous head, and inclined south German Protestantism to closer union with that of Wittenberg. The spring of 1532 brought a new danger to the empire as a whole, that of Turkish invasion. In 1529 the Turks had besieged Vienna, and before their advance religious differences had, in a measure, to give way. On July 23, 1532, the Emperor and the Schmalkaldic league agreed to the truce of

[7] *Ibid.*, pp. 293, 294.   [8] *Ibid.*, p. 296.   [9] Kidd, pp. 298–300.   [10] *Ibid.*, p. 301.

denburg, but though he succeeded in enlarging his territorial possessions, he was too young largely to affect the course of the war.

At last, after infinite negotiation, the "Peace of Westphalia" was made on October 27, 1648. Sweden was firmly settled on the German shore of the Baltic. Most of Alsace went to France. The long-existing independence of Switzerland was formally acknowledged. Brandenburg received the archbishopric of Magdeburg and the bishoprics of Halberstadt and Minden as compensation for surrender of its claims on part of Pomerania to the Swedes. Maximilian of Bavaria kept his title of Elector and part of the Palatinate, while the rest of the Palatinate was restored to Karl Ludwig, son of the unfortunate Frederick V, for whom a new electoral title was created. More important was the religious settlement. Here the ability of the "Great Elector" secured the inclusion of the Calvinists who, with the Lutherans, were regarded as one party as over against the Catholics. German Calvinists at last secured full rights. The Edict of Restitution was fully abandoned and the year 1624 taken as the norm. Whatever ecclesiastical property was then in Catholic or Protestant hands should so remain. While the power of a lay sovereign to determine the religion of his subjects still remained, it was modified by a provision that where divided religious worship had existed in a territory in 1624, each party could continue it in the same proportion as then existed. Between Lutherans and Calvinists it was agreed that the norm should be the date of the Peace, and that a change of the lay ruler to one or the other form of Protestantism thereafter should not affect his subjects. On the other hand, by the insistence of the Emperor, no privileges were accorded to Protestants in Austria or Bohemia.

Neither side liked the Peace. The Pope denounced it. But all were tired of the war, and the Peace had the great merit of drawing the lines between Catholicism and Protestantism roughly, but approximately, where they really stood. As such, it proved essentially permanent, and with it the period of the Reformation on the Continent may be considered closed.

To Germany the Thirty Years' War was an unmitigated and frightful evil. The land had been ploughed from end to end for a generation by lawless and plundering armies. Population had fallen from sixteen millions to less than six. Fields were waste. Commerce and manufacturing destroyed. Above all, intellectual life had stagnated, morals had been roughened and corrupted, and religion grievously maimed. A century after its close the devastating consequences had not been made good. Little evidence of spiritual life was manifested in this frightful time of war; yet to it, in large part, and reflecting the trust of heartfelt piety in its stress, belongs the work of perhaps the greatest of Lutheran hymn-writers, Paul Gerhardt (1607–1676). In its earlier years, also, lie the chief activities of that strange and deep Protestant mystic, Jakob Böhme (1575–1624), of Görlitz.

Socinianism

THE REFORMATION age exhibited a number of departures from traditional orthodoxy regarding the person and work of Christ. Though not characteristic of Anabaptists, in general, their earliest manifestation is to be found among such Anabaptists as Denck and Haetzer (see p. 329). Servetus' radical opinions and tragic fate have already been noted (see pp. 355, 356), but this ingenious thinker founded no school of disciples. The chief anti-Trinitarians of the age came from Italy, where reformed opinions took often radical form, and where the scepticism of the Renaissance and the criticism of the later schoolmen often blended with Anabaptist readiness to see in the meaning of Scripture other than the traditional interpretations. Such Italian radicals were Matteo Gribaldi (?–1564), once professor of law in Padua, whom Calvin drove from Geneva in 1559; and Giovanni Valentino Gentile (1520?–1566), who came to Geneva about 1557, fled from punishment for his views there, and, after a wandering career, was beheaded in Bern in 1566. Of greater importance was Giorgio Biandrata (1515?–1588?), who spent a year in Geneva, but found it wise to leave for Poland in 1558, serving as physician to the ruling families of that land and of Transylvania, helping to found a Unitarian communion in the latter region, which ultimately obtained legal standing.

Those who were destined to give their name to the movement were the two Sozzinis, uncle and nephew. Lelio Sozzini (Socinus, 1525–1562) was of a prominent Sienese family and a student of law. His opinions were at first Evangelical, and he lived for a year, 1550–1551, in Wittenberg, enjoying Melanchthon's friendship. Among other Swiss cities, he was well received in Geneva, and settled in Zürich, where he died. Servetus' execution turned his attention to the problem of the Trinity, but his speculations were not made public in his lifetime. His more distinguished nephew Fausto (1539–1604) was in Lyons in 1561 and Geneva in 1562. Although already a radical and influenced, though less than has often been represented, by his uncle's notes and papers, Fausto conformed outwardly to the Roman Church and lived from 1563 to 1575 in Italy. Thence he removed to Basel, till he went to Transylvania, in 1578, at the instance of Biandrata. The next year saw him in Poland, where he lived till his death in 1604.

preliminary results. He must, if possible, divide the Schmalkaldic league politically; he must ward off danger of French attack; and the ever-threatening perils of Turkish invasion must, for a time at least, be minimized.

The Emperor's purpose of dividing the Protestants was aided by one of the most curious episodes of Reformation history. Landgrave Philip of Hesse, the political genius of the Schmalkaldic league, though sacrificial in devotion to the Protestant cause, was, like most princes of that age, a man of low personal morality. Though married early to a daughter of Duke George of Saxony, who bore him seven children, he had no affection for her. His constant adulteries troubled his conscience to the extent that from 1526 to 1539 he partook of the Lord's Supper but once. He grew anxious as to his soul's salvation, without improving his conduct. For some years he entertained the thought of a second marriage as a solution of his perplexities. The Old Testament worthies had practised polygamy. The New Testament nowhere expressly forbade it. Why should not he? This reasoning was strengthened by acquaintance with Margarete von der Saale, an attractive seventeen-year-old daughter of a lady of his sister's little court. The mother's consent was won on condition that the Elector and the duke of Saxony, and some others should be informed that it was to be a real marriage. Philip's first wife also consented. Philip was fully persuaded himself of the rightfulness of the step, but for the sake of public opinion, he desired the approval of the Wittenberg theologians. He therefore sent for Butzer of Strassburg, whom he partly persuaded, partly frightened with threats of seeking dispensation from the Emperor or the Pope, into full support of his plan. Butzer now became Philip's messenger to Luther and Melanchthon, and to the Saxon Elector, though the matter was presented as an abstract question, without mention of the person with whom marriage was contemplated. On December 10, 1539, Luther and Melanchthon gave their opinion. Polygamy they declared to be contrary to the primal law of creation, which Christ had approved; but a special case required oftentimes treatment which did not conform to the general rule. If Philip could not reform his life, it would be better to marry as he proposed than to live as he was doing. The marriage should, however, be kept absolutely a secret, so that the second wife should appear to be a concubine. The advice was thoroughly bad, though the Wittenberg reformers seem to have been moved by a sincere desire to benefit Philip's soul.

Philip was more honorable than the advice. On March 4, 1540, he married Margarete in what, though private, cannot be called secret fashion. A court preacher performed the ceremony, and Melanchthon, Butzer, and a representative of the Saxon Elector were among the witnesses. Though an attempt was made to keep the affair private, that soon proved impossible. Luther could only advise "a good strong lie"; but Philip was manly enough to declare: "I will not lie."

The scandal was great, both among Protestants and Catholics. Bigamy was prohibited by imperial law. A bigamous prince had to forfeit his crown.

The other Evangelical princes would not defend Philip's act or promise protection from its results. The Emperor saw in it his opportunity. On June 13, 1541, he secured an agreement from Philip, as the price of no worse consequences, that the landgrave would neither personally, nor as representative of the Schmalkaldic league, make alliances with foreign states. The hopeful negotiations with France, England, Denmark, and Sweden, which would have greatly strengthened the power of the Schmalkaldic league against the Emperor, had to be dropped. Worse than that, Philip had to promise not to aid the Evangelically inclined Duke Wilhelm of Cleves, whose rights over Gelders Charles disputed. As the Saxon Elector was Wilhelm's brother-in-law, and determined to support him, a serious division in the Schmalkaldic league was the result, which showed its disastrous consequences when the Emperor defeated Wilhelm, in 1543, took Gelders permanently into his own possession, and forced Wilhelm to repudiate Lutheranism. This defeat rendered abortive a hopeful attempt to secure the great archbishopric of Cologne for the Protestant cause.[13]

Fortune favored Charles in the rest of his program. Paul III was persuaded to call the General Council to meet in Trent, a town then belonging to the empire, but practically Italian, in 1542. War caused a postponement, but in December, 1545, it at last actually began its sessions, which were to run a checkered and interrupted course till 1563. By vague, but indefinite, promises Charles secured, at the Reichstag in Speier in 1544, the passive support of the Protestants, and some active assistance, for the wars against France and the Turks. The campaign against France was brief. The Emperor, in alliance with Henry VIII of England, pushed on nearly to Paris, when, to the surprise of Europe he made peace with the French King, without, apparently, gaining any of the advantages in his grasp. Really, he had eliminated French interference in possible aid of German Protestantism for the immediate future.[14] The Turks, busy with a war in Persia, and internal quarrels, made a truce with the Emperor in October, 1545. All seemed to have worked together for his blow against German Protestantism.

It was while prospects were thus darkening that Luther died on a visit to Eisleben, the town in which he was born, on February 18, 1546, in consequence of an attack of heart-disease or apoplexy. His last years had been far from happy. His health had long been wretched. The quarrels of the reformers, to which he had contributed his full share, distressed him. Above all, the failure of the pure preaching of justification by faith alone to transform the social, civic, and political life about him greatly grieved him. He was comforted by a happy home life and by full confidence in his Gospel. The work which he had begun had passed far beyond the power of any one man, however gifted, to control. He was no longer needed; but his memory must always be that of one of the most titanic figures in the history of the church.

[13] Kidd, pp. 350–354.   [14] *Ibid.*, p. 354.

came to him. He was forced from his strategically situated see, and the territory fully restored to Catholicism. In Austria and Bohemia the situation became steadily more unfavorable for Protestantism; and there as well as elsewhere in the empire the Jesuit propaganda gained many individual converts. It was aggressive and confident of ultimate victory. The situation between Protestants and Catholics was constantly strained.

An event of the years 1606–1607 markedly increased this bitterness. The city of Donauwörth was overwhelmingly Protestant, yet Catholic monasteries had been allowed there. A Catholic procession of 1606 was stoned. On imperial command, Maximilian, the able Catholic duke of Bavaria (1597–1651) occupied the city and began a repression of its Evangelical worship. At the Reichstag of 1608 the Catholics demanded the restitution of all ecclesiastical property confiscated since 1555. For this claim they had the strict letter of the law in the Peace of Augsburg; but many of these districts had become, in the two generations that had elapsed, solidly Protestant in population.

Under these circumstances a number of Protestant princes formed a defensive "Union" on May 4, 1608, headed by the Calvinist Elector Frederick IV of the Palatinate. To it Catholic princes, led by Maximilian of Bavaria, opposed a "League," on July 10, 1609. The strong Lutheran states of northern Germany were unwilling to join the "Union," nor was the Emperor in the "League." Had Henry IV of France lived, war would probably have broken out at this time; but his assassination in 1610 and the uncertainty of the imperial succession in Germany delayed it for a time.

Besides the bitter disputes between Catholics and Lutherans, the condition of Germany was, in many ways, one of unrest. Business was bad. The debased coinage caused great suffering, the country was growing impoverished. The enforcement of unity of belief in Protestant and Catholic territories alike was damaging to the intellectual life of the people; while the witchcraft delusion which cost thousands of lives, and was equally entertained by Catholics and Protestants, was at its worst between 1580 and 1620.

The actual outbreak of the Thirty Years' War came from Bohemia. That then largely Protestant land had wrung from its King, the Emperor Rudolf II (1576–1612), in 1609, a charter—the *Majestätsbrief*—granting a high degree of toleration. Rudolf was succeeded, both as Emperor and King, by his feeble brother Matthias (King, 1611–1619; Emperor, 1612–1619), but he was childless, and in 1617 his cousin, Ferdinand of Styria, a strenuous representative of the Counter-Reformation, succeeded in securing recognition as Matthias' successor from the Bohemian estates. Catholic influences were augmented, and in May, 1618, a party of disaffected Protestants flung the two Catholic regents representing the absent Matthias from a high window in Prague. This act put Bohemia into rebellion and began the war. Its commencement was favorable for the Bohemian insurgents, and in 1619, after the death of Matthias, they elected the Calvinist, Frederick V (1610–1632),

Elector Palatine, their King. The same week Ferdinand of Styria was chosen Emperor as Ferdinand II (1619–1637).

Frederick found little support outside of Bohemia, and now Maximilian of Bavaria and a Spanish force from the Netherlands came to Ferdinand's assistance. Under the command of a Walloon general, Jan Tzerklas, Baron Tilly (1559–1632), this Catholic combination overwhelmed the Bohemian forces, near Prague, on November 8, 1620. Frederick fled the land. The *Majestätsbrief* was annulled, the property of Bohemian Protestants largely confiscated, to the great financial advantage of the Jesuits, and the Counter-Reformation enforced with a high hand in Bohemia, Moravia, and Austria. Among those enriched by the acquisition of confiscated property was one destined to play a great part in the further history of the war, Albrecht von Wallenstein (1583–1634). The "Union" was dissolved. A similar repression of Protestantism now took place in Austria.

Meanwhile Spanish troops, under Spinola, had invaded the Palatinate in 1620, and thither Tilly and the army of the "League" soon followed. The land was conquered, Catholicism enforced, and Frederick's electoral title with a good share of the Palatinate transferred to Maximilian of Bavaria in 1623.

Northwestern Germany, where many bishoprics had become Protestant possessions since the Peace of Augsburg, was now threatened with war, and the disasters to Protestantism which had already happened aroused Protestant foreign powers. Nothing effective was done, however, except by Christian IV of Denmark, to whom England and the Protestant Netherlands sent some slight aid. To the Emperor Ferdinand the enmity of the Danish King seemed formidable, and he therefore turned to Wallenstein to raise a new army as imperial commander-in-chief. This remarkable adventurer, born a Protestant, was nominally a Catholic, and now the richest noble of Bohemia. A natural leader of men, he raised an army in which he asked no questions of race or creed, but simply of capacity to fight, and loyalty to himself. He soon had a force of great efficiency.

On April 25, 1626, Wallenstein defeated the Protestant army under Ernst of Mansfeld, at the Dessau bridge over the Elbe, following the beaten forces to Hungary, whither they retreated in the vain hope of making effective stand in conjunction with the Emperor's enemy, Bethlen Gabor, prince of Transylvania. On August 27, 1626, Christian IV of Denmark was beaten by Tilly and the army of the "League" at Lutter. These successes were followed up by the Catholics in 1627 and 1628. Hanover, Brunswick, and Silesia were conquered, then Holstein, Schleswig, Pomerania, and Mecklenburg. Wallenstein found it impossible to capture the Baltic seaport of Stralsund, which was aided by the Swedes, and thought it wise to make peace before the able Swedish King, Gustavus Adolphus (1611–1632), might interfere. Accordingly, Christian IV was allowed, by a treaty of May, 1629, to keep his territories on condition of no further share in German politics.

ecclesiastical property, heretofore or hereafter secularized. They asked toleration for Lutherans in all Catholic territories, but proposed to grant none to
Catholics in their own. These extreme demands were naturally resisted, and
the result was a compromise, the Peace of Augsburg, of September 25, 1555.[16]
By its provisions equal rights in the empire were extended to Catholics and
Lutherans—no other Evangelicals were recognized. Each lay prince should
determine which of the two faiths should be professed in his territory—no
choice was allowed his subjects—and but one faith should be permitted in a
given territory. This was the principle usually defined as *cujus regio, ejus
religio*. Regarding ecclesiastical territories and properties, agreement was
reached that the time of the Treaty of Passau should be the norm. All then
in Lutheran possession should so remain, but a Catholic spiritual ruler turning
Protestant thereafter should forfeit his position and holdings, thus insuring to
the Catholics continued possession of the spiritual territories not lost by 1552.
This was the "ecclesiastical reservation." To the common man, dissatisfied
with the faith of the territory where he lived, full right of unhindered emigration and a fair sale of his goods was allowed—a great advance over punishment for heresy, but his choice was only between Catholicism and Lutheranism.

So Lutheranism acquired full legal establishment. Germany was permanently divided. Luther's dream of a purification of the whole German
church had vanished, but so had the Catholic conception of visible unity.

The older leaders were rapidly passing. Luther had died nine years
before. Melanchthon was to live till 1560. Charles V was to resign his possession of the Netherlands in 1555, and of Spain a year later, and seek retirement
at Yuste in Spain till death came to him in 1558.

6

The Scandinavian Lands

DENMARK, NORWAY, AND SWEDEN had been nominally united under one
sovereign since the union of Kalmar, in 1397. Since 1460, Schleswig-
Holstein had also been under Danish control. In none of these lands was the
crown powerful. In all, the great ecclesiastics were unpopular as oppressive,

[16] Kidd, pp. 363, 364.

and often foreign-born, and in all they were in rivalry with the nobility. In no portion of Europe, not even in England, was the Reformation to be more thoroughly political. At the dawn of the Reformation the Danish throne was occupied by Christian II (1513–1523), an enlightened despot of Renaissance sympathies. He saw the chief evil of his kingdom in the power of the nobles and ecclesiastics, and to limit that of the bishops by introducing the Lutheran movement he secured a Lutheran preacher in the person of Martin Reinhard, in 1520, and an adviser in Karlstadt for a brief time in 1521. Partially at least through the latter's counsels, a law of 1521 forbade appeals to Rome, reformed the monasteries, limited the authority of the bishops, and permitted priestly marriage. Opposition prevented its execution, and the hostility of the privileged classes, which Christian II had roused in many ways, drove him from his throne in 1523, and made his uncle, Frederick I (1523–1533), King in his stead.

Though inclined to Lutheranism, Frederick was forced by the parties which had put him on the throne to promise to respect the privileges of the nobles and prevent any heretical preaching. Yet Lutheranism penetrated the land. In Hans Tausen (1494–1561), a one-time monk and former Wittenberg student, it found a preacher of popular power from 1524 onward. By 1526, King Frederick took Tausen under protection as his chaplain. The same year the King took the confirmation of the appointment of bishops into his own hands. A law of 1527 enacted this into statute, granted toleration to Lutherans, and permitted priestly marriage.[1] These changes were aided by the support of a large section of the nobility won by the King's countenance of their attacks on ecclesiastical rights and property. In 1530, the same year as the *Augsburg Confession,* Tausen and his associates laid before the Danish Parliament the "Forty-three Copenhagen Articles." The year before, a Danish translation of the New Testament (by Christian Petersen) had been published and was eagerly read. No decision was reached at the time, but Lutheranism made increasing progress till Frederick's demise in 1533.

The death of Frederick left all in confusion. Of his two sons, most of the nobles favored the elder, Christian III (1536–1559), a determined Lutheran, while the bishops supported the younger, Johann. A distracting period of civil conflict followed, from which Christian III emerged the victor in 1536. The bishops were imprisoned, their authority abolished, and church property confiscated for the crown.[2] Christian now called on Wittenberg for aid. Johann Bugenhagen, Luther's associate, came in 1537, and seven new Lutheran superintendents, named by the King, but retaining the title "bishop," were ordained by the German reformer, who was himself a superintendent, namely, of Wittenberg. The Danish church was now reorganized in fully Lutheran fashion.[3]

Norway was a separate kingdom, but by election under the Danish

[1] Kidd, p. 234.   [2] Kidd, pp. 322–328.   [3] *Ibid.,* pp. 328–335.

rising which he had anticipated in England, and which men like Allen and Parsons had predicted, Catholics and Protestants had stood shoulder to shoulder as Englishmen against Spain.

While Philip's larger hopes were thus crushed in 1588, he held as tenaciously as ever to the plan of uprooting Protestantism in France. The death of Henry III's brother, the duke of Anjou, in 1584, left the Huguenot Henry Bourbon of Navarre prospective heir to the throne. To prevent this succession, Philip and the League entered into a treaty, in January, 1585, by which the crown should go to Henry of Navarre's uncle, Charles, Cardinal Bourbon, on Henry III's death. In July, 1585, Henry III was forced by the League to withdraw all rights from the Huguenots, and in September a bull of Sixtus V (1585–1590) declared Henry of Navarre incapable of succeeding to the throne. The eighth Huguenot War was the result—that known as the "War of the Three Henrys," from Henry III, Henry of Guise, the head of the League, and Henry of Navarre. Paris was entirely devoted to Henry of Guise. On May 12, 1588, its citizens compelled Henry III to leave the city. The weak King saw no way to resist the demands of the League and its imperious head and, on December 23, had Henry of Guise treacherously murdered. Thirteen days later Catherine de' Medici closed her stormy life.

Henry of Guise was succeeded in the leadership of the League by his brother Charles, duke of Mayenne. Henry III now made terms with Henry of Navarre, and the two were jointly laying siege to Paris, when Henry III was murdered by a fanatic monk, dying on August 2, 1589. But Henry of Navarre, or as he now became, Henry IV of France (1589–1610), was still far from secure on his new throne. A brilliant victory at Ivry, in March, 1590, defeated the League, but Spanish troops under Parma's able generalship prevented his capture of Paris that year, and of Rouen in 1592. Not till after the death of Parma, on December 3, of the year last named, was Henry IV really master. And now, for purely political reasons, Henry IV declared himself a Catholic, being received into the Roman Church on July 25, 1593, though terms were not concluded with the Pope till more than two years later. However to be criticised morally—and Henry's life, whether as a Protestant or as a Catholic, showed that religious principles had little influence over his conduct—the step was wise. It gave peace to the distracted land. It pleased the vast majority of his subjects. Nor did Henry forget his old associates. In April, 1598, the Edict of Nantes was issued, by which the Huguenots were admitted to all public office, public worship was permitted wherever it had existed in 1597, save in Paris, Rheims, Toulouse, Lyons, and Dijon, and children of Huguenots could not be forced to receive Catholic training. Certain fortified towns were placed in Huguenot hands as guarantees.

The same year (1598) Philip II died, on September 13, convinced to the end that what he had done was for the service of God, but having failed in his great life effort to overthrow Protestantism.

The Huguenot Churches now entered on their most prosperous period. Their organization was completed, and their schools at Sedan, Saumur, Montauban, Nîmes, and elsewhere flourished. They were a political corporation within the state. As such, they were opposed by the centralizing policy of Richelieu, Louis XIII's great minister. In 1628, Rochelle was taken from them, and their political semi-independence ended. By the Edict of Nîmes, in 1629, their religious privileges were preserved, but they suffered increasing attack from Jesuit and other Catholic influences as the century went on, till the revocation of the Edict of Nantes, by Louis XIV, in 1685, reduced them to a persecuted, martyr church, to be proscribed till the eve of the French Revolution, and drove thousands of their numbers into exile, to the lasting gain of England, Holland, Prussia, and America.

13

German Controversies and the Thirty Years' War

IT WAS the misfortune of Lutheranism that it had no other bond of union between its representatives in its several territories than agreement in "pure doctrine," and that differences in apprehension were regarded as incompatible with Christian fellowship. The original Lutheran conception of a faith which constitutes a new personal relationship between God and the believing soul tended to shade off into a belief which, as Melanchthon once defined it, is "an assent by which you accept all articles of the faith." The result was a new Protestant scholasticism.

Melanchthon, influenced by humanistic thought, gradually moved from his original agreement with Luther to some emphases different from those of his greater colleague. By 1527 he had lost sympathy with Luther's denial of human freedom and had reached the conclusion that salvation is only possible through the co-operant action of the will of man—a view to which the name "synergism" is usually given. By 1535 he was emphasizing good works, not as the price of salvation, but as its indispensable evidence. Regarding the Lord's Supper he came to feel that Luther had overemphasized Christ's physical presence and, without quite reaching Calvin's position (see p. 352), to hold that Christ is given "not in the bread, but with the bread," that is, to lay stress on the spiritual rather than the physical reception. These differences never made a breach with Luther, partly because of Luther's

1528 (see p. 323), led the Bernese government to further the introduction of the Reformation into these dependent districts by encouraging the preaching of Guillaume Farel (1489–1565). Farel was a native of Gap, in the French province of Dauphiné. As a student in Paris he came under the influence of the humanistic reformer, Jacques LeFèvre, of Etaples, and by 1521 was preaching under the auspices of the moderately reformatory Guillaume Briçonnet, bishop of Meaux. An orator of fiery vehemence, intense feeling, and stentorian voice, he soon was so preaching the Reformation that he had to leave France. By 1524 he was urging reform in Basel, but his impetuosity led to his expulsion.

The next months were a period of wandering, during which Farel visited Strassburg and won Butzer's friendship; but, in November, 1526, his work in French-speaking Switzerland began in Aigle, where the Bernese government defended him, though not yet itself fully committed to the Reformation.[1] With the complete victory of the newer views in Bern, Farel's work went faster. In 1528 Aigle, Ollon, and Bex adopted the Reformation, destroying images and ending the mass.[2] After vainly attempting to invade Lausanne, he began a stormy attack in Neuchâtel, in November, 1529, which ultimately secured the victory of the Reformation there.[3] Morat followed in 1530;[4] but in Grandson and Orbe, which, like Morat, were under the joint overlordship of Protestant Bern and Catholic Freiburg, he could secure only the toleration of both forms of worship.[5] A visit by invitation in September, 1532, to a synod of the Waldenses in the high valleys of the Cottian Alps resulted in the acceptance of the Reformation by a large section of the body,[6] and was followed in October by an attempt, at first unsuccessful, to preach reform in Geneva.[7] Everywhere Farel faced opposition with undaunted courage, sometimes at the risk of life and at the cost of bodily injury, but no one could be indifferent in his strenuous presence.

Geneva, at Farel's coming, was in the struggle of a revolutionary crisis. Situated on a main trade route across the Alps, it was an energetic business community, keenly alive to its interests and liberties, of rather easy-going moral standards, in spite of its extensive monasteries and ecclesiastical foundations. Genevan liberties were being maintained with great difficulty against the encroachments of the powerful duke of Savoy. At the beginning of the sixteenth century three powers shared the government of the city and its adjacent villages—the bishop; his *vicedominus,* or temporal administrator; and the citizens, who met annually in a General Assembly and chose four "syndics" and a treasurer. Besides the General Assembly, the citizens were ruled by a Little Council of twenty-five, of which the "syndics" of the year and of the year previous were members. Questions of larger policy were discussed by a Council of Sixty appointed by the Little Council, and in 1527 a Council

[1] Kidd, pp. 477–481.   [2] Kidd, pp. 481, 482.   [3] *Ibid.,* pp. 483–489.
[4] *Ibid.,* p. 489.   [5] *Ibid.,* pp. 489–491.   [6] *Ibid.,* pp. 491, 492.
[7] *Ibid.,* pp. 492–494.

of Two Hundred was added, its membership including the Little Council and one hundred and seventy-five others chosen by that inner body. The aggressive dukes of Savoy had appointed the *vicedominus* since 1290, and had controlled the bishopric since 1444. The struggle was therefore one for freedom by the citizens against Savoyard interests, represented by the bishop and the *vicedominus*.

In 1519 the Genevan citizens made a protective alliance with Freiburg, but Duke Charles III of Savoy won the upper hand, and the Genevan patriot Philibert Berthelier was beheaded. Seven years later Geneva renewed the effort, this time entering into alliance with Bern as well as Freiburg. In 1527 the bishop, Pierre de la Baume, left the city, which he could not control, and fully attached himself to the Savoyard interests. The authority of the *vicedominus* was repudiated. Duke Charles attacked the plucky city, but Bern and Freiburg came to its aid in October, 1530, and he had to pledge respect to Genevan liberties.[8] Thus far there was little sympathy with the Reformation in Geneva, but Bern was Protestant and was anxious to see the Evangelical faith there established. Placards criticising papal claims and presenting reformed doctrine were posted on June 9, 1532, but Geneva's ally, Freiburg, was Catholic, and the Genevan government disowned any leanings toward Lutheranism.[9] In October following Farel came, as has been seen, but could get no footing in the city. Farel sent his friend Antoine Froment (1508–1581) to Geneva, who found a place there as a schoolmaster, and propagated reformed doctrine under this protection. On January 1, 1533, Froment was emboldened to preach publicly, though the result was a riot. By the following Easter there were enough Protestants to dare to observe the Lord's Supper, and in December Farel effectively returned. The Genevan government was in a difficult position. Its Catholic ally, Freiburg, demanded that Farel be silenced. Its Protestant ally, Bern, insisted on the arrest of Guy Furbity, the chief defender of the Roman cause.[10] Farel and his friends held a public disputation, and on March 1, 1534, seized a church. Under Bernese pressure the government broke the league with Catholic Freiburg. The bishop now raised troops to attack the city. His action greatly strengthened Genevan opposition, and on October 1, 1534, the Little Council declared the bishopric vacant, though Geneva was still far from predominantly Protestant.[11]

With the following year Farel, emboldened by the successful result of a public debate in May and June, proceeded to yet more positive action. On July 23, 1535, he seized the church of La Madeleine, and on August 8 the cathedral of St. Pierre itself. An iconoclastic riot swept the churches. Two days later the mass was abolished, and speedily thereafter the monks and nuns were driven from the city. On May 21, 1536, the work was completed by the vote of the General Assembly, expressing its determination "to live in this holy Evangelical law and word of God."[12] Meanwhile the duke of Savoy

---

[8] Kidd, pp. 494–500. [9] *Ibid.*, pp. 500–504. [10] *Ibid.*, pp. 504–508.
[11] *Ibid.*, pp. 508–512. [12] Kidd, pp. 512–519.

bull of deposition, issued against Elizabeth by Pope Pius V on February 25, 1570.

In April, 1572, these sea-rovers captured Brill. The northern provinces rose. William of Orange put himself at the head of the movement. On July 15, the leading towns of Holland, Zealand, Friesland, and Utrecht recognized him as Stadholder. Meanwhile, since the peace of 1570, the Huguenots and the opponents of Spain in France had been working for a revival of the older political policy, which made France the rival instead of the ally of Spain. Immediate assistance to the Netherlandish rebels, to be rewarded by accession of some territory to France, was planned, and none favored it more than Coligny, whose influence over Charles IX was now great. To emphasize the reconciliation of parties in France, a marriage was arranged between Henry of Navarre, the Protestant son of the late Antoine of Bourbon, and Charles IX's sister, Marguerite of Valois. For the wedding, on August 18, 1572, Huguenot and Catholic nobles and their followers gathered in the fanatically Catholic city of Paris.

Catherine de' Medici had come to look with fear on the influence now exerted by Coligny over her son, the King. Whether the cause was jealousy regarding her own influence, or fear that the war into which Coligny was leading the King would be disastrous to the French crown, is uncertain. Apparently all that she wanted at first was Coligny's removal by murder. In this she had the hearty sympathy of Henry, Duke of Guise (1550–1588), the son of the murdered Francis, who wrongly charged Coligny with responsibility for his father's death. On August 22 an attempt on Coligny's life failed, and its ill-success carried panic to Catherine. The Huguenots had been alienated without being deprived of their leader. She and her supporters now suddenly decided on a general massacre, for which the Guise party and the fanatical people of Paris furnished abundant means. On August 24, St. Bartholomew's day, the bloody work began. Coligny was killed, and with him a number of victims that has been most variously estimated, reaching not improbably 8,000 in Paris, and several times that number in the whole of France. Henry of Navarre saved his life by abjuring Protestantism.

The news was hailed with rejoicing in Madrid and in Rome, and rightly, if its moral enormity could be overlooked. It had saved the Catholic cause from great peril. The policy of France was reversed. Plans for interference in the Netherlands were at an end. The desperate struggle for Netherlandish freedom was the consequence. Yet the Catholics did not gain in France what they hoped. The fourth, fifth, sixth, and seventh Huguenot Wars, 1573, 1574–1576, 1577, 1580, ran their course of destruction and misery, but the Huguenots were not crushed. Charles IX died in 1574 and was succeeded as King by his vicious brother, Henry III (1574–1589).

A division among the Catholics themselves was developing. There had long been a considerable element which, while Catholic in religion, felt

that the protracted wars were ruining the land and permitting foreign, especially Spanish, intrigue. They believed that some basis of peace with the
Huguenots should be reached, and were known as the *Politiques*. On the
other hand, those who put religion first and were willing to see France
become a mere appanage of Spain, if thereby Catholicism could triumph,
had been for some time organizing associations in various parts of France to
maintain the Roman Church. In 1576 these were developed into a general
"League," led by Henry of Guise and supported by Spain and the Pope. Its
existence drove the *Politiques* more and more into alliance with the Huguenots, who found their political head in Henry of Navarre, he having reasserted his Protestant faith in 1576.

The massacre of St. Bartholomew shattered the hopes of William of
Orange for the speedy expulsion of Spain from the Netherlands. The two
years following were those of intensest struggle, of which William was the
soul. Alva's generalship seemed at first irresistible. Mons, Mechlin, Zutphen,
Naarden, and Haarlem fell before the Spanish forces; but Alkmaar they
failed to take, in October, 1573. Alva was recalled at his own request, and
was succeeded, in November, by Luis de Requesens (1525?–1576), under
whom the Spanish policy was substantially unchanged. But October, 1574,
saw the successful end of the defense of Leyden, and it was evident that the
northern Netherlands could not be conquered by the forces then available
for Spain. In 1576 Requesens died, and the Spanish troops sacked Antwerp,
an event which roused the southern provinces to resistance. The new Spanish
commander, John of Austria (1545–1578), was able to effect little. Elizabeth
aided the revolted Netherlands from 1576. In September, 1577, William was
able to make a triumphal entry into Brussels. John of Austria died, a disappointed man, in October, 1578; but he was succeeded by his nephew,
Alexander Farnese, duke of Parma (1545–1592), a general and a statesman
of commanding talents. Matters went better for the Spanish cause. Parma
played on the jealousies of the Catholic south and the Calvinist north. The
former united in the League of Arras for the protection of Catholicism in
January, 1579; the latter replied the same month by the Union of Utrecht.
Protestants left the south for the north by the thousands, many Catholics went
southward. Ultimately the ten southern provinces were saved by Parma for
Spain, and modern Belgium is his monument. The seven northern states
declared their independence of Spain in 1581, and though much remained
to be done before all dangers were passed, their freedom was so strongly intrenched that not even the murder of William of Orange, on July 10, 1584,
by a fanatic encouraged by Parma, could overthrow it.

During this struggle the Calvinistic churches of the Netherlands had
been shaping. The First National Synod had been held outside of Netherlandish territory, in Emden, in 1571. William of Orange had accepted Calvinism two years later. In 1575 a university was established in Leyden, soon

On November 1, 1533, Cop delivered an inaugural address as newly elected rector of the University of Paris, in which he pleaded for reform, using language borrowed from Erasmus and Luther.[3] That Calvin wrote the oration, as has often been alleged, is improbable, but he undoubtedly sympathized with its sentiments. The commotion aroused was great, and King Francis enjoined action against the "Lutherans." [4] Cop and Calvin had to seek safety, which Calvin found in the home of a friend, Louis du Tillet, in Angoulême. Calvin's sense of the necessity of separation from the older communion was now rapidly developing, and forced him to go to Noyon to resign his benefices on May 4, 1534. Here he was for a brief time imprisoned. Though soon released, France was too perilous for him, especially after Antoine Marcourt posted his injudicious theses against the mass in October, 1534,[5] and by about New Year's following Calvin was safely in Protestant Basel.

Marcourt's placards had been followed by a sharp renewal of persecution, one of the victims being Calvin's friend the Parisian merchant, Estienne de la Forge. Francis I was coquetting for the aid of German Protestants against Charles V, and therefore, to justify French persecutions, issued a public letter in February, 1535, charging French Protestantism with anarchistic aims such as no government could bear. Calvin felt that he must defend his slandered fellow believers. He therefore rapidly completed a work begun in Angoulême, and published it in March, 1536, as his *Institutes of the Christian religion,* prefacing it with a letter to the French King. The letter is one of the literary masterpieces of the Reformation age. Courteous and dignified, it is a tremendously forceful presentation of the Protestant position and defense of its holders against the royal slanders. No French Protestant had yet spoken with such clearness, restraint, and power, and with it its author of twenty-six years stepped at once into the leadership of French Protestantism.[6]

The *Institutes* themselves, to which this letter was prefixed, were, as published in 1536, far from the extensive treatise into which they were to grow in Calvin's final edition of 1559; but they were already the most orderly and systematic popular presentation of doctrine and of the Christian life that the Reformation produced. Calvin's mind was formulative rather than creative. Without Luther's antecedent labors his work could not have been done. It is Luther's conception of justification by faith, and of the sacraments as seals of God's promises that he presents. Much he derived from Butzer, notably his emphasis on the glory of God as that for which all things are created, on election as a doctrine of Christian confidence, and on the consequences of election as a strenuous endeavor after a life of conformity to the will of God. But all is systematized and clarified with a skill that was Calvin's own.

Man's highest knowledge, Calvin taught, is that of God and of himself. Enough comes by nature to leave man without excuse, but adequate knowl-

[3] *Ibid.,* pp. 525, 526.   [4] *Ibid.,* pp. 526–528.   [5] Kidd, pp. 528–532.
[6] *Ibid.,* pp. 532, 533.

edge is given only in the Scriptures, which the witness of the Spirit in the heart of the believing reader attests as the very voice of God. These Scriptures teach that God is good, and the source of all goodness everywhere. Obedience to God's will is man's primal duty. As originally created, man was good and capable of obeying God's will, but he lost goodness and power alike in Adam's fall, and is now, of himself, absolutely incapable of goodness. Hence no work of man's can have any merit; and all men are in a state of ruin meriting only damnation. From this helpless and hopeless condition some men are undeservedly rescued through the work of Christ. He paid the penalty due for the sins of those in whose behalf He died; yet the offer and reception of this ransom was a free act on God's part, so that its cause is God's love.

All that Christ has wrought is without avail unless it becomes a man's personal possession. This possession is effected by the Holy Spirit, who works when, how, and where He will, creating repentance; and faith which, as with Luther, is a vital union between the believer and Christ. This new life of faith is salvation, but it is salvation unto righteousness. That the believer now does works pleasing to God is the proof that he has entered into vital union with Christ. "We are justified not without, and yet not by works." Calvin thus left room for a conception of "works" as strenuous as any claimed by the Roman Church, though very different in relation to the accomplishment of salvation. The standard set before the Christian is the law of God, as contained in the Scriptures, not as a test of his salvation but as an expression of that will of God which as an already saved man he will strive to fulfil. This emphasis on the law as the guide of Christian life was peculiarly Calvin's own. It has made Calvinism always insistent on character, though in Calvin's conception man is saved to character rather than by character. A prime nourishment of the Christian life is by prayer.

Since all good is of God, and man is unable to initiate or resist his conversion, it follows that the reason some are saved and others are lost is the divine choice—election and reprobation. For a reason for that choice beyond the will of God it is absurd to inquire, since God's will is an ultimate fact. Yet to Calvin election was always primarily a doctrine of Christian comfort. That God had a plan of salvation for a man, individually, was an unshakable rock of confidence, not only for one convinced of his own unworthiness, but for one surrounded by opposing forces even if they were those of priests and Kings. It made a man a fellow laborer with God in the accomplishment of God's will.

Three institutions have been divinely established by which the Christian life is maintained—the church, the sacraments, and civil government. In the last analysis the church consists of "all the elect of God"; but it also properly denotes "the whole body of mankind . . . who profess to worship one God and Christ." Yet there is no true church "where lying and falsehood have usurped the ascendancy." The New Testament shows as church officers, pastors, teachers, elders, and deacons, who enter on their charges with the founded a missionary college, he preached throughout southern India, in 1549 he entered Japan and began a work which had reached large dimensions, when its severe repression was undertaken by the native rulers in 1612. Xavier died, in 1552, just as he was entering China. His work was superficial, an exploration rather than a structure, but his example was a contagious influence of far-reaching force. In China the labor which Xavier had attempted was begun, in 1581, by the Jesuit Matteo Ricci (1552–1610), but his desire to be "all things to all men," led him to compromise with ancestor-worship, a relaxation which missionaries of other Catholic orders strongly opposed. In India the converts were almost entirely from outcasts or low-cast ranks. The Jesuit, Roberto de' Nobili (1576?–1656), began a work for those of high caste in Madura, in 1606, recognizing caste distinctions and otherwise accommodating itself to Indian prejudices. Its apparent success was large, but its methods aroused criticism and ultimate prohibition by the papacy. Probably the most famous experiment of Jesuit missions was that in Paraguay. Their work there began in 1586. In 1610, they commenced gathering the natives into "reductions," or villages, each built on a similar plan, where the dwellers were kept at peace and taught the elements of religion and industry, but held in strict and semi-childlike dependence on the missionaries, in whose hands lay the administration of trade and agriculture. Greatly admired, the system fell with the expulsion of the Jesuits, in 1767, and has left few permanent results.

The rivalries of the several orders, and the more effective supervision of missionary labors, induced Pope Gregory XV (1621–1623) to found, in 1622, the *Congregatio de Propaganda Fide,* by which the whole field could be surveyed and superintended from Rome.

12

The Struggle in France, The Netherlands, and England

THE RIVALRIES of France and Spain, with their political and military consequences, had made the growth of the Reformation possible, and had facilitated the division of Germany between Lutherans and Catholics recorded in the Peace of Augsburg of 1555. Henry II (1547–1559) had succeeded Francis I in France, and Charles V had transferred to his son Philip II (1556–1598) the sovereignty of Spain, the Netherlands, and of the Spanish territories in Italy; but the old rivalry continued. In war, however, Philip II at first proved more successful than his father had been, and the battles of St. Quentin in August, 1557, and Gravelines in July, 1558, forced France to the Treaty of Cateau-Cambrésis of April 2, 1559. That treaty was a reckoning point in the history of Europe. France abandoned the long struggle for Italy. Spanish leadership was evidently first in Europe, and had largely bound France to follow, or at least not to oppose, its interests. Protestantism was confronted by a much more politically united Catholicism than it had yet met. The political head of that Catholicism was Philip II of Spain, methodical, industrious, patient, and inflexibly determined, who saw as his God-appointed task the extirpation of Protestantism, and bent every energy to its accomplishment. The next thirty years were to be the time of chief peril in the history of Protestantism.

The point of highest danger was, perhaps, in the year 1559, when after the death of Henry II, in July, the crown passed to Francis II, whose wife was Mary "Queen of Scots," and by her own claim Queen of England also. Yet even Philip's ardent Catholicism was not willing to see a combination so dangerous to Spain as that of France, Scotland, and England under a single pair of rulers. He therefore helped Elizabeth, an action which he must afterward have regretted (see p. 366).

Calvin's influence had increasingly penetrated France, and French Protestants, or Huguenots, as they were known from 1557, multiplied in spite of severe persecution. By 1555 there was a congregation in Paris. Four years later the number of Huguenot Churches in France was seventy-two. That year, 1559, they were strong enough to hold their First General Synod in Paris, to adopt a strongly Calvinistic creed prepared by Antoine de la Roche Chandieu,[1] and a Presbyterian constitution drawn from Calvin's ecclesiastical principles. Popular estimate credited them with 400,000 adherents. Besides these Huguenots of religion, most of whom were from the economically oppressed and discontented artisan classes, the party was soon strengthened by the accession of political Huguenots.

The death of Henry II and the accession of Francis II left the family of Guise, uncles of Francis' Queen, all powerful in his court. The Guises were from Lorraine, and were looked upon by many of the French nobility as foreigners. Strenuously Catholic, the two brothers, Charles (1542–1574), the "cardinal of Lorraine," was head of the French clergy as archbishop of Rheims, while Francis (1519–1563), Duke of Guise, was the best soldier of France. Opposed to the Guise family were the family of Bourbon, of whom the chief in rank was Antoine of Vendôme, titular King of Navarre, a man of weak and vacillating spirit, and his much abler brother, Louis, prince of Condé. Of the house of Châtillon, also opposed to the Guise brothers, the leader was Gaspard de Coligny, known as Admiral Coligny, a man of sterling

[1] Schaff, *Creeds of Christendom*, 3:356–382.

stitution, the *Ordonnances Ecclésiastiques,* now far more definite than the recommendations accepted in 1537. In spite of his successful return, however, he could not have them quite all that he wished. The *Ordonnances* [16] declare that Christ has instituted in His church the four offices of pastor, teacher, elder, and deacon, and define the duties of each. Pastors were to meet weekly for public discussion, examination of ministerial candidates, and exegesis, in what was popularly known as the *Congrégation.* The teacher was to be the head of the Geneva school system, which Calvin regarded as an essential factor in the religious training of the city. To the deacons were assigned the care of the poor and the supervision of the hospital. The elders were the heart of Calvin's system. They were laymen, chosen by the Little Council, two from itself, four from the Sixty, and six from the Two Hundred, and under the presidency of one of the syndics. They, together with the ministers, made up the *Consistoire,* meeting every Thursday, and charged with ecclesiastical discipline. To excommunication they could go; beyond that, if the offense demanded, they were to refer the case to the civil authorities. No right seemed to Calvin so vital to the independence of the church as this of excommunication, and for none was he compelled so to struggle till its final establishment in 1555.[17]

Besides this task, Calvin prepared a new and much more effective catechism,[18] and introduced a liturgy, based on that of his French congregation in Strassburg, which, in turn, was essentially a translation of that generally in use in that German city. In formulating it for Genevan use Calvin made a good many modifications to meet Genevan customs or prejudices.[19] It combined a happy union of fixed and free prayer. Calvin had none of the hostility against fixed forms which his spiritual descendants in Great Britain and America afterward manifested. It also gave full place to singing.

Under Calvin's guidance, and he held no other office than that of one of the ministers of the city, much was done for education and for improved trade; but all Genevan life was under the constant and minute supervision of the *Consistoire.* Calvin would make Geneva a model of a perfected Christian community. Its strenuous Evangelicalism attracted refugees in large numbers, many of them men of position, learning, and wealth, principally from France, but also from Italy, the Netherlands, Scotland, and England. These soon became a very important factor in Genevan life. Calvin himself, and all his associated ministers, were foreigners. Opposition to his strenuous rule appeared practically from the first, but by 1548 had grown very serious. It was made up of two elements, those to whom any discipline would have been irksome; and much more formidable, those of old Genevan families who felt that Calvin, his fellow ministers, and the refugees were foreigners who were imposing a foreign yoke on a city of heroic traditions of independence. That there was a party of religious *Libertins* in Geneva, is a baseless tradition.

[16] Kidd, pp. 589–603. [17] *Ibid.,* p. 647. [18] Extracts, Kidd, pp. 604–615.
[19] Kidd, pp. 615–628.

Calvin's severest struggle was from 1548 to 1555, from the time that some of the older inhabitants began to fear that they would be swamped politically by the refugees, till the refugees, almost all of whom were eager supporters of Calvin, achieved what had been dreaded, and made Calvin's position unshakable. Constantly increasing in fame outside of Geneva, Calvin stood in imminent peril, throughout this period, of having his Genevan work overthrown.

The cases of conflict were many, but two stand out with special prominence. The first was that caused by Jérôme Hermès Bolsec, a former monk of Paris, now a Protestant physician in Veigy, near Geneva. In the *Congrégation* Bolsec charged Calvin with error in asserting predestination. That was to attack the very foundations of Calvin's authority, for his sole hold on Geneva was as an interpreter of the Scriptures. If he was not right in all, he was thoroughly discredited. Calvin took Bolsec's charges before the city government in October, 1551. The result was Bolsec's trial. The opinions of other Swiss governments were asked, and it was evident that they attached no such weight to predestination as did Calvin. It was with difficulty that Calvin procured Bolsec's banishment, and the episode led him to a more strenuous insistence of the vital importance of predestination as a Christian truth than even heretofore.[20] As for Bolsec, he ultimately returned to the Roman communion and avenged himself on Calvin's memory by a grossly slanderous biography.

Calvin was thus holding his power with difficulty, when in February, 1553, the elections, which for some years had been fairly balanced, turned decidedly in favor of his opponents. His fall seemed inevitable, when he was rescued and put on the path to ultimate victory by the arrival in Geneva of Miguel Servetus, whose case forms the second of those here mentioned. Servetus was a Spaniard, almost the same age as Calvin, and undoubtedly a man of great, though erratic, genius. In 1531 he published his *De Trinitatis Erroribus*. Compelled to conceal his identity, he studied medicine under the name of Villeneuve, being the real discoverer of the pulmonary circulation of the blood. He settled in Vienne in France, where he developed a large practice. He was working secretly on his *Restitution of Christianity*, which he published early in 1553. To his thinking, the Nicene doctrine of the Trinity, the Chalcedonian Christology, and infant baptism were the chief sources of the corruption of the church. As early as 1545, he had begun an exasperating correspondence with Calvin, whose *Institutes* he contemptuously criticised.

Servetus's identity and authorship were unmasked to the Roman ecclesiastical authorities in Lyons, by Calvin's friend, Guillaume Trie, who, a little later, supplied further proof obtained from Calvin himself. He was condemned to be burned; though, before sentence, he had escaped from prison in Vienne. For reasons hard to understand he made his way to Geneva, and was there arrested in August, 1553. His condemnation now became a test of strength

[20] Kidd, pp. 641–645.

standpoint, Ignatius Loyola is one of the master figures of the Reformation epoch. Inigo Lopez de Recalde was born of a noble family in northern Spain in 1491. After serving as a page at the court of Ferdinand, he became a soldier. His intrepid firmness was exhibited when Pamplona was besieged by the French in 1521, but he received there a wound that made further military service impossible. During his slow recovery he studied the lives of Christ, St. Dominic, and St. Francis. Chivalrous ideals still lingered in Spain, and he determined that he would be a knight of the Virgin. Recovered, in a measure, he journeyed to Monserrat, and hung his weapons on the Virgin's altar. Thence he went to Manresa, where, in the Dominican monastery, he began those directed visions which were afterward to grow into his *Spiritual Exercises*. It is a work designed to lead man to the realization of his destiny under God. For the sake of the salvation of his soul and the glory of God he is led to make a choice for Christ, to put off his sins, to assume an attitude of "holy disinterestedness" toward this world in order to use all its goods for the glorification of God. The Christian is led to submit wholly to God and to become an utterly disciplined member of the church, resolved to serve it in obedience. The year 1523 saw him a pilgrim in Jerusalem, resolved to serve Christ as a missionary to the Mohammedans, but the Franciscans who were there maintaining the cross with difficulty thought him dangerous and sent him home.

Convinced that if he was to do the work he desired he must have an education, Ignatius entered a boy's class in Barcelona, and went rapidly forward to the Universities of Alcalá and Salamanca. A born leader, he gathered like-minded companions with whom he practised his spiritual exercises. This aroused the suspicion of the Spanish inquisition and his life was in danger. In 1528, he entered the University of Paris, just as Calvin was leaving it. There he made no public demonstration, but gathered round himself a handful of devoted friends and disciples—Pierre Lefèvre, Francis Xavier, Diego Lainez, Alfonso Salmeron, Nicolas Bobadilla, and Simon Rodriguez, mostly from the Spanish peninsula. In the church of St. Mary on Montmartre, in Paris, on August 15, 1534, these companions took a vow to go to Jerusalem to labor for the church and their fellow men, or, if that proved impossible, to put themselves at the disposition of the Pope. It was a little student association, the connecting bond of which was love to God and the church, as they understood it.

The year 1536 saw them in Venice; but Jerusalem was barred by war, and they now determined to ask the Pope's direction. Ignatius was beginning to perceive what his society might become. Italy had seen many military companies in earthly service. His would be the military company of Jesus, bound by a similar strictness of obedience, and a like careful, though spiritual, exercise of arms, to fight the battle of the church against infidels and heretics. In spite of ecclesiastical opposition, Paul III was induced by the favorable attitude of Contarini and the skill of Ignatius to authorize the company on September 27, 1540.[3] The constitution of the society was as yet indefinite, save that it was to have a head to whom full obedience was due, and should labor wherever that head and the Pope should direct. In April, 1541, Ignatius was chosen the first "general"—an office which he held till his death, July 31, 1556.

The constitution of the Jesuits was gradually worked out, indeed it was not completed till after Ignatius' death, though its main features were his work. At the head is a "general," to whom absolute obedience is due; but who, in turn, is watched by assistants appointed by the order, and can, if necessary, be deposed by it. Over each district is a "provincial," appointed by the "general." Each member is admitted, after a careful novitiate, and pledges obedience to the fullest extent in all that does not involve sin. His superiors assign him to the work which they believe him best fitted to do. That that work may be better accomplished the Jesuits are bound to no fixed hours of worship or form of dress as are monks. Each member is disciplined by use of Ignatius's *Spiritual Exercises,*—a remarkable work, in accordance with which the Jesuit is drilled in a spiritual manual of arms, by four weeks of intense contemplation of the principal facts of the life and work of Christ, and of the Christian warfare with evil, under the guidance of a spiritual drill-master. It was a marvellous instrument that Ignatius constructed, combining the individualism of the Renaissance—each man assigned to and trained for his peculiar work—with the sacrifice of will and complete obedience to the spirit and aims of the whole. It stands as the very antithesis of Protestantism.

Though the Jesuit society spread rapidly in Italy, Spain, and Portugal, it was slower in gaining strong foothold in France and Germany, but by the latter half of the sixteenth century it was the advance-guard of the Counter-Reformation. Its chief agencies were preaching, the confessional, its excellent schools—not for the multitude, but for the well-born and well-to-do—and its foreign missions. Under Jesuit influence more frequent confession and communion became the rule in Catholic countries; and, to aid the confessional, the Jesuit moral practice was gradually developed, chiefly after Ignatius's death, and especially in the early part of the seventeenth century, in a fashion that has aroused the criticism not only of Protestants but of many Catholics. In estimating them aright it should be remembered that these moral treatises do not represent ideals of conduct, but the *minima* on which absolution can be given; and, also, that the Jesuit morality emphasized the universal Latin tendency to regard sin as a series of definite acts rather than as a state or attitude of mind.

Naturally a society thus international in character, the members of which were bound to their officers by constant letters and reports, speedily became a force in political life.

With the establishment of the world-wide inquisition and the founda-

[3] Kidd, pp. 335-340.

of Henry VIII's support. That was a strongly developed national consciousness —a feeling of England for Englishmen—that was easily aroused to opposition to all foreign encroachment from whatever source.

Henry VIII, who has been well described as a "tyrant under legal forms," was a man of remarkable intellectual abilities and executive force, well read and always interested in scholastic theology, sympathetic with humanism, popular with the mass of the people, but egotistic, obstinate, and self-seeking. In the early part of his reign he had the support of Thomas Wolsey (1475–1530), who became a privy councillor in 1511, and in 1515 was made lord chancellor by the King and cardinal by Pope Leo X. Thenceforth he was Henry's right hand. When Luther's writings were received in England their use was forbidden, and Henry VIII published his *Assertion of the Seven Sacraments* against Luther in 1521, which won him from Leo X the title "Defender of the Faith." Henry had married Catherine of Aragon, daughter of Ferdinand and Isabella of Spain, and widow, though the marriage had been one in name only, of his older brother, Arthur. A dispensation authorizing this marriage with a deceased brother's wife had been granted by Julius II in 1503. Six children were born of this union, but only one, Mary, survived infancy. By 1527, if not earlier, Henry was alleging religious scruples as to the validity of his marriage. His reasons were not wholly sensual. Had they been, he might well have been content with his mistresses. A woman had never ruled England. The Wars of the Roses had ended as recently as 1485. The absence of a male heir, should Henry die, would probably cause civil war. It was not likely that Catherine would have further children. He wanted another wife, and a male heir.

Wolsey was induced to favor the project, partly from his subservience to the King, and partly because, if the marriage with Catherine should be declared invalid, he hoped Henry would marry the French princess, Renée, afterward duchess of Ferrara, and thus be drawn more firmly from the Spanish to the French side in continental politics. Henry, however, had other plans. He had fallen in love with Anne Boleyn, a lady of his court. A complicated negotiation followed, in which Wolsey did his best to please Henry, while Catherine behaved with dignity and firmness, and was treated with cruelty. Probably an annulment of the marriage might have been secured from Pope Clement VII had it not been for the course of European politics, which left the Emperor Charles V victor in war, and forced the Pope into submission to the imperial policy (see p. 319). Charles was determined that his aunt, Catherine, should not be set aside. Henry, angered at Wolsey's want of success, turned on him, and the great cardinal died, November 30, 1530, on his way to be tried for treason.

Henry now thought well of a suggestion of Thomas Cranmer (1489–1556), then teaching in Cambridge University, that the opinions of universities be sought. This was done in 1530, with only partial success; but a friendship was begun between the King and Cranmer that was to have momentous consequences.

Favorable action from the Pope being now out of the question, Henry determined to rely on the national feeling of hostility to foreign rule, and his own despotic skill, either to break with the papacy altogether, or to so threaten papal control as to secure his wishes. In January, 1531, he charged the whole body of clergy with breach of the old statute of *Præmunire* of 1353 for having recognized Wolsey's authority as papal legate—an authority which Henry himself had recognized and approved. He not only extorted a great sum as the price of pardon, but the declaration by the convocations in which the clergy met, that in respect to the Church of England, he was "single and supreme Lord, and, as far as the law of Christ allows, even supreme head." Early in 1532, under severe royal pressure, Parliament passed an act forbidding the payment of all annates to Rome save with the King's consent.[1] In May following, the clergy in convocation agreed reluctantly, not only to make no new ecclesiastical laws without the King's permission, but to submit all existing statutes to a commission appointed by the King.[2] About January 25, 1533, Henry secretly married Anne Boleyn. In February Parliament forbade all appeals to Rome.[3] Henry used the conditional prohibition of annates to procure from Pope Clement VII confirmation of his appointment of Thomas Cranmer as archbishop of Canterbury. Cranmer was consecrated on March 30; on May 23, Cranmer held court and formally adjudged Henry's marriage to Catherine null and void. On September 7, Anne Boleyn bore a daughter, the princess Elizabeth, later to be Queen.

While these events were occurring Clement VII had prepared a bull threatening excommunication against Henry on July 11, 1533. Henry's answer was a series of statutes obtained from Parliament in 1534, by which all payments to the Pope were forbidden, all bishops were to be elected on the King's nomination, and all oaths of papal obedience, Roman licenses, and other recognitions of papal authority done away.[4] The two convocations now formally abjured papal supremacy.[5] On November 3, 1534, Parliament passed the famous Supremacy Act, by which Henry and his successors were declared "the only supreme head in earth of the Church of England," without qualifying clauses, and with full power to redress "heresies" and "abuses."[6] This was not understood by the King or its authors as giving spiritual rights, such as ordination, the administration of the sacraments and the like, but in all else it practically put the King in the place of the Pope. The breach with Rome was complete. Nor were these statutes in any way meaningless. In May, 1535, a number of monks of one of the most respected orders in England, that of the Carthusians, or Charterhouse, were executed under

---

[1] Gee and Hardy, *Documents Illustrative of English Church History*, pp. 178–186.
[2] *Ibid.*, pp. 176–178.   [3] *Ibid.*, pp. 187–195.   [4] Gee and Hardy, pp. 201–232.
[5] *Ibid.*, pp. 251, 252.   [6] *Ibid.*, pp. 243, 244.

modelled on that of Calvin. It allowed, however, even more use of free prayer, the forms given being regarded as models, the strict employment of which was not obligatory, though the general order and content of the service were definite enough.

Knox was soon obliged to defend what he had gained. King Francis II of France died on December 5, 1560, and in the following August Mary returned to Scotland. Her position as a youthful widow was one to excite a sympathy which her great personal charm increased. She was no longer Queen of France, and that element which had supported Protestantism not by reason of religion but from desire of national independence might well think that the pressing danger of French domination which had induced acquiescence in the religious revolution had passed. Mary behaved, at first, with great prudence. While she made no secret of her own faith, and had mass said in her chapel to the furious disapproval of Knox, who was now minister of St. Giles in Edinburgh, and admired by the burghers of that city, she did not interfere in the religious settlement effected in 1560. She strove to secure recognition as Elizabeth's heir to the English throne, a thing which Elizabeth had no mind to grant. Mary had the sage advice of her half-brother, James Stewart, later to be Earl of Moray (1531?–1570), who had been a leader of the "Lords of the Congregation." She tried by personal interviews of great skill to win Knox, but he refused any overture and remained the soul of the Protestant party. Still the prospect darkened for him. Mary won friends. The Protestant nobles were divided. The mass was increasingly being used. Knox had good reason to fear that Mary would give a Catholic King to Scotland by marrying some great foreign prince. A marriage with the son of Philip II of Spain was seriously discussed. Even more alarming for the Protestant cause in Scotland and England was Mary's actual marriage on July 29, 1565, to her cousin, Henry Stewart, Lord Darnley (1545–1567), with whom she had fallen in love. Darnley's claim to the English throne stood next to that of Mary herself. He was popular with English Catholics, and though he had passed as a Protestant in England, he now avowed himself a Catholic. The marriage increased Elizabeth's danger at home and strengthened the Catholic party in Scotland. Moray opposed it, was driven from court, and soon into exile, and Mary made much progress in subduing, one after another, the Protestant lords who sympathized with Moray. She thus lost her wisest adviser.

Thus far Mary had acted fairly shrewdly, but Scottish Protestantism was now saved by Mary's mistakes and want of self-control. Darnley was certainly disagreeable and vicious. Her feelings for him changed. On the other hand, his jealousy was roused by the favor which Mary showed to David Riccio, an Italian whom Mary employed as a foreign secretary, and who was looked upon by the Protestant lords as their enemy. Darnley and a number of Protestant nobles, therefore, entered into a plot by which Riccio was dragged from Mary's presence and murdered in the palace of Holyrood, on March 9, 1566. Mary behaved with great cunning. Dissembling her anger at the weak Darnley, she secured from him the names of his fellow conspirators, outlawed those who had actually participated in the deed, and took the others back into favor, of course with the knowledge on their part that they were received on sufferance. On June 19, 1566, Mary and Darnley's son was born, the future James VI of Scotland and James I of England. Mary never seemed surer on the Scottish throne.

In reality Mary had never forgiven her husband, and she was now thrown much with a Protestant noble, James Hepburn, Earl of Bothwell (1536?–1578), a rough, licentious, but brave, loyal, and martial man, whose qualities contrasted with those of her weak husband. Bothwell now led in a conspiracy to rid Mary of Darnley, with how much share on the part of Mary herself is still one of the disputed questions of history. Darnley, who was recovering from smallpox, was removed by Mary from Glasgow to a house on the edge of Edinburgh, where Mary spent part of the last evening with him. Early on the morning of February 10, 1567, the house was blown up, and Darnley's body was found near it. Public opinion charged Bothwell with the murder, and it was widely believed, probably with justice, that Mary also was guilty of it. At all events she heaped honors on Bothwell, who succeeded in securing acquittal by a farce of a trial. On April 24, Bothwell met Mary on one of her journeys and made her captive by a show of force—it was generally believed with her connivance. He was married, but he was divorced from his wife for adultery on May 3, and on May 15 he and Mary were married by Protestant rites.

These shameless transactions roused general hostility in Scotland, while they robbed Mary, for the time, of Catholic sympathy in England and on the Continent. Protestants and Catholics in Scotland joined forces against her. Just a month after the wedding Mary was a prisoner, and on July 24, 1567, she was compelled to abdicate in favor of her year-old son, and appoint Moray as regent, while she was herself imprisoned in Lochleven Castle. On July 29 John Knox preached the sermon at James VI's coronation. With Mary's fall came the triumph of Protestantism, which was now definitely established by Parliament in December. Mary herself escaped from Lochleven in May, 1568, but Moray promptly defeated her supporters, and she fled to England, where she was to remain, a center of Catholic intrigue, till her execution for conspiracy against Elizabeth's life, in February, 1587.

Knox's fiery career was about over. On November 24, 1572, he died, having influenced not merely the religion but the character of the nation more than any other man in Scottish history. Knox's work was to be taken up by Andrew Melville (1545–1623), who had taught as Beza's colleague in Geneva, from 1568 to his return to Scotland in 1574. He was the educational reformer of the Universities of Glasgow and St. Andrews and even more disa joint attack by France and Spain on the royal rebel. Henry's diplomacy and mutual jealousies warded it off; but he took several steps of importance to lessen his peril. He would show the world that he was an orthodox Catholic save in regard to the Pope. Accordingly, in June, 1539, Parliament passed the Six Articles Act.[9] It affirmed as the creed of England a strict doctrine of transubstantiation, denial of which was to be punished by fire. It repudiated communion in both bread and wine, and priestly marriage. It ordered the permanent observation of vows of chastity, enjoined private masses, and auricular confession. This statute remained in force till Henry's death. It was not enough, however, that Henry should show himself orthodox. He was a widower, and Cromwell was urgent that he strengthen his position by a marriage which would please the German Protestants, and unite him with those opposed to the Emperor Charles V. Anne of Cleves, sister of the wife of John Frederick, the Saxon Elector, was selected. The marriage took place on January 6, 1540.

Meanwhile Henry had completed the confiscations of all the monasteries in 1539.[10] He was stronger at home than ever. Francis and Charles were evidently soon to be again at war, and the Emperor was beginning to court Henry's assistance. German Protestants looked askance at his Six Articles, and he now no longer needed their aid. Henry had regarded the marriage with Anne of Cleves as a mere political expedient. An annulment was obtained in July, 1540, from the bishops on the ground that the King had never given "inward consent" to the marriage, and Anne was handsomely indemnified pecuniarily. For Cromwell, to whom the marriage was due, he had no further use. A bill of attainder was put through Parliament, and the King's able, but utterly unscrupulous, servant was beheaded on July 28, 1540. These events were accompanied by increasing opposition to the Protestant element, and this Catholic inclination was evidenced in Henry's marriage to Catherine Howard, niece of the duke of Norfolk, shortly after his separation from Anne of Cleves; but the new Queen's conduct was open to question, and in February, 1542, she was beheaded. In July, 1543, he married Catherine Parr, who had the fortune to survive him. On January 28, 1547, Henry died.

At Henry's death England was divided into three parties. Of these, that embracing the great body of Englishmen stood fairly with the late King in desiring no considerable change in doctrine or worship, while rejecting foreign ecclesiastical jurisdiction. It had been Henry's strength that, with all his tyranny, he was fairly representative of this great middle party. There were, besides, two small parties, neither fairly representative—a Catholic wing that would restore the power of the papacy, and a Protestant faction that would introduce reform as it was understood on the Continent. The latter had undoubtedly been growing, in spite of repression, during Henry's last years. It was to be England's fortune that the two smaller and unrepresentative

[9] Gee and Hardy, pp. 303–319.   [10] Ibid., pp. 281–303.

parties should be successively in power during the next two reigns, and that to religious turmoil agrarian unrest should be added, owing to the great changes in property caused by monastic confiscations, and even more to enclosures of common lands by greedy landlords, and the impoverishment of humbler tenants by the loss of their time-honored rights of use.

Edward VI was but nine years of age. The government was, therefore, administered in his name by a council, of which the earl of Hertford, or, as he was immediately created, duke of Somerset, was chief, with the title of Protector. Somerset was the brother of the young King's mother, the short-lived Jane Seymour. He was a man of Protestant sympathies, and of excellent intentions—a believer in a degree of liberty in religious and political questions in marked contrast to Henry VIII. He was, also, a sincere friend of the dispossessed lower agricultural classes. Under his rule the new comparative freedom of religious expression led to many local innovations and much controversy, in which the revolutionary party more and more gained the upper hand. In 1547 Parliament ordered the administration of the cup to the laity.[11] The same year the last great confiscation of church lands occurred —the dissolution of the "chantries," that is, endowed chapels for saying masses. The properties of religious fraternities and guilds were also sequestered.[12] The Six Articles were repealed. Early in 1548 images were ordered removed from the churches. The marriage of priests was made legal in 1549.[13]

The confusion soon became great, and as a means at once of advancing the reforms and securing order, Parliament, on January 21, 1549, enacted an Act of Uniformity,[14] by which the universal use of a Book of Common Prayer in English was required. This book, known as the First Prayer Book of Edward VI, was largely the work of Cranmer, based on the older English services in Latin, with some use of a revised Roman breviary, published in 1535 by Cardinal Fernandez de Quinones, and the Lutheranly inclined tentative *Consultation* of Hermann von Wied, archbishop of Cologne, issued in 1543. In its larger feature it is still the Prayer Book of the Church of England, but this edition preserved much of detail of older worship, such as prayers for the dead, communion at burials, anointing and exorcism in baptism, and anointing the sick, which was soon to be abandoned. In the Eucharist the words used in handing the elements to the communicant were the first clause of the present Anglican form, implying that the body and blood of Christ are really received.

Meanwhile, Somerset was beset with political troubles. To counteract the growing power of France in Scotland he urged the union of the two countries by the ultimate marriage of King Edward with the Scottish Princess Mary, to be "Queen of Scots," and supported his efforts by an invasion of Scotland in which the Scots were terribly defeated, on September 10, 1547, at

---

[11] Gee and Hardy, pp. 322–328.   [12] Gee and Hardy, pp. 328–357.
[13] *Ibid.*, pp. 366–368.   [14] *Ibid.*, pp. 358–366.

bishop of Gloucester and Worcester. Mary was determined to strike the highest of the anti-Roman clergy, Archbishop Cranmer. Cranmer was not of the heroic stuff of which Latimer, Ridley, Hooper, and Rogers were made. He was formally excommunicated by sentence at Rome on November 25, 1555, and Pole was shortly after made archbishop of Canterbury in his stead. Cranmer was now in a logical dilemma. He had asserted, since his appointment under Henry VIII, that the sovereign is the supreme authority in the English church. His Protestantism was real, but that sovereign was now a Roman Catholic. In his distress he now made submission declaring that he recognized papal authority as established by law. Mary had no intention of sparing the man who had pronounced her mother's marriage invalid. Cranmer must die. But it was hoped that by a public abjuration of Protestantism at his death he would discredit the Reformation. That hope was nearly realized. Cranmer signed a further recantation denying Protestantism wholly; but on the day of his execution in Oxford, March 21, 1556, his courage returned. He repudiated his retractions absolutely, declared his Protestant faith, and held the offending hand, which had signed the now renounced submissions, in the flame till it was consumed. His dying day was the noblest of his life.

Philip had left England in 1555, and this absence, coupled with her own childless state, preyed on Mary's mind, inducing her to feel that she had not done enough to satisfy the judgment of God. Persecution therefore continued unabated till her death on November 17, 1558. In all, somewhat less than three hundred were burned—a scanty number compared with the toll of sufferers in the Netherlands. But English sentiment deeply revolted. These martyrdoms did more for the spread of anti-Roman sentiment than all previous governmental efforts had accomplished. It was certain that the accession of the next sovereign would witness a change or civil war.

Elizabeth (Queen 1558–1603) had long passed as illegitimate, though her place in the succession had been secured by act of Parliament in the lifetime of Henry VIII. Of all Henry's children she was the only one who really resembled him in ability, insight, and personal popularity. With a masculine force of character she combined a curious love of personal adornment inherited from her light-minded mother. Of real religious feeling she had none, but her birth and Roman denials of her mother's marriage made her necessarily a Protestant, though under Mary, when her life had been in danger, she had conformed to the Roman ritual. Fortunately her accession had the support of Philip II of Spain, soon to be her bitterest enemy. That favor helped her with English Catholics. Earnest Roman as he was, Philip was politician enough not to wish to see France, England, and Scotland come under the rule of a single royal pair, and if Elizabeth was not Queen of England, then Mary "Queen of Scots," wife of the prince who was in 1559 to become King Francis II of France, was rightfully entitled to the English throne. In her first measures on accession Elizabeth enjoyed, moreover, the aid of one of the most cautious and far-sighted statesmen England has ever produced, William Cecil (1521–1598), better known as Lord Burghley, whom she at once made her secretary and who was to be her chief adviser till his death. For Elizabeth it was a great advantage also that she was thoroughly English in feeling, and deeply sympathetic with the political and economic ambitions of the nation. This representative quality reconciled many to her government whom mere religious considerations would have repelled. No one doubted that she put England first.

Elizabeth proceeded cautiously with her changes. Parliament passed the new Supremacy Act,[19] with much opposition, on April 29, 1559. By it the authority of the Pope and all payments and appeals to him were rejected. A significant change of title appeared, however, by Elizabeth's own insistence. Instead of the old "Supreme Head," so obnoxious to the Catholics, she was now styled "Supreme Governor" of the church in England—a much less objectionable phrase, though amounting to the same thing in practice. The tests of heresy were now to be the Scriptures, the first four General Councils, and the decisions of Parliament. Meanwhile a commission had been revising the Second Prayer Book of Edward VI (see p. 364). The prayer against the Pope was omitted, as was the declaration that kneeling at the Supper did not imply adoration, while the question of Christ's physical presence was left intentionally undetermined by the combination of the forms of delivery in the two Edwardean books (see pp. 363, 364). These modifications were designed to render the new service more palatable to Catholics. The Act of Uniformity [20] now ordered all worship to be conducted, after June 24, 1559, in accordance with this liturgy, and provided that the ornaments of the church and the vestments of its ministers should be those of the second year of Edward VI.

The oath of supremacy was refused by all but two obscurer members of the Marian episcopate, but among the lower clergy generally resistance was slight, the obstinate not amounting to two hundred. New bishops must be provided, and Elizabeth directed the election of her mother's one-time chaplain, Matthew Parker (1504–1575), as archbishop of Canterbury. His consecration was a perplexing question; but there were those in England who had received ordination to the bishopric under Henry VIII and Edward VI. Parker was now consecrated, on December 17, 1559, at the hands of four such—William Barlow, John Scory, Miles Coverdale, and John Hodgkin. The validity of the act, on which the apostolic succession of the English episcopate depends, has always been strongly affirmed by Anglican divines, while attacked by Roman theologians, on various grounds, and declared invalid by Pope Leo XIII in 1896, for defect in "intention." Thus inaugurated, a new Anglican episcopate was speedily established. A definition of the creed, other than implied in the Prayer Book, was purposely postponed; but

[19] Gee and Hardy, pp. 442–458.   [20] Gee and Hardy, pp. 458–467.

in 1563 the Forty-two Articles of 1553 (see p. 364) were somewhat revised, and as the famous Thirty-nine Articles, became the statement of faith of the Church of England.[21]

Thus, by 1563 the Elizabethan settlement was accomplished. It was threatened from two sides: from that of Rome, and, even more dangerously, from the earnest reformers who wished to go further and soon were to be nicknamed Puritans. The remarkable feature of the English revolt is that it produced no outstanding religious leader—no Luther, Zwingli, Calvin, or Knox. Nor did it, before the beginning of Elizabeth's reign, manifest any considerable spiritual awakening among the people. Its impulses were political and social. A great revival of the religious life of England was to come, the earlier history of which was to be coincident with Elizabeth's reign, but which was to owe nothing to her.

10

The Scottish Reformation

AT THE DAWN of the sixteenth century Scotland was a poor and backward country. Its social conditions were mediæval. The power of its Kings was small. Its nobles were turbulent. Relatively its church was rich in land, owning about one-half that of the country, but churchly positions were largely used to supply places for younger sons of noble houses, and much clerical property was in the hands of the lay nobles. The weak monarchy had usually leaned on the church as against the lay nobility. Education was backward, though universities had been founded in the fifteenth century in St. Andrews, Glasgow, and Aberdeen. Compared with continental seats of learning they were weak.

The determining motive of most of Scottish political history in this period was fear of dominance or annexation by England, persuading it to link the fortunes of the land with those of France. Three grievous defeats by the English—Flodden (1513), Solway Moss (1542), and Pinkie (1547)—strengthened this feeling of antagonism, but showed that even English superiority in force could not conquer Scotland. On the other hand, Scotland in alliance with France was a great peril for England, the more serious when

[21] Schaff, *Creeds of Christendom*, 3:487–516.

England had broken with the papacy. Therefore England and France both sought to build up parties and strengthen factions favorable to themselves in Scotland. On the whole the powerful family of Douglas was inclined toward England, while that of Hamilton favored France. France also had strong supporters in Archbishop James Beaton (?-1539) of St. Andrews, the primate of Scotland, and his nephew, Cardinal David Beaton (1494?-1546), his successor in the same see. Though King James V (reigned 1513-1542) was nephew of Henry VIII, and his grandson, James VI, was to become James I of England in 1603 and unite the two crowns after the death of Elizabeth, James V threw in his fortunes with France, marrying successively a daughter of Francis I, and, after her death, Mary of Lorraine, of the powerful French Catholic family of Guise. This latter union, so important in the history of Scotland, was to have as its fruit Mary "Queen of Scots."

Some Protestant beginnings were early made in Scotland. Patrick Hamilton (1504?-1528), who had visited Wittenberg and studied in Marburg, preached Lutheran doctrine, and was burned on February 29, 1528. The cause grew slowly. In 1534 and 1540 there were other executions. Yet, in 1543 the Scottish Parliament authorized the reading and translation of the Bible. It was but a temporary phase, due to English influence, and by 1544 Cardinal Beaton and the French party were employing strong repression. Chief of the preachers at this time was George Wishart (1513?-1546), who was burned by Cardinal Beaton on March 2, 1546. On May 29 Beaton himself was brutally murdered, partly in revenge for Wishart's death and partly out of hostility to his French policy. The murderers gained possession of the castle of St. Andrews and rallied their sympathizers there. In 1547 a hunted Protestant preacher, apparently a convert and certainly a friend of Wishart, of no considerable previous conspicuity, took refuge with them and became their spiritual teacher. This was John Knox, to be the hero of the Scottish reformation.

Born in or near Haddington, between 1505 and 1515, Knox's early career was obscure. He was certainly ordained to the priesthood, but when Wishart was arrested he was with that martyr, and prepared to defend him. French forces sent to reduce the rebels in St. Andrews castle compelled its surrender, and Knox was carried to France to endure for nineteen months the cruel lot of a galley-slave. Released at length, he made his way to England, then under the Protestant government ruling in the name of Edward VI, became one of the royal chaplains, and in 1552 declined the bishopric of Rochester. The accession of Mary compelled his flight in 1554, but the English refugees whom he first joined in Frankfurt were divided by his criticisms of the Edwardean Prayer-Book,[1] and he soon found a welcome in Geneva, where he became an ardent disciple of Calvin, and labored on

[1] Kidd, p. 691.

the Genevan version of the English Bible, later so valued by the English Puritans.

Meanwhile the English had alienated Scotland more than ever by the defeat of Pinkie, in 1547. Mary "Queen of Scots" had been betrothed to the heir to the French throne and sent to France for safety in 1548, while her mother, the Guise, Mary of Lorraine, became regent of Scotland in 1554.

To a large portion of the Scottish nobles and people this full dependence on France was as hateful as any submission to England could have been. Protestantism and national independence seemed to be bound together, and it was in this double struggle that Knox was to be the leader. Knox now dared to return to Scotland, in 1555, and preached for six months; but the situation was not yet ripe for revolt, and Knox returned to Geneva to become the pastor of the church of English-speaking refugees there. He had, however, sowed fruitful seed. On December 3, 1557, a number of Protestant and anti-French nobles in Scotland entered into a covenant to "establish the most blessed Word of God and His congregation"—from which they were nicknamed "The Lords of the Congregation." [2] Additional fuel was given to this dissent by the marriage of Mary to the French heir on April 24, 1558.[3] Scotland now seemed a province of France, for should there be a son of this union he would be ruler of both lands, and the French grip was made doubly sure by an agreement signed by Mary, kept secret at the time, that France should receive Scotland should she die without heirs. Before 1558 was ended Elizabeth was Queen of England, and Mary "Queen of Scots" was denouncing her as an illegitimate usurper, and proclaiming herself the rightful occupant of the English throne.

Under these circumstances the advocates of Scottish independence and of Protestantism rapidly increased and became more and more fused into one party. Elizabeth, moreover, could be expected to assist, if only for her own protection. Knox saw that the time was ready. On May 2, 1559, he was back in Scotland. Nine days later he preached in Perth. The mob destroyed the monastic establishments of the town.[4] This action the regent naturally regarded as rank rebellion. She had French troops at her disposal, and both sides promptly armed for combat. They proved fairly equal, and the result was undecided. Churches were wrecked and monastic property sacked, to Knox's disgust, in many parts of Scotland. On July 10, 1559, Henry II of France died and Mary's husband, Francis II, became King in his stead. French reinforcements were promptly sent to the regent in Scotland. Matters went badly for the reformers. At last, in January, 1560, English help came. The contest dragged. On June 11, 1560, the regent died, but her cause perished with her. On July 6 a treaty was made between France and England by which French soldiers were withdrawn from Scotland, and Frenchmen were debarred from all important posts in its government. The revolution

[2] *Ibid.,* p. 696.   [3] *Ibid.,* p. 690.   [4] Kidd, p. 697.

had triumphed through English aid, but without forfeiting Scottish national independence, and its inspirer had been Knox.[5] In this contest the Scottish middle classes had first shown themselves a power, and their influence was for the newer order.

The victorious party now pushed its triumph in the Scottish Parliament. On August 17, 1560, a Calvinistic confession of faith, largely prepared by Knox, was adopted as the creed of the realm.[6] A week later the same body abolished papal jurisdiction, and forbade the mass under pain of death for the third offense.[7] Though the King and Queen in France refused their approval, the majority of the nation had spoken.

Knox and his associates now proceeded to complete their work. In December, 1560, a meeting was held which is regarded as the first Scottish "General Assembly," in January following the *First Book of Discipline* was presented to the Parliament.[8] It was a most remarkable document, attempting to apply the system worked out by Calvin to a whole kingdom, though the Presbyterian system was far from thoroughly developed as yet. In each parish there should be a minister and elders holding office with the consent of the congregation. Minister and elders constituted the disciplinary board— the later "session"—with power of excommunication. In the larger towns were to be meetings for discussion, out of which "presbyteries" were to grow; over groups of ministers and congregations were synods, and over all the "General Assembly." The need of the times and the inchoate state of the church led to two further institutions, "readers," in places where there were no ministers or the work was large, and "superintendents," without spiritual authority, but with administrative right to oversee the organization of parishes, and recommend ministerial candidates. Besides these ecclesiastical features, the *Book* sketched out notable schemes of national education and for the relief of the poor. Knox would have church, education, and poor supported from the old church property; but here the *Book* met the resistance of Parliament, which did not adopt it, though many of the body approved. The ecclesiastical constitution gradually came into force; but the nobles so possessed themselves of church lands that the church became one of the poorest in Christendom. This relative poverty stamped on it a democratic character, however, that was to make the church of Scotland the bulwark of the people against encroachments by the nobles and the crown.

All observances not having Scriptural authority were swept away. Sunday was the only remaining holy day. For the conduct of public worship Knox prepared a *Book of Common Order*, sometimes called "Knox's Liturgy," which was approved by the "General Assembly," in 1564.[9] It was largely based on that of the English congregation in Geneva, which in turn was

[5] *Ibid.*, pp. 698–700.
[6] *Ibid.*, pp. 700, 704–707; Schaff, *Creeds of Christendom*, 3:437–479.
[7] *Ibid.*, pp. 701, 702.   [8] *Ibid.*, p. 707.   [9] Kidd, pp. 708–715.

modelled on that of Calvin. It allowed, however, even more use of free prayer, the forms given being regarded as models, the strict employment of which was not obligatory, though the general order and content of the service were definite enough.

Knox was soon obliged to defend what he had gained. King Francis II of France died on December 5, 1560, and in the following August Mary returned to Scotland. Her position as a youthful widow was one to excite a sympathy which her great personal charm increased. She was no longer Queen of France, and that element which had supported Protestantism not by reason of religion but from desire of national independence might well think that the pressing danger of French domination which had induced acquiescence in the religious revolution had passed. Mary behaved, at first, with great prudence. While she made no secret of her own faith, and had mass said in her chapel to the furious disapproval of Knox, who was now minister of St. Giles in Edinburgh, and admired by the burghers of that city, she did not interfere in the religious settlement effected in 1560. She strove to secure recognition as Elizabeth's heir to the English throne, a thing which Elizabeth had no mind to grant. Mary had the sage advice of her half-brother, James Stewart, later to be Earl of Moray (1531?–1570), who had been a leader of the "Lords of the Congregation." She tried by personal inter-views of great skill to win Knox, but he refused any overture and remained the soul of the Protestant party. Still the prospect darkened for him. Mary won friends. The Protestant nobles were divided. The mass was increasingly being used. Knox had good reason to fear that Mary would give a Catholic King to Scotland by marrying some great foreign prince. A marriage with the son of Philip II of Spain was seriously discussed. Even more alarming for the Protestant cause in Scotland and England was Mary's actual marriage on July 29, 1565, to her cousin, Henry Stewart, Lord Darnley (1545–1567), with whom she had fallen in love. Darnley's claim to the English throne stood next to that of Mary herself. He was popular with English Catholics, and though he had passed as a Protestant in England, he now avowed himself a Catholic. The marriage increased Elizabeth's danger at home and strength-ened the Catholic party in Scotland. Moray opposed it, was driven from court, and soon into exile, and Mary made much progress in subduing, one after another, the Protestant lords who sympathized with Moray. She thus lost her wisest adviser.

Thus far Mary had acted fairly shrewdly, but Scottish Protestantism was now saved by Mary's mistakes and want of self-control. Darnley was cer-tainly disagreeable and vicious. Her feelings for him changed. On the other hand, his jealousy was roused by the favor which Mary showed to David Riccio, an Italian whom Mary employed as a foreign secretary, and who was looked upon by the Protestant lords as their enemy. Darnley and a number of Protestant nobles, therefore, entered into a plot by which Riccio was dragged from Mary's presence and murdered in the palace of Holyrood, on March 9, 1566. Mary behaved with great cunning. Dissembling her anger at the weak Darnley, she secured from him the names of his fellow conspirators, outlawed those who had actually participated in the deed, and took the others back into favor, of course with the knowledge on their part that they were received on sufferance. On June 19, 1566, Mary and Darnley's son was born, the future James VI of Scotland and James I of England. Mary never seemed surer on the Scottish throne.

In reality Mary had never forgiven her husband, and she was now thrown much with a Protestant noble, James Hepburn, Earl of Bothwell (1536?–1578), a rough, licentious, but brave, loyal, and martial man, whose qualities contrasted with those of her weak husband. Bothwell now led in a conspiracy to rid Mary of Darnley, with how much share on the part of Mary herself is still one of the disputed questions of history. Darnley, who was recovering from smallpox, was removed by Mary from Glasgow to a house on the edge of Edinburgh, where Mary spent part of the last evening with him. Early on the morning of February 10, 1567, the house was blown up, and Darnley's body was found near it. Public opinion charged Bothwell with the murder, and it was widely believed, probably with justice, that Mary also was guilty of it. At all events she heaped honors on Bothwell, who succeeded in securing acquittal by a farce of a trial. On April 24, Bothwell met Mary on one of her journeys and made her captive by a show of force—it was generally believed with her connivance. He was married, but he was divorced from his wife for adultery on May 3, and on May 15 he and Mary were married by Protestant rites.

These shameless transactions roused general hostility in Scotland, while they robbed Mary, for the time, of Catholic sympathy in England and on the Continent. Protestants and Catholics in Scotland joined forces against her. Just a month after the wedding Mary was a prisoner, and on July 24, 1567, she was compelled to abdicate in favor of her year-old son, and appoint Moray as regent, while she was herself imprisoned in Lochleven Castle. On July 29 John Knox preached the sermon at James VI's coronation. With Mary's fall came the triumph of Protestantism, which was now definitely established by Parliament in December. Mary herself escaped from Lochleven in May, 1568, but Moray promptly defeated her supporters, and she fled to England, where she was to remain, a center of Catholic intrigue, till her execution for conspiracy against Elizabeth's life, in February, 1587.

Knox's fiery career was about over. On November 24, 1572, he died, having influenced not merely the religion but the character of the nation more than any other man in Scottish history. Knox's work was to be taken up by Andrew Melville (1545–1623), who had taught as Beza's colleague in Geneva, from 1568 to his return to Scotland in 1574. He was the educational reformer of the Universities of Glasgow and St. Andrews and even more distinguished as the perfector of the Presbyterian system in Scotland and its vigorous defender against the royal and episcopal encroachments of James VI, who compelled him to spend the last sixteen years of his life in exile from his native land.

11

The Roman Revival

*I*T HAS ALREADY been noted (see pp. 287–289) that a generation before Luther's breach with Rome, Spain was witnessing a vigorous reformatory work led by Queen Isabella and Cardinal Ximenes. It combined zeal for a more moral and intelligent clergy, abolition of glaring abuses, and Biblical studies for the learned, not for the people, with unswerving orthodoxy, judged by mediæval standards, and repression of heresy by the inquisition. It was this movement that was to give life and vigor to the Roman revival, often, though rather incorrectly, called the Counter-Reformation. Outside of Spain it had very little influence when Luther began his work. Indeed, the decline of the Roman Church was nowhere more evident than in the feebleness with which it met the Protestant onslaughts during the first quarter century of the Reformation, and the incapacity of the Popes themselves to realize the real gravity of the situation, and to put their interests as heads of the Church above their concerns as petty Italian princes. Though Adrian VI (1522–1523) exhibited a real, though utterly ineffective, reformatory zeal, in the Spanish sense, during his brief and unhappy pontificate, neither his predecessor, Leo X (1513–1521), nor his successor, Clement VII (1523–1534), was in any sense a religious leader, and the political ambitions of the latter contributed materially to the spread of Protestantism.

Yet there were those, even in Italy, who were anxious for reform, though not for revolution. Such a group founded in Rome about 1517 the "Oratory of Divine Love." Among its leaders was Gian Pietro Caraffa (1476–1559), later to be Pope Paul IV (1555–1559), of distinguished Neapolitan parentage, who had lived for a number of years in Spain, and had brought from there an admiration for the Spanish reformation, though no love for the Spanish monarchy. Another member was Jacopo Sadoleto (1477–1547); and in close sympathy, though not one of the Oratory, was Senator Gasparo Contarini (1483–1542) of Venice, who was still a layman. Of these, Caraffa was of unbending devotion to mediæval dogma, while Contarini had much sympathy with Luther's doctrine of justification by faith alone, though not with his rejection of the ancient hierarchy. Pope Paul III (1534–1549), more alive than his predecessors to the gravity of the situation, made Contarini, Caraffa, Sadoleto, and the English Reginald Pole (1500–1558) cardinals early in his pontificate, and appointed them, with others, a commission on the betterment of the church, which made a plain-spoken, but resultless, report in 1538.[1]

These men were far removed from really Protestant views. But there were a considerable number whose sympathies led them much further. In Venice they were particularly numerous, though they produced no real leader there. In that city Bruccioli's Italian translation of the New Testament was printed in 1530, and of the whole Bible in 1532. Ferrara's hospitality, under Duchess Renée, has already been noted in connection with Calvin (see p. 352). The most remarkable of these groups was that gathered in Naples about Juan Valdés, (1500?–1541), a Spaniard of high rank, employed in the service of Charles V and a man of devout, Evangelical mysticism. From his disciple, Benedetto of Mantua, came about 1540 the most popular book of this circle, *The Benefits of Christ's Death*. Among his adherents were Pietro Martire Vermigli (1500–1562), whose father had been an admirer of Savonarola, himself prior of the monastery of St. Peter in Naples, destined to be professor of Protestant theology in Strassburg and Oxford; and Bernardino Ochino (1487–1564), vicar-general of the Capuchin order, later Protestant prebendary of Canterbury, pastor in Zürich, and ultimately a wanderer for erratic opinions. Another friend of this group was Caraffa's own nephew, Galeazzo Caraccioli, marquis of Vico, later to be Calvin's intimate associate in Geneva. These Italian Evangelicals were, however, unorganized and without princely support, save very cautiously in Ferrara, nor did they gain following among the common people. In Italy they were an exotic growth; and the same may be said of the very few Protestants who were to be found in Spain.

Pope Paul III wavered for a time between the method of conciliation advocated by Contarini, who took part in the reunion discussions in Regensburg (see p. 337) as papal legate, and that of Caraffa, who urged stern repression of doctrinal divergence, while advocating administrative and moral reform. Eventually he decided for the latter, and his decision became the policy of his successors. On Caraffa's urgent appeal Paul III, on July 21, 1542, reorganized the inquisition, largely on the Spanish model, on a universal scale,[2] though of course its actual establishment took place only where it had the support of friendly civil authority. Before it, the feeble beginnings of Italian Protestantism rapidly disappeared. One of the main weapons of the Catholic Counter-Reformation was thus forged.

Much more important was a revival of missionary zeal which the fresh genius of Spain contributed to kindle Catholic enthusiasm. Viewed from any

[1] Kidd, pp. 307–318. [2] Kidd, pp. 347–350.

standpoint, Ignatius Loyola is one of the master figures of the Reformation epoch. Inigo Lopez de Recalde was born of a noble family in northern Spain in 1491. After serving as a page at the court of Ferdinand, he became a soldier. His intrepid firmness was exhibited when Pamplona was besieged by the French in 1521, but he received there a wound that made further military service impossible. During his slow recovery he studied the lives of Christ, St. Dominic, and St. Francis. Chivalrous ideals still lingered in Spain, and he determined that he would be a knight of the Virgin. Recovered, in a measure, he journeyed to Monserrat, and hung his weapons on the Virgin's altar. Thence he went to Manresa, where, in the Dominican monastery, he began those directed visions which were afterward to grow into his *Spiritual Exercises*. It is a work designed to lead man to the realization of his destiny under God. For the sake of the salvation of his soul and the glory of God he is led to make a choice for Christ, to put off his sins, to assume an attitude of "holy disinterestedness" toward this world in order to use all its goods for the glorification of God. The Christian is led to submit wholly to God and to become an utterly disciplined member of the church, resolved to serve it in obedience. The year 1523 saw him a pilgrim in Jerusalem, resolved to serve Christ as a missionary to the Mohammedans, but the Franciscans who were there maintaining the cross with difficulty thought him dangerous and sent him home.

Convinced that if he was to do the work he desired he must have an education, Ignatius entered a boy's class in Barcelona, and went rapidly forward to the Universities of Alcalá and Salamanca. A born leader, he gathered like-minded companions with whom he practised his spiritual exercises. This aroused the suspicion of the Spanish inquisition and his life was in danger. In 1528, he entered the University of Paris, just as Calvin was leaving it. There he made no public demonstration, but gathered round himself a handful of devoted friends and disciples—Pierre Lefèvre, Francis Xavier, Diego Lainez, Alfonso Salmeron, Nicolas Bobadilla, and Simon Rodriguez, mostly from the Spanish peninsula. In the church of St. Mary on Montmartre, in Paris, on August 15, 1534, these companions took a vow to go to Jerusalem to labor for the church and their fellow men, or, if that proved impossible, to put themselves at the disposition of the Pope. It was a little student association, the connecting bond of which was love to God and the church, as they understood it.

The year 1536 saw them in Venice; but Jerusalem was barred by war, and they now determined to ask the Pope's direction. Ignatius was beginning to perceive what his society might become. Italy had seen many military companies in earthly service. His would be the military company of Jesus, bound by a similar strictness of obedience, and a like careful, though spiritual, exercise of arms, to fight the battle of the church against infidels and heretics. In spite of ecclesiastical opposition, Paul III was induced by the favorable attitude of Contarini and the skill of Ignatius to authorize the company on September 27, 1540.[3] The constitution of the society was as yet indefinite, save that it was to have a head to whom full obedience was due, and should labor wherever that head and the Pope should direct. In April, 1541, Ignatius was chosen the first "general"—an office which he held till his death, July 31, 1556.

The constitution of the Jesuits was gradually worked out, indeed it was not completed till after Ignatius' death, though its main features were his work. At the head is a "general," to whom absolute obedience is due; but who, in turn, is watched by assistants appointed by the order, and can, if necessary, be deposed by it. Over each district is a "provincial," appointed by the "general." Each member is admitted, after a careful novitiate, and pledges obedience to the fullest extent in all that does not involve sin. His superiors assign him to the work which they believe him best fitted to do. That that work may be better accomplished the Jesuits are bound to no fixed hours of worship or form of dress as are monks. Each member is disciplined by use of Ignatius's *Spiritual Exercises,*—a remarkable work, in accordance with which the Jesuit is drilled in a spiritual manual of arms, by four weeks of intense contemplation of the principal facts of the life and work of Christ, and of the Christian warfare with evil, under the guidance of a spiritual drill-master. It was a marvellous instrument that Ignatius constructed, combining the individualism of the Renaissance—each man assigned to and trained for his peculiar work—with the sacrifice of will and complete obedience to the spirit and aims of the whole. It stands as the very antithesis of Protestantism.

Though the Jesuit society spread rapidly in Italy, Spain, and Portugal, it was slower in gaining strong foothold in France and Germany, but by the latter half of the sixteenth century it was the advance-guard of the Counter-Reformation. Its chief agencies were preaching, the confessional, its excellent schools—not for the multitude, but for the well-born and well-to-do—and its foreign missions. Under Jesuit influence more frequent confession and communion became the rule in Catholic countries; and, to aid the confessional, the Jesuit moral practice was gradually developed, chiefly after Ignatius's death, and especially in the early part of the seventeenth century, in a fashion that has aroused the criticism not only of Protestants but of many Catholics. In estimating them aright it should be remembered that these moral treatises do not represent ideals of conduct, but the *minima* on which absolution can be given; and, also, that the Jesuit morality emphasized the universal Latin tendency to regard sin as a series of definite acts rather than as a state or attitude of mind.

Naturally a society thus international in character, the members of which were bound to their officers by constant letters and reports, speedily became a force in political life.

With the establishment of the world-wide inquisition and the founda-

[3] Kidd, pp. 335–340.

tion of the Company of Jesus, the Council of Trent must be classed as an important agency of the Counter-Reformation. That council had a checkered history. Earnestly desired by Charles V, and reluctantly called by Paul III, it actually met in Trent in December, 1545. In March, 1547, the Italian majority transferred it to Bologna; but in May, 1551, it was back in Trent, where the Spanish minority had all along remained. On April 28, 1552, it adjourned in consequence of the successful Protestant uprising under Moritz of Saxony against the Emperor (see p. 341). Not until January, 1562, did it meet again, and it completed its work on December 4, 1563. The voting was confined to bishops and heads of orders, without division by nations, as at Constance (see p. 276). The majority was therefore in Italian hands. That represented the papal wish that definition of doctrine should precede reform. On the other hand, the Spanish bishops, equally orthodox in belief, stood manfully for the Emperor's desire that reform should precede doctrine. It was agreed that doctrine and reform should be discussed alternately, but all decisions had to have the approval of the Pope, thus strengthening the papal supremacy in the church. No voices were more influential in the council than those of the Pope's theological experts, the Jesuits Lainez, and Salmeron, and their influence steadily supported the anti-Protestant spirit.

The doctrinal decrees of the Council of Trent [4] were clear and definite in their rejection of Protestant beliefs, while often indecisive regarding matters of dispute in mediæval controversies. Scripture and tradition are equally sources of truth. The church alone has the right of interpretation. Justification is skilfully defined, yet so as to leave scope for work-merit. The sacraments are the mediæval seven and defined in the mediæval way. The result is ably expressed, but the church had shut the door completely on all compromise or modification of mediæval doctrine.

Though the reforms effected by the council were far from realizing the wishes of many in the Roman Church, they were not inconsiderable. Provision was made for the public interpretation of Scripture in the larger towns. Bishops were bound to preach and the parish clergy to teach plainly what is needful for salvation. Residence was required and pluralities restrained. Seminaries for clerical training were ordered, and better provision for the moral supervision of the clergy. Regulations were enacted to prevent clandestine marriages. A less praiseworthy step was the approval of an index of prohibited books, to be prepared by the Pope, following the example set by Paul IV in 1559. It resulted in 1571 in the creation by Pius V (1566–1572) of the Congregation of the Index, at Rome, to censure publications.

From a Spanish theologian, influential at Trent, Melchior Cano (1525–1560), came the ablest defense of the Roman position that had yet appeared, in his De Locis Theologicis Libri XII, published three years after his death. Theology, he taught, is based on authority. The authority of Scripture rests

[4] Schaff, Creeds of Christendom, 2:77–206.

on the sifting and approving power of the church, which determines what is Scripture and what not; but as by no means all of Christian doctrine is contained in the Scripture, tradition, handed down and sifted by the church, is another authoritative basis.

The middle of the sixteenth century witnessed a change in the prime interest of the holders of the papacy. They were still Italian temporal princes, but the concerns of the church had now assumed the first place. With Paul IV (Caraffa, 1555–1559) the Counter-Reformation reached the papal throne, with the result that many of the abuses of the curia were done away. Rome was a more somber, a much more ecclesiastical, city than in the Renaissance, and the Popes were now prevailingly men of strict life, religious earnestness, and strenuous Catholicism.

The result of all these influences was that by 1565 Catholic earnestness had been revived. A new spirit, intense in its opposition to Protestantism, mediæval in its theology, but ready to fight or to suffer for its faith, was widespread. Against this renewed zeal Protestantism not merely ceased to make new conquests, its hold on the Rhineland and in southern Germany was soon shaken in considerable measure. Catholicism began to hope to win back all that it had lost.

This Catholic revival was also characterized by a large development of mystical piety, in which, as in so much else, Spain was the leader. The chief traits of this religious life were self-renouncing quietism—a raising of the soul in contemplation and voiceless prayer to God—till a union in divine love, or in ecstasy of inner revelation, was believed to be achieved. Often ascetic practices were thought to aid this mystic exaltation. Conspicuous in this movement were Teresa de Jesus (1515–1582) of Avila and Juan de la Cruz (1542–1591) of Ontiveros, in Spain. François de Sales (1567–1622), nominally bishop of Geneva, to whose efforts the winning for Catholicism of the portions of Savoy near Geneva was due, represented the same type of piety, and it was spread in France by his disciple, Jeanne Françoise Frémyot de Chantal (1572–1641). It was combined with extreme devotion to the church and its sacraments. It satisfied the religious longings of more earnest Catholic souls, and the church, in turn, recognized it by enrolling many of its exemplars among the saints.

Catholic zeal went forth, in full measure, also, in the work of foreign missions. These were primarily the endeavor of the monastic orders, notably the Dominicans and Franciscans, with whom from its foundation the Company of Jesus eagerly shared in the labor. To the work of these orders the Christianity of Southern, Central, and large parts of North America is due. They converted the Philippines. Most famous of these Roman missionaries was Ignatius's original associate, Francis Xavier (1506–1552). Appointed by Ignatius missionary to India, at the request of King John III of Portugal, he reached Goa in 1542 and began a career of marvellous activity. In Goa he founded a missionary college, he preached throughout southern India, in 1549 he entered Japan and began a work which had reached large dimensions, when its severe repression was undertaken by the native rulers in 1612. Xavier died, in 1552, just as he was entering China. His work was superficial, an exploration rather than a structure, but his example was a contagious influence of far-reaching force. In China the labor which Xavier had attempted was begun, in 1581, by the Jesuit Matteo Ricci (1552–1610), but his desire to be "all things to all men," led him to compromise with ancestor-worship, a relaxation which missionaries of other Catholic orders strongly opposed. In India the converts were almost entirely from outcasts or low-cast ranks. The Jesuit, Roberto de' Nobili (1576?–1656), began a work for those of high caste in Madura, in 1606, recognizing caste distinctions and otherwise accommodating itself to Indian prejudices. Its apparent success was large, but its methods aroused criticism and ultimate prohibition by the papacy. Probably the most famous experiment of Jesuit missions was that in Paraguay. Their work there began in 1586. In 1610, they commenced gathering the natives into "reductions," or villages, each built on a similar plan, where the dwellers were kept at peace and taught the elements of religion and industry, but held in strict and semi-childlike dependence on the missionaries, in whose hands lay the administration of trade and agriculture. Greatly admired, the system fell with the expulsion of the Jesuits, in 1767, and has left few permanent results.

The rivalries of the several orders, and the more effective supervision of missionary labors, induced Pope Gregory XV (1621–1623) to found, in 1622, the *Congregatio de Propaganda Fide,* by which the whole field could be surveyed and superintended from Rome.

12

The Struggle in France, The Netherlands, and England

THE RIVALRIES of France and Spain, with their political and military consequences, had made the growth of the Reformation possible, and had facilitated the division of Germany between Lutherans and Catholics recorded in the Peace of Augsburg of 1555. Henry II (1547–1559) had succeeded Francis I in France, and Charles V had transferred to his son Philip II (1556–1598) the sovereignty of Spain, the Netherlands, and of the Spanish territories in Italy; but the old rivalry continued. In war, however, Philip II at first proved more successful than his father had been, and the battles of St. Quentin in August, 1557, and Gravelines in July, 1558, forced France to the Treaty of Cateau-Cambrésis of April 2, 1559. That treaty was a reckoning point in the history of Europe. France abandoned the long struggle for Italy. Spanish leadership was evidently first in Europe, and had largely bound France to follow, or at least not to oppose, its interests. Protestantism was confronted by a much more politically united Catholicism than it had yet met. The political head of that Catholicism was Philip II of Spain, methodical, industrious, patient, and inflexibly determined, who saw as his God-appointed task the extirpation of Protestantism, and bent every energy to its accomplishment. The next thirty years were to be the time of chief peril in the history of Protestantism.

The point of highest danger was, perhaps, in the year 1559, when after the death of Henry II, in July, the crown passed to Francis II, whose wife was Mary "Queen of Scots," and by her own claim Queen of England also. Yet even Philip's ardent Catholicism was not willing to see a combination so dangerous to Spain as that of France, Scotland, and England under a single pair of rulers. He therefore helped Elizabeth, an action which he must afterward have regretted (see p. 366).

Calvin's influence had increasingly penetrated France, and French Protestants, or Huguenots, as they were known from 1557, multiplied in spite of severe persecution. By 1555 there was a congregation in Paris. Four years later the number of Huguenot Churches in France was seventy-two. That year, 1559, they were strong enough to hold their First General Synod in Paris, to adopt a strongly Calvinistic creed prepared by Antoine de la Roche Chandieu,[1] and a Presbyterian constitution drawn from Calvin's ecclesiastical principles. Popular estimate credited them with 400,000 adherents. Besides these Huguenots of religion, most of whom were from the economically oppressed and discontented artisan classes, the party was soon strengthened by the accession of political Huguenots.

The death of Henry II and the accession of Francis II left the family of Guise, uncles of Francis' Queen, all powerful in his court. The Guises were from Lorraine, and were looked upon by many of the French nobility as foreigners. Strenuously Catholic, the two brothers, Charles (1542–1574), the "cardinal of Lorraine," was head of the French clergy as archbishop of Rheims, while Francis (1519–1563), Duke of Guise, was the best soldier of France. Opposed to the Guise family were the family of Bourbon, of whom the chief in rank was Antoine of Vendôme, titular King of Navarre, a man of weak and vacillating spirit, and his much abler brother, Louis, prince of Condé. Of the house of Châtillon, also opposed to the Guise brothers, the leader was Gaspard de Coligny, known as Admiral Coligny, a man of sterling

[1] Schaff, *Creeds of Christendom*, 3:356–382.

character and devoted to Calvinism. These high nobles were moved in large part by opposition to the centralization of power in the King. They represented thus the hostility of the old feudal nobility to royal encroachment. Their interests and those of the humbler middle-class Calvinists coincided in a desire that things in France should not continue as they were. The first step toward a revolution was taken when the badly planned "Conspiracy of Amboise" in March, 1560, failed in its attempt to capture the young King and to transfer the government to the Bourbons. Condé would have been executed had it not been for the death of Francis II on December 5, 1560.

The succession of Charles IX (1560–1574), brother of the late King, brought a new party into the confused struggle. The Guises lost much of their power at court, but were regarded still as the head of Catholic interests in France, and were in constant communication with Philip II of Spain. The chief influence about the new sovereign, who was not yet eleven, was now that of his mother, Catherine de' Medici (1519–1589), able and unscrupulous, determined to maintain the rights of the crown by playing off the two great noble factions of France against each other. She was aided by a statesman of broad and conciliatory views, Michel de l'Hôpital (1505–1573), who became chancellor of France in 1560. Catherine now sought a reconciliation of the factions, released Condé from prison, permitted a public discussion between Catholic and Protestant theologians in Poissy, in September, 1561—in which Beza took part—and followed it, in January, 1562, with an edict permitting the Huguenots to assemble for worship except in walled towns.

Rather than submit, the Catholic party determined to provoke war. On March 1, 1562, the body-guard of the duke of Guise attacked a Huguenot congregation worshipping in Vassy. Three savage wars followed between the Huguenots and Catholics, 1562–1563, 1567–1568, and 1568–1570, with short truces between. Duke Francis of Guise was murdered by a Protestant assassin. Antoine, King of Navarre, and Condé died of wounds. Coligny was left the head of the Huguenot cause. On the whole, the Huguenots held their own, and jealousy of Spanish influence helped their cause, so that in August, 1570, peace was made at St. Germain-en-Laye, by which nobles were given freedom of worship, and two places for services were permitted to the Huguenot common people in each governmental division of France, while four cities were put in Huguenot control as a guarantee.

The situation at this juncture was greatly complicated by the course of events in the Netherlands. The sources of unrest in that region were even more political and economic than religious in their origin, though in the struggle religion assumed a constantly increasing prominence. The Netherlands, which had come to Philip II of Spain from his father, Charles V, in 1555, were a group of seventeen provinces, tenacious of local rights, predominantly commercial and manufacturing, and disposed to resent all that interfered with existing customs or disturbed trade. Lutheranism had early entered, but had been largely displaced by Anabaptism among the lowest stratum of the population, while by 1561 when the Belgic Confession was drafted by Guy de Bray,[2] Calvinism was winning converts among the middle classes. The nobility was as yet hardly touched, and in 1562 the total number of Protestants was reckoned at only 100,000.

Charles V, though strenuously resisting the inroads of Protestantism, had largely respected Netherlandish rights and jealousies. Not so Philip II. He determined to secure political and religious uniformity there similar to that in Spain. In 1559 he appointed his sister, Margaret of Parma, regent, with an advisory committee of three, of which the leading spirit was his devoted supporter, Cardinal Granvella (1517–1586), bishop of Arras. This committee practically usurped the power of the old councils of state, in which the high nobles had shared. The next year Philip secured from the Pope a reconstitution of the ecclesiastical geography of the Netherlands, which had merit in that it freed the Netherlandish bishoprics from foreign ecclesiastical supervision, but aroused jealousy, since the new prelates were Philip's nominees and had places in the Parliament, or "States General," thus greatly strengthening Spanish influence. Philip, moreover, used every power to crush "heresy" —a course that was disliked by the middle classes, because it hurt trade and drove workmen to emigration. Nobles and merchants were, therefore, increasingly restive.

Chief among the opponents of these changes were three eminent nobles, William of Nassau, Prince of Orange (1533–1584), born a Lutheran, but now, nominally at least, a Catholic, to be the hero of Dutch independence; and the Catholic counts of Egmont and Horn. They forced Granvella's dismissal in 1564. Philip now saw in them the chief hindrance to his plans. He demanded the enforcement of the decrees of the Council of Trent and a stricter punishment of heresy. A petition of protest was circulated and presented to the regent on April 5, 1556—the nickname "Beggars" given to its signers on that occasion becoming the name of the party of Netherlandish freedom. Popular excitement was intense. Protestant preaching was openly heard, and in August, 1556, iconoclastic riots, opposed by such men as William of Orange, wrecked hundreds of churches.

To Philip these events were rebellion in politics and religion. He therefore sent the duke of Alva (1508–1582), an able Spanish general, to Brussels with a picked Spanish army and practically as governor. His arrival in August, 1567, was followed by hundreds of executions, among them those of Egmont and Horn. William of Orange escaped to Germany, and organized resistance, but it was beaten down by Alva's skill. Alva, however, completed the alienation of the mercantile classes, in 1569, by introducing the heavy Spanish taxes on sales. Meanwhile William of Orange was commissioning sea-rovers, who preyed on Spanish commerce and found an uncertain refuge in English harbors, where the English Government had been driven into a more strenuous attitude of hostility to all Catholic forces, of which Philip was chief, by the

[2] Schaff, *Creeds of Christendom*, 3:383–436.

bull of deposition, issued against Elizabeth by Pope Pius V on February 25, 1570.

In April, 1572, these sea-rovers captured Brill. The northern provinces rose. William of Orange put himself at the head of the movement. On July 15, the leading towns of Holland, Zealand, Friesland, and Utrecht recognized him as Stadholder. Meanwhile, since the peace of 1570, the Huguenots and the opponents of Spain in France had been working for a revival of the older political policy, which made France the rival instead of the ally of Spain. Immediate assistance to the Netherlandish rebels, to be rewarded by accession of some territory to France, was planned, and none favored it more than Coligny, whose influence over Charles IX was now great. To emphasize the reconciliation of parties in France, a marriage was arranged between Henry of Navarre, the Protestant son of the late Antoine of Bourbon, and Charles IX's sister, Marguerite of Valois. For the wedding, on August 18, 1572, Huguenot and Catholic nobles and their followers gathered in the fanatically Catholic city of Paris.

Catherine de' Medici had come to look with fear on the influence now exerted by Coligny over her son, the King. Whether the cause was jealousy regarding her own influence, or fear that the war into which Coligny was leading the King would be disastrous to the French crown, is uncertain. Apparently all that she wanted at first was Coligny's removal by murder. In this she had the hearty sympathy of Henry, Duke of Guise (1550–1588), the son of the murdered Francis, who wrongly charged Coligny with responsibility for his father's death. On August 22 an attempt on Coligny's life failed, and its ill-success carried panic to Catherine. The Huguenots had been alienated without being deprived of their leader. She and her supporters now suddenly decided on a general massacre, for which the Guise party and the fanatical people of Paris furnished abundant means. On August 24, St. Bartholomew's day, the bloody work began. Coligny was killed, and with him a number of victims that has been most variously estimated, reaching not improbably 8,000 in Paris, and several times that number in the whole of France. Henry of Navarre saved his life by abjuring Protestantism.

The news was hailed with rejoicing in Madrid and in Rome, and rightly, if its moral enormity could be overlooked. It had saved the Catholic cause from great peril. The policy of France was reversed. Plans for interference in the Netherlands were at an end. The desperate struggle for Netherlandish freedom was the consequence. Yet the Catholics did not gain in France what they hoped. The fourth, fifth, sixth, and seventh Huguenot Wars, 1573, 1574–1576, 1577, 1580, ran their course of destruction and misery, but the Huguenots were not crushed. Charles IX died in 1574 and was succeeded as King by his vicious brother, Henry III (1574–1589).

A division among the Catholics themselves was developing. There had long been a considerable element which, while Catholic in religion, felt that the protracted wars were ruining the land and permitting foreign, especially Spanish, intrigue. They believed that some basis of peace with the Huguenots should be reached, and were known as the *Politiques*. On the other hand, those who put religion first and were willing to see France become a mere appanage of Spain, if thereby Catholicism could triumph, had been for some time organizing associations in various parts of France to maintain the Roman Church. In 1576 these were developed into a general "League," led by Henry of Guise and supported by Spain and the Pope. Its existence drove the *Politiques* more and more into alliance with the Huguenots, who found their political head in Henry of Navarre, he having reasserted his Protestant faith in 1576.

The massacre of St. Bartholomew shattered the hopes of William of Orange for the speedy expulsion of Spain from the Netherlands. The two years following were those of intensest struggle, of which William was the soul. Alva's generalship seemed at first irresistible. Mons, Mechlin, Zutphen, Naarden, and Haarlem fell before the Spanish forces; but Alkmaar they failed to take, in October, 1573. Alva was recalled at his own request, and was succeeded, in November, by Luis de Requesens (1525?–1576), under whom the Spanish policy was substantially unchanged. But October, 1574, saw the successful end of the defense of Leyden, and it was evident that the northern Netherlands could not be conquered by the forces then available for Spain. In 1576 Requesens died, and the Spanish troops sacked Antwerp, an event which roused the southern provinces to resistance. The new Spanish commander, John of Austria (1545–1578), was able to effect little. Elizabeth aided the revolted Netherlands from 1576. In September, 1577, William was able to make a triumphal entry into Brussels. John of Austria died, a disappointed man, in October, 1578; but he was succeeded by his nephew, Alexander Farnese, duke of Parma (1545–1592), a general and a statesman of commanding talents. Matters went better for the Spanish cause. Parma played on the jealousies of the Catholic south and the Calvinist north. The former united in the League of Arras for the protection of Catholicism in January, 1579; the latter replied the same month by the Union of Utrecht. Protestants left the south for the north by the thousands, many Catholics went southward. Ultimately the ten southern provinces were saved by Parma for Spain, and modern Belgium is his monument. The seven northern states declared their independence of Spain in 1581, and though much remained to be done before all dangers were passed, their freedom was so strongly intrenched that not even the murder of William of Orange, on July 10, 1584, by a fanatic encouraged by Parma, could overthrow it.

During this struggle the Calvinistic churches of the Netherlands had been shaping. The First National Synod had been held outside of Netherlandish territory, in Emden, in 1571. William of Orange had accepted Calvinism two years later. In 1575 a university was established in Leyden, soon to be famed for its learning in theology and the sciences. The Reformed Church of the Netherlands was, like the Huguenot Church of France, Presbyterian in constitution, though its degree of independence of state control was long a matter of controversy, and varied with the different provinces. The severity of the struggle for national independence, the wish to secure the aid of all who were friendly to it, and the mercantile spirit led the Protestant Netherlands to a larger degree of toleration than elsewhere at the time in Christendom. Catholics were not, indeed, allowed public worship or political office, but they had right of residence and employment. To the Anabaptists William of Orange granted in 1577 the first protection in rights of worship that they anywhere received. This degree of toleration, partial as it was, soon made the Netherlands a refuge for the religiously oppressed and added to the strength of the nation.

Yet the death of their wise leader, William of Orange, brought great peril to the revolted Netherlands. They did not feel able to stand alone, and offered their sovereignty first to Henry III of France and then to Elizabeth of England. Both refused; but Elizabeth sent her favorite, the earl of Leicester, in 1585, with a small army. He now became governor-general, but his rule was a failure, and he returned to England in 1587. It looked as if Parma's skilful generalship might reduce the rebellious provinces; but, fortunately, Philip demanded his attention for a larger enterprise. The Spanish King had determined on nothing less than the conquest of England.

At the beginning of her reign Philip had aided Elizabeth for political reasons (see p. 366) but those reasons soon ceased to apply, and Philip became her enemy, seeing in Elizabeth the head of that Protestantism that it was his chief desire to overthrow. The early part of Elizabeth's reign had been surprisingly free from actual trouble from her Catholic subjects. Mary "Queen of Scots" was the heir to the throne, however, and a constant center of conspiracy. In 1569 a Catholic rebellion broke out in the north of England, aided by Spanish encouragement. It was put down. In 1570 there followed the papal bull declaring Elizabeth excommunicate and deposed. In 1571, a wide-spread plot—that of Ridolfi—aiming at Elizabeth's assassination was uncovered. Elizabeth was saved by the new turn of French affairs just before the massacre of St. Bartholomew (see p. 384) and the outbreak of the Netherlands rebellion. Parliament answered by making attacks on Elizabeth's person, orthodoxy, or title to the throne high treason. For the immediate present, however, England had comparative peace.

During Elizabeth's early years the English Catholics had been left by Rome and their fellow believers on the Continent with surprisingly little spiritual aid or leadership. To remedy this situation, William Allen (1532–1594), an able English exile who became a cardinal in 1587, established a seminary in Douai, in 1568, for training missionary priests for England. His students were soon flocking to England. Their work was almost wholly spiritual, but was looked upon with great hostility by the English authorities. The situation was intensified when, in 1580, the Jesuits began a mission under the leadership of Robert Parsons (1546–1610) and Edmund Campion (1540–1581). Campion was seized and executed, though he seems to have intended no political movement. Not so Parsons. He escaped to the Continent, won Allen for his plans, and began a course of intrigue to bring about a Spanish invasion of England, a Catholic rising there, and the death or dethronement of Elizabeth. His work was most unfortunate for his fellow Catholics. Most of the priests laboring in England are now known to have been free of traitorous designs; but it was not so understood, and the English authorities looked upon them all as public enemies, and executed such as its spies could discover. Their work preserved a Roman Church in England, but it was carried on at frightful cost. Elizabeth now sent an army to the Netherlands, in 1585 (see p. 385), while she encouraged a semipiratical expedition under Sir Francis Drake, the same year, which burned and plundered Spanish settlements on the Caribbean and Gulf of Mexico.

In 1586, a new scheme was hatched against Elizabeth's life—the Babington Plot—in which English spies discovered that Mary "Queen of Scots" was personally involved. As a consequence, she was executed, on February 8, 1587, after a good deal of wavering on the part of Elizabeth. Philip now determined on an invasion of England. Its conquest would establish Catholicism and his own mastery there, and make hopeful the reduction of the rebellious Netherlands. For the work he would collect a great fleet which could hold the North Sea, while Parma brought over his seasoned soldiers from the Netherlands. After infinite trouble, the "Great Armada" got away from Spain on July 12, 1588. The enterprise had appealed to the religious zeal of the nation and men of distinction in unusual numbers had enlisted for it. In the estimate of Europe generally it was believed invincible; but, in reality, it was badly equipped and the sailors inefficient. Moreover, the battle in which it was about to engage was a contest between old and new naval tactics. The Spanish plan of battle was that of grappling and boarding. Their guns were light and few, their vessels slow, though large. England had developed swifter ships, armed with far heavier guns, able to avoid grappling, and to punish the unwieldy Spaniards frightfully. On July 21 the battle was joined off Plymouth. Then followed a week of running fight up the Channel, culminating in a great battle off Gravelines on the 28th. The Spanish fleet, hopelessly defeated, fled north, to escape home around Scotland and Ireland. Any crossing by Parma was impossible. While it is a legend that the Armada was defeated by storms, it really fell before the English gunnery and seamanship, though a week later, on its retreat, storms completed its wreck. England was the rock on which Philip's plans of a victorious Catholicism had shattered, and they had shattered for a cause which he could scarcely have understood. In the contest, instead of the Catholic rising which he had anticipated in England, and which men like Allen and Parsons had predicted, Catholics and Protestants had stood shoulder to shoulder as Englishmen against Spain.

While Philip's larger hopes were thus crushed in 1588, he held as tenaciously as ever to the plan of uprooting Protestantism in France. The death of Henry III's brother, the duke of Anjou, in 1584, left the Huguenot Henry Bourbon of Navarre prospective heir to the throne. To prevent this succession, Philip and the League entered into a treaty, in January, 1585, by which the crown should go to Henry of Navarre's uncle, Charles, Cardinal Bourbon, on Henry III's death. In July, 1585, Henry III was forced by the League to withdraw all rights from the Huguenots, and in September a bull of Sixtus V (1585–1590) declared Henry of Navarre incapable of succeeding to the throne. The eighth Huguenot War was the result—that known as the "War of the Three Henrys," from Henry III, Henry of Guise, the head of the League, and Henry of Navarre. Paris was entirely devoted to Henry of Guise. On May 12, 1588, its citizens compelled Henry III to leave the city. The weak King saw no way to resist the demands of the League and its imperious head and, on December 23, had Henry of Guise treacherously murdered. Thirteen days later Catherine de' Medici closed her stormy life.

Henry of Guise was succeeded in the leadership of the League by his brother Charles, duke of Mayenne. Henry III now made terms with Henry of Navarre, and the two were jointly laying siege to Paris, when Henry III was murdered by a fanatic monk, dying on August 2, 1589. But Henry of Navarre, or as he now became, Henry IV of France (1589–1610), was still far from secure on his new throne. A brilliant victory at Ivry, in March, 1590, defeated the League, but Spanish troops under Parma's able generalship prevented his capture of Paris that year, and of Rouen in 1592. Not till after the death of Parma, on December 3, of the year last named, was Henry IV really master. And now, for purely political reasons, Henry IV declared himself a Catholic, being received into the Roman Church on July 25, 1593, though terms were not concluded with the Pope till more than two years later. However to be criticised morally—and Henry's life, whether as a Protestant or as a Catholic, showed that religious principles had little influence over his conduct—the step was wise. It gave peace to the distracted land. It pleased the vast majority of his subjects. Nor did Henry forget his old associates. In April, 1598, the Edict of Nantes was issued, by which the Huguenots were admitted to all public office, public worship was permitted wherever it had existed in 1597, save in Paris, Rheims, Toulouse, Lyons, and Dijon, and children of Huguenots could not be forced to receive Catholic training. Certain fortified towns were placed in Huguenot hands as guarantees.

The same year (1598) Philip II died, on September 13, convinced to the end that what he had done was for the service of God, but having failed in his great life effort to overthrow Protestantism.

The Huguenot Churches now entered on their most prosperous period. Their organization was completed, and their schools at Sedan, Saumur, Montauban, Nîmes, and elsewhere flourished. They were a political corporation within the state. As such, they were opposed by the centralizing policy of Richelieu, Louis XIII's great minister. In 1628, Rochelle was taken from them, and their political semi-independence ended. By the Edict of Nîmes, in 1629, their religious privileges were preserved, but they suffered increasing attack from Jesuit and other Catholic influences as the century went on, till the revocation of the Edict of Nantes, by Louis XIV, in 1685, reduced them to a persecuted, martyr church, to be proscribed till the eve of the French Revolution, and drove thousands of their numbers into exile, to the lasting gain of England, Holland, Prussia, and America.

13

German Controversies and the Thirty Years' War

*I*T WAS the misfortune of Lutheranism that it had no other bond of union between its representatives in its several territories than agreement in "pure doctrine," and that differences in apprehension were regarded as incompatible with Christian fellowship. The original Lutheran conception of a faith which constitutes a new personal relationship between God and the believing soul tended to shade off into a belief which, as Melanchthon once defined it, is "an assent by which you accept all articles of the faith." The result was a new Protestant scholasticism.

Melanchthon, influenced by humanistic thought, gradually moved from his original agreement with Luther to some emphases different from those of his greater colleague. By 1527 he had lost sympathy with Luther's denial of human freedom and had reached the conclusion that salvation is only possible through the co-operant action of the will of man—a view to which the name "synergism" is usually given. By 1535 he was emphasizing good works, not as the price of salvation, but as its indispensable evidence. Regarding the Lord's Supper he came to feel that Luther had overemphasized Christ's physical presence and, without quite reaching Calvin's position (see p. 352), to hold that Christ is given "not in the bread, but with the bread," that is, to lay stress on the spiritual rather than the physical reception. These differences never made a breach with Luther, partly because of Luther's generous affection for his younger friend, and partly because of Melanchthon's caution in their expression, though they made Melanchthon uncomfortable at times in Luther's presence during that reformer's later years. They were to cause trouble enough in the Lutheran communions.

One chief cause of bad feeling was Melanchthon's reluctant consent to the *Leipzig Interim,* in 1548. To Melanchthon many Roman practices then reintroduced were "non-essentials." To Matthias Flacius Illyricus and Nikolaus von Amsdorf, in the security of Magdeburg, nothing could be "nonessential" in such a time (see p. 341). They attacked Melanchthon bitterly, and perhaps he deserved some of their blame. This strain was soon increased by the feeling of the princes of the old deprived Saxon electoral line that Melanchthon by remaining in Wittenberg, which now belonged to their successful despoiler, Moritz, was guilty of desertion of a family which had faithfully supported him; and they magnified the school in Jena, making it a university in 1558, and appointing Flacius to one of its professorships.

Other theological disputes arose. Andreas Osiander (1498–1552) roused the opposition of all other Lutheran parties by declaring, with Paul, that the sinner receives actual righteousness from the indwelling Christ, and is not simply declared righteous. Georg Major (1502–1574) affirmed, in essential agreement with Melanchthon, the necessity of good works as evidences of salvation. In 1552 he was bitterly assailed by Amsdorf, who went so far as to assert that good works are a hindrance to the Christian life. The same year saw a fierce attack on Melanchthon's doctrine of the Lord's Supper by Joachim Westphal (1510?–1574), as crypto-Calvinism, or Calvinism surreptitiously introduced. It is not surprising that shortly before his death, which occurred on April 19, 1560, Melanchthon gave as a reason for his willingness to depart, that he might escape "the rage of the theologians."

The Protestant situation in Germany was soon after further turmoiled by the victorious advance of Calvinism into the southwest. Frederick III (1559–1576), the excellent Elector Palatine, was led by studies of the discussions regarding the Lord's Supper to adopt the Calvinist position. For his territories the young theologians Kaspar Olevianus (1536–1587) and Zacharias Ursinus (1534–1583) prepared the remarkable Heidelberg Catechism in 1562—the most sweet-spirited and experiential of the expositions of Calvinism.[1] It was adopted by the Elector in 1563. But Calvinism had no protection under the Peace of Augsburg, of 1555, and not only Catholics but Lutherans were soon protesting against its toleration.

The disputes in Lutheranism continued with great intensity. In 1573, Elector August of Saxony (1553–1586), having assumed guardianship over the young princes of ducal Saxony, where the foes of Melanchthon were supreme, drove out their more radical representatives. Thus far electoral Saxony, with its Universities of Wittenberg and Leipzig, had followed the Melanchthonian or "Philippist" tradition. Now, in 1574, the same Elector

[1] Schaff, *Creeds of Christendom,* 3:307–355.

August, influenced by his wife, and by an anonymous volume, believed he had discovered a heretofore unsuspected Calvinist propaganda regarding the Lord's Supper, in his own dominions. He had some of his principal theologians imprisoned, and one even put to torture. "Philippism" was vigorously repressed.

Yet this struggle gave rise, in 1577, to the last great Lutheran creed— the *Formula of Concord.*[2] Prepared by a number of theologians, of whom Jakob Andreæ (1528–1590) of Tübingen, Martin Chemnitz (1522–1586) of Brunswick, and Nikolaus Selnecker (1530–1592) of Leipzig were chief, it was put forth, after infinite negotiation, in 1580, on the fiftieth anniversary of the *Augsburg Confession,* with the approving signatures of fifty-one princes, thirty-five cities, and between eight and nine thousand ministers. A number of Lutheran princes and cities refused their approval; but it undoubtedly represented the decided majority of Lutheran Germany. Not as extreme as Flacius and Amsdorf, it represents the stricter Lutheran interpretation. It is minute, technical, and scholastic in marked contrast to the freshness of the *Augsburg Confession* half a century before. The period of Lutheran high orthodoxy had begun, which was to have its classic exposition in 1622, through the *Loci Theologici* of Johann Gerhard (1582–1637) of Jena. Its scholasticism was as complete as any in the Middle Ages. Under this repression, the Philippists turned increasingly to Calvinism, and Calvinism made larger inroads in Germany. To the Palatinate, Nassau was added in 1577, Bremen by 1581, Anhalt in 1597, and part of Hesse in the same period. The electoral house of Brandenburg became Calvinist in 1613, though most of the inhabitants of Brandenburg remained Lutheran. This transformation was often accompanied by the retention of the *Augsburg Confession.* Yet though these German "Reformed" churches became Calvinist in doctrine and worship, Calvin's characteristic discipline found little foothold among them.

Protestantism in Germany reached its flood-tide of territorial advance about 1566. From that time it began to ebb. The revived Catholicism of the Counter-Reformation became increasingly aggressive, led by the Jesuits and supported by earnest Catholic princes like the dukes of Bavaria. Divided Protestantism could not offer united resistance. In Bavaria, Duke Albert V (1550–1579) vigorously applied the principle *cujus regio, ejus religio,* to crush his Protestant nobility and people. The abbot of Fulda similarly attempted the repression of Protestantism in his territories in 1572. Successfully opposed for a time, he effected his task in 1602. Similar Catholic restorations were effected in the Protestantized territories belonging to the archbishoprics of Mainz and Trier. Under Jesuit leadership similar Catholic advances were made in other bishoprics, the inhabitants of which had embraced Evangelical views. The archbishop of Cologne, Gebhard Truchsess, one of the seven Electors, proposed to marry, in 1582, and embraced Protestantism. Little help

[2] *Ibid.,* 3:93–180.

came to him. He was forced from his strategically situated see, and the territory fully restored to Catholicism. In Austria and Bohemia the situation became steadily more unfavorable for Protestantism; and there as well as elsewhere in the empire the Jesuit propaganda gained many individual converts. It was aggressive and confident of ultimate victory. The situation between Protestants and Catholics was constantly strained.

An event of the years 1606–1607 markedly increased this bitterness. The city of Donauwörth was overwhelmingly Protestant, yet Catholic monasteries had been allowed there. A Catholic procession of 1606 was stoned. On imperial command, Maximilian, the able Catholic duke of Bavaria (1597–1651) occupied the city and began a repression of its Evangelical worship. At the Reichstag of 1608 the Catholics demanded the restitution of all ecclesiastical property confiscated since 1555. For this claim they had the strict letter of the law in the Peace of Augsburg; but many of these districts had become, in the two generations that had elapsed, solidly Protestant in population.

Under these circumstances a number of Protestant princes formed a defensive "Union" on May 4, 1608, headed by the Calvinist Elector Frederick IV of the Palatinate. To it Catholic princes, led by Maximilian of Bavaria, opposed a "League," on July 10, 1609. The strong Lutheran states of northern Germany were unwilling to join the "Union," nor was the Emperor in the "League." Had Henry IV of France lived, war would probably have broken out at this time; but his assassination in 1610 and the uncertainty of the imperial succession in Germany delayed it for a time.

Besides the bitter disputes between Catholics and Lutherans, the condition of Germany was, in many ways, one of unrest. Business was bad. The debased coinage caused great suffering, the country was growing impoverished. The enforcement of unity of belief in Protestant and Catholic territories alike was damaging to the intellectual life of the people; while the witchcraft delusion which cost thousands of lives, and was equally entertained by Catholics and Protestants, was at its worst between 1580 and 1620.

The actual outbreak of the Thirty Years' War came from Bohemia. That then largely Protestant land had wrung from its King, the Emperor Rudolf II (1576–1612), in 1609, a charter—the *Majestätsbrief*—granting a high degree of toleration. Rudolf was succeeded, both as Emperor and King, by his feeble brother Matthias (King, 1611–1619; Emperor, 1612–1619), but he was childless, and in 1617 his cousin, Ferdinand of Styria, a strenuous representative of the Counter-Reformation, succeeded in securing recognition as Matthias' successor from the Bohemian estates. Catholic influences were augmented, and in May, 1618, a party of disaffected Protestants flung the two Catholic regents representing the absent Matthias from a high window in Prague. This act put Bohemia into rebellion and began the war. Its commencement was favorable for the Bohemian insurgents, and in 1619, after the death of Matthias, they elected the Calvinist, Frederick V (1610–1632),

Elector Palatine, their King. The same week Ferdinand of Styria was chosen Emperor as Ferdinand II (1619–1637).

Frederick found little support outside of Bohemia, and now Maximilian of Bavaria and a Spanish force from the Netherlands came to Ferdinand's assistance. Under the command of a Walloon general, Jan Tzerklas, Baron Tilly (1559–1632), this Catholic combination overwhelmed the Bohemian forces, near Prague, on November 8, 1620. Frederick fled the land. The *Majestätsbrief* was annulled, the property of Bohemian Protestants largely confiscated, to the great financial advantage of the Jesuits, and the Counter-Reformation enforced with a high hand in Bohemia, Moravia, and Austria. Among those enriched by the acquisition of confiscated property was one destined to play a great part in the further history of the war, Albrecht von Wallenstein (1583–1634). The "Union" was dissolved. A similar repression of Protestantism now took place in Austria.

Meanwhile Spanish troops, under Spinola, had invaded the Palatinate in 1620, and thither Tilly and the army of the "League" soon followed. The land was conquered, Catholicism enforced, and Frederick's electoral title with a good share of the Palatinate transferred to Maximilian of Bavaria in 1623.

Northwestern Germany, where many bishoprics had become Protestant possessions since the Peace of Augsburg, was now threatened with war, and the disasters to Protestantism which had already happened aroused Protestant foreign powers. Nothing effective was done, however, except by Christian IV of Denmark, to whom England and the Protestant Netherlands sent some slight aid. To the Emperor Ferdinand the enmity of the Danish King seemed formidable, and he therefore turned to Wallenstein to raise a new army as imperial commander-in-chief. This remarkable adventurer, born a Protestant, was nominally a Catholic, and now the richest noble of Bohemia. A natural leader of men, he raised an army in which he asked no questions of race or creed, but simply of capacity to fight, and loyalty to himself. He soon had a force of great efficiency.

On April 25, 1626, Wallenstein defeated the Protestant army under Ernst of Mansfeld, at the Dessau bridge over the Elbe, following the beaten forces to Hungary, whither they retreated in the vain hope of making effective stand in conjunction with the Emperor's enemy, Bethlen Gabor, prince of Transylvania. On August 27, 1626, Christian IV of Denmark was beaten by Tilly and the army of the "League" at Lutter. These successes were followed up by the Catholics in 1627 and 1628. Hanover, Brunswick, and Silesia were conquered, then Holstein, Schleswig, Pomerania, and Mecklenburg. Wallenstein found it impossible to capture the Baltic seaport of Stralsund, which was aided by the Swedes, and thought it wise to make peace before the able Swedish King, Gustavus Adolphus (1611–1632), might interfere. Accordingly, Christian IV was allowed, by a treaty of May, 1629, to keep his territories on condition of no further share in German politics.

The Catholics had determined to reap the fruits of their great victories. On March 6, 1629, an imperial "Edict of Restitution" ordered the restoration to Catholic possession of all ecclesiastical property which had come into Protestant hands since 1552, the expulsion of Protestants from territories ruled by Catholics, and no recognition of any Protestants save Lutherans, thus depriving the Calvinists of any rights whatever. The events of the next few years prevented its full execution, but five bishoprics, a hundred monasteries, and hundreds of parish churches were, for a time, thus transferred. Many more would have been had Catholic success continued, and had not the Catholics themselves quarrelled over the spoils. These disputes, and the jealousy of the "League," headed by Maximilian of Bavaria, by reason of the great increase in imperial power which Wallenstein had effected, now led to a successful demand by the "League" that Wallenstein be dismissed. In September, 1630, the Emperor was compelled to part with his able general.

Even before Wallenstein's dismissal an event of prime importance had occurred, though its consequences were not immediately apparent. Gustavus Adolphus of Sweden with a small army had landed on the German coast on June 26, 1630. Two motives induced his interference in the war. He came undoubtedly as a champion of the Protestant faith; but he also desired to make the Baltic a Swedish lake, and he saw in the imperial attacks on the German Baltic seaports an immediate danger to his own kingdom. Should they be held by a hostile power, Sweden would be in great peril. Gustavus soon succeeded in driving the imperial forces out of Pomerania; but he moved slowly, since he had no adequate allies. In January, 1631, however, he entered into a treaty with France, then under the masterful leadership of Louis XIII's great minister, Armand du Plessis, Cardinal Richelieu (1585–1642), by which considerable financial subsidies were granted. Richelieu had resumed the historic hostility of France to the Habsburgs of Spain and Austria, and the ancient French policy of aiding their enemies for the political advantage of the French monarchy, even if those enemies were Protestants. Gustavus' next important and difficult work was to secure the alliance of Brandenburg, which, though Protestant, had been imperialist, and of Saxony, which had been neutral. On May 20, 1631, Tilly captured Magdeburg, the inhabitants being treated with brutal ferocity.

This loss of a great Protestant stronghold was followed by an alliance in June between Gustavus and the Elector of Brandenburg, and in August Saxony threw off its neutrality and joined the Swedes. On September 17, 1631, Gustavus, with little real help from the Saxons, won a great victory over Tilly at Breitenfeld, close by Leipzig. The imperial power in northern Germany crumbled, and the Swedish King marched victoriously to the Rhine, establishing himself in Mainz, while the Saxons took Prague. In his extremity, the Emperor called on Wallenstein once more to raise an army, and in April, 1632, that general was at the head of a redoubtable force.

Gustavus now marched against Maximilian of Bavaria, defeating Tilly in a battle near Donauwörth, in which that commander was mortally wounded. Munich, the Bavarian capital, had to surrender to the Swedish King. Meanwhile Wallenstein had driven the Saxons out of Prague, and marched to meet Gustavus. For some weeks the two armies faced each other near Nürnberg, but the fighting was indecisive, and Wallenstein marched northward to crush Saxony. Gustavus followed him, and defeated him at Lützen, near Leipzig, on November 16, 1632, in a fierce battle in which Gustavus was slain. His work was enduring. He had made the Edict of Restitution a dead letter in northern Germany, and his memory is deservedly cherished by German Protestantism.

The control of Swedish affairs passed to the able chancellor, Axel Oxenstjerna, though the most capable Protestant general was now Bernhard of Saxe-Weimar (1604–1639). In November, 1633, Bernhard captured the important south German city of Regensburg, and opened the line of the Danube to Protestant advance. Meanwhile Wallenstein had remained comparatively inactive in Bohemia, partly jealous of large Spanish forces which had been sent to southern Germany, and partly intriguing with Saxony, Sweden, and France. Just what he had in mind is uncertain, but the most probable supposition is that he aimed to secure for himself the crown of Bohemia. His failure to relieve Regensburg was the last straw in rousing the suspicious hostility of the Emperor, and on February 25, 1634, he was murdered by his own soldiers as a result of imperial intrigue.

On September 5 and 6, 1634, Bernhard and the Swedish troops were badly defeated at Nördlingen, by combined imperial and Spanish forces. In its way the battle was as decisive as Breitenfeld nearly three years before. That had shown that northern Germany could not be held by the Catholics; this that southern Germany could not be conquered by the Protestants. The war ought now to have ended; on June 15, 1635, peace was made at Prague between the Emperor and Saxony. November 12, 1627, was taken as the normal date. All ecclesiastical properties should remain for forty years in the hands of those who then held them, and their ultimate fate should be decided by a court composed equally of Catholic and Protestant judges. No mention was made of privileges for Calvinists. To this peace most of Protestant Germany agreed in the next few weeks.

Yet no peace was to be had for the wretched land. For thirteen years more the war continued as savagely as ever. Its original aims were practically lost, and it became a struggle, fought out on German soil with the aid of German parties, for the aggrandizement of Spain, France, and Sweden, in which France gained most. Ferdinand II was succeeded by his son, Ferdinand III (1637–1657), but the change brought no real alteration of the situation. Germany lacked men of real leadership, the only conspicuous exception being Frederick William, the "Great Elector" (1640–1688) of Brandenburg, but though he succeeded in enlarging his territorial possessions, he was too young largely to affect the course of the war.

At last, after infinite negotiation, the "Peace of Westphalia" was made on October 27, 1648. Sweden was firmly settled on the German shore of the Baltic. Most of Alsace went to France. The long-existing independence of Switzerland was formally acknowledged. Brandenburg received the arch-bishopric of Magdeburg and the bishoprics of Halberstadt and Minden as compensation for surrender of its claims on part of Pomerania to the Swedes. Maximilian of Bavaria kept his title of Elector and part of the Palatinate, while the rest of the Palatinate was restored to Karl Ludwig, son of the un-fortunate Frederick V, for whom a new electoral title was created. More important was the religious settlement. Here the ability of the "Great Elector" secured the inclusion of the Calvinists who, with the Lutherans, were regarded as one party as over against the Catholics. German Calvinists at last secured full rights. The Edict of Restitution was fully abandoned and the year 1624 taken as the norm. Whatever ecclesiastical property was then in Catholic or Protestant hands should so remain. While the power of a lay sovereign to determine the religion of his subjects still remained, it was modified by a provision that where divided religious worship had existed in a territory in 1624, each party could continue it in the same proportion as then existed. Be-tween Lutherans and Calvinists it was agreed that the norm should be the date of the Peace, and that a change of the lay ruler to one or the other form of Protestantism thereafter should not affect his subjects. On the other hand, by the insistence of the Emperor, no privileges were accorded to Protestants in Austria or Bohemia.

Neither side liked the Peace. The Pope denounced it. But all were tired of the war, and the Peace had the great merit of drawing the lines be-tween Catholicism and Protestantism roughly, but approximately, where they really stood. As such, it proved essentially permanent, and with it the period of the Reformation on the Continent may be considered closed.

To Germany the Thirty Years' War was an unmitigated and frightful evil. The land had been ploughed from end to end for a generation by law-less and plundering armies. Population had fallen from sixteen millions to less than six. Fields were waste. Commerce and manufacturing destroyed. Above all, intellectual life had stagnated, morals had been roughened and corrupted, and religion grievously maimed. A century after its close the devastating con-sequences had not been made good. Little evidence of spiritual life was mani-fested in this frightful time of war; yet to it, in large part, and reflecting the trust of heartfelt piety in its stress, belongs the work of perhaps the greatest of Lutheran hymn-writers, Paul Gerhardt (1607–1676). In its earlier years, also, lie the chief activities of that strange and deep Protestant mystic, Jakob Böhme (1575–1624), of Görlitz.

Socinianism

*T*HE REFORMATION age exhibited a number of departures from traditional orthodoxy regarding the person and work of Christ. Though not characteristic of Anabaptists, in general, their earliest manifestation is to be found among such Anabaptists as Denck and Haetzer (see p. 329). Servetus' radical opinions and tragic fate have already been noted (see pp. 355, 356), but this ingenious thinker founded no school of disciples. The chief anti-Trinitarians of the age came from Italy, where reformed opinions took often radical form, and where the scepticism of the Renaissance and the criticism of the later schoolmen often blended with Anabaptist readiness to see in the meaning of Scripture other than the traditional interpretations. Such Italian radicals were Matteo Gribaldi (?–1564), once professor of law in Padua, whom Calvin drove from Geneva in 1559; and Giovanni Valentino Gentile (1520?–1566), who came to Geneva about 1557, fled from punishment for his views there, and, after a wandering career, was beheaded in Bern in 1566. Of greater importance was Giorgio Biandrata (1515?–1588?), who spent a year in Geneva, but found it wise to leave for Poland in 1558, serving as physician to the ruling families of that land and of Transylvania, helping to found a Unitarian communion in the latter region, which ultimately obtained legal standing.

Those who were destined to give their name to the movement were the two Sozzinis, uncle and nephew. Lelio Sozzini (Socinus, 1525–1562) was of a prominent Sienese family and a student of law. His opinions were at first Evangelical, and he lived for a year, 1550–1551, in Wittenberg, enjoying Melanchthon's friendship. Among other Swiss cities, he was well received in Geneva, and settled in Zürich, where he died. Servetus' execution turned his attention to the problem of the Trinity, but his speculations were not made public in his lifetime. His more distinguished nephew Fausto (1539–1604) was in Lyons in 1561 and Geneva in 1562. Although already a radical and influenced, though less than has often been represented, by his uncle's notes and papers, Fausto conformed outwardly to the Roman Church and lived from 1563 to 1575 in Italy. Thence he removed to Basel, till he went to Transylvania, in 1578, at the instance of Biandrata. The next year saw him in Poland, where he lived till his death in 1604.

Thanks to the labors of Fausto Sozzini and others in Poland the party gained considerable foothold, and expressed its belief effectively in the Racovian Catechism, on which Fausto had labored, published in 1605, in Rakow, the city from which it took its name and in which these "Polish Brethren" had their headquarters. The catechism is a remarkable combination of rationalistic reasoning and a hard supernaturalism. The basis of truth is the Scriptures, but confidence in the New Testament is based primarily on the miracles by which its promulgation was accompanied and especially by the crowning miracle of the resurrection. The New Testament, thus supernaturally attested, guarantees the Old Testament. The purpose of both is to show to man's understanding the path to eternal life. Though there may be in them matters above reason, there is nothing of value contrary to reason. The only faith that they demand is belief that God exists and is a recompenser and a judge. Man is by nature mortal and could not find the way to eternal life of himself. Hence God gave him the Scripture and the life and example of Christ. Christ was a man, but one who lived a life of peculiar and exemplary obedience, filled with divine wisdom, and was therefore rewarded with a resurrection and a kind of delegated divinity, so that He is now a hearer of prayer. The Christian life consists in joy in God, prayer and thanksgiving, renunciation of the world, humility and patient endurance. Its consequences are forgiveness of sins and eternal life. Baptism and the Lord's Supper are to be retained as commanded by Christ and possessing a certain symbolic value. Man's essential freedom is asserted, and original sin and predestination denied.

The most successful portion of the Socinian polemic was its attack on the satisfaction theory of the atonement, which the reformers had universally accepted. Satisfaction is no demand of God's nature. Forgiveness and satisfaction are mutually exclusive conceptions. It is absolute injustice that the sins of the guilty be punished on the person of the innocent. Christ's death is a great example of the obedience which every Christian should, if necessary, manifest; but that obedience was no greater than He owed for Himself, and He could not transfer its value to others. Could it be so transferred, in so far as a man felt himself thereby relieved from moral effort for righteousness, character would thereby be weakened.

The relation of Socinianism to the later Scholasticism, especially that of Scotus, is undoubted; but unlike that mediaeval system, it rejected all authority of the church and found its source in the Scriptures, interpreted by reason. It rebelled against the prevailing views of human inability and total depravity. It did not a little to free religion from the bondage of dogma and to favor the unprejudiced study of Scripture; but it had almost no conception of what religion meant to Paul, Augustine, or Luther—a new, vital personal relationship between the believing soul and God through Christ.

Suppressed, largely through the efforts of the Jesuits in Poland, Socinianism found some supporters in the Netherlands and even more in England, where it was to have no little influence.

15

Arminianism

THE RIGOR of Calvinism produced a reaction, especially in Holland, where humanistic traditions had never died out and where Anabaptism was widely spread. It manifested itself in an emphasis on the more practical aspects of religion, a disinclination toward sharp creedal definitions, and a more tolerant attitude. Such a thinker was the Dutch scholar Dirck Coornhert (1522–1590); but it came to its fullest expression in the work of Jacobus Arminius (1560–1609) and his disciples.

Arminius, whose relatives were killed in the Netherland struggle for independence, was educated by friends at the University of Leyden, from 1576 to 1582. He was then sent to Geneva at the expense of the merchant's guild of Amsterdam. In 1588, he entered on a pastorate in Amsterdam, winning distinction as a preacher and pastor of irenic spirit. In 1603 he was chosen to succeed the eminent Franz Junius (1545–1602), as professor of theology in Leyden, where he remained till his death. Though indisposed to controversy, he was appointed in 1589 to reply to Coornhert and to defend the "supralapsarian" position against two ministers of Delft. The discussion last named had to do with the order of the divine purposes. Did God "decree" election and reprobation, and then permit the fall as a means by which the decree could be carried out (*supra lapsum*)? Or did He foresee and permit that man would fall, and then decree election as the method of saving some (*infra lapsum*)? As he studied the questions involved, Arminius came to doubt the whole doctrine of unconditional predestination and to ascribe to man a freedom, which, however congenial to Melanchthon (see p. 389), had no place in pure Calvinism. A bitter controversy sprang up between Arminius and his supralapsarian colleague in the university, Franz Gomarus (1563–1641), and soon the Protestant Netherlands were widely involved.

After Arminius' death, in 1609, the leadership of the party was taken by the court preacher Johan Wtenbogaert (1557–1644) and by Simon Episcopius (1583–1643), Arminius' friend and pupil, and soon to be professor of theology in Leyden. By them "Arminian" views were systematized and developed, and both opposed the current emphasis on minutiæ of doctrine, viewing Christianity primarily as a force for moral transformation. In 1610, they and other sympathizers to the number of forty-one, at the instance of the eminent Dutch statesman, Johan van Oldenbarneveldt (1547–1619), a lover of religious toleration, drew up a statement of their faith called the "Remonstrance," [1] from which the party gained the name "Remonstrants." Over against the Calvinist doctrine of absolute predestination, it taught a predestination based on divine foreknowledge of the use men would make of the means of grace. Against the doctrine that Christ died for the elect only, it asserted that He died for all, though none receive the benefits of His death except believers. It was at one with Calvinism in denying the ability of men to do anything really good of themselves—all is of divine grace. Hence the Arminians were not Pelagians (see p. 168). In opposition to the Calvinist doctrine of irresistible grace, they taught that grace may be rejected, and they declared uncertainty regarding the Calvinist teaching of perseverance, holding it possible that men may lose grace once received.

All the Protestant Netherlands were speedily filled with conflict. The vast majority of the people were Calvinists, and that view had the support of the Stadholder Maurice (1588–1625). The Remonstrants were favored by Oldenbarneveldt, the leader of the province of Holland, and by the great jurist and historian, the founder of international law, Hugo Grotius (1583–1645). The dispute soon became involved in politics. The Netherlands were divided between the supporters of "states rights," which included the wealthier merchant classes and of which Oldenbarneveldt and Grotius were leaders, and the national party of which Maurice was the head. The national party now wished a national synod to decide the controversy. The province of Holland, under Oldenbarneveldt, held that each province could decide its religious affairs and resisted the proposal. Maurice, by a *coup d'état* in July, 1618, overthrew the "states-rights" party. Oldenbarneveldt, in spite of his great services, was beheaded on May 13, 1619, and Grotius condemned to life imprisonment, from which he escaped in 1621.

Meanwhile a national synod, called by the states-general, held session in Dort from November 13, 1618, to May 9, 1619. Besides representatives from the Netherlands, delegates from England, the Palatinate, Hesse, Bremen, and Switzerland shared in its proceedings. By the synod of Dort, Arminianism was condemned and "canons," aggressively Calvinistic in tone, adopted, which, together with the Heidelberg Catechism, and the Belgic Confession (see pp. 383, 390) became the doctrinal basis of the Dutch Church.[2] Not so extreme as individual Calvinists—it did not adopt Gomarus's supralapsarian views—the synod of Dort reached the high-water mark of Calvinistic creed-making.

Immediately after the synod of Dort the Remonstrants were banished, but on the death of Maurice, in 1625, the measures against them became dead letters. They returned, though they were not to receive official recognition till 1795. In the Netherlands the party grew slowly, and still exists. Its type of

---

[1] Schaff, *Creeds of Christendom*, 3:545–549.   [2] Schaff, *Creeds of Christendom*, 3:550–597.

piety in the home land was prevailingly intellectual and ethical, and was somewhat affected by Socinianism. Arminianism was to have even greater influence in England than in its home land, and was to prove, in the person of John Wesley, its possibility of association with as warm-hearted and emotional a type of piety as any interpretation of Christian truth can exhibit.

Out of this controversy there emerged from the pen of Grotius, in 1617, an important theory of the atonement. The view of Anselm had looked upon Christ's death as the satisfaction of the injured divine honor (see p. 239). The reformers had viewed it as the payment of penalty for sin to outraged divine justice on behalf of those for whom Christ died, and had represented the exaction of penalty as a fundamental demand of God's nature, who may be merciful but must be just. To Calvinistic conception, Christ's sacrifice was sufficient for all, but efficient only for the elect in whose behalf He died. The Socinians had subjected these views to a radical criticism, denying that God's nature demanded punishment, or that the penalty due to one could justly be met by the sufferings of another (see p. 398). To the Socinian criticism Grotius now replied. God is a great moral ruler. Sin is an offense against His law. Like a wise earthly governor He may pardon if He chooses; but to pardon without making evident the regard in which He holds His law would be to bring that law into contempt. Hence Christ's death was not a payment for man's sin—that is freely forgiven—but a tribute to the sanctity of the divine government, showing that while God remits the penalty, He vindicates the majesty of His divine government. In that sense the sacrifice of Christ is no injustice. It is the divine tribute to offended law. Like a wise earthly ruler, God may offer pardon to all who will receive it on such terms as He chooses, for example, on condition of faith and repentance. The ingenuity of this theory is undeniable. It relieved the embarrassment of the Arminians caused by their assertion that Christ died for all. If that sacrifice was for all, and not for the elect only, and was a payment of the penalty for sin, why then were not all saved? Grotius gave answer by denying the payment of penalty. He also gave, in reply to the Socinians, a definite reason for the great sacrifice. Yet, of all the theories of the atonement this is the most theatrical and least satisfactory, for the message of the Gospel is that in some true sense Christ died, not for general justice, but for *me*.

16

Anglicanism, Puritanism, and the Free Churches in England. Episcopacy and Presbyterianism in Scotland

QUEEN ELIZABETH'S POSITION, at the beginning of her reign, was one of exceeding difficulty. Her relations to Roman Catholics have been elsewhere considered (see p. 386). With her people far from united in religious belief, with plots at home and enemies abroad, it was only by political maneuvering of extreme skilfulness that she was able to steer a successful course. Her difficulties were increased by the divisions which appeared, soon after the beginning of her reign, among those who accepted her rejection of Rome. These were augmented, as that reign advanced, by the quickened popular religious life which was transforming a nation that had been previously rather spiritually apathetic during the changes under Henry VIII, Edward VI, and Mary.

Elizabeth purposely made the acceptance of her religious settlement as easy as possible. The church, in its officers and services, resembled the older worship as fully as Protestant sentiment would tolerate. All but a fragment of its parish clergy conformed, and Elizabeth was well satisfied to leave them undisturbed in their parishes, provided they remained quiet, though their hearty acceptance of Protestantism was often doubtful and their capacity to preach or their spiritual earnestness often dubious. From a political point of view her policy was wise. England was spared such wars as devastated France and Germany.

From the first, however, the Queen was faced by a more aggressive Protestantism, which did not find her idea of a broad, national, comprehensive church sufficiently "reformed." Many who had been exiles under Mary had come under the influence of Geneva, Zürich, or Frankfort and returned home filled with admiration for their thoroughgoing Protestantism. They were men prevailingly of deep religious earnestness, upon whom Elizabeth must depend in her conflict with Rome. But the Queen believed that, if they could introduce the changes which they desired, they would disturb a situation kept at best at peace with difficulty.

From a religious point of view, the desires of these men are quite easily understandable. For them the Bible was the basic authority, superseding any claim of the church as interpreter or custodian of authoritative tradition. They would purge from the services what they believed to be remnants of Roman superstition, and procure in every parish an earnest, spiritual-minded, preaching minister. In particular, they objected to the prescribed clerical dress as perpetuating in the popular mind the thought of the ministry as a spiritual estate of peculiar powers and hence not consistent with the priesthood of all believers, to kneeling at the reception of the Lord's Supper as implying adoration of the physical presence of Christ therein, to the use of the ring in marriage as continuing the estimate of matrimony as a sacrament, and to the use of the sign of the cross in baptism as superstitious. Because they thus desired to purify the church, these men came to be called the "Puritans" by the early 1560's. In 1563 they attempted to get their reform program through the Convocation of the clergy of the province of Canterbury, the legislative body for most of the Church of England, but lost by a single vote.

Many Puritans had already begun to adopt simpler practices in worship and vestment on their own. Led by Laurence Humphrey (1527–1590), president of Magdalen College, Oxford, and Thomas Sampson (1517–1589), dean of Christ Church, Oxford, both Marian exiles, a vigorous Puritan discussion concerning the use of the prescribed garments was conducted—the "Elizabethan Vestiarian Controversy." Cambridge University sympathized largely with the Puritans. But in this matter the Queen's policy was strongly opposed to modification, and in 1566 Archbishop Matthew Parker issued his "Advertisements," [1] by which all preachers were required to secure fresh licenses from the bishops, controversial sermons forbidden, kneeling at communion required, and clerical dress minutely prescribed. Under these regulations a number of Puritan clergy were deprived of their positions, including Sampson, who was for a time imprisoned.

Among men who had learned in Reformed centers on the continent to feel that any worship for which Biblical warrant could not be found is an insult to the divine majesty, this led to a further position—a question whether an ecclesiastical system which deposed ministers who refused to use vestments and ceremonies that were not delineated in Scripture was what God had intended for His church. Furthermore, as they read their New Testament through Genevan spectacles, some Puritans saw there a definite pattern of church government quite unlike that existing in England, in which effective discipline was maintained by elders, ministers were in office with the consent of the congregation, and there was essential spiritual parity between those whom, as Calvin said, the Scriptures in describing them as "bishops, presbyters, and pastors," "uses the words as synonymous." [2] It was the same conviction as to the essential equality of those in spiritual office that nerved Scottish Presbyterianism to its long fight with "prelacy."

The representative and leader of this development within Puritanism was Thomas Cartwright (1535?–1603). As Lady Margaret professor of di-

[1] Gee and Hardy, *Documents Illustrative of English Church History*, pp. 467–475.
[2] *Institutes*, 4:3, 8.

vinity in Cambridge University in 1569, he advocated the appointment of elders for discipline in each parish, the election of pastors by their people, the abolition of such offices as archbishops and archdeacons, and the reduction of clergy to essential parity. That was practical Presbyterianism, and the more radical Puritans moved henceforth in the Presbyterian direction. Cartwright's arguments aroused the opposition of the man who was to be the chief enemy of the early Puritans, John Whitgift (1530–1604). Against Cartwright's assertion of *jure divino* Presbyterianism, Whitgift was far from asserting a similar authority for episcopacy. To him it was the best form of church government, but he denied that any exact pattern is laid down in the Scriptures, and affirmed that much is left to the judgment of the church. In 1572, Whitgift was able to have Cartwright, who had been removed from his professorship nearly two years before, finally deprived of his fellowship also. Cartwright thenceforth lived a wandering and persecuted life, much of the time on the Continent, laboring indefatigably to further the Presbyterian Puritan cause.

The changes advocated by Cartwright were presented in an extreme but popularly effective pamphlet entitled *An Admonition to the Parliament*, written by two London ministers, John Field (?–1588) and Thomas Wilcox (1549?–1608), in 1572. To it Whitgift replied, and was answered, in turn, by Cartwright. Some Puritans were more moderate than Cartwright, and felt that relatively little alteration of the existing churchly constitution was required. The obnoxious ceremonies could be discarded, the Prayer Book revised, elders instituted in parishes, and the bishops preserved as presiding officers of the churches of each diocese organized as a synod, *primi inter pares*. But the Presbyterian spirit was growing, and in the 1570's various Presbyterian experiments were attempted within the framework of the Establishment. Meetings of ministers and devout laymen for preaching and discussion, called "prophesyings," were undertaken. In some cases—first at Wandsworth near London in 1572—congregations voluntarily organized themselves into a kind of parochial presbytery. The Presbyterian position was advanced by the publication in 1574 of *A Full and Plain Declaration of Ecclesiastical Discipline* by a former Cambridge scholar, Walter Travers (1548?–1635). All this was aided by the succession to the archbishopric of Canterbury, on Parker's death, in 1576, of Edmund Grindal (1519?–1583), who sympathized with the Puritans and was suspended for his conscientious objections to the Queen's orders to forbid the prophesyings.

Cartwright and his fellow Puritans opposed all separation from the Church of England. Their thought was to introduce as much of Puritan discipline and practice as possible, and wait for its further reformation by the government. Such a hope did not seem vain. Within a generation, the constitution and worship of the church of the land had been four times altered. Might it not soon be changed for a fifth time into what the Puritans deemed a more Scriptural model? They would agitate and wait. This remained the program of the Puritans generally.

There were some, however, to whom this delay seemed unjustifiable. They would establish what they conceived to be Scriptural at once. These were the Separatists, among whom proponents of congregational polity appeared. On June 19, 1567, the authorities in London seized and imprisoned some of the members of such a Separatist congregation, assembled for worship ostensibly to celebrate a wedding. This company believed it could no longer freely follow the Word of God within the framework of the Church of England, and had chosen its own officers, with Richard Fitz as minister. Besides this "Plumbers' Hall" group there were other non-conformist bodies, but in the early Puritan period separatist activities were of a fugitive and temporary character.

The first really conspicuous advocate of Separatist views in England was Robert Browne (1550–1633), a student in Cambridge in the troublous time of Cartwright's brief professorship, and a graduate there in 1572. At first an advanced Presbyterian Puritan, he came to adopt Separatist principles by about 1580, and in connection with a friend, Robert Harrison, founded an independent gathered congregation in Norwich in 1581. As a result of his preaching he found himself several times in prison. He and the majority of his congregation sought safety in Middelburg, in the Netherlands. Here in Middelburg Browne had printed, in 1582, a substantial volume containing three treatises. One, directed against the Puritans who would remain in the Church of England, bears its burden in its title: *A Treatise of Reformation without Tarying for anie, and of the Wickednesse of those Preachers which will not reforme . . . till the Magistrate commaunde and compell them.* Another, *A Booke which sheweth the Life and Manners of all true Christians,* pictured the true church as composed of believers gathered together of their own volition. According to Browne, the only church is a local body of experiential believers in Christ, united to Him and to one another by a voluntary covenant. Such a church has Christ as its immediate head, and is ruled by officers and laws of His appointment. Each is self-governing and chooses a pastor, a teacher, elders, deacons, and widows, whom the New Testament designates; but each member has responsibility for the welfare of the whole. No church has authority over any other, but each owes to other brotherly helpfulness.

Browne's congregational approach resembles Anabaptist views (see p. 330) at certain points. But there was no organized Anabaptist effort in England until the next century; Browne displayed no conscious indebtedness to the Anabaptists, nor did he reject infant baptism. English separatism arose out of the Puritan movement chiefly. Browne did not remain its champion very long. His stay in Holland was brief. His church was turbulent and after a period in Scotland he returned to England, where he conformed, outwardly at least, to the Established Church in October, 1585, and spent his long remaining life, from 1591 to 1633, in its ministry.

Meanwhile, under Grindal's archbishopric, many of the main body of Puritan ministers, who remained within the Established Church, ceased to use the Prayer Book in whole or in part. Stress was placed on the establishment of "Holy Discipline"—Walter Travers prepared a second work on this theme as a guide for Puritan practice. Grindal was succeeded, however, from 1583 to 1604, in the see of Canterbury by Whitgift. A Calvinist in theology, he was a martinet in discipline, and in this had the hearty support of the Queen, who was implacably hostile to the Puritan movement. He promptly issued articles enjoining full approval and use of the Prayer Book, prescribing clerical dress, and forbidding all private religious meetings.[3] Thenceforth the hand of repression rested heavily on the Puritans. This hostility was embittered by the secret publication of a telling satire against the bishops, coarse and unfair, but extremely witty and exasperating, plainly of Puritan origin, though disliked by the Puritans generally. Issued in 1588–1589, and known as the "Martin Marprelate Tracts," their authorship has never been fully ascertained, though probabilities point to Job Throckmorton (1545–1601), a Puritan layman.

Puritan and Separatist assertion of the divine character of their systems was now rapidly strengthening a change of attitude in the leaders of their opponents, the Anglicans. In his sermon at Paul's Cross, in London, in 1589, Richard Bancroft (1544–1610), to be Whitgift's successor as archbishop, not merely denounced Puritanism, but affirmed a *jure divino* right for episcopacy. Adrian Saravia (1531–1613), a Walloon theologian domiciled in England, advocated the same view a year later, as did Thomas Bilson (1547–1616), soon to be bishop of Winchester, in his *Perpetual Government of Christ's Church,* in 1593. Less extreme was the learned Richard Hooker (1553?–1600), in his *Laws of Ecclesiastical Polity,* of 1594 and 1597. He believed that episcopacy was grounded in Scripture, but his chief argument in its favor was its essential reasonableness, over against the extreme Biblicism of the Puritans. The foundations of a high-church party had been laid.

The repression of Puritanism and Separatism was greatly aided by the court of the High Commission. From Henry VIII's time it had been a favorite royal expedient to control ecclesiastical affairs or persons by commissions appointed to investigate and adjudicate without being bound by the ordinary processes of law. The system was a gradual growth. Elizabeth developed it, and made it more permanent; but it did not become thoroughly effective as an Ecclesiastical Commission till Bancroft had become one of its members in 1587. By 1592 it had fully attained its powers. The presumption of guilt was against the accused, and the nature of proof was undefined. It could examine

[3] Gee and Hardy, pp. 481–484.

and imprison anywhere in England, and had become the right arm of episcopal authority.

Separatism had waned after Browne's return to the Church of England,
but soon reappeared. In 1587 Henry Barrow (1550?–1593), a lawyer of London, and John Greenwood (?–1593), a clergyman, were arrested for holding
Separatist meetings in London. From their prison they smuggled manuscripts
which appeared as printed treatises in Holland, attacking Anglicans and
Puritans alike, and advocating strict Separatist principles more radical than
those of Browne. A number were won, including Francis Johnson (1562–
1618), a Puritan minister. In 1592 a Separatist congregation was formally
organized in London with Johnson as pastor and Greenwood as teacher. On
April 6 of the next year Barrow and Greenwood were hanged for denying the
Queen's supremacy in ecclesiastical matters. The same year Parliament passed
a statute proclaiming banishment against all who challenged the Queen's
ecclesiastical authority, refused to go to church, or were present at some "conventicle" where other than the lawful worship was employed.[4] Under its
terms most of the London congregation were compelled to seek refuge in
Amsterdam, where Johnson, after release from prison, continued as their
pastor while Henry Ainsworth (1571–1623) became their teacher.

The closing years of Elizabeth's reign also saw the beginnings of a reaction from the dominant Calvinism. By 1595 a controversy broke out in Cambridge, where Peter Baro (1534–1599) had been advocating the liberal doctrines of Arminius. This discussion led to the publication, under Whitgift's
auspices, of the strongly Calvinistic "Lambeth Articles"; [5] but the tendency
to criticise Calvinism, thus started, increased, and thorough opposition to
Puritanism was to become more and more characteristic of the Anglican party.

Elizabeth's long reign ended on March 24, 1603. She was succeeded by
Mary "Queen of Scots'" son, James I (1603–1625), who had already held
the Scottish throne since 1567 as James VI. All religious parties in England
looked with hope to his accession, the Catholics because of his parentage, the
Presbyterian Puritans by reason of his Presbyterian education, and the Anglicans on account of his high conceptions of divine right and his hostility to
Presbyterian rule, which had developed in his long struggles to maintain the
power of the crown in Scotland. Only the Anglicans read his character correctly. "No bishop, no King," was his favorite expression. In claim and action
he was no more arbitrary than Elizabeth, but the country would bear much
from a popular and admired ruler which it resented from a disliked, undig-
nified, and unrepresentative sovereign.

On his way to London, in April, 1603, James I was presented with the
"Millenary Petition," [6] so-called because it professed to represent more than

[4] Gee and Hardy, pp. 492–498.   [5] Schaff, *Creeds of Christendom*, 3:523.
[6] Gee and Hardy, pp. 508–511.

a thousand Englishmen, though no signatures were attached. It was a very moderate statement of the Puritan desires. As a consequence, a conference was held at Hampton Court, in January, 1604, between bishops and Puritans, in the royal presence. The leading Anglican disputant, besides the King himself, was Bancroft, now bishop of London. No changes of importance desired by the Puritans were granted, except a new translation of the Bible, which resulted in the "Authorized" or "King James Version" of 1611. They were ordered to conform. This Anglican victory was followed by the enactment by convocation, with royal approval, in 1604, of a series of canons elevating into church law many of the declarations and practices against which the Puritans had objected. The leading spirit here was Bancroft, who was soon to succeed Whitgift in the see of Canterbury (1604–1610). The Puritans were now thoroughly alarmed, but Bancroft was more considerate in government than his declarations and previous conduct would have prophesied, and only a relatively small number of ministers were actually deprived. Anglicanism was gaining strength, also, from a gradual improvement in the education and zeal of its clergy, which Whitgift and Bancroft did much to foster —a conspicuous example being the learned, saintly, and eloquent Lancelot Andrewes (1555–1626), who became bishop of Chichester in 1605.

Bancroft's successor as archbishop was George Abbot (1611–1633), a man of narrow sympathies and strong Calvinism, unpopular with the mass of the clergy, and himself in practical disgrace in the latter part of his episcopate. The loss of such strong hands as those of Whitgift and Bancroft was felt by the Anglicans, and under these circumstances, not only Puritanism but Separatism made decided progress.

A Separatist movement of far-reaching ultimate consequences had its beginnings early in the reign of James I when John Smyth (?–1612), a former clergyman of the establishment, adopted Separatist principles and became pastor of a gathered congregation at Gainsborough. Soon adherents were secured in the adjacent rural districts, and a second congregation gathered in the home of William Brewster (1560?–1644) at Scrooby. Of this Scrooby body William Bradford (1590–1657) was a youthful member. It enjoyed the leadership of the learned and sweet-tempered John Robinson (1575?–1625), like Smyth a former clergyman of the Church of England, and like him led to believe Separatism the only logical step. The hand of opposition being heavy upon them, the members of the Gainsborough congregation, led by Smyth, were self-exiled to Amsterdam, probably in 1608. The Scrooby congregation, under Robinson and Brewster's leadership, followed the same road to Holland, settling finally in Leyden in 1609.

At Amsterdam Smyth engaged in controversy with Francis Johnson, and on the basis of his own study of the New Testament became convinced that the apostolic method of admitting members to church fellowship was by baptism on profession of repentance towards God and faith in Christ. In 1608 or 1609 he therefore baptized himself by pouring, and then the others of his church, forming the first English Baptist church, though on Dutch soil. Smyth also became an Arminian, believing that Christ died not only for the elect but for all mankind. His new emphases brought him close to the Anabaptist position, and some of his congregation finally did affiliate with the Dutch Mennonites, though Smyth himself died of tuberculosis in 1612 before the transfer had been completed. A remnant of his congregation, however, clung to the English Baptist position under the leadership of Thomas Helwys (1550?–1616?) and John Murton (?–1625?). They returned to England in 1611 or 1612, becoming the first permanent Baptist congregation on English soil. Arminian in viewpoint, they were known therefore as "General Baptists." They were ardent champions of religious toleration.

In these same years a new Puritan position was shaped by Henry Jacob (1563–1624), who had been a member of Robinson's congregation in Leyden, William Ames (1576–1633), prominent theologian exiled to Holland, and William Bradshaw (1571–1618), leading Puritan writer. These men enunciated the Independent, or non-separatist Congregational position, from which modern Congregationalism has directly stemmed. Striving to avoid separation from the Church of England, they worked toward a nation-wide system of established Congregational churches. Henry Jacob founded a church in Southwark in 1616, the first Congregational church to remain in continuous existence.

In the 1630's, however, a small group from Jacob's church became convinced that believers' baptism was the Scriptural norm. Separating from Jacob's congregation, they started a second Baptist line in England, called the "Particular" or Calvinistic Baptists because they believed in particular or restricted atonement, confined to the elect. By them immersion was adopted as the proper mode of baptism about 1641, and thence spread to all English Baptists.

The chief event in the history of the congregation at Leyden was the decision to send its more active minority to America. Robinson, who had been largely won to the non-separatist Congregational position by Jacob and Ames, reluctantly stayed with the majority. In 1620, after much tiresome negotiation, the "Pilgrim Fathers" crossed the Atlantic in the *Mayflower,* under the spiritual leadership of their "elder," William Brewster. On December 21 they laid the foundations of the colony of Plymouth, of which William Bradford was soon to be the wise and self-forgetful governor. Congregationalism was thus planted in New England.

Meanwhile under Abbot's less vigorous government, Puritanism was developing its "lectureships," the successors of the old-time "prophesyings." In parishes where the legal incumbent was hostile, or unwilling, or unable to preach, Puritan money was financing afternoon preachers of strongly Puritan cast. This was a time-tested Puritan device to allow preachers who could not conscientiously administer the sacraments in the prescribed manner to proclaim their message. Puritanism had always laid stress on a strict observance of Sunday, and its Sabbatarian tendencies were augmented by the publication, in 1595, by Nicholas Bownde (?–1613) of his *Doctrine of the Sabbath,* urging the perpetuity of the fourth commandment in Jewish rigor. Much Puritan hostility was, therefore, roused—and that of Archbishop Abbot also—when James I issued his famous *Book of Sports* in 1618, in which he commended the old popular games and dances for Sunday observance. To the Puritans it seemed a royal command to disobey the will of God. The growth of Puritanism was further stimulated by political considerations. The King's arbitrary treatment of Parliament, his failure to support effectively the hard-pressed Protestants of Germany in the opening struggles of the Thirty Years' War, and above all, his ultimately unsuccessful attempts to procure marriage with a Spanish princess for his heir, were increasingly resented, and drove the Commons into a steadily growing political sympathy with Puritanism, all the more as the Anglicans were identified largely with the royal policies. By the end of his reign, in 1625, the outlook was ominous.

Nor was James's policy in his northern kingdom less fraught with future mischief. During James's childhood the Regent Morton, in 1572, had secured the nominal perpetuation of the episcopate largely as a means of getting possession of church lands. There were, therefore, bishops in name in Scotland. Their power was slight. In 1581, under the lead of Andrew Melville, the General Assembly had given full authority to presbyteries as ecclesiastical courts, and had ratified the Presbyterian *Second Book of Discipline.* In spite of James's opposition, the King and the Scottish Parliament had been compelled to recognize this Presbyterian system as established by law in 1592.

Yet James was determined to substitute a royally controlled episcopacy for this largely self-governing Presbyterianism. He had the means at hand in the nominal bishops. By 1597 he was strong enough to insist that he alone had the right to call general assemblies, and his encroachments on Presbyterianism steadily grew. Melville and other leaders were exiled. The year 1610 saw a strong royal advance. James established two high commission courts for ecclesiastical cases in Scotland, similar to that of England, and each with an archbishop at its head; and he procured from the English bishops episcopal consecration and apostolical succession for the hitherto irregular Scottish episcopate. A packed Parliament, in 1612, completed the process by giving full diocesan jurisdiction to these bishops. Thus far there had been no changes in worship, but nine years later the King forced through a cowed General Assembly, and then through Parliament, provisions for kneeling at communion, confirmation by episcopal hands, the observation of the great church festivals, private communion and private baptism. Scotland was seething with religious discontent when James died.

James I was succeeded, in England and Scotland, by his son Charles I

(1625–1649). A man of more personal dignity than his father, of pure family life, and of sincere religion, he was quite as exalted as James in his conceptions of the divine right of Kings, arbitrary in his actions, and with no capacity to understand the drift of public sentiment. He was also marked by a weakness that easily laid him open to charges of double-dealing and dishonesty. From the first he enjoyed the friendship and support of one of the most remarkable men of the time, William Laud (1573–1645).

Laud had been, under James, a leader among the younger Anglicans. A vigorous opponent of Calvinism, he had argued as early as 1604 "that there could be no true church without bishops." In 1622, in contest with the Jesuit, Fisher, he had held that the Roman Church was a true church, and a branch of the Catholic Church universal, of which the Church of England was the purest part. In many respects he was a pioneer of what later was known as the Anglo-Catholic tradition, but it is not to be wondered that both the Puritans and the Roman authorities, to whom such views were then novel, believed him a Roman Catholic at heart. Twice he was offered a cardinalate. So to class him was, however, not fair to his true position. Laud was intent on uniformity in ceremony, dress and worship. He was industrious and conscientious, but with a rough tongue and overbearing manner that made him many enemies. To the Puritans, he became a symbol of all they hated. At bottom, with all his narrowness of sympathy, he had a real piety of the type, though not of the winsomeness, of Lancelot Andrewes. In 1628 Charles made Laud bishop of the strongly Puritan diocese of London, and in 1633 archbishop of Canterbury. To all intents he was Charles's chief adviser also in political affairs after the murder of the Duke of Buckingham in 1628.

The country gentry, who formed the backbone of the House of Commons, were strongly Calvinist in their sympathies, and disposed politically to resent the arbitrary imposition of taxes without parliamentary consent. Charles soon put himself in disfavor in both respects. Under Laud's guidance he promoted Arminians to church preferments. To prevent Calvinistic discussion, in 1628 he caused a declaration to be prefixed to the Thirty-nine Articles, that no man shall "put his own sense," on any Article, "but shall take it in the literal and grammatical sense." [7] Parliament resented these actions. [8] Charles had proceeded to forced taxation, imprisoning some who refused to pay. Roger Manwaring (1590–1653), a royal chaplain, argued that as the King ruled as God's representative, those who refused taxes imposed by him were in peril of damnation. Parliament condemned Manwaring, in 1628, to fine and imprisonment, but Charles protected him by pardon and rewarded him by ecclesiastical advancement, ultimately by a bishopric. Questions of royal right to imprison without statement of cause, and of taxation, as well as of religion, embittered the relations of King and Parliament, and after dismissing the Parliament of 1629, Charles determined to rule without parliamentary aid.

[7] Gee and Hardy, pp. 518–520.   [8] Ibid., pp. 521–527.

No Parliament was to meet till 1640. The weakness of the Anglican party was that it had identified itself with the arbitrary policy of the King.

Laud, with the support of the King, enforced conformity with a heavy hand. Lectureships were broken up. Puritan preachers were silenced. The *Book of Sports* was reissued. Under these circumstances many Puritans began to despair of the religious and political outlook, and planned to migrate to America. It was no abstract religious liberty that they sought, but freedom to preach and organize as they desired. By 1628, emigration to Massachusetts had begun. In 1629, a royal charter for Massachusetts was secured, and a church formed in Salem. The year 1630 saw the arrival of many immigrants under the leadership of John Winthrop (1588–1649). Soon there were strong churches about Massachusetts Bay, under able ministerial leaders, of whom John Cotton (1584–1652) of Boston, and Richard Mather (1596–1669) of Dorchester, were the most conspicuous. Connecticut colony was founded in 1636, with Thomas Hooker (1586–1647) as its chief minister at Hartford; and New Haven colony in 1638, under the spiritual guidance of John Davenport (1597–1670). These men were clergy of the English establishment. They had no fondness for Separatism. But as staunch Puritans, they looked on the Bible as the sole law of church organization, and they firmly believed it taught Congregational polity. They were able to do in New England what their fellow non-separatist Congregationalists longed to do in old England—set up their Congregational system under the law of the state as the sole established church. Till 1640, the Puritan tide to New England ran full, at least twenty thousand crossing the Atlantic.

Charles's period of rule without Parliament was a time of considerable prosperity in England, but taxes widely believed to be illegal, such as the famous "ship-money," and enforced religious uniformity, kept up the unrest. It was in Scotland, however, that the storm broke. James I had succeeded in his overthrow of Presbyterianism largely by securing the support of the nobles by grants of church lands. At the beginning of his reign Charles, by an act of revocation that was just, though impolitic, ordered the restoration of these lands, to the lasting advantage of the Scottish church, though the command was imperfectly executed. Its political effect, however, was to throw the possessors of church lands and tithes largely on the side of the discontented Presbyterians. There was now a relatively united Scotland, instead of the divisions which James had fomented to his profit.

Great as were the changes effected by James I, he had not dared alter the larger features of public worship (see p. 410). But now, in 1637, in a fatuous desire for uniformity, Charles, inspired by Laud, ordered the imposition of a liturgy which was essentially that of the Church of England. Its use, on July 23, in Edinburgh, led to riot. Scotland flared in opposition. In February, 1638, a National Covenant to defend the true religion was widely signed. In December, the General Assembly deposed the bishops, and repudiated the whole ecclesiastical structure which James and Charles had erected. This was rebellion, and Charles raised forces to suppress it. So formidable was the Scottish attitude that an agreement patched up a truce in 1639; but in 1640 Charles determined to bring the Scots to terms. To pay the expenses of the war in prospect Charles was at last compelled to call an English Parliament in April, 1640. The old parliamentary grievances in politics and religion were at once presented, and Charles speedily dissolved the "Short Parliament." But in the brief war that followed, the Scots successfully invaded England. Charles was forced to guarantee the expenses of a Scottish army of occupation till the treaty should be completed. Of course, the English Parliament had to be summoned again, and in November, 1640, the "Long Parliament" began its work. It was evident at once that Presbyterian Puritanism was in the majority. Laud was cast into prison. In July, 1641, the High Commission was abolished. In January, 1642, the attempt of the King to seize five members of the Commons, whom he accused of treason, led finally to the outbreak of the civil war. In general, the North and West stood for the King, the South and East for Parliament.[9]

Parliament passed an act early in 1643 which abolished episcopacy before the year was out. Provision had to be made for the creed and government of the church, and therefore Parliament called an assembly of one hundred and twenty-one clergymen and thirty laymen, named by it, to meet in Westminster on July 1, 1643, to advise Parliament, which kept the power of enactment in its own hands. The Westminster Assembly, thus convened, contained a few Congregationalists and Episcopalians, but its overwhelming majority was Presbyterian Puritan. Meanwhile the war had begun ill for Parliament, and to secure Scottish aid the Solemn League and Covenant, pledging the largest possible uniformity in religion in England, Scotland, and Ireland, and opposing "prelacy," was accepted by Parliament in September, 1643, and was soon imposed on all Englishmen over eighteen years of age. Scottish commissioners, without vote, but with much influence, now sat in the Westminster Assembly. The Assembly presented to Parliament a *Directory of Worship* and a thoroughly Presbyterian system of church government in 1644. In January following, Parliament abolished the Prayer Book and substituted the *Directory,* which provided an order of worship substantially that used in conservative Presbyterian and Congregational Churches for generations. It struck a balance between a prescribed liturgy and extemporaneous prayer. Parliament was hesitant to establish Presbyterian government, but finally ordered it in part in 1646 and 1647. The work was, however, very imperfectly set in operation. In January, 1645, Laud was executed under a bill of attainder—an act which must be judged one of vindictiveness. The Assembly next prepared its famous confession,[10] which it laid

[9] For the important documents illustrative of this period, see Gee and Hardy, pp. 537–585.
[10] Schaff, *Creeds of Christendom*, 3:598–673.

before Parliament late in 1646. Adopted by the General Assembly of Scotland on August 27, 1647, it remains the basic standard of Scottish and American Presbyterianism. The English Parliament refused approval till June, 1648, and then modified some sections. In 1647, the Assembly completed two catechisms, a Larger, for pulpit exposition, and a Shorter,[11] for the training of children primarily. Both were approved by the English Parliament and the Scottish General Assembly in 1648.

The *Westminster Confession* and catechisms, especially the Shorter, have always ranked among the most notable expositions of Calvinism. In general, they repeat the familiar continental type. On the question of the divine decrees they are infralapsarian (see p. 399). One of their chief features is that in addition to the familiar derivation of original sin from the first parents as "the root of all mankind," they emphasize a "covenant of works" and a "covenant of grace." In the former, Adam is regarded as the representative head of the human race, to whom God made definite promises, which included his descendants, and which he, as their representative, forfeited by his disobedience for them as well as for himself. The "covenant of works" having failed, God offered a new "covenant of grace" through Christ. The roots of this covenant, or federal, theology can be traced back to Zwingli, though its fullest exposition was to be in the work of Johann Cocceius (1603–1669), professor in Franeker and Leyden. It was an attempt to give a definite explanation of sin as man's own act, and to show a real human responsibility for his ruin. Another characteristic of these symbols is an emphasis on the Sabbath consonant with the Puritan development of this doctrine (see p. 410).

While these theological and ecclesiastical discussions were in progress the civil war had run its early course. On July 3, 1644, the royal army had been defeated on Marston Moor near York, largely by the skill of a member of Parliament of little military experience, Oliver Cromwell (1599–1658), whose abilities had created a picked troop of "religious men." Not quite a year later, on June 14, 1645, Cromwell cut to pieces the last field army of the King near Naseby. The next year Charles gave himself up to the Scots, who, in turn, surrendered him to the English Parliament. The "new model" army, as created by Cromwell, was a body of religious enthusiasts, in which little question was raised of finer distinctions of creed. So long as they opposed Rome and "prelacy," Puritans of all stripes were welcome in it. The Independents emerged as the dominant group, with Baptists and sectaries ever more in evidence. But the rigid Presbyterianism of the parliamentary majority was becoming as distasteful to the army as the older rule of bishops, and Cromwell fully shared this feeling. The army was soon demanding a large degree of toleration. Puritanism had appealed to the Bible and experience, and now men on spiritual pilgrimages—many of them in the army—were demanding the freedom to follow their convictions.

[11] *Ibid.,* pp. 676–703.

This attitude of the army prevented the full establishment of Presbyterianism which Parliament sanctioned. This displeased the Scots. Charles now used this situation to intrigue with the Scots to invade England in his interest, inducing them to believe that he would support Presbyterianism. On August 17–20, 1648, the invading Scottish army was scattered by Cromwell near Preston. This victory left the army supreme in England. On December 6, "Pride's Purge" expelled from Parliament the Presbyterian members, leaving the "Rump Parliament." Charles I was then tried and condemned for his alleged treasons and perfidies, and was beheaded on January 30, 1649, bearing himself with great dignity. Cromwell next subjugated Ireland in 1649, reduced Scotland the next year, and overthrew Charles's son, the later Charles II (1660–1685), near Worcester in 1651. Opposition had been everywhere put down.

Cromwell, though not identified wholly with any one Puritan strand, was inclined toward the Independents. Under his Protectorate a large degree of toleration was allowed,[12] and moderate Episcopalian Puritans, Presbyterians, Independents and some Baptists were included in a broad establishment. Since the beginning of the war, however, about two thousand Episcopal clergymen had been deprived, and had suffered great hardship. Then as in earlier and later changes it is evident, nevertheless, that the great majority of the clergy either were undisturbed or managed to adjust themselves to the new state of affairs. Able, conscientious, and statesmanlike as Cromwell was, his rule was that of military authority, and was, as such, disliked, while the bickerings of rival religious bodies were equally distasteful to a great majority of the people of England who could, as yet, conceive of only one established form of faith. Till his death, on September 3, 1658, Cromwell suppressed all disaffection.

Oliver Cromwell was succeeded by his son, Richard, as Protector; but the new ruler was a man of no force, and practical anarchy was the result. Royalists and Presbyterians now combined to effect a restoration of the monarchy. On April 14, 1660, Charles II issued a declaration "of liberty to tender consciences," from Breda,[13] and on May 29 he entered London. But if the Presbyterians had just hopes of being included in the new religious settlement, they were doomed to bitter disappointment.

Charles II may have intended some comprehension of Presbyterians in the national church. Edward Reynolds (1599–1676), heretofore a decided Puritan, was made bishop of Norwich. The saintly Richard Baxter (1615–1691), one of the most eminent of the Presbyterian party, was offered a bishopric, but declined. A conference between bishops and Presbyterians was held by government authority at the Savoy Palace in 1661,[14] but led to little result. Charles II was unscrupulous, immoral, weak, and indifferent in religion. Little reliance could be placed on his promises. But had he been a better or a stronger man, it is doubtful whether he could have stemmed

[12] Gee and Hardy, pp. 574–585.   [13] *Ibid.*, pp. 585–588.   [14] Ibid., pp. 588–594.

the tide of national reaction against Puritanism. The first Parliament chosen after his restoration was fiercely royalist and Anglican. The Convocations of Canterbury and York met in 1661, and some six hundred alterations were made in the Prayer Book, but none looking in the Puritan direction. In May, 1662, the new Act of Uniformity received the royal assent. By it [15] the use of any other service than those of the revised Prayer Book was forbidden under heavy penalties, and each clergyman was required, before August 24, to make oath of "unfeigned assent and consent to all and everything contained and prescribed" therein; and also, "that it is not lawful, upon any pretense whatsoever, to take arms against the King."

These provisions were intended to bar the Puritans from the church, and as such they were effectual. Some eighteen hundred ministers gave up their places rather than take the prescribed oaths. The Puritan party was now, what it had not been before, one outside the Church of England. Nonconformity had been forced to become Dissent. Presbyterians and Independents, the latter now organized along Congregational lines, were forced outside the establishment. Severer acts soon followed, induced in part by fear of conspiracy against the restored monarchy. By the First Conventicle Act, of 1664, fine, imprisonment, and ultimate transportation were the penalties for presence at a service not in accordance with the Prayer Book, attended by five or more persons not of the same household. By the "Five Mile Act" [16] of the next year, any person "in Holy Orders or pretended Holy Orders," or who had preached to a "conventicle," and did not take the oath condemning armed resistance to the King and pledging no attempt at "any alteration of government either in church or state," was forbidden to live within five miles of any incorporated town or within the same distance of the former place of his ministry. Such persons were also forbidden to teach school—about the only occupation readily open to a deprived minister. These and other acts of the so-called "Clarendon Code" were impossible of strict enforcement, but they led to a great deal of persecution of the Dissenters. The Second Conventicle Act, [17] of 1670, made penalties for unlawful attendance at Dissenting services less severe, but ingeniously provided that the heavy fines on preacher and hearers could be collected from any attendant, in case poverty prevented their payment by all. Yet, in spite of this repression, Dissenting preaching and congregations continued.

Charles II, though a man of no real religion, sympathized with the Roman faith, which he professed on his death-bed, and his brother, the later James II, was an acknowledged and earnest Catholic from 1672. Moreover, Charles was receiving secret pensions from the strongly Catholic Louis XIV of France. On March 15, 1672, with a design of aiding the Catholics and securing Dissenting favor to that end, Charles issued, on his own authority,

[15] *Ibid.*, pp. 600–619.   [16] *Ibid.*, pp. 620–623.   [17] *Ibid.*, pp. 623–632.

a Declaration of Indulgence, by which Protestant Dissenters were granted the right of public worship, the penal laws against the Catholics remitted, and their worship permitted in private houses. To Parliament this seemed an unconstitutional favor to Rome. It forced the withdrawal of the Indulgence, in 1673, and passed the Test Act,[18] which, though aimed at Catholics, bore hard on Protestant Dissenters. All in military or civil office, with few minor exceptions, living within thirty miles of London, were required to take the Lord's Supper according to the rites of the Church of England or forfeit their posts. This statute was not to be repealed till 1828. The repression of Dissent, therefore, continued till the death of Charles II, in 1685.

For James II (1685–1688) it must be said that he saw in the establishment of Catholicism his chief aim, and his measures toward that end were vigorous but tactless. He ignored the Test Act, and appointed Catholics to high office in military and civil service. He brought in Jesuits and monks. He secured from a packed Court of the King's Bench, in 1686, an acknowledgment of his right "to dispense with all penal laws in particular cases." He re-established a High Commission Court. On April 4, 1687, he issued a Declaration of Indulgence,[19] granting complete religious toleration. In itself it was a well-sounding, and from the modern standpoint, a praiseworthy act. Yet its motives were too obvious. Its ultimate aim was to make England once more a Roman Catholic country, and all Protestantism was alarmed, while lovers of constitutional government saw in it a nullification of the power of Parliament by arbitrary royal will. The vast majority of Dissenters, though relieved thereby from grievous disabilities, refused to support it, and made common cause with the churchmen. When, in April, 1688, James II ordered the Indulgence read in all churches, seven bishops protested. They were put on trial and, to the delight of the Protestants, acquitted. James had taxed national feeling too greatly. William of Orange (1650–1702), the Stadholder of the Netherlands, who had married Mary, James's daughter, was invited to head the movement against James. On November 5, 1688, he landed with an army. James fled to France. The Revolution was accomplished, and on February 13, 1689, William (III) and Mary were proclaimed joint sovereigns of England.

The clergy of the Restoration had asserted too long the doctrines of the divine right of Kings and of passive obedience to royal authority to make this change palatable. Seven bishops, headed by William Sancroft (1617–1693), refused the oath of allegiance to the new sovereigns, and with them about four hundred clergy. To them James II was still the Lord's anointed. They were deprived, as Anglicans and Dissenters had been before, and they bore themselves with equal courage. Many of them were men of earnest piety.

---

[18] *Ibid.*, pp. 632–640.   [19] *Ibid.*, pp. 641–644.

They formed the Nonjuror party, part of which took refuge in Scotland, there to make a genuine liturgical contribution to the Episcopal Church in that country.

Under the circumstances of the Revolution of 1688, toleration could no longer be denied to Protestant Dissenters. By the Toleration Act [20] of May 24, 1689, all who swore, or affirmed, the oaths of allegiance to William and Mary, rejected the jurisdiction of the Pope, transubstantiation, the mass, the invocation of the Virgin and saints, and also subscribed the doctrinal positions of the Thirty-nine Articles, were granted freedom of worship. It was a personal toleration, not a territorial adjustment as in Germany at the close of the Thirty Years' War. Diverse forms of Protestant worship could now exist side by side. The Dissenters may have amounted to a tenth of the population of England, divided chiefly between the "three old denominations," Presbyterians, Congregationalists, and Baptists. They were still bound to pay tithes to the establishment, and had many other disabilities, but they had won essential religious freedom. In time they became known as the English free churches. No such privileges as they won were granted to deniers of the Trinity or to Roman Catholics. The effective relief of the latter did not come till 1778 and 1791, and was not completed till 1829.

In Scotland, the Restoration was a time of great turmoil and suffering. The Parliament of 1661 annulled all acts favorable to the Presbyterian Church since 1633. Episcopacy was, therefore, restored as in the time of Charles I. In September, 1661, four bishops were appointed, chief of them James Sharp (1618–1679) as archbishop of St. Andrews. Consecration was obtained from England. Sharp had been a Presbyterian minister, but had betrayed his party and his church. All office-holders were required by Parliament to disown the covenants of 1638 and 1643. In 1663 Parliament enacted heavy fines for absence from the now episcopally governed churches, though even it did not dare introduce a liturgy. Many Presbyterian ministers were now deprived, especially in southwestern Scotland. When their parishioners absented themselves from the ministration of the new appointees, they were fined, and if payment was not forthcoming, soldiers were quartered on them. In 1664 a High Commission Court was added to the instruments of repression. Two years later some of the oppressed supporters of the covenants of 1638 and 1643, or Covenanters, engaged in the Pentland Rising. It was ruthlessly crushed, and the Presbyterian element treated with increasing severity. On May 3, 1679, in belated retaliation, Sharp was murdered. This crime was speedily followed by an armed rising of Covenanters; but on June 22 the revolt was crushed at Bothwell Bridge and the captured insurgents treated with great cruelty. Six months later the King's brother, James—the later James II of England—was practically put in charge of Scottish affairs. The extremer and uncompromising Presbyterians were now a proscribed and

[20] *Ibid.*, pp. 654–664.

hunted folk, known as Cameronians—from one of their leaders, Richard Cameron (1648?–1680).

The accession of James II, or VII, as he was numbered in Scotland, but intensified at first the repression of the Cameronians. His first year was the "killing time"; and the Parliament of 1685 made death the punishment for attendance at a "conventicle." James, however, soon pursued the same course as in England. He filled his council with Catholics, and in 1687 issued Letters of Indulgence granting freedom of worship. As in England, this release of Catholics from penalty aroused the hostility of all shades of Protestants. Episcopalians and Presbyterians were alike opposed; and when William and Mary mounted the throne of England they had many friends in the northern kingdom. Scotland was more divided than England, however. The Stewarts were Scottish, and though Episcopalians disliked the Catholicism of James they distrusted the Calvinism of "Dutch William," whom the Presbyterians favored. The Revolution triumphed, however, and on May 11, 1689, William and Mary became rulers of Scotland. In 1690 Parliament restored all Presbyterian ministers ejected since 1661, ratified the Westminster Confession (see p. 414), and declared Presbyterianism the form recognized by the government. This legal establishment of the Presbyterian Church was opposed by the Cameronian laity, who continued their hostility to any control of the church by civil authority and condemned the failure to renew the covenants, and by the Episcopalians, who were strong in northern Scotland. In 1707 England and Scotland were united into one kingdom of Great Britain; but the independent rights of the Church of Scotland were safeguarded. Under Queen Anne, in 1712, two important acts were passed by Parliament. By one the status of a tolerated communion was given to episcopacy, then strongly intrenched in northern Scotland. The other, destined to be the source of infinite trouble, permitted "patrons," usually the crown or the great landlords, to force appointments of Presbyterian ministers on hostile parishioners (see pp. 463–464).

17

The Quakers

DURING THE TURMOIL of the 1640's and 1650's in England a number of sect movements multiplied. Some of these, like the Levellers and the Diggers, were religio-political sects. Others exhibited a strong millennial emphasis, especially the Fifth Monarchy Men. Mystical tendencies were strong in some, such as the Seekers and the Finders. By far the most significant of these movements, and one of the most remarkable products of the period of the civil wars, was the Society of Friends, or Quakers. George Fox (1624–1691) was one of the few religious geniuses of English history. Born in Fenny Drayton, the son of a weaver, he grew up earnest and serious-minded, having "never wronged man or woman." At nineteen a drinking bout, to which he was invited by some nominal Christians, so disgusted him by the contrast between practice and profession that he was set on a soul-distressing search for spiritual reality. Shams of all sorts he detested. His transforming and always central experience came to Fox in 1646. Out of it came the firm conviction that every man receives from the Lord a measure of light, and that if this "Inner Light" is followed, it leads surely to the Light of Life and to spiritual truth. Revelation is not confined to the Scriptures, though they are a true Word of God—it enlightens all men who are true disciples. The Spirit of God speaks directly through them, gives them their message, and quickens them for service.

In 1647 Fox began his stormy ministry. Since God gives inner light where He will, the true ministry is that of any man or woman that He deigns to use. A professional ministry is to be rejected. The sacraments are inward and spiritual verities. The outward elements are not merely unnecessary but misleading. Oaths are a needless corroboration of the truthful word of a Christian. Servility in speech or behavior is a degradation of the true Christian respect of man to man. Artificial titles are to be rejected— Fox did not deny legal titles like King or judge. War is unlawful for a Christian; slavery abhorrent. All Christianity to be true must express itself in a transformed, consecrated life. The sincerity and spiritual earnestness of Fox's beliefs, his hatred of all that savored of formalism, and his demand for inward spiritual experience were immensely attractive forces. He drew followers from among the various Puritan parties, and from the sects that had proliferated on Puritan soil. By 1652 the first Quaker community was gathered in Preston Patrick in northern England. Two years later the Friends had spread to London, Bristol, and Norwich. Fox's most eminent early convert was Margaret Fell (1614–1702), whom he married after she became a widow, and her home, Swarthmore Hall, furnished a headquarters for his preachers.

In the circumstances of English life such a movement met with fierce opposition. Before 1661 more than three thousand Friends, including Fox himself, had suffered imprisonment. A missionary zeal was early manifested which sent Quakers to proclaim their faith to as far distant points as Jerusalem, the West India Islands, Germany, Austria, and Holland. In 1656, they entered Massachusetts, and by 1661 four had been hanged. There was some explanation, though no justification, for this severity in the extravagant conduct of a good many of the early Quakers, which would have aroused police interference in any age.

These extravagances were made possible by the early want of organization, as well as belief in the immediate inspiration of the Spirit. Fox saw the necessity of order, and by 1666 the main features of the Quaker discipline were mapped out, though in the face of considerable opposition. "Monthly Meetings" were established, by which strict watch could be kept over the life and conduct of the membership. Before Fox died, in 1691, the body had taken on the sober characteristics which have ever since distinguished it.

The laws against Dissenters at the Restoration bore with peculiar severity on the Quakers, since they, unlike the Presbyterians and Congregationalists, made no effort to conceal their meetings, but defiantly maintained them in the face of hostile authority. About four hundred met their deaths in prison, and many were ruined financially by heavy fines. To this period, however, belongs their most eminent trophy and their great colonial experiment. William Penn (1644–1718), son of Admiral Sir William Penn, after inclinations toward Quakerism as early as 1661, fully embraced its beliefs in 1666 and became at once one of the most eminent preachers and literary defenders of the faith. He determined to find in America the freedom denied Quakers in England. After aiding in sending some eight hundred Quakers to New Jersey in 1677–1678, Penn obtained from Charles II the grant of Pennsylvania, in 1681, in release of a debt due from the crown to his father. In 1682 Philadelphia was founded, and a great colonial experiment begun.

The Toleration Act of 1689 (see p. 418) relieved the Quakers, like other Dissenters, of their more pressing disabilities, and granted them freedom of worship.

Period Seven

✻

MODERN CHRISTIANITY

1

The Beginnings of Modern Science and Philosophy

THE QUESTION has been much controverted whether the Reformation is to be reckoned to the Middle Ages or to modern history. Not a little may be urged in support of either position. Its conceptions of religion as to be maintained by external authority, of the dominance of religion over all forms of educational and cultural life, of a single type of worship as alone allowable, at least within a given territory, of original sin, of evil spirits and witchcraft, of the immediacy and arbitrariness of the divine relations with the world, and of the other-worldliness of religious outlook, all link the Reformation to the Middle Ages. So, too, the problems primarily discussed, however different their solution from that characteristic of the Middle Ages, were essentially mediæval. Sin and grace had been, since the time of Augustine, if not rather of Tertullian, the very heart problems of Latin theology. They were so of the Reformation. However Luther himself might reject Aristotle, the older Protestant philosophy was thoroughly Aristotelian. Nor, though monasticism was repudiated, was the ascetic view of the world rejected, least of all by Calvinism.

On the other hand, the Reformation as a religious movement represented a new apprehension of the meaning of Christian faith. It broke the dominance of the sacramental system which had controlled Christianity for so many centuries. Baptism and the Lord's Supper were preserved and highly valued, but they were now regarded more as seals to the divine promises, not as exclusive channels of grace. The Holy Spirit, who works when and how and where He will, uses them for His gracious purposes doubtless, but not to the exclusion of other means. One comes to faith through the written or preached Word of God. Salvation is a direct and personal relationship, wrought by God, bringing the presence of the living Christ to the believer. Faith in Christ, who is experienced as both forgiveness and power, is a gift of God. Man's relationship to God is not one of debt and credit, of evil acts to be purged and merit to be acquired, but a state of reconciliation of which good works are the natural fruits. Nor was the Protestant estimate of the normal relations and occupations of life as the best fields for service to God a less radical departure from the Middle Ages. These characteristics link the

Reformation with the modern world; indeed they have contributed not a little to the shaping of the modern period. Yet if one strikes a balance, and remembers, also, how largely the worldly tendencies of humanism were suppressed by the Reformation, the movement in its first century and a half must be reckoned in great measure a continuance of the Middle Ages. After that, though great religious bodies still used the Reformation formulas and bore names then originating, they no longer moved in the same atmosphere.

To assign an exact line of demarcation for this change is impossible. The alteration was not due to a single leader or group of leaders. It modified Christian thought unevenly but pervasively. The transformation was aided by a great variety of causes. One of these was the steady secularization of culture since the middle of the seventeenth century. The mediæval and Reformation pattern of a church-dominated state and society gave way to the drive for a religiously neutral civilization.[1] Another important factor has been the rise of the professional, mercantile, and laboring classes to constantly increasing educational and political influence. In the Reformation age leaders of thought and sharers in government were few, but in the modern period their number and independence steadily expanded. This growth helped to bring about, and, in turn, was aided by, an increasing toleration on the part of the state, which made possible both the enormous subdivision of Protestantism and the rise of many groups of thinkers not directly associated with, or opposed to, organized religion.

The most potent instruments in effecting this change of atmosphere were the rise of modern science and philosophy, with the immense consequent transformations in outlook upon the universe and upon man's position in it, and the subsequent development of the historic method of examining and interpreting thought and institutions.

The early Reformation period conceived of the universe in Ptolemaic fashion. This earth was viewed as the center about which sun and stars revolve. The Renaissance had revived in Italy Greek speculations of a heliocentric system, and these were elaborately developed by Nicolaus Copernicus (1473–1543), of Thorn in Poland, and published in the year of his death. At the time, they excited slight attention and that mostly unfavorable. But astronomic science made progress. Tycho Brahe (1546–1601), though but partially accepting the Copernican system, multiplied observations. Johann Kepler (1571–1630), a Copernican, developed these into brilliant generalizations. Both were pursuing, though uninfluenced directly by him, the new method of Sir Francis Bacon (1561–1626), by which inductive experiment was made the basis of hypothetical generalization. Galileo Galilei (1564–

---

[1] James Hastings Nichols, in his *History of Christianity, 1650–1950: Secularization of the West* (New York, 1956), believes that the Peace of Westphalia (1648), which ended the Thirty Years' War, is as good a date as any to represent the transition to the new phase in politics, for at that time national and dynastic considerations pushed aside theological and confessional ones. P. 6.

1642), of Pisa, gave to the world the thermometer, developed the pendulum, put mechanical physics on a new basis by experiment, and, above all, applied the telescope to the study of the heavens. To him the real triumph of the theory of Copernicus was due. But its explication, especially in his *Dialogue* of 1632, led to bitter philosophical and ecclesiastical opposition, and he was compelled to abjure it by the inquisition the year following. The real popular demonstration of the Copernican theory was, however, the work of Sir Isaac Newton (1642–1727). His *Principia* of 1687 made a European sensation, showing as it did by mathematical demonstration that the motions of the heavenly bodies are explainable by gravitation. The effect of Newton's conclusions was profound. To thinking men, the physical universe no longer appeared a field of arbitrary divine action, but a realm of law, interpretable, such was the conclusion of the science of that age, in strict terms of mechanical cause and effect. This earth was no longer the center of all things, but a mere speck in a vast realm of bodies, many of infinitely greater size, and all moving in obedience to unchangeable law. Newton himself was deeply religious and much interested in theology, but his scientific findings were used by some as a means of disregarding Christianity.

While science was thus revealing a new heaven and a new earth, philosophy was no less vigorously challenging the claims of authority in the name of reason. René Descartes (1596–1650), a native of France and a devout Catholic, spent most of his active intellectual life in the Netherlands. There he wrote his *Discourse on Method* of 1637, his *First Philosophy* of 1641, and his *Principia* of 1644. To his thinking, only that is really knowledge which the mind fully understands. Mere erudition is not intelligence. The objects and ideas which present themselves to the mind are so involved and so dependent one on another that they must be analyzed and separated into simplicity to be really understood. Hence the beginning of all knowledge is doubt; and no real progress can be made till a basis, or point of departure, can be found which cannot be doubted. That Descartes found, with Augustine, in his own existence as a thinking being. Even in doubting, "I think, therefore I am." If we examine the contents of this thinking I, we find in it ideas greater than it could of itself originate, and since nothing can be without an adequate cause, there must be a cause great enough and real enough to produce them. Hence we are convinced of the existence of God, and His relation to all our thinking. In God thought and being are united. Our ideas are true and Godlike only as they are clear and distinct with a logical clarity like the demonstrations of geometry. Matter, though equally with mind having its source in God, is in all things the opposite of mind. In the last analysis it has only extension and the purely mechanical motion imparted to it by God. Hence animals are merely machines, and the relations between human bodies and minds caused Descartes great perplexities.

Yet, influential as the Cartesian philosophy was, it was not its details which profoundly affected popular thought, but its assertion that all conceptions must be doubted till proved, and that any adequate proof must have the certainty of mathematical demonstration. These two principles were to have momentous consequences.

The influence of the Netherlandish Hebrew, Baruch Spinoza (1632–1677) was strongly on the side of the principles of Descartes. In later centuries both Pietists and Romanticists were to draw on Spinoza's work, with its monistic and pantheistic tendencies. He taught that all is an infinite substance, all is God or nature, known in two modes or attributes, thought and extension, of which all finite persons or attributes are the expression. In the debates of his time, however, Spinoza's contribution strengthened a developing rationalism.

But *how* do men know? One influential answer came from the German mathematician, historian, statesman, and philosopher, Gottfried Wilhelm Leibnitz (1646–1716), for the last forty years of his life librarian in Hanover, and an earnest seeker of the reunion of Catholicism and Protestantism. Unlike Spinoza, who saw in the universe one substance, Leibnitz believed substances infinite in number. Each is a "monad," an indivisible center of force. Each mirrors the universe, though the degree of consciousness in differing monads varies from practical unconscious to the highest activity. The greater and clearer the consciousness, the nearer the monad approaches the divine. God is the original monad, to whose perception all things are clear. All ideas are wrapped up in the monad, are innate, and need to be drawn out to clearness. Here again is the characteristic test of truth, which Descartes and Spinoza had presented. No monad influences another; but all that seems mutual influence is the working of pre-established harmony, like perfect clocks pointing to the same hour. Nor do the aggregations of monads which constitute bodies really occupy space. Each monad is like a mathematical point, and time and space are simply the necessary aspects under which their groupings are perceived. God created the world to exhibit His perfection, and therefore, of all possible worlds, chose the best. What seems evil is imperfection, physical pain, and limitation, or moral wrong, which is nevertheless necessary in the sense that God could not have made a better world. Leibnitz's answer was, therefore, that men know by the elucidation of their innate ideas.

Very different was the answer given by the most influential English thinker of the close of the seventeenth and opening of the eighteenth centuries, John Locke (1632–1704). In his famous *Essay Concerning Human Understanding* of 1690 Locke denied the existence of innate ideas. The mind is white paper, on which sensation writes its impressions, which the mind combines by reflection into ideas, and the combination of simple ideas gives rise to more complex ideas. Locke's purpose was to show that all that claims to be knowledge is justly subject to criticism as to its reasonableness judged by reason based on experience. Thus tested, he finds the existence of God demonstrated by the argument from cause and effect; morality is equally demonstrable like the truths of mathematics. Religion must be essentially reasonable. It may be above reason—beyond experience—but it cannot be contradictory to reason. These views Locke developed in his *Reasonableness of Christianity* of 1695; the Scriptures contain a message beyond the power of unaided reason to attain, attested by miracles; but that message cannot be contrary to reason, nor could even a miracle attest anything essentially unreasonable. Hence, though sincerely Christian, Locke had little patience with mystery in religion. For him it was enough to acknowledge Jesus as the Messiah, and practise the moral virtues which He proclaimed, and which are in fundamental accord with the dictates of a reason which is hardly distinguishable from enlightened common sense.

Locke was no less influential as an advocate of toleration and opponent of all compulsion in religion. Religion's only proper weapon is essential reasonableness. Nor was Locke less formative of political theory in England and America. He had indeed been preceded in this field, in various directions, by Grotius (1583–1645), Hobbes (1588–1679), and Pufendorf (1632–1694). In his *Treatises on Government* of 1690 Locke urged that men have natural rights to life, liberty, and property. To secure these, government has been established by the consent of the governed. In such a state the will of the majority must rule, and when that will is not carried out, or fundamental rights are violated, the people have the right of revolution. The legislative and executive functions should be carefully discriminated. The legislative is the superior. However inadequate and fanciful this may be as a historic explanation of the origin of the state, its influence in the development of English and American political theory can hardly be overestimated.

Of considerable significance in the theory of morals was the view developed by the Earl of Shaftesbury (1671–1713) in his *Characteristics of Men* of 1711. Hobbes had attempted to find the basis of morality in man's constitution, but had discovered there nothing but pure selfishness. To Locke the basis which reason discovers is the law of God. Though entirely reasonable, morality is still positive to Locke, a divine command. Shaftesbury now taught that, since man is a being having personal rights and social relationships, virtue consists in the proper balancing of selfish and altruistic aims. This harmony is achieved, and the value of actions determined, by an inward "moral sense." Shaftesbury thus based right and wrong on the fundamental constitution of human nature itself, not on the will of God. This gave a reason why even one who rejected the divine existence—which was not the case with Shaftesbury—was nevertheless bound to maintain moral conduct. It removed the hope of reward or fear of punishment as prime motives for moral conduct. Atheist and rejector of morality could no longer be considered, as they had generally been, equivalent terms.

These developments in science and philosophy provided the foundations for that movement which characterized the atmosphere of the eighteenth century, the Enlightenment. The Enlightenment was the conscious effort to apply the rule of reason to the various aspects of individual and corporate life. Its fundamental principles—autonomy, reason, pre-established harmony—deeply influenced the thought and action of the modern world and conditioned the atmosphere into which Christianity moved.

2

The Transplantation of Christianity to America

*A*MERICAN CHRISTIANITY is primarily an importation from the Old World. As the colonization of America represented many races of Europe, so the various types of European Christianity were reproduced on the new continent. Where, as in South and Central America, the immigration was of a homogeneous people, imposing their civilization on the natives, a single type of Christianity—the Roman Catholic—has been dominant, however extensively its control has been contested by secularist influences. Where, as in North America, many stocks have contributed to the population, though one form of Christianity was here and there dominant in colonial beginnings, the result has been great variety and necessary mutual toleration, which contributed much to the rise of full religious liberty. In North America especially, where contact between various types has been constant, and where the principle of independence from state control has been dominant since the Revolution, there has been much modification from European forms, especially in church government—what may be called an Americanization. The transition to the new environment produced subtle changes, so that the similarities among American denominations have often appeared more striking than the historic differences. Most of the European churches soon sank their roots into the American soil, thus successfully withstanding the shock of transplantation. While American Christianity should be viewed in a general way as an integral part of the religious developments of European Christendom, the early appearance of its "American" aspects must not be minimized.

An important aspect of the Spanish conquest of Central and South America was the establishment of Roman Catholicism. For the European settlers, secular priests working in the context of elaborate hierarchical structures were provided. The conversion of the native populations was largely the work of the monastic orders, strongly supported by the Spanish Crown (the Portuguese for Brazil). Successfully protesting against the enslavement of the Indians, the monks developed the mission system. In theory an agent of the expansion of church and culture soon to be replaced by normal structures, the somewhat paternalistic system often endured for long periods. Franciscans, Dominicans, and Jesuits were especially active in the conversion of South and Central America.

In the first half of the sixteenth century, Franciscans had undertaken work in Venezuela, Mexico, Peru, and Argentina. They were the first to labor in Brazil. By the end of the century, they had founded Christian communities in what is today New Mexico and Texas. In 1770 Franciscans developed extensive mission centers in California, where their work flourished for half a century.

The Franciscans found worthy competitors in the Dominicans. By 1526 they were in Mexico. Soon after they were laboring in Colombia, Venezuela, and Peru.

Even more extensive was the activity of the Jesuits. From 1549 they developed extensive work in Brazil. Colombia soon proved to be one of their most successful fields. They were in Peru by 1568. In 1572 they began a great work in Mexico. The seventeenth century witnessed their extensive activities in Ecuador, Bolivia, and Chile, and saw the development of their much discussed, paternally controlled Indian villages in Paraguay. These armies of monastic missionaries reproduced with fidelity the Spanish Roman Catholic Christianity to which they were so devoted.

Universities were founded in Lima and in Mexico City in 1551—the most venerable institutions of higher learning in the New World. Elementary education was kept at a minimal level, so that there was widespread illiteracy, especially among the natives, throughout the Spanish period.

The real beginnings of French Canada were made in 1604. At first there was considerable Huguenot influence, but it was soon all but displaced by a dominant Catholicism. Serious efforts were made to convert the Indians by religious orders, led by the Jesuits. The story of their heroism and sacrificial spirit is one of the classics of missionary history. In 1673 a Jesuit missionary, Jacques Marquette (1637–1675), discovered the Mississippi. A series of mission stations through the Mississippi valley, as far south as Louisiana, followed. Few permanent results accompanied this vigorous missionary thrust, however. Contrary to the pattern of South America, the tribes resisted settlement in agricultural communities, and were ravaged by disease, drink, and intertribal war. The growth of the church in New France was the result of immigration. The molder of French Canadian Roman Catholicism was the aggressive François de Laval (1623–1708), first bishop of Quebec.

The Spanish and French colonies in the New World thus saw the importation of one dominant religious tradition, but to the English colonies a number of church bodies were drawn. The Church of England was transplanted to Virginia at its permanent founding in 1607, and remained established by law throughout the colonial period. The lack of a resident bishop throughout the entire colonial period seriously handicapped the church, however. In the absence of adequate supervision, lay vestries often assumed control of given parishes, and tended to administer them in the interests of the local aristocracy. The bishop of London exercised nominal jurisdiction over the colonial establishment; by the appointment of commissaries some effort to fulfil these responsibilities was made. James Blair (1656–1743) served as commissary in Virginia from 1685 till his death. His most noteworthy achievement was the founding of William and Mary College in 1693. But the commissaries lacked much real authority; the church suffered from some incompetent and a few unworthy clergymen. Furthermore, some of the parishes were vast in extent, and there were usually not enough clergymen to fill them all. Hence the establishment was not a strong one, and could not effectively resist the spread of dissenting groups.

Virginia's northern neighbor, Maryland, the first English proprietary colony in what is now the United States, was chartered to Lord Baltimore, a Roman Catholic, in 1632. Anxious to secure a place of refuge and freedom under the sovereignty of England for his fellow believers, Baltimore established religious toleration. Protestants outnumbered the Catholics from the start. In 1691 Maryland was made a royal colony, and, largely through the efforts of Commissary Thomas Bray (1656–1730), the Church of England was established by law. Bray was actually in the colony only a few months, but his services, especially through the organization of the Society for Promoting Christian Knowledge (S.P.C.K.) in 1699 and the Society for the Propagation of the Gospel in Foreign Parts (S.P.G.), in 1701 (see pp. 434, 471), were invaluable. The establishment did not secure the affections of the majority of the population, however; Quakers, Presbyterians, and Baptists steadily spread. As for the Roman Catholics, they were subject to legal disabilities as in other colonies; in Catholic history the eighteenth century, up to the Revolution, was the "penal period."

After 1689, efforts were made by the mother country to secure establishment of the Church of England where possible. The first fruit of this policy was the Maryland law; then came establishments in South and North Carolina, in 1706 and 1715 respectively. The mixed religious character of their population, including Huguenots, Scotch-Irish Presbyterians, Baptists, and Quakers, rendered these establishments largely ineffective, though they were well served by missionaries of the S.P.G., and Charleston had a distinguished succession of rectors. Church of England work began in Georgia with the founding of the colony in 1733, but establishment of the church was not effected until 1758. The policy of toleration early attracted various other Protestant groups there, and the establishment was largely nominal.

The settlement of the English Pilgrims and Puritans in New England, beginning in 1620, and the steps which led to the erection, between then and 1638, of the Congregational colonies of Plymouth, Massachusetts Bay, Connecticut, and New Haven have already been noted (see p. 412). With the able leaders of Massachusetts Bay pointing the way, serious effort to establish a holy commonwealth on earth, solidly based on the "plain law" of the Bible, was undertaken. Making the charter of their commercial company in effect the constitution of a state, for over half a century they labored to build their theocratic Bible commonwealth. Believing that their educated ministers had correctly read the Scriptures, they hastened to found Harvard College (1636) so that educated leaders might never be lacking. Nor was effort neglected for the conversion of the Indians. The work of John Eliot (1604–1690), begun in 1646, led to the formation, in 1649, of the first missionary society in England, the Society for the Propagation of the Gospel in New England (see p. 471). These early Congregationalists of New England did not differ theologically from their Puritan brethren in Great Britain—they welcomed the appearance of the Westminster Confession (see p. 414), adopted it in substance, and stressed the federal, or covenant, theology. For their first century their controversies dealt more with the developments of polity than with questions of doctrine. By 1631, in Massachusetts and speedily in the other Puritan colonies, Congregationalism was established by law, and the full meaning of "non-separatist Congregationalism," which vigorously insisted on religious uniformity and sought to restrain or exclude all dissidents became clear. The religious establishments of the Puritan colonies (Connecticut and New Haven were merged, 1662–1665; Massachusetts Bay and Plymouth were merged in 1691; New Hampshire became independent from Massachusetts in 1680) survived longer than in any other part of the country (see p. 473).

Dissent from the established order soon appeared, however. There were occasional Baptists in the Massachusetts colony almost from the beginning, and in spite of governmental repression they organized a church in Boston in 1665, and spread slowly in New England. Quakers arrived in the Bay in 1656, anxious to testify against the Puritan church-state. Within five years four of them were hanged on Boston Common, until Charles II ordered such proceedings stopped. The restoration government in England sought to curb the stubborn Puritans, and finally had the Massachusetts Bay charter vacated (1684). With the assertion of royal control, Church of England worship finally got a permanent foothold in New England, beginning in Boston in 1687. The new charter of 1691 replaced the religious with a property qualification for the franchise, and a measure of toleration for religious minorities was granted, though various irritations, such as enforced payments for the established churches, were continued. In Massachusetts and Connecticut, exemption from taxation for the support of Congregationalism was granted to certain groups, under somewhat onerous conditions, between 1727 and 1729.

The decline of Puritan hopes for a monolithic holy commonwealth was not effected by outside forces alone, for the zeal of the founders was often not matched by their children and grandchildren. The original hope had been for a church of elect members, "proved saints" only, but soon the bars had to be lowered some by the Half-way Covenant (1657–1662). Liberal trends appeared at Harvard toward the end of the century, and the founding of the then radical Brattle Street Church in Boston in 1699 showed how far some of the descendants of the Puritan settlers had departed from the original faith. Connecticut Congregationalists, who had tended to move toward a semi-presbyterian position, were distressed by these trends in Massachusetts, and the founding of Yale College (1701) was a partial reaction to them. But dissenting groups troubled Connecticut, too; Baptists, Quakers, and an unusual sect called the Rogerenes began to be heard from. Episcopalians secured a foothold in Stratford in 1707, and advanced colorfully in 1722 when a small group of Congregational leaders went over to episcopacy, led by the rector, or president, of Yale, Timothy Cutler (1684–1765), and Samuel Johnson (1696–1772), who later (1754) became the first president of what is now Columbia University. The growth of the Church of England was greatly assisted by the work of the Society for the Propagation of the Gospel in Foreign Parts, which sent the bulk of its missionaries to the colonies where the Episcopal Church was weakest.

A highly distinctive development in New England was the settlement of Rhode Island. Providence was begun in 1636 by Roger Williams (1604?–1683), then under banishment from Massachusetts, and an opponent of coercion in matters of religion on the basis of theological principle. Rhode Island became a refuge for those seeking freedom of religious expression. In 1639 the first Baptist Church in America was founded. Williams was a member of this church for a short time, spending his later life as a "Seeker" in quest of the true church. In spite of many internal troubles from an intense individualism, the broad principles of religious liberty on which Rhode Island was founded were well maintained. The Quakers, in particular, found in it a home. Williams strongly disliked and mistrusted them, but would never violate his principles in seeking to use the arm of the state to curb them.

Thus Anglicanism was established by law in the southern colonies, and Congregationalism in New England (except Rhode Island), with dissenting groups soon in evidence both south and north. But in the middle colonies, extensive religious diversity was present early, and whatever hopes for religious establishments may have been held soon faded. New Netherland was permanently settled as a Dutch trading post in 1624. By 1628 its first Dutch Reformed Church, the earliest representative of the presbyterian polity in America, was formed at New Amsterdam on Manhattan Island; Jonas Michaelius (1584–?) came from Holland as its first minister. This and other Reformed churches were established by law, but by 1644 the religious population of Manhattan included also Lutherans, Mennonites, English Puritans, and Roman Catholics. Attempts were made to prevent other worship than that of the Reformed Church of Holland during the administration of Governor Peter Stuyvesant (1647–1664), though concessions were made to the presbyterially inclined Puritans. The Quakers especially were objects of repression. Dutch control ceased in 1664, when the colony passed to the English as New York. The English leaders secured the passage of a ministry act in 1693, and then attempts were made to interpret it as establishing the Church of England in New York. But the area over which the act was effective was limited, and it did not establish the Episcopal Church there in the sense of the establishments in the southern colonies. A few churches, especially Trinity beginning in 1697, did receive public funds for the support of their clergy under the act for many years, but the Dutch Reformed were protected by liberal charters, and growing toleration provided opportunities for other denominations. In 1709 a large German Reformed immigration from the Palatinate came into the colony.

The Quakers first came to America in 1656 as missionaries; persecution was their lot almost everywhere. They soon won a measure of toleration, and steadily they grew and developed their meetings. The visit of George Fox to the colonies in 1672 greatly aided in the stabilization of the movement. The main area of Quaker growth soon became the middle colonies. The first important Quaker experiment in government began in West Jersey, where a charter of 1677, "Laws, Concessions and Agreements," provided for religious liberty. East Jersey early had settlers representing English Puritan Presbyterianism, the Dutch Reformed, and Scotch Presbyterianism; it too passed for a time into Quaker hands, though the Presbyterian element remained the strongest religious force. Before the two Jerseys were merged to form New Jersey in 1702, Quaker control had been lost.

Mention has already been made of the grant of Pennsylvania to William Penn, in 1681, and its settlement by Quakers in the following year (see p. 421). The Quaker policy of religious freedom attracted representatives of other forms of faith. Hence no other colony presented such a variety of religious bodies as Pennsylvania. Baptists, many from England and Wales, were soon more strongly represented than elsewhere in the colonies. In 1707 the Philadelphia Baptist Association, destined to play a major role in intercolonial affairs, was organized. Mennonites from Germany and Switzerland seeking refuge flooded into Pennsylvania. Various other German bodies, such as the German Baptists (Dunkers, founded in 1708), migrated to the inviting refuge. In the eighteenth century, a great wave of German Lutherans poured in. The first Lutheran groups in America had been Swedish, in connection with the brief Swedish effort to found a colony on the Delaware River;

the second period of Lutheran development had been the Dutch, focusing in the New York area. But in the eighteenth century the German immigration centering in Pennsylvania introduced what soon became by far the most conspicuous element in colonial Lutheranism. Numbers of German Reformed came also; they enjoyed close relationship with the Dutch Reformed leaders.

In the early eighteenth century another wave of immigration, destined to be of great religious, economic, and political importance, brought Scotch-Irish settlers not only to the middle colonies but also to other colonies. The Scotch-Irish, from the Scottish settlements in northern Ireland, were, like most of the Scots who came at this time, devotedly Presbyterian. They found a leader and an organizer in Francis Makemie (1658–1708), to whose initiative the first American presbytery, that of Philadelphia, in 1706, was due. In this presbytery, and in many Presbyterian congregations, English Puritan Presbyterians worshipped together with Scottish and Scotch-Irish followers of Calvin. Down to the outbreak of the Revolution the Scotch-Irish migration continued, until their presence was felt in almost every colony. Many of them pushed to the frontier, and to this energetic race the settlement of what is now West Virginia, western North Carolina, and ultimately Kentucky and Tennessee, as well as large sections of South Carolina, Georgia, and Alabama, was largely due. So fast was their growth, that ten years after the formation of the first presbytery a synod was formed, including the presbyteries of Long Island (later New York), New Castle (Delaware), and Philadelphia.

Episcopal work had been started in the middle colonies before the beginning of the eighteenth century, but its spread there in that century was largely the work of the missionaries of the S.P.G.

Thus by the end of the first quarter of the eighteenth century, the middle colonies especially exhibited a great diversity in religion, though the multiplicity of religious bodies was felt in all the colonies. No one communion was dominant in the colonies as a whole. While particular denominations were intrenched in particular colonies, no church could become that of all the colonies. The churches that spread in America were clearly transplanted churches. But in the new environment, and especially for churches which had been established in Europe but were not in the colonies, there was confusion and hesitation, because familiar practices and procedures often did not work well. Many church members who had been faithful in the Old World did not (or for reasons of distance could not) retain their religious ties in the New. The established bodies were also troubled, both by the decline in fervor of their own members, and by the spread of dissidents in their midst. Furthermore, the effects of the rationalism and Deism of the Age of Reason were beginning to be felt in the churches, and many outside them were indifferent or even hostile to religion. Despite the growth of churches through immigration, a situation in which a steadily increasing segment of the population had no religious connections was spreading.

3

Deism and Its Opponents. Scepticism

ONE OF THE IMPORTANT consequences of the spread of the spirit of the Enlightenment (see p. 430) in the late seventeenth and early eighteenth centuries was the development of rationalism in religion. The Newtonian conception of the universe was of a realm of law, created by a "first cause," and operating in a mechanical order. The new knowledge of long-established civilizations and of other religions enlarged men's horizons and confronted them with other than Christian culture. Locke's test of truth was reasonableness, in the sense of conformity to common sense. He viewed morality as the prime content of religion. A powerful spur to the development of religious rationalism was moral reaction against the passions and brutalities of the age of the religious wars. All these influences led to the significant departure of rationalism in English religious thought. In its milder form this emerged as "rational supernaturalism," but in its central development it took the form of a full Christian Deism, while its radical wing turned against organized religion as anti-Christian Deism.

The pioneer Deist was Edward Herbert of Cherbury (1583–1648), who as early as 1624 had enumerated the articles of belief alleged to constitute natural religion, held by all mankind in primitive unspoiled simplicity, as: God exists; He is to be worshipped; virtue is His true service; man must repent of wrong-doing; and there are rewards and punishments after death. But few rationalists went that far in the seventeenth century. Locke himself reserved a place for revelation in his interpretation of Christianity, though he insisted that what was revealed was basically simple and always reasonable. Not greatly dissimilar was the rational supernaturalist faith of John Tillotson (1630–1694), famous preacher, Archbishop of Canterbury, and leader of the Latitudinarian party in the Church of England. For him natural religion must be supplemented by revelation, as a divine sanction for morality is necessary. But John Toland (1670–1722), though still keeping some place for divine revelation, was moving towards a full Deist position, and his book, *Christianity not Mysterious,* published in 1696, opened the Deistic controversy in England. Those who held to a concept of revelation defended themselves by arguing that it was attested to by prophecy and miracle. But in

1713 Anthony Collins (1676–1729) issued his *Discourse of Freethinking* in which he attacked the argument from prophecy, while Thomas Woolston (1669–1733) subjected the miracles to searching criticism. In 1730 appeared Matthew Tindal's (1657–1733) *Christianity as Old as the Creation,* often called the Deist Bible. In the writings of these men the main features of the Deistic position were set forth. All that is acknowledged beyond or above reason is really held on belief without proof, they argued. To be rid of superstition is to be free, hence the only rational thinker is a freethinker. The worst enemies of mankind are those who have held men in bondage to superstition, and the chief examples of these are "priests" of all sorts. All that is valuable in revelation had already been given men in natural reasonable religion, hence "Christianity"—that is, all that is of worth in Christianity—is "as old as creation." All that is obscure or above reason in so-called revelation is superstitious and worthless or worse. Miracles are no real witness to revelation; they are either superfluous, for all of value in that to which they witness reason already possesses; or they are an insult to the perfect workmanship of a Creator who has set this world running by most perfect mechanical laws and does not now interfere with its ongoing. Deism thus seemed to destroy all historic Christianity and authoritative revelation. It was widely denounced as atheism, yet destructive as it was, not justly. In the thought of its advocates it was a rescue of religion from bondage to the superstitious and a return to primitive rational simplicity and purity.

From a later standpoint the weakness of Deism is evident. Its primitive universal, rational religion is as much a figment of the imagination as the primitive unspoiled social and political state of the unspoiled child of nature so dear to the eighteenth century. Its assertion that "whatever is," that is, whatever is natural, "is right," is shallow optimism. It had no sense of the actual facts of the historic religious development of the race. Its God was afar off, a being who once for all established certain religious principles, essentially rules of morality, and set a wonderfully contrived mechanical world in motion with which He has nothing now to do. Despite its profession of being grounded solidly in self-evident truth, it was itself based on a position of faith. Its merit was that it contributed to a generally higher level of ethical awareness and humanitarian concern.

Deism called out many replies, and the chief proof of its power is that, relatively mediocre men as most of the Deists were, most of its opponents attempted to meet it by rational argument, often admitting a considerable share of its method, though not its results. Some few met it by a flat denial of any power of reason in the realm of religion. Such was the answer of the excellent Nonjuror William Law (1686–1761) in his reply to Tindal, entitled *The Case of Reason* (1732). Reason, Law argued, not merely does not find truth in religion; "it is the cause of all the disorders of our passions, the corruptions of our hearts." God is above the power of man to comprehend, "His own will is wisdom and wisdom is His will. His goodness is arbitrary."

Less directly designed as an answer to Deism but believed by himself to be destructive of all "atheism" was the philosophy of George Berkeley (1685–1753), a man of most generous impulses, who attempted to found a missionary college in Bermuda for the evangelization of the American Indians, lived for a time in Rhode Island, and in 1734 became bishop of Cloyne in Ireland. To Berkeley's thinking nothing really exists but minds and ideas. There is no other knowledge of what is called matter but an impression in our minds, and since like can only affect like, our minds must be affected only by other minds. Since ideas are universal and constant, they must be the product in our minds of a universal, eternal, and constantly working mind. Such a mind is God, and to Him all our ideas are due. But ideas exist not merely subjectively in our minds. In some sense what we call nature is a range of ideas in the divine mind, impressed in a definite and constant order on our minds, though their reality to us is only in our perception of them in our own minds. By thus denying the reality of matter Berkeley would destroy that whole conception of the world as a huge mechanism—a magnified watch—made once for all by an all-wise Maker, who has nothing now to do with its ongoing, which Deism had held. For it he would substitute a universal constant divine spiritual activity. Though this conception of Berkeley has always enjoyed high philosophic respect, it is too subtle and too contrary to the evidences of his senses for the average man.

More famous in its own time, yet of far less philosophic ability or permanent value, was a work of Joseph Butler (1692–1752), a Presbyterian by descent who had early entered the Church of England and become bishop of Bristol in 1738, and of Durham in 1750. His *Analogy of Religion* of 1736 was a work of immense labor, candor, and care. In answer to the Deists he starts from the premises, held equally by the Deists and their opponents, that God exists, that nature moves in a uniform course, and that human knowledge is limited. God is admittedly the author of nature: if the same difficulties can be raised against the course of nature as against revelation, the probability is that both have the same author. Their positive resemblances also lead to the same conclusion. Immortality is at least strongly probable. As present happiness or misery depend on conduct, it is probable that future will also. Every man is now in a state of "probation" as regards his use of this life; it is probable that he is also now on "probation" as to his future destiny. Our limited knowledge of nature does not warrant a declaration that revelation is improbable, much less impossible, and whether there has actually been a revelation is a historic question to be tested by its attestation by miracles and fulfilment of prophecy. Believed widely in its time an unanswerable answer to Deism, and as such long required in English and American universities, Butler's cautious balance of probabilities utterly fails to meet modern questions, and has been well criticised as raising more doubts than it answers. Its most attractive feature is its moral fervor in its exaltation of the divine regnancy of conscience over human action.

A noteworthy attack alike on Deism and on much of the current defenses of Christianity against it was made by the acutest British philosopher of the eighteenth century, David Hume (1711–1776). Born in Edinburgh, he died in that city. He lived in France for some years, saw some public employment, wrote a popular but highly Tory *History of England,* and won deserved fame as a political economist. During his last years he was regarded as the friendly, kindly head of the literary and intellectual circles of his native city. His philosophical system was ably set forth in his *Treatise of Human Nature* of 1739; but this rather youthful publication attracted little notice. Very different was it when the same ideas were recast in his *Philosophical Essays* of 1748 and his *Natural History of Religion* of 1757. Philosophically, Hume was one of the keenest of reasoners, standing on the basis of Locke, but with radical and destructive criticism of Locke's theories and with most thoroughgoing religious scepticism. Experience gives us all our knowledge, but we receive it as isolated impressions and ideas. All connection between our mental impressions as related by cause and effect, or as united and borne by an underlying substance, are simply the inveterate but baseless view-points of our mental habit. They are the ways in which our minds are accustomed to act. What we really perceive is that in our limited observation certain experiences are associated. We jump to the conclusion that there is a causal relation between them. So, too, substance is "feigned." If therefore cause and effect are ruled out, the argument for a God founded thereon is baseless. The denial of substance leaves no real permanent I behind my experiences, and leaves no philosophical basis for immortality. Hume, in whom a dawning of historic criticism manifested itself, also held that history shows that Polytheism preceded Monotheism in human development, and thus history gives no support to the doctrine of the one originally recognized God of Deism, or to the existence of the simple primitive, rational religion of nature which Deists claimed. Most of Hume's criticisms were too subtle and too radical to be very fully understood by either Deists or their orthodox opponents in his day, against whom they were equally directed.

Hume's greatest sensation was his criticism of miracles, then looked upon as the main defense of revelation and Christianity. His argument was twofold. Experience is the source of all our knowledge. Our experience witnesses to the uniformity of nature much more strongly than to the infallibility of human testimony. Hence the probability that error, mistake, or deception has led to the report of a miracle is vastly greater than that the uniform course of nature has really been interrupted. Yet, granted that testimony may prove that unusual events have occurred, that would not prove that they established anything, unless it could be further proved that they were wrought for that special purpose by divine power, which is an even more difficult task. The positions here assumed have had lasting effect. Few who now affirm miracles view them, as the eighteenth century did, as the prime proofs of Christianity. Rather, the revelation is regarded as carrying faith in the miracles far more than their lending support to it. Those who accept miracles now largely regard the revelation as so supernatural and divine as to render miracles not unfitting as its accompaniment. Since Hume's criticism, the question of miracles has been increasingly felt to be one of peculiar difficulty. Hume's work was the most powerful expression of one result of the Deistic controversy in England—the emergence of scepticism.

A sceptical criticism on the early history of Christianity advanced by the historian Edward Gibbon (1737–1794) in the fifteenth and sixteenth chapters of his great *History of the Decline and Fall of the Roman Empire* (1776) deserves notice, not for its inherent importance, but for the controversy that it aroused, and the light that it throws on the thought of the time. In accounting for the spread of Christianity, Gibbon gave as reasons its zeal inherited from the Jews, its teaching of immortality, its claim to miraculous gifts, its strict morality, and its efficient organization. No modern historian would probably object to any of these explanations, as far as they go. What would impress him is their absolute want of comprehension of the nature of religion, whether Christian or other, and of the forces by which religion makes conquests. But that was an ignorance equally shared by Gibbon's critics in the eighteenth century. The usual orthodox explanation had been that the first disciples had been so convinced of the truth of the Gospel by miracles that they were willing to hazard their lives in its behalf. The excitement roused by Gibbon's rather superficial explanation was that it supplied other causes, less directly supernatural, for the spread of Christianity. Its one permanent result was to aid, with other influences, toward the historical investigation of the Scriptures and Christian origins, which was to be so largely the work of the nineteenth century.

The general attitude of the period, and also the general rationalizing of even orthodox Christian presentation in England, at the close of the eighteenth century is best illustrated in the work of William Paley (1743–1805). His *View of the Evidences of Christianity* of 1794 and *Natural Theology* of 1802 were written with remarkable clearness of style and cogency of reasoning, and long enjoyed high popularity. From a watch, he argues, we infer a maker, so from the wonderful adaptation of the human body, the eye, the hand, the muscles, we infer an almighty Designer. These arguments, therefore, prove the existence of God. God has made His will the rule of human action and revealed it to men. The purpose of revelation is "the proof of a future state of rewards and punishments." That revelation was given by Christ, and its convincing force to the first disciples was in the miracles by which it was accompanied. "They who acted and suffered in the cause acted and suffered for the miracles." Paley then proceeds to definition. "Virtue is the doing good to mankind, in obedience to the will of God, and for the sake of everlasting happiness." This prudential and self-regarding estimate of virtue is characteristic of Paley's age, as were his emphases on the evidential character of miracles and on a mechanical demonstration of the divine existence which the theory of evolution has since largely robbed of force. Yet it is pleasant to note that Paley's thought of "doing good to mankind" led him to strenuous opposition to human slavery. In many ways, Deism exerted a more profound influence through its stimulation of Christian apology on the one hand and of sceptical philosophy on the other than by its own direct efforts.

English Deism on the whole was a cautious, Christian Deism, largely restricted in influence to the upper classes. But a radical anti-Christian Deism, militant in its attack on organized Christianity, though with few supporters, accompanied it. Peter Annet (1693–?) employed a crude and iconoclastic kind of Biblical criticism in his attack. Toward the end of the century, anti-Christian Deism had a powerful popular presentation in the militant, passionate work of Thomas Paine (1737–1809), the son of an English Quaker. His *Common Sense* of 1776 did great service to the American Revolution; his *Rights of Man* of 1791 was no less effective in defense of the principles underlying the French Revolution. In 1795 came his *Age of Reason,* in which Deism was presented in its most aggressive anti-Christian form.

English Deism influenced the development of rationalism elsewhere, in Germany, but most directly in France, where it had many advocates and became fashionable among upper classes. Chief of these French Deists was François Marie Arouet, or, as he called himself, Voltaire (1694–1778). He had become familiar with Deism in England during a trip there from 1726 to 1729, and was much influenced by the writings of Peter Annet. In Voltaire eighteenth-century France had its keenest wit. No philosopher, vain, self-seeking, but with genuine hatred of tyranny, especially of religious persecution, no one ever attacked organized religion with a more unsparing ridicule. Such a contest was, of necessity, more sharply drawn in France than in Great Britain. In the latter country a certain degree of religious toleration had been achieved, and great divergence of religious interpretation was practically allowed. In France dogmatic Roman Catholicism was dominant. The contest was, therefore, between Deism or Atheism, on the one hand, and a single assertive type of Christianity, on the other. Voltaire was a true Deist in his belief in the existence of God and of a primitive natural religion consisting of a simple morality; also in his rejection of all that rested on the authority of Bible or church. Of the extent and significance of his work in influencing the French mind in directions that were to appear in the French Revolution there can be no question. Deism affected the eighteenth century widely. It was substantially the creed of Frederick the Great of Prussia (1740–1786); of Joseph II, the Holy Roman Emperor (Austria, 1765–1790); and of the marquis of Pombal (1699–1782), the greatest of Portuguese statesmen of the century.

In the English colonies of North America, the deistic controversy was followed with great interest, and native exponents of the three main rationalist positions appeared. Massachusetts pastors Ebenezer Gay (1696–1787) and Jonathan Mayhew (1720–1766) were basically rational supernaturalists, while Benjamin Franklin (1706–1790) and Thomas Jefferson (1743–1826) were essentially Deistic. Anti-Christian Deism was expressed by the author of *Reason the Only Oracle of Man* (1784), Ethan Allen (1737–1789), revolutionary general, and by the blind crusader, Elihu Palmer (1764–1806).

4

Unitarianism in England and America

IT HAS ALREADY been pointed out that on the Continent anti-Trinitarian views were represented by some Anabaptists (see p. 329) and by the Socinians (see pp. 397–398). Both types penetrated into England. Under Elizabeth "Arian Baptists" from the Netherlands were burned in 1575. Under James I, Bartholomew Legate (1575?–1612) and Edward Wightman (?–1612), of similar views, have the distinction in 1612 of being the last Englishmen burned for their faith. With the controversies of the civil-war period anti-Trinitarian views became more evident. In John Biddle (1615–1662), an Oxford graduate, Socinianism had a more learned representative, who suffered much imprisonment. The great Puritan poet, John Milton (1608–1674), inclined to Arianism in his later years. Biddle's chief convert was Thomas Firmin (1632–1697), a London layman, who furthered the publication of anti-Trinitarian tracts.

With the dawn of the eighteenth century, with its rationalizing impulses both in orthodox and Deistic circles, and its inclination to see in morality the essence of religion, these anti-Trinitarian tendencies were greatly strengthened. The Presbyterian minister Thomas Emlyn (1663–1741) published his widely read *Inquiry into the Scripture Account of Jesus Christ* in 1702. In 1712 Samuel Clarke (1675–1729), rector of St. James, Westminster, and deemed the most philosophical of the Anglican clergy, published his *Scripture Doctrine of the Trinity,* in which he sought to demonstrate Arian views by a painstaking examination of the New Testament. It was, however, among the Dissenters, especially the Presbyterians and General Baptists, that anti-Trinitarian views won the largest following. In 1717 Joseph Hallett (1691?–1744) and James Peirce (1674?–1726), Presbyterian ministers in Exeter, sought to find a median position between orthodoxy and Arianism. The most learned of the eighteenth century Dissenters, Nathaniel Lardner (1684–1768), held similar views, and the movement spread. On the whole, the Congregationalists and the Particular Baptists were little affected, and in consequence grew in numbers as the century went on, surpassing the Presbyterians, who at the time of the Toleration Act had been the most numerous Non-Conformist body.

The Arian trend paved the way for the development of a separately organized Unitarianism in England. The movement was precipitated when a clergyman of the establishment, Theophilus Lindsey (1723–1808), who had adopted a Unitarian position, circulated a petition which received some two hundred and fifty signatures asking that clergymen be relieved from subscription to the Thirty-nine Articles, to pledge their fidelity to the Scriptures alone. Parliament in 1772 refused to receive it. In 1773 Lindsey withdrew from the establishment, and the next year organized a Unitarian Church in London. Closely associated with Lindsey was Joseph Priestley (1733–1804), a Dissenting clergyman, an eminent chemist, the discoverer of oxygen, a sympathizer with the American and French Revolutions, who spent the last ten years of his life in Pennsylvania. Parliament in 1779 amended the Toleration Act by substituting profession of faith in the Scriptures for the required acceptance of the doctrinal part of the Thirty-nine Articles, and removed all penal acts against deniers of the Trinity in 1813. This older English Unitarianism was formal and intellectual, clear in its rejection of "creeds of human composition," and insistence on salvation by character. It was often intellectually able, but had little influence on popular religious life.

English Unitarianism had some effect in producing a similar movement in New England, though that grew also out of the general rationalizing tendencies of the eighteenth century. The presence in the colonies of Priestly and of William Hazlitt (1737–1820) helped to precipitate its emergence as an independent movement. King's Chapel, the oldest Episcopal Church in New England, became the first openly Unitarian Church in 1785 under the leadership of its pastor, James Freeman (1759–1835). Many Congregationalists were in sympathy with Unitarianism, but not until the nineteenth century did the Unitarian schism occur (see p. 511).

5

Pietism in Germany

THE DEVELOPMENT of a scholastic Lutherianism has already been noted (see p. 391). Though based on the Scriptures, it assumed the form of a fixed dogmatic interpretation, rigid, exact, and demanding intellectual conformity. Emphasis was laid on pure doctrine and the sacraments, as constituting the sufficient elements of the Christian life. For that vital relationship between the believer and God which Luther had taught had been substituted very largely a faith which consisted in the acceptance of a dogmatic whole. The layman's role was largely passive: to accept the dogmas which he was assured were pure, to listen to their exposition from the pulpit, to partake of the sacraments and share in the ordinances of the church—these were the practical sum of the Christian life. Some evidences of deeper piety existed, of which the hymns of the age are ample proof, and doubtless many individual examples of real and inward religious life were to be found, but the general tendency was external and dogmatic. It was the tendency often, though only partially justly, called "dead orthodoxy." This Protestant scholasticism was in some respects narrower than that of the mediæval period, for it had unwittingly been influenced by the spirit of rationalism against which it struggled, so that it became akin to the new rationalistic currents both in temper and in method. Hence it shared in the reactions against rationalism.

Pietism was a breach with these scholastic tendencies, an assertion of the primacy of feeling in Christian experience, a vindication for the laity of an active share in the upbuilding of the Christian life, and a stress upon a strict ascetic attitude toward the world. Many influences contributed to the rise of the movement, and it is difficult to trace them all with certainty. The best approach to an understanding of the background and nature of the Pietist revival is through its central figure, Philipp Jakob Spener (1635–1705), one of the most notable religious figures of the seventeenth century, in whose teaching and example Pietism had its immediate source.

Born in Rappoltsweiler, in Upper Alsace, he was educated at Strassburg, where he became versed in Biblical exegesis, and saw there a church discipline and a care in catechetical instruction far beyond what is customary in most Lutheran circles. Further studies at Basel and Geneva acquainted him with Reformed emphases without weaning him from Lutheranism. His mental and spiritual development was shaped by many factors. At Strassburg, he had studied carefully Luther's theology. He was especially stimulated by the famous work of the mystically-inclined Johann Arndt (1555–1621), *True Christianity*, which had been published 1605–1609. It is not clear how far the religious poetry of Paul Gerhardt (1607–1676) impressed him. Nor is it known just how much he was indebted to the movement in Reformed churches sometimes called "Dutch Pietist" or "Dutch Precisianist." Willem Teelinck (1579–1629), Gisbert Voet (1589–1677), and Jodocus van Lodensteyn (1620–1677) were leaders in this movement, which has often been identified with English Puritanism, for the latter deeply fertilized it. But there is no doubt that Spener himself was strongly influenced by Puritan writings, most especially by the German translation of Lewis Bayly's (?–1631) widely read *The Practice of Pietie*, also by some of the translated works of Richard Baxter.

In 1666 Spener became chief pastor in the prosperous commercial city of Frankfort. He felt the need of church discipline, but found himself hindered, because all authority was in the hands of the city government. Under such leadership as was permitted him, catechetical instruction speedily improved. His first considerable innovation occurred in 1670, when he gathered in his own house a little group of like-minded people for Bible reading, prayer, and the discussion of the Sunday sermons—the whole aiming at the deepening of the individual spiritual life. Of these circles, to which the name *collegia pietatis* was given (hence Pietism), the first was that in Spener's home.

These plans for cultivating a warmer Christian life Spener put forth in his *Pia desideria* of 1675. The chief evils of the time he pictured as governmental interference, the bad example of the unworthy lives of some of the clergy, the controversial interpretation of theology, and the drunkenness, immorality, and self-seeking of the laity. As measures of reform he proposed the gathering within the various congregations of circles—*ecclesiolæ in ecclesia*—for Bible reading; and since all believers are priests—a Lutheran contention which had been practically forgotten—for mutual watch and helpfulness. Christianity is far more a life than an intellectual knowledge. Controversy is unprofitable. Better training for the clergy is desirable. An experimental knowledge of religion, and a befitting life should be demanded of them. A new type of preaching should be practised, designed to build up the Christian life of the hearers, not primarily controversial or exhibitory of the argumentative abilities of the preacher. That only is genuine Christianity which shows itself in the life. Its normal beginning is a spiritual transformation, a conscious new birth. Spener also showed certain ascetic tendencies, like the English Puritans, inculcating moderation in food, drink, and dress, and rejecting the theatre, dances, and cards, which contemporary Lutheranism regarded as "indifferent things." Spener's efforts encountered bitter opposition, and aroused enormous controversy. He was accused of heresy. Falsely so, as indicating any intentional departure from Lutheran standards; but rightly so in the sense that his spirit and ideals were quite unlike those of contemporary Lutheran orthodoxy. His work involved a shift of emphasis from the creeds to the Scriptures. His feeling that, if "the heart" was right, differences of intellectual interpretation were relatively unimportant, was sharply opposed by those who put the emphasis on "pure doctrine." Spener undoubtedly greatly popularized familiarity with the Bible, and undermined the authority of confessional standards, as giving in final logical form what the Scriptures had to teach. A result of this Biblical study was to prepare the way for, rather than to effect, an investigation of the nature and history of the Scriptures themselves. Spener greatly improved the religious instruction of youth, and achieved his purpose of introducing a more strenuous, Biblically fed, and warmer popular Christian life.

At Frankfort some of Spener's disciples, in spite of his protests, withdrew from church worship and the sacraments. Spener's meetings consequently met with police opposition, and he was glad, in 1686, to accept a call to Dresden as court preacher.

Meanwhile, the Pietist movement had spread to the University of Leipzig. In 1686 one of the younger instructors, August Hermann Francke (1663–1727), and a few associates, founded there a *collegium philobiblicum* for the study of the Scriptures. Its members were at first instructors, its method scientific, and it had the approval of the university authorities. But in 1687 Francke experienced what he regarded as a divine new birth while in Lüneburg and engaged in writing a sermon on *John* 20:31. A couple of months' stay with Spener, in Dresden, completed his acceptance of Pietism. In 1689 Francke was back in Leipzig, lecturing to the students and to the townspeople with great following. Leipzig was soon in a good deal of turmoil. An electoral edict soon forbade the meeting of citizens in "conventicles." Undoubtedly Francke's lectures led some students to neglect other studies and to assume a critical attitude. Under the leadership of the Leipzig professor of theology, Johann Benedict Carpzov (1639–1699), the university authorities limited Francke's work. Carpzov became one of the most unwearied of Spener's opponents. Francke's position became so uncomfortable that he was glad, in 1690, to accept a call to Erfurt as "deacon."

Meanwhile Spener's path in Dresden was not easy. The Saxon clergy looked upon him as a stranger; the two Saxon universities, Leipzig and Wittenberg, opposed him. His meetings for spiritual upbuilding developed criticism. The Elector, John George III (1647–1691), took offense at Spener's pastoral reproof of his drunkenness. When, therefore, an invitation to Berlin came from the Elector of Brandenburg, Frederick III (1688–1701), who was to become King Frederick I of Prussia (1701–1713), Spener willingly accepted it in 1691. Though Spener never won his new sovereign for personal Pietism, he had much support from Frederick, and his years in Berlin, to his death, on February 5, 1705, were his happiest and most successful.

While in Berlin Spener was able to do his greatest service to Pietism. Christian Thomasius (1655–1728), a rationalist in the sense of Locke, a critic of the theological hair-splitting of the day, a creator of German jurisprudence, the first to substitute German for Latin as the language of the university instruction, a defender of religious toleration, a sceptic regarding witchcraft, the opponent of the judicial use of torture, had been driven from Leipzig in 1690 by the hostility of the theologians. His popularity in the student body was great. Thomasius was no Pietist, though he disliked the persecution of the Pietists, and had done his utmost to aid Francke in the contest with the Leipzig authorities. The Elector of Brandenburg, long desirous of having a university of his own, improved the exile of Thomasius to found a university in Halle, in 1691, which was formally opened in 1694, and in which Thomasius was to lead the faculty of law till his death.

Meanwhile Francke had many difficulties in Erfurt. His energetic introduction of Pietistic measures roused the opposition of the clergy of the city. Carpzov's hostility pursued him, and in 1691 he was expelled by the authorities. Spener now procured for him from the Elector appointment to a professorship in Halle, and the pastorate of the neighboring village of Glaucha, and also the appointment of colleagues of Pietistic sympathies. From the first Francke dominated the theological methods and instruction in Halle, though he did not become formally a member of the theological faculty till 1698. Till his death, in 1727, Francke made and kept Halle a center of Pietism.

Francke was a man of unbounded energy and organizing genius. His parish of Glaucha was a model of pastoral faithfulness. His lectures in the university were largely exegetical and experiential; and his combination of the classroom and parish practice was highly helpful for his students. In 1695 he began a school for poor children, and such was its fame that children from outside were offered to him in such numbers that he soon established his famous fitting school, the *Paedogogium,* and also a Latin school. These educational foundations were soon renowned, and all were managed in the spirit of Pietism. At his death two thousand two hundred children were under instruction. At about the same time he founded his famous Orphan House, which numbered a hundred and thirty-four inmates when he died. All these foundations, most of which have continued to the present, were begun almost without means, and Francke sincerely believed were maintained in answer to prayer. Gifts flowed in from all parts of Germany. Without doubting Francke's faith, it is but just to note that he understood the art of honorable publicity, and of enlisting friends. The number of nobles who were patrons of his foundations was really remarkable. One further foundation may be called almost his own. That was the Bible Institute, established in 1710 by his friend, Karl Hildebrand, Freiherr von Canstein (1667–1719), for the publication of the Scriptures and their circulation in inexpensive form. The institute has done a noble work to the present day.

One notable feature of these activities in Halle was the zeal for missions there aroused. At a time when Protestants generally still failed to recognize the missionary obligation, Francke and his associates were awake to it. When Frederick IV (1699–1730), of Denmark, wished to send the first Protestant missionaries to India, in 1705, establishing them in 1706 in Tranquebar, then belonging to Denmark, he found them among Francke's students in Halle, Bartholomäus Ziegenbalg (1683–1719) and Heinrich Plütschau (1678–1747). During the eighteenth century not less than sixty foreign missionaries went forth from the University of Halle and its associated foundations, of whom the most famous was Christian Friedrich Schwartz (1726–1798), who labored, from 1750 to his death, in India. Certainly Francke's name deserves high place on the roll of missionary leadership.

Pietism's influence was felt also in the German Reformed churches of the lower Rhine region, where a fusion of Reformed and Lutheran pietistic emphases was exemplified by Theodore Untereyck (1635–1693) and Joachim Neander (1650?–1680). The Pietist leaven penetrated the Lutheran churches of Norway, Sweden, and Denmark, where it stimulated much religious zeal among the people. And many of the German settlers in America had been deeply affected by the movement.

In Germany, by the time of Francke's death in 1727, Pietism had passed its high-water mark. It produced no further leaders equal in ability to Spener and Francke. It continued to spread in Germany, notably in Württemberg under the leadership of Johann Albrecht Bengel (1687–1752). A statistical estimate is difficult, as Pietists did not separate from the Lutheran Churches; but Pietism undoubtedly affected Germany very widely and for good. It fostered a more vital type of piety. It greatly improved the spiritual quality of the ministry, preaching, and the Christian training of the young. It increased the share of the laity in the life of the church. It greatly augmented familiarity with the Bible, and the devotional study of the Scriptures. Its shadows were its insistence on a conscious conversion through struggle as the only normal method of entrance into the kingdom of God, its ascetic attitude toward the world, illustrated in Francke's severe repression of play among the children in his foundations, its censorious judgments on those who were not Pietists as irreligious, and its neglect of the intellectual elements in religion. It produced very few intellectual leaders. But, on the whole, the judgment on Pietism is predominantly favorable. It did a service of great value for the religious life of Protestant Germany.

One fruit of Pietism deserves notice in a contribution of value made to the interpretation of church history by one of the most radical of the Pietists, Gottfried Arnold (1666–1714), a friend of Spener, for a short time a professor in Giessen, and thenceforward living in comparative retirement in Quedlinburg. Since the Reformation church history had been polemic and had regarded all thinkers as to be rejected whom the church of their own age rejected. In his *Unparteiische Kirchen und Ketzer-Historie* of 1699 and 1700 Arnold introduced a new conception. He had read much of the ancient heretics. No man is to be deemed a heretic because his own age so deemed him. He is to be judged on his own merits, and even the views of so-called heretics have their place in the history of Christian thought. As is always a danger to a man who has conceived a fruitful idea, Arnold pushed his interpretation rather to the conclusion that there had been more truth with the heretics than with the orthodox. Yet he gave to church history a forward step of decided importance.

6

Zinzendorf and Moravianism

ONE OF THE MOST notable results of the Pietistic awakening, though far from approved by the Pietists in general, was the reconstitution of the Moravian Brethren, under the leadership of Count Nicolaus Ludwig von Zinzendorf. Zinzendorf was born in Dresden, on May 26, 1700. His father was a high official of the Saxon electoral court and a friend of Spener. Zinzendorf's father died shortly after his son's birth, the mother married again, and the boy was brought up, rather solitary and introspective, by his grandmother, the pietistic Baroness Henrietta Catherine von Gersdorf. Even as a boy he was marked by the trait that was to dominate his religious life—passionate personal devotion to Christ. From the time he was ten till his seventeenth year he studied in Francke's *Paedagogium* in Halle. Its rigor repelled him, but he gradually came to appreciate Francke's zeal, and his religious nature was quickened in 1715 in connection with his first communion. The insistence of his family that he should enter public employment sent him to Wittenberg from 1716 to 1719 to study law. Though a decided Pietist, his experiences in Wittenberg gave him a kindlier feeling than before toward orthodox Lutheranism. In 1719 and 1720 he took a long journey to Holland and France, forming the acquaintance of many distinguished men, and making his religious principles clearly, though tactfully, evident. On his return journey through Castell he fell in love with his cousin, but he thought Count Heinrich XXIX von Reuss a more favored suitor, and resigned his pretensions, believing that God thereby had indicated some work for him to do. He ultimately married, in 1722, Count Heinrich's sister, Erdmuth Dorothea, who made him a most sympathetic wife.

The wishes of his relatives led him to enter the electoral service in Dresden in 1721. Yet he was primarily interested in cultivating the "heart-religion," in the Pietistic sense, among his friends in Dresden, and even more on his estate of Berthelsdorf, about seventy miles east of Dresden, where as patron he appointed his like-minded friend, Johann Andreas Rothe, to the pastorate. Here in wholly unlooked-for fashion his life-work was to meet him.

The old Hussite church of Bohemia had fallen on evil days. Part had found refuge in Poland, where it had long maintained its episcopal constitution, but finding the difficulties increasing, had preserved it by persuading

Frederick III's Calvinistic court preacher in Berlin, Daniel Ernst Jablonsky, of the Moravian Brethren by ancestry and training, to accept ordination to the bishopric in 1699. The consequences of the Thirty Years' War to Bohemian Protestantism had been destructive, and it had persisted in Bohemia and the neighboring province of Moravia only in concealment and under persecution. As early as 1722 the German-speaking Moravians began to seek a refuge in Saxony under the leadership of the carpenter, Christian David (1690–1751). Zinzendorf allowed them to found a village on his Berthelsdorf estate, which they named Herrnhut, and where they collected in considerable numbers. They were joined by many native German Pietists and other religious enthusiasts. Zinzendorf at first paid little attention to these settlers besides allowing them a refuge, but by 1727 he began their spiritual leadership. The task was hard at first. The refugees were divided, their aim was a separate church, while that of Zinzendorf and Rothe was incorporation in the Saxon Lutheran state church, though with special additional meetings as in Spener's plan of *collegia pietatis*. On the other hand, local customs permitted an organized village to give itself a secular organization and make its own rules. Under these customs Herrnhut chose "elders" for its secular direction in 1727. Zinzendorf, as lord of the estate, had a certain indefinite right of leadership, and all this was sealed by a communion service of such spiritual power in Berthelsdorf on August 13, 1727, that that date has generally been reckoned that of the rebirth of the Moravian Church.

Out of these institutions for the leadership of the village of Herrnhut, originally secular, a spiritual organization soon grew. An executive committee of four developed from the eldership, and by 1730 was regarded as exercising ministerial functions. A general eldership was formed, of which the first holder was Leonhard Dober (1706?–1766), who returned from the mission field in 1734 to assume the rôle. To Zinzendorf the Herrnhut society soon seemed a body of soldiers of Christ, to advance His cause at home and abroad—a new Protestant monasticism without vows or celibacy, but bound to their Lord by daily prayer and worship. The young men and the young women were separated from ordinary family life by 1728, and each class placed under strict superintendence. Children were brought up away from their parents—after the manner of the Halle Orphan House. The community even attempted to regulate choices in marriage. The ideal was that of a community separate from the world, yet ready to send forces to work anywhere for Christ's kingdom. Yet two tendencies confused this development. The Moravian element would gladly have seen the establishment of a separate denomination, a full revival of the ancient Moravian Church. Zinzendorf clung firmly to the Pietistic idea of an *ecclesiola in ecclesia*. He would keep them part of the Lutheran state church, only a special group within it, where a warmer spiritual life, a "heart-religion," should be fostered. The movement soon met much opposition, not merely from orthodox Lutherans, but from Pietists, both by reason of Herrnhut's peculiarities, and as separatist. On the whole, the separatist tendencies slowly won the upper hand, yet without fully displacing the other trend.

The Moravian willingness to go anywhere in the service of Christ soon gave a noble missionary development to the movement which it has never lost. No Protestant body had been so awake to the duty of missions, and none is so consecrated to the service in proportion to its numbers to the present day. A journey to Copenhagen to attend the coronation of Christian VI (1730–1746) of Denmark brought Zinzendorf into contact with natives of the Danish West India Islands and of Greenland. Zinzendorf returned to Herrnhut aflame with missionary enthusiasm. As a result Leonhard Dober and David Nitschmann (1696–1772) began a mission to the West Indies in 1732, and Christian David and others to Greenland in 1733. Two years later a considerable party, led by August Gottlieb Spangenberg (1704–1792), began labors in Georgia. For this outreaching work Nitschmann was ordained a bishop—the first of the modern Moravian succession—by Jablonsky in 1735.

Meanwhile Zinzendorf's relations with the Saxon government were becoming strained. The Austrian authorities complained, without ground, that he was enticing their subjects. Ecclesiastical complaints were renewed, and on March 20, 1736, he was banished from Saxony. Zinzendorf found opportunity to carry on his work in Ronneburg in western Germany and in the Baltic provinces. In 1737 he was ordained bishop by Jablonsky in Berlin. In 1738–1739 he journeyed to the West India Islands; in 1741 he was in London, where Moravian work had been several years in progress. By December, 1741, Zinzendorf was in New York, and on Christmas Eve he named the settlement which Moravians from Georgia were beginning to effect in Pennsylvania, Bethlehem—a town destined to become the American headquarters of the movement.

Zinzendorf's sojourn in America was full of activities. He made great efforts to gather the scattered German Protestant forces of Pennsylvania into a spiritual unity to be known as "the Church of God in the Spirit." He began missions to the Indians; he organized seven or eight Moravian congregations and planted schools. Itineracy was established under the superintendence of Peter Böhler (1712–1775). In January, 1743, Zinzendorf sailed for Europe, and in December, 1744, Spangenberg was put in charge of all the American work as bishop. Its most famous Indian missionary was David Zeisberger (1721–1808), who worked among the Creeks of Georgia from 1740, and from 1743 to his death in labor for the Iroquois.

Herrnhut thus became a hive of missionary activity. Missions were begun in Surinam, Guiana, Egypt, and South Africa. In 1771, after repeated attempts, a permanent mission was established in Labrador. The names of its early mission fields show one characteristic of Moravian effort. They were prevailingly hard places, requiring peculiar patience and devotion, and this trait characterizes Moravian missionary labors to the present.

Meanwhile, in spite of Zinzendorf's dislike of separatism, Moravianism was becoming more fully a church. In 1742 it was so recognized in Prussia by the government. By 1745 the Moravian Church was thoroughly organized with bishops, elders, and deacons, though its government was, and still is, more Presbyterian than Episcopal. The English Parliament by a law of 1749 recognized it as "an ancient Protestant Episcopal Church." Yet Zinzendorf did not give up his theory of an *ecclesiola in ecclesia*. Negotiations with the Saxon authorities resulted in his recall from banishment in 1747, the acceptance of the Augsburg Confession by the Moravian body the next year, and its recognition in 1749 as a portion of the Saxon state church, with its own special services. By this time Moravianism was developing a liturgy of much beauty and a hymnody of rich fulness. The Moravian Church remained small, but its influence spread widely through the outreach of the "diaspora" in Europe. Religious societies under Moravian auspices influenced many people whose membership in the regular state churches was not disturbed.

During the time of his banishment Zinzendorf and some of the Moravians developed certain theological and cultural peculiarities that were the source of deserved criticism. His emphasis on the atoning death of Christ turned in a distorted direction, focusing on a morbid concentration and wordplay upon the blood and wounds of the crucified Christ. This fanciful and sentimental trend was encouraged by Moravians in Wetteravia, where the movement centered at Ronneburg, Marienborn, and Herrnhaag during the banishment period, and by Zinzendorf's son, Christian Renatus (1727–1752). Zinzendorf's insistence that Christians must become as little children to enter the kingdom of God led to much puerility of expression. The peculiarities were at the height of their manifestation between 1747 and 1749, but in large measure they corrected themselves. Zinzendorf himself turned away from them. This period is called by the Moravians themselves "the sifting time." These tendencies should be regarded at the most as but blemishes on the character of one who could say of his devotion to Christ, as few can: "I have one passion. It is He."

Zinzendorf's life from 1749 to 1755 was spent mostly in England. His property had been spent unstintedly for the Moravians, and he now found himself almost bankrupt. His debts were assumed, as was fitting, by the Moravian body, and gradually discharged. This financial need led to a growth in Moravian constitutional development. A collegiate directorate was established, which soon became a board of control, by which Moravian affairs were superintended, and the taxes paid by the several congregations soon led to their representation in a general synod, meeting at regular intervals.

Zinzendorf's last few years were spent chiefly in pastoral activities. His strength had been lavishly spent, and he was bereaved of his wife and only son. On May 9, 1760, he died in Herrnhut.

The Moravian Church, which Zinzendorf had done so much to renew and inspire, was firmly grounded, so that his death made no serious breach.

It was fortunate, however, that its practical leadership fell to Spangenberg, who was called back from America in Herrnhut in 1762, and continued his guidance to his death, thirty years later. Not a man of genius and enthusiasm like Zinzendorf, he was marked by equal devotion, great practical sense, and high organizing abilities. Under his strong, wise guidance Moravianism strengthened and grew; its criticized peculiarities were generally discarded. His work was quiet and unpicturesque but wholly useful. The Moravian Church took its accredited place among the families of Christendom, exerting wide influence through its missionary zeal and diaspora work.

7

The Evangelical Revival in Great Britain. Wesley and Methodism

THE TRENDS in religious thought and life in England in the early part of the eighteenth century have already been described (see p. 437). The end of the struggles of the seventeenth century had been marked by a general spiritual lethargy in the Established Church of England and among Dissenters alike. Rationalism had penetrated all classes of religious thinkers, so that even among the orthodox, Christianity seemed little more than a system of morality supported by divine sanctions. Joseph Butler (see p. 439) may stand as typical. His frigid probabilities may have convinced some intellects, but they can have led few men to action. There were able preachers, but the characteristic sermon was the colorless essay on moral virtues. Outreaching work for the unchurched was but scanty. The condition of the lower classes was one of spiritual destitution. Popular amusements were coarse, illiteracy wide-spread, law savage in its enforcement, jails sinks of disease and iniquity. Drunkenness was more wide-spread than at any other period in English history.

Furthermore, Great Britain stood on the eve of the industrial revolution that was to transform it in the last third of the eighteenth century from agriculture to manufacture. James Watt (1736–1819) patented the first really effective steam-engine in 1769. James Hargreaves (?–1778) patented the spinning-jenny in 1770. Richard Arkwright (1732–1792) brought out the spinning-machine in 1768. Edmund Cartwright (1743–1823) invented the power-loom in 1784. Josiah Wedgwood (1730–1795) made the Staffordshire potteries effective from 1762 onward. The industrial and social changes, and problems consequent upon the changes, were of the widest importance, and of themselves involved readjustments of immense practical religious consequence.

There were not wanting men and movements, early in the eighteenth century, looking toward better things. William Law was not only a vigorous opponent of Deism but his *Serious Call to a Devout and Holy Life* of 1728 profoundly influenced John Wesley, and remains one of the monuments of English hortatory literature, though it is to be feared now seldom read. The Congregationalist, Isaac Watts (1674–1748), long since forgotten as a theologian, has well been called "the founder of modern English hymnody." His *Hymns* of 1707 and *The Psalms of David, Imitated in the Language of the New Testament* of 1719 broke down the prejudice on both sides of the Atlantic then existing in non-prelatical English-speaking circles against the use of all but rhymed passages of Scripture. They express a deep and vital piety.

Some combined efforts of significance were being made for a warmer religious life. Such were the "religious societies," the earliest of which was formed by a group of young men in London about 1678, for prayer, reading the Scriptures, the cultivation of a religious life, frequent communion, aid to the poor, soldiers, sailors, and prisoners, and encouragement of preaching. They spread rapidly. By 1700 there were nearly a hundred in London alone, and they were to be found in many parts of England and even in Ireland. One of these societies was formed by John Wesley's father, Samuel Wesley, in Epworth in 1702. In many ways they resembled Spener's *collegia pietatis* (see p. 446), but they had no Spener to further them. They were composed almost exclusively of communicants of the establishment. Many of the clergy looked upon the movement as "enthusiastic," or as would now be said "fanatical," and after 1710 it measurably declined, though the "societies" were to continue and be of importance in the beginnings of Methodism.

Yet these efforts were at best local and partial in their influence. The mass of the people of England was in spiritual lethargy, yet blindly conscious of sin and convinced of the reality of future reward and retribution. Emotions of loyalty to Christ, of salvation through Him, of a present transforming faith had not been aroused. It needed the appeal of vivid spiritual earnestness— directed to conviction of the heart rather than to considerations of prudence or cold logical argument. That a profound transformation was effected in England, the results of which flowed in beneficent streams to all English-speaking lands, was primarily the result of the Evangelical Revival. The first signs of an awakening appeared early in the eighteenth century. In Scotland, under the leadership of Ebenezer (1680–1754) and Ralph (1685–1752) Erskine, an evangelical movement developed in the early years of the century; Ebenezer was forced to preach in a field adjacent to his church by 1714 to accommodate the crowds. Three years later an anonymous seventeenth-century Puritan work, probably by Edward Fisher, *The Marrow of Modern Divinity,* was republished at the instigation of Thomas Boston (1677–1732) of Ettrick, a zealous popular preacher. Despite censure by the General Assembly in 1722, the "Marrow Men" with their warm evangelical spirit won much sympathy. They organized "praying societies" also suggestive of Spener's *collegia pietatis.* In Wales, Howel Harris (1714–1773) and Daniel Rowlands (1713–1790) were leaders in a revival that broke out in the mid-1730's. But only with the emergence of its three great leaders—John and Charles Wesley, George Whitefield—did the Evangelical Revival swell into a mighty tide. For four decades it advanced in three identifiable but closely related strands, all related to the established Church of England: the Methodist societies under the Wesleys, the Calvinistic Methodists under Whitefield, and the Anglican Evangelicals who operated along more traditional parish lines. Not until 1779 did the first formal separations of any of these strands from the Church of England occur.

The parents of the Wesley brothers were of Non-Conformist ancestry. Both grandfathers had been among the ejected clergy of 1662. Their father, Samuel Wesley (1662–1735), had preferred the ministry of the establishment, and was, from 1696 to his death, rector of the rough country parish of Epworth. A man of earnest religious disposition, he was somewhat unpractical, a writer of a *Life of Christ in Verse* and of a commentary on the book of *Job.* Their mother, Susanna (Annesley), was a woman of remarkable strength of character, like her husband a devoted Anglican. The sons took much from either parent, but perhaps more of force from the mother. In a household of nineteen children, even if eight died in infancy, hard work and stringent economy were perforce the rule. Of this large brood John was the fifteenth and Charles the eighteenth.

John Wesley was born on June 17, 1703, Charles on December 18, 1707. Both were saved with difficulty from the burning rectory in 1709, an event that made an ineffaceable impression on the mind of John, who thenceforth regarded himself as literally "a brand snatched from the burning." In 1714 John entered the Charterhouse School, in London, and Charles the Westminster School two years later. Both boys distinguished themselves for scholarship. In 1720 John entered Christ Church College, Oxford, whither Charles followed him six years after, and such was John's intellectual attainment that, in 1726, he was chosen a Fellow of Lincoln College. To become a candidate for that honor John must be in holy orders, and therefore, on September 25, 1725, he was ordained a deacon. With his ordination the spiritual struggles began which were to last till his conversion, in 1738, and perhaps in a sense beyond that time.

From 1726 to 1729 John Wesley was for the most part his father's assistant. On September 22, 1728, he was ordained a priest. During his absence from Oxford, by the spring of 1729, Charles Wesley and two fellow students, Robert Kirkham and William Morgan, formed a little club, primarily for progress in their studies, but which soon engaged in reading helpful books and frequent communion. On his return to Oxford in November, 1729, John Wesley became the leader of the group, which soon attracted other students. Under his guidance it sought to realize William Law's ideals of a consecrated life. Under Morgan's influence it began visitation of the prisoners in the Oxford jail in August, 1730. The members fasted. Their ideals were high-churchly. They were derided by the university. They were called the "Holy Club," and finally some student hit upon a nickname that stuck, the "Methodists"—though the name had been in currency in the previous century. They were very far as yet from what Methodism was to be. They were still a company painfully bent on working out the salvation of their own souls. As matters then were, they more resembled the Anglo-Catholic movement of the nineteenth century than the Methodism of history.

An important accession to the club, early in 1735, was George White-field. Born in Gloucester on December 16, 1714, the son of an inn-keeper, he had grown up in poverty, entering Oxford in 1733. A severe illness in the spring of 1735 brought a crisis in his religious experience, from which he emerged in joyous consciousness of peace with God. In June, 1736, White-field sought and received episcopal ordination, and at once, young as he was, began his marvellous career as a preacher. No Anglo-Saxon of the eighteenth century showed such pulpit power. A man largely without denominational consciousness, in an age when such feelings were usually intense, he was ready to preach anywhere, and in any pulpit open to him. Sometimes censorious as to the genuineness of religious experiences unlike his own, his nature was in the highest degree simple and unself-seeking. His message was the Gospel of God's forgiving grace, and of peace through acceptance of Christ by faith, and a consequent life of joyful service. His few printed sermons give little sense of his power. Dramatic, pathetic, appealing, with a voice of marvellous expressiveness, the audiences of two continents were as wax melted before him. A large part of his active ministry was spent in America. In 1738 he was in Georgia. In 1739 he was back in America, and his preaching in New England in 1740 was accompanied by the greatest spiritual upheaval ever there witnessed (see p. 466); nor was his success less in the middle colonies, though there and in New England there was great division of feeling as to the permanent spiritual value of his work. The years 1744 to 1748 saw him again on this side of the Atlantic, once more in 1751 and 1752; again in 1754 and 1755. His sixth visit was from 1763 to 1765. In 1769 he came for his last preaching tour, and died in Newburyport, Mass., on September 30, 1770. He had given himself unstintedly to the service of the American churches of every Protestant family. He was no organizer. He left no party to bear his name, but he awakened thousands.

None of the leaders of the Methodist Club was destined long to remain in Oxford, nor did their movement have much influence on the university, which was then in scholastic and religious ebb. The death of their father on

April 25, 1735, whom John Wesley would gladly have succeeded, if possible, in Epworth, left the Wesleys less bound to home, and both now gained employment as missionaries to the new colony of Georgia, the settlement of which had been begun by General Oglethorpe, in 1733. They sailed in October, 1735. On the voyage they were unremitting in religious exercises and efforts for their fellow passengers; but in the ship was a company of twenty-six Moravians, headed by Bishop David Nitschmann. The cheerful courage of this company in a storm convinced John Wesley that the Moravians had a trust in God that was not yet his. From them he learned much. Soon after reaching Savannah he met Spangenberg (see pp. 452–454), who asked him the embarrassing question: "Do you know Jesus Christ?" Wesley answered: "I know He is the Saviour of the world." Spangenberg responded: "True, but do you know He has saved you?"

The Wesleys' labors in Georgia were strenuous, yet most unsuccessful. Charles Wesley returned home in disgust and ill health in 1736. John continued. He showed his marvellous linguistic abilities by conducting services in German, French, and Italian. In 1736 he founded a little society in Savannah for cultivating the warmer religious life. He worked indefatigably, yet with little peace of mind or comfort to others. He was a punctilious high-churchman. He lacked tact. A conspicuous case was that of Sophy Hopkey, a woman in every way suitable to be his wife. He gave her and her friends every encouragement to believe his intentions earnest, but he seesawed up and down between clerical celibacy and possible matrimony. A vein of superstition always present in Wesley, which led him to decide important questions by the first verse of Scripture to which he should open, or by drawing lots, led him now to the latter method of decision as to the marriage. The lot fell adverse, and Wesley naturally aroused the resentment of the young woman and of her relatives. In a pique she married hastily another suitor. The husband objected to her continuance in attendance on Wesley's intimate religious discussions. Wesley now felt that she was not making proper preparation for communion, and refused her the sacrament. No wonder her friends charged that this was the act of a disgruntled suitor. Wesley's influence in Georgia was at an end. Suits were started against him. He decided to leave the colony for home. On February 1, 1738, John Wesley was back in England. As on his outward voyage, he had feared death. In his bitterness of disappointment he could only say: "I have a fair summer religion." Yet he was a preacher of marked power, he had labored unsparingly. He had made a good many mistakes, but they were not those which show lack of Christian consecration.

Fortunately for their distressed state of mind, within a week of John Wesley's return both brothers were in familiar intercourse with a Moravian, Peter Böhler, delayed in London till May on his way to Georgia. Böhler taught a complete self-surrendering faith, an instantaneous conversion, and a joy in believing. But though before sailing Böhler organized a "society," later to be known as the "Fetter-Lane Society," of which John Wesley was one of the original members, neither brother was as yet at peace. That experience, his "conversion," came to Charles Wesley, then suffering from a serious illness, on May 21, 1738. On Wednesday, May 24, the transforming experience came to John. That evening, as he recorded, he went unwillingly to an Anglican "society" in Aldersgate Street, London, and heard Luther's preface to the *Commentary on Romans* read. "About a quarter before nine, while he [Luther] was describing the change which God works in the heart through faith in Christ, I felt my heart strangely warmed. I felt I did trust in Christ, Christ alone, for salvation; and an assurance was given me, that He had taken away my sins, even mine, and saved me from the law of sin and death." Of the far-reaching significance of this experience there can be little question. It determined thenceforth Wesley's estimate of the normal mode of entrance on the Christian life. It was the light of all his theologic insight. Yet it was in some measure gradually, even after it, and by preaching and observing a similar work in others and by communion with God, that he entered into full freedom from fear and complete joy in believing.

John Wesley determined to know more of the Moravians, who had helped him thus far. Less than three weeks after his conversion he was on his way to Germany. He met Zinzendorf in Marienborn, spent two weeks in Herrnhut, and in September, 1738, was back in London. It was a happy visit for Wesley. He saw much to admire. Yet he was not pleased with all. He felt that Zinzendorf was treated with too great deference, and that Moravian piety was not without its subjective limitations. Much as he owed to the Moravians, Wesley was too active in religious attitude, too little mystical, too outreaching to men in their wider needs, to be fully a Moravian.

John and Charles Wesley now preached as opportunities offered, finding many pulpits closed to their "enthusiasm," and speaking chiefly in the "societies" in and about London. Early in 1739 Whitefield was developing a great work in Bristol, and there on February 17 he began preaching in the open to the coal miners of Kingswood. He now entered into friendly relations with Howel Harris, who had been working with great success, since 1736, as a lay preacher in Wales. Whitefield now invited John Wesley to Bristol. Wesley hesitated about field-preaching; but the opportunity to proclaim the Gospel to the needy was irresistible, and on April 2 he began in Bristol what was thenceforth to be his practice for more than fifty years, as long as strength permitted. Charles Wesley soon followed his example. While without Whitefield's dramatic power, John Wesley was a preacher with few equals in popular effectiveness—earnest, practical, fearless. Thenceforward he was to tour England, Scotland, and Ireland. Attacked, especially in the early part of his ministry, in peril from mob violence, no danger could daunt him, or interruption could check him. Under his preaching, as under that of Whitefield, remarkable exhibitions of bodily excitement were frequent. Men and women cried out, fainted, were torn with convulsions. To both preachers these seemed the working of the Spirit of God, or the visible resistance of the devil. They are the frequent accompaniments of great religious excitement among the ignorant and uncontrolled, and the disfavor with which they were regarded accounts for much of the opposition which these preachers encountered from the regular clergy.

John Wesley's gifts as an organizer were pre-eminent. Yet the creation of Methodism was a gradual work—an adaptation of means to circumstances. In Bristol he founded in 1739 his first really Methodist "society," and began the erection of the first chapel there on May 12, 1739. Late that year he secured in London an old "foundery," which became the first chapel there.

Thus far, in London, the Methodists had also joined in the Moravian Fetter-Lane Society, which Peter Böhler had founded in 1738. Wesley's ideals were leading him away from Moravianism. This separation was increased when, in October, 1739, Philipp Heinrich Molther (1714–1780), just come from Zinzendorf, asserted in Fetter-Lane that if any man had doubts he had no true faith, and should absent himself from the sacraments and prayer, awaiting in silence till God should renew his religious hope. Such teaching found little sympathy from Wesley's strenuous activity. The Fetter-Lane Society was divided. Wesley and his friends withdrew and founded a purely Methodist "United Society" in the Foundery, on July 23, 1740. Wesley continued on friendly terms with some of the Moravians, but thenceforth the movements were independent of each other.

Wesley had no desire or intention of breaking with the Church of England. He did not, therefore, found churches, but took up into service the device of the long-existing "religious societies," but these should now consist only of converted persons. These "societies" were from the first divided into "bands," or groups, within the society, for mutual cultivation of the Christian life. This was a Moravian device; but experience soon showed Wesley something more efficient. Soon after the Bristol society was formed Wesley hit on the plan of giving "society tickets" to those whom he found sufficiently grounded to be full members, and receiving others on trial. These tickets were renewable quarterly, and furnished a ready means of sifting the society. The debt on the Bristol chapel led to a yet more important arrangement. On February 15, 1742, the members were divided into "classes" of about twelve persons, each under a "class leader," charged to collect a penny weekly from each member. This system was introduced in London on March 25. Its advantages for spiritual oversight and mutual watch were soon even more apparent than its financial merits. It soon became one of the characteristic features of Methodism, though the older "bands," also, long continued.

Wesley would have preferred to have all preaching by ordained men, but few of the clergy were sympathetic with the movement. A lay preacher, Joseph Humphreys, was helping him as early as 1738; but extensive use was not made of this agency till 1742, when Thomas Maxfield became regularly the earliest of what soon became a considerable company. The growth of the movement developed other lay officers, "stewards," to care for property, teachers for schools, "visitors of the sick," for the duties which their names implied. At first Wesley visited all "societies," which were chiefly in the regions of London and Bristol, but the task soon became too great. In 1744 he had the preachers meet him in London—the first of the "Annual Conferences." Two years later the field was divided into "circuits," with travelling preachers and more stationary leaders to "assist chiefly in one place." Soon an "assistant," later called a "superintendent," was placed in charge of each "circuit." Wesley endeavored by suitable publications to aid the intellectual development of his lay preachers and secured study as far as possible. He tried in vain to obtain episcopal ordination for them; but would not allow the sacraments to be administered by unordained men.

While Wesley stood theologically on the common basis of Evangelical doctrinal tradition and regarded his "societies" as part of the Church of England, two disputes led to considerable controversy. One was regarding perfection. Wesley believed it possible for a Christian to attain right ruling motives—love to God and to his neighbor—and that such attainment would free from sin. To Wesley's cautious and sober judgment this was an aim rather than a frequently completed achievement—however it may have appeared to some of his followers. No man was ever more positive than he that salvation evidences itself in a life of active, strenuous obedience to the will of God.

A second dispute was regarding predestination. Wesley, like the Church of England generally of his time, was Arminian, but he had derived a special parental hostility to Calvinism, which seemed to him paralyzing to moral effort. Whitefield was Calvinistic. A hot interchange of letters took place between the two Evangelists in 1740 and 1741. Their good personal relations were soon restored in large measure. Whitefield found a supporter, in 1748, in Selina, Countess of Huntingdon (1707–1791), a wealthy widow, a convert to Methodism, but far too dominant a character to yield to Wesley's insistent leadership. She would be her own Wesley, and, like Wesley, founded and superintended "societies" and chapels—the first in Brighton in 1761—thus beginning the "Lady Huntingdon's Connection." She made Whitefield her chaplain. Her "Connection" was Calvinist. In 1769 the predestinarian controversy broke out with renewed intensity. At the "Conference" of 1770, Wesley took a strongly Arminian position, and was defended by his devoted disciple, the Swiss John William Fletcher (1729–1785), who had settled in England and accepted a living in the established church at Madeley, where he did notable work. The effect of the controversy was to confirm the Arminian character of Wesleyan Methodism. Yet "Lady Huntingdon's Connection" of Calvinistic Methodists must be regarded as a parallel rather than as a hostile movement. Its fundamental spirit was essentially the same as that of the Wesleys.

The Wesleyan Methodist movement grew enormously. John Wesley had many friends and assistants, but few intimates who shared his responsibilities. His brother Charles long had part in his constant travels, but Charles had not the iron constitution of John. After 1756 Charles itinerated seldom. He labored in Bristol, and from 1771 to his death on March 29, 1788, he preached in London. He was always more conservative than John, and more Anglican. His great service was as the hymn-writer, not merely of Methodism, but of all English-speaking Christianity. John's unwise marriage to a widow, Mrs. Mary Vazeille, in 1751, was unhappy. He devoted himself all the more unreservedly to his work. Over all the multitudinous concerns of Methodism he exercised a wise but absolute authority. Naturally, as the "societies" grew and preachers multiplied, pressure rose for authority to administer the sacraments. This Wesley resisted long, but episcopally ordained men were few, and the force of events made the pressure irresistible in spite of Wesley's insistence that his movement was within the establishment.

Wesley won many sympathizers whose focus remained in the established Church of England. These Anglican Evangelicals were generally in agreement with his religious emphases—conversion, confident faith, a religious life manifested in active work for others. On the other hand, they adopted few of his peculiar methods, and in general were marked theologically by a moderate Calvinism rather than by Arminianism. Whitefield was the spiritual father of many of them. Not very closely organized, they developed into the Evangelical party within the Church of England. A pioneer in this position was William Grimshaw (1708–1763), Vicar of Haworth, who underwent a conversion experience in 1734 which transformed him and set his feet on Evangelical paths. He kept on good terms with Wesley and Whitefield. Conspicuous among the Evangelicals was John Newton (1725–1807), once a slave-dealing shipmaster. Converted, he became one of the most helpful of preachers, first in Olney and then as rector of St. Mary Woolnoth in London. His hymns express his cheerful, confident faith. Another Evangelical renowned for his hymns was Augustus Toplady (1740–1778), author of "Rock of Ages."

Thomas Scott (1747–1821), Newton's successor in Olney, was best known for his *Family Bible with Notes*—a commentary of immense popularity on both sides of the Atlantic. Richard Cecil (1748–1810) in later life was one of the most influential preachers in London. Joseph Milner (1744–1797) made Hull an Evangelical stronghold and won much influence through his *History of the Church of Christ,* continued after his death by his brother, Isaac, in which he emphasized the development of Christian biography rather than the disputes of Christianity. Isaac Milner (1750–1820) was long a professor in Cambridge and aided in making the tone of that university largely Evangelical, a work which was continued there in power by Charles Simeon (1759–1836).

Several not in clerical ranks were instrumental in the spread of Evangelical opinions. Such was William Cowper (1731–1800), the greatest English poet of the latter half of the eighteenth century, and Newton's warm friend. In Hannah More (1745–1833) Evangelicalism had a supporter personally acquainted with the literary, artistic, and theatrical circles of London, a writer of tracts and stories of unbounded popularity and herself of generous and self-denying philanthropy.

The Anglican Evangelicals remained within the Church of England, but the two Methodist strands finally separated from it. In 1779 the Countess of Huntingdon and those associated with her separated from the Church of England; in time the connection became the Welsh Methodist Church. The Wesleyan Methodists separated from the Establishment by degrees, and finally only after the death (1791) of John Wesley, who wished his followers might avoid separation. Yet in 1784 two important steps had been taken. On February 28, Wesley entered the "Deed of Declaration" which provided for the continuance of the movement after his death by naming a "Conference" of one hundred members to hold the property and assume the direction of the movement. It was a step toward the self-government of Methodism. On September 1, Wesley joined with other presbyters of the Church of England to ordain presbyters and a superintendent for America (see p. 471). This was, indeed, a breach with the Church of England, though Wesley did not then see it as such. The final separation of the Wesleyan Methodists is perhaps best marked by the "Plan of Pacification" of 1795, which stabilized the now independent church.

Wesley's strength and activities continued unabated almost to the end. On March 2, 1791, he died in London, having done a work which had largely revolutionized the religious condition of the English lower and middle classes, and was even more largely to affect America.

In Scotland, actual separations from the established Presbyterian Church occurred much earlier, largely because of the "patronage" system, by which the patron could force the appointment of a minister on a reluctant congregation (see p. 419). In 1733 Ebenezer Erskine of Stirling denounced such limitation of the power of the congregation to chose its minister. He was disciplined by his synod, and he and several associates were deposed by the General Assembly in 1740. Before these censures were completed they had founded the first Scottish free church, ultimately known as the Secession Church. It grew rapidly, but was soon turmoiled over the question whether the burgesses of the Scottish cities could properly swear to support "the true religion . . . authorized by the laws" of Scotland. In 1747 the Secession Church divided into Anti-Burgher, or Nonjuror, and Burgher sections. Further subdivisions occurred, but most of the Anti-Burghers and Burghers united, in 1820, as the United Secession Church.

The question of patronage continued divisive. Thomas Gillespie (1708–1774), of Carnock, refused to participate in the installation of a minister over an unwilling congregation, and was deposed by the General Assembly in 1752. In 1761 he and like-minded ministers founded the organization which became the Relief Church. These various secessions won large popular support, especially among the more earnest-minded. By 1765 they counted one hundred and twenty congregations, and one hundred thousand adherents.

Under these circumstances the state church was robbed of a good deal of its spiritual strength. Rationalistic thought penetrated Scotland as the eighteenth century advanced, as contemporaneously in England and Germany. Hume's speculations (see p. 440) were not without influence. The result was the growth of what was called Moderatism, which was controlling in the latter half of the eighteenth century, and influential well into the nineteenth. To the Moderates generally Christianity was largely ethical rather than strongly experiential or doctrinal. It was believed that the patronage system favored the appointment of Moderates, where congregations would often have chosen men of more Evangelical type. For by no means all of the awakening spirit was to be found in the separated bodies in Scotland. Within the establishment was also a "Popular" party in which there was a strong Evangelical current; John Witherspoon (1723–1794), later to become president of Princeton (1768), penned his powerful satire *Ecclesiastical Characteristics* (1753) against the Moderates. But it was the latter who dominated the Church of Scotland in the closing decades of the eighteenth century—in some respects the secessions had only strengthened their hold.

8

The Great Awakening

THE MOST FAR-REACHING and transforming movement in the eighteenth-century religious life of America was the Great Awakening, a revival that had many phases and lasted for over half a century. Coming at a time when the familiar patterns of Christian outreach were not proving very effective, and at a time of spreading rationalism and cultural confusion, the awakening not only led to a tremendous quickening of the Christian life, but also changed the conceptions of entrance upon that life in a way that profoundly affected the majority of American churches. In this respect, the Great Awakening was the analogue of Pietism in Germany and the Evangelical Awakening in Britain. Emphasis was placed on a transforming regenerative change, a "conversion," as the normal method of entrance into the church. That view of the church which emphasizes its importance as a company of experiential

Christians was widely extended; primary attention was not given to Christian nurture. Strict morality and earnest piety were inculcated by the movement was a whole.

The Awakening began in 1726 in the Raritan Valley of New Jersey in Dutch Reformed circles under the leadership of Theodore J. Frelinghuysen (1691–1748). Formalism and loss of vitality marked many of the Reformed churches; many of the Dutch were content to think of their churches as symbols of their nationality and heritage. But Frelinghuysen had become acquainted with Puritan emphases in Holland, where he had been educated and ordained, and he sought to awaken his people to a deeper, more experiental knowledge of Christian faith. After some half-dozen years of effort on his part, a revival movement broke out in the churches under his care. It attracted much attention. Frelinghuysen was invited to preach at many points, others adopted his emphases, many new members were brought into the churches. But many disliked the intensity and emotionalism of the revival and opposed it—especially the New York pastors were disturbed. Despite the opposition of some, however, revival waves continued to influence the Dutch Reformed churches for many years.

Among those who were attracted to the revival was a group of Presbyterian leaders. William Tennent, Sr. (1673–1745), a man of Puritan convictions, had trained a number of young men, including three of his four sons, for the pastorate. His educational work so expanded that he finally (1736) erected a "Log College" north of Philadelphia—one of the ancestors of Princeton. His son Gilbert (1703–1764) adopted the revivalist approach, and as Presbyterian pastor at New Brunswick became the central figure in an awakening movement in his denomination. Two strong parties were then active in Presbyterianism—one representing English Puritan concern for experiential faith, the other the Scotch-Irish insistence on correct doctrine. The Tennent group stressed the Puritan emphases, but were in the territory where the other view was dominant, so in 1738 they organized their own, the New Brunswick, presbytery. The "Old Side" excluded this "New Side" presbytery from the synod, and from 1745 Presbyterianism was divided into two synods, the New York, representing Puritan and revivalist emphases, and the Philadelphia, adhering to the Scotch-Irish views, strict on strict subscription of ministers to the Westminster Confession. The trend of the times favored the growth of growth of the New Side; the fervent preaching of George Whitefield during his American tours (see p. 457) assisted the revivalists very much. When Presbyterianism reunited in 1758, the awakening group had modified some of its more extreme positions, but had won a secure place for itself in the life of the church. Thus the Awakening, controversial enough to divide a denomination for a number of years, left its permanent stamp upon it.

The Great Awakening reached New England when a remarkable revival swept the town of Northampton, Massachusetts, in 1734–1735. It attracted great attention, especially when its leader, Jonathan Edwards (1703–1758), Congregational pastor at Northampton, described it in a revivalist classic, *A Faithful Narrative of the Surprising Work of God in the Conversion of Many Hundred Souls* . . . (1737). In 1739 the revival erupted again, spreading widely in New England. Congregational leaders were assisted in the work by Gilbert Tennent and George Whitefield, the latter then at the height of his youthful enthusiasm. Everywhere throngs hung on his words; faintings and outcries attended his sermons. As the awakening spread, hundreds were permanently changed. The spiritual condition of many communities was transformed. But the New England awakening was as controversial as the middle colony movement. Whitefield was often denunciatory of those who did not agree with him as unconverted, and some who were influenced by him were even more censurious and uncharitable. The revival was further troubled by the disruptive activities of the unstable James Davenport (1716–1757), who preached long, unprepared, ranting discourses in which he attacked by name many of the leading ministers as unconverted. Separate Congregational churches were formed. In protest, the "Old Lights," under the leadership of the pastor of the First Church of Boston, Charles Chauncy (1705–1787), attacked the "New Lights," who saw in the revivals a work of God. Reaction against the awakening contributed to the spread of Arminian and ultimately Unitarian thought in Congregationalism. Reaction against the revival was such that the awakening was no longer a potent force in the established Congregational churches after mid-century, though it continued strongly among the Baptists, who were now spreading rapidly in New England, profiting greatly from the awakening patterns.

The Great Awakening spread to the southern colonies, too, there contributing to the growth of the Dissenting bodies. In the 1740's and 1750's Presbyterianism expanded rapidly in Virginia and southward, especially under the fervent preaching of Samuel Davies (1723–1761). Soon after 1750, revivals among the Baptists were touched off in Virginia by awakeners from New England, who formed many Separate Baptist churches when the Regulars resisted. High emotional enthusiasm was stirred by these revivals, and persecution at the hands of the colonial authorities only served to advance the cause. Though it is true that the Great Awakening as an intercolonial phenomena of major proportions can be said to have terminated when the concerns of the Revolution became so absorbing, in Baptist and Methodist circles the awakening motifs strongly continued.

Methodism was late in reaching America—not until 1766 did work begin. At about the same time, Philip Embury (1728–1773) and Robert Strawbridge (?–1781) began Methodist activities in New York and Maryland respectively. A vigorous early lay preacher was Captain Thomas Webb (1724–1796) of the British army. In 1769 Wesley sent the first of eight officially appointed lay missionaries, the only one of which to remain active in American Methodism during and after the Revolution was Francis Asbury (1745–1816). During the 1770's, Methodism mushroomed chiefly in Maryland and Virginia, as a society movement loosely tied to the Church of England, as in the mother country. The first American "Conference" was held in Philadelphia in 1773. Growth continued during the Revolution, and a number of native lay preachers were drawn into the movement.

Except for the Methodist societies, there was little interest in the awakening in the Episcopal churches—in the South the rationalist current was strong (Latitudianarianism), in the North the High Church tendency of S.P.G. missionaries was not receptive of revival trends. The most conspicuous Episcopal evangelical was Devereux Jarratt (1733–1801), a rector in Virginia who had been converted under New Light Presbyterian preaching but had joined the Church of England because Wesley and Whitefield were within it. He did much to aid the Methodist societies before their organization into an independent church in 1784.

The Lutheran bodies were not directly much affected by the Great Awakening. Their growth in this period was largely because of the influx of German settlers. There was considerable pietistic feeling among them, however. Their outstanding leader, Henry Melchior Muhlenberg (1711–1787), had been encouraged to come to the colonies by the leaders at Halle. He himself represented a balance between pietist and orthodox emphases, and was vigorous in organizing new churches among German Lutherans, who had become the largest religious group in Pennsylvania by the middle of the eighteenth century. In 1748 he organized the first Lutheran synod to enjoy permanent existence. Among some of the smaller German bodies, the pietist spirit was much more in evidence.

Out of the discussions occasioned by the Great Awakening there emerged in New England the most considerable contribution that eighteenth century America had to make to theology—the work of Jonathan Edwards and his school. Born in a pastor's home in Connecticut in 1703, Edwards graduated from Yale in 1720. After a brief Presbyterian pastorate in New York, he became tutor at Yale. In 1727 he became associate pastor at Northampton, then full pastor when his grandfather, Solomon Stoddard (1643–1729) died. Brilliant in intellect, Edwards read widely in the philosophic and scientific works of his time, steeping himself in the writings of Locke and Newton. Early convinced of the classic Calvinist emphases on the sovereignty of God and of predestination, Edwards shaped his theological position boldly, using as grist for his mill the most recent discoveries of the age of reason. A leader in the revivals, he defended what he felt to be true revivalism, a work of God, against those who rejected all emotionalism in religion on the one hand and those who exploited it on the other. In 1746 appeared *A Treatise Concerning Religious Affections,* a theological defense of what he believed to be genuine revival, in which Edwards utilized psychological insights derived in part from Locke. A pastor and churchman, he was a champion of higher standards for church members, believing that only the saints—the true elect —should be members in full communion. When he acted on the basis of this position, no longer abiding by the laxer view, he was dismissed from his pulpit in 1750, despite a careful treatise on the subject which had appeared the year before, *Qualifications Requisite for Full Communion.*

Edwards became missionary to the Indians at Stockbridge, Massachusetts, where he found leisure to devote his theological and philosophical powers to the defense of Calvinism against Arminianism, under which term he characterized the liberal theological trends of the eighteenth century. In his famous *Treatise on the Will* (1754), he held that while all men have natural ability to turn to God, they lack moral ability—that is, the inclination—so to do. This determining inclination is the transforming gift of God's grace, though its absence is no excuse for sin. A systematic theologian, Edwards planned a massive work setting forth his entire position. Actually he finished only a few fragments of it, though some of his earlier treatises were apparently to be fitted into it. One of the fragments was *The Nature of True Virtue,* posthumously published in 1765. To Edwards' thinking, virtue is love to intelligent Being in general. But God has infinitely the greatest share of existence, he is infinitely the greatest Being, so true virtue must essentially and radically consist in supreme love to God. Such true virtue cannot be found through reason and understanding, for it is of the affections and the disposition; it arises from the ascendancy of the supreme passion, love, over self-love. "Disinterested benevolence" is one of its tests, and it is wholly a gift of God. But Edwards' systematic work was left largely unfinished. Called to serve as president of Princeton, he submitted to inoculation during a small-pox epidemic, contracted the disease and died a few weeks after assuming his new duties.

Edwards' views were championed by a group of followers, Joseph Bellamy (1719–1790), Samuel Hopkins (1721–1803), Jonathan Edwards, Jr. (1745–1801), and Nathaniel Emmons (1745–1840). This Edwardean group set the pattern of theological discussion in New England for many decades; they continued to debate the issues that he had raised, engaging in arguments with the Old Calvinists, followers of the federal or covenant theology. Though the Edwardeans were competent scholars and industrious workers, they lacked the poetic insights and breadth of vision that had characterized the master. Hopkins especially handled some of the Edwardean positions with harsh logic, yet in stressing the theme of "disinterested benevolence" he unwittingly prepared the way for some of the theological shifts of the nineteenth century.

9

The Impact of the Evangelical Revival. The Rise of Modern Missions

THE IMPACT of the Evangelical Revival in Britain was felt far beyond the range of its nominal adherents. Its influence on the older Non-Conformist bodies was stimulating, though unequal. Their condition in the first half of the eighteenth century was one of decay. Their leaders looked askance at Wesley and Whitefield at first; but as the revival continued the younger men caught its zeal. This was especially the case among the Congregationalists, who profited most of all. Their preaching was quickened, their zeal revived, their numbers rapidly increased. Many accessions came to them from those awakened by Methodism to whom the Methodist discipline was irksome. Many came to them from parishes of the establishment. By 1800 the Congregationalists occupied a very different position in England from that of 1700. The Particular Baptists also shared in this growth, as did the General Baptists, in spite of a considerable leaven of Arian thought. In 1770 an Evangelical wing separated as the General Baptist New Connection, in protest against the Unitarian tendency. The Presbyterians, on the other hand, were almost unaffected. Arianism and Socinianism were dominant among them. Their numbers dwindled. Nor were the Quakers much moved. Their noble humanitarian zeal was never more manifest, but the revival methods were too foreign to their spirit to make much impression.

The Methodist movement was forward-looking in its philanthropic sympathies, and the Evangelicals shared this trait. Methodism, under Wesley's leadership, sought to aid its poorer members financially, to provide work, to care for the sick, to furnish schools and cheap reading, and to overcome the coarseness and brutality of the lower classes.

The awakening of the new spirit of humanitarianism had one of its noblest illustrations in John Howard (1726–1790), a quiet, religious, country landlord, interested in schools and model cottages, a worshipper in Congregational and Baptist congregations; Howard was chosen high sheriff of Bedford in 1773. He was inexpressibly shocked at the moral and physical filth of the jails, their officers supported by what they could wring from the prisoners, not by salaries; no proper separation of prisoners, no release for those acquitted till their fees were discharged. Thorough in all that he did,

Howard visited practically all the jails of England, and laid the horrible results before Parliament in 1774. He then did a similar work for Scotland, Ireland, and the Continent. Much remained to be done, but he deserves the title of the "father of prison reform." His last years were devoted to equally self-sacrificing efforts to ascertain methods to prevent the spread of the plague. His devotion cost him his life in southern Russia.

A group which distinguished itself for devotion to good causes gathered around Henry Venn (1725–1797), rector of Huddersfield, and his son John (1759–1813), rector of Clapham. This group, chiefly of wealthy Anglican Evangelical laymen, was dubbed "the Clapham Sect." Its members were especially influential in ridding Britain and the dominions of slavery. That evil had received John Wesley's severest condemnation. It had been vigorously opposed by the Quakers. In the early nineteenth century, the Claphamites led the successful drive to eliminate it. Zachary Macaulay (1768–1838), father of the historian, once booked passage on a slave ship to observe conditions first hand. The most effective leader in the crusade was one of the most eminent of Evangelical laymen, William Wilberforce (1759–1833). Wealthy, popular, and a member of Parliament, he was "converted" in 1784 through the instrumentality of Isaac Milner. In 1797 he published his *Practical View of the Prevailing Religious System of Professed Christians in the Higher and Middle Classes in this Country Contrasted with Real Christianity*. It proved one of the most popular of Evangelical treatises. In 1787 he began his lifelong battle with slavery, resulting in the abolition of the slave trade in 1807, and of slavery itself throughout the British dominions in 1833.

In carrying out their religious, humane, and charitable efforts, Evangelicals of various types frequently worked together through voluntary societies. The revival movement gave a great impulse to the diffusion of Christian literature. Wesley published constantly through the Society for Promoting Christian Knowledge, which had been founded in 1699 (see p. 432). In 1799 the interdenominational Religious Tract Society was formed in London. Pietism had set the example of extensive and cheap publication of the Bible through Baron Canstein's great foundation in Halle, in 1710 (see p. 448). In 1804 the British and Foreign Bible Society was founded in London through the efforts of Evangelicals. Similar societies in Ireland, Scotland and the United States (see p. 509) were soon found; by their work the present enormous diffusion of the Scriptures has been possible.

Some form of religious teaching of children is probably as old as organized religion, and the Reformation age made much of catechetical instruction. Though attempts were made even earlier, the first systematic and successful efforts to reach the poor and unschooled with a Christian training on a large scale were in the Sunday schools, founded in 1780 by Robert Raikes (1735–1811), an Evangelical layman of the establishment, of Gloucester. In the absence of public education, he sought to give the ignorant training in the three "R's," and in Christian fundamentals by means of paid teachers, on the only day, Sunday, when the children were free. Attendance at church was also required. Raikes was proprietor of the *Gloucester Journal,* which published accounts of these activities. The work spread with great rapidity. Wesley and the Non-Conformists favored them. A Society for Promoting Sunday Schools throughout the British Dominions, was organized in London in 1785. A similar society was formed in Philadelphia in 1791. Though the growth of the movement was as rapid as it was permanent, it was not without clerical opposition, partly on account of its novelty and partly as a desecration of Sunday. The secular instruction rapidly decreased, and the paid teacher gave place to the voluntary leader. No Christian agency has become more fully part of normal modern church life.

One of the most important consequences of the Evangelical Revival was the rise of modern Protestant missions. The development of Roman Catholic missions in the Reformation age had been rapid and fruitful (see pp. 379–380). But lack of geographical contact coupled with certain internal problems and theological convictions long deterred equivalent Protestant efforts. However, with Dutch conquests work was begun in Ceylon, Java, and Formosa in the seventeenth century. The first English foreign missionary organization, the Society for the Propagation of the Gospel in New England, came into existence by act of Parliament in 1649, in response to the efforts among the Massachusetts Indians of John Eliot (see p. 433). At its expense his Indian Bible and other works, were printed. The Society for the Propagation of the Gospel in Foreign Parts was organized in 1701 (see p. 432). German Pietism produced the Halle-Danish missions from 1705 onward (see p. 448). In 1732 the notable missionary career of the Moravians began (see p. 452). Quakers had made some missionary efforts.

Interest in non-Christian peoples was aroused in Great Britain by the voyages of discovery in the Pacific, under government auspices, conducted by Captain James Cook (1728–1779), from 1768 to his death. These discoveries awakened the missionary zeal of William Carey (1761–1834), a shoemaker, then a Baptist preacher, and who was to show himself a man of remarkable talents as a linguist and a botanist, as well as of unquenchable missionary devotion. The result of his thought was his *Enquiry into the Obligation of Christians to use Means for the Conversion of the Heathens* of 1792. In October of that year this book and Carey's sermon on *Isaiah* 54:2, 3 induced the organization of the Baptist Society for Propagating the Gospel among the Heathen. Carey was its first missionary, and his letters from India proved a powerful stimulus to other missionary endeavor. In 1795 the London Missionary Society was formed, as an interdenominational enterprise, largely through the efforts of David Bogue (1750–1825), a Congregational minister of Gosport, and of Thomas Haweis (1734–1820), the Evangelical rector of Aldwinkle. Its first missionaries were sent in 1796 to Tahiti. It had long been

Congregational. The growing sense of missionary obligation led in 1799 to the organization of the Church Missionary Society, representative of the Evangelical wing of the establishment, through the agency of John Venn, rector of Clapham, and Thomas Scott, editor of the *Family Bible*. The Wesleyan Methodist Missionary Society of England was founded in 1817–1818. After small local beginnings in Scotland, as early as 1796, the Church of Scotland Mission boards came into being in 1825. This deepening of British missionary obligation roused interest widely in other lands. The early nineteenth century was to see the organization of extensive missionary societies, both denominational and interdenominational, in the United States and on the Continent (see pp. 506, 509).

10

The Revolutionary Epoch in the United States

THE THIRTEEN ENGLISH COLONIES in North America broke free from the mother country to become an independent nation during the last quarter of the eighteenth century, the Revolutionary Epoch in America. The attention of many men was turned from the strenuous interest in religion that had marked the Great Awakening by a long series of political and military events of absorbing concern. Increasing friction between colonies and crown led to the outbreak of the Revolution in 1775, the Declaration of Independence in 1776, the destructive war till 1783, and the protracted discussions concerning the framework of the new nation which did not terminate till the establishment of government under the Constitution of the United States in 1789. The revolutionary philosophy tended to be rationalistic in its attitude to religion, minimizing the prestige of the churches. Many of the trusted political leaders were influenced by the Deism of England or France (see p. 442). Thus for more than a generation men were absorbed in questions of revolutionary thought and action, and religion was at a low ebb.

The event of greatest significance for religion in this period in America was the achievement of religious freedom. This was a revolutionary step, for it marked a radical departure from the principles of uniformity and establishment that had marked western civilization for over a thousand years. Toleration had been granted in some European countries, notably the Netherlands and England, but the acceptance of religious freedom as a national principle was new. It was brought about by the interworking of many factors. The very multiplicity of religious organizations served to check the advance of any one church, and to prevent it from securing a majority of the population as its supporters. The breadth of the ocean was not conducive to the maintenance of vigorous colonial branches of European state churches; the sheer immensity of the continent made the maintenance of ecclesiastical establishments in it difficult. The desire for economic prosperity in colonies where laborers were scarce encouraged the overlooking of religious differences. The rise of toleration in England checked efforts to maintain rigorous uniformity, as when Charles II prohibited Massachusetts Bay officials from hanging any more Quakers in 1662. Of great importance was the witness of a number of religious groups stemming from the left wing of the Reformation—Mennonites, Dunkers—and the left wing of Puritanism—Baptists, Quakers. These groups believed in religious freedom on religious principles. During the exciting days of the civil wars in England, there were forged in certain Puritan circles strong arguments for religious freedom based on broadly orthodox, classical Christian premises. In Rhode Island and Pennsylvania, representatives of these positions had opportunity to put their ideas to work and to prove that an orderly civil state could be maintained without religious uniformity or establishment. The Great Awakening further stimulated the desire for freedom in religion, and its practical effect was to contribute heavily to the growth of unestablished bodies. Then, the representatives of rationalist views in religion were firm believers in religious liberty; they often served as leaders in drives for disestablishment.

These various factors combined in various ways in the different areas to secure religious liberty. Some of the most vigorous struggles came at the state level, in places where there had been strong establishments. In Virginia, after long years of political debate, the Virginia Statute for Religious Freedom, of which the original draft had been written by Thomas Jefferson, was passed in 1785, rationalists and Dissenters teaming up in the struggle. In New England, the rising tide of sentiment for religious liberty, coupled with the growing strength of the nonestablished bodies, led to the end of the Congregational establishments, in Connecticut in 1818, New Hampshire in 1819, and Massachusetts in 1833. At the national level, the various factors combined to bring about religious freedom from the beginning. Article VI of the Constitution provided that "No religious test shall ever be required as a qualification to any office or public trust under the United States." The First Amendment (1791) to the Constitution declared that "Congress shall make no law respecting an establishment of religion, or prohibiting the free exercise thereof; . . ." Thus the patterns of establishment and uniformity were given up, and, with the disappearance of the last state establishment, all churches survived as voluntary associations, equal before the law.

The attainment of American independence thrust new problems upon all American denominations. Some of which had been branches of European churches now found it necessary to reorganize on an independent basis. No

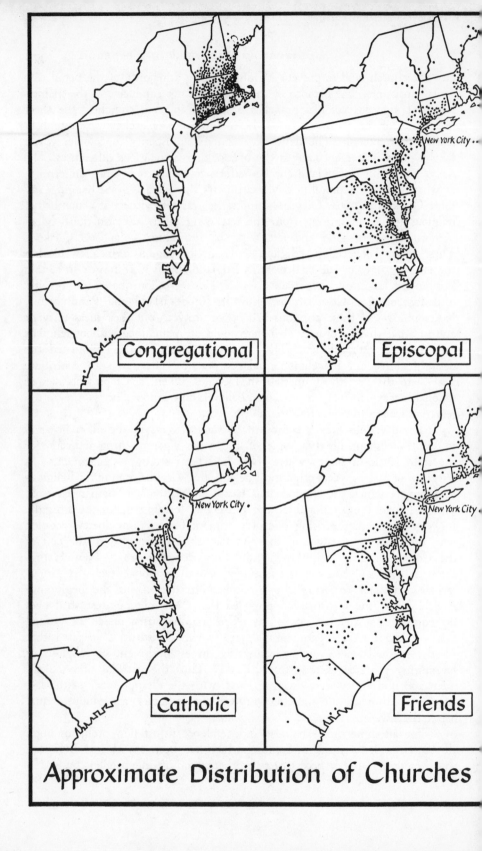

Congregational

Episcopal

New York City

Catholic

New York City

Friends

New York City

Approximate Distribution of Churches

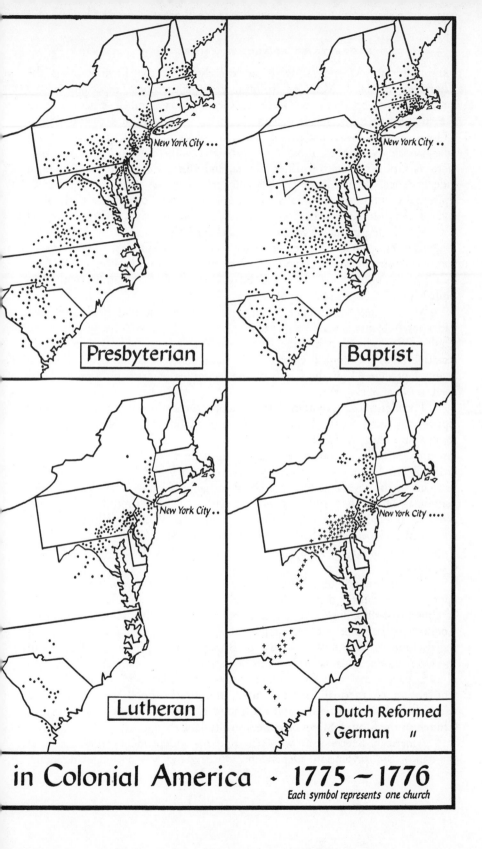

Presbyterian

Baptist

New York City ...

New York City ..

Lutheran

New York City .

New York City ....

• Dutch Reformed
+ German   "

in Colonial America ᐧ 1775 – 1776

Each symbol represents one church

communion in America suffered so severely from the Revolution as the Church of England. Many of its ministers and members, especially in the north, were sympathetic with the mother country, and it emerged from the struggle in ruins. Its very name seemed unpatriotic, and that of "Protestant Episcopal" was first suggested by a conference of clergy and laity of Maryland in November, 1780. Two years later William White (1748–1836), rector of Christ's Church in Philadelphia, and a hearty supporter of American independence, sketched out the plan under which the American Protestant Episcopal Church was essentially to be organized, in independence of the state and of English ecclesiastical control, with representative bodies composed not only of clergy but of laymen. He believed the prospect of securing an American episcopate remote. In accordance with White's suggestions, a voluntary convention, representative of eight states, met in New York City in October, 1784, and called the First General Convention to gather in Philadelphia in September, 1785.

Meanwhile, the Episcopal clergy of Connecticut had held aloof and had chosen Samuel Seabury (1729–1796) as bishop, and he had gone to England for ordination in June, 1783. Finding it impossible to receive consecration from the English episcopate in the absence of action by Parliament, Seabury procured it at the hands of the Nonjuror Scottish bishops in Aberdeen in November, 1784.

The General Convention of 1785 adopted a constitution for the Protestant Episcopal Church in the United States, largely the work of William White. It also appealed to the English bishops for the ordination of bishops for America. Seabury's Scottish ordination might be valid, but the derivation of orders from the parent English body was desired. The local Episcopal conventions of the several states were asked to name bishops. The General Convention reconvened in 1786 was able to report that the English bishops had procured an enabling act from Parliament, and that William White had been chosen bishop of Pennsylvania and Samuel Provoost (1742–1815) of New York. On February 4, 1787, they were consecrated by the archbishop of Canterbury.

Bishop Seabury and Bishops White and Provoost, who had stood on opposite sides during the Revolution and who represented different traditions of churchmanship, looked upon each other at first with some antagonism. Connecticut had not yet been represented in the General Convention, but the decision to have both a House of Bishops and a House of Deputies in the Convention, thus satisfying the demands for both clerical and lay emphases, paved the way for the adjustment of difficulties. In the General Convention of 1789 all parties united, the Prayer Book was revised and adapted to American needs, and the foundation of the Protestant Episcopal Church in the United States of America fully laid.

American Methodism was also ripe for independent organization at the end of the Revolution. Dependence on England was no longer desirable, nor was the continued relationship with the Episcopal Church very promising, in view of the latter's weakness, and inability to provide the sacraments, especially in places where Methodism was rapidly moving, as on the frontier. Wesley had tried in vain, in 1780, to procure ordination for clergymen for America from the bishop of London. He had long been convinced that bishops and presbyters in the ancient church were one order. He therefore, as a presbyter, felt empowered to ordain in case of necessity. At Bristol, on September 1, 1784, he, Thomas Coke (1747–1848), and James Creighton, all presbyters of the establishment, ordained Richard Whatcoat and Thomas Vasey deacons, and on the next day ordained them as presbyters or elders for America. On that day, too, Wesley, "assisted by other ordained ministers" "set" Coke "apart as a superintendent" for the same work. Wesley sent word to the American Methodists that he had appointed Francis Asbury, who had been active among them throughout the Revolution, as well as Coke "superintendents." But Asbury knew the American temper, and realized that the lay preachers must meet, freely accept Wesley's plan, and elect him and Coke as superintendents. Thus, beginning on December 24, 1784, the "Christmas Conference" at Baltimore did just that, forming the Methodist Episcopal Church. Asbury was ordained deacon, elder, and superintendent on successive days; a dozen other preachers were ordained as elders. A discipline was prepared. Coke and Asbury, much to Wesley's annoyance, soon began to call themselves "bishop," and in 1787 this was made official. The first General Conference met in 1792, guiding the growth of the rapidly expanding, fully independent new church.

The dependence on Holland of the Dutch and German Reformed Churches had long been weakening, and the severing of the ties completely, in 1792 and 1793 respectively, was largely a formality.

The Roman Catholics, of course, did not become independent, but they did redefine their relationships and achieved a national organization. They were still a tiny minority at the time of American independence, but their position was much improved as a result of the growing tradition of religious liberty and the patriotic activities of many of them during the Revolution. They had been under the vicar apostolic of London, but with independence this was no longer feasible. In 1784 the much-respected John Carroll (1735–1815) of Maryland was appointed prefect apostolic for the United States by Pius VI (1774–1799). Internal problems soon made it highly advisable to have a bishop, but the American Catholics feared being placed under a foreign bishop, and the priests petitioned Rome for the right to elect their own. This was granted, and in 1790 Carroll was consecrated bishop of Baltimore in London. In 1791 the first Roman Catholic synod in the United States was held at the cathedral city. In 1808 Baltimore, under Carroll, was made the seat of an archbishopric, while bishoprics were established in New York, Boston, Philadelphia, and Bardstown (Kentucky). By the year of Carroll's death the foundations of Roman Catholicism in the United States were strongly established, and the priesthood numbered more than one hundred, though the immigration that was so enormously to augment this communion was yet in the future.

The Moravians also retained close ties with the European center at Herrnhut. In 1775, indeed, a new policy of centralization was adopted so that the American Moravians were more than ever dependent on overseas control. It was an unfortunate move, for overseas leaders continued to think in European state-church terms, and misunderstood the opportunity offered by the freedom of the American scene. The Moravian impact soon diminished. Not until later in the nineteenth century did the American Moravian Church become autonomous.

Some of the denominations—Congregational, Baptist, Quaker—were already independent, and the Revolution did not directly affect them organizationally. Presbyterians were also independently organized, but they seized the opportunity to reorganize. During the 1780's they drew up a new constitution, which provided for a full Presbyterian structure, headed by the General Assembly, which first met in Philadelphia in 1789. Lutherans, also, had been autonomous, but during the Revolutionary epoch they began to develop organizationally. Muhlenberg (see p. 467), prepared a model constitution for his Philadelphia congregation in 1762, by which all officers were chosen by the congregation itself. The two basic features of American Lutheran polity were thus sketched—congregational in respect to the local congregation, presbyterian in respect to the standing of ministers in the synod. The synodical system spread slowly. The ministerium of New York was organized in 1786. A third synod was soon after formed in North Carolina. In 1820 a General Synod was formed, but only a portion of the Lutherans supported it. Nationality and theological tensions kept the Lutherans from any over-all national unity.

A religious body new in America that developed during the period of struggle for national independence was that of the Universalists. Belief in the salvation of all occasionally appeared in eighteenth-century America as elsewhere as a sporadic speculation. The father of organized Universalism was John Murray (1741–1815), who had been touched by Whitefield's preaching in his native England, and by the writings of James Relly (1722?–1778), who had passed from the status of one of Whitefield's preachers to that of an advocate of universal salvation. It was as a disciple of Relly that Murray came to America in 1770, and began an itinerating ministry, chiefly in New England. A Calvinist, Murray believed that Christ had made full payment not for the sins of a restricted group of the elect, but for all men, and immediate blessedness would be theirs at the judgment, when all unbelief in God's mercy would vanish. For those who fully believe, the divinely promised blessedness begins now.

A further impulse was given to Universalism when in 1780 Elhanan

Winchester (1751–1797), a Baptist minister of Philadelphia, independently of Murray, adopted Universalist views, which he advocated with eloquence. Unlike Murray, his general opinions were Arminian. Salvation is based on the ultimate free submission of all to God; but will not be achieved in the case of the unrepentant till their spirits have been purified by protracted, but not eternal, suffering. Even more influential was Hosea Ballou (1771–1852), long a pastor in Boston. Murray and Winchester had been Trinitarians. Ballou was an Arian, and in this Unitarian direction American Universalism has followed him. The purpose of the atonement was moral—to set forth God's love to men. Sin brings punishment, here or hereafter, till men turn from it to God.

By 1790 the Universalists were sufficiently numerous to hold a convention in Philadelphia. Three years later a New England convention was organized which in 1803 met in Winchester, New Hampshire, and adopted a brief creed which stated the basic tenets of the new denomination. The early converts to Universalism were prevailingly, though not always, from the humbler walks of life.

11

The German Enlightenment (Aufklärung)

*E*NGLAND had well advanced in its Deistic, rationalistic, and Unitarian development before the rise of Methodism. There the two streams long ran parallel. If the Evangelical Awakening, theologically, was in part a return to older doctrinal conceptions, it was even more an appeal to the strong, deep religious feelings of the nation. In Germany Pietism, with its emphasis on feeling, preceded the Enlightenment (Aufklärung), though continuing to run parallel to the latter movement when that developed. Pietism broke the grasp of confessional orthodoxy, but it raised up no theological leaders to take the place of the older dogmatic theologians. The critical, rationalist spirit of the eighteenth century, the works of the English Deists and their opponents, the radical popular modification of Deism in France—all these invaded Germany and found the intellectual field largely barren. The result was the rapid growth of the Enlightenment, as it styled itself. Strongly rationalistic, it sheltered many shades of opinion. More than in England or in France, by its critical and constructive work it prepared the way for a significant shift in theology, which, in the nineteenth century, was to spread widely throughout Protestant lands.

Leibnitz's speculations (see p. 428) were too deep to produce a powerful impression on his own age, though later they were of powerful effect. Thomasius (see p. 447) spread a rationalistic spirit, without working out a system. His influence was marked in developing an attitude of mind, so that he has not untruly been described as the "road-breaker of the Enlightenment." Its great protagonist, however, was Christian Wolff (1679–1754). Not a creative genius, it was Wolff's fortune so to embody and give expression to the unformed and inarticulate thought of his age, as to become the philosophical and theological leader of two generations of his countrymen. Skilled in mathematics, like most of the philosophers of his and the preceding century, he began lecturing on mathematics in Halle in 1707. Here his philosophy rapidly developed, in close connection with that of Leibnitz, whose deeper thoughts, however, he never grasped. That alone is true, Wolff held, which can be demonstrated by logical certainty akin to mathematics. Truth must thus rationally be deduced from the innate contents of the mind —the "pure reason." All that comes by experience is merely contingent and confirmatory. The world is composed of an infinite multitude of simple substances, each endowed with force, though not with all the qualities of Leibnitz's monads (see p. 428). Bodies are aggregations of these substances. The world is a huge machine, ruled by mechanical laws. The soul is that in us which is conscious of itself and of other objects. It is endowed with capacities of knowledge and desire. Their completeness of fulfilment is pleasure, their incompleteness, pain.

Since the world is contingent, it must have a cause. Hence God exists and has made the world. The laws of all rational thinking and acting give us the divine attributes. Since completeness is the highest aim of all being, all that aims at the completeness of ourselves and other men must be virtue. Hence the principles of right action are embodied, as with the Deists, in the fundamental divinely appointed constitution of man. Wolff did not deny that there was revelation, but declared that it could not contain anything in disagreement with reason. He felt that miracles were not impossible, though improbable, and that each would imply two acts of equal power, the interruption of the order of nature and its restoration after the event. Wolff's view of man was optimistic. He is going on individually, and socially, to larger completeness. Here was a breach with the older theology, both of orthodoxy and of Pietism, and one that came to its age with the conclusiveness of a logical demonstration. God, natural religion, originally implanted morality, and progress toward individual and racial perfection, not supernatural revelation or supernatural rescue from sin and ruin, are the proper objects of religious regard, even if Wolff allows a little standing room to revelation and miracle. Nor is man the hopeless or incapable being of the older theology.

Wolff's views aroused the hostility of his Pietistic colleagues in Halle. They procured from King Frederick William I (1713–1740) his removal. The royal sentence was even to them surprisingly strenuous. Wolff was ordered, in 1723, to leave the university within forty-eight hours, or be hanged. He found a refuge in Marburg, and was honorably restored to Halle in 1740 by Frederick the Great. His work had, however, become common property, and he added little to his achievements during the fourteen years in Halle till his death. His thought had become that of a large section of Germany. The sway of Pietism in Halle was over.

Less radical, but influential in aiding the new attitude of German thought, was Johann Lorentz von Mosheim (1694?–1755), professor in Helmstädt and finally in Göttingen. The most admired preacher of his time, master of a style of brilliancy in Latin or in German, he was basically a rational supernaturalist. He had no sympathy with the dogmatism of the orthodox. The emphases of the Pietists awakened no response in him; nor could he support the extreme rationalism of Wolff. He touched most fields of religious thought, and his influence, on the whole, favored the spread of the Enlightenment. His chief service was in the field of history. His *Institutiones Historiæ Ecclesiasticæ,* first issued in 1726 and in final form in 1755, embraced the whole story of the church. In his *Commentarii de rebus Christianorum ante Constantinum* of 1753, he treated the earlier centuries in ampler fashion. Mosheim well deserves the name of "the father of modern church history." He desired to be free of all partisan bias, and succeeded in remarkable measure at the expense of some colorlessness. His is the first church history which aimed to tell events exactly as they happened, without a cause to defend. As such, and by reason of its learning and style, his work long survived his death.

More extreme rationalism soon found its representatives in Germany. Hermann Samuel Reimarus (1694–1768), long a highly reputed professor of Oriental languages in Hamburg, and the leader in scholarly circles there, had travelled in England in early life, and had there adopted Deist views, in defense of which he wrote much, though his works were not issued till after his death, when they were put forth by Lessing between 1774 and 1778 as fragments found in the library of Wolfenbüttel—hence *Wolfenbüttel Fragments,* the publication of which aroused immense discussion. As with the Deists, all that is true is that natural religion which teaches the existence of a wise Creator, a primitive morality, and immortality—all ascertainable by reason. The world itself is the only miracle and the only revelation—all others are impossible. The writers of the Bible were not even honest men, but were moved by fraud and selfishness. It is a curious commentary on the condition of thought in Germany that Reimarus' writings, though widely criticised, were no less valued by others as a defense of religion against materialism and atheism.

Gotthold Ephraim Lessing (1729–1781), to whom the publication of Reimarus' religious writings was due, eminent as a dramatist and a literary and artistic critic, himself ranking as a German classic writer with Goethe and Schiller, though not agreeing wholly with Reimarus, presented in his *Education of the Human Race* of 1780 a theory of much plausibility. As the individual passes through the successive stages of childhood, youth, and manhood, so does the race. The Scriptures have been given by God to meet these needs. Childhood is moved by immediate rewards and punishments. For men in that condition the Old Testament is a divine book of training, with its promises of long life and temporal blessings for obedience. Youth is ready to sacrifice present ease and lesser goods for future success and happiness. For it, or for men in that state, the New Testament with its present self-surrender and eternal rewards is a fitting guide. But manhood is ruled by duty, without hope of reward or fear of punishment as its motives. Its guide is reason, though perhaps God may yet send some further revelation as its aid. Lessing's work spread wide the feeling in educated Germany that the historic Christian religion belonged to a past or to an inferior present stage of human development.

The effect of the Enlightenment was a wide diffusion of the views that what alone were valuable in the Scriptures were the truths of natural religion and its morality, divested of miracle or the supernatural. Jesus was a moral teacher rather than a personal center of faith. This was rationalism, and was characteristic of much of the strongest theological thinking of Germany by 1800, and was to continue powerful in the nineteenth century. Side by side with it, confessional orthodoxy and Pietism continued, though with decreasing intellectual appeal, and much, also, which may be called semi-rationalism. Yet the age was characterized, also, by vigorous polemic against superstitions, and a large development of voluntary and popular beneficence, and provision for popular education.

The eighteenth century was also marked, and nowhere more than in Germany, by the development of textual and historical studies of the Bible which initiated the modern period of criticism. The English scholar, John Mill (1645–1707), published a Greek Testament, based on a careful collation of manuscripts, in the year of his death. Jean le Clerc (1657–1736), brought up in Geneva, later an Arminian in Amsterdam from 1684 to his death, won fame as an exegete, through his attempts to explain the teaching of the Scriptures without dogmatic prepossessions—approaching them not to discover proof texts, but their actual meaning. Johann Albrecht Bengel (see p. 449), long head of the theological seminary in Denkendorf, in Württemberg, a man of Pietistic leanings, was the first to recognize that New Testament manuscripts may be grouped in families, and to establish the generally accepted critical canon that a more difficult reading is to be preferred. His *Gnomon,* or Index, of the New Testament, of 1742, was the most remarkable commentary thus far produced. Nothing, he declared, should be read into the Scripture, and nothing there contained omitted, which could be drawn out by the most rigid application of grammatical principles. Wesley made it the basis of his *Notes upon the New Testament* of 1755. Contemporaneously Johann Jakob Wettstein (1693–1754), of Basel and Amsterdam, spent nearly a lifetime of labor on his *Greek New Testament with Various Reading,* published in 1751–1752. Textual criticism and sound exegesis were thus given a great advance.

To Jean Astruc (1684–1766), royal professor of medicine in Paris, was due the announcement, in his *Conjectures* of 1753, of the composite character of *Genesis.* The theory won essential support in 1781 from Johann Gottfried Eichhorn (1752–1827), later the rationalistic professor in Göttingen, often called "the founder of Old Testament criticism," but it is only in the latter part of the nineteenth century that Astruc's discovery won extensive recognition.

In Johann August Ernesti (1707–1781), professor in Leipzig from 1742, Germany had a teacher who not only aided greatly that awakening of classical thought and ideals which affected German intellectual life in the closing years of the eighteenth century, but one who carried to New Testament interpretation the same principles which he applied to classical literature. The meaning is to be ascertained by the same grammatical and historical methods in the one field as in the other. Reimarus (see p. 481), in his seventh Fragment, published by Lessing in 1778, for the first time subjected the life of Christ to rigid historic methods, like those applied to secular history. His total rejection of the supernatural, the mythical, or the legendary left his results barren enough, but he raised questions of method and conclusion which have constituted the problems of this investigation, in large measure, ever since. Johann Salomo Semler (1725–1791), professor in Halle from 1752, was of Pietistic training, though in manhood a conservative rationalist. His importance was in the paths he indicated rather than in the results he achieved. He distinguished between the permanent truths in Scripture and the elements due to the times in which the several books were written. He denied the equal value of all parts of Scripture. Revelation, he taught, is in Scripture, but all Scripture is not revelation. The creeds of the church are a growth. Church history is a development. In particular he made a distinction between Petrine, Judaizing parties, in the early church, and Pauline, anti-Judaic, that was to play a great rôle in later discussions.

12

Trends in Nineteenth Century Protestant Thought in Germany

NOTHING SEEMED more characteristic of the earlier half of the eighteenth century than the dominance of "reason," or common sense. The age was unemotional, intellectual. It did a remarkable work in questioning that which had been accepted on tradition, in sweeping away ancient superstitions and abuses, and demanding the rightfulness of that which claimed authority. But it was cold and one-sided. It was met, as the eighteenth century went on, by an immense opposition. The claims of feeling asserted themselves, voiced in a "return to nature," that was too often a nature conjured up by the imagination, but accompanied by a renewed appreciation of the classical and the mediæval, and the revival of a sense of the supernatural in religion, often vague and obscure, but creating a totally different atmosphere in which man's claims as a feeling, rather than as a purely thinking, being were asserted.

Its most effective early apostle was Jean Jacques Rousseau (1712–1778); but the movement was manifested throughout Europe. Nowhere was it more evident than in Germany. Lessing shared it. Its most conspicuous literary representatives there were Johann Wolfgang von Goethe (1749–1832) and Johann Christoph Friedrich von Schiller (1759–1805). The older rationalism was not, indeed, swept from the field, but radically different patterns of life and thought, usually referred to under the generic term Romanticism, contended on more equal terms for mastery.

Philosophy, in the eighteenth century, had seemed to lead to no thoroughfare. Leibnitz had taught that all knowledge was an elucidation of that which was wrapped up innate in the monad. Wolff had affirmed the power of "pure reason" to give the only certainties. On the other hand, Locke had taught that all comes by experience, and though Hume had pushed to scepticism all conclusion based on cause and substance, he had viewed, like Locke, all knowledge as founded on experience. The British and the German tendencies were apparently mutually destructive. It was to be the work of Kant to combine and supersede both, on a new basis which should be the starting-point of modern philosophy, and to give a value to feeling which neither earlier parties had recognized. On the one hand, Kant was the climax and fulfilment of rationalistic, Enlightenment religion. But on the other hand, he was also the critic of the Enlightenment, laying bare its weaknesses and limitations, thus undermining its hold upon men, and revealing the need for fresh approaches, which came into their own in the early nineteenth century.

Immanuel Kant (1724–1804) was a native of Königsberg, where all his life was spent. His paternal ancestry, he believed, was Scotch. His earliest influences were Pietist. In 1755 Kant became a teacher in the University of Königsberg. His development was slow. He held at first to the school of Leibnitz-Wolff. Study of Hume awakened doubts as to its adequacy, though he did not become Hume's disciple. Rousseau profoundly influenced him with the "discovery of the deep hidden nature of man." In 1781 came Kant's epoch-making work, the *Critique of Pure Reason*—a blow struck primarily at the then dominant philosophy of Wolff. His formative treatises rapidly followed, and his thought was soon powerful in Germany. By 1797 his mental and physical powers had begun a decline which was to end in pitiful ruin. A little man in physical stature, never married, of strict moral uprightness, he devoted himself to his task with singular simplicity and fidelity.

Kant's system is in many respects a theory of knowledge. With the school of Locke and Hume he held that in our knowledge something, or some stimulus—the content—comes to the mind from without. With Leibnitz and Wolff he maintained that the mind has certain innate qualities, transcendent in the sense that they do not come by experience, which condition and give form to that which comes from without. Time and space are subjective conditions under which perception is possible. The mind classifies what comes to it from without under its own laws. These are the categories. Knowledge is, therefore, the product of two elements—a content from without, to which form is given by the laws of the mind. These two elements give us experience; but they do not give us knowledge of what things are in themselves, only of what our minds make of what has come into them from without. Such a demonstration from "pure reason," as Wolff had attempted of God, natural religion, and the constitution of the universe, is intellectually impossible. We cannot thus demonstrate the nature of these existences as they are in themselves. Nature may be studied as the realm of exact law, but the law is simply that of our own thinking.

While absolute knowledge of that beyond experience is, therefore, unattainable by purely intellectual processes, man is conscious of a feeling of moral obligation when he asks what he ought to do. This subject was developed in Kant's *Critique of the Practical Reason* of 1788. When man answers the question as to conduct, he feels within the "categorical imperative"—an imperative because a command; and categorical because without conditions. It is so to act that the principles of action may become those of universal law—in a phrase, do your duty. That moral law within is the noblest of man's possessions, it shows him as a personality and not as a machine.

With this "categorical imperative" three postulates, or inseparable thoughts, are united. The most evident is, that if man ought to do his duty, he can. Hence man must have freedom. And freedom gives us a glimpse of a supersensuous realm of moral purpose—of a sphere of moral order. A second postulate is that of immortality. If life should be subjected to the categorical imperative it must last long enough for that result to be accomplished. Closely connected is the third postulate. Virtue should result in happiness. Experience does not give that union. Hence its accomplishment demands a power that can unite the two. The third postulate is, therefore, God. His existence is in the "pure reason" only a hypothesis; but in the postulates of the practical reason it becomes a conviction.

When Kant set forth his own religious ideas, on the basis of practical rather than theoretical or pure reason, it was the familiar rationalistic Enlightenment faith that was presented. His *Religion Within the Bounds of Reason Only* (1793) emphasized morality as the prime content of the practical reason, and reduced religion practically to theistic ethics. Evil and the categorical imperative contest for the obedience of man. One ruled by this principle of moral good—the categorical imperative—is pleasing to God, is a son of God. Of this sonship Christ is the highest illustration. The invisible church is the ideal union of all those obedient to moral law. The visible church is a union to develop this obedience. Its complete achievement will be the kingdom of God. Kant's contribution to Christian theology was not his rationalizing interpretation of doctrines, but his vindication of man's profoundest feelings as bases of practical religious conviction and moral conduct. Romanticists soon developed this lead in quite a different direction than Kant's.

A decided impulse to the historical interpretation of the Bible was given by Johann Gottfried von Herder (1744–1803), in early life an intimate with Goethe, influenced by personal contact with Kant, and an eager supporter of the romantic movement. From 1776 to his death he was court preacher in Weimar. His *Spirit of Hebrew Poetry* appeared in 1782–1783. His *Philosophy of the History of Mankind* in 1784–1791. Religion, especially Christianity, is the embodiment of that which is deepest in the feelings of mankind. The Scriptures are to be understood in the light of the views and feelings of the times in which the several books were written. They are, therefore, essentially a religious literature. What is true and permanent in them must be distinguished from the temporary and local.

Out of this romantic movement came the most influential German theologian of the opening nineteenth century, and one whose work has moulded religious thought far outside the borders of his native land— Friedrich Daniel Ernst Schleiermacher (1768–1834). The son of a Prussian army chaplain, he was educated by the Moravians, fell under the influence of the views of Wolff and Semler, and was then greatly impressed by Plato,

Spinoza, Kant, and Romanticism. In 1796 he became hospital chaplain in Berlin, then a center of the Enlightenment, and there published in 1799 his remarkable *Addresses on Religion,* directed to the "cultured despisers" of religion. In these his fundamental thoughts, deeply influenced by romantic currents, were set forth. From 1804 to 1807 he was professor in Halle. In the last-named year he settled once more in Berlin, becoming a little later pastor of the Trinity Church. In 1810, on the founding of the University of Berlin, he was appointed professor of theology, a post which he occupied till his death in 1834. In 1821–1822 he set forth his mature views in his *Christian Faith According to the Principles of the Evangelical Church.*

Schleiermacher's prime significance is that he took up into his own system the results of previous tendencies, and gave to theology a new basis, and to the person of Christ a meaning largely ignored in his age. Orthodoxy and rationalism had both made religion essentially acceptance of an intellectual system and an externally authoritative rule of conduct. To the orthodox religion was based on assent to the truths of revelation and obedience to the will of God. To the rationalists it was acceptance of natural theology and of universal morality ascertained by the reason. Both parties in the eighteenth century looked upon religion and morality as primarily means for securing a happy immortality. To Schleiermacher religion belongs to the realm of "feeling." In itself religion is neither a body of doctrines, revealed or rationally certified, nor a system of conduct, though both belief and conduct flow from religion.

Schleiermacher took much from Spinoza, Leibnitz, and Kant. In our experience we perceive the antithesis of the manifold and changing over against a principle of unity and permanency. These antitheses give us the Absolute and eternal—God—without whom all would be chaos; and the world, without which all would be empty. The Absolute is throughout all. God is therefore immanent in His world. Man is, in himself, as with Leibnitz, a microcosm, a reflection of the universe. As contrasted with that which is universal, absolute, and eternal, he feels himself finite, limited, temporary— in a word, dependent. This feeling of dependence is the basis of all religion. To bridge over the gulf between the universal and the finite, to bring man into harmony with God, is the aim of all religions. The worth of each religion is to be measured by the degree in which this result, which is the aim of all, is accomplished. Hence religions are not to be divided into true and false, but into relative degrees of adequacy. All advances in religion throughout history are in a true sense revelations, a fuller manifestation to human consciousness of the immanent God. Of all religions thus far known to men, Christianity is the best, since it most fully accomplishes what it is the aim of all religions to achieve. Its problems are those most fundamental to all religion, sin and pardon, separation and reconciliation. And in the Christian religion the person of Christ is the central element. He is Himself the reconciliation of the finite with the universal, the temporal with the eternal, the union of God and man. He is, therefore, the Mediator of this reconciliation to others. Hence Schleiermacher was strongly Christocentric. The life thus uniting the temporal and the eternal—man and God—is now immortal. An immortality in duration is a great hope, but true immortality is a quality of life rather than a mere question of duration.

Doctrines are these fundamental religious experiences defining and interpreting themselves intellectually; but these explanations have only a relative and secondary value. They have changed and may change. They are simply the forms in which abiding truth from time to time expresses itself.

In Schleiermacher's view, morality is the result of the proper understanding of that of which man is a part, the family, the community, the state, the world. Such an enlarging view of his real place in these relations will drive out selfishness and self-centering. Morality is not religion, nor religion morality; but religion is the indispensable friend and advocate of morality. It asks the question insistently, what ought to be, in the light of the Christian consciousness.

Schleiermacher was condemned by the orthodox of his day as too radical, by the rationalists as too visionary; but no one influenced religious thinking in Protestant circles in the nineteenth century more, or more variously.

Kant's system contained two evident points of difficulty. It denied the power of intellectual processes to give knowledge of things as they are in themselves, and it did not explain how mental processes are necessarily the same in all individuals. Philosophy was developed in the clarification of both these difficulties, under the influence of Romanticism, into idealism, by Johann Gottlieb Fichte (1762–1814), Friedrich Wilhelm Joseph von Schelling (1775–1854), and especially by Georg Wilhelm Friedrich Hegel (1770–1831). A native of Stuttgart, educated at Tübingen, Hegel taught in Jena, with scanty following, from 1801 to 1807. From 1808 to 1816 he was the head of the gymnasium school in Nürnberg. The year 1818 saw his appointment to a professorship in Berlin, where his fame rapidly rose to that of the first philosopher of his day in Germany. He died of cholera, at the height of his reputation and activity, in 1831. This distinction was in spite of his uninteresting and obscure manner of presentation in the classroom.

To Hegel the universe is a constant development of the Absolute, that is, God, through struggle and effort. The Absolute in Spirit, and its development is in accordance with the laws by which Mind thinks itself out logically. These always involve three stages, a movement in one direction—a thesis. This proceeds till it encounters its opposition or its limitation—the antithesis. But the two are but aspects of the one Absolute, and both thesis and antithesis unite in a higher union, the synthesis. Over against the "idea," the thesis, as its antithesis, is nature—but the two unite in higher synthesis in man, who is the union of both mind and matter. Since all is the Absolute developing in accordance with the laws of all thought, the laws of thought are the laws of things; and since our thinking is a fragment of that of the Absolute, in so far as it is true, it gives us true knowledge of the things outside our minds, and is the same in all minds since a part of the one Absolute. Since we are portions of the Absolute come to consciousness, a prime duty of the finite spirit is to realize its relation to the Absolute—such realization is religion. Religion may, indeed, begin, as with Schleiermacher, in feeling; but to be true it must become real knowledge. Every religion is an attempt thus to know God, of which Christianity is the most complete realization. God is always striving to reveal Himself; yet this outworking must always be through the three necessary stages of development. Thus the Father is the divine unity—the thesis. He objectifies Himself in the Son—the antithesis. The uniting love is the Holy Spirit—the synthesis. The whole process gives the Trinity. So regarding the incarnation. God is the thesis. He is distinguished from finite humanity, the antithesis. Both unite in the higher synthesis, the God-man. Hegel's system did much to substitute for the older sharp distinction between the divine and the human, the sense of their fundamental unity so prevalent in nineteenth-century Protestant theology.

The breadth, power, and ingenuity of Hegel's synthesis won for him great popularity; his system became the most influential in the philosophical circles of his day, and had great impact in the world of thought generally. Though Hegel was philosopher of religion and not theologian, his approach deeply influenced theology. His views were soon sharply challenged, but they continued to attract interpreters, especially in Great Britain and America, throughout the latter half of the nineteenth century.

Hegel's theory of development had a significant application to New Testament criticism in the work of Ferdinand Christian Baur (1792–1860), professor in Tübingen from 1826 to his death, and founder of the new Tübingen school in theology. The essential features of his interpretation were sketched by Baur in his account of the parties in the Corinthian Church, published in 1831, and were thenceforward developed in a series of brilliant studies, which won many disciples. All historical progress, Baur felt, with Hegel, must be through the three stages of thesis, antithesis, and synthesis. Semler (see p. 483) had already taught the existence of Petrine (Judaizing) and Pauline parties in the early church. These gave the elements of the Hegelian triad. Christianity, so Baur taught, began as essentially a Messianic Judaism. This—the thesis—was the position of all the original Apostles. The necessary antithesis inevitably arose and was Pauline Christianity. Petrine and Pauline views struggled far into the second century; but the inevitable synthesis came eventually, in the Old Catholic Church, which honored both Peter and Paul, and was unconscious that they had ever stood in serious opposition.

The most debated use made by Baur of this reconstruction of the early history of the church was a redating of the books of the New Testament. They must display the biases of the various aspects of this development—

that is, they must show "tendencies." Applying this test, Baur found only *Romans, Galatians,* and the *Corinthian* epistles genuinely Pauline, since they alone showed traces of the conflict. The others did not reveal the struggle, and hence must be dated later, when it had become a forgotten story. *Revelation* was early and Judaizing. In 1847 Baur turned to the investigation of the Gospels by the same methods. *Matthew* reveals Judaizing tendencies, and is the oldest. *Luke* is probably a reworking of Marcion's (see p. 54) gospel. *Mark* sought to hide the conflict, and is later, while *John* is not only irenic but betrays familiarity with controversies of the later half of the second century. The greater part of the New Testament was, therefore, written in the second century.

Baur's discussion aroused advocates and opponents in great numbers. Its ultimate effect on New Testament investigation was most fruitful. These debates immensely enlarged the knowledge of the early church and of its literature. Their results have been, however, the best answer to Baur's own theories. He had no adequate conception of the significance of Christ in the development of the early church. There were important differences between Judaic and Pauline Christianity; but to reduce the intellectual reactions of nascent Christianity to these only is far too simple. There were many other shades of unlikeness. Above all, an increasing knowledge of the second century, and an appreciation of its atmosphere impossible in Baur's time, makes it inconceivable that the books which he assigns to it could, for the most part, have been then written. They are not of that age and outlook.

By the time that Baur began his work, and for the next generation, German theologians were divided into three main groups. On one extreme stood the rationalists, the continuation of the type of the closing eighteenth century. Among them none was of greater influence than Heinrich Eberhard Gottlob Paulus (1761–1851), professor from 1789 in Jena, who spent the latter part of his long life (1811–1844) as professor in Heidelberg. An opponent of all supernaturalism, his *Life of Jesus* of 1828 is typical of the woodenness of the rationalism of his period. Christ's walking on the water, he explains as a misunderstanding of the disciples, viewing Christ through the mist as He walked on the shore. The feeding of the five thousand was accomplished by the generous freedom with which Christ bestowed the little food He had, thus awakening the generosity of those in the throng who had a larger supply. Christ's death was no real event. He revived in the tomb, aroused by the earthquake, and returned to His disciples.

Confessional orthodoxy of the most uncompromising pattern had a notable representative in Ernst Wilhelm Hengstenberg (1802–1869), professor in Berlin from 1826 to his death. He began under rationalist influence, but then for a time became leader in Pietist circles. By 1840 he emerged as a vigorous champion of strict Lutheran orthodoxy.

Between the two extremes stood a "mediating" school, largely influenced by Schleiermacher, sharing his warmth of Christian feeling, perhaps generally intensified, strongly devoted, like him, to the personal Christ, but disposed to accept many of the results of criticism, especially regarding the Biblical inspiration and narratives.

Most influential of these "mediating" theologians was Johann August Wilhelm Neander (1789–1850). Of Hebrew parentage, originally David Mendel, he took the name by which he is known at baptism in 1806, to signify his new birth. A student under Schleiermacher in Halle, it was his teacher's influence that secured for him a professorship in Berlin in 1813, which he filled with distinction till his death in 1850. Neander turned his attention to church history with a series of remarkable monographs, and in 1826 published the first volume of his *History of the Christian Religion and Church,* at which he labored for the rest of his life. Distinguished by thorough use of the sources, Neander's conception of the history of the church was that of a divine life gaining increasing control over the lives of men. That life is manifested in individuals. Hence, Neander's work was a series of striking biographical portraits. Its weakness was its over-emphases on the influence of individuals, and its scanty appreciation of the institutional or corporate life of the church. Yet it put church history on a new plane of achievement. Quite as significant as his writings were the influence of Neander's personal intercourse with his students, and his childlike, unaffected Christian trust. "The heart makes the theologian," was frequently on his lips, and expresses his character. Few men have been more personally helpful or more beloved.

A similar personal influence was exercised by Friedrich August Gottreu Tholuck (1799–1877), who became a professor in Berlin in 1823, but held a chair in Halle from 1826 to his death. A man of Pietistic sympathies, yet with acceptance of the critical views in many features, he turned Halle from the rationalism which had dominated since the time of Wolff to the Evangelicalism which characterized it in the nineteenth century. As a preacher he was distinguished. His kindness to English and American students was unwearied.

A third important representative of the "mediating" school was Isaac August Dorner (1809–1884), a student in Tübingen from 1827 to 1832, and an instructor there in 1834. After service in a number of German universities he closed his career as professor in Berlin from 1862 to his death in 1884. Dorner's most important early publication was his *Doctrine of the Person of Christ* of 1839. His completed theology was formulated in fulness, late in life, in his *System of the Doctrines of Faith* of 1879–1881. Theology and philosophy are truly akin, but both embody themselves in a progressive historic development. Christian belief thus finds its attestation in the Christian consciousness, which in turn recognizes the validity of the spiritual experience recorded in the Scriptures, and has had its growing clarification in Christian history. The central doctrine of Christianity is the incarnation in which Christ is the revelation of what God is, and of what man may be—the Head of humanity. Dorner had much influence in Great Britain and America.

This "mediating school," by reason of its warm Christian faith, and its partial, though cautious, acceptance of critical positions, had considerable following in the Christian world. Its mediating approach, however, was not able to deal with the intellectual revolutions of the nineteenth century, and in Germany it hardly survived its principal leaders, as other positions came to dominance.

The most epoch-making book in German theological development came not from any of these schools, but from a young scholar of twenty-seven at the University of Tübingen, in 1835, David Friedrich Strauss (1808–1874). Strauss had made himself at home in the Hegelian philosophy. He was familiar with the earlier positions of Baur. He was, also, acquainted with the interpretation as mythical which the historian and statesman Barthold Georg Niebuhr (1776–1831) had made of the early story of Rome. These principles he now applied to the life of Christ. He was far from denying that much could be known of Jesus' earthly career; it must be viewed, however, as moving wholly in the realm of the human, like other historical events. Of the Gospel sources, he regarded that bearing the name of *John* as most removed in time and of the least historical worth, thus differing from much of the scholarship immediately before him which, notably that of Schleiermacher, had preferred *John* to the others. Strauss gave the first place to *Matthew,* but none of the Gospels were by eye-witnesses. Miracles are inherently impossible; but the Gospels are full of them. The ordinary rationalistic interpretations, like those of Paulus (see p. 490), are ridiculous; the assertions of the ultra-rationalists, like Reimarus (see p. 481), that they were recounted with intent to deceive, are impossible. The only adequate explanation is that the simple, natural facts of Christ's life are covered over with myth. The men of that time were expecting a Messiah who would be a wonder-worker; they were looking for the fulfilment of Old Testament prophecy; they had great true ideas, such as that the race is partly divine and partly human, that it rises above death by union with God. These were attributed to, or regarded as impersonated in, Christ. Jesus lived; but the Christ of the New Testament is therefore, essentially, in all His superhuman characteristics a creation of myth.

Strauss's book aroused an enormous controversy. He had attacked the views of every party in contemporary Germany, the orthodox, the rationalists of all shades, the "mediating" theologians. He met unsparing denunciation. He was debarred all further theological employment, and lived an embittered existence. Yet his work placed the investigation of the life of Christ on a new plane, he answered conclusively the older rationalists, and the discussions which he inaugurated were productive for religious scholarship. Two fundamental criticisms of his approach have proven especially telling. Either the church created that which is important in the figure of Christ, albeit unconsciously, or Christ is the source of the church. If Strauss and those who shared his essential position were right, the former conclusion is true—but serious theological scholarship has found the other view prevailingly preferable. Nor has the purely human historical interpretation of the life of Christ led to the construction of a really plausible picture that could long be maintained. Albert Schweitzer (1875—), in his famous *The Quest of the Historical Jesus* (1910), showed how such efforts end in what is essentially failure.

The most potent influence both in theology and in the interpretation of the history of the early church in Germany in the latter half of the nineteenth century was Albrecht Ritschl (1822–1889), pioneer of liberalism and theologian of moral values. At a time when the approaches of Schleiermacher and Hegel were losing their appeal, Ritschl's effort was to frame a new apologetic synthesis between Christian faith and the new knowledge contributed by scientific and historical scholarship. A disciple at first of the school of Baur, he broke with its main contentions when he published the second edition of his *Origin of the Old Catholic Church* in 1857. Baur's Hegelian Petrine thesis and Pauline antithesis are not adequate explanations of the growth of the early church. There were differences, but all parties had a greater fundamental unity in owning the mastery of Jesus. Nor are the unlikenesses of early Christianity resolvable into two sharply antagonistic parties. There were many shades of opinion. Christianity came into no empty world, but one filled with religious, philosophical, and institutional ideas. By them, especially on Gentile soil, the simple, primitive truths of Christianity were profoundly modified, resulting in the theology and institutions of the Old Catholic Church. Ritschl advocated the full use of the tools of historical criticism in order to understand fully the primitive Christian community and the historical Jesus. Stressing the centrality of Jesus and the given nature of the first century church, Ritschl won a large following among Protestant scholars, in America as well as in Europe.

Ritschl began teaching in the University of Bonn in 1846. In 1864 he became professor in Göttingen, where he remained till his death. Here he published, in 1870–1874, his chief theological work, *The Christian Doctrine of Justification and Reconciliation*. Ritschl had few personal disciples, but the propagating influence of his writings was great.

Ritschl was much influenced by Kant's assertion of moral feeling as the basis of practical certainty and denial of absolute intellectual knowledge, and by Schleiermacher's affirmation of religious consciousness as the foundation of conviction. Yet Schleiermacher's assertion of the normative value of religious consciousness was, to his thinking, too individual. The real consciousness is not that of the individual, but that of the Christian community, the church. Nor is that consciousness a source of abstract speculative knowledge. It has to do with eminently practical, personal relationships—those of God and the religious community—sin and salvation. Hence "natural" or speculative philosophic theology is valueless. Philosophy may give, as with Aristotle, a "first cause"; but that is far from a loving Father. Such a practical revelation is made to us only through Christ. That revelation is mediated to us through the consciousness of the first disciples. Hence the Old Testament, as revealing their religious background, and especially the New Testament, as recording their consciousness of Christ and His Gospel, are of supreme value. To ascertain the religious consciousness recorded in the Old and New Testaments, no theory of inspiration is necessary, only normal historical investigation.

Though Ritschl thus rejected metaphysics as an aid to Christian truth, he made much use of a theory of knowledge advocated by the philosopher Rudolf Hermann Lotze (1817–1881). While it is true, Lotze held with Kant, that things as they are in themselves cannot be known, he affirmed that they are truly known in their attributes or activities. A brick pavement is known, and truly known, to me as a sidewalk. To the ants whose mounds of sand rise between the bricks it may be a home. What it is abstractly or in itself I have no means of knowing. If that knowledge in its attributes is one affecting my conduct it is a "value judgment." So Ritschl held that to those who came in contact with Him in the first Christian community, Christ was truly a revelation of what God is in love, the pattern of what man may be, the bearer of God's moral authority over men, and the Founder of the kingdom of God. As such He was truly known; but to ask whether He was pre-existent, was of two natures, or was one person of a Trinity, is to ask what the experience of the early church could not answer, and what only metaphysics could assert or deny. This recognition of what Christ is and signifies, arouses faith in men, that is trust and love toward God through Christ. This new attitude is accompanied by the forgiveness and removal of sin, which constituted the barrier between man and God—justification—and the new relationship expresses itself in desire to do the will of God and to live the life of the kingdom —reconciliation. The Christian life is essentially social, hence Redeemer, redeemed, and the redeemed community are inseparable conceptions. The Gospel is an ellipse with two foci: justification and reconciliation, and the kingdom of God. These ideas of salvation, Ritschl believed, have never been more clearly formulated, in later church history, than by Luther.

Among the prominent Ritschlians were Wilhelm Herrmann (1846–1922) and Adolf von Harnack (1851–1930). Herrmann, professor of theology at Marburg, was a leading exponent of liberal theology. Of greatest influence in liberalism was Harnack of Berlin, prince of church historians. His outstanding work was the *History of Dogma,* which appeared in a seven-volume English edition between 1894 and 1899. His *What is Christianity?* (1901) was a classic statement of advanced liberal theology. The Ritschlian spirit, with its earnest piety and devotion to truth, had a great vogue in Germany, England, and America in the closing years of the nineteenth and opening years of the twentieth centuries.

In the 1890's, however, the Ritschlian approach was challenged by the "history of religions" school. This school sought to universalize the historical approach to religion by putting Christianity in its context with the other religions of the ancient Near East. What Ritschl had done so forcefully in tracing the historical *development* of Christian doctrine, it tried to do for the *beginnings* of Christianity itself, accusing him of provincialism in not following out his method fully. Its most distinguished exponent was Ernst Troeltsch (1865–1923). His historical work was brilliant, especially his *Social Teachings of the Christian Churches* (1912), but the relativism of the *Religionsgeschichtliche* school contributed to the crisis of liberalism.

13

British Protestantism in the Nineteenth Century

*E*NGLISH RELIGIOUS LIFE in the opening years of the nineteenth century was dominated by the spiritual awakening of the Evangelical revival, which was leading to much separation from the establishment (see p. 463). In the establishment that revived zeal was represented by the Evangelical party, which in the nineteenth century became the low-church party, in opposition to revived high-church emphases. The Evangelicals, like the Methodists, were keenly alive to works of practical and missionary activity (see p. 470). The Anglican Evangelicals increased in importance in ecclesiastical affairs; they won their first bishopric in 1815, and by mid-century were the leading party of the church, with great strength among the laity. But the nineteenth century saw the shaping of a new liberal, broad-church movement, and the revivification of the high-church tradition.

The broad-church impulse arose out of the dissatisfaction with the current theological formulations. Intellectually, all parties in the Church of England at the opening of the nineteenth century stood on the basis of the rather provincial discussions of the eighteenth century. Theology was looked upon in the same rationalistic fashion—a system of intellectual demonstration, or of authoritative revelation, or both combined. The stirrings of new intellectual forces were being felt however. English poetry flowered into splendid blossoming with the opening years of the nineteenth century. Romanticism, as powerfully as in Germany (see p. 484), was beginning to produce an intellectual atmosphere wholly unlike that of the preceding age. The novels of Sir Walter Scott are familiar illustrations of this new outlook. A new humanitarianism, largely due to the Methodist revival, was developing, and was to be manifested multitudinously in reformatory movements. All the tendencies were sure to affect theological thinking and religious ideals.

Probably the most stimulating force in the religious thinking of the first quarter of the nineteenth century was that of Samuel Taylor Coleridge (1772–1834), eminent as a poet, literary critic, and philosopher. A Neo-Platonist in his early sympathies, he studied in Germany, in 1798 and 1799, which led to acquaintance not only with the masters of German literature but with the thought of Kant, Fichte, and Schelling, and a philosophical outlook then largely unfamiliar in England. Coleridge never worked out a rounded system. His most significant volume was his *Aids to Reflection* of 1825. Over against the rationalizing of Paley he held to a distinction between "reason" and "understanding." To Coleridge "reason" was a power of intuitive perception, an "inward beholding," by which religious truths are directly perceived. This "moral reason" has, as its associate "conscience," which is an unconditional command, and has as its postulates the moral law, a divine lawgiver, and a future life. Religious certainty is thus based not on external proofs but on religious consciousness. Hence, he has been called the "English Schleiermacher." In most respects Coleridge was the forerunner of the broad-church way of thinking; but in his emphasis on the church as a divine institution, higher and nobler than anything "by law established," he prepared the way for the high-church party.

The work of Coleridge in its religious aspects was continued by Thomas Arnold (1795–1842), who began his famous mastership of Rugby in 1828. A man of profound and simple Christian faith, his helpfulness to his pupils was great. His views much resembled those of Herder (see p. 486). The Bible is a literature, to be understood in the light of the times in which it was written, but its divine truth finds us.

Biblical criticism was furthered, in a very moderate fashion, by Henry Hart Milman (1791–1868), dean of St. Paul's, London, from 1849, by his *History of the Jews* in 1829, in which he applied critical methods to the Old Testament. His most valuable work was his *History of Latin Christianity* of 1855.

Not willing to be reckoned to the broad-church school, yet contributing much to its spread, was John Frederick Denison Maurice (1805–1872). The son of a Unitarian minister, he conformed to the establishment, and became chaplain of Guy's Hospital in London. In 1840 he was appointed to a chair in King's College, of which he was deprived for his opinions in 1853. The year after he founded the Working Men's College, and was instrumental in inaugurating a Christian socialist movement. In 1866 he was appointed to a professorship in Cambridge. To Maurice's thinking, Christ is the Head of all humanity. None are under the curse of God. All are sons, who need no other reconciliation than a recognition by them of their sonship, with the filial love and service to which such recognition will naturally lead. Presumably all will ultimately be brought home to God and none forever lost.

Not very unlike Maurice in his theology, but primarily a great preacher, was Frederick William Robertson (1816–1853), educated under Evangelical influences, then passing through a period of intense questioning to a broad-church position. From 1847 to his early death he was minister in Brighton. No English sermons of the last century were so influential on both sides of the Atlantic as those of Robertson. Spiritual truth must be spiritually discerned rather than intellectually proved. The nobility of Christ's humanity attests and leads to faith in His divinity.

Much influence in the spread of broad-church opinions was wielded by Charles Kingsley (1819–1875), rector of Eversley, the novelist, and by Alfred, Lord Tennyson (1809–1892), whose *In Memoriam* of 1850 was fully a broad-church poem. Similarly to be reckoned were Arthur Penrhyn Stanley (1815–1881), dean of Westminster, and Frederic William Farrar (1831–1903), dean of Canterbury. Great commotion was caused in 1860 by the *Essays and Reviews,* in which a group of Oxford scholars tried to present Christianity in the light of contemporary science and historical criticism, and by the trial of Bishop John William Colenso (1814–1883) of Natal for his Pentateuchal criticism published in 1862. Important contributions to Biblical scholarship were made by three Cambridge scholars, Brooke Foss Westcott (1825–1901), Joseph Barber Lightfoot (1828–1889), and Fenton John Anthony Hort (1828–1892). Westcott and Hort's critical text of the Greek New Testament, published in 1881 after nearly thirty years of scholarly labor, became standard. The broad-church movement was, however, never, strictly speaking, a party. Its numbers were not large, but its influence on English religious thought was widespread.

A highly significant, deeply devout and intensely self-conscious development within the Church of England in this period was the Oxford, or Tractarian, movement, out of which came the Anglo-Catholic party. The movement gave new life and direction to the high-church tradition, which had become somewhat arid. The early years of the second quarter of the nineteenth century saw several significant breaches in the exclusive privileges of the establishment. The Test (see p. 417) and Corporation Acts were repealed in 1828. Roman Catholics were made eligible to the House of Commons and to most public offices in 1829. The July Revolution of 1830 in France stimulated a demand for reform in parliamentary representation, which triumphed, after heated struggles, in 1832, and transferred power largely from the landed gentry to the middle classes, thus increasing Non-Conformist influence. To many conservative churchmen it seemed that the foundations of church and state were being removed. They were disposed to raise the question of the nature of the church itself. Is it an essentially unalterable divine institution, or may it be altered, as so often since the Reformation, by government enactment? The form their answer took was to be determined largely by the romantic revival of interest in the primitive and mediæval.

During these discussions several young clergymen, mostly associated with Oriel College, Oxford, were led to take the steps that inaugurated the "Oxford movement," as it was often called. Probably the most influential of the group, while his brief life lasted, was Richard Hurrell Froude (1803–1836). To him the church is in possession of the truth, important elements of which primitive endowment were repudiated by the reformers. A revival of fasting, clerical celibacy, reverence for the saints and "Catholic usages" he deemed imperative. Closely associated with Froude was a man of great pulpit and intellectual abilities, whose early training had been Evangelical, but who had come to share Froude's feelings, John Henry Newman (1801–1890). A third of the Oriel group was John Keble (1792–1866), of Nonjuror ancestry, and already distinguished as the author of the most popular volume of religious poetry that was issued in the nineteenth century, *The Christian Year* of 1827. In hearty sympathy stood a Cambridge scholar, Hugh James Rose (1795–1838), who founded the *British Magazine* in 1832, to further faith in the divine authority and essential unchangeableness of the church. To all these men the course of recent political events seemed menacing. The formal beginning of the movement is usually associated with Keble's sermon of July 14, 1833, in Oxford, on "National Apostasy." In September of that year Keble formulated the principles for which he and his associates stood. The way to salvation is through reception of the body and blood of Christ in the Eucharist, which is validly administered only through those in apostolical succession. This is the treasure of the church—a church which must in all ways be restored to the purity of its undivided early centuries.

The same month Newman began the publication of the famous *Tracts for the Times,* which gave to the movement they fostered the name "Tractarianism." By 1835 these associates had won the support of one who, next to Newman, and fully after Newman's defection, was to be its leader, Edward Bouverie Pusey (1800–1882). A man of great earnestness and piety, Pusey was so fully ultimately to become the head of the Anglo-Catholic movement, that it was largely called "Puseyism"—to Pusey it was the revival of primitive Christianity.

Of these *Tracts,* of which ninety were issued, Newman wrote twenty-three. Keble, Pusey, and Froude, with others, also contributed. To Newman the Church of England was the golden mean, the *via media,* between Protestantism and Rome; but as the series went on the writers emphasized increasingly those doctrines and practices which, though undoubtedly ancient, are popularly identified with Rome. Thus, Pusey taught the regenerative nature of baptism and the sacrificial aspect of the Lord's Supper. Confession was commended. Reserve was to be practised in the use of the Bible and the proclamation of religious truth. It was the ninetieth *Tract* by Newman, in 1841, that aroused most controversy. Newman held that the Thirty-nine Articles did not intend to teach anything other than the Catholic faith and was not in conflict with genuine Roman Catholicism, even in its Tridentine form. Very few scholars or churchmen could accept this interpretation, which seemed plainly wrong, and the bishop of Oxford now forbade the continuation of the *Tracts.*

Newman was at the height of his influence when *Tract Ninety* was published. The Anglo-Catholic movement numbered hundreds of followers among the clergy. Newman was doubting, however, the catholicity of the Church of England, and on October 9, 1845, he made his submission to Rome. Several hundred clergy and laymen followed him into the Roman communion, of whom the most distinguished was Henry Edward Manning (1808–1892), who conformed to Rome in 1851, and was created a cardinal in 1875. Great excitement was caused in 1850 by the re-establishment in England by Pope Pius IX of the Roman Catholic diocesan episcopate, which had been in abeyance since the Reformation. Manning became an extreme ultramontane supporter of papal claims, unlike Newman, who was always moderate, and who, though the most eminent of English Roman Catholics, was not given a cardinalate till 1879.

These conversions to Rome ended the Oxford movement as such, but the Anglo-Catholic party which grew out of it weathered the storm under Pusey's able leadership, and rapidly matured into an important element within the establishment. As its doctrinal modifications became accepted, it concerned itself increasingly with the "enrichment" of the liturgy, by the introduction of usages which Protestantism had discarded. These changes encountered much popular and legal opposition, but the modifications desired by the ritualists were largely secured. Any estimate of the Anglo-Catholic movement would be erroneous that failed to recognize its profound religious zeal. It not only brought a fresh Catholic emphasis into the worship and theology of the church, it also showed genuine devotion to the poor, neglected, and unchurched. It did much to regain the hold of the church on the lower classes. In 1860 the English Church Union was organized to support high-church faith and practice, and to expand the influence of this significant awakening movement within the Church of England.

The sister Protestant state church of Ireland, always an anomaly in that it was the governmentally supported church of a minority of the population, was disestablished in 1869, but the even tenor of its way was not much disturbed by the change.

The nineteenth century was marked by the steady expansion and increasing proliferation of Non-Conformity, in which Evangelical influence was strong. Probably quite early in the century, the number of active Non-Conformists came to surpass the number of practicing Anglicans. Methodism, for example, increased four-fold from 1800 to 1860, even though it lost a number of factions through schisms. The other large and growing Non-Conformist bodies were the Congregational and the Baptist, while Quakers and Unitarians persisted as small minorities, and Presbyterianism was revivified, largely by migration from Scotland. Non-Conformist strength was in the middle classes. Non-Conformity produced preachers of great power, and had its scholars and social workers, but in its scholarship and in work for the unchurch it was less eminent than the Church of England.

Of great importance in English life was the steady diminution of the disabilities resting on Non-Conformists. In 1813 the Unitarians obtained relief by the repeal of penal acts against deniers of the Trinity. The Test and Corporation Acts were abolished in 1828. Marriages were permitted in dissenting places of worship in 1836. Non-Conformists were freed from taxes for the benefit of the establishment in 1868. In 1871 all religious tests, save for degrees in theology, were abolished at the Universities of Oxford, Cambridge, and Durham. In 1880 Non-Conformist services were permitted at burials in churchyards.

In the latter half of the century, Non-Conformity profited by what has often been called the "Second Great Evangelical Awakening," a chief feature of which was the work of the American evangelist, Dwight L. Moody (1837–1899). Anglican Evangelicals also profited from these later awakenings; their centers at Mildmay and Keswick contributed to them.

Non-conformists not only expanded in the nineteenth century, they also proliferated a number of new bodies. Three movements are of special interest. Edward Irving (1792–1834) was a Scottish Presbyterian minister in London, of eloquence and mystic tendencies. By 1828 he had become persuaded that the "gifts" of the apostolic age would be restored if faith was sufficient. Though no claimant to them himself, he believed by 1830 that his hopes had been fulfilled in others. In 1832 he was deposed from his Presbyterian ministry. Soon after, six Apostles were believed to be designated by prophecy, which number was similarly completed to twelve in 1835. The body thus led took the name Catholic Apostolic Church. In 1842 an elaborate ritual was adopted. The Apostles were regarded as organs of the Holy Spirit. The speedy coming of Christ was long expected, but the last Apostle died in 1901. The church has spread also to Germany and the United States.

A second movement grew out of reaction against the unspirituality of the establishment in the early years of the nineteenth century. Groups of "brethren," who claimed faith and Christian love as their only bonds, gathered in Ireland and western England. Their great increase was through the labors of John Nelson Darby (1800–1882), formerly a clergyman of the (Anglican) Church of Ireland, in the vicinity of Plymouth about 1830. They are therefore generally nicknamed "Plymouth Brethren." To their thinking all believers are priests, and hence formal ministries are to be rejected. Creeds are to be refused. The Holy Spirit guides all true believers, and unites them in faith and worship after the apostolic model. Though professedly rejecting all denominationalism, the "brethren" found themselves speedily compelled to corporate acts of discipline, and are divided into at least six groups. Darby was an indefatigable propagandist. Through his efforts the "brethren" were planted in Switzerland, France, Germany, Canada, and the United States. Among their eminent adherents were George Müller (1805–1898), whose remarkable orphan houses in Bristol were supported, he believed, largely in direct answer to prayer; and Samuel Prideaux Tregelles (1813–1875), an eminent student of the Greek text of the New Testament.

The most important of these new organizations was the Salvation Army. Its creator, William Booth (1829–1912), was a New Connection Methodist minister, who, after successful revival work in Cardiff, began similar labors in London in 1864, out of which an organization in military form, with military obedience, developed in 1878, to which the name Salvation Army was given in 1880. Always strongly engaged in practical philanthropy as well as street evangelism, the philanthropic work was developed on a great scale from 1890 onward, when Booth published his *In Darkest England and the Way Out*. In spite of its autocratic military form, the Salvation Army is in many respects a church. Though open to the charge of occasional arbitrariness, it has done an immense and beneficent work for the defective and delinquent, and has extended to all English-speaking lands, as well as to France, Germany, Switzerland, Italy, the Scandinavian lands, and the Orient.

In the last half of the nineteenth century, English Christians of various denominations and traditions became more concerned with the acute social problems of the time. Evangelicals had long engaged in charitable activities and reform movements, while churchmen like Maurice and Kingsley had pioneered in Christian Socialism at mid-century. But toward the close of the century, a wider concern for social justice and the direct facing of social issues was felt. In Anglican circles, the Christian Social Union was founded in 1889 under the leadership of Bishop Westcott, Henry Scott Holland (1847–1918) and Charles Gore (1853–1932). Strongly Anglo-Catholic in tone, it strove to apply the moral truths of Christianity to social and economic difficulties. In Non-Conformist circles, the social concern manifested itself especially in liberal political activity. The "Non-Conformist conscience" became a force to be reckoned with in English life; its outstanding voices were Congregationalist Robert William Dale (1829–1895) of Birmingham and Methodist Hugh Price Hughes (1847–1902) of West London.

As in England, so in Scotland the story of Christianity in the nineteenth century begins with spiritual awakening. As in England, the reaction against the French Revolution, the rise of Romanticism, and the general revolt from the rationalism of the eighteenth century prepared the way for Evangelical revival north of the Tweed. Early leaders in the awakening were Robert (1764–1842) and James Alexander (1768–1851) Haldane, laymen who became active evangelists and organizers of societies to promote further revival. From 1815, when he entered on a memorable pastorate in Glasgow, the most eminent of the Evangelical party was Thomas Chalmers (1780–1847), distinguished as a preacher, a social reformer, a mathematician, a theological teacher, and an ecclesiastical statesman. Under his leadership, and in the changed spirit of the times, the Evangelical party rapidly grew in strength. Under Chalmers' guidance a great campaign to meet the needs of the growing population of Scotland was inaugurated, which resulted by 1841 in the erection of two hundred and twenty new churches by popular gifts. The old question of patronage still continued burning. In 1834 the growing Evangelical party secured the passage by the General Assembly of a "veto" rule, by which presbyteries were forbidden to proceed to installation where a majority of the congregation were opposed to the candidate. This rule soon involved legal controversy. The courts held that the General Assembly had exceeded its powers. Parliament was asked for relief, which was refused. Under Chalmers' leadership, therefore, some four hundred and seventy-four ministers formally withdrew from the state church in 1843 and founded the Free Church of Scotland. They gave up parishes and salaries. All had to be provided anew; but the enthusiasm and sacrifice of the new body was equal to the task. In general, it was a withdrawal of the Evangelical element from the already considerably modified but less zealous and spiritual "Moderates." A third, and that the most active part, of the state church had gone out in the Disruption. Yet the example of the seceders worked ultimately for a quickening of zeal in the state church itself. In 1874 the rights of patronage, the original ground of division, were abolished by law.

The vigor of British Evangelicalism, in both established and Non-Conformist forms, was reflected in the great missionary surge of nineteenth-century Protestantism. English-speaking Evangelicals seized the initiative in Protestant missions at the end of the eighteenth century, and held it throughout the "Great Century" [1] of Protestant missionary outreach. The rapid expansion of foreign missions in the nineteenth century brought Protestantism to almost every country of the globe, making it truly world-wide in scope. This missionary campaign centered in Great Britain, with the United States close behind. Its beginnings at the end of the eighteenth century have already been noted (see p. 471); throughout the nineteenth century the crusade steadily expanded in extent and complexity, and the organization of missionary agencies of many types continued.

The movement was led by a number of famous missionary pioneers, who followed the example of William Carey, first of the modern missionary vanguard. Those from Great Britain went especially, though by no means exclusively, into the parts of the world where the British Empire had territorial claims. In India, Anglican Evangelical Henry Martyn (1781–1812) burned himself out at an early age in his vigorous missionary efforts. The first Church of Scotland foreign missionary, Alexander Duff (1806–1878), devoted himself especially to educational work, seeking to attract the cultured classes of India. Samuel Marsden (1764–1838), another Anglican of Evangelical

---

[1] The term has been popularized by a leading historian of missions, Kenneth Scott Latourette. In his seven-volume *A History of the Expansion of Christianity* (New York, 1937–45), he took three volumes to get to 1815, and then three volumes to cover the period 1815–1914, the "Great Century."

stamp, labored for more than four decades in planting Christianity in Australia, New Zealand, and the Pacific islands. In Africa, Robert Moffat (1795–1883) and David Livingstone (1813–1873), both Scotsmen serving the London Missionary Society, brought the gospel to South Africa. That Society also sent Robert Morrison (1782–1834) as the first Protestant missionary to China in 1807. The efforts of these pioneers, heroic as they were, did not seem to yield many results at first—their task was to open doors, to found schools and stations, and above all to translate the Scriptures. But where they led, hundreds of missionaries followed. As the century progressed, other lands opened to Protestant effort—Japan, Korea, the Philippines. In all these lands, the missionaries brought not only the gospel, but western literature and educational methods, modern medical knowledge and hospitals, improved techniques of agriculture and forestry. The denominational missionary societies mushroomed into vast agencies with large and complex staffs. In addition, there were nondenominational "faith missions," such as the China Inland Mission, founded in 1865 by J. Hudson Taylor (1832–1905). By the end of the century, usually small but significant Protestant minorities had developed in land after land that had had no Protestant witness before. In India and China especially, these tiny Protestant communities were an important ferment in swift-changing cultures. The missionary efforts changed the religious map of the world, and extended the influence of English-speaking Evangelicalism around the world. Through this missionary impulse, the foundations of the so-called "Younger Churches," indigenous churches in non-Christian lands, were laid.

14

Continental Protestantism in the Nineteenth Century

W HAT WAS PROBABLY the most significant development in Continental Protestantism in the nineteenth century has already been considered—the movements of Christian thought in Germany. But there were also important trends in the life of the churches, for in the nineteenth century surges of life that to a considerable extent cut across confessional and national lines swept through the Christian churches on the continent of Europe. This nineteenth-century awakening had many aspects. Of especial importance in the early part of the century was the "Réveil," the emergence of Evangelical and Pietistic currents reminiscent of the earlier awakenings. But in addition to this resurgence, movements of renewal stressing romantic, sacramental, and confessional elements can also be distinguished. The various aspects of the nineteenth-century awakening might thus be styled as low church, broad church, high church, and orthodox.

In Germany, the awakening began in the central state of Prussia during the Napoleonic occupation. The theologian Schleiermacher, preacher at Berlin's Trinity Church, led people to find depths in the Christian tradition that had long been obscured. In the 1820's and 1830's a more Pietistic movement, spearheaded by Hengstenberg's *Evangelische Kirchenzeitung,* became influential. Hengstenberg (see p. 490) stood firmly for the infallibility of the Bible and the alliance of Christianity with the conservative feudal party in German politics. Still another current in the awakening was intensely confessional. It was in part a reaction against the Prussian Union of 1817, in which the Lutheran and Reformed churches were merged at the impulse of King Frederick William III (1797–1840). Similar unions were effected in some of the other German states. But staunchly orthodox Lutherans, cherishing a bitter hostility toward the Calvinists, refused to become a part of such a union. These "Old Lutherans" were subjected to considerable persecution, and not until the 1840's were they even allowed to emigrate. When they could break away, many of them came to the United States to form such conservative synods as Buffalo and Missouri. Not all the strongly confessional tendencies were to be found among the Old Lutherans, however. Hengstenberg himself broke with the Pietistic movement about 1840 and himself became a champion of strict Lutheran orthodoxy, and there were many similarly disposed. Allied with this confessional trend was a high-church movement. Central figures in this development were Wilhelm Loehe (1808–1872) of Bavaria and Theodor Kliefoth (1810–1895) of Mecklenberg. These "New Lutherans" sought to stress the transmission of the saving grace of God objectively through peoples and institutions, and to revive ancient liturgical traditions.

The vitality released through these awakening currents found an outlet in the "inner mission," a multitude of evangelistic and charitable efforts reminiscent of the activities at Halle in the early days of Pietism. Johann Hinrich Wichern (1808–1881), brought up under pietistic auspices, in 1833 founded a home for underprivileged boys. Under his organizational skill, a vast network of hundreds of agencies to reach seamen, the unemployed, prisoners, and neglected children was spread. Above all, serious efforts to reach the masses through Sunday schools, city missions, lodging houses, and the dissemination of literature were undertaken. Many laymen were drawn into the movement, and orders of deaconesses were formed. The inner mission was supported by Protestants under the influence of various of the awakening elements, though its pietistic stamp remained strong. It also found strong response from South Germany and the lower Rhine region, where the Reformed tradition remained an important force.

Scandinavian Protestantism was also penetrated by the awakening. In Denmark, the response to the various aspects of the revival stimulated a genuinely creative period. The pietistic emphasis with its "inner mission" was welcomed into the established Lutheran church. A tendency more akin to the Romantic motifs, more "broad-church," was represented by Bishop J. P. Mynster (1775–1854), court preacher, theological professor, and primate of the Church of Denmark. The high-church aspect was represented by Nicolai Frederick Severin Grundtvig (1783–1872), who found as his rock the Apostles' Creed, and who stressed the living tradition and the sacramental focus of the church. One of the products of this creative period reacted strongly against the Christianity he knew—Søren Kierkegaard (1813–1855). Stressing the paradoxical and existential aspects of Christian faith, Kierkegaard made little impression on his own time, but was to be rediscovered in the twentieth century.

In Norway, the pietistic aspect of the awakening was especially felt. Hans Nielsen Hauge (1771–1824), itinerant lay evangelist, assailed the coldness of the state church, and was imprisoned for almost a decade. Later, the movement he had inspired was brought into closer relation to the established Lutheran church through the efforts of Gisle Johnson (1822–1894). Both confessional and clerical emphases were evident in the work of this professor of theology at the University of Christiana. In Sweden also the revival had a variety of aspects, but the influence of Henrik Schartau (1757–1825), pastor at Lund, was especially important. Originally under Moravian influence, he developed a high-church and sacramental bent, stressing the antiquity of the church's tradition and the real presence in the Eucharist.

The influence of the nineteenth-century Protestant awakening was also strongly felt in the Reformed churches of the Continent. In the late eighteenth century, the impact of rationalism had been very great in the Calvinist communions of Switzerland, France, and the Netherlands. The beginnings of revival can be traced in part to the Evangelical movement in Scotland, for Robert Haldane was instrumental in stimulating an awakening in France and French Switzerland in 1816. A conspicuous convert to the new emphases was H. A. César Malan (1787–1864), who became a leading itinerant evangelist and writer of many hymns. In the Netherlands, an important figure in the revival was a converted Jew, Isaac de Costa (1798–1860). As in Britain, the awakening currents produced a network of voluntary societies to conduct evangelistic, missionary, and charitable undertakings. And in all these lands, exponents of the "Réveil" found themselves opposed by church leaders of rationalist leanings, and kept out of positions of power. In Holland the tension between rationalism and awakening, represented in this case by a young pastor, Hendrik de Cock (1801–1842), who also stood for high Calvinism and strict adherence to the findings of the Synod of Dort, led to a schism. When de Cock was deposed in 1834, a number of congregations founded the Christian Reformed Church. Many of Evangelicals, however, remained within the state church. In Switzerland, a disruption was led by Alexander Vinet (1797–1847), the "Schleiermacher of French Protestantism." Vinet at first had been repelled by what he felt to be the crudity of the Réveil, but attracted by the emphases of the more moderate Evangelicals and by Romantic currents, and disturbed over the efforts of the rationalists to repress the Evangelicals, he himself espoused the Réveil, and became an outspoken advocate of the separation of church and state. In 1845 he led a group, including a majority of the ministers and most of the theological faculty at Lausanne, out of the state church to form the Free Church of Vaud.

The churches of the Continent, stimulated by the currents of awakening, contributed not a little to the missionary drive of nineteenth-century Protestantism. Many societies were organized to channel the energies stirred by revival into missionary channels. The Basel Evangelical Missionary Society dates from 1815; the Danish Missionary Society from 1821; the Berlin and the Paris Societies from 1824; the Rhenish Missionary Society from 1828; the Leipzig Evangelical Lutheran Mission and the North German Missionary Society from 1836—these societies were but the more conspicuous of hundreds which sent missionaries abroad. Protestant missionaries from the Continent were especially active in the Dutch East Indies, where the greatest concentration of Protestants in the Far East developed, and in South Africa.

In the later nineteenth century, the social interpretation of Christianity was advanced in certain quarters. The Evangelical Union Church in Prussia, the largest Protestant church in the world at the time, was in many ways administered conservatively and in the interests of the state, while the inner mission had cooled to a system of organized charity. In 1874, Adolf Stöcker (1835–1909) came to Berlin as court preacher. He shared the Junker outlook, despising liberal parliamentarianism, but was greatly concerned with the alienation of the industrial masses by the forces of socialism and secularism. He advocated labor legislation and social insurance, unfortunately mingling anti-semitic elements in his messages. But Stöcker was too politically minded for conservative Lutheran understanding of the separation of spiritual and political spheres, and he lost his post. A more liberal middle-class social Christian message was preached by Friedrich Naumann (1860–1919), but he, too, found that the political consequences of a social ethic were difficult for Lutherans to accept, and he resigned from the ministry. Meanwhile, a "social gospel," somewhat academic in nature, was advocated by such liberal theologians as Harnack and Hermann (see p. 494).

In the Reformed churches, social Christianity found more fertile soil. Conspicuous leaders in the movement were Leonhard Ragaz (1868–1945), advocate of pacifism, cooperatives, folk-schools and settlements, and Hermann Kutter (1863–1931), author of *They Must!* (1905), a theological interpretation of socialism that also influenced developments in social Christianity in England and the United States. Though the interest of the mass of Christians in social questions never developed to the degree social Christian leaders hoped, still significant changes in the way Protestants confronted social issues were effected, and thereafter narrowly individualistically ways of thinking were permanently challenged.

15

American Protestantism in the Nineteenth Century

JUST AS THE STORY of nineteenth-century Protestantism in Great Britain and on the Continent began with Evangelical awakening, so did the story of religion in the United States in the same period. In America, the pietistic, evangelistic, low-church current of revival became largely dominant in church life. Although there were some evidences suggestive of the other aspects of the British and Continental revival, and although some communions resisted the revivalist tide, on the whole an Evangelical conception of Christian faith with characteristic attention to the winning of souls set the pace in American Protestantism. Led by men who shared in the Pietist and Evangelical traditions, it regarded a conscious and often emotional conversion as the normal way of entering the Christian life. The internal situation—church life was at a low ebb during the Revolutionary period, and at the opening of the new century less than ten per cent of the population were church members—emphasized the need for awakening. The external situation—a country which about tripled in territorial extent and increased some five times in population in half a century—played its part in focusing Christian attention on the winning of converts.

Beginning at the very end of the eighteenth century, a mighty reawakening of religious interest swept the land. In New England, what was sometimes called the "Second Great Awakening" showed its first signs as early as 1792. By 1800, revival was in full tide. Congregationalist leaders were determined that some of the excesses that had led to the decline of the earlier Great Awakening should not be repeated. Hence in their churches the new revivals were somewhat restrained, taking place largely within the normal patterns of church life. Conspicuous in leading the movement were the brilliant Yale president, Timothy Dwight (1752–1817), and the men he trained to carry on the work: Congregational preacher Lyman Beecher (1775–1863) and Yale theologian Nathaniel W. Taylor (1786–1858). The awakening

was by no means limited to the Congregational churches, for Baptists flourished in an awakening atmosphere, and the Methodists, seeking a securer
foothold in New England, freely used revivalistic practices.

The awakening also swept the Middle Atlantic states, the South, and
the frontier. The easterners did their part in seeking to extend the revival
westward. In 1801 the Congregational General Assembly of Connecticut and
the Presbyterian General Assembly entered into the "Plan of Union," providing for the virtual merger of the denominations in frontier areas. Soon the
other New England Congregational associations joined in the scheme, and
many "Presbygational" churches were planted, especially in New York and
Ohio. But often the westerners were impatient with the restraint of eastern
revivalism, and impatient with the stress on an educated clergy. It was in the
frontier states of Tennessee and Kentucky that the most emotional and spectacular manifestations of the awakening occurred. There the "camp meetings" began in 1800, and there the revivals, especially at first, were marked
by emotional outcries and bodily manifestations. On the whole, however, the
new revival movement, which continued to ebb and flow for decades, was less
marked than the eighteenth century awakenings by these symptoms of over-
wrought excitement. The impact of the revival was evident in the decline of
"infidelity," the lifting of the moral level of the frontier, and the steady
growth of Baptist, Methodist, and Presbyterian churches.

A product of the awakening, destined to become the outstanding exponent of revivalism through a long career, was a young lawyer of upstate
New York, Charles Grandison Finney (1792–1875). Converted in 1821, he
set out on evangelistic tours, and despite lack of college or formal theological
training, was ordained under Presbyterian auspices. Soon great revivals broke
out under his fervent and intense preaching. He brought revival methods into
an ordered pattern which became known as the "new measures." The measures—such as "unseasonable hours" for services, "protracted" meetings, the
use of harsh and colloquial language, the specific naming of individuals in
prayer and sermon, inquiry meetings, the "anxious bench"—were really not
new, of course. It was the shaping of them into a system designed to produce
results that was the novel feature. Despite the opposition of those who feared
the emotionalism of frontier and "new measures" evangelism, Finney soon
invaded the eastern cities. His tested methods soon came to be widely accepted
and copied. The intensity and frequency of the revivals declined in the 1840's,
but burst out again in new crescendo in 1857–1858, when a nationwide revival swept thousands in the churches. Daily prayer meetings, often at unusual hours, and lay leadership were features of this great peak in revival
history.

Meanwhile, from the beginning of the century, the energies produced
by the revivals were being channeled into Evangelical causes through a steadily
expanding network of voluntary societies. Often organization began at the
local level, then the small units banded together in state societies, and finally

the great national societies completed the pattern. When the concern of these voluntary societies was for home or foreign missions, they often followed denominational lines. Thus, when a group of Williams College students under the leadership of Samuel J. Mills (1783–1818) offered their services to Congregational authorities as missionaries for India, the formation of the American Board of Commissioners for Foreign Missions in 1810 was precipitated. This was basically a Congregationalist society, though Presbyterians and Reformed supported it for a time. It dispatched its first five missionaries in 1812. En route to India, two of them, Adoniram Judson (1788–1850) and Luther Rice (1783–1836), came to the conclusion that believers' baptism by immersion was the Scriptural way. This, in turn, precipitated the organization of the General Missionary Convention of the Baptist Denomination of the United States of America for Foreign Missions. Other denominations also founded missionary societies: Presbyterians in 1817, Methodists in 1818, Episcopalians in 1820. The American Home Missionary Society was instituted in 1826 to implement the operation of the Plan of Union.

Voluntary societies were also organized for the distribution of Bibles and tracts, the promotion of educational interests and Sunday schools, and for the direction of charitable and reform efforts. These great national societies were usually nondenominational—they sought the support of Evangelicals of various backgrounds. Among the societies were the American Education Society (founded 1815), the American Bible Society (1816), the American Sunday School Union (1817–1824), and the American Tract Society (1825). The pattern of organization was consciously influenced by the British example. In the 1830's these agencies mushroomed in size and increased in support and effectiveness. Their annual meetings, the "May anniversaries," came to be held at the same time in New York City. Their membership and their directorates were overlapping, so that they formed what has been called a "benevolent empire." Control was largely in the hands of a group of wealthy laymen, predominantly Presbyterian or Congregational, among whom Arthur (1786–1865) and Lewis (1788–1873) Tappan were central. These men recognized Finney's power, enlisted him in their causes, and when ill health necessitated the curtailment of his travels, had him called to a New York pastorate. In 1834 and 1835 he published his *Lectures on Revivals of Religion,* spelling out his proven ways of promoting revival. In the latter year he went to the new Oberlin College in Ohio, where as professor of theology and later president, he became at once the leading exponent and the major theoretician of American revivalism. His voluminous *Lectures on Systematic Theology,* first published 1846–1847, presented a theology of revival, in which a test for any doctrine was whether or not it would contribute to salvation. Finney was a leader with many followers—hosts of revivalists put his methods to work.

Vitalities stimulated by revivalism were poured directly into the benevolent empire. Never relaxing their missionary passion, its leaders utilized the voluntary society pattern to remake society by conducting great moral and humanitarian crusades. It was hoped that such evils as vice, licentiousness, juvenile delinquency, and Sabbath-breaking might be eliminated, and such causes as temperance, peace, and the abolition of slaves be promoted. Temperance, for example, had aroused the efforts of the Presbyterian General Assembly and the Congregational Associations of Connecticut and Massachusetts in 1811. Lyman Beecher's sermons against drunkenness in 1813—repeated and published in 1827—attracted great attention. In 1826 the American Society for the Promotion of Temperance was added to the circle of benevolent voluntary societies. The results of all this activity was a permanent change in the drinking habits of professed Christians. Efforts then turned toward the promotion of temperance among those not actively of the church. The Washingtonian movement of 1840 sought the reformation of drunkards. Prohibition by legislation was enacted in Maine in 1846. The history of legislative prohibition, thus backed by strong Christian support, was checkered, but in the twentieth century was to culminate in the experiment of national prohibition (1919–1933).

The American Peace Society was organized in 1828. The greatest of the reform crusades, however, was for abolition. Before the nineteenth century there had been some sentiment against slaveholding, especially among Quakers. The work of John Woolman (1720–1772) had been especially important. Increasing antipathy toward slavery was spreading in the country in the early nineteenth century. But about 1830 a great change came over the South, because of the supposed industrial necessities of the plantation system, the fear of slave uprising, and deepening resentment against the uncompromising attacks of such northern abolitionists as William Lloyd Garrison (1805–1879). In the North, however, the abolition movement gave a cutting edge to the rather general but vague emancipation interests. In 1833 the American Anti-slavery Society was organized as part of the benevolent empire; Finney convert Theodore Dwight Weld (1803–1895) became its most powerful figure in spreading abolition sentiment among Evangelicals. As the reform concerns of northern Protestants became increasingly funneled into the abolition drive, the gulf between northern and southern Evangelicals steadily widened.

Thus through the revivals, through missionary organizations and voluntary societies, an evangelistic, pietistic interpretation of Christian faith became widely disseminated in America in the nineteenth century. The denominations that employed the revival pattern most fully grew to be the giants in this period of national expansion. Methodists, a scant fifteen thousand strong at the time of their independent organization in 1784 (see p. 477), were well past the million mark by 1850. The Baptists, about one hundred thousand in number at the opening of the century, had increased eightfold by the mid-century mark. Congregationalists and Presbyterians, among whom the nineteenth-century revival had appeared so early, continued to gain from the awakening, but internal resistance in both bodies to revival emphases inhibited them, and they fell behind in comparative denominational strength, dropping from the commanding place they had held at the dawn of the century. The second awakening greatly strengthened those Massachusetts Congregationalists who considered themselves orthodox, but the "liberal" party, the rise of which has already been noted (see p. 444), was deeply opposed to it. In 1805, the liberals succeeded in placing Henry Ware (1764–1845) as Hollis professor of divinity at Harvard. Meanwhile, William Ellery Channing (1780–1842) had begun a greatly respected and widely influential pastorate in Boston, where he was preaching a high Arian Christology. Increasing division, caused in part by the orthodox attack upon the liberals, led in 1815 to the adoption of the Unitarian name by the liberals. But even more characteristic of them than the denial of the doctrine of the Trinity were their criticism of the doctrine of original sin, of the Calvinistic theory of predestination, and an insistence on salvation by character. A sermon by Channing in 1819 at the installation of Jared Sparks (1789–1866) in Baltimore was widely regarded as the authoritative statement of the liberals, and gave to Channing henceforth an unofficial leadership in early American Unitarianism. In 1825 the American Unitarian Association was formed. The allegiance of some of the oldest Congregational churches and most eminent men of eastern Massachusetts was won to the new denomination. But the orthodox, spurred by the energetic Lyman Beecher, who became pastor of the Hanover Street Church in Boston in 1826, made renewed use of revivals, and succeeded in arresting Unitarian advance, and in confining them largely to eastern New England.

In Connecticut there was no such open break, but the more conservative Calvinists feared that the New Haven theology had gone too far in modifying Calvinism to support revivalism and meet Unitarian objections. Hence a new "orthodox" ministerial association was formed in 1833, and a new seminary founded at Hartford in 1834. Both the Connecticut parties continued to employ revivals, however. It was a brilliant pastor, Horace Bushnell (1802–1876), who thoughtfully criticized the revival system in his most influential publication, *Christian Nurture,* which first appeared in 1847. He urged the quiet unfolding of the Christian nurture of the child, under appropriate influences, as the normal mode of entrance into the kingdom of God, instead of the struggling conversion which Pietist and Methodist traditions had considered the only legitimate experience. An able theologian, Bushnell did much to shift the emphasis from exact dogma, to be demonstrated to the intellect, to religious feeling, to which men's hearts and minds should be stirred. These ideas, influenced by Romanticism and reflecting the work of Samuel Taylor Coleridge (see p. 496) were presented in such books as *God in Christ* (1849) and *Nature and the Supernatural* (1857).

The Presbyterians were also torn by controversy. Those, often of Scotch-Irish background, who held firmly to confessional standards and to traditions of an educated ministry were sore troubled by frontier revivalists whose doctrinal emphases and ordination standards were more lax. Attempts to curb them, however, led only to schism. In 1803, Barton W. Stone (1772–1844) led a group of evangelistic Presbyterians out of the Synod of Kentucky. These "New Lights" soon dropped all "sectarian" names, seeking to be known simply as "Christians." Several years later, attempts to discipline Cumberland (Kentucky) Presbytery revivalists led to open break, and the formation of what became the Cumberland Presbyterian Church. Some of the smaller Presbyterian bodies suffered schism too. Thomas Campbell, a Seceder Presbyterian minister in the north of Ireland, came to America in 1807, and began work in western Pennsylvania. Here his freedom in welcoming Presbyterians of all parties to communion aroused criticism, and he was disciplined by the Seceder Presbytery of Chartiers. Campbell felt it his duty to protest against such sectarianism, and to assert as the standard of all Christian discipleship the literal terms of the Bible alone, as he understood it. Thomas Campbell now broke with the Seceder Presbyterians, but continued to labor in western Pennsylvania, announcing as his principle: "Where the Scriptures speak, we speak; and where the Scriptures are silent, we are silent." It was not a new denomination that he planned, but a union of all Christians on this Biblical basis, without added tests of creed or ritual. In August, 1809, Thomas Campbell organized The Christian Association of Washington—so-called from the Pennsylvania county of its origin—and for it he prepared the "Declaration and Address" which has since been regarded as a fundamental document of what was to be known as the Disciples movement. The same year Thomas Campbell's son, Alexander (1788–1866), emigrated to America, and was soon to outstrip his father in fame as an advocate of the former's views.

In spite of their deprecation of sectarianism, the Campbells organized a church in Brush Run, Pennsylvania, in May, 1811. The Lord's Supper was observed each Sunday from the beginning. But doubts now arose as to the Scriptural warrant of infant baptism. In 1812 the Campbells and a number of their associates were immersed. A year later the Brush Run church became a member of the Redstone Association of Baptist Churches. Points of disagreement with the Baptists developed. The Campbells disliked the Baptists' strenuous Calvinism. To the Campbells the Old Testament was far less authoritative than the New. To the Baptists baptism was a privilege of the already pardoned sinner; to the Campbells it was a condition of forgiveness. Moreover, the Campbells, without being in any sense Unitarians, refused to employ other than Scriptural expressions regarding the Father, Son, and Holy Spirit. The result was a withdrawal from the Baptists, which may be said to have been completed by 1832, when the followers of Campbell merged with the bulk of the followers of Barton Stone to form the Disciples of Christ. Perhaps 25,000 strong at that time, they passed the million mark before the turn of the century.

The loss of the extremer revivalists from the main body of Presbyterians by no means ended the tension over revivalism within that communion. The "New School" Presbyterians who looked with favor on the New Haven theology and worked wholeheartedly with the benevolent empire, were strengthened by the operation of the Plan of Union, which brought men of Congregational background into Presbyterian judicatories. In 1837 the "Old School" Presbyterians were strong enough to rule the suspected Presbyteries out of the church, thereby dividing it almost in two. Theological tension and controversy of the voluntary societies, which were not under direct church control, were central issues in the division.

The Society of Friends was also split. An Evangelical movement favoring certain revivalistic emphases and techniques was led by an English Quaker, Joseph John Gurney (1788–1846), while the liberal reaction found as its central figure Long Islander Elias Hicks (1748–1830). The "Great Separation" occurred in 1828–1829, ending in separate "Orthodox" and "Hicksite" meetings.

The resurgence of revivalism also produced controversy in Lutheran circles. The leading voice in Lutheranism in the first half of the nineteenth century was Samuel Simon Schmucker (1799–1873). He favored an "American Lutheranism" in which certain revivalistic practices would be accepted. Confessionally inclined Lutherans were troubled, and the General Synod (see p. 478), in which he was conspicuous, suffered through dissensions and withdrawals, especially as the waves of German and Scandinavian immigration brought many Lutherans who felt that the American churches had departed from the true Lutheran tradition. As the immigration strengthened confessional resurgence, Schmucker's influence declined. The General Synod came to be rivalled by the General Council in 1867, and Schmucker's seminary at Gettysburg (founded 1826) was matched by one at Mt. Airy, Pennsylvania (1864). Central figure in the latter developments was Charles Porterfield Krauth (1823–1883), author of *The Conservative Reformation and its Theology* (1871).

In some denominations there were no overt schisms over revivalism, but there was considerable inner tension created. In German Reformed churches there was spirited resistance to the spread of the "system of the revival" by exponents of the "system of the catechism," chiefly theologian John W. Nevin (1803–1886) and church historian Philip Schaff (1819–1893) of the seminary at Mercersburg, Pennsylvania. But the Mercersburg theology made little direct contribution; its larger significance was rediscovered only in the twentieth century. In the Protestant Episcopal Church there was little revivalism as such, but there was a strong, Evangelical, low-church party in which Bishop Alexander Viets Griswold (1766–1843) of the Eastern diocese was conspicuous. The early years of the century saw the renaissance of the high-church party under the leadership of Bishop John

Henry Hobart (1775–1830), a trend which the rise of Anglo-Catholicism (see p. 499) was to strengthen. The Episcopal Church was small in these years, but steadily grew, especially in the urban centers, throughout the nineteenth century.

The most extensive nineteenth century denominational schisms occurred in connection with the struggle over slavery. Growing antipathy to slavery led to the organization, in 1843, of the Wesleyan Methodist Church of America on the basis of no slaveowning membership. The question was thus in the foreground when the General Conference of the Methodist Episcopal Church met in 1844, and an immediate struggle arose over the retention of a slaveholding bishop. Northern and Southern sentiment was hopelessly divided. The Conference adopted a report permitting the division of the church, with the result that the Methodist Episcopal Church, South, was constituted, in 1845.

Contemporaneously a similar division separated the Baptists of North and South. The Alabama State Convention of Baptists demanded, in 1844, that the Foreign Mission Board make no discrimination against slaveholders in missionary appointments. The board declared that it would take no action implying approval of slavery. The result was the formation of the Southern Baptists Convention in 1845 and the cleavage of the churches.

As the Civil War (1861–1865) approached, other churches divided. The New School Presbyterian Church split in 1857 and the Old School in 1861. The two southern wings merged in 1864 as the Presbyterian Church in the United States, and the two northern wings united in 1869–1870 as the Presbyterian Church in the United States of America. The Protestant Episcopal Church was divided only during the war itself, and was reunited at its close. The churches supported their respective sections through the war. Following the struggle, the great majority of Negro Christians became members of their own independently organized bodies, chiefly the National Baptist Convention, and the smaller African Methodist Episcopal and African Methodist Episcopal Zion Churches. Some of the major white denominations had significant Negro minorities, and there was a considerable growth in the number of Negro sects, especially in metropolitan areas.

The founding of many new colleges and seminaries was stimulated by the religious awakening, the controversies, and the rise of new denominations. The nineteenth century saw the beginnings of hundreds of denominational colleges, many of them short-lived. A major purpose of these schools was to help prepare men for the ministry. But the need for specialized further preparation for the ministry was increasingly felt. In 1784 the (Dutch) Reformed Church instituted ministerial training, ultimately removed to New Brunswick, New Jersey, which has often been called the oldest American theological seminary. The Associate (later United) Presbyterians in 1794 were beginning theological instruction in a seminary later to find a home in

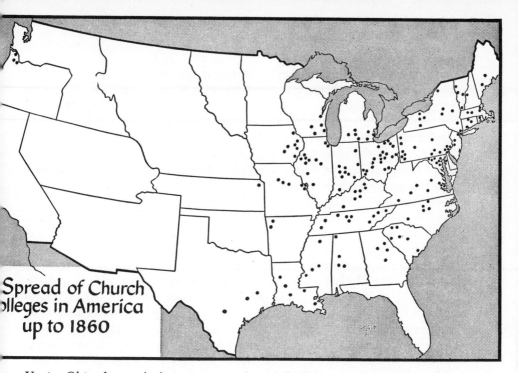

Spread of Church Colleges in America up to 1860

Xenia, Ohio, from which it was named, and finally in Pittsburgh. The Lutherans founded such an institution in 1797, to be located in Hartwick, New York. In 1807, the Moravians established a theological school in Nazareth, Pennsylvania, later relocated at Bethlehem. The most elaborately equipped theological seminary, and in many ways the inaugurator of a new era, was that opened by the Congregationalists in Andover, Massachusetts, in 1808. Four years later the Presbyterians founded a seminary at Princeton, New Jersey. Bangor Theological Seminary, in Maine, was founded by Congregationalists in 1814, and five years later the Divinity School of Harvard University was opened under Unitarian influence. The Baptists began a seminary at Hamilton, New York, in 1820, while the Presbyterians established a school at Auburn, New York, at about the same time. In 1822 the Congregationalists opened the Divinity School of Yale University. Then the institutions for ministerial training, some of which have been mentioned, multiplied rapidly; by 1860 they had increased to fifty.

In the first part of the nineteenth century, in the emotional climate stimulated by awakening, there emerged several movements which represented significant departures or distortions of the Evangelical Protestant pattern. A peculiar development of prophetical interpretation was that of William Miller (1782–1849), a Baptist farmer of Low Hampton, New York. From 1831 onward he preached widely, asserting on the basis of calculations from the book of *Daniel* that the second coming and the inauguration of the millennial reign of Christ would occur in 1843–1844. He won thousands of followers. In spite of the failure of his prediction, his disciples held a general conference of Adventists, as they styled themselves, in 1845, and have persisted to the present, some holding to the observance of the seventh day. The most conspicuous such body was the Seventh-day Adventists, formally organized in 1863. The Adventist faith, often coupled with pentecostal or perfectionist (holiness) emphases, played an important rôle in the formation of new sects in America in the latter nineteenth and early twentieth centuries. The movement that later became known as Jehovah's Witnesses, a peculiar outgrowth of adventist teaching, began in the late 1870's under the leadership of Charles Taze Russell (1852–1916).

A movement nurtured in the revivalist atmosphere of the "burned-over" district of upstate New York but which soon went in its own highly distinctive direction was Mormonism. It was founded by Joseph Smith (1805–1844), who claimed to have dug up, near Manchester, New York, in 1827, a volume of gold plates, the *Book of Mormon,* supplementary to the Bible, written in mysterious characters which he was able to translate by means of a pair of magic spectacles, but the original of which was removed by angelic agency. In this book Smith is proclaimed a prophet. The first Mormon Church was organized in 1830, in Fayette, New York. It was soon largely recruited in the neighborhood of Kirtland, Ohio. Here Brigham Young (1801–1877) became a member. In 1838 the Mormon leaders removed to Missouri, and in 1840 founded Nauvoo, Illinois. In spite of the monogamy enjoined by the *Book of Mormon,* Smith claimed to have received a revelation, in 1843, establishing polygamy. Popular hostility led to his murder by a mob the next year. The church now came under the leadership of Brigham Young, an organizer and leader of the highest ability. Under him the Mormons marched to Salt Lake, in Utah, and a community of great material prosperity was inaugurated. Under pressure from the government, polygamy was officially abandoned in 1890. The Mormons have been indefatigable missionaries, and they have recruited many from Europe, and planted their church overseas. Their system of economic and social supervision has been remarkable. Their unique theological system is based upon three sources of revelation: the Bible, the *Book of Mormon,* and the books recording the progressive direct revelations claimed to have been received by Joseph Smith from God, especially the *Doctrines and Covenants.* Besides the main Church of Jesus Christ of Latter Day Saints, with headquarters at Salt Lake City, Utah, there is a much smaller group with its center at Independence, Missouri.

In the period between the Civil War and the first World War, the revival emphasis of American Protestantism was strongly continued. Lay evangelist Dwight L. Moody (1837–1899) was its most conspicuous exponent. Tireless organizer and aggressive pulpiteer, Moody was a powerful force in Protestant life. His revival methods were widely copied, and his missionary enthusiasm contributed significantly to the continued growth of the foreign missionary enterprise. But the intellectual atmosphere of the late nineteenth century was swift-changing, and many new views sharply challenged ideas cherished by conservative Protestants. The impact of the revolutions in scientific and historical thought was remaking the reigning concepts of the nature of the world and its history. Those who were reared in the traditional Biblical views of creation were shaken by the new ideas coming from the geologists on the one hand and the Biblical critics on the other. Many Protestants reacted by holding to their views of Biblical infallibility with greater rigidity. They founded a series of important Bible conferences in defense of their views—Niagara, Winona, Rocky Mountain. At the Niagara Conference in 1895 was prepared the statement which became known as the "five points of fundamentalism." It stood for the verbal inerrancy of Scripture, the deity of Jesus, the virgin birth, the substitutionary atonement, and the physical resurrection and bodily return of Christ. The conservative cause was strengthened by prophetic conferences, the founding of Bible schools, and the activities of many itinerant revivalists.

Other Protestants reacted in quite another way, seeking to retain the Evangelical orientation, but to recast their faith so as to be in touch with the scientific and historical thought of the time. Deriving many of their ideas from the Ritschlian movement in Germany and the broad-church movement in England (see pp. 493, 497), they fought two long battles for the acceptance of evolutionary thought and the critical approach to the Bible. Many seminaries championed the liberal approach; the "progressive orthodoxy" of Andover, for example, proved to be but a transition to liberalism.

A series of heresy trials marked the emergence of liberal theology. Especially conspicuous was the suspension of Professor Charles A. Briggs (1841–1913) of Union Theological Seminary, New York, by the Presbyterian General Assembly in 1893. Union severed its link with the Presbyterians, and emerged as a champion of the liberal way. By the dawn of the twentieth century, the liberals had won a place for themselves in many denominations. In the early decades of the new century militant conservatives made a resolute drive to oust them in the bitter fundamentalist-modernist controversy. Largely failing by 1930, they tended to withdraw into independent churches and splinter denominations. Conspicuous leadership was provided for the fundamentalists by Presbyterian professor J. Gresham Machen (1881–1937), and for the liberals by Baptist minister Harry Emerson Fosdick (1878—).

The 1865–1914 period witnessed an ever-enlarging recognition of the work of women in the Protestant Churches. A Woman's Board of Foreign Missions was founded among the Congregationalists in 1868. The Methodist Episcopal Church, North, followed in 1869; the Northern Presbyterians in 1870; and the Protestant Episcopal Church in 1871. Similar organizations for home and foreign missions became well-nigh universal in American Protestantism. Women have long been eligible to the representative conventions of the Baptist and Congregational Churches. They won the right of election to the Methodist general conferences in 1900. A number of denominations ordained them to the ministry, notably Baptists, Congregationalists, Disciples, Unitarians, and Universalists.

The same period was also marked by an increasing attention on the part of the churches to their young people. The nondenominational Christian Endeavor movement was founded by Congregationalist Francis E. Clark (1852–1927) in 1881. The denominations adopted the idea, and in 1889 the Epworth League was organized by the Methodists, the Baptist Young People's Union was formed in 1891, and the Luther League for Lutheran young people was set up in 1895.

An important feature of religious life after the Civil War was the steady increase in the demand for an educated ministry in those bodies which formerly had laid little stress on such training. This demand was met by constantly increasing provision, as the older theological seminaries steadily enlarged their facilities by augmented faculties and extension of the curriculum, and many new seminaries were founded. By 1900, over one hundred Protestant theological schools were functioning.

The late years of the nineteenth century saw the rise of deep social concern on the part of many Christians. Under the leadership of such liberal ministers as Washington Gladden (1836–1918) and Walter Rauschenbusch (1861–1918) the "social gospel" was advanced. It drew on British and Continental social Christianity (see pp. 501, 506), as well as on American progressive social thought. Early nineteenth-century Protestantism had expressed its social concerns largely in individualistic terms, stressing charity and moral reform, but the social gospel focused attention on the corporate aspects of modern life and on the achievement of social justice. Great attention was devoted to the relations between capital and labor, and the movement influenced the shortening of the working day. Dedicated to the building of the kingdom of God on earth, the social gospel was especially prominent in the life and work of the Presbyterians, Baptists, and Methodists of the North, and among Congregationalists and Episcopalians. Courses on social ethics were added to seminary curricula, and denominational departments of social action were founded under social Christian influence. A number of social settlements in underprivileged areas were founded under Protestant auspices, and many institutional churches to bring social services to the urban masses were erected. The social emphasis was strongly felt on the mission field, where agricultural, medical, and educational missions were expanded.

16

Roman Catholicism in the Modern World

THE COUNTER-REFORMATION had spent its force by the middle of the seventeenth century. Its strength had been in the might of Spain and the zeal of the Jesuit order. Spain had emerged from the Thirty Years' War shorn of its power. The Jesuits, though more potent than ever in the counsels of the Roman Church, had become more worldly, and had kept little of their earlier spiritual zeal. None of the Popes of the seventeenth or eighteenth centuries were men of commanding force. Several, like Innocent XI (1676–1689), Innocent XII (1691–1700), or Benedict XIV (1740–1758), were of excellent character and intentions, but they were not rulers of men. The course of the Roman Church was one of increasing feebleness in the face of the growing claims of the Catholic civil governments. A really effective attack upon Protestantism was no longer possible, save where it existed, as in France, in predominantly Roman lands. In seventeenth-century France, the Catholic position was strengthened by the attainment of a high level of Catholic piety. In 1611, Pierre de Bérulle (1575–1629) founded the French congregation of the Oratory, a great inspirer of spirituality. Bérulle's work influenced such founders of new orders and authors of spiritual writings as Saint Francis de Sales (1567–1622) and Saint Vincent de Paul (1576?–1660).

Under Louis XIV (1643–1715) the French monarchy pursued a policy dictated by the King's absolutism. As against papal claim he asserted possession by the crown of all income of vacant bishoprics, and favored the proclamation by the French clergy in 1682 of the "Gallican liberties," that civil rulers have full authority in temporal affairs, that general councils are superior to the Pope, that the usages of the French church limit papal interference, and that the Pope is not infallible. The resulting quarrel was compromised in 1693 in such wise that the King kept the disputed income but agreed to be less insistent on the statement of the Gallican liberties, though it could still be held and taught.

As against his own subjects, Louis XIV's policy was determined by his conception of national unity and Jesuit influence, especially after his marriage to Madame de Maintenon in 1684. In 1685 he revoked the Edict of Nantes (see p. 388), and made Protestantism illegal under the severest penalties. The ultimate result was disastrous for France. Thousands of its most industrious citizens emigrated to England, Holland, Germany, and America. The former alliances with Protestant Powers were ruptured, contributing much to the military failures of the latter years of Louis XIV's reign.

Jesuit influence led to equally disastrous opposition by the King and Pope to Jansenism. Cornelius Jansen (1585–1638), bishop of Ypres, an earnest Catholic, was a thoroughgoing Augustinian, convinced that the semi-Pelagian Jesuit interpretations of sin and grace must be combated. His chief work, *Augustinus*, was published in 1640, after his death. Jansen's book was condemned by Pope Urban VIII (1623–1644) in 1642, but Jansen's views found much support among the more deeply religious Catholics of France, notably in the nunnery of Port Royal, near Paris. The most influential opponent of the Jesuits was Blaise Pascal (1623–1662), especially in his *Lettres Provinciales* of 1656–1657. Louis XIV supported the Jesuit hostility to Jansenism, and persecuted its followers. In 1710 the buildings of Port Royal were torn down. Jansenism had found a new leader of power in Pasquier Quesnel (1634–1719), who had to seek safety in the Netherlands. His devotional commentary, *Moral Reflections on the New Testament,* of 1687–1692, aroused bitter Jesuit hostility, and through their efforts Pope Clement XI (1700–1721), by the bull *Unigenitus* of 1713, condemned one hundred and one of Quesnel's statements, some taken literally from Augustine. Louis Antoine de Noailles (1651–1729), cardinal archbishop of Paris, protested and appealed to a general council. Opposition was, however, vain. The Jesuits, supported by the French monarchy, ultimately triumphed.

Partly through this Jansenist controversy, and partly by reason of quarrels between the Jesuits and the older Roman clergy, a division occurred in Utrecht, in the Netherlands, from which in 1723 a small, independent, so-called Jansenist Catholic Church originated, which still exists, with an archbishop in Utrecht, and bishops in Haarlem and Deventer.

For France the expulsion of the Huguenots and the triumph of the Jesuits were great misfortunes. While much variety of religious interpretation was possible in England, Germany, and Holland, within the bounds of Christianity, in eighteenth-century France the choice was only between Romanism of the narrow Jesuit type, which many of its own noblest sons condemned, and the rapidly rising tide of the new rationalism of a Voltaire and his associates (see p. 442). Thousands preferred the latter, and the destructive results were to be obvious in the French Revolutionary treatment of the church.

Elsewhere in Catholic circles in Europe, sentiment corresponding to the Gallican spirit in France was on the increase in the eighteenth century. In Germany it took a conciliar form, and was called "Febronianism," from the pseudonym "Justinus Febronius" taken by its most articulate exponent,

Nicholas von Hontheim (1701–1790), auxiliary bishop of Trier. In Austria it took a monarchical form, and was called "Josephism," from the ecclesiastical policies of Emperor Joseph II (1765–1790).

The latter half of the eighteenth century brought to the Jesuits their greatest catastrophe. They had largely engaged in colonial trade, in spite of its prohibition in their own constitutions; their political influence was notorious, and they had the hostility of the radical rationalism of the age. In this latter force they found their most determined foes. The powerful minister of King Joseph of Portugal (1750–1777), the marquis of Pombal (1699–1782), was a man of rationalistic sympathies. He was angered by Jesuit resistance to his policy in Paraguay. He opposed the free-trade attitude of the Jesuits. In 1759 he enforced the deportation of all Jesuits from Portuguese territory with ruthless high hand. In France, too, sentiment against the Jesuits increased. The controlling force in the French government was that of the duke of Choiseul (1719–1785), a sympathizer with the Enlightenment. He was also aided by Madame de Pompadour, the mistress of Louis XV (1715–1774). A large part of the French clergy were also hostile to the Jesuits. In 1764 the Jesuits were suppressed in France. Spain and Naples expelled them in 1767. The rulers of these lands now forced from Pope Clement XIV (1769–1774) the abolition of the order in July, 1773. These events attested the weakness of the papacy. The Jesuits continued existence in non-Roman Russia and in Protestant Prussia.

The tremendous storm of the French Revolution was about to break and to sweep away the church, with the nobility, the throne, and kindred ancient institutions. The Revolutionary leaders were filled with the rationalistic spirit. They viewed the churches as religious clubs. In 1789 church lands were declared national property. In 1790 the monasteries were abolished. The same year the Civil Constitution of the Clergy overthrew the old ecclesiastical divisions, made each "department" a bishopric, and provided for the election of all priests by the legal voters of their communities. The constitution of 1791 pledged religious liberty. Then in 1793 came a royalist and Catholic uprising in La Vendée, and in retaliation the Jacobin leaders sought to wipe out Christianity. Hundreds of ecclesiastics were beheaded. After the "terror" was over, in 1795, religious freedom was once more proclaimed, though the state, as such, was to be without religion. It was, in reality, strongly antichristian. This situation was extended by French conquests to the Netherlands, northern Italy, and Switzerland. In 1798 Rome was made a republic by French arms, and Pope Pius VI (1775–1799) carried a prisoner to France, where he died.

The military events of 1800 led to the election of Pius VII (1800–1823) and the restoration of the States of the Church. Napoleon, on attaining power, though himself without religious feeling, recognized that a majority of the French people were Roman Catholics, and that the church might be used by him. The result was the Concordat with the papacy in 1801 and the Organic Articles of 1802. By the former, the church surrendered all confiscated lands not still held by the government. Those in government possession were restored to it. Appointment of bishops and archbishops were to be by the Pope on nomination by the state. Lower clergy were appointed by bishops, but the state had a veto power. Clergy were to be paid from the state treasury. By the Organic Articles no papal decrees were to be published or French synods held without governmental allowance. To Protestants full religious rights were accorded, at the same time, and the pay of their ministers and control of their affairs assumed by the state. Napoleon, who crowned himself Emperor in 1804, soon quarrelled with Pius VII, annexed the States of the Church in 1809, and held the Pope a prisoner from that time till 1814. Napoleon's Concordat was to rule the relations of France and the papacy for more than a century. Intended to place the French Catholic Church under the control of the government, and accomplishing that result under Napoleon, its real effect was to make the French clergy look to the Pope as their sole aid against the state. By ignoring all ancient local rights, it really ruined all Gallican claims to partial freedom, and opened the door to that Ultramontane spirit characteristic of French Catholicism throughout the nineteenth century.

The wars of the republican and Napoleonic periods resulted in farreaching changes in Germany. The old ecclesiastical territories practically ceased to exist in 1803, and were divided between the secular states. In 1806 Francis II (1792–1835) resigned the title Holy Roman Emperor. He had already assumed that of Emperor of Austria. It was the passing of a venerable institution, the Holy Roman Empire, which had, indeed, been long but a shadow, but which was bound up with mediæval memories of the relations of church and state.

Napoleon's downfall in 1815 was followed by universal reaction. The old seemed of value by its antiquity. It was to be years before the real progress effected by the Revolutionary age was to be manifest. This reaction was aided by the rise of Romanticism with its new appreciation of the mediæval and rejection of that spirit of the eighteenth century which had been dominant in the Revolution. François Rene de Chateaubriand (1768–1848) in his *Génie du Christianisme* of 1802 showed how Catholicism could profit from Romanticist currents, and contributed to the beginnings of a Catholic revival. The papacy profited by all these impulses and soon developed a strength greater than it had shown for a hundred years. A characteristic evidence of this new position of the papacy was the restoration, by Pius VII, in August, 1814, of the Jesuits, who speedily regained their old ascendancy in papal counsels, and their wide extended activities, though not their former political power. They have, in turn, been foremost in the development and support of papal authority. At the same time the restoration of the power of the Roman Church was accompanied and made possible by a real revival of piety that has continued to characterize it to the present day.

Roman development during the nineteenth century has been in the direction of the assertion of papal supremacy, called Ultramontanism— *i. e.,* beyond the mountains from the point of view of northern and western Europe—that is, Italian. The Ultramontane position with its magnification of the place of pope and king was strengthened by the writings of the "three prophets of traditionalism," Joseph Marie de Maistre (1754–1821), Louis Gabriel Ambroise de Bonald (1754–1840) and especially Hugues Félicité Robert de Lamennais (1782–1854). To this Ultramontane tendency to exalt the papacy above all national or local ecclesiasticism the Jesuits have powerfully contributed. Pius VII's successor, Leo XII (1823–1829), was reactionary, condemning, like his predecessor, the work of Bible societies. Gregory XVI (1831–1846) was a patron of learning, but reactionary toward modern social and political ideals. This essentially mediæval outlook and refusal to make terms with the modern world led to the formation, in the first half of the nineteenth century, of clerical and anticlerical parties in Catholic countries, whose contests largely determined the politics of those lands. An attempt on the part of the brilliant Lamennais to form an alliance of Catholicism and liberalism, especially for lands where Catholicism was in the minority, only brought about his condemnation and excommunication by Gregory.

The Ultramontane tendencies found their conspicuous illustration in the papacy of Pius IX (1846–1878). Beginning his pontificate at a time when the States of the Church were on the edge of revolt because the leading political offices were held by the clergy, he was at first a political reformer; but the task proved too much for him and he adopted a reactionary political policy which made it necessary to seek the support of foreign soldiery and rendered the people dissatisfied with his political rule. In religion he was sincerely convinced that in the papacy is a divinely appointed institution to which the modern world can appeal for the decision of its vexed religious problems. He desired to make this evident. In December, 1854, after consultation with the bishops of the Roman Church, he proclaimed the immaculate conception of the Virgin—that is, that Mary shared in no taint of original sin. The question had been in discussion since the Middle Ages, though the balance of Catholic opinion in the nineteenth century was overwhelmingly in favor of the view approved by the Pope. He elevated it, by his own act, into a necessary dogma of faith.

In 1864 a Syllabus of Errors, prepared under papal auspices, condemned many things which most Christians oppose; but also repudiated much which is the foundation of modern states, like the separation of church and state, non-sectarian schools, toleration of varieties in religion, and concluded by condemning the claim that "the Roman Pontiff can and ought to reconcile himself to, and agree with, progress, liberalism, and civilization as lately introduced."

The crowning event of Pius IX's pontificate was the Vatican Council. Opened on December 8, 1869, with a remarkably large attendance from all over the Roman world, its most important result was the affirmation, on July 18, 1870, of the doctrine of papal infallibility by a vote of five hundred and thirty-three to two. It was far from asserting that all papal utterances are infallible. To be so the Pope must expound, in his official capacity, "the revelation or deposit of faith delivered through the Apostles." "The Roman pontiff, when he speaks *ex cathedra*, that is, when in discharge of the office of pastor and doctor of all Christians, by virtue of his supreme apostolic authority, he defines a doctrine regarding faith or morals to be held by the universal church, by the divine assistance promised to him in blessed Peter, is possessed of that infallibility with which the divine Redeemer willed that His church should be endowed." Thus the Vatican Council sealed the triumph of Ultramontanism. It was the completion of the absolute papal monarchy, and the overthrow of that doctrine of the supremacy of a general council which had loomed so large in the fifteenth century (see pp. 274–280), and had not been without its representatives since.

Though undoubtedly the logical outcome of centuries of papal development, this doctrinal definition encountered considerable opposition, especially in Germany. The most eminent refuser of conformity was the distinguished Munich historian, Johann Joseph Ignaz von Döllinger (1799–1890), but though excommunicated, he declined to initiate a schism. What he refused, others achieved, and the result was the organization of the Old Catholics, who received episcopal ordination from the Jansenist Church of Utrecht (see p. 520). Their chief spread has been in Germany, Switzerland, and Austria, where they still number more than a hundred thousand adherents. They have even, though very feebly, reached the United States. Yet the Old Catholic movement would seem to have little future. Its departures from Rome, though important, were not vital enough to serve as a long-continuing basis of a branch of the Christian Church.

Meanwhile the tide of Italian national unity had been rising. The war carried on jointly by the kingdom of Sardinia, under Victor Emmanuel II (1849–1878), and France, under Napoleon III (1852–1870), against Austria, supplemented by Italian enthusiasm led by Giuseppe Garibaldi (1807–1882), resulted in the establishment of the kingdom of Italy under Victor Emmanuel in 1861, and the inclusion in it of the greater part of the old States of the Church. Rome and its vicinity were preserved to the Pope by the Ultramontane policy of Napoleon III. On the outbreak of the war between France and Germany in 1870, the French troops were withdrawn. On September 20, 1870, Victor Emmanuel captured Rome, and the inhabitants of the district voted one hundred and thirty-three thousand to one thousand five hundred for annexation to Italy. To the Pope the Italian Government guaranteed the privileges of a sovereign, and absolute possession of the Vatican, the Lateran, and Castel Gandolfo. Thus came to an end the States of the Church, the oldest continuous secular sovereignty then existing in Europe. Pius IX protested, declared himself the "prisoner of the Vatican," and excommunicated Victor Emmanuel. For half a century, until the Concordat with Mussolini settled the "Roman question" in 1929, the papacy refused to accept the loss of its temporal possessions. Yet it had its advantages. It aroused sympathy for the Pope, and the contributions that flowed in from the Catholic world more than made up for the financial loss. It removed from the papacy a secular task which it was ill adapted to meet, and the attempted accomplishment of which laid it open to well-grounded charges of maladministration. It gave to the papacy unhindered scope for the development of its spiritual functions, and ultimately increased papal moral prestige.

These advantages did not immediately appear, however. For many years it appeared that the church was retreating before the forces of the modern world, withdrawing within its own circle. In Italy, for example, Pius IX forbade Italian Catholics to participate in the political life of the kingdom of Italy. The consequence of this policy of *non expedit* was largely to strengthen the influence of radicals and socialists. In Germany in the 1870's occurred the *Kulturkampf* which set the Catholic Church against Bismarck's State; in the struggle Catholics were often cut off from their accustomed contacts and sources of support, and forced to consolidate their interests in a distinctive way.

Pius IX was succeeded by a statesman Pope, Leo XIII (1878–1903). He concluded the conflicts between the papacy and the imperial government of Germany. The church had won, but at the apparent cost of becoming something of an enclave. He urged French Catholics to support the republic, but the effects of the Dreyfus case largely undid his efforts, and the struggle between church and state in France reached a climax under his successor. In Italy, Leo continued to seek the restoration of the States of the Church, and the tension between church and state continued. But he developed policies of great significance for the future. The relations of labor and capital and the interests of working men enlisted his attention. His famous encyclical of 1891, *Rerum novarum,* awoke wide Catholic concern with the issues of social justice. Leo urged the formation of a network of clerically led Catholic associations for social, benevolent, economic, and political purposes. This pattern of "Catholic Action" became an important source of strength in the twentieth century. Leo was a man of scholarly tastes, who urged the study of the Scriptures, and declared that Aquinas (see p. 245) was the standard of Roman Catholic instruction. He opened the treasures of the Vatican to historical scholars. He sought the reunion of the Roman and the Eastern churches, but declared Anglican orders invalid in 1896. He was a skillful and zealous pope, who reigned in a difficult time in the life of the church.

The nineteenth century was a "great century" for Roman Catholic as well as for Protestant missions, though they were a few years later in arising, and were not quite so conspicuous. The main missionary base was France, and the missionary force, chiefly monks and clergy, was strengthened by a marked increase in the number of monks serving as missionaries. Many orders and societies, some of them newly founded, participated in the movement. New movements for the support of missions, such as the Society for the Propagation of the Faith, founded at Lyons in 1822, contributed to a new interest in missions on the part of the laity. The revived missionary thrust, which drew much of its power from the Ultramontane revival, revivified the Catholic minorities in India and Indochina. In China, Catholic converts, often of the peasant classes, tended to be somewhat withdrawn from vigorous participation in the common life, so that the larger Catholic community made less general impact than did the Protestant. In central Africa, many were won to the faith by the missionary thrust.

Pius X (1903–1914) was, in many ways, a contrast to Leo XIII. The latter was of noble birth. Pius X was of humble origin. Leo XIII was of great diplomatic ability and far-sighted vision. Pius X was a faithful parish priest whose parish had become world-wide. He was called to handle two questions of great difficulty. The first had to do with the relations of church and state in France. In spite of the efforts of Leo XIII, the majority of French Catholics were regarded as lukewarm toward the republic. Relations had long been growing strained. In 1901 religious orders not under state control were forbidden to engage in instruction. The refusal of conformity by some was followed in 1903 by the suppression of many monasteries and nunneries, and the confiscation of their properties. In 1904 President Loubet of France paid a state visit in Rome to the King of Italy. Pius X, regarding the Italian sovereign as in wrongful possession of Rome, protested. France withdrew its ambassador from the papal court, and soon after broke off all diplomatic intercourse. In December, 1905, the French Government decreed the separation of church and state. All governmental aid was withdrawn from Catholics and Protestants. All churches and other church property were declared the possession of the state, to be rented for use by state-responsible local associations for worship, preference being given to those representative of the faith by which the property had last been employed. Though many French bishops were ready to form such organizations, Pius X forbade. The result was a deadlock. Support had to be provided by voluntary gifts. Not until the 1920's was the church to have a legal basis in France.

The second problem was occasioned by the rise of the Modernists. In spite of growing Ultramontanism, modern historical criticism, Biblical investigation, and scientific conceptions of growth through development, found a foothold, though scanty, in the Roman communion. To some earnest and thoughtful men some reinterpretation of Catholicism in terms of the modern intellectual world seemed imperative. Such were Hermann Schell (1850–1906) in Germany, Alfred Loisy (1857–1940) in France, George Tyrrell (1861–1909) in England, and quite a group in Italy. Modernism was confined to no country. Against this movement Pius X set his face. By a decree, *Lamentabili,* and an encyclical, *Pascendi,* both in 1907, Modernism was condemned, and stringent measures were taken for its repression. Loisy and Tyrrell were excommunicated. The impression that Catholicism was retreating from the modern world was heightened.

The period of the first World War, during which Benedict XV (1914–1922) was Pope, saw a marked improvement in Catholic fortunes. Catholic charitable institutions gave a good account of themselves in the struggle. The improved moral and spiritual prestige of the papacy now began to count. Rome had fought the cultural developments of the nineteenth century, but as these came into crisis during the war and after, the stand of the church appeared less anachronistic. The organizations of Catholic Action gave to Roman Catholicism an effective instrument for growth and survival in pluralistic societies.

The pontificate of able and scholarly Pius XI (1922–1939) was marked by a decided Catholic revival. Revived theological interest, a significant liturgical movement, and continued missionary interest were evident. The "Roman question" was finally settled in 1929 by the Lateran Pacts, by which the Pope accepted the loss of the former States of the Church in exchange for a large sum, and received the domain of the Vatican City as his own. The church sought to consolidate her new gains in Europe through a series of concordats with various governments, including agreements with Fascist Italy (1929) and Nazi Germany (1933). When those governments broke faith, Pius protested in his vigorous encyclicals, *Non abbiamo bisogno* (1931) and *Mit brennender Sorge* (1937).

Roman Catholicism in the United States grew steadily throughout the nineteenth and early twentieth centuries, for the tides of immigration brought millions of that faith to American shores. In the first half of the nineteenth century, one of the chief internal problems was the desire of certain lay trustees of Catholic parishes to take on themselves the episcopal prerogative of appointing and dismissing their pastors. Schisms over "trusteeism" in some cases lasted for many years, but the bishops succeeded in securing full control. The chief external problem was the recrudescence of anti-Catholic feeling, heightened by the influx of the militantly Roman Catholic Irish in the 1840's. Meanwhile, by developing parochial schools, institutions of charity, and a Catholic press, vigorous effort to hold the loyalty of the incoming foreigners was made.

The second half of the century was a period of naturalization and Americanization for the Catholic Church. The calling of the First Plenary Council in Baltimore in 1852 was a step toward consolidating Catholic gains, and toward securing a larger place in the life of the nation. By that time, Catholics were nearly two million strong—the largest single religious body in the land. The central figure in this period was James Gibbons (1834–1921), who was consecrated bishop in 1868, made archbishop in 1877, and elevated to the cardinalate in 1886. He did much to make his church at home in America, and to ease the tensions against Catholics. He believed that the separation of church and state was best for America, and supported it heartily. He championed the rights of working men, at a time when the shift in the main sources of immigration to southern Europe was pouring ever greater number of people of Catholic background into the urban centers. There were those who feared that the Roman Catholic Church in the United States was becoming *too* American in this age of Gibbons, and in 1899 a papal letter, *Testem benevolentiae,* warned against such dangers.

In the early twentieth century, Catholicism came of age in America. In 1908, the American church was removed from the jurisdiction of the Sacred Congregation for the Propagation of the Faith, its missionary status ended. The participation of Catholics in the first World War established its "Americanism" beyond any doubt, and served further to diminish surviving tensions between ethnic groups. Furthermore, the National Catholic War Council (1917) proved to be such an effective instrument of consolidation and advance that it was retained as the National Catholic Welfare Conference, an instrument of the hierarchy, and the dynamic center of "Catholic Action" in the United States. Increased Roman Catholic strength in America was accompanied by some increased resistance on the part of both Protestants and "other" Americans.

17

The Eastern Churches in Modern Times

THE IMPRESSION of many Westerners that Eastern Christianity has had an uneventful history in modern times probably merely reflects the fact that the study of Eastern church history has been neglected in the West. The "Florentine Union" was quickly repudiated by the major Eastern churches. The Greek Metropolitan Isidore of Kiev was expelled when he attempted to proclaim it at Moscow, and from 1448 the Russian church was fully autonomous. At Constantinople the Union lasted in form until the fall of the city, but was definitely repudiated by a Synod in 1472. Under the Sultans the Patriarchs rose to a dangerous eminence as civil heads of the "Rum millet," the Orthodox subjects of the Turks. Subjected to heavy exactions and frequently deposed, they lost one ancient church after another until settled after 1603 at St. George's in the Phanar quarter of Istanbul. Other Orthodox prelates became dependent on the Œcumenical Patriarchate, although the Serbian and Bulgarian churches retained some autonomy until their Patriarchates were suppressed in 1766–1767. From 1461 an Armenian Patriarch at Istanbul had a similar position as civil representative of the Monophysites.

After 1453 the Muscovite principality replaced the Byzantine Empire as the great Orthodox state. Some ecclesiastics advanced the theory that since Old Rome had fallen into heresy and New Rome had been conquered, Moscow with its Orthodox princes and prelates was the New Rome which would never fail. Monasteries such as the great Troitsky Lavra (Trinity Monastery) near Moscow founded by St. Sergius in the fourteenth century were the main centers of piety, learning, and church life. An interesting monastic controversy of the late fifteenth century was between the "non-possessioners" headed by Nil Sorssky, who emphasized the life of prayer and monastic poverty at the expense of limiting activities to the strictly religious, and the "possessioners" headed by Joseph of Volokolamsk who accepted social and political responsibilities and welcomed wealth and property as a means of discharging them. The bestowal of patriarchal rank on the Metropolitans (1589), like the earlier assumption of the title Tsar by the Grand Dukes, merely gave formal recognition to an existing situation.

In the sixteenth and seventeenth centuries the Eastern churches had to come to terms with Western influences, both Catholic and Protestant. Luther and other Reformers appealed to the Eastern example of a non-Roman Catholicism. But when the theologians of Tübingen opened a correspondence with the Patriarch Jeremiah II (1574–1584), his replies stated clearly the divergence of the Greek church from the Lutheran teaching on authority, faith, grace, and the sacraments. Under obscure circumstances the remarkable Cyril Lucar (Patriarch five times between 1620 and 1638) issued a Confession of a strongly Reformed character; while in the Union of Brest, 1596, the Metropolitan of Kiev and other prelates in what was then Polish territory accepted the Florentine terms—local autonomy and liturgical independence, subject to ultimate Roman authority in doctrine and discipline. From the Polish word "unia" this Church of the Ukraine ("borderland") is popularly called Uniat, a term often applied (somewhat improperly) to other Eastern-Rite Catholics. Under Peter Mogila, who became Metropolitan in 1632, Kiev itself returned to the Orthodox Communion. His own Confession and Catechism are documents of importance in this controversy, which ends with the decrees of the Synod of Bethlehem, held under Patriarch Dositheus of Jerusalem in 1672. Though Orthodox in substance, these "confessional books" show Western influence in their form. Western methods were also used in Mogila's Theological Academy of Kiev (which was in

Russian territory after 1665), where the language of instruction was neither Greek nor Slavonic, but Latin. Through the eighteenth-century, Russian theological schools, organized on the Kiev model, followed this system.

In the sphere of influence of Catholic powers (first Portugal, later France and Austria, as well as Poland) other "Uniat" Churches were formed. Ethiopia was in formal union with Rome from 1624–1632. In India the Syrian Christians of Malabar suffered considerable Latinization under Archbishop Menezes (Synod of Diamper, 1599). In 1653 a large section renounced the Roman Communion, later securing the episcopal succession from the Syrian Jacobites, the Nestorians, with whom they had once been connected, being out of reach. A section of Nestorians were united with Rome as "Chaldeans" in the sixteenth century, and a section of Syrian Orthodox (to whom the Arabic name of the whole group, "Melkite" or royalist, *i. e.,* Byzantine, has come to be restricted) in the eighteenth. Other "Uniat" groups parallel the Copts, Jacobites, and Armenians.

In Russia the church was a focus of national loyalty during the wars and invasions of the "Time of Troubles" which followed the extinction of the ancient dynasty of Rurik. The defence of the Troitsky Lavra against the Poles in 1612 was one of the turning points of the period. When the new dynasty began with Michael Romanov in 1613, his father, who had been forced to take monastic vows during the wars, practically reigned with him as Patriarch Philaret. The Patriarch Nicon (1652–1666), vigorous to the point of roughness, introduced practical reforms, which included a correction of the service-books from the Greek. Nicon was deposed with the assent of other Patriarchs, but the reforms remained in effect. Opponents were forced into schism, as Old-Believers (properly Old-Ritualists) or separatists (Raskolniki). The importance of the liturgy in Orthodox faith and life stiffened their loyalty to the details of rite and ceremonial which represented to them the strict Orthodoxy of Russia. Peter the Great's westernizing reforms intensified the difference. The Russian sects form three groups—1) the Old Believers proper, of whom some (*popovtsi*) accepted priests who came over from the established Church, and in 1849 secured, irregularly from a Greek Bishop, their own episcopate, while others (*bez-popovtsi,* that is "priestless") hold that apostasy had destroyed the Orders of the Church, and limit themselves to such rites as laymen can administer, using consecrated Wine and Chrism maintained by dilution: 2) a variety of extreme or eccentric groups, some picking up survivals of paganism or ancient heresies—the pacifist Doukhobors ("spirit-wrestlers") who have migrated to Canada are the best known: and 3) since the nineteenth century, Protestant groups who have found their way into Russia in various ways.

Planning to organize church administration on the lines of a government department, Peter left the Patriarchate vacant after 1700, and in 1721 replaced it by the "Holy Governing Synod." This was composed of a few bishops and other clergy summoned by the Emperor, who also appointed its lay secretary and executive, the "Ober-Procuror." In English he is usually called Procurator, but the barbarous title, not even good German, expresses the revolutionary character of the institution. The Patriarch who might seem to rival the Tsar was thus replaced by an administration clearly subject to him. Although the established church was not without outstanding examples of piety, learning, charity, and missionary zeal, the deepest devotion flowed in unofficial channels. The eighteenth century saw a renewal of the old monastic tradition of straightforward piety and spiritual guidance among the monks of Mount Athos, one of whom, Paisi Velichkovsky (1722–1794), later an Abbot in Moldavia near the Russian border, brought this tradition back into Russian church life. The two most modern saints canonized by the Russian Church represent the same tendency, comparable in some ways to the pietist reaction against official Protestantism—the Bishop Tikhon Zadonsky, and the hermit of the northern woods, Seraphim of Sarov (d. 1835). One of the "elders" (*startsi*) or spiritual directors, of the Optina Monastery near Moscow is depicted in the Father Zossima of Dostoievsky's *Brothers Karamazov*.

The rise of nationalism and modern intellectual and spiritual movements have confronted the Eastern churches with new situations, the traditional close union of people and church expressing itself in new forms. The Greek Revolution was launched at the Peloponnesian monastery of Megaspelaion (and Patriarch Gregory V, though he formally condemned the insurgents, was hanged as a Greek leader in front of his residence at the Phanar in 1821). With political independence the Church of Greece renewed its intellectual life and assumed ecclesiastical autonomy, which the Patriarch of Constantinople recognized in 1851. Similar action was taken in Serbia, Romania, and Bulgaria. In 1870 the Bulgarian Exarch claimed jurisdiction over Bulgars everywhere, even at Istanbul—this was condemned as "philetism ["over-nationalism," perhaps], the heresy of our age," and produced a schism between Greeks and Bulgars from 1872 to 1945. Church life in the Balkans has continued to be unhappily involved in national conflicts. In Syria the Arab Christians became restive under Greek hierarchs. Since 1898 there have been Syrian Patriarchs of Antioch at Damascus, but the Patriarchate of Jerusalem continues to be controlled by the Brotherhood of the Holy Sepulchre (almost entirely Greek). Missionary interest helped to bring modern education to the Near East, but at the expense of further ecclesiastical divisions. The work of Eastern Catholics was extended by Latin missionaries, and small Protestant groups came into being among Greeks, Armenians and Syrians, and a larger Evangelical Church among the Copts. In India the Anglican missionaries of the C.M.S. worked for a time among the Syrian Christians, an ultimate result of their influence being the separation of a more Evangelical wing as the Mar Thoma Church.

The reaction against westernizing influences, whether religious or antireligious, led to the presentation of traditional Orthodoxy in more vigorous and up-to-date forms. Westernizing and strictly Orthodox trends have competed in the theological faculties of the Balkans and among the Christian thinkers of Russia. In the later nineteenth century the Greek Church was stimulated by the vigorous if eccentric ultra-Orthodox lay theologian Apostolos Makrakis. Since that time voluntary organizations have done much to revive preaching, organize religious education, and encourage the social activity of the Church—the Zoë Brotherhood, a confraternity of celibate *theologoi* (that is, graduates in theology), lay and clerical, is the best known of these. In Russia the Slavophils turned to the corporate and spiritual traditions of Orthodoxy, as against both the dullness of the repressed and repressing official Church (at its worst perhaps under Nicholas I, 1825–1855) and the secular trends of reformers and revolutionaries. The layman Alexis Khomiakov (1804–1860) is an early leader of the school. Others are less churchly if equally religious in their interests, such as the novelist Dostoievsky and the philosopher Soloviev, whose longing for spiritual unity led him to claim the right to enter the Roman Communion without abandoning his standing in the ancient Orthodox Church. The semi-official missionary activity of the Russian Church, often heroic, was at least encouraged because of its possible effect in consolidating the Empire or extending its influence, as in the work of the Imperial Palestine Society and the patronage of a Russian monastery on Mount Athos. But there was missionary work which rose beyond any political connections in Alaska, a Russian outpost till 1867, and under Bishop Nicholas of Tokyo (in Japan 1860–1912), founder of Japanese Orthodoxy.

The wars and revolutions of the twentieth century have brought further changes. After the Balkan Wars most of the dioceses of "new Greece" were in effect transferred from the jurisdiction of Constantinople to that of Athens. Somewhat later the Albanian Church became autonomous. After the first World War, Serbs and Rumanians who had been under separate jurisdictions in Austria-Hungary were restored to their native lands and native Churches; the Serbian Patriarchate was restored in 1920, and the Rumanian Church raised to patriarchal rank in 1925. The Œcumenical Patriarch's immediate jurisdiction was reduced to the immediate neighborhood of Istanbul by the exchange of populations between Greece and Turkey in 1923. But the Greek parishes of Europe and America are under his jurisdiction, and his undefined primacy among Orthodox hierarchs is from time to time appealed to. Considerable feeling (and some schism) was caused in the 1920's by the adoption of the Gregorian Calendar, somewhat improved, by Greeks, Syrians, and Rumanians for fixed festivals—though for the sake of unity all Orthodox still follow the Julian for the calculation of Easter.

The shift of Russia from Orthodox Empire to Marxist state was a blow to the church comparable to that of the Moslem conquest. In 1917 a church assembly met at Moscow which revived the Patriarchate and otherwise planned for the freedom of the church. But the movement from establishment to persecution was rapid under the Bolshevik regime. Though in principle tolerating "religious profession and anti-religious propaganda," the Soviet government actively promoted the latter and barely permitted the former. Many bishops and priests disappeared in prison or exile, monasteries were dissolved and most of the churches closed, church administration was impeded, and for some years the radical reforming groups commonly called the "Living Church" received relative encouragement as a further divisive factor. But the church lived on in the hearts of believers, and its leaders managed to retain some form of organization. In 1923 Patriarch Tikhon declared his political loyalty to the regime, and was allowed some freedom till his death in 1925, after which Metropolitan Sergius became guardian of the patriarchal throne. Periods of anti-religious pressure alternated with periods of relative calm, until the undoubted loyalty of Russian Orthodox to their country in the second World War led to a more settled relation. A patriarchal election was allowed in 1943, and under Sergius and his successor Alexis (1944—) the Russian Church has functioned more normally. Facilities are provided for its activities within the strictly religious sphere (worship, and instruction in homes when invited), and some institutions have been revived—a few monasteries and convents, seminaries, and theological academies at the Troitsky Lavra, Leningrad and Kiev. The church and its leaders are of course expected to manifest political loyalty—and Marxist leaders still expect religion to die out in time, but have abandoned their frontal attack. The Georgian Church had been absorbed by the Russian after the country was annexed in 1801 (to this resented status may partly be due the disaffection found in its ecclesiastical schools, such as that in which the future Joseph Stalin studied), but in 1917 it again became autonomous under its own Catholicos-Patriarch, and was so recognized by the Russian Church in 1944. Other churches in the Soviet Union have a status similar to that of the Orthodox Patriarchate—the Old Believers (at least the *popovtsi*), the Armenians, whose Supreme Catholicos resides at Etchmiadzim in Soviet Armenia, the Russian Baptists and the Lutherans of the Baltic Republics. In the 1920's the Orthodox Churches of areas formerly Russian but then independent received recognition of autonomous status from the Œcumenical Patriarch. This has been extinguished in Estonia (except for congregations in exile) and Latvia, but survives in Poland and Finland. In the Ukraine an autocephalous Church was formed during the brief period of independence during the Revolution, which now only survives among the Ukrainians of the United States and Canada.

Russian Orthodox outside Russia have fallen into three main groups. Some remain loyal to the Patriarchate in ecclesiastical matters. Others follow the lead of a group of exiled Bishops headed originally by Metropolitan Anthony of Kiev, who maintain that Tikhon and his successors have been slaves of the Soviet regime and that their Russian Orthodox Church outside

Russia is the true heir of its traditions. Its Synod was long established at Karlovtsi in Yugoslavia, but after the second World War moved to Munich and then to the United States. The third group seeks to avoid political involvement by insisting on autonomy in matters of administration and Church government, at least for the present, while remaining loyal to the traditions of Russian Orthodoxy. The main body of Russian Orthodox in the United States, the Russian Orthodox Greek Catholic Church of North America, belongs in this group, as does an important section of the Russian Church in Western Europe. In the latter an important center of theology and church life was established in 1925, the Academy of St. Sergius at Paris, headed for many years by the distinguished theologian Sergius Bulgakov (1871–1944).

A brief survey of present conditions and problems may conclude this section. The remnant of the Nestorian, or Assyrian, Church suffered greatly in both World Wars, and has largely taken refuge in Syria. The patriarchal family, in whom the dignity is hereditary, have been in exile, and the present Catholicos, Mar Shimun XXIII, has established his headquarters in California. The Syrian Christians of Malabar have suffered another division since 1910, between the Patriarch's party, willing to accept Syrian jurisdiction, and the Catholicos party desiring complete autonomy. Of other churches of the Monophysite or Jacobite Communion, the Ethiopian under Haile Selassie has at last secured its independence of the Coptic, and efforts are being made to prepare it to meet the educational and other responsibilities of a national church. The Armenians have recovered remarkably from the massacres and exiles of 1915–1916. Their second hierarch, the Catholicos of Cilicia, once in Turkey, is established with his flock in Lebanon—but political movements for or against Soviet Armenia affect the life of the Church.

The list of functioning Eastern Orthodox Churches includes the ancient Patriarchates of Constantinople, Alexandria (whose flock has been increased in modern times by the settlement of Greeks and Syrians in Egypt), Antioch, and Jerusalem; the later Patriarchates of Russia, Serbia, Rumania, Bulgaria, where the title has recently been revived, and Georgia; the autocephalous Churches of Cyprus (so recognized since the Council of Ephesus, prominent in recent years through the leadership of its Bishops in the national movement for union with Greece)—Greece, Poland, Finland, Albania, and Czechoslovakia—and the independent Monastery of Mount Sinai. Before 1917 the Russian bishopric—moved from Alaska to San Francisco in 1872, and to New York in 1905 (under Bishop Tikhon, later Patriarch)—was the only organized Orthodox jurisdiction in America, and supervised other national parishes except the Greek (which were formed into an archbishopric under Constantinople in 1922). Since 1920 the Syrians, Serbians, Rumanians, Bulgars and Albanians have established American dioceses. The rise of the American-born younger generation among laity and clergy (for whom the

Greeks and Russians have seminaries) marks the naturalization of Orthodoxy in America. English is increasingly used for instruction, and in varying degrees for the Liturgy, and in due time one may expect the national groups to join in an American Orthodox Church. There is also an Armenian Prelacy in America, and groups of Assyrian and Syrian Jacobite parishes.

Until recently the largest body of Eastern Catholics were the survivors of the Union of Brest in Galicia (after the partition of Poland, Austrian; after 1918, again Polish territory) and the related Carpatho-Russians (formerly in Hungary, after 1918 in Czechoslovakia). The Uniat Dioceses in Russian Poland were reunited to the Russian Church in 1840 and 1875. A famous leader among the Galician Ukrainians was Andrew Szepticky (Metropolitan of Lvov 1900–1944), one of the Eastern Catholics who have endeavored to represent within the papal obedience the less formalized spirit of Eastern Christian piety. The Soviet occupation of these lands in 1946 was followed by the reunion of Ukrainians and Carpatho-Russians with the Patriarchate of Moscow, and the Ukrainian "Unia" survives primarily in the "Apostolic Exarchates" established in the United States and Canada for immigrants from Galicia and Carpatho-Russia who have remained loyal to it.

Confident of the correctness of their own traditions, Eastern Christians have nevertheless been able to establish friendly contacts with others whenever the relation has not been complicated by controversy or proselytism. Friendly exchanges of various kinds have been carried on since the seventeenth century—most often though by no means exclusively with the Anglican Communion, and since 1870 with the Old Catholics, who arrived by a different route at a position very similar to that of the Orthodox Churches. Eastern Churches have participated in the Ecumenical Movement since the Stockholm and Lausanne Conferences of 1925 and 1927—a step prepared by the Synodical Encyclical of 1920 (issued by the Synod of Constantinople during a vacancy in the Patriarchate) which urged conference between churches on matters of practical concern. The Russian Church was unhappily not able to share in such discussions in the 1920's and the 1930's. But its interest was shown in the Moscow Conference of 1948, succeeding the celebrations of the 500th anniversary of its autocephaly, and attended by most of the non-Greek Orthodox Churches—although the immediate decisions had a rigid sound, conspicuous items being a denunciation of Vatican policy, a rejection at that time of cooperation in the World Council of Churches, and a reservation of judgment on Anglican Orders, which had been conditionally recognized by the Œcumenical Patriarchate and several other Orthodox Churches between 1922 and 1935. In 1961, however, the Russian Orthodox Church became a member of the World Council of Churches, so that almost every major autocephalous national Orthodox Church came into full membership in that ecumenical body.

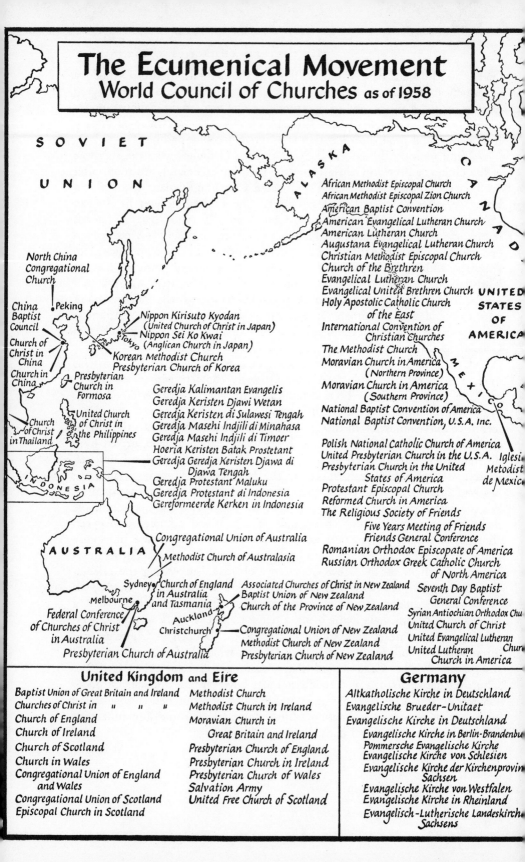

The Ecumenical Movement
World Council of Churches as of 1958

SOVIET UNION

ALASKA

North China Congregational Church

China Baptist Council
Peking

Church of Christ in China

Church in China

Church of Christ in Thailand

Presbyterian Church in Formosa

Nippon Kirisuto Kyodan
(United Church of Christ in Japan)
Nippon Sei Ko Kwai
(Anglican Church in Japan)
Korean Methodist Church
Presbyterian Church of Korea

Tokyo

United Church of Christ in the Philippines

Geredja Kalimantan Evangelis
Geredja Keristen Djawi Wetan
Geredja Keristen di Sulawesi Tengah
Geredja Masehi Indjili di Minahasa
Geredja Masehi Indjili di Timoer
Hoeria Keristen Batak Prostetant
Geredja Geredja Keristen Djawa di
Djawa Tengah
Geredja Protestant Maluku
Geredja Protestant di Indonesia
Gereformeerde Kerken in Indonesia

INDONESIA

AUSTRALIA

Congregational Union of Australia

Methodist Church of Australasia

Sydney — Church of England in Australia and Tasmania
Melbourne
Federal Conference of Churches of Christ in Australia
Presbyterian Church of Australia

Auckland
Christchurch

Associated Churches of Christ in New Zealand
Baptist Union of New Zealand
Church of the Province of New Zealand
Congregational Union of New Zealand
Methodist Church of New Zealand
Presbyterian Church of New Zealand

African Methodist Episcopal Church
African Methodist Episcopal Zion Church
American Baptist Convention
American Evangelical Lutheran Church
American Lutheran Church
Augustana Evangelical Lutheran Church
Christian Methodist Episcopal Church
Church of the Brethren
Evangelical Lutheran Church
Evangelical United Brethren Church
Holy Apostolic Catholic Church
of the East
International Convention of
Christian Churches
The Methodist Church
Moravian Church in America
(Northern Province)
Moravian Church in America
(Southern Province)
National Baptist Convention of America
National Baptist Convention, U.S.A. Inc.

Polish National Catholic Church of America
United Presbyterian Church in the U.S.A.
Presbyterian Church in the United
States of America
Protestant Episcopal Church
Reformed Church in America
The Religious Society of Friends
Five Years Meeting of Friends
Friends General Conference
Romanian Orthodox Episcopate of America
Russian Orthodox Greek Catholic Church
of North America
Seventh Day Baptist
General Conference
Syrian Antiochian Orthodox Chu
United Church of Christ
United Evangelical Lutheran
United Lutheran Chur
Church in America

UNITED STATES OF AMERICA

Iglesi
Metodist
de Mexica

CANADA

MEXICO

United Kingdom and Eire

Baptist Union of Great Britain and Ireland
Churches of Christ in " " "
Church of England
Church of Ireland
Church of Scotland
Church in Wales
Congregational Union of England
and Wales
Congregational Union of Scotland
Episcopal Church in Scotland

Methodist Church
Methodist Church in Ireland
Moravian Church in
Great Britain and Ireland
Presbyterian Church of England
Presbyterian Church in Ireland
Presbyterian Church of Wales
Salvation Army
United Free Church of Scotland

Germany

Altkatholische Kirche in Deutschland
Evangelische Brueder-Unitaet
Evangelische Kirche in Deutschland
Evangelische Kirche in Berlin-Brandenbu
Pommersche Evangelische Kirche
Evangelische Kirche von Schlesien
Evangelische Kirche der Kirchenprovin
Sachsen
Evangelische Kirche von Westfalen
Evangelische Kirche in Rheinland
Evangelisch-Lutherische Landeskirch
Sachsens

France
Eglise de la Confession d'Augsbourg d'Alsace et de Lorraine
Eglise Evangelique Lutherienne de France. Eglise Reformee de France
Eglise Reformee d'Alsace et de Lorraine

Evangelisch-Lutherische Landeskirche Hannovers
Evangelisch-Lutherische Kirche in Bayern
Evangelisch-Lutherische Kirche in Thuringen
Evangelisch-Lutherische Landeskirche Schleswig-Holsteins
Evangelisch-Lutherische Landeskirche in
   Hamburgischen Staate
Evangelisch-Lutherische Landeskirche Mecklenburgs
Braunschweigische Evangelisch-Lutherische Landes-
Evangelisch-Lutherische Kirche in Lübeck   kirche
Evangelisch-Lutherische Landeskirche in
   Schaumburg-Lippe
Evangelische Landeskirche in Württemberg

Evangelisch-Lutherische Kirche in Oldenburg
Evangelisch-Lutherische Landeskirche Eutin
Evangelische Kirche in Hessen und Nassau
Evangelische Landeskirche in Kurhessen-Waldeck
Vereinigte Evangelisch-Protestantische Landeskirche Badens
Vereinigte Protestantische Kirche der Pfalz
Evangelische Landeskirche Anhalts
Bremische Evangelische Kirche
Evangelisch-Reformierte Kirche in Nordwestdeutschland
Lippische Landeskirche
Vereinigung der Deutschen Mennonitengemeinden

18

The Ecumenical Movement

THE HISTORY of the Christian Church has constantly been marked by two major drives, toward expansion and toward integration. In the nineteenth century, especially in the Protestant world, the theme of expansion was dominant, but in the twentieth century the movements toward consolidation have been the most conspicuous. The concern for the reintegration of Christendom has manifested itself in many ways. The term "ecumenical movement" is a generic one which refers to a whole range of movements and tendencies toward reunion, not all of them wholly consistent with each other. Of greatest importance in Protestant affairs, the ecumenical movement has also involved most of the Eastern Orthodox Churches. The Roman Catholic Church for a long time took no official part in ecumenical discussion or action. The encyclical *Mortalium Animos* (1928) declared that the only way in which the unity of Christianity could be fostered would be "by furthering the return to the one true Church of Christ of those who are separated from it," which would involve their believing in "the infallibility of the Roman Pontiff in the sense of the Œcumenical Vatican Council with the same faith as they believe in the Incarnation of Our Lord." This uncompromising attitude kept the door to Catholic participation in the ecumenical movement closed until a dramatic reversal took place during the pontificate of John XXIII (see chap. 19).

The ecumenical movement became prominent in the twentieth century, but its historical roots run deep, indeed back to the sixteenth century itself. It was in the nineteenth century, however, that there were launched specific movements in half a dozen areas of Protestant life and thought which were to flower into world interdenominational agencies and stimulate a number of organic church unions in the twentieth century.

The first and in many ways the most important of these areas was the missionary enterprise. On the mission fields the evils of competitive denominationalism and the need for coordination became especially obvious. The missionary thrust of the nineteenth century had many interdenominational features from the beginning, for many of the missionary societies drew support from Christians across denominational lines. On the field, gatherings of missionaries for fellowship and discussion developed early. The first such meetings on a world scale took place in New York and in London in 1854, to be followed by others at irregular intervals. The eighth in the series of gatherings was the World Missionary Conference held at Edinburgh in 1910. The affair differed from its predecessors, however, in that most of those who attended came not only as deeply interested individuals, but also as official delegates of the various missionary societies. A feature of the assembly was its thorough advance preparation, including the preliminary circulation of carefully prepared study volumes. Representatives of the missionary or younger churches were present, giving a good account of themselves. At Edinburgh, many individuals who were to play an important rôle in the many areas of twentieth-century ecumenical development received inspiration and direction.

The conference marked the great turning point in ecumenical history. A Continuation Committee, set up to preserve the gains made at Edinburgh, grew by 1921 into the International Missionary Council. Its first chairman was the American Methodist layman who had presided at Edinburgh, John Raleigh Mott (1865–1955). Membership in the Council was held chiefly by the national and regional interdenominational missionary organizations, such as the Committee of the German Evangelical Missions (1885), the Foreign Missions Conference of North America (1893), and the Conference of Missionary Societies of Great Britain and Ireland (1912). It encouraged the development of National Christian Councils in the lands of the younger churches, especially in India, China, Japan, the Congo, and the Near East. This period of growing missionary cooperation was also a period of rapid devolution in the missionary enterprise, so that by mid-twentieth century some ninety per cent of the personnel in Protestant mission fields were nationals. The increasing significance of the younger churches was reflected in the World meetings of the I.M.C. at Jerusalem in 1928 and Madras in 1938. At the former, the younger church leaders constituted about a quarter of the delegation, but at the latter, slightly more than half.

A second area of growing ecumenical activity was that of youth work and Christian education. A pioneer, nondenominational agency of considerable ecumenical significance was the Young Men's Christian Association, founded in London by George Williams (1821–1905) in 1844, and since spread through the world. The World's Alliance of the Y.M.C.A. was established in 1855. That same year the Young Women's Christian Association was organized in London, and the World's Y.W.C.A. was formed in 1894. Another important movement among young people was the Student Volunteer Movement for Foreign Missions, organized in 1886 at one of Dwight L. Moody's summer conferences. John R. Mott served as its organizer and for many years as its chairman. Under his leadership, the World's Student Christian Federation was created in Sweden in 1895. The Student Christian Movement was characterized by prophetic and pioneering aspects; it served as a training ground for men and women who later became conspicuous in the various areas of ecumenical life. These world student fellowships were predominantly lay movements, and the World Christian Education movement also was strongly lay in character. World's Sunday School Conventions met regularly beginning in 1889. In 1907 the World's Sunday School Association was formed. It became in 1924 a federation of national and interdenominational Christian Education agencies, and then was renamed the World Council on Christian Education and Sunday School Association (1947, 1950).

A third area of ecumenical development was that of federation for Christian service and common ethical action, the area that came to be called "Life and Work." A pioneer of this general approach was Samuel S. Schmucker (see p. 513), who published his *Fraternal Appeal to the American Churches: With a Plan for Catholic Union, on Apostolic Principles* in 1838. His was a federal plan, in which the existing denominations, practically intact, would become branches of the Apostolic Protestant Church. Though the time was scarcely ripe for the serious discussion of such plans, they did contribute to the longing for some fuller unity. An early organizational expression in this area, though composed wholly of interested individuals, was the Evangelical Alliance, organized in London in 1846. It sponsored world conferences and served as a sounding board of evangelical opinion. It was especially active in the defense of religious liberty, and accomplished much in this field. But it was not in official relationship with the communions, and as the century progressed, this was seen to be desirable. The last conspicuous secretary of the American branch of the Evangelical Alliance (organized in 1867), was Josiah Strong (1847–1916), but he resigned in 1898 to take an active part in the organization of the Federal Council of the Churches of Christ in America. Founded finally in 1908, it had about thirty American denominations as members, including many, but not all, of the major bodies. The professed objects of the Federal Council were: (1) to express the fellowship and catholic unity of the Christian Church; (2) to bring the Christian bodies of America into united service for Christ and the world; (3) to encourage devotional fellowship and mutual counsel concerning the spiritual life and religious activities of the Churches; (4) to secure a larger combined influence for the Churches of Christ in all matters affecting the moral and social condition of the people, so as to promote the application of the law of Christ in every relation of human life; and (5) to assist in the organization of local branches of the Federal Council to promote its aim in their communities. In 1950, it merged with a number of other interdenominational agencies of the United States—those concerned with home and foreign missions, with missionary and religious education, with higher education, stewardship, and women's work—to form the National Council of the Churches of Christ in the U.S.A. In other lands, similar organizations were formed; for example, in France in 1905, Switzerland in 1920, Britain in 1942, Canada in 1944.

On the world scene, the federative approach found its most conspicuous champion in Nathan Söderblom (1866–1931), Swedish Lutheran pastor and scholar, later Archbishop of Uppsala. Veteran of the Student Christian Movement, he was convinced that the churches could serve together in common ethical action despite deep doctrinal differences. His driving energy led to the first Universal Christian Conference on Life and Work at Stockholm in 1925. The conference made a rapid survey of the social needs of the world, appealed to the conscience of the Christian world, and indicated possible lines of advance. A Continuation Committee grew into the Universal Christian Council for Life and Work in 1930. It called a second world gathering, the Conference on Church, Community, and State at Oxford in 1937. The theological foundations of ethical action, which had been "overlooked" at Stockholm, were carefully explored, and the distinctive rôle of the Church in the world was given attention.

A fourth area of ecumenical activity was in some ways the most precarious, for it involved the frank facing of the most crucial doctrinal differences, which often did not need to be directly confronted in the other areas. The original Protestant ecumenical discussions in the sixteenth century had broken down just at such points of "Faith and Order," and there was hesitation in raising them again. Yet specific proposals for Christian unity in any full sense involved such confrontation of doctrinal issues. For example, when American Episcopalian William Reed Huntington (1838–1918) sought to state the minimum "essentials" of Anglicanism as a basis for reunion discussion, he named four items: (1) the Holy Scriptures as the Word of God; (2) the primitive Creeds as the rule of faith; (3) the two Sacraments ordained by Christ himself; and (4) the historic episcopate as the keystone of governmental unity. Approved with slight modifications by the American Episcopal House of Bishops and the Anglican Lambeth Conference in the 1880's, the "Chicago-Lambeth Quadrilateral" clearly showed how central in unity discussions matters of faith and order were. It was an American Episcopal missionary bishop, Charles H. Brent (1862–1929), who caught a new vision at Edinburgh in 1910—a vision of a reunited church, but which could come about only through discussion of doctrinal matters which had been omitted at Edinburgh. He called on his own communion to take the lead in the area of "Faith and Order." After years of preparation, the first World Conference on Faith and Order met at Lausanne in 1927. Over four hundred delegates represented over one hundred churches. Some of the deepest issues between the communions were given full discussion, surprisingly large areas of agreement were found, and a spirit of friendship prevailed. A Continuation Committee carried on the movement, summoning the next conference for Edinburgh in 1937. That gathering prepared a remarkable statement on "The Grace of our Lord Jesus Christ," prefaced with the judgment, "There is in connection with this subject no ground for maintaining division between Churches." But with respect to "The Ministry and Sacraments" very deep differences were revealed, pointing to the matters that needed further illumination. Yet the generalization seemed generally accepted that in the doctrinal realm, the agreements between the churches cover eighty-five per cent of the ground.

Many suggestions had been advanced for the uniting of Life and Work with Faith and Order into a World Council of Churches. The two 1937 conferences had been planned to meet in sequence. Both conferences voted for integration, and at Utrecht in 1938 a provisional structure for the World Council was prepared. The Basis of the Council which was adopted was: "The World Council of Churches is a fellowship of Churches which accept our Lord Jesus Christ as God and Saviour." Taking the lead in these developments was William Temple (1881–1944), then Archbishop of York and later (1942) of Canterbury. Philosopher, theologian and churchman, Temple had played important rôles in the Student Christian Movement, the International Missionary Council, Life and Work, and Faith and Order. Now he became chairman of the Provisional Committee of the World Council of Churches "in process of formation." Because of interruption by war, it remained in this stage for ten years. In those difficult years its service in providing for orphaned missions, caring for prisoners of war, and helping with refugees was outstanding. Finally, at Amsterdam in 1948, one hundred and forty-seven churches from forty-four countries participated in the completion of the organization of the World Council, approving the Basis. It was made clear that the Council could have no constitutional authority over the member churches. Most of the major Protestant bodies of Europe and the British Isles, the majority of those of America and Australasia, and several of the Orthodox communions became members. Most of the younger churches of Asia and Africa also joined.

The International Missionary Council merged with the World Council of Churches at New Delhi in 1961. The World Council kept close ties with the World's Alliance of the Y.M.C.A., the World's Y.M.C.A., and the World's Student Christian Federation. The World Conferences of Christian Youth, held at Amsterdam in 1939, Oslo in 1947, and Travancore in 1952, were initiated jointly by those world bodies.

A fifth area of ecumenical concern is that of organic church union. Some of the specific unions have been intra-confessional, or within a denominational family. Conspicuous among such achievements were the Presbyterian reunions in Scotland. The United Secession and Relief Churches (see p. 463) had combined as the United Presbyterian Church in 1847. In 1900 the latter body combined with the majority of the Free Church of Scotland, the result of the Disruption of 1843, to form the United Free Church of Scotland. A small minority of the old Free Church (the "Wee Frees") refused to enter the union. In 1874, the rights of patronage, the original ground of the divisions, had been abolished by law. But it took many years of discussion to clear the way for the larger reunion. In 1921 Parliament passed a bill allowing the church to legislate for itself in all matters of doctrine and practice without interference by the state, but also declaring that it was the duty of the nation to render homage to God and seek to promote his kingdom. In 1929 the union was consummated, and ninety per cent of the Presbyterians of the country—probably more than two-thirds of the population—became members of the established Church of Scotland.

In the United States, there have been a number of denominational reunions. In 1918, the Lutheran General Synod and General Council merged with the United Synod of the South to form the United Lutheran Church. In 1930, the synods of Buffalo, Iowa, and Ohio united as the American Lutheran Church. A series of mergers in the early 1960's brought almost all Lutherans in the United States into three major bodies, the Lutheran Church in America (including the United and Augustana churches), the Lutheran Church—Missouri Synod, and The American Lutheran Church (including the American, Evangelical, and Lutheran Free churches).

The northern Presbyterian Church united with the major part of the Cumberland Presbyterian Church in 1906, and in 1958 joined with the United Presbyterian Church to form the United Presbyterian Church in the United States of America. The Unitarian and Universalist churches came together in 1961 as the Unitarian Universalist Association.

The Methodist Church was the result in 1939 of the reunion of the Methodist Episcopal Church, the Methodist Episcopal Church South, and the Methodist Protestant Church (which had broken away from the larger body of Methodists over a century earlier). Seven years later two groups of German Methodist background united as the Evangelical United Brethren Church. This church in turn joined with the Methodists in 1968 to form the United Methodist Church.

Church unions across denominational lines, trans-confessional, have also taken place. In Canada, diverse Protestant beginnings had meant for much complexity of organization. The nineteenth century was a period of denominational consolidation. In Presbyterianism there were nine unions, culminating in 1875 when four bodies came together to form the Presbyterian Church in Canada. Methodism saw eight unions climaxing in 1884, when again four bodies came together to compose the Methodist Church of Canada. Much small Congregationalism found unity as three strands came together in 1906 and 1907. But in a land of vast territory and scattered population, the need for closer Protestant accord was great, and the movement for a united church began at the turn of the century. A "Basis of Union" drew from the Presbyterian standards and the Methodist Twenty-five Articles, and the plan of government combined features from the various traditions. It was soon recognized that Anglicans and Baptists would not be included, and that a large Presbyterian minority was opposed to union. Only after long years of work and many bitter exchanges was the United Church of Canada brought into being in 1925, a little more than a third of the Presbyterians remaining out.

In the lands of the younger churches occurred one of the most important unions, involving Congregational, Presbyterian, and Episcopal polities. In 1908 the South India United Church had brought together Presbyterian and Congregational missions. This was but the beginning; soon Methodists and Anglicans became involved in union negotiations that went on for years. The basic agreement that paved the way for larger union was that all ministers at the time of union would be accepted with equal rights and status, though congregations would be safeguarded against having thrust upon them ministries they were not prepared to accept. Then, for thirty years, all ordinations would be carried out by bishops with the assistance of presbyters. In 1947 the Church of South India was inaugurated. Five Anglican bishops were re-elected, and nine new bishops elected and consecrated. A million Indian Christians were brought together into one independent, indigenous communion.[1]

In the United States, the formation of the United Church of Christ in 1957 brought four different denominational traditions together. The Congregational and Christian churches (the latter originated in the frontier revivalist movement of the early nineteenth century) had united in 1931. Three years later, the German Reformed Church and the Evangelical Association (formed in the 1840's when groups of pietistic German-speaking immigrants of Lutheran and Reformed backgrounds began to work together) united as the Evangelical and Reformed Church. Efforts to bring these two communions together in the United Church of Christ were sharply opposed by minorities, but, in 1961, the union of 1957 was ratified by an overwheming majority of the congregations on both sides. In time, a still larger united church may develop. In 1962, the Consultation on Church Union began its work. Nine denominations were participating by the end of the decade, including those of congregational, connectional, and episcopal polities, and involving three Negro communions of Methodist background.

A sixth area of ecumenical activity was the formation of world denominational fellowships. At times these seem to work at cross purposes to other areas of ecumenical concern, but in general they continue on the principle that such bodies as the World Council of Churches cannot be stronger than the churches which are its members. In some respects the Lambeth Conference of Anglican Bishops was the first (1867) such denominational world organization, though as a meeting of bishops it is quite different from the others, except perhaps the Conference of Old Catholic Bishops (1889). The Alliance of Reformed Churches throughout the World holding the Presbyterian System was organized in 1875, the World Methodist Council in 1881, the International Congregational Council in 1891, the Baptist World Alliance in 1905, the Lutheran World Federation in 1923, the World Conven-

---

[1] A table of the many plans for union and reunion, 1910–1952, including both those completed and those in prospect, can be found in Ruth Rouse and Stephen C. Neill (eds.), *A History of the Ecumenical Movement, 1517–1948* (2nd ed.; Philadelphia, 1967), pp. 496–505.

tion of the Churches of Christ in 1930, the International Association for Liberal Christianity and Religious Freedom in 1930, and the Friends' World Committee for Consultation in 1937. Most of these bodies entered into a consultative relationship with the World Council.

The Protestant world was influenced in the twentieth century not only by the ecumenical movement, but also by a theological revival. In the early years of the century attention to theological issues was somewhat generally minimized. But fresh attention to Biblical and systematic theology arose soon after the first World War in Europe. The most powerful spokesmen for the new "dialectical" or "crisis" theology were H. Emil Brunner (1889–1966) and especially Karl Barth (1886–1968), Reformed pastor and theologian, author of the influential *Church Dogmatics* (13 vols., 1932–1967). Criticizing the schools of Schleiermacher and Ritschl for their subjectivism and relativism, Barth put great emphasis on the otherness of God, the centrality of revelation, and the sinful nature of man. His many works have been controversial, but have contributed to a wide and serious discussion of theological questions. The theological renaissance was further stimulated by churchly resistance to Nazi totalitarianism; the German "Barmen Declaration" of 1934 insisted that Jesus Christ is the only Word of God that men are to hear, trust, and obey.

In the United States, the change in theological atmosphere began in the 1930's, as "Christian realism" criticized what it saw as the idealistic assumptions and utopian illusions of much American theology, and mediated the new theological currents to the American scene. Central figures in this development were the Niebuhr brothers and Paul Tillich. The persistent search for a sound theological basis for social ethics led Reinhold Niebuhr (1892—) to produce works of major importance, especially *The Nature and Destiny of Man* (1941–1943). H. Richard Niebuhr (1894–1962) combined theological, sociological, and ethical analyses in his lifetime of creative work; a characteristic volume was *Christ and Culture* (1951). Tillich (1886–1965) came to America as a refugee from Hitler's Germany, and became an important influence in the theological and intellectual worlds; his mature thought is presented in the three-volume *Systematic Theology* (1951–1963).

The ecumenical movement, especially as it was focused in the World Council of Churches, reflected the theological contributions of these and other biblically-oriented theologians, and in turn served as a transmitter of them. A liturgical renaissance was also at work in world Protestantism, significantly changing levels of understanding and practice in worship. A number of communions revised their liturgies, while the free churches tended to incorporate certain liturgical elements into their worship. The interest of a number of Catholic and Protestant scholars in biblical study and liturgical reform helped to prepare the way for a remarkable ecumenical breakthrough in the 1960's.

19

The Church in the World

*I*N MANY AREAS of the world immediately following World War II, the Christian churches, especially in the West, seemed to be institutionally quite stable and were hopeful of continued advance. The establishment of the United Nations (1945) provided an international forum for dealing with tensions between nations and maintaining peace. The Roman Catholic Church under the leadership of Pope Pius XII (1939–1958) outwardly maintained its centralized and conservative stance. The promulgation in 1950 of the dogma of the bodily assumption into heaven of the Blessed Virgin Mary was consistent with the spirit of the dominant nineteenth-century currents in the Church, while the encyclical *Humani generis* (1950) warned against major departures in philosophical or theological thought.

The Protestant and Orthodox churches in many lands showed significant institutional resilience. In North America there was an unexpected postwar revival of religion, while in Germany there was a notable resurgence of the laity, especially through the Evangelical Academies, in which laymen planned strategies for Christian witness in their daily vocations, and through the great *Kirchentag* gatherings which drew vast numbers into annual week-long periods of study and renewal.

The closing of mainland China to missionary work and the isolation of the remaining churches was a serious loss to world Christianity, but in other parts of the world most churches seemed to be successfully making the transition to indigenous and autonomous patterns. The World Council of Churches, under the leadership of its first general secretary, Dutch-born Willem A. Visser 't Hooft (1900—), enjoyed a steadily increasing membership throughout the world. At the Third Assembly of the World Council in New Delhi, India (1961) the total membership in the council was 197 churches from 50 nations, including for the first time the Russian Orthodox Church and also two Pentecostal bodies. Though there were many theological currents flowing through the ecumenical world, the influence of revelational, Christocentric biblical theology was pervasive.

In many parts of the Christian Church, however, there was a deep restlessness. As nation after nation of Asia and Africa became independent and threw off the bonds of colonialism, there often arose in the churches of those lands a questioning of Western ways of worshiping God, organizing churches, and formulating theologies. There surged up a conviction in the "third world" that the rich nations of Europe and North America, both capitalist and communist, especially the United States and the Soviet Union, were growing richer while the poor nations were growing relatively poorer. The institutional self-centeredness and complacency of many Western churches fell under considerable attack, both from within them and from the outside, for there was increasing conviction that churches should show much more concern than they had with the plight of the world's poorer and less powerful people, many of whom were black, or brown, or yellow.

Growing sensitivity to the world's injustices and imbalances, combined with increasing irritation over the use of military force in the world led to deepening criticism of the high institutional barriers among Catholic, Orthodox, and Protestant Christians, for these hindered effective cooperation for human good. Collaboration between Catholics and Protestants in opposition to totalitarianism in the 1930's had provided some precedents which were not forgotten. A longing for renewal and reform at deeper levels than the postwar revival of religion had offered was frequently expressed; dissatisfactions with traditional styles of piety and organization in the church emerged. Among laymen and youth, especially, there arose considerable overt as well as covert criticism.

The impetus for renewal and reform in the Roman Catholic Church, however, came unexpectedly from the top. When Angelo Giuseppe Roncalli was elevated to the pontificate in 1958 and took the name John XXIII[1] (1958–1963), many felt that his was to be a "caretaker" administration. But as a church diplomat he had had considerable experience with social and political movements of various kinds. His assignments in Bulgaria, Turkey, France, and Germany had brought him into contact with Orthodox and non-Catholic worlds, and with many types of political groupings. As Pope he manifested a determination to guide his church toward a reconsideration of its patterns of faith and life in view of the world's needs, and also toward genuine ecumenical relations with other Christian churches. Early in 1959 he announced that he would convoke the Twenty-first Ecumenical Council (Vatican II), to which would be gathered the bishops of the Church from all over the world. In 1960 he established the Secretariat for Promoting Chris-

[1] No pope had used the name John since 1415, when the earlier John XXIII, one of the three rival popes at the end of the great schism, had sullied the name and had been deposed at the Council of Constance (see p. 276). By selecting it, Pope John restored for the papacy a name which has been much loved in Christian history, and which had been taken by more popes than any other.

tian Unity and named Augustin Cardinal Bea (1881–1968) as its head, thus providing an effective channel for dialogue with other churches. The Pope named five official observers to attend the Third Assembly of the World Council of Churches, and invited Protestant and Orthodox communions to send observers to Vatican II; many did send such observers.

John XXIII's concern for human needs and world problems was reflected in two notable encyclicals. *Mater et magistra* (1961) was an updating of Catholic social teaching in the tradition of *Rerum novarum* and *Quadragesimo anno,* issued on the 70th and 30th anniversary of those documents. *Pacem in terris* (1963) was devoted to establishing conditions which could lead to universal peace in truth, justice, charity, and liberty. It declared that "all men are equal in their natural dignity," and called for the end of the arms race, stressed the growing interdependence of national economies, and instructed Catholics to work with people of other faiths for the common good.

After more than three years of preparation, Vatican II opened on October 11, 1962 in St. Peter's Basilica in Rome. It soon became apparent that the desired "updating" (*aggiornamento*) of the Church would not be easy, for progressive and reactionary forces among the more than two thousand bishops present disagreed on many particulars. The spirit of reformism and ecumenism did break through during the first session, though it adjourned on December 8 with no appreciable completed results.

John XXIII died the following June. His successor, Giovanni Battista Montini, Paul VI (1963—), determined to complete and implement the Council, which met for three more sessions, each fall. Pope Paul did not emerge as the charismatic figure his predecessor had been, but his concern for reconciliation with others was dramatized by his ecumenical journey to the Holy Land early in 1964, during which he met with the Patriarch of Constantinople. An outcome was the issuance later (December 7, 1965) of identical statements from Rome and Constantinople regretting the offensive words and reprehensible gestures on both sides accompanying the sad events of the separation of 1054, and removing the sentences of excommunication.

The first completed work of Vatican II was the Constitution on the Sacred Liturgy.[2] Building on the work of the liturgical movement, it provided for the revision of the rite of the Mass, and for its more communal celebration.

Sixteen texts were adopted by the council fathers, varying in length from the Declaration on the Relationship of the Church to Non-Christian Religions, which ran just over a thousand words, to the Pastoral Constitution on the Church in the Modern World, of more than twenty-three thousand words. The former referred primarily to the sensitive area of Jewish-Christian relations and has been criticized as weak in part and as somewhat abstruse. It did

[2] For the texts adopted by the Council in English translation, see Walter M. Abbott, S. J. (ed.), *The Documents of Vatican II* (N. Y., 1966).

deplore any form of anti-Semitism or any discrimination or harassment of men because of race, color, condition of life, or religion, and it encouraged dialogue with members of non-Christian religions and cooperation with them for the common good.

The Pastoral Constitution on the Church in the Modern World was addressed not only to the faithful but to "the whole of humanity," and consciously directed the Church to the service of the family of man. It instructed clergy and laity to collaborate in a ministry of service, so that a more human and humane world may emerge despite the dehumanizing aspects of technological society. Many overtones of John XXIII's "social encyclicals" echoed in the text.

One of the unfinished tasks of Vatican I was the completion of a Constitution on the Church—the abrupt end of that council left only the chapters on the papacy enacted. Meanwhile, some significant statements on the Church had been produced, especially Pius XII's important encyclical on the mystical body of Christ, *Mystici corporis Christi* (1943). Much preparation went toward Vatican II's Dogmatic Constitution on the Church; the draft was revised many times during the sessions. Widely held to be the masterpiece of the council, the text moved away from hierarchical and juridical emphases to a more biblical, historical, and dynamic position. Of central importance was the stress on collegiality, on the priestly role of all bishops who, with the Pope, collectively form a "college" responsible for guiding the Church. A final chapter on the Blessed Virgin was placed in this text so that Mariology would not be isolated from other theological and ecclesiological matters. Affirming the various titles which had been accorded Mary by the Church, the Constitution on the Church declared that "they neither take away from nor add anything to the dignity and efficacy of Christ the one Mediator" (III, 62).

Pastoral and ecumenical, this constitution opened the way for fruitful ecumenical dialogue with Orthodox, Anglican, and Protestant theologians. Some of its positions were speedily implemented; early in the final session of the council Paul VI instituted a Synod of Bishops, in which representatives of the episcopate throughout the world meet regularly at Rome.

Vatican II produced two fundamental theological documents, the Dogmatic Constitution on the Church and the Dogmatic Constitution on Divine Revelation. The latter text was much informed by general ecumenical scholarship on revelation and its transmission, and moved away from earlier attitudes toward Scripture and Tradition as "sources of revelation." It took modern methods of biblical interpretation seriously, in keeping with the tone of a forward-looking encyclical of Pius XII, *Divino Afflante Spiritu* (1943). It viewed revelation as God's manifestation of himself, of his will and intentions, publicly granted to men. Scripture *contains* revelation in the form of a written record, along with accounts of its effects and of men's reactions to it.

The biblical writings are read and interpreted by the living community of the Church with its ongoing tradition of understanding and explanation under the leadership of the Church magisterium guided by the Holy Spirit. The document closed by emphasizing the importance of easy access to Scripture by all the faithful, in suitable and correct translations. "And if, given the opportunity and the approval of Church authority, these translations are produced in cooperation with the separated brethren as well, all Christians will be able to use them" (VI, 22). One result of this judgment was the approval for Catholic use of the Revised Standard Version of the Bible, which had been prepared primarily by Protestant scholarship.

Of particular interest to the non-Catholic world was the council's Decree on Ecumenism. Down to the pontificate of John XXIII, Catholic ecumenism had meant largely work for the return of all Christians to the Roman Catholic Church, and that communion did not join officially in the many aspects of the ecumenical movement. The Decree on Ecumenism formally marked a remarkable about-face, and put the Roman Catholic Church squarely in the ecumenical movement, calling on the faithful to take an active part in the work of ecumenism. Admitting that the divisions among Christians have been the result of sin on both sides, the text spoke of those outside the Roman Church as "separated Churches and Communities" which suffer from certain defects of doctrine, discipline or structure and yet which "have by no means been deprived of significance and importance in the mystery of salvation" (I, 3). Cooperation with them by Catholics should be encouraged especially in regions where social and technical evolution is taking place, and dialogue on matters of faith should be undertaken. Under certain special circumstances, corporate prayer is deemed desirable. Protestant comment on this decree was generally favorable, though there was some uneasiness concerning the continuing tension between its sincere ecumenical spirit and the assumption that the Roman Catholic is the only true Church.

Originally a part of the draft of the Decree on Ecumenism was a section that became the Declaration on Religious Freedom. It touched off an intensive, vigorous, often emotional debate at the council, for it affirmed positions on religious freedom which had been rejected in such statements as the Syllabus of Errors. The declaration unequivocally declared that "all men are to be immune from coercion on the part of individuals or of social groups and of any human power, in such wise that in matters religious no one is to be forced to act in a manner contrary to his own beliefs" (I, 2). It is affirmed that religious freedom has its foundation in the dignity of the person, which can be known both by human reason through historical experience and by revelation. The document contributed significantly to a new straightforwardness in Catholic relations with other churches and in secular affairs. But in opening up a topic for continued attention—the theological meaning of Christian freedom—the decree in time may prove to have unexpected ramifications.

Most of the other conciliar documents were decrees dealing largely with practical matters of church life, such as the episcopal office, priestly formation, the renewal of the religious life, the ministry and life of priests, missions, and education. On December 8, 1965, the council was formally closed. Prophetically, the last message of the council was to the youth of the world, who must live in it "at the period of the most gigantic transformations ever realized in its history." They were exhorted to open their hearts to the dimensions of the world, to place their energies at the service of their brothers, to build in enthusiasm a better world than their elders had.

Vatican II was accorded much attention by the press; it was a major event in world as in church history. Its impact quickly began to be felt, within the fold and in the ecumenical movement. Liturgical reform came quickly, with the very extensive use of the vernacular in the Mass. The structures of the national hierarchies were reorganized in many instances. In the United States, for example, a National Conference of Catholic Bishops was organized in 1966; it became responsible for the United States Catholic Conference, a continuation of the National Catholic Welfare Conference.

More dramatic was the rapid escalation of ecumenical contacts between Catholics and other Christians. A joint "working group" of the Secretariat for Promoting Christian Unity and the World Council of Churches was established in 1965. Official Catholic representation in the Faith and Order Commission of the World Council was begun, and the possibility of formal Roman Catholic membership in the Council was publicly discussed.

In various countries, depending on the situation, parallel manifestations developed. In the United States, a joint working group was established by the National Council of Churches and the Bishops' Committee for Ecumenical and Interreligious Affairs. The latter agency has been responsible for the initiation of a number of bi-lateral theological dialogues between Catholics and representatives of other traditions: Baptist, Disciples, Episcopal, Lutheran, Methodist, Reformed and Presbyterian, Orthodox. Various Catholic parishes and dioceses joined or began to cooperate with local or regional councils of churches, which sometimes were reorganized to meet new needs. At local levels, dialogues between Catholic and other Christian laymen developed impressively.

The epochal changes in Catholicism did raise some serious problems. A number of the faithful were bewildered by the changes and troubled by the minimization of past customs. Others had their hopes for rejuvenation and freedom raised so high that the bureaucratic reformism that was offered appeared much too slow and authoritarian. Some drifted into "free" or "underground" churches.

Pope Paul's traditional stand on birth control in the encyclical *Humanae vitae* (1968) in which all forms of artificial birth control were absolutely proscribed, despite the majority opinion of the special commission which had been called to give advice had advocated change. Many Catholic theologians and laymen took strong exception to the encyclical, finding that it was not in keeping with the expectations created by the Pastoral Constitution on the Church in the Modern World. A new freedom was being expressed within the Church; statements even from the highest sources were being read critically. Tension over the rule of clerical celibacy was also experienced; some hoped that the long-standing rule might be relaxed.

Despite the differences of opinion as to how far and fast the Church should be renewed, Vatican II meant that a significant new step which observers called largely irreversible had been taken. The determination to focus on complex contemporary world problems inevitably meant that many new tensions would arise. To carry out a sweeping program of reform in a time of world turmoil, when many longed for the security of the familiar and the permanent, while others were anxious to experiment with the revolutionary, proved to be difficult. The Church at the end of the decade of amazing change found itself in a time of testing as difficult as any in its history.

To summarize trends in the Protestant and Orthodox worlds for the stormy sixties is in some ways more difficult because there was no one center for the many communions involved, bodies with quite different traditions and styles throughout the world, most of them deployed in autonomous national structures. The World Council of Churches, however, which by the time of the Fourth Assembly at Uppsala in 1968 included most of the major and a number of the smaller Protestant and Orthodox churches and with which Roman Catholicism was in growing cooperation and dialogue, was an arena which mirrored the various tendencies and tensions of the churches. There was an observable trend through the decade toward deepening concern for the world, toward service to those in need and those unable to speak effectively for themselves.

The move toward involvement with the secular world displayed itself in many ways, most of them debatable and controversial. In ecumenical gatherings, attention to the world and its problems absorbed increasing attention. This did not mean that questions of theology and churchmanship were neglected.

The World Council always strove to keep the interests of life and work and of faith and order in creative balance. In the first dozen years of its life many historic misunderstandings among the member churches had to be overcome, and a considerable emphasis on theological and ecclesiastical questions was necessary. Much attention continued to be given to such matters in the sixties, yet more was devoted to the demands of ministry and service to the world.

The shift was felt early in the decade. At the Third Assembly in New Delhi, familiar theological questions about the nature of the church and the realization of ecclesiastical unity were much debated. One of the three main sections of the assembly considered "witness," and an important part of its report dealt with "Reshaping the Witnessing Community." The section on "unity" approved the famous paragraph that became known as the "New Delhi Statement":

> We believe that the unity which is both God's will and his gift to his Church is being made visible as all in each place who are baptized into Jesus Christ and confess him as Lord and Savior are brought by the Holy Spirit into ONE fully committed fellowship, holding the one apostolic faith, preaching the one Gospel, breaking the one bread, joining in common prayer, and having a corporate life reaching out in witness and service to all and who at the same time are united with the whole Christian fellowship in all places and all ages in such wise that ministry and members are accepted by all, and that all can act and speak together as occasion requires for the tasks to which God calls his people.

Many of the theological concerns of the World Council's early years were reflected in that paragraph; the section's commentary on it referred freely to past ecclesiological discussion.

The Third Assembly took place in India, and that location helped to dramatize the facts of hunger and poverty in much of the world. The section on "service" insisted that many of the familiar Christian forms of philanthropy and service were so dated as to be of little use in contemporary society. New ways of expressing the obedience of the servant Church in the modern world had to be found, it was declared.

Theological inspiration for much of the impulse toward "worldly Christianity" in the World Council and its members was drawn in considerable part from the unfinished work of Dietrich Bonhoeffer (1906–1945), a young German theologian who was martyred in prison in the closing months of World War II. Some of the advocates of "secular ecumenism," especially among the younger churchmen, were impatient with older styles of faith and order discussions. The latter were continued, but on a broader and more diversified basis. The Fourth World Conference on Faith and Order was held at Montreal in 1963, with Orthodox theologians in full participation, Catholic observers present, and conservative evangelicals contributing to the debates.

The shift in ecumenical emphasis toward service to the world became more pronounced as the decade wore on. In 1966 the Church and Society department of the World Council sponsored a conference in Geneva on "Christians in the Technical and Social Revolutions of Our Time." It was a unique gathering in that a larger portion of participants came from Africa, Asia and Latin America than any previous such conference had collected. It was also the first major ecumenical conference in which a majority of the participants were laymen. The new Roman Catholic ecumenical stance was demonstrated by the presence of official observers and several main speakers.

Other denominations not in World Council membership were represented. The "third world" point of view, critical of the imbalance of power by which the Soviet Union and the United States exercised such decisive sway over the entire world, was forcefully presented. The vast chasm between the rich and poor nations, between the developed and the undeveloped, was dramatized in many ways; such a situation, it was agreed, should not continue, especially in view of the fact that technological means to provide enough for all were now at hand.

There was much discussion of the relationship between the revolutionary nature of the gospel and social revolution in the contemporary world. Some espoused Christian participation in revolutionary activity, involving violence if necessary. A section report observed that in some cases where small *élites* rule at the expense of the welfare of the majority, Christians should participate in political movements which work toward the achievement of a just social order as quickly as possible. In such cases, the report declared, Christians need not rule out the use of revolutionary methods *a priori,* for "it may very well be that the use of violent methods is the only recourse of those who wish to avoid prolongation of the vast covert violence which the existing order involves." [3]

In general, the conference agreed that the church should be on the side of social revolution against serious injustice, though it was divided about the appropriate use of violence in revolution. It was emphasized that the role of Christians and churches is to work within the secular orders to humanize them, to reform society for the sake of man. They work always from a Christian perspective, sensitive to divine judgments on human affairs. The working group on theology and social ethics explained that "the discernment by Christians of what is just and unjust, human and inhuman in the complexities of political and economic change, is a discipline exercised in continual dialogue with biblical resources, the mind of the Church through history and today, and the best insights of social scientific analysis. But it remains a discipline which aims not at a theoretical system of truth but at action in human society. Its object is not simply to understand the world but to respond to the power of God which is recreating it." [4]

The findings of a conference under World Council auspices are of quite different nature from those of a Vatican Council. The gatherings are very brief in comparison (the Geneva Conference lasted two weeks) and only a few of the ranking officials of the churches participate. Hence such meetings cannot speak officially for the World Council or for its member churches. But in speaking *to* them, the Geneva Conference revealed a strong emerging

[3] P. R. Abrecht and M. M. Thomas (eds.), *The World Conference on Church and Society* (Geneva, 1967), p. 143.
[4] *Ibid.,* p. 201.

concern in the churches for the serious social, economic, and political issues of the day.

On racial matters the unambiguous statements of previous World Council assemblies and conferences against all forms of segregation or discrimination were restated; churches were urged to oppose, openly and actively, the perpetuation of the myth of racial superiority as it finds expression in social conditions and in human behavior as well as in laws and social structures.

A high point of the gathering was a sermon by Martin Luther King, Jr. (1929–1968), prominent nonviolent leader of the civil rights movement in the United States. Founder of the Southern Christian Leadership Conference, King played an important role in the increasing church and ecumenical support of the Negro search for justice in America. Unable to be present at Geneva because of riots in Chicago, King's sermon, eschewing senseless violence and pointing out the irony of a nation founded on the principle of freedom having to undergo a continuing struggle for human rights, was taped and flown to Geneva in time for the service. In less than two years, King, a modern Christian martyr, was to fall by the hand of an assassin.

An important convergence of Catholic, Protestant and Orthodox concern about the church in the world was dramatized by the Beirut Conference on World Cooperation for Development in 1968. Jointly planned and convened by the Roman Catholic Church and the World Council of Churches, it brought together experts on world economic and political problems to develop a "strategy for development" consistent with a theological rationale. The bases for discussion were the Geneva report and an encyclical of Paul VI on development and aid to the third world, *Populorum progressio* (1967), in which it was maintained that "the new word for peace is development." The conference findings urged Christians to be politically active on an ecumenical basis in ways relevant to particular local situations, ways which might include lobbying, marches, meetings and other pressures to focus governmental responsibility for undeveloped nations. It was recommended that a joint Roman Catholic–World Council Exploratory Committee on Society, Development and Peace (SODEPAX) be continued.

The Fourth Assembly of the World Council at Uppsala, Sweden in 1968 continued many of these lines of thought and action. It accepted the Geneva report and responded favorably to the recommendations of the Beirut conference. Characteristically seeking to keep in creative balance theological concerns with attention to action and service in the world, the conference put greater time and energy on the latter. Such matters as war and peace, human rights, selective conscientious objection to war, racism, refugees, economic justice, nationalism and regionalism, international structures and taxation, world hunger and world development were discussed and recommendations drafted.

In a statement adopted by the Assembly, one section declared that "to be complacent in the face of the world's need is to be guilty of practical heresy." [5] World Council members were urged to cooperate actively at every level with non-member churches, non-church groups, representatives of other religions and men of good will everywhere for the good of mankind, and to give sacrificially for development. The American military intervention in Vietnam was sharply criticized, by American opponents of the war as well as by others. The youth participants at Uppsala reminded the delegates pointedly that they were impatient with high-sounding reports followed by little action, tired of timidity and a "business as usual" attitude in the face of the unjust and inhuman treatment accorded much of the world's population.

The Fourth Assembly was an exciting, crowded, somewhat stormy affair. Earlier assemblies were not without their drama, but their tone was calmer than this one with its frank speeches and jarring encounters. Efforts to serve the needs of the world in relevant ways brought something of the turmoil of the world into church life.

Such gatherings as have been described reflected many of the pressing concerns and dominant directions of the Christian Church throughout the world as the last third of the twentieth century began. In many areas, of course, Christian churches went their way little influenced if at all by what was said in world assemblies. Churches in many parts of the world were struggling with problems unique to their situations.

Regional ecumenical associations to deal with church relations in particular areas were developing—the East Asia Christian Conference was founded in 1959, the Continuation Committee of the Pacific Church's Conference in the same year, the All Africa Conference of Churches in 1963, and the Conference of European Churches in the following year. In Africa, for example, the proliferation of independent prophetic movements continued, some related to the mainstream of Christian life, others moving outside of anything recognizable Christian, posed certain problems. By the late 1960's it was reported that in South Africa there were over two thousand independent churches with over a million followers. But for many churches of Africa, as in other areas, there was a growing relationship to the ecumenical movement, along with a clear determination to encourage the development of indigenous patterns of Christian worship and organization.

In many communist lands, organized religion generally continued to decline, yet showed surprising persistence, especially in less traditional forms. In many congregations of Europe and America there was little real awareness of world needs or even of neighborhood problems, but rather an internal institutional focus, often mixed with a nostalgia for earlier and calmer days.

In theological thought there were many new trends. Unconventional and radical theological positions were articulated, some of them attracting con-

[5] N. Goodall (ed.), *The Uppsala Report, 1968* (Geneva, 1968), p. 51.

siderable attention. Efforts to frame theologies of hope and of the future were more representative. Informed by the long history of biblical and theological reflection and shaped in the crucibles of the encounter of the church with the modern world, they were moving in the stream of life that has flowed through some of the most creative periods of the church's history.

The long story of the Christian Church is a panorama of lights and shadows, of achievement and failure, of conquests and divisions. It has exhibited the divine life marvellously transforming the lives of men. It has also exhibited those passions and weaknesses of which human nature is capable. Its tasks have seemed, in every age, almost insuperable. They were never greater than at present when confronted by a materialistic interpretation of life, and when the threat of atomic war endangers the whole fabric of civilization. Yet no Christian can survey what the church has done without confidence in its future. Its changes may be many, its struggles great. But the great hand of God which has led it hitherto will guide it to larger usefulness in the advancement of the kingdom of its Lord, and toward the fulfilment of His prediction that if He be lifted up He would draw all men unto Him.

BIBLIOGRAPHICAL
SUGGESTIONS

Bibliographical Suggestions

GENERAL ENCYCLOPEDIAS

The Oxford Dictionary of the Christian Church, ed. F. L. CROSS, Oxford, 1957.

The New Schaff-Herzog Encyclopedia of Religious Knowledge, New York, 1908–12.

Twentieth Century Encyclopedia of Religious Knowledge, Grand Rapids, 1955.

Encyclopaedia of Religion and Ethics, ed. J. HASTINGS, New York, 1917–27.

The Catholic Encyclopaedia, New York, 1907–22.

The New Catholic Encyclopedia, New York, 1967.

Dictionary of Christian Ethics, ed. J. MACQUARRIE, Philadelphia, 1967.

A Dictionary of Christian Theology, ed. A. RICHARDSON, Philadelphia, 1969.

SOURCE BOOKS

BETTENSON, H., *Documents of the Christian Church*, Oxford, 1947. Brief, weighted on Anglicanism.

SCHAFF, P., *The Creeds of Christendom*, New York, 4th ed., 1905.

DENZINGER, H. J. D., *The Sources of Catholic Dogma*, tr. R. J. Deferrari, St. Louis, 1957.

AYER, J. C., *A Source Book for Ancient Church History, from the Apostolic Age to the Close of the Conciliar Period*, New York, 1913. The standard work.

KIDD, B. J., *Documents Illustrative of the History of the Church*, 3 vols., London, 1920–41. Vol. 1., to 313 A.D.; Vol. 2., 313 to 461 A.D.; Vol 3., 500 to 1500 A.D.

PETRY, R. C., *A History of Christianity: Readings in the History of the Early and Medieval Church*, Englewood Cliffs, N.J., 1962. A varied selection with helpful introductions, illustrated.

BINDLEY, T. H., *The Oecumenical Documents of the Faith*, rev. F. W. Green, London, 1950. Contains the Greek and Latin texts, with introductions and translations, of the early conciliar documents.

GRANT, F. C., *Hellenistic Religions*, New York, 1953. A useful collection of materials which illustrate the religious world into which Christianity was born.

LEWIS, N. and REINHOLD, M., *Roman Civilization*, Vol. 2, *The Empire*, New York, 1955. Documents illustrating all phases of the Roman world from Augustus.

HENDERSON, E. F., *Select Historical Documents of the Middle Ages*, London, 1912.

THATCHER, O. J., and McNEAL, E. H., *A Source Book for Medieval History*, New York, 1905.

McNEILL, J. T. and GAMER, H. M., *Medieval Handbooks of Penance*, New York, 1938.

GILES, E., *Documents Illustrating Papal Authority, A.D. 96–454*, London, 1952.

SHOTWELL, J. T., and LOOMIS, L. P., *The See of Peter*, New York, 1927. Papal documents to the end of the 4th century.

MIRBT, C., *Quellen zur Geschichte des Papsttums und des Römischen Katholizismus,* 5th ed., Tübingen, 1934. Latin texts of the whole papal development.

ROBINSON, J. H., *Readings in European History,* New York, 1906.

ELTON, G. R., *Renaissance and Reformation, 1300–1648,* New York, 1963. A collection of basic documents, with some contemporary comments.

KIDD, B. J., *Documents Illustrative of the Continental Reformation,* Oxford, 1911. In Latin and French; the German is translated into English.

GEE, H., and HARDY, W. J., *Documents Illustrative of English Church History,* London, 1896.

BELL, G. K. A., *Documents on Christian Unity,* 4 vols., Oxford, 1929–58.

SOURCES IN ENGLISH TRANSLATION

The Library of Christian Classics, ed. J. BAILLIE, J. T. MCNEILL, and H. P. VAN DUSEN, Philadelphia, 1953–69. Twenty-six volumes cover the main theological writings from the early Fathers through the Reformation.

The Fathers of the Church, founder L. SCHOPP, ed. R. J. Deferrari, New York, 1947—. A Roman Catholic series which will eventually comprise all the patristic literature in new translation. Approximately 100 volumes are projected.

Ancient Christian Writers, ed. J. QUASTEN and J. C. PLUMPE, Westminster, Md., 1946—. Another Roman Catholic Series of translations, more specialized and with fuller introductions and notes.

The Ante-Nicene Fathers, Edinburgh ed. revised by A. C. COXE, Buffalo, 10 vols., 1884–86.

The Nicene and Post-Nicene Fathers, First Series, 14 vols., New York, 1886–94; Second Series, 12 vols., New York, 1890–95. These three series are still indispensable, although in many instances the texts and translations have been superseded. Eusebius' *Ecclesiastical History,* ed. A. C. MCGIFFERT, is invaluable. It is the first volume of the First Series of N.P.N.F.

The Apostolic Fathers, ed. K. LAKE, 2 vols., New York, 1925–30. A useful work with the Greek and English on opposite pages.

Basic Writings of St. Augustine, ed. W. J. OATES, 2 vols., New York, 1948. See also under Reformation section: *Works of the Reformers.*

BEDE, *The Ecclesiastical History of England,* tr. A. M. Sellar, London, 1907; Books I and II tr. by M. Maclagan, Oxford, 1949.

ATLASES

WRIGHT, G. E. and FILSON, F. V., *Westminster Atlas of the Bible,* Philadelphia, 1945.

SHEPHERD, W. R., *Historical Atlas,* 7th ed., New York, 1929.

HEUSSI, K., and MULERT, H., *Atlas zur Kirchengeschichte,* Tübingen, 1919.

MEER, F. VAN DER, *Atlas of Western Civilization,* 2nd ed., Princeton, 1960.

HISTORIES OF THOUGHT AND PHILOSOPHY
I. GENERAL

MCGIFFERT, A. C., *A History of Christian Thought,* 2 vols., New York, 1931. Chapters on the leading writers down to Erasmus.

FISHER, G. P., *A History of Christian Doctrine,* New York, 1896. Out of date, but still a useful, comprehensive survey.

SEEBERG, R., *Textbook of the History of Doctrines,* tr. C. E. Hay, Philadelphia, 1905. Somewhat out of date, but a solid survey through the Reformation.

HARNACK, A., *A History of Dogma,* tr. N. Buchanon, 7 vols., London, 1894ff. A fundamental work from a special point of view, through the Reformation.

NEVE, D. L., *A History of Christian Thought,* 2 vols., Philadelphia, 1946. Useful, but uneven in quality.

TILLICH, P., *A History of Christian Thought,* ed. C. E. Braaten, New York, 1968. A clarifying survey of Christian thought to the nineteenth century from Tillich's distinctive systematic viewpoint.

LOHSE, B., *A Short History of Christian Doctrine,* tr. F. E. Stoeffler, Philadelphia, 1966. Highly selective, concise, illuminating.

COPLESTON, F., *A History of Philosophy,* 8 vols., London, 1946–66. Lucid and thoroughly up to date.

TROELTSCH, E., *The Social Teachings of the Christian Churches,* tr. O. Wyon, London, 1931. A standard work.

NYGREN, A., *Eros and Agape,* 2 vols., London, 1932–39.

II. SPECIAL PERIODS

BETHUNE-BAKER, J. F., *An Introduction to the Early History of Christian Doctrine,* 5th ed., Cambridge, 1933. The standard work.

TIXERONT, J., *History of Dogmas,* tr. H. L. B., 3 vols., St. Louis, 1923ff. Clear and exact French work on the patristic period.

CADOUX, C. J., *The Early Church and the World,* Edinburgh, 1925. A careful and well-documented study of early Christian ethics and eschatology.

COCHRANE, C. N., *Christianity and Classical Culture,* New York, 1940.

MELLONE, S. H., *Western Christian Thought in the Middle Ages,* London, 1935. A useful, brief introduction.

DE WULF, M., *A History of Medieval Philosophy,* tr. E. C. Messenger, 2 vols., New York, 1925–26; rev. ed., Edinburgh, 1952.

GILSON, E., *A History of Christian Philosophy in the Middle Ages,* New York, 1955.

BUSSELL, F. W., *Religious Thought and Heresy in the Middle Ages,* London, 1918.

THOMAS, E. C., *A History of the Schoolmen,* London, 1941.

GILSON, E., *The Spirit of Mediaeval Philosophy,* New York, 1936.

TAYLOR, H. O., *The Medieval Mind,* 2 vols., 4th ed., Cambridge, Mass., 1949.

CURTIUS, E. R., *European Literature and the Middle Ages,* New York, 1953.

MISSIONS

LATOURETTE, K. S., *A History of the Expansion of Christianity,* 7 vols., New York, 1937–45. The standard work.

HARDY, E. R., *Militant in Earth,* Oxford, 1940. A brief introduction to the spread of Christianity through twenty centuries.

HARNACK, A., *The Expansion of Christianity in the First Three Centuries,* tr. J. Moffatt, 2 vols., New York, 1904–05. Still an invaluable work.

THE PREPARATION FOR CHRISTIANITY: JUDAISM

ANDERSON, B. W., *Understanding the Old Testament,* Englewood, New Jersey, 1957.

PFEIFFER, R. H., *Introduction to the Old Testament,* New York, 1941.

—— *A History of New Testament Times,* New York, 1949. This title is a little misleading. The work is really an introduction to inter-testamental Judaism.

MOORE, G. F., *Judaism,* 3 vols., Cambridge, Mass., 1930–32. A standard study of the age of the Tannaim.

SCHÜRER, E., *A History of the Jewish People in the Times of Jesus Christ,* Eng. tr., 3 vols., Edinburgh, 1885–90. Monumental, standard work.

OESTERLEY, W. O. E., and Box, G. H., *A Short Survey of the Literature of Rabbinical and Medieval Judaism,* London, 1920. A useful, brief handbook.

BAAB, O. J., *Theology of the Old Testament,* New York, 1949.

RINGGREN, H., *The Messiah in the Old Testament,* Chicago, 1956.

MOWINCKEL, S., *He that Cometh,* tr. G. W. Anderson, New York, 1957. A study of the Messiah in the O.T.

KLAUSNER, J., *The Messianic Idea in Israel,* tr. W. F. Stinespring, New York, 1955.

WOLFSON, H. A., *Philo,* 2 vols., Cambridge, Mass., 1948.

BURROWS, M., *The Dead Sea Scrolls,* New York, 1955. The best general account of this subject.

GASTER, T. H., *The Dead Sea Scriptures,* New York, 1956. The most complete translation of the available material with notes.

STENDAHL, K. (ed.), *The Scrolls and the New Testament,* New York, 1957. A collection of important essays by different scholars.

MACGREGOR, G. H. C., and PURDY, A. C., *Jew and Greek: Tutors unto Christ,* London, 1936. A useful brief account of the Jewish and Greek background of the N.T.

KRAELING, C. H., *John the Baptist,* New York, 1951.

THE PREPARATION FOR CHRISTIANITY: HELLENISTIC

WILLOUGHBY, H. R., *Pagan Regeneration,* Chicago, 1929. A careful study of the Mystery Religions.

NOCK, A. D., *Conversion,* Oxford, 1933. A study of conversion and initiation in the mysteries.

ANGUS, S., *The Mystery-Religions and Christianity,* London, 1925.

DILL, S., *Roman Society from Nero to Marcus Aurelius,* London, 1911.

ROSTOVTZEFF, M., *A History of the Ancient World,* Vol. 2, *Rome,* Oxford, 1927.

—— *The Social and Economic History of the Hellenistic World,* 3 vols., Oxford, 1941.

MOORE, F. G., *The Roman's World,* New York, 1936. An account of the home and social life of the Roman, especially in imperial times.

FESTUGIÈRE, A. J., *Personal Religion among the Greeks,* Berkeley, California, 1954.

NILSSON, M. P., *Geschichte der griechischen Religion,* 2 vols., Munich, 1941–50.

GRANT, F. C., *Hellenistic Religions,* New York, 1953. A short source book.

GLOVER, T. R., *The Conflict of Religions in the Early Roman Empire,* London, 1909.

THE BEGINNINGS OF CHRISTIANITY

KEE, H. C., and YOUNG, F. W., *Understanding the New Testament,* Englewood, New Jersey, 1957.

GOGUEL, M., *The Life of Jesus,* tr. O. Wyon, New York, 1946.

—— *The Birth of Christianity,* tr. H. C. Snape, New York, 1954.

BULTMANN, R., *Primitive Christianity in its Contemporary Setting,* tr. R. H. Fuller, New York, 1956.

—— *Theology of the New Testament,* 2 vols., tr. K. Grobel, New York, 1951–55.

TAYLOR, N., *The Names of Jesus,* New York, 1953. Succinct account of the origin and meaning of the titles given to Jesus.

DIBELIUS, M., *Jesus,* tr. C. B. Hedrick, and F. C. Grant, Philadelphia, 1949.

MAJOR, H. D. A., MANSON, T. W., and WRIGHT, C. J., *The Mission and Message of Jesus,* New York, 1938.

SCHWEITZER, A., *The Quest of the Historical Jesus,* Eng. tr., London, 1910.

KNOX, J., *Christ the Lord,* New York, 1945.

GRANT, F. C., *An Introduction to New Testament Thought,* New York, 1950.

DODD, C. H., *The Apostolic Preaching and Its Development,* New York, 1950.

NOCK, A. D., *St. Paul,* London, 1938.

DIBELIUS, M. and KUEMMEL, W. C., *Paul,* Philadelphia, 1953.

DAVIES, W. D., *Paul and Rabbinic Judaism,* London, 1948.

CULLMANN, O., *Peter,* tr. F. V. Filson, Philadelphia, 1953. A study of Peter in the New Testament and with reference to the Vatican excavations.

FOAKES-JACKSON, J. F. and LAKE, K. (eds.), *The Beginnings of Christianity,* 5 vols., London, 1920–33. Fundamental study of the *Acts of the Apostles:* a mine of information on primitive Christianity.

JAMES, M. R., *The Apocryphal New Testament,* Oxford, 1924. Careful translations of all the extra-canonical material.

THE CHURCH IN THE ROMAN EMPIRE
DICTIONARIES

Dictionary of the Apostolic Church, ed. J. HASTINGS, 2 vols., Edinburgh, 1915–18.

Dictionary of Christian Biography, ed. W. SMITH and H. WACE, 4 vols., London, 1877–88.

Dictionnaire d'archéologie chretienne et de liturgie, ed. F. CABROL and H. LECLERCQ, Paris, 1907—.

Real lexicon für Antike und Christentum, Leipzig, 1941—.

MANUALS OF EARLY CHRISTIAN LITERATURE

QUASTEN, J., *Patrology,* 3 vols., Westminster, Md., 1950–60.

ALTANER, B., *Patrologie,* 2nd ed., Freiburg, 1950.

GOODSPEED, E. J., *A History of Early Christian Literature,* Chicago, 1942.

STANDARD GENERAL HISTORIES

KIDD, B. J., *A History of the Church to 461 A.D.,* 3 vols., Oxford, 1922. A mine of information and carefully documented.

LIETZMANN, H., *The Beginnings of the Christian Church,* tr. B. L. Woolf, New York, 1937.

—— *The Founding of the Church Universal,* tr. B. L. Woolf, New York, 1938.

—— *From Constantine to Julian,* tr. B. L. Woolf, New York, 1950.

—— *The Era of the Church Fathers,* tr. B. L. Woolf, New York, 1951. These four volumes tell the story down to the end of the fourth century.

LEBRETON, J., and ZEILLER, J., *The History of the Primitive Church,* tr. E. C. Messenger, 2 vols., New York, 1949. Roman Catholic treatment. Very conservative on N.T. material, careful and precise on patristic history.

PALANQUE, J. R., and DE LABRIOLLE, P., *The Church in the Christian Empire,* 2 vols., tr. E. C. Messenger, London, 1949–52. A continuation of the preceding work, down to the end of the fourth century.

ELLIOTT-BINNS, L. E., *The Beginnings of Western Christendom*, London, 1948. Carries the story down to Constantine.

DUCHESNE, L., *The Early History of the Christian Church*, tr. from 4th French ed., 3 vols., London, 1909–24. A liberal Roman Catholic treatment to the end of the fifth century.

CHADWICK, H., *The Early Church*, Baltimore, 1967. A very readable introduction, with emphasis on thought.

DANIÉLOU, J. and MARROU, H., *The First Six Hundred Years.*, tr. Vincent Cronin, London, 1964. The first volume of a series, The Christian Centuries: A New History of the Catholic Church.

Cambridge Ancient History, ed. S. A. COOK, *et al.*, vols. 11 and 12, Cambridge, 1936–39.

Cambridge Medieval History, ed. M. M. GWATKIN, and J. P. WHITNEY, vol. 1, Cambridge, 1924. These volumes have excellent background material, and many essays directly on Christianity.

THE PERSECUTIONS

WORKMAN, H. B., *Persecution in the Early Church*, 3rd ed., London, 1911.

HARDY, E. G., *Christianity and the Roman Government*, 3rd ed., London, 1910.

MASON, A. J., *The Historic Martyrs of the Primitive Church*, London, 1905.

GRANT, R. M., *The Sword and the Cross*, New York, 1955.

ORGANIZATION OF THE CHURCH

GORE, C., *The Church and the Ministry*, rev. by C. H. TURNER, London, 1936. Anglo-Catholic treatment.

KIRK, K. E. (ed.), *The Apostolic Ministry*, London, 1946. Essays from Anglo-Catholic viewpoint.

MANSON, T. W., *The Church's Ministry*, London, 1948. Protestant reply to preceding work.

LINDSAY, T. M., *The Church and Ministry in the Early Centuries*, 3rd ed., London, 1907. Presbyterian viewpoint.

STREETER, H. B., *The Primitive Church*, New York, 1929. Liberal Anglican viewpoint.

CAMPENHAUSEN, H. VON, *Ecclesiastical Authority and Spiritual Power in the Church in the First Three Centuries*, tr. J. A. Baker, Stanford, Calif., 1969.

CHRISTIAN WORSHIP

DIX, G., *The Shape of the Liturgy*, London, 1944.

SRAWLEY, J. H., *The Early History of the Liturgy*, 2nd. ed., Cambridge, 1947.

ART AND ARCHITECTURE

LOWRIE, W., *Art in the Early Church*, New York, 1947.

DAVIES, J. G., *The Origin and Development of Early Christian Church Architecture*, London, 1952.

CHURCH ORDERS AND PENANCE

DIX, G., *The Apostolic Tradition of St. Hippolytus*, London, 1937. Latin text, translation, reconstruction and notes.

MACLEAN, A. J., *The Ancient Church Orders*, Cambridge, 1910.

WATKINS, O. D., *The History of Penance*, 2 vols., London, 1920.

CREEDS AND COUNCILS

KELLY, J. N. D., *Early Christian Creeds,* New York, 1950.

HEFELE, C, J., *A History of the Councils of the Church,* tr. from German, 5 vols., Edinburgh, 1871–96. The new French ed., *Histoire des Conciles,* ed. H. LECLERCQ, 20 vols., Paris, 1907–52, is much more up to date.

LANDON, E. H., *A Manual of the Councils of the Holy Catholic Church,* 2 vols., Edinburgh, 1909.

SELLERS, R. V., *The Council of Chalcedon,* London, 1953.

EARLY CHRISTIAN THOUGHT

(Note the previous section on *Histories of Thought and Philosophy*)

PRESTIGE, G. L., *God in Patristic Thought,* London, 1936.

——— *Fathers and Heretics,* London, 1940.

MELLONE, S. H., *Leaders of Early Christian Thought,* London, 1954.

RAWLINSON, A. E. J. (ed.), *Essays on the Trinity and Incarnation,* New York, 1933.

SPENCE-LITTLE, V. A., *The Christology of the Apologists,* London, 1934.

TURNER, H. E. W., *The Patristic Doctrine of Redemption,* London, 1952.

CHADWICK, H., *Early Christian Thought and the Classical Tradition: Studies in Justin, Clement and Origin,* New York, 1966.

KELLY, J. N. D., *Early Christian Doctrines,* New York, 1959.

PELIKAN, J., *Development of Christian Doctrine: Some Historical Prolegomena,* New Haven, Conn., 1969.

WOLFSON, H. A., *The Philosophy of the Church Fathers,* Cambridge, Mass., 1956.

JEWISH CHRISTIANITY

SCHOEPS, H. J., *Theologie und Geschichte des Judenchristentums,* Tübingen, 1949. English summary in *Journal of Theological Studies,* Oct. 1953, pp. 219–24.

DANIÉLOU, J., *The Theology of Jewish Christianity,* tr. J. A. Baker, Chicago, 1964.

GNOSTICISM

BURKITT, F. C., *The Church and Gnosis,* Cambridge, 1932.

QUISPEL, G., *Gnosis als Weltreligion,* Zürich, 1951.

CROSS, F. L., (ed.), *The Jung Codex,* London, 1955. Studies on the new Chenoboskion finds.

BUONAIUTI, E., *Gnostic Fragments,* London, 1924.

BLACKMAN, E. C., *Marcion and His Influence,* London, 1948.

GRANT, R. M., *Gnosticism and Early Christianity,* New York, 1959.

——— *Gnosticism: A Source Book of Heretical Writings from the Early Christian Period,* New York, 1961.

ORIGEN

BUTTERWORTH, G. W. (ed.), *Origen On First Principles,* London, 1936. The best English version with introduction and notes.

CHADWICK, H. (ed.), *Origen's Contra Celsum,* Cambridge, 1953. The best English version with extensive notes.

CADIOU, R., *Origen, His Life at Alexandria,* tr. J. A. Southwell, St. Louis, 1944.

DANIÉLOU, J., *Origen,* tr. W. Mitchell, New York, 1955.

BIGG, C., *The Christian Platonists of Alexandria,* Oxford, 1913.

AUGUSTINE

BATTENHOUSE, R. W., (ed.), *A Companion to the Study of St. Augustine,* Oxford, 1955.

BURNABY, J., *Amor Dei,* London, 1938.

SPARROW-SIMPSON, W. J., *St. Augustine's Conversion,* London, 1930.

HERESY AND SCHISM

GREENSLADE, S. L., *Schism in the Early Church,* London, 1953.

TURNER, H. E. W., *The Pattern of Christian Truth,* London, 1954.

THE SEE OF ROME

KIDD, B. J., *The Roman Primacy to A. D. 461,* London, 1936.

JALLAND, T. G., *The Church and the Papacy,* London, 1944.

MONASTICISM

WORKMAN, H. B., *The Evolution of the Monastic Ideal,* London, 1913.

HANNAH, I. C., *Christian Monasticism,* London, 1925.

The Lausiac History of Palladius, tr. W. K. L. Clarke, London, 1918. A fundamental source for early monasticism.

CELTIC CHURCH

GOUGAUD, L., *Christianity in Celtic Lands,* tr. M. Joynt, New York, 1932.

RYAN, J., *Irish Monasticism: Origins and Early Development,* New York, 1931.

BIELER, L. (ed.), *The Works of St. Patrick,* Westminster, Md., 1953.

HUGHES, K., *The Church in Early Irish Society,* London, 1966.

DAILY LIFE AND LETTERS

DAVIES, J. G., *Daily Life in the Early Church,* London, 1952. Attractive study of figures from Clement of Alexandria to Cassian, with detailed background of daily life.

BROOKE, D., *Private Letters, Pagan and Christian,* London, 1929. Well-selected letters in translation.

THE EASTERN CHURCHES AND BYZANTIUM

KIDD, B. J., *The Churches of Eastern Christendom,* London, 1928. Detailed, carefully annotated.

OSTROGORSKY, G., *History of the Byzantine State,* Oxford, 1956. Best general survey.

HUSSEY, J. M., *The Byzantine World,* London, 1957. A useful, up-to-date sketch.

DIEHL, C., *Byzantium: Greatness and Decline,* tr. N. Walford, New Brunswick, 1957. Brief sketch.

GUERDAN, R., *Byzantium: Its Triumph and Tragedy,* tr. D. L. B. Hartley, New York, 1957. Brief sketch.

VASILIEV, A. A., *History of the Byzantine Empire,* tr. from Russian, 2 vols., Wisconsin, 1928–29. Standard work.

RUNCIMAN, S., *Byzantine Civilization,* London, 1933.

———— *The Eastern Schism,* Oxford, 1955.

EVERY, G., *The Byzantine Patriarchate, 451–1204,* London, 1946.

FRENCH, R. M., *The Eastern Orthodox Church*, New York, 1951. Useful, brief sketch.

ZERNOV, N., *Eastern Christendom: A Study of the Origin and Development of the Eastern Orthodox Church*, New York, 1961. A clarifying general introduction with illustrations and bibliography.

SCHMEMANN, A., *The Historical Road of Eastern Orthodoxy*, tr. L. W. Kesich, New York, 1963. A stimulating interpretation from a Russian Orthodox viewpoint.

BAYNES, N. H., *Byzantine and Other Studies*, London, 1955. Essays on various themes.

GRABAR, A., *Byzantine Painting*, tr. S. Gilbert, Geneva, 1953. Brief text; wonderful color reproductions.

HUSSEY, J. M., *Church and Learning in the Byzantine Empire, 867–1185*, Oxford, 1937.

THE CHURCH IN THE MIDDLE AGES
CHURCH HISTORIES

DEANSLEY, M., *A History of the Medieval Church, 590–1500*, 5th ed., London, 1947. The best brief history.

SCHAFF, D., *The Middle Ages*, Parts 1 and 2 of Vol. 5 of SCHAFF, P., *A History of the Christian Church*, New York, 1907–10. A fuller history, but somewhat wooden and out of date.

FLICK, A. C., *The Decline of the Medieval Church*, 2 vols., New York, 1930. Deals with the later medieval period.

ELLIOTT-BINNS, J., *History of the Decline and Fall of the Medieval Papacy*, London, 1934.

LAGARDE, A., *The Latin Church in the Middle Ages*, New York, 1915.

GENERAL MEDIEVAL HISTORIES

THOMPSON, J. W., and JOHNSON, E. N., *An Introduction to Medieval Europe, 300–1500*, New York, 1937.

The Cambridge Medieval History, ed. M. M. GWATKIN, and J. P. WHITNEY, 6 vols., Cambridge, 1911–29. Indispensable; many Church History topics fully treated.

PIRENNE, H., *A History of Europe from the Invasions to the XVI Century*, tr. B. Miall, New York, 1939.

DEANSLEY, M., *A History of Early Medieval Europe, 476–911*, London, 1956.

DAWSON, C., *The Making of Europe*, New York, 1935. Deals with the early middle ages.

PIRENNE, H., *Mohammed and Charlemagne*, New York, 1939.

STEPHENSON, C., *Medieval History: Europe from the Second to the Sixteenth Century*, 3rd ed., New York, 1951.

MEDIEVAL RELIGION AND THOUGHT

(Note the previous section on *Histories of Thought and Philosophy*)

DAWSON, C., *Medieval Religion*, New York, 1934. A slight but highly suggestive volume.

—— *Religion and the Rise of Western Culture*, New York, 1950.

TAYLOR, H. O., *The Medieval Mind*, 2 vols., 4th ed., New York, 1925.

COULTON, G. G., *Five Centuries of Religion*, 4 vols., Cambridge, 1929–50. A mine of information and materials on medieval religion.

POOLE, R. L., *Illustrations of the History of Medieval Thought and Learning*, 2nd. ed., London, 1920.

ARTZ, F. B., *The Mind of the Middle Ages*, New York, 1953.

KNOWLES, D., *The Evolution of Medieval Thought*, London, 1962.

OBERMAN, H. A. (ed.), *Forerunners of the Reformation: The Shape of Late Medieval Thought, Illustrated by Key Documents,* New York, 1966.

GENERAL LIFE

POWER, E., *Medieval People* (reprint), London, 1937. Lively account of some typical characters.

COULTON, G. G., *Medieval Panorama,* New York, 1938. Studies of the English scene.

—— *Life in the Middle Ages,* 4 vols., Cambridge, 1929–30. Anthology of medieval materials.

HOYT, R. S. (ed.), *Life and Thought in the Early Middle Ages,* Minneapolis, Minn., 1968.

HUIZINGA, J., *The Waning of the Middle Ages* (reprint), New York, 1954.

VOSSLER, K., *Medieval Culture: An Introduction to Dante and His Times,* New York, 1929.

MOREY, CHARLES R., *Medieval Art,* New York, 1942.

PANOFSKY, ERWIN, *Gothic Architecture and Scholasticism,* New York, 1957.

RASHDALL, H., *The Universities of Europe in the Middle Ages,* 3 vols., rev. ed., Oxford, 1936.

THE MEDIEVAL PAPACY

GREGOROVIUS, F., *History of the City of Rome,* Eng. tr., 8 vols., London, 1894–1902. A classic treatment.

GRISAR, H., *History of Rome and the Popes in the Middle Ages,* tr. L. Cappadelta, 3 vols., St. Louis, 1911–13.

BARRY, W., *The Papal Monarchy from St. Gregory the Great to Boniface VIII (590–1303),* London, 1902.

ELLIOTT-BINNS, J., *Innocent III,* London, 1931.

MANN, H. K., *The Lives of the Popes in the Middle Ages,* 18 vols., London, 1925–32.

PASTOR, L., *The History of the Popes from the Close of the Middle Ages,* 36 vols., London and St. Louis, 1902–1950.

CHURCH AND STATE

GAVIN, F., *Seven Centuries of the Problem of Church and State,* Princeton, 1938.

BRYCE, J., *The Holy Roman Empire,* 5th ed., London, 1904. A classic treatment.

BROOKE, Z. N., *Lay Investiture and Its Relation to the Conflict of Empire and Papacy,* London, 1939. A short but highly informative lecture.

TELLENBACH, G., *Church, State and Christian Society at the Time of the Investiture Contest,* tr. R. F. Bennett, Oxford, 1940.

R. W. and A. J. CARLYLE, *A History of Medieval Political Theory in the West,* 6 vols., Edinburgh, 1903–1938.

THE CRUSADES

RUNCIMAN, S., *A History of the Crusades,* 3 vols., Cambridge, 1951.

MUNRO, D. C., *The Kingdom of the Crusades,* New York, 1935.

Chronicles of the Crusader, ed. H. G. B., London, 1900. Translations of the earliest chronicles.

MONASTICISM

WORKMAN, H. B., *The Evolution of the Monastic Ideal,* London, 1913.

HANNAH, I. C., *Christian Monasticism,* London, 1925.

BUTLER, C., *Benedictine Monasticism*, London, 1924.

SMITH, L. M., *Cluny in the Eleventh and Twelfth Centuries*, London, 1930.

EVANS, J., *Monastic Life at Cluny, 910–1157*, London, 1931.

HUBER, R. M., *A Documented History of the Franciscan Order*, Milwaukee, 1948.

BENNETT, R. F., *The Early Dominicans*, Cambridge, 1937.

KNOWLES, D., *The Religious Orders in England*, 3 vols., Cambridge, 1948–59.

BOEHMER, H., *The Jesuits*, Philadelphia, 1928.

BRODRICK, J., *The Origins of the Jesuits*, London, 1940.

—— *The Progress of the Jesuits*, London, 1947.

McCANN, *Saint Benedict*, London, 1924.

WILLIAMS, W. W., *Studies in St. Bernard of Clairvaux*, London, 1927.

JAMES, BRUNO S., *St. Bernard of Clairvaux*, New York, 1957.

"The Little Flowers" and The Life of St. Francis (Everyman's Library), London, 1910.

SABATIER, PAUL, *Life of St. Francis of Assisi*, New York, 1909.

PETRY, RAY C., *Francis of Assisi*, Durham, N. C., 1941.

MANDONNET, P., *St. Dominic and His Work*, St. Louis, 1945.

The Spiritual Exercises of St. Ignatius of Loyola, tr. J. Rickaby, London, 1923.

VAN DYKE, P., *Ignatius Loyola*, New York, 1926.

DUDON, F. P., *St. Ignatius of Loyola*, Milwaukee, 1950.

THE SCHOLASTICS

McCRACKEN, GEORGE E. (ed.), *Early Medieval Theology* (Library of Christian Classics, vol. ix), Philadelphia, 1957.

PEGIS, A. C. (ed.), *The Wisdom of Catholicism*, New York, 1949.

PIEPER, J., *Scholasticism: Personalities and Problems of Medieval Philosophy*, tr. R. and C. Winston, New York, 1960.

FAIRWEATHER, EUGENE R. (ed.), *A Scholastic Miscellany: Anselm to Occam* (Library of Christian Classics, vol. x), Philadelphia, 1956. Contains the best English translations of the Works of Anselm of Canterbury.

CHURCH, R. W., *Saint Anselm*, London, 1905.

MacINTYRE, J., *St. Anselm and His Critics*, London, 1954.

The Story of Abelard's Adversities, tr. J. T. Muckle, Toronto, 1954.

Abailard's Ethics, tr. J. R. McCallum, Oxford, 1935.

SIKES, J. G., *Peter Abailard*, Cambridge, 1932.

WADDELL, HELEN, *Peter Abelard:* a novel, London, 1933.

GILSON, E., *Heloise and Abelard*, Chicago, 1951.

Breviloquium by St. Bonaventura, tr. E. E. Nemmers, St. Louis, 1946.

GILSON, E., *The Philosophy of St. Bonaventura*, London, 1938.

Basic Writings of St. Thomas, ed. A. C. PEGIS, New York, 1945.

THOMAS AQUINAS, *The Summa contra Gentiles*, tr. the English Dominican Fathers, 4 vols., London and New York, 1924–29.

—— *The Summa Theologica*, tr. the Fathers of the English Dominican Province, 19 vols., 2nd ed., London, 1912–36.

FARRELL, W., *A Companion to the Summa*, 4 vols., New York, 1945–49.

GILSON, E., *The Philosophy of St. Thomas Aquinas*, St. Louis, 1929.

GRABMANN, M., *Thomas Aquinas, His Personality and Thought*, New York, 1929.

SERTILLANGES, A. D., *St. Thomas Aquinas and His Work*, London, 1933.

LONGERGAN, B. J. F., *Verbum: Word and Idea in Aquinas*, ed. D. B. Burrell, Notre Dame, 1967.

DUNS SCOTUS, *Tractatus de primo principio*, ed. E. ROCHE, St. Bonaventura, New York, 1949.

GILSON E., *Jean Duns Scot: Introduction à ses positions fondamentales*, Paris, 1952.

HARRIS, C. R. S., *Duns Scotus*, 2 vols., Oxford, 1927.

BUESCHER, G. N., *The Eucharistic Teaching of William Ockham*, St. Bonaventura, New York, 1950.

MOODY, E. A., *The Logic of William of Ockham*, London, 1935.

THE INQUISITION

TURBERVILLE, A. S., *Medieval Heresy and Inquisition*, London, 1920. Best, balanced account.

MAYCOCK, A. L., *The Inquisition from Its Establishment to the Great Schism*, New York, 1927. Roman Catholic treatment.

COULTON, G. G., *Inquisition and Liberty*, London, 1938.

MEDIEVAL MYSTICISM

JONES, R. M., *The Flowering of Mysticism*, New York, 1939.

SEESHOLTZ, A. G., *Friends of God*, New York, 1934.

PETRY, RAY C. (ed.), *Late Medieval Mysticism* (Library of Christian Classics, vol. xiii), Philadelphia, 1957.

BUTLER, DOM CUTHBERT, *Western Mysticism*, 2nd ed., London, 1926.

UNDERHILL, EVELYN, *Mysticism*, 12th ed., London, 1930.

CLARK, J. M., *The Great German Mystics: Eckhart, Tauler and Suso*, Oxford, 1949.

BLAKNEY, R. B., *Meister Eckhart, A Modern Translation*, New York, 1941.

HYMA, A., *The Brethren of the Common Life*, Grand Rapids, Mich., 1950.

BETT, H., *Nicholas of Cusa*, London, 1932.

DE GANDILLAC, M., *La philosophie de Nicolas de Cues*, Paris, 1941 (2nd rev. ed.: *Nikolaus von Cues*, Düsseldorf, 1953).

ADVOCATES OF REFORM

SPINKA, M. (ed.), *Advocates of Reform: From Wyclif to Erasmus* (Library of Christian Classics, vol. xiv), Philadelphia, 1953.

FLICK, A., *The Decline of The Medieval Church*, 2 vols., New York, 1930.

GEWIRTH, A. (ed. and tr.), *Marsilius of Padua: The Defender of Peace*, 2 vols., New York, 1951–56.

CONNOLLY, J. L., *John Gerson, Reformer and Mystic*, Louvain, 1928.

McCOWAN, JOHN T., *Pierre d'Ailli and the Council of Constance*, Washington, 1936.

WORKMAN, H. B., *John Wyclif*, 2 vols., London, 1926.

SCHAFF, D. S., *John Hus*, New York, 1915.

——— (tr.), *John Hus' De ecclesia*, New York, 1915.

SPINKA, MATTHEW, *John Hus and the Czech Reform*, Chicago, 1941.

MILLER, E. W. and SCUDDER, J. W. (eds. and trs.), *Wessel Gansfort, Life and Writings*, 2 vols., New York, 1917.

RENAISSANCE AND HUMANISM

GILMORE, M. P., *The World of Humanism, 1453–1517*, New York, 1952.

HYMA, A., *The Christian Renaissance*, Grand Rapids, Mich., 1924.

HUIZINGA, J., *The Waning of the Middle Ages*, London, 1928.

BURCKHARDT, JACOB, *The Civilization of the Renaissance*, New York, 1909, etc.

HULME, E. M., *The Renaissance, The Protestant Reformation, and the Catholic Reformation*, New York, 1914.

FERGUSON, W. K., *The Renaissance in Historical Thought*, Boston, 1948.

KRISTELLER, PAUL O., *Studies in Renaissance Thought*, Rome, 1956.

——— *The Classics and Renaissance Thought*, Cambridge, Mass., 1955.

——— *The Philosophy of Marsilio Ficino*, New York, 1943.

RANDALL, J. H., JR., *The Making of the Modern Mind* (rev. ed.), Boston, 1940.

CASSIRER, E., KRISTELLER, P. O., RANDALL, J. H. (eds.), *The Renaissance Philosophy of Man*, Chicago, 1948.

RENAUDET, A., *Preréforme et Humanisme à Paris (1494–1517)*, 2nd ed., Paris, 1954.

MARRIOTT, J. A. R., *The Life of John Colet*, London, 1933.

HUNT, ERNEST W., *Dean Colet and His Theology*, London, 1956.

CHAMBERS, R. W., *Thomas More*, London, 1934.

ROUTH, E. M. G., *Sir Thomas More and His Friends*, London, 1934.

SMITH, PRESERVED, *Erasmus*, New York, 1923.

HUIZINGA, J., *Erasmus*, London, 1924 (Phaedon ed., New York, 1952).

ALLEN, P. S. (ed.), *Opus Epistolarum Des. Erasmi Roterodami*, 11 vols., Oxford, 1906–47. The most important work on Erasmus and his contemporaries.

BAINTON, R. H., *Erasmus of Christendom*, New York, 1969.

ENGLISH CHURCH HISTORY

MOORMAN, J. R. H., *A History of the Church of England*, London, 1953.

PATTERSON, M. W., *A History of the Church of England*, 2nd ed., New York, 1925.

STEPHENS, W. R. W., and HUNT, W. (eds.), *A History of the English Church*, 8 vols. in 9, London, 1899–1910. A standard work, now a little out of date.

OLLARD, S. L., CROSSE, G., and BOND, M. F. (eds.), *Dictionary of English Church History*, 3rd ed., London, 1948.

TREVELYAN, G. M., *History of England*, 2nd ed., London, 1937. Concise and scholarly.

——— *English Social History*, 2nd ed., New York, 1946.

MAYNARD-SMITH, H., *Pre-Reformation England*, London, 1938.

USEFUL HANDBOOKS

PAETOW, J. L., *A Guide to the Study of Medieval History*, New York, 1931. Bibliographical.

PHILIPS, C. H., *Handbook of Oriental History: the European Inheritance*, ed. E. BARKER, London, 1954.

CRUMP, C. G., and JACOB, E. F. (eds.), *The Legacy of the Middle Ages*, Oxford, 1926.

THE REFORMATION
BIBLIOGRAPHIES

SCHOTTENLOHER, KARL, *Bibliographie zur deutschen Geschichte im Zeitalter der Glaubens-paltung*, 6 vols., Leipzig, 1933–66. Current bibliographical surveys are to be found in the following journals: *Luther Jahrbuch; Archiv für Reformations-geschichte; Church History; Revue Historique.*

GENERAL BOOKS

RITTER, GERHARD, *Die Neugestaltung Europas im 16. Jahrhundert*, Berlin, 1950.

SMITH, PRESERVED, *The Age of the Reformation*, New York, 1920.

GRIMM, HAROLD J., *The Reformation Era, 1500–1650*, New York, 1954.

GREEN, V. H. H., *Renaissance and Reformation*, London, 1952.

BAINTON, R. H., *The Reformation of the Sixteenth Century*, 2nd ed., Boston, 1965.

HARBISON, E. HARRIS, *The Age of the Reformation*, Ithaca, New York, 1955.

HILLERBRAND, H. J. (ed.), *The Reformation: A Narrative History Related by Contemporary Observers and Participants*, New York, 1964.

——— *The Protestant Reformation*, New York, 1968.

CHADWICK, O., *The Reformation*, Baltimore, 1964.

ELTON, G. R., *Reformation Europe, 1517–1559*, London, 1963.

DANIEL-ROPS, H., *The Protestant Reformation*, tr. A. Butler, New York, 1961.

JOACHIMSEN, PAUL, *Die Reformation als Epoche der deutschen Geschichte*, München, 1951.

LORTZ, JOSEPH, *Die Reformation in Deutschland*, 2 vols., Freiburg, 1939. The best Roman Catholic treatment.

OECHSLI, W., *Switzerland Since 1499*, London, 1922.

DUNCKLEY, *The Reformation in Denmark*, London, 1948.

BERGENDOFF, C., *Olavus Petri and the Ecclesiastical Transformation in Sweden*, New York, 1928.

BLOK, P. J., *A History of the People of the Netherlands*, 5 vols., New York, 1898–1912. Vol. III deals with the Reformation.

GEYL, P., *The Revolt of the Netherlands, 1555–1609*, London, 1937.

VIÉNOT, J., *Histoire de la Réforme française des origines a l'édit de Nantes*, Paris, 1926.

BAIRD, H. M., *The History of the Rise of the Huguenots of France*, 2 vols., New York, 1900.

WILKENS, C. A., *Spanish Protestants in the Sixteenth Century*, London, 1897.

BROWN, C. K., *Italy and the Reformation to 1500*, Oxford, 1930.

CHURCH, F. C., *The Italian Reformers*, New York, 1932.

CONSTANT, G. Q. M., *The Reformation in England*, 2 vols., New York, 1935–42.

POWICKE, F. M., *The Reformation in England*, New York, 1941.

PARKER, T. M., *The English Reformation*, New York, 1951.

HEWISON, J. K., *The Covenanters, A History of the Church in Scotland from the Reformation to the Revolution*, 2 vols., 2nd ed., Glasgow, 1913.

WORKS OF THE REFORMERS

Martin Luther's Werke, WEIMAR, 1883— (now almost complete).

Luther's Works, ed. JAROSLAV PELIKAN and HELMUT T. LEHMANN, St. Louis and Philadelphia, 1955–68. This American edition in 54 vols. is based on the text of the WEIMAR ed.

Works of Martin Luther, 6 vols. Philadelphia, 1915–32. New York, 1915.

SMITH, P. and JACOBS, G. M., *Luther's Correspondence,* 2 vols.

The works of PHILIP MELANCHTHON are published in *Corpus Reformatorum,* Vols. I–XXVIII. Halle, 1834–60 and in *Supplementa Melanchthonia,* Leipzig, 1910–1968. A critical edition has been edited by R. Stupperich, *Melanchthons Werke in Auswahl,* Gütersloh, 1951–65. Only parts of Melanchthon's writings are in English translation; see C. L. Hill (tr. and ed.), *The Loci Communes of Philip Melanchthon,* Boston, 1944, and *Melanchthon: Selected Writings,* Minneapolis, 1962.

Martin Bucer's Works are being published in modern critical editions; his Latin writings (by French editors) in Paris, 1954—, and his German writings (by German editors) in Gütersloh, 1960—. *De Regno Christi,* ed. F. WENDEL, was published as vol. XV of the *Opera Latina,* Paris, 1955.

ZWINGLI, H., *Sämtliche Werke,* ed. E. EGLI *et al.,* Leipzig and Zürich, 1926—.

——— *The Latin Works and Correspondence together with Selections from his German Works,* ed. S. M. JACKSON, New York, 1912.

CALVIN, J., *Opera quae supersunt omnia* (Corpus Reformatorum. vols. XXIX–LXXXVII) 59 vols. Braunschweig, 1863–1900. *Works,* 51 vols. Edinburgh, 1844–56. *Letters,* ed. J. BONNET, 4 vols., Philadelphia, 1858. *Opera Selecta,* ed. PETER BARTH and W. NIESEL, 5 vols., München, 1926–55. *The Institutes of the Christian Religion,* tr. J. Allen, 7th American ed., Philadelphia, 1936.

The works of the Anglican Reformers are collected in *The Publications of the Parker Society,* 55 vols., Cambridge, 1843–55.

BIOGRAPHIES AND INTERPRETATIONS OF THE REFORMERS

MACKINNON, JAMES, *Martin Luther and the Reformation,* 4 vols., London, 1925–30.

E. G. SCHWIEBERT, *Luther and His Times,* St. Louis, 1950.

BAINTON, R. H., *Here I Stand: The Life of Martin Luther,* New York, 1950.

BOEHMER, H., *Road to Reformation,* Philadelphia, 1946.

FIFE, R. H., *The Revolt of Martin Luther,* New York, 1957.

LAU, F., *Luther,* tr. R. H. Fischer, Philadelphia, 1963.

ALTHAUS, P., *The Theology of Martin Luther,* tr. R. C. Schultz, Philadelphia, 1966.

WATSON, P. S., *Let God be God,* London, 1947.

RUPP, E. G., *The Righteousness of God,* London, 1953.

RICHARDSON, J. W., *Philip Melanchthon,* New York, 1907.

HILDEBRANDT, F., *Melanchthon, Alien or Ally,* New York, 1946.

MANSCHRECK, CLYDE, *Melanchthon, the Quiet Reformer,* New York, 1957.

STUPPERICH, R., *Melanchthon,* tr. R. H. Fischer, Philadelphia, 1965.

EELLS, H., *Martin Bucer,* New Haven, 1931.

HOPF, C., *Martin Bucer and the English Reformation,* Oxford, 1946.

JACKSON, S. M., *Huldreich Zwingli,* New York, 1901.

FARNER, OSKAR, *Zwingli the Reformer,* New York, 1952.

McNEILL, J. T., *The History and Character of Calvinism,* New York, 1954. Contains excellent biographies of Zwingli and Calvin.

WALKER, WILLISTON, *John Calvin,* New York, 1906.

HUNT, R. N. C., *Calvin,* London, 1933.

WENDEL, F., *Calvin: The Origins and Development of his Religious Thought,* tr. P. Mairet, New York, 1963.

HUNTER, A. M., *The Teaching of Calvin,* 2nd ed., Glasgow, 1950.

DOWEY, EDWARD A., *The Knowledge of God in Calvin's Theology,* New York, 1952.

BAIRD, H. M., *Theodore Beza,* New York, 1899.

POLLARD, A. F., *Thomas Cranmer,* London, 1904.

BROWN, P. H., *John Knox,* 2 vols., London, 1895.

PERCY, E., *John Knox,* London, 1937.

THE RADICAL REFORMERS, PARTICULARLY THE ANABAPTISTS

The Mennonite Quarterly Review (Goshen, Ind., 1932—) is a mine of information on Anabaptist history and has made available many primary sources in English translation. *The Mennonite Encyclopedia* gives full (though uneven) information on all phases of the Radical Reformation. In vol. 25 of the Library of Christian Classics, *Spiritual and Anabaptist Writers* (ed. GEORGE H. WILLIAMS and ANCEL M. MERGAL, Philadelphia, 1957), one will find not only selected Anabaptist texts in translation, but also a most informative essay on the whole movement written by G. WILLIAMS. The same writer reviews modern research on the movement in *Church History,* vol. XXVII (1958): "Studies in the Radical Reformation (1517–1618)." See also his *The Radical Reformation,* Philadelphia, 1962.

BAX, E. B., *Rise and Fall of the Anabaptists,* London, 1903.

BURRAGE, H. S., *History of the Anabaptists in Switzerland,* Philadelphia, 1891.

DOSKER, H. E., *The Dutch Anabaptists,* Philadelphia, 1921.

LITTELL, FRANKLIN, *The Anabaptist View of the Church,* rev. ed., Boston, 1958.

SMITHSON, R. J., *The Anabaptists,* London, 1953.

PAYNE, E. A., *The Anabaptists of the Sixteenth Century,* London, 1949.

HORSCH, J., *The Mennonites in Europe,* Scottsdale, Pa., 1942.

JONES, R. M., *Spiritual Reformers of the Sixteenth Century,* London, 1914.

BENDER, H. S., *Conrad Grebel: The Founder of the Swiss Brethren,* Scottsdale, Pa., 1950.

BENDER, H. S., and HORSCH, J., *Menno Simons: Life and Writings,* Scottsdale, Pa., 1936.

COUTTS, A., *Hans Denck,* Edinburgh, 1922.

VEDDER, H. C., *Balthasar Hubmaier,* New York, 1905.

SCHULTZ, S. G., *Caspar Schwenckfeld,* Norristown, Pa., 1947.

WILBUR, EARL M., *History of Unitarianism,* 2 vols., Cambridge, Mass., 1945–52.

BAINTON, R. H., *Hunted Heretic* (Servetus), Boston, 1953.

GENERAL AND SPECIAL ASPECTS OF THE REFORMATION

REID, J. K. S., *The Authority of Scripture,* London, 1957.

REU, M., *The Augsburg Confession,* Chicago, 1930.

McNEILL, JOHN T., *Unitive Protestantism,* rev. ed., Richmond, Va., 1964.

ALLEN, J. W., *A History of Political Thought in the Sixteenth Century,* London, 1928.

WEBER, MAX, *The Protestant Ethic and the Spirit of Capitalism,* London, 1930.

TAWNEY, R. H., *Religion and the Rise of Capitalism,* New York, 1926.

BAINTON, R. H., *The Travail of Religious Liberty*, Philadelphia, 1951.

PAUCK, WILHELM, *The Heritage of the Reformation*, 2nd ed., Glencoe, Ill., 1961.

HARBISON, E. HARRIS, *The Christian Scholar in the Age of the Reformation*, New York, 1950.

SPITZ, L. W., *The Religious Renaissance of the German Humanists*, Cambridge, Mass., 1963.

LECLER, J., *Toleration and the Reformation*, tr. T. L. Westow, 2 vols., New York, 1960.

BEARDSLEE, J. W., III, *Reformed Dogmatics: J. Wollebius, G. Voetius, F. Turretin* (A Library of Protestant Thought), New York, 1965.

THE CATHOLIC REFORMATION

The works of Catholic theologians who engaged in controversy with the Protestant Reformers are published in *Corpus Catholicorum*, Münster, 1919—.

JANELLE, P., *The Catholic Reformation*, Milwaukee, 1949.

JEDIN, HUBERT, *A History of the Council of Trent*, tr. E. Graf, 2 vols., New York, 1957–61.

THE THIRTY YEARS' WAR

GARDINER, S. R., *The Thirty Years' War*, 2nd ed., London, 1912.

WEDGEWOOD, C. V., *The Thirty Years' War*, London, 1938.

MODERN AND AMERICAN CHRISTIANITY — GENERAL SURVEYS

BRAUER, J. C., *Protestantism in America, A Narrative History*, rev. ed., Philadelphia, 1965. A popular, readable introduction.

—— (ed.), *Reinterpretation in American Church History* (Essays in Divinity, vol. v), Chicago, 1968. A useful collection, combining assessments of new trends in the study of American religious history with essays on particular topics.

BURR, N. R., *A Critical Bibliography of Religion in American* (Religion in American Life, ed. J. W. Smith and A. L. Jamison, vol. iv), Princeton, 1961. An indispensable narrative bibliography, useful for all aspects of the study of religion in America.

CLEBSCH, W. A., *From Sacred to Profane America: The Role of Religion in American History*, New York, 1968. A study by an intellectual historian of the social function of religion in America.

DILLENBERGER, J., and WELCH, C., (eds.), *Protestant Christianity Interpreted Through Its Development*, New York, 1954. A rapid, interpretative survey with focus on developments in thought.

DRUMMOND, A. L., *German Protestantism Since Luther*, London, 1951. A readable survey, with major attention to developments in theology and tensions between church and state.

ELLIS, J. T., (ed.), *Documents of American Catholic History*, Milwaukee, 1956. A well-balanced selection, carefully introduced.

FRAZIER, E. F., *The Negro Church in America*, New York, 1964. A brief, helpful introduction from a sociological viewpoint.

GAUSTAD, E. S., *Historical Atlas of Religion in America*, New York, 1962. A valuable reference tool.

HUDSON, W. S., *Religion in America*, New York, 1965. The best one-volume introduction to American religious history.

LATOURETTE, K. S., *A History of Christianity*, New York, 1953. Covers the whole field of church history, with 500 pages on the modern period.

—— *Christianity in a Revolutionary Age: A History of Christianity in the Nineteenth and Twentieth Centuries*, 5 vols., New York, 1958–62. A comprehensive, country by country survey, with useful bibliographies.

MANSCHRECK, C. L. (ed.), *A History of Christianity: Readings in the History of the Church from the Reformation to the Present*, Englewood Cliffs, N.J., 1964. Documents in an interpretive framework, dealing primarily with Western Europe.

McNEILL, J. T., *Modern Christian Movements*, Philadelphia, 1954. Excellent brief interpretations of Puritanism, Pietism, Evangelicalism, Tractarianism, Ecumenicity, modern Catholicism.

MEAD, S. E., *The Lively Experiment: The Shaping of Christianity in America*, New York, 1963. A stimulating collection of essays interpreting Protestant experience.

NICHOLS, J. H., *History of Christianity 1650–1950: Secularization of the West*, New York, 1956. A solid, detailed, over-all survey from a Protestant point of view.

NIEBUHR, H. R., *The Kingdom of God in America*, Chicago, 1937. A perceptive interpretation of American Christian developments.

MAYER, F. E., *The Religious Bodies of America*, St. Louis, 1954. A survey of the American churches from a conservative Lutheran viewpoint.

NORWOOD, F. A., *The Development of Modern Christianity Since 1500*, New York, 1956. A brief survey which focuses on the rise of the many denominations.

SMITH, H. S., HANDY, R. T., and LOETSCHER, L. A., *American Christianity: An Historical Interpretation with Representative Documents*, 2 vols., New York, 1960–63. Basic sources in an interpretive framework covering the whole period of American church history.

SWEET, W. W., *The Story of Religion in America*, rev. ed., New York, 1950. The most characteristic single volume of a major contributor to American church history.

WALSH, H. H., *The Christian Church in Canada*, Toronto, 1956. The first over-all survey, competent.

PURITANISM, NON-CONFORMITY, THE FREE CHURCHES

BURRAGE, C., *The Early English Dissenters in the Light of Recent Research, 1550–1641*, 2 vols., Cambridge, 1912.

COLLINSON, P., *The Elizabethan Puritan Movement*, London, 1967.

DAVIES, H., *The English Free Churches*, 2nd ed., New York, 1963.

HALLER, W. E., *The Rise of Puritanism*, New York, 1938.

—— *Liberty and Reformation in the Puritan Revolution*, New York, 1955.

HENSON, H. H., *Puritanism in England*, London, 1912.

KNAPPEN, M. M., *Tudor Puritanism*, Chicago, 1939.

MILLER, P., *The New England Mind*, 2 vols., New York, 1939–1953.

—— and JOHNSON, T. H., *The Puritans*, New York, 1938.

PAYNE, E. A., *The Free Church Tradition in the Life of England*, rev. ed., London, 1951.

RUSSELL, E., *The History of Quakerism*, New York, 1942.

SCHNEIDER, H. W., *The Puritan Mind*, New York, 1930.

SIMPSON, A., *Puritanism in Old and New England*, Chicago, 1955.

TORBET, R. G., *A History of the Baptists*, rev. ed., Valley Forge, Pa., 1963.

WALZER, M., *The Revolution of the Saints: A Study in the Origins of Radical Politics*, Cambridge, Mass., 1965.

WOODHOUSE, A. S. P., *Puritanism and Liberty*, 2nd ed., Chicago, 1951.

PIETISM AND MORAVIANISM

ADDISON, W. G., *The Renewed Church of the United Brethren, 1722–1930*, New York, 1932.

GOLLIN, G. L., *Moravianism in Two Worlds: A Study of Changing Communities*, New York, 1967.

HEPPE, H. L. J., *Geschichte des Pietismus und der Mystik in der Reformierten Kirche*, Leiden, 1879.

KNOX, R. A., *Enthusiasm*, Oxford, 1951.

LANGTON, E., *History of the Moravian Church: The Story of the First International Protestant Church*, London, 1956.

RITSCHL, A., *Geschichte des Pietismus*, 3 vols., Bonn, 1880–1886.

SESSLER, J. J., *Communal Pietism among Early American Moravians*, New York, 1933.

STOEFFLER, F. E., *The Rise of Evangelical Pietism* (Studies in the History of Religions, vol. ix), Leiden, 1965.

WEINLICK, J. R., *Count Zinzendorf*, New York, 1956.

THE ENLIGHTENMENT

CRAGG, G. R., *From Puritanism to the Age of Reason*, Cambridge, 1950.

GAY, P., *The Enlightenment, An Interpretation: The Rise of Modern Paganism*, New York, 1966.

KOCH, G. A., *Republican Religion*, New York, 1933, republished as *Religion of the American Enlightenment*, New York, 1968.

MANUEL, F. E., *The Eighteenth Century Confronts the Gods*, Cambridge, Mass., 1959.

PALMER, R. R., *Catholics and Unbelievers in Eighteenth Century France*, Princeton, 1939.

STROMBERG, R. N., *Religious Liberty in Eighteenth-Century England*, London, 1954.

THE EVANGELICAL REVIVAL

BALLEINE, G. R., *A History of the Evangelical Party in the Church of England*, new ed., London, 1951.

CAMERON, R. M., *The Rise of Methodism: A Source Book*, New York, 1954.

CELL, G. C., *The Rediscovery of John Wesley*, New York, 1935.

CHURCH, L. F., *The Early Methodist People*, London, 1948.

CURNOCK, N. (ed.), *The Journal of John Wesley*, 8 vols., New York, 1909–1916.

ELLIOTT-BINNS, L. E., *The Early Evangelicals: A Religious and Social Study*, Greenwich, Connecticut, 1953.

GARBER, P. N., *The Methodists of Continental Europe*, New York, 1945.

HOWSE, E. M. F., *Saints in Politics: The "Clapham Sect" and the Growth of Freedom*, Toronto, 1952.

LINDSTRÖM, H., *Wesley and Sanctification: A Study in the Doctrine of Salvation*, Stockholm, 1946.

OUTLER, A. C. (ed.), *John Wesley* (A Library of Protestant Thought), New York, 1964.

PARKER, P. L. (ed.), *The Heart of John Wesley's Journal*, New York, 1903.

WORKMAN, H. B., et al., A New History of Methodism, 2 vols., London, 1909.
ZABRISKIE, A. (ed.), Anglican Evangelicalism, Philadelphia, 1943.

REVIVALISM IN AMERICA

BARNES, G. H., The Antislavery Impulse, 1830–1844, New York, 1933.
BILLINGTON, R. A. The Protestant Crusade, 1800–1860, New York, 1938.
CLEVELAND, C. C., The Great Revival in the West, 1797–1805, Chicago, 1916.
CROSS, W. R., The Burned-over District: The Social and Intellectual History of Enthusiastic Religion in Western New York, 1800–1850, Ithaca, New York, 1950.
ELSBREE, C. W., The Rise of the Missionary Spirit in America, 1780–1815, Williamsport, Pennsylvania, 1928.
GEWEHR, W. M., The Great Awakening in Virginia, Durham, North Carolina, 1930.
HEIMERT, A. and MILLER, P. (eds.), The Great Awakening: Documents Illustrating the Crisis and Its Consequences, Indianapolis, 1967.
JOHNSON, C. A., The Frontier Camp Meeting, Religion's Harvest Time, Dallas, Texas, 1955.
KELLER, C. A., The Second Great Awakening in Connecticut, New Haven, Connecticut, 1942.
MAXSON, C. H., The Great Awakening in the Middle Colonies, Chicago, 1920.
McLOUGHLIN, W. G., Modern Revivalism: Charles Grandison Finney to Billy Graham, New York, 1959.
SCHNEIDER, C. E., The German Church on the American Frontier, St. Louis, 1939.
SMITH, T. L., Revivalism and Social Reform in Mid-Nineteenth Century America, New York, 1957.
SWEET, W. W., Revivalism in America: Its Origins, Growth, and Decline, New York, 1945.
TEWKSBURY, D. G., The Founding of American Colleges and Universities before the Civil War, With Particular Reference to Religious Influences Bearing upon the College Movement, New York, 1932.
TRINTERUD, L. J., The Forming of an American Tradition: A Re-examination of Colonial Presbyterianism, Philadelphia, 1949.

RELIGIOUS LIBERTY

BAINTON, R. H., The Travail of Religious Liberty: Nine Biographical Studies, Philadelphia, 1951.
BATES, M. S., Religious Liberty: An Inquiry, New York, 1945.
BLAU, J. L. (ed.), Cornerstones of Religious Liberty in America, rev. ed., New York, 1964.
DUNCAN-JONES, A. S., The Struggle for Religious Freedom in Germany, London, 1938.
GREENE, E. B., Religion and the State, New York, 1941.
HOWARD, G. P., Religious Liberty in Latin America, Philadelphia, 1944.
HOWE, M. D., The Garden and the Wilderness, Chicago, 1965.
JORDAN, W. K., The Development of Religious Toleration in England, 4 vols., London, 1932–1940.
KELLER, A., Church and State on the European Continent, Chicago, 1936.
PFEFFER, L., Church, State, and Freedom, Boston, 1953.
SANDERS, T. G., Protestant Concepts of Church and State: Historical Backgrounds and Approaches for the Future, New York, 1964.
STOKES, A. P., Church and State in the United States, 3 vols., New York, 1950.

CHRISTIAN THOUGHT IN THE MODERN PERIOD

AHLSTROM, S. E. (ed.), *Theology in America: The Major Voices from Puritanism to Neo-Orthodoxy*, Indianapolis, 1967.

CAUTHEN, K., *The Impact of American Religious Liberalism*, New York, 1962.

DORNER, J. A., *History of Protestant Theology, Particularly in Germany*, Edinburgh, 1871.

ELLIOTT-BINNS, L. E., *The Development of English Theology in the Later Nineteenth Century*, London, 1952.

GROFF, W. E. and MILLER, D. E., *The Shaping of Modern Christian Thought*, Cleveland, 1968.

HAMMAR, G., *Christian Realism in Contemporary American Theology*, Uppsala, 1940.

HORTON, W. M., *Contemporary Continental Theology*, New York, 1938.

MACKINTOSH, H. R., *Types of Modern Theology, Schleiermacher to Barth*, New York, 1937.

MACQUARRIE, J., *Twentieth-Century Religious Thought: The Frontiers of Philosophy and Theology*, New York, 1963.

MOORE, E. C., *An Outline of the History of Christian Thought Since Kant*, New York, 1912.

NICHOLS, J. H. (ed.), *The Mercersburg Theology* (A Library of Protestant Thought), New York, 1966.

NIEBUHR, R. R., *Schleiermacher on Christ and Religion: A New Introduction*, New York, 1964.

PFLEIDERER, O., *The Development of Theology in Germany Since Kant, and Its Progress in Great Britain Since 1825*, New York, 1890.

SELBIE, W. B., *Schleiermacher, A Critical and Historical Study*, New York, 1913.

SMITH, H. S., *Changing Conceptions of Original Sin: A Study in American Theology Since 1750*, New York, 1955.

——— (ed.), *Horace Bushnell* (A Library of Protestant Thought), New York, 1965.

TILLICH, P., *Perspectives on 19th and 20th Century Protestant Theology*, ed. C. E. Braaten, New York, 1967.

TULLOCH, J., *Movements of Religious Thought in Britain During the Nineteenth Century*, New York, 1886.

VIDLER, A. R., *The Modernist Movement in the Roman Church: Its Origins and Outcome*, Cambridge, 1934.

WELCH, C. (ed.), *God and Incarnation in Mid-Nineteenth Century German Theology: Thomasius, Dorner, Biedermann* (A Library of Protestant Thought), New York, 1965.

ANGLICANISM AND THE OXFORD MOVEMENT

BRILIOTH, Y. T., *The Anglican Revival: Studies in the Oxford Movement*, New York, 1925.

——— *Three Lectures on Evangelicanism and the Oxford Movement*, London, 1934.

BROWN, F. K., *Fathers of Victorians and the Age of Wilberforce*, Cambridge, 1961.

CARPENTER, S. C., *Church and People, 1789–1889*, London, 1933.

CHADWICK, O. (ed.), *The Mind of the Oxford Movement*, London, 1960.

CRAGG, G. R. (ed.), *The Cambridge Platonists* (A Library of Protestant Thought), New York, 1968.

DAVIES, H., *Worship and Theology in England*, 3 vols., Princeton, 1961—.

DE MILLE, G. E., *The Catholic Movement in the American Episcopal Church*, Philadelphia, 1941.

FAIRWEATHER, E. R. (ed.), *The Oxford Movement* (A Library of Protestant Thought), New York, 1964.

MORE, P. E., and CROSS, E. L. (eds.), *Anglicanism*, Milwaukee, Wisconsin, 1935.

OLLARD, S. Y., *A Short History of the Oxford Movement*, Milwaukee, Wisconsin, 1915.

STEWART, H. L., *A Century of Anglo-Catholicism*, London, 1929.

MODERN ROMAN CATHOLICISM

ABBOTT, W. M. (ed.), *The Documents of Vatican II*, New York, 1966.

BERKOUWER, G. C., *The Second Vatican Council and the New Catholicism*, tr. Lewis B. Smedes, Grand Rapids, Mich., 1965.

BURY, J. B., *History of the Papacy in the Nineteenth Century*, New York, 1930.

CROSS, R. D., *The Emergence of Liberal Catholicism in America*, Cambridge, Mass., 1958.

ELLIS, J. T., *American Catholicism*, rev. ed., Garden City, New York, 1965.

GEFFCKEN, F. H., *Church and State: Their Relations Historically Developed*, 2 vols., London, 1877.

GURIAN, W., and FITZSIMONS, M. A., *The Catholic Church in World Affairs*, South Bend, Indiana, 1954.

HUSSLEIN, J. (ed.), *Social Wellsprings: Fourteen Documents by Pope Leo XIII*, Milwaukee, Wisconsin, 1940.

MACCAFFREY, J., *History of the Catholic Church in the Nineteenth Century, 1789–1908*, 2 vols., St Louis, 1909.

NIELSEN, F. K., *The History of the Papacy in the Nineteenth Century*, 2 vols., New York, 1906.

PHILLIPS, C. S., *The Church in France, 1789–1848: A Study in Revival*, London, 1929.

—— *The Church in France, 1848–1907*, London, 1936.

SCHILLEBEECKS, E., *The Real Achievement of Vatican II*, tr. H. J. J. Vaughan, New York, 1967.

MODERN EASTERN ORTHODOXY

ANDERSON, P. B., *People, Church and State in Modern Russia*, New York, 1944.

ATTWATER, D., *The Christian Churches of the East*, Milwaukee, Wisconsin, 1947–1948.

BENZ, E., *The Eastern Orthodox Church: Its Thought and Life*, tr. R. and C. Winston, Chicago, 1963.

BOLSHAKOFF, S., *Russian Nonconformity, The Story of "Unofficial" Religion in Russia*, Philadelphia, 1950.

BROWN, L. W., *The Indian Christians of St. Thomas*, Cambridge, 1956.

BULGAKOV, S., *The Orthodox Church*, London, 1935.

CURTISS, J. S., *Church and State in Russia, 1900–1917*, New York, 1940.

—— *The Russian Church and the Soviet State*, Boston, 1953.

FEDOTOV, G. P. (ed.), *A Treasury of Russian Spirituality*, New York, 1948.

FRERE, W. H., *Some Links in the Chain of Russian Church History*, London, 1918.

MEYENDORFF, J., *The Orthodox Church: Its Past and Its Role in the Church Today*, tr. J. Chapin, New York, 1962.

SPINKA, M., *The Church in Soviet Russia,* New York, 1956.

TIMASHEFF, N. S., *Religion in Soviet Russia, 1917–1942,* New York, 1942.

WARE, T., *The Orthodox Church,* Baltimore, 1963.

ZANKOV, S., *The Eastern Orthodox Church,* Milwaukee, Wisconsin, 1930.

ZERNOV, N., *The Russians and Their Church,* London, 1945.

—— *Orthodox Encounter: The Christian East and the Ecumenical Movement,* London, 1961.

SOCIAL CHRISTIANITY

ABELL, A. I., *American Catholicism and Social Action: A Search for Social Justice, 1865–1950,* Garden City, New York, 1960.

—— (ed.), *American Catholic Thought on Social Questions,* Indianapolis, 1968.

BINYON, G. C., *The Christian Socialist Movement in England: An Introduction to the Study of Its History,* London, 1931.

CARTER, P. A., *The Decline and Revival of the Social Gospel: Social and Political Liberalism in American Protestant Churches, 1920–1940,* Ithaca, New York, 1956.

HANDY, R. T. (ed.), *The Social Gospel in America, 1870–1920: Gladden, Ely, Rauschenbusch* (A Library of Protestant Thought), New York, 1966.

HOPKINS, C. H., *The Rise of the Social Gospel in American Protestantism, 1865–1915,* New Haven, Conn., 1940.

JONES, P. D' A., *The Christian Socialist Revival, 1877–1914: Religion, Class, and Social Conscience in Late-Victorian England,* Princeton, 1968.

MAY, H. F., *Protestant Churches and Industrial America,* New York, 1949.

MCNEILL, J. T., *Christian Hope for World Society,* Chicago, 1937.

MEYER, D. B., *The Protestant Search for Political Realism, 1919–1941,* Berkeley, 1960.

NICHOLS, J. H., *Democracy and the Churches,* Philadelphia, 1951.

RECKITT, M. B., *Maurice to Temple: A Century of the Social Movement in the Church of England,* London, 1947.

REIMERS, D. M., *White Protestantism and the Negro,* New York, 1965.

SHANAHAN, W. O., *German Protestants Face the Social Question,* Notre Dame, Indiana, 1954.

VISSER 'T HOOFT, W. A., *The Background of the Social Gospel in America,* Haarlem, 1928,

WARD, L. R. (ed.), *The American Apostolate: American Catholics in the Twentieth Century,* Washington, Maryland, 1952.

WEILL, G., *Histoire du Catholicisme-libéral en France, 1828–1908,* Paris, 1909.

THE ECUMENICAL MOVEMENT

BROWN, R. M. *The Ecumenical Revolution: An Interpretation of the Catholic-Protestant Dialogue,* Garden City, New York, 1967.

BROWN, W. A., *Toward A United Church: Three Decades of Ecumenical Christianity,* New York, 1946.

CAVERT, S. M., *The American Churches in the Ecumenical Movement, 1900–1968,* New York, 1968.

CROW, P. A., JR., *The Ecumenical Movement in Bibliographical Outline,* New York, 1965.

GAINES, D. P., *The World Council of Churches, A Study of Its Background and History,* Peterborough, N. H., 1966.

GOODALL, N., *The Ecumenical Movement: What It Is and What It Does,* New York, 1961.

HOGG, W. R., *Ecumenical Foundations: A History of the International Missionary Council and Its Nineteenth-century Background,* New York, 1952.

HORTON, W. M., *Toward a Reborn Church,* New York, 1949.

HUTCHISON, J. A., *We Are Not Divided: A Critical and Historical Study of the Federal Council of the Churches of Christ in America,* New York, 1941.

MACFARLAND, C. S., *Steps Toward the World Council: Origins of the Ecumenical Movement as Expressed in the Universal Christian Council for Life and Work,* New York, 1938.

NEILL, S. C., *The Church and Christian Union,* New York, 1968.

ROUSE, R., and NEILL, S. C. (eds.), *A History of the Ecumenical Movement, 1517–1948,* 2nd ed., Philadelphia, 1967.

SILCOX, C E., *Church Union in Canada,* New York, 1933.

SLOSSER, G. J., *Christian Unity: Its History and Challenge in All Communions, in All Lands,* New York, 1929.

VAN DUSEN, H. P., *World Christianity: Yesterday—Today—Tomorrow,* New York, 1947.

––––––– *One Great Ground of Hope: Christian Missions and Christian Unity,* Philadelphia, 1961.

VISCHER, L. (ed.), *A Documentary History of the Faith and Order Movement, 1927–1963,* St. Louis, 1963.

INDEX